Regulating Long-Term Care Quality

The number of elderly people relying on formal long-term care services is dramatically increasing year after year, and the challenge of ensuring the quality and financial stability of care provision is one faced by governments in both the developed and developing world. This edited book is the first to provide a comprehensive international survey of long-term care provision and regulation, built around a series of case studies from Europe, North America and Asia. The analytical framework allows the different approaches that countries have adopted to be compared side-by-side and readers are encouraged to consider which quality assurance approaches might best meet their own country's needs. Wider issues underpinning the need to regulate the quality of long-term care are also discussed. This timely book is a valuable resource for policy makers working in the healthcare sector, researchers and students taking graduate courses on health policy and management.

VINCENT MOR is the Florence Pirce Grant Professor of Community Health in the School of Public Health, Department of Health Policy and Practice at the Brown University School of Public Health. He is also Senior Health Scientist at the Providence Veterans Administration Medical Centre (Health Services Research Service). His research focuses on the organizational and healthcare delivery system factors associated with variation in use of health services, and outcomes experienced by frail and chronically ill persons.

TIZIANA LEONE is a lecturer in demography in the Department of Social Policy at the London School of Economics and Political Science. Dr Leone's research interests focus on demography and health policy. She is particularly interested in reproductive and health systems in developing countries as well as health and ageing in Europe.

ANNA MARESSO is a research officer at LSE Health and the European Observatory on Health Systems and Policies at the London School of Economics and Political Science. Her research focuses on the healthcare systems of western Europe and comparative health policy.

Health Economics, Policy and Management

Series Editor

Professor Elias Mossialos, London School of Economics and Political Science

This series is for scholars in health policy, economics and management. It publishes texts that provide innovative discourses, comprehensive accounts and authoritative approaches to scholarship. It also creates a forum for researchers to participate in interdisciplinary conversations on contemporary issues in healthcare. Concerns in health policy, economics and management will be featured in the context of international healthcare practices and ongoing discussions on the latest developments in scholarly research and theoretical issues from a variety of perspectives.

Presenting clear, concise and balanced accounts of topics, particularly those that have developed in the field in the last decade, the series will appeal to healthcare scholars, policy makers, practitioners and students.

PUBLISHED TITLES:

Performance Measurement for Health System Improvement:
Experiences, Challenges and Prospects
Edited by Peter C. Smith, Elias Mossialos, Irene Papanicolas and Sheila Leatherman

Health Systems Governance in Europe:
The Role of European Union Law and Policy
Edited by: Elias Mossialos, Govin Permanand, Rita Baeten and Tamara K. Hervey

FORTHCOMING TITLES:

Private Health Insurance and Medical Savings Accounts:
History, Politics, Performance
Edited by Sarah Thomson, Elias Mossialos and Robert G. Evans

Regulating Long-Term Care Quality

An International Comparison

Edited by
VINCENT MOR
Brown University, Rhode Island
TIZIANA LEONE
London School of Economics and Political Science
ANNA MARESSO
London School of Economics and Political Science

Shaftesbury Road, Cambridge CB2 8EA, United Kingdom

One Liberty Plaza, 20th Floor, New York, NY 10006, USA

477 Williamstown Road, Port Melbourne, VIC 3207, Australia

314–321, 3rd Floor, Plot 3, Splendor Forum, Jasola District Centre, New Delhi – 110025, India

103 Penang Road, #05–06/07, Visioncrest Commercial, Singapore 238467

Cambridge University Press is part of Cambridge University Press & Assessment, a department of the University of Cambridge.

We share the University's mission to contribute to society through the pursuit of education, learning and research at the highest international levels of excellence.

www.cambridge.org
Information on this title: www.cambridge.org/9781107042063

© Cambridge University Press & Assessment 2014

This publication is in copyright. Subject to statutory exception and to the provisions of relevant collective licensing agreements, no reproduction of any part may take place without the written permission of Cambridge University Press & Assessment.

First published 2014

A catalogue record for this publication is available from the British Library

ISBN   978-1-107-04206-3   Hardback
ISBN   978-1-107-66535-4   Paperback

Cambridge University Press & Assessment has no responsibility for the persistence or accuracy of URLs for external or third-party internet websites referred to in this publication and does not guarantee that any content on such websites is, or will remain, accurate or appropriate.

Contents

List of tables, figures and boxes	*page*	viii
List of contributors		xii
Foreword		xvii

PART I: Introduction — 1

Chapter 1   A framework for understanding regulation of long-term care quality — 3
VINCENT MOR

PART II: Long-term care quality systems based on 'professionalism' — 29

Chapter 2   Performance measurement in long-term care in Austria — 33
KAI LEICHSENRING, FRÉDÉRIQUE LAMONTAGNE-GODWIN, ANDREA SCHMIDT, RICARDO RODRIGUES AND GEORG RUPPE

Chapter 3   Monitoring the quality of long-term care in Germany — 67
VJENKA GARMS-HOMOLOVÁ AND REINHARD BUSSE

Chapter 4   Quality monitoring and long-term care in Switzerland — 102
GUIDO BARTELT, RUEDI GILGEN, DANIEL GROB AND THOMAS MÜNZER

Chapter 5   Japan's long-term care regulations focused on structure – rationale and future prospects — 121
NAOKI IKEGAMI, TOMOAKI ISHIBASHI AND TAKASHI AMANO

PART III: Long-term care quality systems based on regulatory inspection frameworks 145

Chapter 6   Regulating long-term care quality in Australia 149
LEN C. GRAY, DAVID J. CULLEN AND HAROLD B. LOMAS

Chapter 7   Regulating the quality and safety of long-term care in England 180
JULIETTE MALLEY, JACQUETTA HOLDER, RACHAEL DODGSON AND SAMANTHA BOOTH

Chapter 8   Quality monitoring of long-term care for older people in The Netherlands 211
JOS M. G. A. SCHOLS, DINNUS H. M. FRIJTERS, RUUD G. I. J. M. KEMPEN AND JAN P. H. HAMERS

Chapter 9   The regulatory structure of Spanish long-term care: the case of Catalonia's service structures and quality assurance systems 240
SERGIO ARIÑO BLASCO, MERITXELL SOLÉ, GLORIA RUBERT, JOSÉ M. SANJUAN AND JOAN GIL

PART IV: Long-term care quality systems based on data measurement and public reporting 265

Chapter 10   Monitoring the quality of long-term care in Finland 269
HARRIET FINNE-SOVERI, TEIJA HAMMAR, ANJA NORO, SARI ANTTILA AND PÄIVI VOUTILAINEN

Chapter 11   Regulation of long-term care in the United States 289
DAVID STEVENSON AND JEFFREY BRAMSON

Chapter 12   Long-term care for the elderly in Canada: progress towards an integrated system 324
JOHN P. HIRDES AND VAHE KEHYAYAN

Chapter 13   Regulating the quality of long-term aged care in New Zealand 357
BRIGETTE MEEHAN AND NIGEL MILLAR

Contents vii

PART V: Long-term care quality systems and developing regulatory systems 383

Chapter 14   Quality monitoring of long-term care in the Republic of Korea 385

HYE-YOUNG JUNG, SOONG-NANG JANG, JAE EUN SEOK AND SOONMAN KWON

Chapter 15   Long-term care in China: reining in market forces through regulatory oversight 409

ZHANLIAN FENG, XINPING GUAN, XIAOTIAN FENG, CHANG LIU, HEYING JENNY ZHAN AND VINCENT MOR

PART VI: Conclusion 445

Chapter 16   Regulating quality of long-term care – what have we learned? 447

TIZIANA LEONE, ANNA MARESSO AND VINCENT MOR

Index 477

Tables, figures and boxes

Tables

2.1	Staffing ratio and staffing structure in Austrian residential care facilities by region	*page* 44
2.2	Selected features of care home inspection stipulated by Austrian regions	49
2.3	Overview of the E-Qalin model to assess and improve the quality of care homes in Austria	57
3.1	Obligations and competences of the Medical Review Boards at the state level (MDK) and the Medical Review Board of the Federal Association of Sickness Funds (MDS)	78
3.2	Examples of external quality certificates and audits used in the German long-term care sector	90
4.1	Population growth and trends in long-term care institutions and home-based long-term care in Switzerland, 2000–2009	104
5.1	Expansion in number of LTCI service users in Japan, May 2001–May 2009	125
5.2	Staffing regulations for institutional care in Japan	127
5.3	Facility regulations for institutional care in Japan	128
5.4	Regulations for home- and community-based care agencies in Japan	130
6.1	Residential and community care quality regulation in Australia	164
7.1	Numbers of providers in England by ownership and type of service at 31 March 2010 (percentage shown in brackets)	183
7.2	The Essential Standards of Quality and Safety and their relationship to the regulations in England	186

Tables, figures and boxes   ix

7.3 Findings from CQC reviews of compliance for care homes in England by home type and standard, October 2010 to March 2011   195
7.4 Findings from CQC reviews of compliance of home care agencies in England by standard, October 2010 to March 2011   198
7.5 Number of inspections or reviews conducted by CQC in England across ASC providers per year, 2002/03 to 2010/11   202
8.1 Healthcare, social services, and housing for older people in The Netherlands   213
8.2 Health and long-term care legislation in The Netherlands   220
8.3 Main aspects of long-term care organizations' quality of care in The Netherlands   224
8.4 Overview of quality indicators in long-term care developed by the Steering Group on Responsible Care, The Netherlands   229
9.1 Socio-demographic indicators and some long-term care services characteristics in Spain and Catalonia, 2010   243
9.2 Global staffing ratio per resident in the nursing home sector in Spain – regional government average in 2008 and mandated ratios in 2011   248
9.3 Results from PLAENSA survey on the level of residents' satisfaction with skilled nursing facilities in Catalonia, 2003, 2007, 2010   253
9.4 Quality indicators related to long-term care in the Catalan Outcomes Centre's data set   257
11.1 US State variation in nursing home deficiencies and complaints   305
11.2 Information available on the Nursing Home Compare public reporting website, USA   311
14.1 Assessment grades for long-term care eligibility status in South Korea   390
14.2 Residential care benefits and home care limits in South Korea, 2011   392
14.3 Domains of long-term care evaluation and weighted scores in South Korea   399
15.1 Officially classified types of elder care facilities in China   427
16.1 Classification of countries by broad regulatory approach   448

x   *Tables, figures and boxes*

16.2 Centralization and decentralization in the regulation of
     public long-term care   455
16.3 Long-term care regulatory function undertaken by
     countries   464

Figures

2.1 Responsibilities of the federal and regional governments
     in long-term care in Austria   41
3.1 Legal responsibilities within the long-term care sector in
     Germany   73
4.1 Relative number of beds in nursing homes per 100 people
     aged 80 or over (expressed as a percentage) by Swiss
     canton, 2008   105
4.2 'Prevalence of severe pain' quality indicator in the City of
     Basel canton, 2003–11   116
4.3 Prevalence of restraint use in Ticino canton, 2006–11   116
6.1 Australian agencies involved in residential aged care
     quality regulation   157
7.1 An example QRP for Standard 13 in England   192
9.1 Dependency Assessment Process in Spain   246
9.2 Quality indicators and dimensions for nursing homes in
     Catalonia, 2010   250
9.3 Extract from first public reporting exercise on skilled
     nursing facilities with mid-term care beds in Catalonia,
     November 2010   258
10.1 Provision of long-term care services in Finland, 2009 and
     2010   271
10.2 Number of municipalities in Finland using interRAI
     instruments, 2000–12   282
10.3 Number of bi-annually assessed older people in Finland
     according to long-term care setting, 2000–12   282
10.4 Use of hypnotic drugs in long-term care units in Finland,
     2001–12   283
11.1 Graphical representation of some of the entities involved
     in long-term care regulation in the United States   297
14.1 Trends in the number of long-term care recipients in
     South Korea, 2005–11   389

Tables, figures and boxes xi

14.2 Assessment process in South Korea to determine long-term care needs 391

14.3 Trends in the number of long-term care providers in South Korea, 2005–11 393

14.4 The qualification process for certified care workers in South Korea 403

15.1 Growth of elder care homes in selected Chinese cities, 1952–2009 416

15.2 Administrative and regulatory structure of aged care services in China 423

Boxes

3.1 Long-term care decision-making powers by different levels of government in Germany 72

7.1 Explanation of the Quality and Risk Profile and underlying intelligence sources, England 191

10.1 Government recommendations in Finland for long-term care coverage of those aged 75 or older according to type of care 271

Contributors

TAKASHI AMANO, Research Scientist, Dia Foundation for Research on Ageing Societies, Tokyo, Japan.

SARI ANTTILA, Senior Medical Officer, National Supervisory Authority for Welfare and Health (Valvira), Helsinki, Finland.

SERGIO ARIÑO-BLASCO, Associate Professor in Geriatric Medicine at Universitat Internacional de Catalunya and Director of the Geriatrics Department at the Granollers General Hospital, Barcelona, Spain.

GUIDO BARTELT, BBP Healthcare Consultants and Partner at Q-Sys AG, Switzerland.

SAMANTHA BOOTH, Analysis Development Manager, Intelligence Directorate, Care Quality Commission, United Kingdom.

JEFFREY BRAMSON, Harvard Law School Class of 2012, Cambridge MA, United States.

REINHARD BUSSE, Professor and Department Head for Healthcare Management at the University of Technology Berlin and Associate Head of Research Policy at the European Observatory on Health Systems and Policies.

DAVID J. CULLEN, Adjunct Senior Fellow, Australian Centre for Economic Research on Health, Australian National University and Assistant Secretary, Strategic Policy Unit, Australian Department of Health and Ageing, Canberra, Australia.

RACHAEL DODGSON, Head of Regulatory Design, Care Quality Commission, United Kingdom.

XIAOTIAN FENG, Professor and Chair, Department of Sociology, Nanjing University, China.

List of contributors

ZHANLIAN FENG, Senior Research Public Health Analyst, Aging, Disability and Long Term Care, RTI International, USA.

HARRIET FINNE-SOVERI, Adjunct Professor in Geriatric Medicine, Chief of Aging and Services Unit, National Institute for Health and Welfare, Helsinki, Finland.

DINNUS H. M. FRIJTERS, Institute for Health and Care Research, Department of Nursing Home Medicine, VU University Medical Center, Amsterdam, The Netherlands.

VJENKA GARMS-HOMOLOVÁ, Professor for Healthcare Management, Alice Salomon University of Applied Sciences, Berlin, Germany.

JOAN GIL, Associate Professor, Department of Economic Theory and Centre for Economic Analysis and Social Policy (CAEPS), University of Barcelona, Spain.

RUEDI GILGEN was a leading gerontologist in Switzerland. He passed away during the writing of this book. His chapter co-authors and the editors are extremely appreciative of his contribution to this volume and for sharing his substantial knowledge and expertise.

LEN C. GRAY, Professor and Director, Centre for Research in Geriatric Medicine and Director, Centre for Online Health, The Masonic Chair in Geriatric Medicine, The University of Queensland, Australia.

DANIEL GROB, Medical Director, Waid Hospital, Zurich, Switzerland.

XINPING GUAN, Professor and Chair, Department of Social Work and Social Policy, Nankai University, Tianjin, China.

JAN P. H. HAMERS, Professor in the Care of Older People, School for Public Health and Primary Care (CAPHRI), Department of Health Services Research, Maastricht University, The Netherlands.

TEIJA HAMMAR, Senior Researcher, Aging and Services Unit, National Institute for Health and Welfare, Helsinki, Finland.

JOHN P. HIRDES, Professor, School of Public Health and Health Systems, University of Waterloo, Ontario, Canada.

JACQUETTA HOLDER, Research Fellow, Personal Social Services Research Unit, University of Kent at Canterbury, United Kingdom.

NAOKI IKEGAMI, Professor and Chair, Department of Health Policy and Management, Keio University School of Medicine, Japan.

TOMOAKI ISHIBASHI, Director of Research, Dia Foundation for Research on Ageing Societies, Tokyo, Japan.

SOONG-NANG JANG, Professor, Department of Nursing, Chung-Ang University, Seoul, South Korea.

HYE-YOUNG JUNG, Professor, Department of Public Health, Weill Cornell Medical College of Cornell University, USA.

VAHE KEHYAYAN, Adjunct Assistant Professor, School of Public Health and Health Systems, University of Waterloo, Ontario, Canada.

RUUD G. I. J. M. KEMPEN, Professor of Social Gerontology, School for Public Health and Primary Care (CAPHRI), Department of Health Services Research, Maastricht University, The Netherlands.

SOONMAN KWON, Professor of Health Economics and Policy, School of Public Health, Seoul National University, South Korea.

FRÉDÉRIQUE LAMONTAGNE-GODWIN, Researcher, European Centre for Social Welfare Policy and Research, Vienna, Austria (2008–2011).

KAI LEICHSENRING, Associate Senior Researcher, European Centre for Social Welfare Policy and Research, Vienna, Austria.

TIZIANA LEONE, Senior Research Fellow in Health Policy at LSE Health and Lecturer in Demography in the Department of Social Policy, The London School of Economics and Political Science, United Kingdom.

CHANG LIU, Assistant Professor, Program in Health Services and Systems Research, Duke–NUS Graduate Medical School, Singapore.

HAROLD B. LOMAS, Australian Department of Industry, Innovation, Science, Research and Tertiary Education (formerly Director, Aged Care Reform Taskforce, Australian Department of Health and Ageing), Canberra.

JULIETTE MALLEY, Research Fellow, Personal Social Services Research Unit, The London School of Economics and Political Science, United Kingdom.

List of contributors

ANNA MARESSO, Research Officer, LSE Health, The London School of Economics and Political Science and European Observatory on Health Systems and Policies, United Kingdom.

BRIGETTE MEEHAN, interRAI Programme Manager, New Zealand Ministry of Health, New Zealand.

NIGEL MILLAR, Chief Medical Officer, Canterbury District Health Board, New Zealand.

VINCENT MOR, Florence Pirce Grant Professor of Community Health, Department of Health Policy and Practice, Brown University School of Public Health, and Senior Health Scientist at the Providence Veterans Administration Medical Centre (Health Services Research Service), USA.

THOMAS MÜNZER, Chief of Geriatrics and Long Term Care, Geriatrische Klinik St Gallen Kompetenzzentrum Gesundheit und Alter St Gallen, and Lecturer in Geriatrics, University of Bern Medical Faculty, Bern, Switzerland.

ANJA NORO, Research Director, Aging and Services Unit, National Institute for Health and Welfare, Helsinki, Finland.

RICARDO RODRIGUES, Research Fellow, European Centre for Social Welfare Policy and Research, Vienna, Austria.

GLORIA RUBERT, Associate Professor, Department of Economic Theory and Centre for Economic Analysis and Social Policy (CAEPS), University of Barcelona, Spain.

GEORG RUPPE, since 2011 CEO and Researcher at the Austrian Interdisciplinary Platform on Ageing/ÖPIA, Vienna, Austria. Previously, Researcher, European Centre for Social Welfare Policy and Research, Vienna, Austria.

JOSÉ M. SANJUAN, Ph.D. candidate and Researcher at the University of Barcelona, Spain.

ANDREA SCHMIDT, Researcher, European Centre for Social Welfare Policy and Research, Vienna, Austria.

JOS M. G. A. SCHOLS, Professor of Old Age Medicine, School for Public Health and Primary Care (CAPHRI), Department of General

Practice and Department of Health Services Research, Maastricht University, The Netherlands.

JAE EUN SEOK, Professor, Department of Social Welfare, Hallym University, South Korea.

MERITXELL SOLÉ, Ph.D. candidate and Researcher at the University of Barcelona and CREB, Spain.

DAVID STEVENSON, Associate Professor, Department of Health Policy, Vanderbilt University School of Medicine, Nashville, USA.

PÄIVI VOUTILAINEN, Dr Sc. (Healthcare), Ministerial Counsellor, Social Affairs, Ministry of Social Affairs and Health, Finland.

HEYING JENNY ZHAN, Associate Professor, Department of Sociology, Georgia State University, USA.

Foreword

A key but neglected issue in long-term care is how different countries ensure that nursing homes, home care agencies and residential care facilities provide good-quality care. Although countries employ a number of strategies to accomplish this goal, the most common approach is regulation – to establish mandatory, government or government agent-imposed quality standards (Wiener et al., 2007a, 2007b). In most cases, these government regulations or other standards set the minimum quality that providers must meet to operate or to receive government funding. The role of government regulation in long-term care varies widely across countries, within countries and across services. In most countries, long-term care is heavily financed by the public sector (European Commission, 2012; OECD, 2005). Thus, governments have a fiduciary responsibility to ensure that the public's money is well spent. This book fills an important gap by analysing how a large number of countries around the world regulate the quality of long-term care services and the extent to which they make the results of their inspections and other information on quality available to the public.

Although some countries, such as the United States, have well-established regulatory systems, others, such as China, do not. But having a well-established regulatory system does not guarantee that all providers establish high quality. For example, in the United States, 23 per cent of nursing homes in 2010 were cited for causing actual harm or placing residents in jeopardy (Harrington et al., 2011). Moreover, during that same year, the US Administration on Aging received 157,962 complaints from nursing home residents or their families about poor quality of care, problematic quality of life and violations of resident rights (US Administration on Aging, 2011). Additionally, almost nothing is known about the quality of residential care facilities

xvii

because these providers are regulated at the state level using highly variable standards and the provision of personal care by home care agencies and individual providers is hardly regulated.

The regulatory process has three components: (1) rules that establish the standards or norms that providers must meet; (2) inspections or other means of collecting data to assess whether the providers are meeting the rules or performance norms; and (3) enforcement or other remedies to address problems identified during the inspection or other discovery process. How countries implement these three activities varies widely. Reflecting the historical emphasis on institutional care, such as nursing homes, regulation of institutions is more common than regulation of home- and community-based services.

Although ensuring quality of long-term care has always been important, its salience will grow rapidly in the coming years because many more people will receive long-term care services and because government expenditures to pay for those services will increase substantially (European Commission, 2012; Johnson et al., 2007; OECD, 2006). Throughout the world, the population is aging. People aged 80 and older, who are most likely to be disabled and need long-term care services, are among the fastest-growing segments of the population. For example, for the twenty-seven countries in the European Union, the population aged 80 and older is projected to increase 2.6-fold as a proportion of the total population, from 4.7 per cent of the population in 2010 to 12.1 per cent of the population in 2060 (European Commission, 2012). The ageing of the population in the developed countries is well known; much less appreciated is that the population in middle-income countries is also ageing rapidly. Indeed, the proportion of the population aged 85 and older in Brazil, China, India, Mexico, and Russia will more than quadruple between 2010 and 2050, bringing them to at least the 2010 level of the United States or higher (US Census Bureau, 2009).

The critical role of government regulation in long-term care is related to the types of services provided and the people who use those services. Regulation is used cautiously in most free-market-oriented economies, yet quality assurance for long-term care is an area dominated by regulation. The rationale for the prominent role of regulation in free-market economies is market failure such that consumers cannot effectively use their market power to improve quality.

Foreword xix

First, many people using long-term care services are severely ill and disabled, and some of these individuals may not have the ability to complain about the care they are receiving or to 'vote with their feet' and use another provider. Moreover, many people who require long-term care services have cognitive impairments that make it difficult for them to make decisions. For example, in the United States, 41 per cent of nursing home residents in 2009 had moderate to severe cognitive impairment and 68 per cent of nursing home residents had some level of cognitive impairment (US Centers for Medicare and Medicaid Services, 2010). Finally, some people using long-term care services have no close family or friends to act on their behalf for their care and protection, if needed.

Second, nursing homes and other residential settings, in particular, are 'total institutions', where individuals live twenty-four hours a day and where many aspects of life are controlled by others (Goffman, 1961). Fear of physical abuse and other retribution from staff may prevent residents from complaining, and difficulty finding other placements may prevent them from leaving. Even for home care, people with severe disabilities may suffer adverse consequences if they are left with a gap in service caused by 'firing' their personal care worker (LaPlante et al., 2004).

Third, although a great deal of long-term care is non-technical help with activities of daily living or instrumental activities of daily living, many providers serve individuals with substantial healthcare needs that require medical skills that laypersons are unlikely to be able to evaluate (Walsh et al., 2012). Fourth, high occupancy rates in nursing homes and a shortage of home and community-based services providers in many countries may mean that providers are able to operate at near capacity without having to compete based on quality of care. This may be especially true of providers serving beneficiaries of programmes designed for the poor, which often have lower reimbursement rates. In these situations, consumers cannot choose another, higher-quality provider because there are none available.

Finally, decisions about the appropriate type of care and which provider to use are often made more difficult by the need to make decisions quickly while under substantial stress. Thus, placement in nursing homes is often done during a rushed period when hospitals are seeking to discharge patients so that they can free up beds, making the choice of long-term care services less deliberative and careful. In addition, because relatives often want services provided at a geographic location close to them, the choice of facilities or other services may actually be quite limited, again lessening the amount of effective competition.

Issues in the design of a long-term care regulatory system

In designing regulatory systems for long-term care, countries must address a number of important issues, including defining what is meant by quality, deciding which providers will be subject to the regulation, establishing quality standards, providing incentives for providers to do more than meet minimum standards, obtaining timely information about the quality of care provided, enforcing regulations in a way that obtains compliance and deciding what information about regulatory performance should be made available to the public.

Given the characteristics of long-term care, the domains of quality are often divided into quality of care and quality of life. Although related, these domains are analytically separate and address separate parts of the care experience. In terms of quality of care, a major focus of long-term care regulation in the United States is on health and safety, including potential markers of poor quality such as dehydration, urinary tract infections, malnutrition, bedsores, excessive use of hypnotics and anti-psychotic medications, undertreatment of depression, weight loss and uncontrolled pain. For example, quality of care assessments include whether nursing homes carefully help residents with eating, whether there is adequate staffing to assist residents at mealtime and whether residents maintain an appropriate weight. The vast majority of existing regulations and quality measures focus on quality of care.

In contrast, quality of life refers to much more intangible factors, such as autonomy, dignity, individuality, comfort, meaningful activity and relationships, a sense of security, and spiritual well-being (National Citizens' Coalition for Nursing Home Reform, 1985; Noelker and Harel, 2000). These factors are, by definition, subjective, but they are critical to living a good and meaningful life. For example, quality of life refers to the tastiness of the food, the ability to choose meals that fit with personal preferences and ethnic heritage, the friendliness and patience of the staff helping with feeding and the willingness of the staff to let residents feed themselves to the extent possible, even if it takes additional time.

Foreword xxi

An important hypothesis articulated by some advocates of assisted living and consumer-directed services is that there may be a trade-off between quality of care and quality of life (Kane, 2001, 2003). Kane (2001) argues that for most people a meaningful quality of life is more important than health and safety. Thus, for example, an individual with diabetes at the end of life may want to eat candy because it tastes good, even though doing so is medically undesirable. The negotiated risk agreements in some assisted living facilities in the United States, where informed consumers or their agents explicitly accept risks and the possibility of adverse outcomes to achieve quality of life goals, are an effort to address these trade-offs (Jenkens et al., 2006).

Almost all countries devote far greater resources to monitoring nursing homes and other institutional providers than they allocate to home care and other community services. Reflecting funding limitations and the greater vulnerability of people in institutions, it also reflects the greater difficulty of regulating quality in home- and community-based services: the range of services is great with a great multiplicity of types of providers; users are, by definition, highly geographically dispersed, making data collection difficult and expensive; and there is less consensus on what the standards should be. In the United States, this lack of consensus is exacerbated by a belief by some policy analysts that nursing home standards are rigid and interfere with quality of life; thus, there is a strong policy desire not to replicate those standards in the home- and community-based setting (Kane, 2001).

A key task is establishing the quality standards that providers must meet. In the United States, federal and state regulations emphasize inputs, manuals, paperwork and structural capacity rather than resident outcomes. Critics contend that regulations are usually not evidence-based and do not measure what is important. These observers blame much of the poor quality of life in nursing facilities on rigid regulations, which force a 'medical model' on nursing homes.

A major element of the political economy of regulation is that many proposals for improving the quality of long-term care – for example, requiring higher staffing levels – require substantially more financial resources than governments are willing to spend. Thus, providers contend that it is unfair for governments to insist on high-quality care when they are unwilling to pay for the staffing and other inputs necessary to make it happen.

Most regulations establish the minimum that providers must do; in other words, they set a floor on provider activity. Opponents of stricter regulation also argue that detailed rules stifle innovation, with few incentives for doing more than the minimum. The dilemma is how to give good-quality facilities more flexibility while still requiring substandard facilities to meet adequate standards.

Setting standards is important, but standards are meaningless unless regulators are able to monitor how providers are performing against them. In many countries, regulators often do not have adequate resources to even visit all providers on a regular basis. The United States, for example, had 15,678 nursing facilities in 2012 (American Health Care Association, 2013), 31,100 residential care facilities in 2010 (Park et al., 2011), 10,581 home health agencies in 2009 (National Association for Home Care, 2010), and an unknown but large number of non-skilled home care agencies and consumer-hired individual personal care providers, making just visiting providers a daunting task. Infrequent visits mean that providers may perform when visited by regulators, but provide substandard care when government inspectors are not around. Limited funding for inspections in many countries means that providers are visited infrequently, raising questions of how effective the monitoring oversight can be. The infrequency of the inspections has led consumer advocates to argue for more resources and to search for strategies that do not depend on the constant presence of inspectors.

Different countries have adopted varying strategies to enforce regulations. However, without enforcement, the standards are meaningless. For some countries, such as the United States and England, enforcing regulations is a classic policing function in which providers who do not meet the regulatory requirements are identified and punished. In other countries, the relationship between providers and inspectors is more collaborative and the role of inspectors is more to work with providers to resolve problems. Advocates of strong government regulation argue that enforcement remains too weak and that stronger regulation would greatly improve quality of care.

Although regulatory sanctions are meant to punish the owners or administrators of poor-quality nursing facilities, it is hard to avoid 'punishing' the residents at the same time. For example, closing a facility may require the relocation of a large number of residents, which is hard to achieve because of relatively high nursing home occupancy rates in most countries, and which will cause disruption to residents' lives and

Foreword   xxiii

social relations. Likewise, 'intermediate sanctions', such as freezing new admissions or imposing civil fines, may result in reduced cash payments to facilities that may need to be spending more money on staff and other services. This inability to separate nursing homes from their residents is a major constraint on the willingness of regulators to impose tough sanctions on poor-quality facilities.

One increasingly prominent approach to improving quality of care is to provide more information to consumers, their families, providers, hospital discharge planners and others about the quality of individual long-term care providers (US Centers for Medicare and Medicaid Services, 2012). The underlying premise is that the lack of information on quality results in a market failure. The basic assumption of this approach is that, armed with more information about quality of care, consumers will choose high-quality providers and avoid poor-quality providers. Thus, in theory, market competition for residents and clients would force poor-performing providers to improve their quality of care or go out of business. Hospital discharge planners, case managers and others involved in the placement process could also use the information to advise individuals needing services and their families. Providers could also use the information to identify areas for improvement. Many countries are now exploring this strategy, although providers generally resist releasing information to the public about the performance of individual providers. Although there is widespread support for providing more information to consumers, the research literature on the consumer response to quality of care information for long-term care finds only modest positive effects (US Centers for Medicare and Medicaid Services, 2012).

Conclusion

For people who use long-term care services, the quality of the care they receive is critically important, and in some cases can be the difference between life and death. Too often, quality of care is like what we ourselves would want to receive if we needed care. Government regulation is one strategy to try to ensure that all providers supply at least a minimally adequate level of care. Throughout the world, these strategies are evolving, and in many countries expanding to home- and community-bases services that were never before regulated. This book provides an invaluable examination of how fourteen countries regulate the quality of long-term care services. The hope of cross-national analyses is that countries will learn from each other and improve services to people with functional and cognitive impairments who need long-term care services.

Joshua M. Wiener, PhD
Distinguished Fellow and Program Director for Aging, Disability and Long-Term Care at RTI International.[1]

References

American Healthcare Association (2013). LTS Stats: nursing facility operational characteristics report, December 2012. Washington, DC. Available at: www.ahcancal.org/research_data/oscar_data/Nursing per cent20Facility per cent20Operational per cent20Characteristics/LTC +STATS_PVNF_OPERATIONS_2012Q4_FINAL.pdf.

European Commission (2012). The 2012 aging report: economic and budgetary projections for the 27 EU member states (2010–2060). Brussels: European Union. Available at: http://ec.europa.eu/economy_finance/publications/european_economy/2012/2012-ageing-report_en.htm.

Goffman, E. (1961). Asylums: Essays on the Social Situation of Mental Patients and Other Inmates. New York: Random House.

Harrington, C., Carrillo, H., Dowdell, M., Tang, P.P. and Blank, B.W. (2011). Nursing facilities, staffing, residents and facility deficiencies, 2005 through 2010. San Francisco: University of California, San Francisco. Available at: www.theconsumervoice.org/sites/default/files/OSCAR-2011-final.pdf.

Jenkens, R., O'Keeffe, J., Carder, P. and Brown-Wilson, K. (2006). A study of negotiated risk agreements in assisted living facilities: Final report. Washington, DC: Office of the Assistant Secretary for Planning and Evaluation. Available at: http://aspe.hhs.gov/daltcp/reports/2006/negrisk.htm.

Johnson, R.W., Toomey, D., and Wiener, J.M. (2007). Meeting the long-term care needs of the baby boomers: how changing families will affect paid helpers and institutions. Washington, DC: The Urban Institute. Available at: www.urban.org/UploadedPDF/311451_Meeting_Care.pdf.

Kane, R.A. (2001). Long-term care and a good quality of life: bringing them closer together. *The Gerontologist*, 41(3): 293–304.

---

[1] RTI International is a large, non-profit research institute in the United States.

Foreword

(2003). Definition, measurement, and correlates of quality of life in nursing homes: Toward a reasonable practice, research, and policy agenda. *The Gerontologist*, 43 (Special Issue II): 28–36.

LaPlante, M., Kaye, H. S., Kang, T. and Harrington, C. (2004). Unmet need for personal assistance services: estimating the shortfall in hours of help and adverse consequences. *Journal of Gerontology B: Psychological and Social Sciences*, 59(2): S98–S108.

National Association for Home Care (2010). Basic statistics about home care. Washington, DC. Available at: www.nahc.org/assets/1/7/10HC_Stats. pdf.

National Citizens' Coalition for Nursing Home Reform (1985). A Consumer perspective on quality care: the residents' point of view. Washington, DC: National Citizens' Coalition for Nursing Home Reform. Available at: www.theconsumervoice.org/sites/default/files/resident_pers.pdf.

Noelker, L. S., and Harel, Z. (eds.) (2000). Quality of Life and Quality of Care in Long-Term Care. New York: Springer Publishing Company.

Organization for Economic Co-operation and Development (2005). Long-Term Care for Older People. Paris: OECD.

(2006). Projecting OECD health and long-term care expenditures: What are the main drivers? Economics Department Working Paper No. 477. Paris: Organization for Economic Co-operation and Development. Available at: www.oecd.org/tax/public-finance/36085940.pdf.

Park-Lee, E., Caffrey, C., Sengupta, M., Moss, A. J., Rosenoff, E., Harris-Kojetin, L. D. (2011). Residential care facilities: a key sector in the spectrum of long-term care providers in the United States. NCHS data brief, no 78. Hyattsville, MD: National Center for Health Statistics. Available at: www.cdc.gov/nchs/data/databriefs/db78.pdf.

US Administration on Aging (2011). 2010 National Ombudsman Reporting System data tables. Washington, DC. Available at: www.aoa.gov/aoa_p rograms/elder_rights/Ombudsman/National_State_Data/2010/Index. aspx.

US Census Bureau (2009). International database. Washington, DC. Available at: www.census.gov/ipc/www/idb/index.php.

US Centers for Medicare and Medicaid Services (2010). Nursing home data compendium, 2010 edition. Baltimore, MD. Retrieved from: www.cms. gov/Medicare/Provider-Enrollment-and-Certification/Certificationand Complianc/downloads/nursinghomedatacompendium_508.pdf.

(2012). Report to Congress: Plan to implement Medicare skilled nursing facility value-based purchasing program. Available at: www.cms.gov/ Medicare/Medicare-Fee-for-Service-Payment/SNFPPS/Downloads/SNF-VBP-RTC.pdf.

Walsh, E. G., Wiener, J. M., Haber, S., Bragg, A., Freiman, M., and Ouslander, J. G. (2012). Potentially avoidable hospitalizations of dually eligible Medicare/Medicaid beneficiaries from nursing facility and home- and community-based services waiver programs. *Journal of the American Geriatric Society*, 60(5): 821–9.

Wiener, J. M., Freiman, M. P., and Brown, D. (2007a). Strategies for improving the quality of long-term care. Washington, DC: National Commission for Quality Long-Term Care. Available at: www.newschool.edu/ltcc/pdf/NCQLTC_QualityReport_RTI_Final.pdf.

Wiener, J. M., Tilly, J., Cuellar, A. E., Howe, A., Doyle, C., Campbell, J., and Ikegami, N. (2007b). Quality assurance for long-term care: the experiences of England, Australia, Germany, and Japan. Washington, DC: AARP Public Policy Institute. Available at: http://assets.aarp.org/rgcenter/il/2007_05_ltc.pdf.

PART I

Introduction

1 A framework for understanding regulation of long-term care quality

VINCENT MOR

1.1 Introduction

Periodically, in most developed countries there are scandals reported in the press regarding poor treatment of frail elders living in residential care settings purportedly supervised by governmental authorities. While far more prevalent in the aggressive and adversarial legal environment in the US, scandals have been documented in England, Switzerland, Japan, Korea and China (Xinhua, 2005, 2007, 2008; Ferguson, 2012; Association TP, 2012). These instances represent an indictment of the regulatory bodies charged with insuring that adequate standards of care are maintained but also reflect the public outrage associated with authorities' 'allowing' such scandalous situations. Indeed, the outrage is as strong in countries where the regulation of elder care services is new as it is in societies where it is more established.

Such scandals violate social norms of filial piety, which are strong in most societies, but they also violate our expectations that the social institutions and arrangements we have come to trust have let us down, with significant consequences for the lives of the frail elderly who depend upon society for their care. Whether these expectations are warranted or not is not the point. However, they call into question our assumptions about how society should be meeting the needs of the frail and the elderly. Social commentaries on these scandals tend to have a particularly parochial perspective, assuming that the structure of regulation, oversight and financing of long-term care services that exist within a country are necessarily unique. Since failures to adequately care for the most vulnerable among us often are used as an excuse to make political or ideological points, the resulting discussions are often superficial without any real analysis of the fundamental assumptions underlying regulatory structures that govern long-term care service providers. However, demography and the different approaches that countries have adopted vis-à-vis financing long-term care have conspired to bring the issue of how societies assure the quality of those services to the forefront.

This chapter provides a framework for understanding the origins and regulatory structure of each of the country case studies included in this volume. After considering the historical basis of regulation in this sector, I review the functions any system of elder care regulation must address, followed by a discussion of the alternative regulatory philosophies and their application in long-term care. Since regulation is a quintessential government function, where the agency charged with regulating long-term care is situated with respect to the levers of power is an important characteristic of societies' investment in regulation, as is the extent to which it enlists the assistance of other social institutions like the professions and relevant non-governmental organizations in pursuing its agenda of assuring quality of care. Since the role of the market as a self-regulating force has received increasing attention in many circles, the chapter closes with a discussion of how market forces can reinforce, or counteract, the actions of the regulator.

1.2 Historical basis for the regulation of elder care

Conceptually, a regulatory apparatus consists of rules governing which entities, individuals or organizations can provide services of a particular type (Day and Klein, 1987). Most modern states govern which kinds of individuals and groups of individuals are allowed to assume responsibility for frail and impaired individuals thought to be unable to protect themselves from unscrupulous groups who might take advantage of their weaknesses. The state assumes responsibility for protecting such individuals for the same reasons it protects the public by requiring physicians to have a licence before they can minister to the sick by diagnosing, prescribing and operating. The informal caregiving network of family and friends need not have a licence to perform caregiving precisely because the state assumes that these informal relationships will have the best interest of the frail and impaired individual at heart. Things become more ambiguous when neighbours and others, not formally licensed to provide long-term care services, assume caregiving roles in exchange for either short-term or long-term economic considerations. Regardless of such ambiguity, the state has an interest in the regulation of transactions between individuals or organizations that purport to serve frail and impaired individuals since those individuals and their families may not be able to advocate for themselves (Braithwaite, 2002).

Historically, caring for the frail has been a family, or tribal, responsibility. Up until the time of the epidemiological transition and the beginning of population ageing, the prevalence of frail older persons in society was low and their survival time limited since neither the existing social structure nor medical knowledge were conducive to the extended survival of the elderly once they became frail (National Research Council, 1988).[1] As more older people survived to become frail, the challenge of caring for them inevitably fell to women of the younger generation as a universal obligation with innumerable exemplars from world literature. Only wealthier families were able to employ others to assist in this caregiving function. The notion that states would regulate who was hired to care for a family member was as unheard of as the state regulating the hiring and firing of domestic workers.

It is only with migration and population ageing, causing elders to be left behind to fend for themselves, that formal caregiving organizations arose. Obviously, societies have always included childless individuals, those incapable of earning their keep and/or who became impoverished due to illness, mental or physical. The Anglo-Saxon tradition of the 'poor house' or other community institutions filled that role as governmental or quasi-governmental entities serving a charitable function (Talbott, 1981; Brundage, 2002). In other European countries religious societies served this charitable function and even in the early years of communist China, local governments were charged with the responsibility of caring for the destitute, who were unable to work and who had no families. Societies' expectations of these facilities were quite limited and it was widely acknowledged that these were undesirable places, housing the least fortunate, who were, nonetheless, lucky to be receiving the minimal levels of care provided (Sherwood and Mor, 1980).

The rise of specialized facilities serving the frail elderly whose families could not care for them emerged largely from sectarian traditions in most Western societies (www.elderweb.com/book/export/html/2806). Catholic charities, Lutheran homes and Jewish homes for the aged,

---

[1] The epidemiological transition began when infectious diseases were no longer the primary cause of death and chronic illnesses such as diabetes and heart disease became more prevalent as a higher proportion of the population reached advanced age.

along with various 'benevolent societies', emerged in the latter part of the nineteenth century, providing culturally focused residential services sustained by community philanthropy and private fees paid from residents' savings and families' income. In Switzerland, local monasteries operated 'hospices' which included care for the elderly but gradually local communities (cantons) took over these functions. Like hospitals which preceded them, the emergence of this class of service providers was accompanied by the development of some form of licensure, even if only because the facilities served meals and had to comply with public health and hygiene laws. In parallel with this more formalized approach to elder care, in most communities an informal market of caregivers arose among landladies or boarding home operators, who increased their level of service as their elderly boarders grew more frail, or among housekeepers, who provided personal care in addition to cooking and cleaning. To the extent that such informal arrangements became more public or commercial, they could have been subject to licensure, but rarely were.

Societal ageing, falling birth rates and geographic and economic mobility among the young, particularly to urban centres from villages, resulted in elders increasingly living alone. In Spain, over the last several decades, the proportion of the elderly population living alone has nearly doubled and China's one-child policy has only reinforced this natural tendency toward urban migration. The net result is that the elderly are increasingly living outside of traditional multi-generational households in rapidly modernizing countries like South Korea, Japan and China. Even in Germany and other European countries that went through the demographic transition some time ago, the proportion of the population over 65 has exceeded 20 per cent and many of these individuals live alone.

While not universally true, the movement from informal arrangements to more formalized regulatory structures seems to be accelerated when governments begin to finance these services. Financing can refer to either construction assistance or operating subsidies in the form of payments to residents (and therefore to providers) or both. For example, in the US, when state and federal governments wanted to stimulate the supply of nursing home beds, low-interest loans were made available and the cost-based reimbursement system served to encourage many to enter the market as long-term care providers. Interestingly, China, which has a limited institutional long-term care system which the government would like to expand, also offers two approaches to supporting nursing home providers: first by offering a financial subsidy per bed built and secondly by subsidizing providers per occupied bed, irrespective of the wealth or need of the resident. Regardless of type of financing support, social expectations of these services change because of the change in the behaviour of providers in response to the availability of funding for activities that had previously been undertaken informally. Indeed, the impact of public financing alters the market quite dramatically; in most societies that have instituted some form of public financing for long-term care a new group of providers enters the mix and the existing providers alter their activities in order to become eligible for public support. This growth of long-term care providers has generally been the stimulus for wholesale revisions to regulations designed to assure the quality of care frail older persons receive, at least partially, to insure that public funds are properly spent.

1.3 The structure of regulatory functions

A useful heuristic device is to divide the regulatory functions that govern long-term care providers into three broad domains: 1) standard setting and initial inspection and licensure; 2) ongoing surveillance and enforcement; and 3) reporting and/or rewarding performance. Each function has various components, which vary both in structure and approach, as will be evident in the country studies included in this volume. The structure of a country's regulatory function is informed by a philosophical or ideological position regarding whether the regulator acts as the police monitoring compliance or as a partner striving to achieve the ultimate goal of assuring quality.

Establishing Provider Standards determines what it takes to be able to offer long-term care services to the public and includes how the provider goes about obtaining a licence. In many professional fields like medicine and nursing, the state delegates to the profession the task of setting standards precisely because they have the expertise to determine what the standards should be (Kovner and Jonas, 2002). Thus, medical professionals are generally granted licensure upon completion of the agreed-upon educational requirements that were established by the profession itself. Since historically elder care was a social and/or residential service rather than a medical service, setting standards for long-term care services was not delegated to established medical professions. Rather, regulations governing standards for issuing a licence were formulated by a combination of professionals, advocates, engaged politicians and representatives of the provider community. While national regulation of long-term care is relatively young, England has had regulation since 1927 under a social welfare model. However, as the needs of those receiving long-term care evolved and become increasingly medically complex, the weight given to clinical issues versus social issues often changes the standards and requirements for being a long-term care provider. In some instances, different regulations apply for different kinds of providers depending on the types of residents served and the range of services provided.

Standards commonly address the structural features a provider must meet in order to obtain licensure. These include aspects of the physical environment ranging from fire and safety concerns to room size and services and common space available as well as the number, training and education of the staff caring for the service recipients. Standards may also dictate specific processes of care that providers must ensure, generally related to the documentation of services rendered. These can take the form of documenting the frequency with which staff apply creams and/or turn bed-bound residents to prevent pressure ulcers. In some instances standards may also offer patient outcomes to which providers should aspire, such as the 'maximum rehabilitation potential' enshrined in the US Nursing Home Reform Act of 1987 (Institute of Medicine, Committee on Nursing Home Regulation, 1986). Patient outcome domains of salience can range from clinical care provided, such as the occurrence of skin pressure ulcers or uncontrolled pain, to quality of life or even satisfaction with the quality of patients and/or their family members' experience. In this way the patients' experience can become an integral part of the quality assessment process, in spite of the many technical challenges associated with doing this well (Mor, 2005).

In addition to establishing standards that providers must meet, regulations also stipulate how applications to become licensed providers are reviewed and inspections are to be undertaken as part of the licensure and certification process. In some cases the first step in obtaining licensure is to prove that there is a need for the service, irrespective of whether standards are met. Depending upon numerous factors, in some instances the state may have an interest in restraining the supply of services, either to minimize duplication or to stimulate demand, that is thought to ultimately end up costing the state more than would otherwise be the case (Rivlin et al., 1988). While the wisdom of policies designed to constrain supply has been questioned, the state does have an interest in ensuring that only qualified providers receive licensure and/or certification. As such, the application process along with the associated review and on-site inspection can be prolonged with multiple steps in the process. In those countries in which licensure or certification carries with it the right to seek reimbursement for eligible service recipients, the oversight and review process necessary before a licence is granted may be even more tightly controlled. Indeed, in countries like Germany, Japan, England and the US requirements for payment are commensurate with quality regulations.

In some instances licensure or certification may be provisional for some period of time to allow for ongoing observation of how the provider operates and meets residents' needs. In order to begin serving frail older persons an operator must have a licence but inspectors can only observe care being delivered *after* the licence is issued, making it reasonable to grant provisional licences. The rush of applications that frequently accompany wholesale regulatory changes can result in a backlog of provider applications which, without a provisional licence, means that providers' investments in staff and facilities cannot be recouped since no residents can be admitted. In England, there is a requirement that the regulatory agency must conduct a complete inspection within a fixed period of time following the filing of the application, but in actuality this can be more prolonged.

Nonetheless, once a service is operational it is as difficult to close it even after only several months of operation as it is after several years, since individual service recipients will necessarily experience the disruption of a transition to a new provider. Unfortunately, since a flood of new providers often enters the market immediately following the introduction of long-term care financing, the time and effort needed to scrutinize prospective providers are frequently unavailable just when they are needed most. It is for this reason that standards are often adhered to more rigidly in the initial application process than in subsequent inspections. This means that there can be a fine line between standard setting and initial inspection and the next stage of ongoing monitoring and enforcement.

Ongoing Monitoring and Enforcement represents a broad range of functions and choices, ranging from the frequency and scope of inspections to the means by which sanctions are applied and whether and how they can be appealed. Monitoring of providers' compliance with standards theoretically begins as soon as the licence is issued, but in actuality it begins when the first repeat inspection is undertaken. The frequency with which inspections are conducted is generally explicitly mandated in regulations. In some instances, inspectors have the discretion to inspect providers that have a good record less often and to inspect chronically poor performing providers more often. In view of the substantial costs incurred by the regulator and provider in preparing for and executing an inspection under most regulatory regimes, more frequent inspection is viewed as a significant adverse event.

The composition and character of the inspection team is also relevant. While most inspections are conducted by teams, almost invariably one of these individuals is an experienced nurse familiar with long-term care services. Other professionals included might be someone with a background in environmental engineering or a dietician or long-term care pharmacist. It is often the case that inspections are supposed to be unannounced, even though they tend to occur around the anniversary of the previous one. In some cases it is desirable to alter the composition of the inspection team between inspections to insure a 'fresh' pair of eyes, but that may depend on the enforcement philosophy and the range of alternatives available.

The literature on regulation differentiates between compliance-based and deterrence-based regulation, with the latter focused on rigid adherence to the precise strictures of standards while the former adopts more of an informal dispute resolution approach (Day and Klein, 1987). It is during the inspection process that this difference in philosophy is most apparent since adherents to the deterrence approach would necessarily follow a much more formalized inspection protocol. Indeed, the centralized US Medicare/Medicaid nursing home recertification inspection process (even though delegated to the states) has become increasingly proscriptive over the last several decades, precisely to minimize individual inspector discretion. While the advantage of this approach is greater specificity and explicit focus, some believe that it results in compliance with the 'letter' of the law rather than with its spirit since the latter cannot be 'observed and documented'. Indeed, some would argue that the natural result of the deterrence approach is a counting game that serves no real purpose and does not necessarily translate into superior quality (Day and Klein, 1987). On the other hand, the disadvantage of

A framework for understanding regulation of long-term care quality   11

the compliance-based approach is precisely the degree of variability in what constitutes an infraction that is reported or which stimulates a fine. Major changes to the documentation of inspections and adherence to the regulations in England have largely been associated with differences of opinion regarding how much discretion inspectors should have.

In addition to regularly scheduled inspections, most regulations include a complaint process, one aspect of which is to require timely complaint investigations. Complaint systems are highly variable and in some cases may be completely independent of the regular inspection process. However, since anyone can lodge a complaint, including 'disgruntled' staff, regulators first authenticate all but the most extreme complaints before investing in the effort to launch an inspection (Stevenson, 2006). How the results of complaint-based inspections are integrated into those emanating from regularly scheduled inspections is another important consideration since the basis for the two kinds of inspections may be quite different. That is, inspections stimulated by a complaint are for 'cause' and have more focus than regularly scheduled reinspections. Complaint-based inspections focus on the source of the complaint and seek to substantiate it and to document it and to find problems related to the same domain of performance as the complaint. Complaint systems in England draw in a local government ombudsman, who is independent of the regulatory authority, which has no role in dispute resolution related to consumers' complaints.

Having identified regulatory non-compliance or violations of standards during inspections, the next significant question is how the regulator responds. Ultimately, violations of the rules may be grounds for decertification or revocation of the operating licence. However, this drastic step is rarely taken unless there is chronic poor performance and indications of malfeasance (Angelelli et al., 2003). Theoretically, there exists a wide suite of alternative and graduated sanctions possible in response to failures observed during inspection. Fines can be imposed, solutions to observed quality problems can be mandated within a certain period, the facility can be closed to new admissions and/or reimbursements withheld (in those countries which have public financing). Braithwaite (2002) advocates the use of the 'regulatory pyramid' as a model to guide the imposition of sanctions. The base of the pyramid, or most common action, is for the regulator to persuade the operator to comply with the standard they violated, after which, if still not in compliance, they are sent a warning letter followed by a civil penalty, such as a fine. Only after the imposition of fines are legal proceedings instituted with an eye toward revoking the provider's licence.

While this graduated approach seems quite reasonable, in fact each step can take considerable time and effort on the regulators' part since each complaint must be documented and, depending upon the processes stipulated in the regulations and the litigiousness of the society, there may be appeals to administrative judges at each step. The result may be that regulators can only proceed down the formal path of warnings and legal action for the most egregious quality problems observed among providers with a history of poor performance. Otherwise, actions taken in response to 'minor' violations may be merely negotiated as part of a persuasion process.

In light of the high cost of regulatory action, theorists have suggested 'risk-based regulation', which conditions the intensity and frequency of inspections on the past performance of the provider (Phipps et al., 2011). Operating on the assumption that the best predictor of the future is the past, a risk-based approach to regulation sets a threshold of risk that allows regulators to skip a regularly scheduled inspection if a provider has not exhibited any significant quality deficits during an earlier inspection. Additionally, other factors such as leadership or ownership changes might alter the provider's risk profile, overriding prior positive reinforcement. Risk-based regulation necessarily relies upon historical inspection data and, as such, resembles giving good performers a 'good driver' discount, which is a common practice in setting automobile insurance premiums. This requires retaining the data from prior inspections and using it to stratify the intensity of subsequent inspections or other regulatory actions. Additionally, it requires having exceptions built into the laws on which the regulations are based and is supported by the existence of explicit criteria as to what constitutes performance that is so good the provider can be exempted from future inspections. The term 'risk-based' is apt since the volatility of leadership tenure in the long-term care arena and the critical importance of leadership in setting the tone vis-à-vis quality of care means that past performance by no means perfectly predicts the future. It is likely, but not known, that in regulatory structures that permit considerable local discretion, such risk-based monitoring occurs naturally.

Reporting and Rewarding Performance is a relatively recent tool in the regulators' repertoire. Reporting providers' quality performance implicitly relies upon social forces that are extra-legal in nature. Public reporting of providers' quality problems or the results of recent inspections means that prospective consumers and their advocates might rely upon this information in selecting a long-term care provider. Use of this information to shape choices brings market forces to bear, which can reinforce the regulators' perceptions and inspection-based actions. Even if consumers and their advocates neither understand nor use this information to select providers, the reports can still change provider behaviour since peer pressure is such that most providers do not want to be publicly shamed. Indeed, there is some evidence that socially induced competition is as powerful as is market competition (Werner and Liang, 2012).

A prerequisite to reporting provider performance is documentation, either the results of inspections or other systematically collected quality measures. While almost all countries with long-term care providers have some form of regulatory structure, even among the more longstanding or sophisticated regulatory systems, it is not necessarily the norm to consistently record the detailed results of inspections. For example, in England, while there are national standards and guidelines, even in the face of the repeated changes in the regulatory structure over the last decade, until recently there has been no change in the longstanding practice of allowing local health authorities considerable leeway in how the results of inspections are documented (Day and Klein, 1987).

Consistent reporting requires a consistent inspection protocol and a consistent interpretation of what constitutes the violation of a standard. As such, focus on documentation of the inspection process and its results in a manner that could stand up to the scrutiny to which it would be subjected were the information publicly reported necessarily means that local, and even individual, inspector discretion cannot be tolerated. Since the consultative and negotiated change approach is predicated on such discretion, it may not be a surprise that public reporting of performance on inspections is not widely used, at least in the countries included in this volume.

It is possible to assemble systematic data about aspects of the providers' performance that is not based upon inspection results. The outcome measurement movement in some countries has introduced systematic assessment of care recipients primarily to inform the caregivers about the services frail older people need. However, this information, if systematically coded, can be used to create aggregated measures of the proportion of individual service recipients who are, for example, in pain, or have a pressure ulcer. Since these systems must be standardized across providers in a district or country, it is possible that providers can be compared on the basis of such aggregated performance measures, irrespective of whether these measures are correlated with inspection results (Mor, 2004). Indeed, some have argued that such quality measures are a more valid and consistent approach to measuring quality than are the results of inspections (Kane et al., 1998). Nonetheless, in Switzerland and Finland, both of which have voluntary systems for measuring residents' outcomes, there has been little appetite among providers to make these data public. In Canada and New Zealand, such outcome-based systems are in place but, to date, there has been relatively little movement towards making these data public.

In those countries that provide public financing for long-term care providers' services, it is possible to use information about quality performance to reward those providers that achieve the highest performance, or which exhibit the greatest improvement in quality, or some combination of the two. This is a relatively new endeavour and there have only been a relatively small number of experiments, generally in the US, although the US is not the only country that has the information upon which to base a 'pay-for-performance' programme (Mor et al., 2009). Clearly, basing financial rewards on quality scores with known measurement error that can never completely account for differences in the mix of frail older persons served carries with it considerable risk, both technical and political. In the various experiments undertaken in the US using this kind of approach, it is interesting that, in the end, the rewards were less substantial than originally planned since the level of new funding made available was ultimately viewed as having been extracted from what would have been a larger industry-wide inflation-adjusted increase in reimbursement levels (Werner and Lang, 2012).

1.4 The role of regulated professionals in long-term care regulation

Regulation of the 'professions' is often incorporated into countries' long-term care regulatory structure by reference. The domain of professional regulation is generally delegated to professional societies of physicians, nurses, accountants, etc. and this often evolves in conjunction with the emergence of formalized professional education to which government regulation cedes the authority for certifying competence as

A framework for understanding regulation of long-term care quality 15

a prerequisite for licensure. Society has an interest in ceding oversight of professional behaviour to groups of similar professionals vested with the knowledge to judge what is and is not outside the norm of professional standards for that profession. By ceding this authority, society signals that it trusts the professionals and their specialized institutions to serve society's interests and not merely their own. Since care homes for the frail and elderly were often not seen as entailing a 'skilled' or 'professional' set of tasks and functions, associations of providers were more likely to have been viewed representing the industry and its commercial interests, and, as such, were less trusted than the professionals. Nonetheless, as skilled professions were incorporated, by reference, into long-term care regulations, some societies reframed their trust of elder care services, trusting that the professional ethics of those in charge would serve to uphold the high standards of their profession in the context of the long-term care service sector as it does in a hospital.

In Japan, professional associations of nurses have had extensive influence over long-term care regulations, setting minimum staffing standards, stipulating the kinds of training those working in long-term care had to have and differentiating the roles of the different kinds of institutional long-term care providers that are regulated in the country. In Austria, national efforts at quality assurance and quality improvement in regulated homes for the aged depend almost entirely on the initiative of the professional associations of nurses and of facility administrators.

With greater credence placed upon the role of professionals in the operation and management of elder care services, it might seem presumptuous if regulations were too proscriptive since this would implicitly question the judgement of the professionals in charge. Since there is a long tradition of granting discretion to professionals in the face of ambiguous clinical decisions where evidence of what the correct approach is does not exist, the more that professionals are incorporated into the structure of the long-term care service sector, the more likely the regulations will resemble those in hospitals, with more focus on documentation of decisions rather than merely compliance with externally proscribed rules.

Thus, comparing countries' different approaches to regulating the quality of long-term care requires that one understand the relative importance of professionals in setting standards and the level of trust each society attributes to these professionals. In countries like the US, Canada, New Zealand and Australia, where long-term care is considered to be 'second class' among the nursing and medical professionals and there is a stronger commercial tradition around the provision of long-term care services, government is less likely to delegate discretionary care decisions to professionals than is the case in hospitals and physicians' practices.

1.5 Organization of elder care service regulations

In formulating a regulatory structure to govern how long-term care providers are licensed and inspected, governments face numerous choices and challenges in terms of which bureaucracy has the authority, the requisite skills and experience and the level of control to adequately assure the quality of care provided to frail older persons. In the paragraphs below, the framework for each of these alternatives is discussed.

Centralization vs. Decentralization is a choice that is generally consistent with the overall structure of a country's government. Most countries have explicit regional authorities and in many cases this includes states, provinces, regions or cantons with considerable autonomy, along with authority structures that often replicate the organization of government departments at the national level. This is often enshrined in the national constitution and reflects the cultural heterogeneity of the country, with each region having some historical uniqueness. Regardless of whether these politically defined regions are constitutionally guaranteed or merely a long-standing administrative convenience, it is critical to understand their role in the formulation and implementation of regulations governing the licensure of long-term care services.

The interrelationship between the national and regional governmental levels as it applies to long-term care regulation can be highly varied. It is possible that 'guidelines' are set at the national level with each region being free to develop detailed regulations sensitive to their unique conditions and situation. Alternatively, the national government may establish regulations and standards that serve as a template for individualization by certain regions that may not have the experience or skill to develop laws and associated regulations anew but allows for substantial local autonomy. Finally, the nation state may be the source of regulatory authority, although regions are given the freedom and discretion to implement these national rules in a manner that is sensitive to local supply and demand circumstances.

A framework for understanding regulation of long-term care quality 17

The balance between centralization and decentralization of licensure authority and enforcement of the regulations can vary over time in the same way that federal authority may wax and wane relative to states' or regional rights. In some instances this may come about in response to scandals related to quality problems that catapult the issue of long-term care to the level of a national debate. This level of attention may be the stimulus for a rewrite of the laws, or a change in administrative procedures that emphasize greater national homogeneity of practice in order to avoid future scandals. This happens routinely in the US and seems to be at least partially in response to negative newspaper attention (Miller et al., 2013). Similar changes in the balance between centralized control and regional autonomy have been observed in England and Australia, where long-term care regulation became a federal responsibility some time ago.

In many countries financing long-term care is a national, or largely national, enterprise, but quality regulation may be a more complicated regional responsibility. Germany's mandatory long-term care insurance system is administered by health insurers but those applying do so within the constraints of the states' system and only state-approved providers can be reimbursed by the insurers. Less centralized, the national government in China establishes service development goals and approaches to funding existing and new facilities, but the regions are responsible for implementing and paying providers in a manner that is consistent with their resources. Obviously, less centralized systems will have greater variability than more centralized systems.

Adversarial vs. Consensual approaches to enforcement of regulations represents another important dimension by which regulatory structures can be characterized. Adversarial approaches tend to be associated with strict interpretations of standards and a 'letter of the law' approach. Inspections are guided by strict protocols from which regulators are not supposed to deviate in order to make sure that their ratings and associated sanctions are not overturned on appeal. The entire enterprise is infused with a legalistic quality. Indeed, inspectors might even be rotated in order to make sure that they do not become too familiar with the providers they inspect. In some jurisdictions in the US, the branch of the regulatory agency that includes the inspectors is housed separately (including in regional offices) from the office where case managers who support the clients served by the licensed providers are situated, precisely to keep the enforcement and client-support functions separate.

In England, the application of a risk-based approach to inspections means that local areas may be left to work out the quality problems identified by inspectors who do not have the detailed information necessary to document the deficiencies and to be able to defend them from appeal.

On the other side of the ledger, the consensual approach minimizes conflict and seeks to convince the provider to do the 'right thing' by adopting organizational and care practices that are consistent with the regulations. Inspectors offer consultation by drawing upon their experience of seeing numerous providers performing well. Under a consensual approach they offer this information to providers having difficulty adhering to the requisite standards. The goal is to improve care for the client and enforcing adherence to the regulations is done in such a way as to minimize disruption for the client, while maximizing the chance of improving care quality. Such a consultative approach places considerable discretion in the hands of the inspector or local regulator. This, in turn, means that there is considerably less consistency from district to district. This lack of consistency may reduce the ability of the regulatory authority to make enforcement sanctions 'stick' if they are appealed to an administrative law judge. Thus, the advantages of the consensual approach may evaporate when regulators are confronted with a provider who is unwilling or unable to adhere to the standards.

The long-term care regulatory structure in the Netherlands operates on a quasi-consultative model since inspectors have as their first response to a non-compliant provider the possibility of advising the provider and suggesting approaches that might be taken to overcome the quality problems observed during the inspection. While financial penalties and regulatory sanctions are also available, regulators begin with the premise that the providers want to improve the quality of their care.

Social Welfare vs. Healthcare Regulation. Another important issue is the determination of which bureaucracy is responsible for setting the standards and implementing the regulations, regardless of the level of government. The choice of whether to make the Health or Social Welfare Ministries responsible for long-term care services regulation is crucial in terms of the philosophy, skill set and relative importance of quality of care vs. quality of life. Historically, long-term care emerged from a social welfare model since the services rendered substituted for family care and support as well as for the income necessary to purchase services independently. In the US, prior to the advent of Medicare and

Medicaid financing of nursing home and home healthcare, some states licensed nursing homes from the same office that licensed hospitals while in other states this was done by the social welfare organizations that regulated foster homes or abuse cases (Mor et al., 1986). In China, which has many prodromal qualities that harken back to where many more developed countries were a half century ago, elder care homes are regulated by the Ministry of Social Welfare nationally and in each region and city. On the other hand, the many thousands of hospitals in China and the innumerable medical clinics operate under the auspices of the Department of Health. Since many community hospitals in China have extended lengths of stay of older patients who cannot return home, many of these hospitals have populations that look very much like those residing in Ministry of Social Welfare elder care homes. As can be seen in the country cases, there continues to be ambiguity about whether long-term care is predominantly a medical (health) service or a social service. Where a society stands on this particular issue may have profound implications for the approach to regulation and enforcement and certainly influences the relative importance of some provisions of the regulations more than others.

When long-term care is regulated by social welfare agencies there is likely to be less emphasis on clinical care requirements and the regulations are likely to be silent on the role of the physician and what the providers' responsibilities are vis-à-vis insuring that physicians' orders are carried out, since those are fundamentally medical care requirements. In Japan, while both nursing homes and homes for the aged have extensive requirements governing nurse and aide staffing levels, there is little in the way of requirements covering medical care. In the US, after Medicare/Medicaid began financing nursing home services, most states gradually began to shift the responsibility for regulation of nursing homes to the Department of Health, if it was not already located there. As another example of this split, it is still the case in many US states that Assisted Living Facilities (non-medical living arrangements offering personal care and supervision for which government financing is not available) are often regulated by the social welfare agency rather than the Department of Health.

With respect to the regulation of residential long-term care, there is considerable debate regarding the appropriateness of regulation by health or social service authorities. Advocates of the social welfare model note that regulation under the auspices of a healthcare authority 'medicalizes' what is otherwise a social service, placing safety and standardized medical care delivery over the value of autonomy and quality of life. On the other hand, as the average medical acuity and complexity of the resident population increases, the role of medical and nursing personnel takes precedence and the personnel required to care for the sicker patients are often more comfortable emphasizing medical rather than social values.

Regulation through Purchasing Power can have a profound effect on the nature of the relationship between regulator and regulated entity. The agency that reimburses the provider for many of the services rendered can have considerably more clout in enforcing compliance than is the case for an entity whose only authority lies in the licence that the service provider holds. The power of the purse affords the regulator a wide array of graduated financial sanctions otherwise unavailable to a regulator without reimbursement control. The results of quality inspections in the Netherlands go to the insurer, which could drop a provider from the list of authorized facilities, effectively closing them. Similarly, in Germany, insurers will not pay institutional providers under the long-term care insurance plan unless they are certified to have met quality standards for the state. In the US, Medicaid/Medicare regulations include orders to cease admitting new patients funded by these two payment sources.

The higher the proportion of revenue that is derived from the regulator the more dependent the provider is and the more responsive they must be. Interestingly, the authority of the purchaser is not always clear unless performance standards are written into the purchasing contracts or the conditions of participation in the programme. For example, it is possible that providers are licensed by a health authority but some of their clients are eligible for the service by virtue of social welfare eligibility. In this instance, if the social welfare agency discovers quality problems they may not have the authority to affect the provider's licence. Rather, they may be restricted to removing their client from the provider's service, which can be traumatic for the client and not be that consequential for the provider. Indeed, only if the social welfare agency supports a majority of the provider's clients does it have much influence over provider quality-related behaviour. The subtleties of the interrelationships between purchaser and regulator can be very influential and must be considered if one is to understand the impact of quality regulations on provider behaviours.

1.6 The role of extra-governmental regulators

State licensure is often conceived of as a 'minimal' standard to which all providers must conform. In a competitive market many providers aspire to be able to differentiate themselves from other providers. Austria, Germany, the Netherlands and Switzerland, among others, have seen the emergence of private, third-party associations to accredit, certify or rate the quality of providers. These groups claim expertise that the government regulatory authority does not have and their stamp of approval, which is voluntary, offers a quality ranking that government licensure does not offer. Some of these private, voluntary, quality rating agencies undertake inspections which form the basis for certification as a high-performing provider. As private entities, these organizations charge providers for the inspections. Some have argued that this makes it impossible for them to be impartial. Others argue that since these voluntary standards exceed those government licensure standards in terms of comprehensiveness and stringency, there is no need for government inspections if a provider has already obtained voluntary accreditation. In the US, the Joint Commission for the Accreditation of Health Care Organizations has acquired this kind of 'deemed' status for hospitals but not for nursing homes.

Provider organizations, or associations, are another source of self-regulation and offer staff training and other quality-improvement functions. However, as membership associations, they are not in a position to sanction members for poor performance. Indeed, since one of the primary functions of such associations is to intercede with government on behalf of its membership (generally advocating for higher reimbursement) their mission is to advocate for the entire membership. This is not to say that educational and quality improvement consortia which provider associations undertake are not useful – rather that they are incapable of serving a regulatory role as do the voluntary accreditation organizations.

Professional associations also play a role in enhancing care quality by focusing on continuing education of professionals and even creating professional certification. For example, nurses, the dominant professional group caring for long-term care clients, are served by nursing associations, often with specialty groups focused on long-term care nurses. These organizations offer regular continuing education, which is required to maintain licensure as a nurse in many countries, and in some locations specialty certification in long-term care nursing. In the case of nursing homes, managers who are not already nurses by profession may be required to have special training or certification as a qualified administrator. This is the case in Japan, Austria and Germany where nursing home standards for licensure require that the administrator carry certification in the same way that licensure requires a minimum number of nurses on staff and the type of nurses required are specified in nurse licensure laws. This cross-referencing of agency licensure standards and professional licensure requirements is another example of the interlocking nature of regulatory controls that often link government and extra-governmental standards.

In societies where there is limited 'trust' in government or a long history of scandals, advocacy groups and other watchdog groups have emerged to insure that government regulators are enforcing regulations or to push for new regulations and policies. These needn't be politically based organizations, although they generally favour more intensive enforcement. Rather, these are non-governmental organizations with a mission to protect the rights of the frail and disenfranchised who are unable to advocate for themselves. In some instances, local chapters of these organizations will field a cadre of volunteers to visit long-term care residents and file complaints on their behalf if conditions are inadequate. As noted, such complaints often stimulate inspections, which can be very costly for providers. Since providers must allow advocates entry to the facility, their presence acts as another form of quality assurance since it is in providers' interests to ensure that care meets regulatory standards. Indeed, some have argued that the best way to assure care quality is to have the buildings open to visitors and advocates who can observe how care is provided on an ongoing basis.

The importance attributed to having extra 'eyes and ears' monitoring care quality is institutionalized in some countries. In England, there is a government-funded, but independent, ombudsman who visits facilities and has private conversations with residents and has the authority to lodge independent complaints. A similar structure exists in the US with states funding individuals who advocate for the needs of the frail elderly in institutional care. This entails state agencies employing individuals as advocates for the elderly who fulfil these functions. In essence the ombudsman programme reinforces the inspectors' roles, partially 'checking' on them and partially extending their observational reach (Estes et al., 2012).

A framework for understanding regulation of long-term care quality   23

In summary, in addition to explicit governmental roles, there are a variety of different 'interest groups' that contribute to the political context in which the regulation of care for the frail and elderly occurs. In some instances, government actually funds these extra-governmental forces as an explicit antidote to the complacency that often arises among inspectors charged with enforcing regulations.

1.7 Transparency, public scrutiny and the role of the market

Historically government regulators have not published the results of their inspections of provider quality. This means that there is limited public information about the range of quality among providers, reducing the need for providers to compete on quality. The rationale behind publicly reporting the results of inspections is to provide information to consumers and their advocates that could be useful in their choice of provider. Obviously, this is only useful if the information reported is more detailed than merely indicating whether the provider 'passed' the inspection! However, as noted earlier, this is precisely the problem: reporting greater detail requires that the information be consistent, otherwise providers presented in a bad light may challenge the results as being idiosyncratic.

In spite of concerns about consistency, transparent reporting of quality problems such as the results of inspections, the numbers of complaints or even more detailed performance reporting opens providers to 'shame and blame'. Being subject to public scrutiny may possibly make them more responsive to negotiated settlements under a collaborative enforcement model, particularly if poor performance scores are made public even while they are appealed. However, the details may be difficult to work out in this manner, depending upon whether the legal system favours the government or those making the appeals.

Public reporting of quality engenders competition amongst providers first because they do not want to be perceived to be worse than their neighbours and second because the public might actually use these data to make a decision about which provider to select. These initiatives have been most widely adopted in the US and echo efforts in the healthcare arena to measure and report 'quality performance' in the form of league tables. Other countries are watching these developments closely.

England has a public website which can be used to learn more about the adequacy of long-term care providers based upon their structural characteristics and some basic information from the most recent inspections. In the Netherlands there is also a website that summarizes information about facility quality performance along a number of different dimensions that was designed for use by consumers and their advocates explicitly to enhance choice of facility. Other countries, and several provinces in Canada, Finland and New Zealand, have the data to be able to make this kind of a resource available to the public, but there is not yet consensus as to the best way to present this kind of information.

As the reader will observe in the current volume, provider groups and/or governments in a number of countries have introduced voluntary quality measurement systems. Unlike the US, for the most part, these serve the purpose of internal quality improvement. For example, in Finland, providers form consortia in order to learn from one another how it is that they are able to solve chronic quality problems. Such exchanges of 'trade craft' are highly valued, but providers may be much less willing to reveal their secrets in a competitive environment in which quality performance is publicly reported. Nor might they be as willing to admit to their need for remediation in certain areas were the consortia sponsored by the regulatory agency rather than an association of their peer providers. How to achieve this balance of openness necessary to truly engage in quality improvement while also publicly reporting remains a challenge.

1.8 Summary and structure of the country case study chapters

We have proposed a framework for characterizing the structure of long-term care regulation and enumerated the conceptual and operational problems that the various approaches may have as they are implemented. Regulatory structures must set standards, establish application processes and inspection protocols in order to grant licensure to an entity interested in serving the public by providing care for frail older people. Once providers are operational, the regulatory authority must institute quality monitoring on an ongoing basis, applying sanctions as necessary. While it is possible to contrast and compare countries' regulatory structures, this may tell us nothing of the actual quality of care experienced by the frail older persons, ostensibly the ones being protected by the regulations. As Day and Klein (1987) have noted:

A framework for understanding regulation of long-term care quality   25

Not only is quality itself an elusive and difficult notion, which is precisely why the regulation of standards is problematic. But it is also the product of a complex, ill-understood process in which social, organizational, and economic dynamics may be just as important as the regulatory system, and, at present, we lack the understanding needed to separate out the contributions of these factors.

It is unfortunate that so little attention has been devoted to understanding the impact of different regulatory structures and approaches on the quality of care experienced by frail long-term care service recipients. In spite of the volumes written about the differences between the rigid compliance-oriented enforcement approach versus the consultative, deterrent approach, there is no evidence available to indicate which is the more effective, not to speak of efficient, in assuring the quality of care that clients receive. While at the extremes, both approaches may be inefficient and/or ineffective, it is generally not the case that the extremes are what is actually observed; rather significant shades of grey exist and it would be useful to know which approach is superior and under which conditions that is the case. The cost of implementing stringent regulatory controls over long-term care facilities is high, for both the regulator and the regulated (Mukamel et al., 2011). While there are many who have asked whether this investment in stringent regulatory control is 'worth it', until recently, there have been no studies that have tried to empirically test that proposition (Mukamel et al., 2012). Unfortunately, the amount of consistent data collected over a long period of time necessary to address this issue is only available in the US setting at this juncture, currently making cross-national comparisons impossible.

This volume consists of fourteen specially commissioned chapters describing the structure of long-term care regulation in each of the North American, European and East Asian countries with well-developed or rapidly developing long-term care systems. After summarizing the demographic circumstances in the country followed by a description of the approach to long-term care financing and how it relates, or is separate from, regular healthcare financing in the country, each chapter describes in detail the regulatory control structures in place to assure long-term care quality. In some cases, because of the differences between residential and community based long-term care, the emphasis is on one rather than the other. Furthermore, since the long-term care financing and regulatory control systems vary substantially regionally, some chapters focus only on one region with brief forays referring to what goes on in other regions, or at the national level. To the extent that each country has policies related to the three components of the regulatory structure described in this introductory chapter, the case studies focus on standard setting and licensure followed by enforcement and quality monitoring and finally any public reporting and/or outcome measurement system that might be present.

The volume ends with a synthesis of the case studies that relies upon the structure outlined here in the first chapter. That is, drawing upon the information contained in each chapter, the final chapter compares the approaches to standard setting, quality monitoring and public transparency adopted across the countries included in the volume. While it would have been desirable to adopt a quantitative approach to address the question of what regulatory features are most conducive to achieving high-quality long-term care, the level of specificity about each country is not sufficient to even frame that question. Most importantly, at present there is no consensus as to what constitutes quality long-term care nor is there any common framework for measuring it from country to country. Since international comparisons of acute and ambulatory care quality are not much more advanced, there is still a long way to go before we are in a position to systematically learn from one another. We hope that this current volume is a step in the right direction.

References

Angelelli, J., Mor, V., Intrator, O., Feng, Z. and Zinn, J. (2003). Oversight of nursing homes: pruning the tree or just spotting bad apples? *The Gerontologist*, 43(2): 67–75.

Association TP (2012). Essex nursing home accused of neglect. *Nursingtimes* Available at: twittweb.com/news+essex+nursing+home-15644985.

Braithwaite, J. (2002). Rewards and regulation, *Journal of Law and Society*, 29(1): 12–26.

Brundage, A. (2002). *The English Poor Laws, 1700–1930*. Basingstoke: Palgrave Macmillan.

Day, P. and Klein, R. (1987). The regulation of nursing homes: a comparative perspective, *The Milbank Quarterly*, 65(3): 303–47.

Estes, C., Goldberg, S. P. L. S., Grossman, B. R., Nelson, M., Koren, M. J. and Hollister, B. (2012). Factors associated with perceived effectiveness of local long-term care Ombudsman Programs in New York and California, *Journal of Aging and Health*, 22(6): 772–803.

Ferguson, G. P. (2012). Nursing home abuse – a sobering reality, Ezine Articles. Available at: http://ezinearticles.com/?Nursing-Home-Abuse-A-Sobering-Reality&id=7196084.

Institute of Medicine, Committee on Nursing Home Regulation (1986). *Improving the Quality of Care in Nursing Homes*. Washington, DC: National Academy Press.

Kane, R. A., Kane, R. L. and Ladd, R. C. (1998). *The Heart of Long-Term Care*. New York: Oxford University Press.

Kovner, A. R. and Jonas, S. (2002). *Healthcare Delivery in the United States*. 7th edn. New York: Springer Publishing Company.

Miller, E. A., Tyler, D. A. and Mor, V. (2013). National newspaper portrayal of nursing homes: tone of coverage and its correlates. *Medical Care*, 51(1): 78–83. doi: 10.1097/MLR.0b013e318270baf2.

Mor, V. (2004). A comprehensive clinical assessment tool to inform policy and practice: applications of the minimum data set. *Medical Care*, 42(4): III50–9.

(2005). Improving the quality of long-term care with better information, *The Milbank Quarterly*, 83(3): 333–64.

Mor, V., Finne-Soveri, H., Hirdes, J., Gilgen Rand DuPasquier, J.-N. (2009). *Long Term Care Quality Monitoring Using the InterRAI Common Clinical Assessment Language in Performance Measurement for Health System Improvement: Experiences, Challenges and Prospects*. Cambridge University Press.

Mor, V., Sherwood, S. and Gutkin, C. (1986). A national study of residential care for the aged, *The Gerontologist*, 26(4): 405–17.

Mukamel, D. B., Li, Y., Harrington, C., Spector, W. D., Weimer, D. L. and Bailey, L. (2011). Does state regulation of quality impose costs on nursing homes? *Medical Care*, 49(6): 529–34.

Mukamel, D. B., Weimer, D. L., Harrington, C., Spector, W. D., Ladd, H. and Li, Y. (2012). The effect of state regulatory stringency on nursing home quality. *Health Services Research*, 47(5): 791–813.

National Research Council (1988). *The Aging Population in the Twenty-First Century: Statistics for Health Policy*. Washington, DC: National Academy Press.

Phipps, D. L., Noyce, P. R., Walshe, K., Parker, D. and Ashcroft, D. M. (2011). Risk-based regulation of health care professionals: what are the implications for pharmacists? *Health, Risk and Society*, 13(3): 277–92.

Rivlin, A. M., Wiener, J. M., Hanley, R. J. and Spence, D. A. (1988). *Caring for the Disabled Elderly: Who will Pay?* Washington, DC: The Brookings Institution.

Sherwood, S. and Mor, V. (1980). Mental health institutions and the elderly. In J. Birren and R. Sloan (eds.), *Handbook of Mental Health and Aging*. New Jersey: Prentice Hall, pp. 854–84.

Stevenson, D. G. (2006). Nursing home consumer complaints and quality of care: a national view. *Medical Care Research and Review*, 63(3): 347–68.

Talbott, J. A. (1981). *The Chronic Mentally Ill: Treatment, Programs, Systems*. New York: Human Sciences Press.

Werner, R. T. K. and Liang, K. (2012). State adoption of nursing home pay-for-performance, *Medical Care Research and Review*, 67(3): 364–77.

Xinhua (2005). Beijing encourages private nursing homes. Available at www.china.org.cn/english/Life/126277.html.

  (2007). More personnel needed in Chinese nursing homes. *People's Daily* Available at: http://english.peopledaily.com.cn/200701/23/eng200701 23_344000.html.

  (2008). Fire killed 7 in a Wenzhou senior apartment alleged in operation illegally. Available at: http://news.xinhuanet.com/society/2008-12/04/content_10454544.htm.

PART II

Long-term care quality systems based on 'professionalism'

This first set of country case studies includes Austria, Germany, Switzerland and Japan. All have universal long-term care insurance, although the structure of the insurance system and how the funds are disbursed varies substantially between these countries. All have long traditions of federal and state (regional) partnership in implementing social welfare and health policies and this sharing of responsibility creates certain conflicts and barriers to the operation of systematic quality assurance systems. Like most of the countries described in this volume, these four have relatively standardized approaches to determining which institutions and agencies can become licensed to provide services to the frail elderly; however, the standards that emerged have generally been the product of a negotiated settlement between various segments of the interested parties, with particular emphasis on the role of the organizations of professionals involved in caring for those requiring long-term care. In a sense the 'institution' of the health professions assumed a significant role in the setting of standards for long-term care quality which the professionals were assumed to police themselves in much the same way that physicians are almost always the arbiters of what constitutes quality care which is determined by local practice standards, largely based upon medical boards. Society accepts this notion of professionals policing themselves and in some of the countries included in this segment it is clear that government actually delegates the authority for regulatory oversight to the professional organizations.

In Austria conditions for licensure of institutions and home care agencies are largely based on structural criteria like staffing and physical facilities. There are no federal quality standards even though the central government is paying a base proportion of all care. The state has looked to professional organizations to provide input into setting care standards, as was done in the acute care sector, but there has been no comparable national effort in long-term care. Large regional variation in the level of regulatory oversight and the accompanying expression of public concern has led to a provider-led initiative to institute quality improvement programmes that was undertaken in conjunction with local professional organizations; but, these are only reaching a minority of long-term care users.

The Long Term Care Act in Germany stipulates that providers are responsible for maintaining and assuring their own quality and they must adhere to expert guidelines developed by the stakeholders that are uniquely German in their emphasis on achieving consensus as part of negotiating. Historically, German regulations governing long-term care have been focused on structural aspects, particularly stipulating the number and the level of training of staff. An emphasis on expert standards promulgated by the clinical leadership of the nursing professions began to be incorporated by reference into selected regulations. Nonetheless, these standards have not been universally adopted, meaning that regional variation in how quality standards are monitored is substantial, leading to considerable public concern about provider quality.

In Switzerland the Federal Health Insurance Regulation Act formally invests power in the federal government but allows the development of regulations to be delegated to long-term care provider professional organizations and those devoted to the professionals. This delegation of standard setting applies to things as basic as the numbers of staff of each professional licensure type and to the range of service and treatments that should be available and how they should be delivered. Since the healthcare professionals have an incentive to have higher staffing levels while the provider organizations have the opposite incentive, local differences may prevail resulting in considerable regional variation in standards, quality monitoring frequency and approach.

While the emphasis on structural quality characteristics is similar in Japan to these other countries, the history of having different kinds of settings meeting the needs of long-term care patients has created some unique circumstances. However, professional organizations have been very influential in pushing for higher staff standards and even higher mandatory training levels among the traditionally unskilled nurses and home care aides. Even though the providers have tended to oppose increases in staffing minimum standards, government reimbursement models reflect the negotiated settlement and have been increasing to accommodate the higher staffing levels.

As the reader considers the history and description of each of these countries, it will be useful to take note of the interplay between federal

Long-term care quality systems based on 'professionalism' 31

and regional power and accountability sharing, which is key due to the federal role in paying for long-term care. Of interest is the role of the professions and the providers, along with the various levels of regional government, in negotiating quality standards and making sure they can be paid for implementing them. Based upon the authors' reviews of the available evidence however, the net result is considerable regional variation in how quality monitoring and inspection is actually done.

2 Performance measurement in long-term care in Austria

KAI LEICHSENRING,
FRÉDÉRIQUE LAMONTAGNE-GODWIN,
ANDREA SCHMIDT, RICARDO RODRIGUES
AND GEORG RUPPE

2.1 The emerging Austrian long-term care system in the context of a federal constitution

In Austria, long-term care started to become acknowledged as a specific field of social and health policies during the 1980s, when a debate about long-term care allowances was initiated by people with disabilities acquired during their working age. The ensuing reform was marked by the legacies of the traditional Austrian welfare regime, by the federal constitution and the clear-cut distinction between the health and social care systems. The decentralized governance of health and social care in Austria has been based on two distinct principles. On the one hand, healthcare is a part of the social insurance system that is primarily regulated by the federal government, financed by contributions and administered by the self-governed health insurance agencies at federal and regional levels. The regional governments (*Bundesländer*) are involved as planners, managers and co-financers of hospitals (Hofmarcher and Quentin, 2013). On the other hand, the principle of subsidiarity has been applied to the areas of disability, social and long-term care with respective responsibilities assigned by constitutional law to the nine regional governments. Their activities are funded from general taxes that are centrally levied and distributed according to defined criteria. In practice, this means that, if patients have been assessed as being in need of long-term care, they have to rely on their own assets and/or means-tested social assistance from the local or regional authorities (Ganner, 2008).

With the rising need for long-term care due to an ageing population, regional governments began to find it difficult to shoulder the increasing demand for social care during the 1980s. To overcome this shortcoming, in 1993 Austria became one of the first countries in Europe to introduce universal coverage of long-term care allowances as a key instrument to finance long-term care. Indeed, this scheme blurred the traditional subsidiarity principle as described above, requiring a treaty between the regions and the federal state to alter constitutional inconsistencies. The reasons for introducing a comprehensive long-term care allowance system, rather than investing only in services-in-kind, were twofold. First, there were already several types of cash benefits intended to top-up old-age or disability pensions in case of need and people with disabilities at working age thus called for equal treatment and a standardization of these payments. Secondly, the payment of long-term care allowances served to indirectly acknowledge the importance of informal (family) care as the allowance would, in many cases, become part of the total family's household budget. In any case, the Austrian long-term care allowance (*Pflegegeld*) is conceived as a non-means-tested cash benefit. Its eligibility is verified by an individual needs assessment carried out by specialized medical doctors or nurses. Needs are assessed as the amount of time needed to help with activities of daily living (ADL) and selected instrumental activities of daily living (IADL). Benefits are paid at fixed rates to the individual beneficiary together with his/her pension or social assistance payment according to seven levels (Level 1 being the lowest) from about €154 to €1,655 per month. Considering that the threshold to become eligible for Level 1 is currently at sixty hours of care needs per month, it becomes obvious that the allowance contributes no more than €2.50 to each hour of care needed. Considering also that the median income of employed women is currently about €1,500 per month, monthly payments at the higher levels of about €902 (Level 5) to about €1,655 (Level 7)[1] might nevertheless be qualified as an incentive to provide informal care.[2]

In 2011, about 440,000 people in need of care, more than 80 per cent of whom were above the age of 65, were entitled to a long-term care allowance. Applied to about 5 per cent of the population, the coverage rate of this scheme is one of the highest in the world. The rising

---

[1] To qualify for Levels 5–7 of the long-term care allowance scheme, applicants have to be in need of 180 hours or more of care, with additional needs that call for permanent attendance, e.g. due to incontinence, hazardous behaviour, etc.

[2] According to the only evaluation research concerning the long-term care allowance (Badelt et al., 1997), about 15 per cent of family carers of working age (mainly female) stated that they had left formal employment due to the allowance.

purchasing power of users has certainly influenced the quantitative extension of services and facilities. However, the allowance has not been sufficient to trigger competition between providers in terms of prices and quality that continue to be regulated by rationing and supply-driven bureaucratic mechanisms. Concerning transparency and quality assurance, the Austrian long-term care system is still searching for ways to improve methods and regulations – with a persistent fear of public reporting.

Furthermore, the allowance also contributed to the emergence of a 'grey' or 'black' market of care, fuelled by the opportunity to reach out to migrant carers from neighbouring countries who are ready to provide twenty-four-hour care in the home of the beneficiary at affordable prices (€800-€1,500 per month). An estimated 5–7 per cent of the 440,000 or so beneficiaries of the long-term care allowance rely on this form of care. The legal caveats linked with this phenomenon have been partly amended by varied reforms of the labour law, organizational support and financial incentives to 'legalize' the employment of migrant carers (Schmidt et al., 2013). However, from the perspective of quality assurance, performance measurement or transparency, this area of provision continues to remain, in general, unregulated and 'informal' (see Section 2.3).

This chapter seeks to provide an overview of the existing regulatory framework to define, assess and control quality in the area of community or home care and in residential care facilities (care homes) as well as the efforts currently underway to extend and further differentiate this framework. It will thus focus primarily on the formal long-term care system. The chapter is organized as follows: Section 2.2 will depict the current provision of formal long-term care services in Austria in the wake of a reform in 1993, while Section 2.3 will address the regulatory framework emerging from these developments. Section 2.4 highlights incentives and disincentives for providers to become more transparent in terms of quality assessment and to implement quality improvement on a voluntary basis. Respective initiatives at the level of providers and regulators are presented and analysed. Finally, Section 2.5 will conclude with challenges for quality assurance, quality management and performance measurement in the emerging Austrian long-term care system, in particular in relation to links and interfaces between health and social care, to human resource management and to methods to improve performance measurement.

2.1.1 A note on terminology

For the purpose of this chapter, the realm of long-term care comprises all policies, services and facilities that address people of all ages with needs for assistance, social care and healthcare due to restricted physical, cognitive or mental capabilities over an extended period of time, independently of whether this help with ADL or IADL is provided by formal or informal carers, and whether it is provided in residential or community settings (OECD, 2005; WHO, 2000; http://interlinks.euro.centre.org). As older people are the largest group of people with long-term care needs, this chapter will focus on selected services and facilities for this target group. Informal carers provide the bulk of long-term care services, mainly as family carers, but also as volunteers and as 'paid' informal carers. Women constitute the majority of 'migrant' informal carers (in Austria called 'twenty-four-hour-carers' or 'domestic assistants'). In the formal care sector, the terms 'residential care' and 'care homes' refer to all facilities that provide long-term accommodation for residents in an institutional setting, be it in 'traditional' old-age homes, providing mainly housing and accommodation or in nursing homes that also provide more intensive nursing care. The term 'home care' encompasses home help (social care) and home nursing care (healthcare). While in many countries these services are provided by two distinct organizations, in Austria, although these are carried out by distinct professional groups, almost all organizations offering home nursing care also employ home helpers.

2.2 The extent of formal long-term care services in Austria

Care at home is still the main type of long-term care arrangement. To maintain and facilitate such arrangements has been the key aim of policies and reforms that have slowly developed over the past two decades. About 5.5 per cent of Austrians over the age of 65 live in an old-age or nursing home but the average age of residents in these facilities is, similar to other European countries, above the age of 80 (Biwald et al., 2011). More than 80 per cent of those older people in need of care who live at home receive care predominantly from relatives. Only 9 per cent of these receive help and support exclusively from professional caregivers (Schneider et al., 2006).

2.2.1 Home care and intermediary care services

Although the organization, coverage, regulation and financing differ across the nine regions, the take-up rate of home care services depends mainly on local supply, personal information and the cost of out-of-pocket contributions, rather than on individual needs. For instance, most regional governments have decided that no more than a total of thirty hours of home nursing and eighty hours of home help per month or other services will be provided to an individual user at a subsidized rate. Additional service hours would have to be paid at full cost. People needing more than two hours of care per day (Levels 3 to 7 according to the regular assessment) thus face difficulties in having their needs covered by these services, while for those with assessed care needs of between 60 and 119 hours per month (Levels 1 and 2), the long-term care allowance of about €300 will usually not suffice to cover the costs. Still, on average, out-of-pocket contributions to home care services cover only about 25 per cent of total costs (BMASK, 2012).

In Austria, health and social care services for people living at home are almost entirely provided by third-sector organizations, mainly affiliated to the churches or to political parties. Although the share of some small commercial providers has increased in Vienna following the introduction of the long-term care allowance, 'market shares' in the regions have remained relatively stable. Users are completely free to choose between different providers. Generally, across the board the availability and accessibility of services, semi-residential (day care, short-term care facilities) and residential care facilities has increased significantly over the past ten years, in particular the supply of home care has more than doubled in some regions, though from a very low base (Leichsenring et al., 2009). Notwithstanding this positive development, there are still considerable regional differences so that community care services – home help, home nursing, geriatric aides – remain inadequate to meet needs (Biwald et al., 2011). This may best be illustrated by the fact that the average number of hours provided per user per week is less than one hour in Upper Austria but reaches a maximum of 4.3 hours in Lower Austria (both well below the sixty hours of care per month considered necessary for Level 1 of care). A particular challenge for home care services remains alpine and border regions with difficult accessibility and long distances between the agencies' headquarters. However, while the capital area (Vienna) traditionally has had one of the highest rates of service provision, other regions are catching up. Still, services are also increasingly targeted towards a smaller number of clients with more important care needs and no available family carer. Indeed, only about 25 per cent of long-term care allowance beneficiaries with a family carer are making use of complementary community care services, mainly home nursing. Only a small proportion of these caring households are using day care facilities (3.4 per cent) or short-term care (5.1 per cent). Lack of information, unavailability of services and mainly the lack of financial means to (co-)pay for these services were the main reasons given by carers for not considering these respite services (Pochobradsky et al., 2005), as the means-tested out-of-pocket payment per service hour (subject to a maximum of €25 per hour) amounts to about 1 per cent of income (reduced by expenditure on heating and housing costs). As a consequence of this pattern of supply and demand, informal (family) care remains the key resource for people with care needs living at home, in the majority of cases without respite or support from formal care services.

2.2.2 Residential care facilities

About 71,000 places[3] in about 800 old-age and nursing homes are available in Austria. About 55 per cent of these are publicly owned and managed while about 21 per cent are managed by commercial providers and the remaining 24 per cent by private non-profit organizations (Schneider et al., 2006). These shares have remained relatively stable over the past 15 years. Modernization, physical restructuring and the transformation of traditional old-age homes into nursing homes, as well as the conversion of large institutions into smaller units have been the main aims of reforms to improve the structural basis of this sector over the past decade. During this period, and notwithstanding the general focus on trying to promote community care, some regions have witnessed remarkable growth rates also in the number of residential care places available. For instance, in Carinthia the number

---

[3] In Austria, the term 'place' is used in relation to care homes for older people as normatively, these elderly people should have a 'place to live', rather than a 'hospital bed'.

Performance measurement in long-term care in Austria 39

of nursing places has increased by 30 per cent within a short four-year period, between 2002 and 2006 (Pochobradsky et al., 2008: 17).

Residents' payments for a place in a care home come from individual pensions and long-term care allowances and from potential assets, although residents are entitled to keep 20 per cent of their individual pension and about €44 per month from the long-term care allowance.[4] These payments from pensions, attendance allowances and assets cover an estimated 28–50 per cent of total costs, indicating that individual out-of-pocket payments usually do not suffice and have to be topped-up in many cases by regions and municipalities from social assistance funds. Since the long-term care allowance has only been increased twice since 1995, net expenditures of regions and municipalities for residential care have quadrupled during the same period (Biwald et al., 2011: 53). This has led regional governments to define a threshold of care needs (at least Level 3 of the long-term care allowance scheme) to qualify for access to residential care.

Some care homes are offering short-term stays as a 'respite care' arrangement for family carers. However, these services are facing difficulties due to a lack of information and incentives. Indeed, many older people with care needs tend to remain in hospitals, where they can stay for the most part free of charge[5] rather than enter a nursing home. Moreover, for carers, it is more convenient to make use of a hospital stay for their family member in need, rather than paying for short-term stays in a care home which would have to be paid with up to 80 per cent of the older person's income per month (Vienna) or between about €70 and €150 per day according to the level of care needs (Lower Austria).[6]

---

[4] Depending on the region, a defined amount of assets (between about €3,600 in Tyrol and about €11,000 in Lower Austria) has to remain at the disposal of the resident and in 2008, family members were principally exempted from payments, although since then some regions have reintroduced claims for recourse from children.

[5] According to the Federal Audit Commission, the number of these so-called 'procuratio patients' in Viennese hospitals had fallen by about 25 per cent between 2005 and 2008 when still about 1,000 'procuratio patients' were registered with an average length of stay between eighty-four and 102 days (Rechnungshof, 2011b).

[6] Information provided by the relevant websites: www.noe.gv.at/bilder/d30/InfoblattTarifeKurzzeitpflege.pdf?12193; http://sozialinfo.wien.gv.at/content/de/10/Institutions.do?liid=2&senseid=310.

2.3 The regulatory framework for quality assurance and performance measurement of long-term care services in Austria

2.3.1 *The regulatory structure for residential facilities and community-based services*

Following the care reform in 1993 that introduced long-term care insurance it became apparent that both providers and purchasers of services had to search for mechanisms to define, monitor and ensure the quality of care they provided and purchased, respectively. However, since then the federal constitution, the arbitrary but strict division between health and social care (Ganner, 2008), the small size of municipalities and the long tradition of private non-profit providers, which are affiliated to either political parties or religious organizations, continue to produce a mixed bag of regulations and standards – and a lack of transparent data, rather than a public reporting system that would help users to take informed decisions.

Under the Austrian constitution, regional governments are the main bodies responsible for planning, funding, regulating and controlling long-term care services and facilities, traditionally based on social assistance legislation (see Figure 2.1 for an overview). Any interference in this area by the federal state thus requires for a 'state treaty' between the latter and the nine regions. Such a treaty was signed in 1993, stipulating that the federal government would finance the long-term care allowance through general taxes, while regional governments set up development plans for the long-term care sector over a period of fifteen years (1996–2011) with the aim of providing more equal long-term care across the country.[7] For the first time, this treaty also outlined some quality criteria concerning the delivery of long-term care services and facilities, though it failed to define standards and methods to assess structural, process and outcome quality measures. It then took more than a decade for all regional governments to implement specific legal regulations concerning institutional care, e.g. specifying education and training for managers of nursing homes, contracts with residents

---

[7] BGBl 866/1993. Development plans were produced in all regions between 1996 and 1999, but have since become outdated and, in most regions, were superseded by real developments and/or continuous planning.

	Federal Government	State Treaties	9 Regional Governments (*Bundesländer*)
Framework	LTC Allowance Act (needs-tested cash benefits)	**Regions:**	Regional Social Welfare Acts (in-kind benefits)
Responsibilities	Federal LTC allowance Regulation of healthcare (staff training, quality requirements)	1. Develop social care services 2. Development plans 3. Set minimum standards	Social assistance (means-tested) Regulation of social care (eligibility, financing, means-testing, staff training, quality requirements, monitoring)
Financing	LTC allowance: general taxes. Healthcare: contributions (social insurance based)	**Federal government:** Transfer of financial resources	Social care: general taxes (regional budgets and transfer from 'Long-term Care Fund') and user charges

Figure 2.1 Responsibilities of the federal and regional governments in long-term care in Austria.

Source: update of Rodrigues, 2010; Leichsenring et al., 2009.

Note: State treaties between the federal state and the regional governments were signed in 1993 and in 2011 to redefine responsibilities for long-term care as funding is now being guaranteed by the federal state (since 2011) through a Long-term Care Fund, which provides additional funding for regional governments to cover expenditures for long-term care services and facilities; the treaty also stipulated that eventually the entire administration of the long-term care allowance would be centralized at the federal level with reimbursement from the regional governments.

defining rights and duties and some structural requirements concerning space, staffing or the maximum number of places.

Finally, issues concerning residents' rights were eventually regulated in 2004–5 as an issue of 'consumer protection' by the federal Care Home Treaty Act (Heimvertragsgesetz), which regulates minimum standards for contracts between residents and care home providers, and the Care Home Habitation Act (Heimaufenthaltsgesetz) which stipulates procedures and principles concerning the restriction of freedom (physical and medical restraints) for residents and patients in all types of residential care facilities, including care homes for older people, for people with disabilities and patients in hospitals (Barth and Engel, 2004).[8]

---

[8] BGBl 11/2004 and BGBl 12/2004. With these two pieces of legislation the federal government in practice 'overruled' the primary responsibility of regions for care homes based on its responsibility for issues concerning civil law and consumer protection.

As for community care services, regulations concerning quality are even more sparse. However, regional governments have issued legal guidelines for the delivery of home help and home nursing care (community care) concerning authorization (see Section 2.3.2) and to guarantee minimum standards (see Section 2.3.3). As all regions mainly rely on the traditional non-profit organizations that have developed and provided these services hitherto, the focus of quality criteria has been on standards of education and training of staff, on care documentation and on the user's rights ('care contract').

2.3.2 Application and authorization

All providers of care homes or community-based services have to apply for authorization according to the regional regulations with the respective regional or district authorities. Even if private providers decide not to apply for public funding (as their target group may be clients who can cover all the costs through their own resources), they still have to comply with general legal guidelines as soon as they host more than five people with care needs. Applications for new care homes will only be considered if they are in accordance with local or regional authorities' development plans and quality standards that are described below (Section 2.3.3). For this reason, in most cases, public authorities rather than private entities plan and construct new care homes. However, the three largest private for-profit providers have increased their market share over the past few years, both by applying for new care homes and by taking over formerly public facilities following a tendering process or direct commissioning. To become an authorized provider of care homes it is sufficient to prove compliance with the general terms and conditions stipulated by legal regulations (mainly staffing and structural standards).

Apart from the few quality standards in relation to staffing and structural criteria, only a few regional regulations have stipulated an upper limit of places per care home, e.g. in Upper Austria no more than 120 places per care home are allowed (since 2002; OÖ LGBl 29/1996). In Carinthia, when a regulation for care homes was eventually approved in 2005, an upper limit of fifty places per care home was decided. However, because of complaints by providers that maintained that care homes with fewer than seventy places would not be economically viable, this upper limit was recently increased to seventy-five places. Other regional regulations define only the upper limit of places per ward: in Styria, the Tyrol and Salzburg this limit is fifty. In Vienna, the Care Home Act stipulates that newly constructed care homes must not have more than 350 places, with individual wards not exceeding twenty-eight, while in exceptional cases thirty-six places is the maximum (Wr LGBl 2005/31).

Home care organizations have to apply for authorization at least three months before starting their activity; this is the maximum period usually needed to accomplish the authorization process. For instance, the Viennese Act on home help services stipulates that a provider organization, in order to receive authorization, has to prove its ability to carry out home help services by describing its care concept, its economic viability and its human resources concept, in particular by ensuring the number of qualified staff (Wiener Heimhilfeeinrichtungengesetz (WHEG) LGBl, 2008/08, §3).

2.3.3 Quality standards

As already mentioned, no binding quality standards have been defined at the federal level. The state treaty of 1993 enumerated the following issues for (newly built) *care homes* (BGBl 866/1993):

- their size should be 'manageable and arranged in family-like structures';
- all rooms should be 'equipped with an accessible toilet and a bathroom'; primarily there should be single rooms;
- residents 'must have the right to receive visitors at any time';
- there should be rooms for therapies, day care and rehabilitation services as well as for other services such as, for instance, a hairdresser or foot care that may be provided in-house, but also by external companies or individuals;
- the care home 'should be situated within the borough to facilitate external relationships' not only with family and friends, but also with the community.

Regional regulations for care homes, which had hitherto been regulated by general social assistance legislation, were developed and implemented rather late, namely between 1998 and 2005. There are vast differences in general structural quality requirements defined in the regional legal regulations for care homes with respect to staffing standards, as exemplified in Table 2.1. Even if evidence for an optimal

Table 2.1 *Staffing ratio and staffing structure in Austrian residential care facilities by region*

Region	Staffing ratio	Staffing structure	Comments
Burgenland	Specific model, depending on number of places, weekly hours, day/ night-shift etc.	50 per cent registered nurses, 50 per cent assistant nurses	
Carinthia	1 FTE: 2.4 residents	40 per cent registered nurses, 50 per cent assistant nurses, 10 per cent others (trainees)	1:12 in units without nursing care needs, but at least 2 registered nurses
Lower Austria	Depending on residents' level of care needs, e.g. Level 1 (lowest): 1:20; Level 3: 1:10; Level 7 (highest): 1:1.4	45 per cent registered nurses, 55 per cent assistant nurses	
Upper Austria	Depending on residents' level of care needs, e.g. Level 1 (lowest): 1:24; Level 3: 1:4; Level 7 (highest): 1:1.5	20 per cent registered nurses, 50 per cent geriatric assistant nurses (*Altenfachbetreuer*), 30 per cent geriatric assistant nurses (*Altenbetreuer*)	No differentiation between nursing ward and units without nursing
Salzburg	To be defined by each care home	To be defined by each care home	No legally defined staffing ratio or structure*
Styria	Depending on residents' level of care needs, e.g. Level 1 (lowest): 1:12; Level 3: 1:4; Level 7 (highest): 1:2	20 per cent registered nurses, 60 per cent assistant nurses /geriatric assistant nurses (*Altenbetreuer*), 20 per cent others	

Performance measurement in long-term care in Austria 45

Table 2.1 (*cont.*)

Region	Staffing ratio	Staffing structure	Comments
The Tyrol	Day-time: depending on residents' level of care needs, e.g. Level 1 (lowest): 1:10; Level 3: 1:3; Level 7 (highest): 1:1.9 Night-time: 2.75–3.2 staff per 30 residents with at least Level 3 care needs.		In units with residents without care needs: 1 FTE: 50 residents
Vienna	Depending on residents' level of care needs, e.g. Level 1 (lowest): 1:20; Level 3: 1:2; Level 7 (highest): 1:1	40 per cent registered nurses, 45 per cent assistant nurses, 15 per cent home helpers	

Source: Adapted from Riess et al., 2007: Annex (Table A6).
Note: *The regional regulations of Salzburg require that providers of care homes ensure 'a sufficient number of qualified care staff to guarantee assistance according to the number of residents and the type and extent of services needed' (Salzburger LGBl 52/2000, §18).

staffing standard in care homes is lacking, the differences in regulations – with a heavy impact on facility operating costs – are striking. In most regions the prescribed staff ratio depends on the resident structure by levels of care needs, but different standards apply. In one region (Salzburg), no staffing standards have been defined at all – it is up to care home management to decide upon the staffing structure – thus far, with no negative impact on the quality of care, according to local authorities. Indeed, some care homes in this region have been incentivized by this 'legal leeway' to develop innovative types of participative leadership and shared responsibilty between staff.

There are also differences in the definition of 'professional carer' – in Burgenland 50 per cent of staff have to be registered nurses, but only 20 per cent in Styria and Upper Austria where so-called *Altenfachbetreuer* (geriatric aides) are employed, a professional profile that does not exist in other regions (Schneider et al., 2006: 11). However, the new comprehensive, modular education system for social carers that was introduced by another state treaty signed between the federal and the regional governments in 2005 will amend this situation (BGBl 55/2005). Under the treaty, the regional governments, which are principally responsible also for education in social care, are committed to implementing a comprehensive, modular education system for social carers.[9] Training courses were initiated by several providers of social carer education in all regions in 2007. It will take some time before the impact of this reform becomes apparent.

Other differences in structural quality standards of care homes concern the size of rooms – ranging from 14 m^2 in Styria and Vienna to 18 m^2 in Upper Austria and Carinthia – or the extent to which double rooms may be provided (Scholta, 2008: 396). The regional regulations are also quite vague in specifying that care should be provided in an adequate manner, following current professional standards. In this context, it should be mentioned that Austrian care home regulations do not stipulate the employment of physicians. Only in the City of Vienna and in Lower Austria have some larger care homes (providers) employed physicians with a geriatric specialization. Usually, an agreement is made between the care home and one or several local GPs to hold surgery at defined hours in the care home, but if residents prefer their former GP they are completely free to arrange visits. In this context, there is also an incipient debate on whether the introduction of 'nursing home doctors' could improve quality of care in terms of reducing multi-medication, (re-)admissions to hospitals and uncoordinated prescription of medications by GPs, who are seldom specialized in geronto-psychiatric care (Fasching, 2007) but as mentioned, so far, there is no specific requirement for care homes to employ physicians.

Only in the region of Salzburg is there a stipulation that care should strive to 'maintain and regain the abilities and autonomy of clients

---

[9] Home helpers should receive a minimum of 200 hours of training and 200 hours of practice. This might be supplemented with another 1,000 hours of training and another 1,000 hours of practice within two years to become a 'professional social carer' (*Fach-Sozialbetreuer*). With an additional 600 hours of training and 600 hours of practice during a third year they might then receive a diploma as social carers (*Diplom-Sozialbetreuer*).

Performance measurement in long-term care in Austria 47

as much as possible' (Salzburger LGBl 52/2000, §3). However, over the past few years, process quality criteria and the requirement for quality assurance or even quality management have been introduced in many regions. For instance, the Viennese Care Home Act (WWPG, Wr LGBl 2005/15, resp. 31) calls for proper care documentation and quality management to provide care that complies with the scientific state of the art and measures to improve structural, process and outcome quality. This regulation also stipulates the introduction of the Viennese Care Home Commission, an independent expert committee whose tasks include consulting with the city council, regularly assessing care standards (yearly reporting) and supporting the rights and interests of residents and families. In addition, in the Tyrol legislation stipulates the documentation required, the need for a service charter and that quality management frameworks need to be implemented (LGBl 23/2005).

In *community care*, which has emerged from initiatives by private non-profit organizations since the late 1970s, specific regulations are developing even more slowly than in residential care. The state treaty only mentioned the following issues (BGBl 866/1993, Anlage A):

- users should have a choice[10] between services according to the general principles of social assistance regulations;
- services should be delivered 'in an integrated (holistic) manner', and regional governments have to facilitate the 'networking necessary to generate smooth transitions between community and residential care services';
- 'basic services must also be available at weekends and holidays'; and
- regional governments are obliged to cater for 'professional quality assurance and control of services and their degree of expansion', details of which are to be shown in regional plans concerning needs and development of care services.

It took some time for the regional governments to develop and produce their plans that initially were to expand the quantity of available services. Legal regulations remain relatively vague with respect to quality standards. Vienna is an exception, as providers of community care services, most of which offer both nursing home care and home

---

[10] In this context 'user's choice' would mean both the choice between different providers of the same service and the choice between different types of service, e.g. between a care home and a community-based service.

help services, have to become members of the Federation of Viennese Health and Social Care Services and adhere to the procedures and structural prerequisites it has defined. The organization has developed a model contract and quality guidelines (expert standards for nursing care) for home care in cooperation with experts and the Vienna Social Funds (Fonds Soziales Wien, FSW). The FSW is the Municipality of Vienna's purchasing unit for social care and also regulates provision by means of case managers who assess care needs and stipulate the type and number of subsidized service hours to which each client will be entitled. The FSW also negotiates prices with individual providers and administers client's out-of-pocket contributions.

With regard to the expanding phenomenon of migrant 'twenty-four-hour home assistants' from neighbouring central and eastern European countries, legal amendments made during 2008 also sought to influence the quality of these services (Prochazkova and Schmid, 2009). This was done mainly by linking eligibility for additional means-tested subsidies – between €800 and €1,100 monthly as a contribution to cover additional expenses for social insurance expenditures – to a precondition that seeks to ensure adequate training or experience. This precondition takes one of three forms: i) hired home assistants must have completed training provided by various schools and agencies – usually according to the training guidelines for home helpers (about 200 hours); or ii) they must prove that they have already successfully carried out assistance over a period of more than six months; or iii) they must prove that they have specific education and related practice in the area of health or social care. In the meantime, many non-profit organizations providing home care now also act as brokers for domestic care assistants, but the vast majority of them are formally self-employed. In any case, no further quality criteria or regulations in this context have been stipulated.

2.3.4 Quality assurance, monitoring and inspection

Debates about quality assurance, monitoring and inspection, to the extent that they are considered at all, have concentrated on residential care. Therefore, this section will mainly focus on this area by starting, again, with the regional differences in terms of stakeholders, approaches and methods. Table 2.2 shows an overview of regional

Performance measurement in long-term care in Austria

Table 2.2 *Selected features of care home inspection stipulated by Austrian regions*

Region	Responsible unit for inspection	Frequency of control	Potential fines and penalties in case of continued infringement
Burgenland	District authorities for smaller care homes, otherwise regional authorities	Once in twenty-four months unannounced	Up to €2,200
Carinthia	Regional government appoints a team of three authorized healthcare experts and a building expert	Once in twenty-four months, unannounced	Max. €7,500
Lower Austria	Regional government: 'Pflegeaufsicht' – this unit of the regional government is an interdisciplinary team responsible for care inspection in health and social care facilities	Not specified by law (in practice, about once per year with pre-announcement)	n/a
Upper Austria	Regional government appoints a team consisting of healthcare professionals, a lawyer, administrative staff, a medical doctor and a building expert	Not specified by law (aim: once per year, currently from time to time, according to inducement)	n/a
Salzburg	Regional government appoints a team of three healthcare professionals	Once per year (but not always possible); unannounced	Up to €10,000
Styria	District authority; two inspectors (officer for social care; authorized expert for healthcare)	Twice per year; unannounced	Up to €5,000

Table 2.2 (*cont.*)

Region	Responsible unit for inspection	Frequency of control	Potential fines and penalties in case of continued infringement
Tyrol	District authority	n/a	Up to €2,000
Vorarlberg	District authority appoints a team that consists of the responsible officer for social care, one officer of the building administration, experts for healthcare, fire protection, hygiene and food control	Once every three years; announced	Up to €2,000
Vienna	Local Authority (*Magistrat*) appoints Care Home Commission of three to eight experts, including a registered nurse and a responsible officer, medical doctors, technicians, etc. upon request	Once per year; not always announced	Up to €10,000

Source: Authors' compilation based on Regional Care Home Acts and Fischbacher, 2011.

legislation concerning responsibilities, approaches to and intensity of inspections. While all regions stipulate specified procedures in case of imminent danger for residents, regular inspection varies greatly between regions and in Upper Austria it is possible that a care home will not be inspected for as long as five years after undergoing an inspection that satisfied the inspection team. In all regions, there is an inspection team of about three authorized experts to carry out the assessment; in some cases this team can include up to eight members, in particular authorized healthcare experts as well as lawyers, building and hygiene experts.

According to the regional regulations, inspection teams address the requirements defined by the legal framework in existence in each region. Content, protocols and methods thus differ from region to region. Generally, methods include a mix of interviews with management, staff and residents, checklists, observation and document analysis (care documentation) to check whether requirements are met. Where possible, interviews with selected residents are carried out or 'typical care situations' are observed. In some cases, indicators for process and outcome quality are used, e.g. the prevalence of decubitus ulcers, the number of residents who have been physically restrained, end-of-life care planning and other items from the care documentation (for randomly selected residents) or the number of hours of further training of staff.

Interviews or written questionnaires carried out with seven out of the nine regional government inspection units revealed quite a number of characteristics of these inspections (Fischbacher, 2011). According to this research, after inspection there was usually a feedback meeting, and written reports were sent back to the care home management with suggestions for improvement or required amendments (if inspection was triggered by a complaint the report was also sent to the complainant). This reflected a modus operandi where enforcement was seldom used and inspectors relied on trying to find solutions with providers on a consensual basis. The interviews also revealed no evidence that public, private non-profit or for-profit providers were being inspected differently. Data collected through these inspections is used neither for regional benchmarking nor for comparisons over time. Public disclosure of inspection results is currently not being considered, neither are data available about enforcement measures (fines) in case of non-compliance. During inspection procedures older people are not given a specific voice, apart from what emerges in interviews and observation of residents. Only in Lower Austria has there been a regional survey that gathered data on the satisfaction levels of residents, their family members and staff carried out recently. Altogether, sixty-six care homes participated in the survey and about 10,000 questionnaires were analysed. The results reveal that 96 per cent of family members report that the care home satisfies their expectations, and 98 per cent of residents are completely or rather satisfied with the care they receive (NÖ LAK/ZeSG, 2010). However, it has to be underlined that interviews were carried out by care staff.

In general, the residents' voice is represented in all regions by the 'Patient and/or Resident Advocate'. This organization usually focuses on acute care patients but has developed, for instance in Vienna, as an advocate for residents of care homes. Furthermore, many regions' care home legislation stipulates that a residents' council should be established as well as complaints procedures that may be used by residents, their friends or family members. It should be mentioned that the Viennese Care Home Commission has started to influence the long-term care sector by means of recommendations, studies and model projects derived from expert knowledge and direct contact with residents and their families. Although evidence for tangible improvements, e.g. in terms of evaluation studies, has not yet been produced, some recommendations such as training and employment of discharge managers or small housing units for people with dementia have been implemented to improve performance (Wiener Heimkommission, 2010; 2011).

Two additional types of institutions should be mentioned when it comes to monitoring performance in the long-term care sector. On the one hand, federal and regional audit commissions have audited the care home sector in selected regions (Rechnungshof, 2011a) and/or individual public care homes (Steiermärkischer Landtag/ Landesrechnungshof, 2002), mainly to check their organizational efficacy, economic viability and accountability. As an example of the findings of the federal and regional audit commissions, a comparison of financial and administrative practices in two regions, provided by the Federal Audit Commission (Rechnungshof, 2011a), revealed shortcomings in terms of planning, funding and quality assurance. For instance, only 15 per cent of Carinthian care homes complied with defined staffing levels – with up to 20 per cent lacking registered nurses – while in Tyrol there were still care homes that had never been inspected over the past five years, although the law stipulates inspections every two years. Another report about care for older people in Carinthia (Rechnungshof, 2008) criticized the fact that the public funder had hardly any influence on the services provided and that it was up to the non-profit providers of home care services to decide on the needs and services provided to the user.

On the other hand, the Working Group for Long-Term Care, which was installed at the Ministry of Social Affairs in the context of the care reform in 1993, comprises representatives of all regional governments. It compiles yearly statistical reports on the number of long-term care allowance recipients, services and facilities and thus provides an important, though incomplete, database in this sector. Notwithstanding some progress, the working group has still not succeeded in streamlining reporting systems, so data are barely comparable. Reports do not systematically monitor quality issues, nor do they include findings and results from inspections. However, in 2009, registered nurses visited more than 17,000 beneficiaries of long-term care allowances living at home (about 4 per cent of all recipients) to assess their general care conditions, which, in 99 per cent of all visits, were qualified as good or very good; only six cases of poor care conditions and neglect were detected (BMASK, 2012).

2.3.5 *Quality assurance in acute healthcare*

Compared to the scattered approach to quality assurance in long-term care, a more engaged policy discourse can be observed with respect to quality thinking in acute healthcare settings. In the context of health reforms carried out in 2004–5, a specific Health Quality Act was adopted to promote a 'systematic quality approach' based on the principles of patient orientation, transparency, efficacy and efficiency (BGBl 179/2004) and thus a nationwide quality system is to be developed. The Federal Minister for Health may define quality standards and has been supported since 2006 by the purposely-established Federal Institute for Quality in Healthcare (BIQG), which is currently working primarily on standards for disease management (diabetes, dementia, Parkinson's, discharge management). In addition, in 2006, a Federal Healthcare Agency (Bundesgesundheitsagentur/BGA), and similar regional agencies (Landesgesundheitsfonds/LGF) were established to improve planning, management and financing of the health system. The regional healthcare funds should implement the guidelines at the regional level by pooling the financial resources from social health insurance, the federal government and the regional hospital funds (Hofmarcher and Röhrling, 2006). The different stakeholders meet regularly in the framework of regional 'Health Platforms' which also design, tender and select projects to improve the coordination of services between in-patient and out-patient services. Each regional healthcare fund used to earmark 1 per cent of its funds, altogether about €130 million per year, to support these so-called 'reform pool projects' (Hofmarcher et al., 2007). However, due to a lack of interest and political will, this voluntary instrument was halted in 2013.

In any case, these efforts have thus far not produced an important spill-over effect onto long-term care provision. The 2005 Healthcare Reform is a good example of the neglect of the long-term care sector in the context of health policy. Although the aim of optimizing management and coordination at the interfaces between different care providers has been an explicit goal of the reform, long-term care providers have not been considered as relevant stakeholders to be involved.

2.4 Quality management and quality development at the provider level – a voluntary bottom-up approach

The professionalization of long-term care providers and management, both in residential and community care only really began during the 1990s with some structural innovations such as the foundation of a Federation of Care Homes (Lebenswelt Heim) in 1994, when directors of care homes started to follow specific training courses for care home management on a voluntary basis – conceived along with the European Association for Directors and Providers of Residential Care Homes for the Elderly (EDE). In addition, a federation of non-profit organizations providing social care (Bundesarbeitsgemeinschaft Freie Wohlfahrt) was founded in 1995 to join the forces of hitherto divided entities affiliated to the churches or political parties. It developed quality criteria for community-based care[11] – such as, for instance, having a service charter, documentation and monitoring of professional processes, further training of staff, user orientation, etc. – and has been involved in debates on recent care reforms (see below). In the context of the Austrian system of social partnership it is also important to mention that a voluntary federation of employers in social and healthcare (Berufsvereinigung von Arbeitgebern für Gesundheits- und Sozialberufe) was founded in 1997 with the main aim to establish a commonly agreed collective bargaining process for social care workers, with respective standards and levels of payment (www.bags-kv.at).

---

[11] This document defines structural and process indicators for all community-based care services (www.freiewohlfahrt.at).

While national, regional and local authorities slowly began to commission research studies and pilot projects in the area of long-term care (Bahr and Leichsenring, 1995; Kaltenbrunner and Kattnigg, 2008; Pass and Hofer, 2009), it is evident that public authorities remained hesitant to regulate quality measurement, for instance by requiring all care homes to obtain a quality certificate on the free market of certification agencies (as in Switzerland). Moreover, the German approach towards centrally defined inspection procedures and public reporting by means of indicators and grades was not adopted by Austrian regulators and policy makers.

The extent to which and the way in which quality assurance or quality management should be applied, if at all, has emerged primarily via highly variable special by-laws. As a result, a bottom-up process concerning the development of quality management in long-term care has developed as some providers started to voluntarily introduce ISO 9000[12] or QAP,[13] an adaptation of EFQM,[14] while others joined the development of an initiative to create a specific quality management system for care homes under the title E-Qalin (see Section 2.4.1). Still, in 2010, no more than about 20 per cent of Austrian care homes had a certified quality management system (Steuerungsgruppe NQZ, 2010) and, with the exception of Lower Austria and Vienna, no specific methods or standards have been defined by public authorities in relation to how and what kind of quality management should be applied. In Vienna, the Federation of Viennese Health and Social Care Services, which also includes many providers of residential care, has published a 'quality programme' to develop quality assurance based on the Viennese legal framework for care homes and on acknowledged expert standards (Schrems et al., 2007). In Lower Austria, where it has become legally binding for all care homes to introduce E-Qalin as a

[12] The ISO 9000 family of standards is published by the International Organization of Standards (ISO) and deals with the fundamentals of quality management systems (www.iso.org/iso/iso_9000_essentials).

[13] 'Quality As Process' (QAP) was one of the first quality management systems in German-speaking Europe to translate the EFQM standards into the area of health and social care. It has now been developed into 'Go4Excellence' (see www.swexs.com).

[14] The European Foundation for Quality Management (EFQM) was founded in 1988 by leading industrial corporations to develop a management tool to increase the competitiveness of European organizations by means of an excellence model that is widely used in all kinds of economic sectors (www.efqm.org).

quality management system, a care inspection unit has been established that is complemented by an expert group on care. Apart from inspection and control, the aim has also been to develop and implement expert standards and an overall concept of care for the region.

2.4.1 European Quality Improvement and Innovative Learning (E-Qalin)

The outlined situation may explain why the Federation of Care Homes became engaged in the development of a project proposal by the Austrian Institute for Training and Education in Public Health to construct a transnational quality management system for residential care, involving, among others, the Ministry for Social Affairs and Consumer Protection and the European Association for Directors and Providers of Long-Term Care Services for the Elderly. This project was co-financed (2004–7) by the European Union Leonardo da Vinci Programme and involved almost thirty organizations from seven member states and thirty 'pilot care homes' in Austria, Germany, Italy, Luxembourg and Slovenia under the title 'European Quality Improvement and Innovative Learning in Residential Care for Older People' (E-Qalin). The result of this initiative was a full-fledged quality management system for care homes that has been introduced in about 150 care homes (about 18 per cent of all providers) in Austria, while in Lower Austria the regional government has made the implementation of E-Qalin compulsory and has funded the training of E-Qalin process managers for all care homes.[15]

The E-Qalin quality management system supports initiatives to map the reality in residential care facilities by accompanying representatives of all stakeholders to assess and improve structures, processes and results (Table 2.3). E-Qalin seeks to enable stakeholders by means of specific training modules to enhance communication, social competence and systems-thinking within the organization. E-Qalin process managers are trained to guide the self-assessment process within the care home, to set up a steering group with representatives of all stakeholders (whenever possible also including residents, relatives and other external

---

[15] Whilst initially developed for care homes, E-Qalin models also have been issued for community care services, for services and facilities for people with disabilities and for general social work.

Performance measurement in long-term care in Austria 57

Table 2.3 *Overview of the E-Qalin model to assess and improve the quality of care homes in Austria*

Structures and Processes (66 criteria = 50 per cent)	Results (25 partial results assessed by key performance indicators = 50 per cent)
Five Perspectives	Five Perspectives
• Users, e.g. biographical approach, privacy, care process	• Users, e.g. quality of care, user satisfaction (quality of life)
• Staff, e.g. working time arrangements, cooperation, communication, incentives	• Staff, e.g. satisfaction with working conditions, staff-turnover
• Leadership, e.g. corporate policies, organization, financial management	• Leadership, e.g. economic viability, financing, costs
• Social context, e.g. relationships with families, partners, media	• Social accountability, e.g. satisfaction of family and friends, attractiveness as employer
• Learning organization, e.g. learning, transfer of knowledge, assessment	• Future orientation, e.g. sustainability, education and training

Source: Authors' compilation based information on the E-Qalin website: www.e-qalin.net.

stakeholders), to coordinate assessment groups consisting of representatives of all staff involved, and to steer the organizational development process linked to the introduction of E-Qalin. In addition, E-Qalin facilitators are trained to guide these groups in assessing criteria from a user and staff perspective.

The E-Qalin model does not prescribe standards or key performance indicators to be chosen, but organizations are supported to work with those key performance indicators that are most suited to their current status and that improve transparency. While in the area 'structures and processes' the assessment of individual criteria follows the classic PDCA (plan-do-check-act) cycle of quality management (plus INVOLVEMENT), key performance indicators in the area of 'results' are assessed and analysed with respect to their changes over time and the way they are used to steer quality and to implement measures for achieving defined targets.

An evaluation study with participating pilot care homes (nine in Austria, six in Germany, six in Luxembourg, two in Italy, six in Slovenia) showed that, for the huge majority, E-Qalin helps to identify and analyse shortcomings, to develop new solutions and to implement improvement projects (Rosenbaum and Schlüter, 2007). The experience of E-Qalin also revealed that only a few managers and staff in care homes are used to working with these kinds of tools, in particular with controlling and results-oriented indicators. With the introduction of E-Qalin, a rising number of care homes in Austria (as also in Luxembourg, Germany and Slovenia) have learned to identify key performance indicators and to use these as a tool for strategic management and steering processes. The skills achieved by stakeholders also led to an increased awareness of the usefulness of mutual exchange of data, 'benchmarking' and learning from each other. While care homes in Slovenia have made results public and have even started benchmarking processes, in Austria and Germany E-Qalin care homes have still not disclosed their results, in spite of generally positive feedback.

2.4.2 The National Quality Certificate (NQZ) for care homes

In parallel to the development of E-Qalin, and widely based on the experiences during the project, the Austrian Ministry for Social Affairs and Consumer Protection started an initiative to develop a National Quality Certificate (NQZ) as a tool for the voluntary external certification of care homes that already have in place an acknowledged quality management system. Although all of these systems already stipulate an external audit, the NQZ is conceived as a supplementary external audit to complement the self-assessment process at a national level, with a specific focus on the characteristics of care homes.[16] The aim is to make the quality of care homes visible and transparent, and to provide incentives for quality improvement by exchanging good practice and provide visibility to certified providers. As clients are free to choose between providers and between types of service, the NQZ might

---

[16] This solution was chosen as the federal ministry cannot, and did not want to, prescribe a particular type of quality management system for care homes. Therefore the NQZ was conceived as an overarching instrument that is accessible and feasible for all care homes that have introduced any kind of accredited quality management system.

Performance measurement in long-term care in Austria 59

improve their information base and the market position of certified care homes.

In 2008, a first pilot phase with fourteen care homes and the training of external auditors (quality managers, care home managers with quality management experience) was launched. An evaluation showed broad satisfaction with the certification tools and procedures, independent of the quality management system used by the pilot homes (Steuerungsgruppe NQZ, 2010). The NQZ is currently being prepared for a general roll-out over the next few years. It is supported by a broad coalition, including most regional governments, the Federation of Care Homes and user organizations. This initiative will remain on a voluntary basis as experience has shown that organizational improvement only works if management and staff are engaged in quality management, rather than perceiving it as yet another bureaucratic exercise to please funders, regulators or purchasers. The intrinsic motivation of management and staff will thus be supported by integrating standards for palliative care or specific geriatric care and the exchange of 'good practice' examples. Finally, a legal regulation of NQZ procedures and an 'NQZ organization' to administer and coordinate certifications were established in 2013. In a mid-term perspective, this initiative could also become the basis for meaningful public reporting of certified care homes' performance.

2.5 Challenges for transparency and performance management of long-term care in Austria

This chapter has provided an overview of efforts that have been made in Austria over the past few years concerning the development of quality assurance, quality management and related issues to further improve quality, but also to overcome the lack of transparency and public acknowledgement of long-term care. While the developments described here have not yet resulted in public reporting and thus might appear slow and cumbersome, one should bear in mind that only fifteen years ago the majority of care homes was managed by directors with no specific education or knowledge in care for older people and residents could be physically restrained without any legal decision. Residents had no written rights as their stay was not based on a contract between them and the care home provider and many facilities still had 'visiting hours' for friends or family members rather than twenty-four-hour access. Certainly some of these shortcomings continue to exist, including generally low educational standards of staff and a broad unease concerning transparent assessments and comparisons. The employment of social workers is still a novelty in Austrian care homes. Graduates from masters courses for health and social care management or nurses with a Ph.D. – the first chair of nursing sciences was established only in 1999 – do not easily find suitable jobs as more scientific approaches to care still face difficulties. Thus, a first challenge will be to generally increase training for management and staff – with respective implications for payment levels and resources needed within the entire sector.

It has been argued in the context of the Austrian healthcare system that the lack of competition might be one reason for the difficulty of implementing major reforms (Laimböck, 2008). The same might apply also to long-term care, although it is likely that cooperation and coordination, key issues for providing quality in long-term care, might be further hampered by the introduction of more market mechanisms (Leichsenring et al., 2013). In any case, during the past few years most tenders to manage hitherto public care homes or new facilities in Austria have been won by private for-profit providers, and most often due to lower costs, rather than based on defined quality criteria. In community care, users may choose between different non-profit providers in almost all regions (except Tyrol and Vorarlberg), but both capped prices and the capped numbers of subsidized service hours available are creating a highly regulated quasi-market. Competition between home care and residential care providers can be observed in only a few areas as it is still mainly (deficient) supply structures that determine access.

Governance mechanisms that find a balance between market-based mechanisms and social planning will thus be a second challenge to be addressed. In Austria, this will include a reform of the vertical distribution of responsibilities (state, regions, municipalities) that goes beyond the recent agreement concerning the introduction of a 'Long-term Care Fund'. Local, regional and national decision makers conceived this fund with the main objective of closing the funding-gap that regions and municipalities face in relation to expenditures for care homes and home care services. In the context of respective negotiations between federal and regional governments, the following measures were agreed upon:

Performance measurement in long-term care in Austria 61

- Between 2011 and 2014, the federal government will support regional governments with an earmarked transfer of €685 million to cover expenditures for long-term care services and facilities.
- The federal government will take over all administrative and financial burdens for those beneficiaries of long-term care allowances which had hitherto been administered by the regional governments, with a respective reimbursement of the former by the latter.[17]
- The 280 different offices that had been involved in the administration of the long-term care allowance at all levels will be reduced to eight, also in order to create a consistent and informed database of beneficiaries.

This shift in responsibilities was not contingent upon the adoption of any measures concerning the quality of services or to any improved ability of the federal government to steer quantitative and/or qualitative developments in the regions. No conditions were formulated by the federal government that would link additional funding to more transparency, quality development or evidence-based improvements. The debates about the long-term care fund also revealed that regional and local governments are not interested or willing to use their position as purchasers and regulators to improve quality measurement and public reporting. In many cases this may be because policymakers worry that quality improvement would require additional investments that would increase costs. Although originally the Long-term Care Fund was viewed as an interim solution, it now seems to be considered the main instrument to steer the further development of the long-term care system in Austria.

In this context, with a general lack of incentives – as fines for non-compliance are low and rarely enforced and the market on the supply side is heavily regulated – it may even seem surprising that many care home providers have started to engage in quality management with an intrinsic, professional motivation, and the awareness that quality management serves to also improve economic performance. In principle, users are free to choose between providers and types of care

---

[17] Regional governments hitherto administered and financed attendance allowances for social assistance recipients who were also in need of care. From now on all beneficiaries of attendance allowances will be centrally administered, but regional governments will reimburse the federal state for beneficiaries without a pension entitlement.

provision, but they lack publicly available information about quality of care – and they prefer, in general, to stay at home as long as possible. It is thus likely that their choice remains mainly based on the mere availability of services, proximity to the family, word of mouth and/or the affiliation of the care provider to the political or religious preferences of clients (Bahr and Leichsenring, 1995).

The lack of competition may be one reason why providers' investments in quality improvement are still rather low. When it comes to setting priorities, structural investments, e.g. in fire protection or other safety requirements, will win over investments in transparency and quality control. In the long run, however, both political and administrative strategies, as well as further efforts by providers to create a more transparent system of quality reporting, will be needed since future generations of users are likely to be far more demanding about the services or facilities they will choose. In this respect, developments in the Open Method of Coordination[18] and other initiatives at the EU level (for instance, SPC, 2010) could serve to raise awareness of the value of public reporting on quality (see also Nies et al., 2013).

The same might apply to initiatives in the healthcare system that could trigger a spill-over effect in long-term care, in particular once claims for 'more coordination and cooperation' are heard. In this case, there will also be a need to develop quality assurance and quality management systems, as well as appropriate outcome indicators, across providers and with a focus on the interfaces at system and organizational boundaries – which is still an area without any experience to draw on (Hoffmann and Leichsenring, 2011). In the meantime, while the healthcare sector invests in expert standards and performance measurement, standards in long-term care will improve slowly with the introduction of different quality management systems, mainly pushed by the most 'enlightened' providers and managers. It is still too early to say whether these initiatives have been able to improve quality as no empirical studies have yet been conducted. However, management and staff who were not previously used to working with indicators at all have now started to deal with data and to monitor trends that, in general, seem to be positive for individual care homes.

---

[18] www.peer-review-social-inclusion.eu/peer-reviews/2010/achieving-quality-long-term-care-in-residential-facilities

Cooperation between community care and care home providers, the provision of integrated care packages, not to mention continuity of care between hospital in-patient care and community care, will nevertheless remain a challenge for the future, in particular when it comes to assessing, measuring and reporting on outcomes of inter-agency working.

While this still shaky, fragmented and not sufficiently needs-oriented system of formal long-term care is developing, many older people in need of such care and their carers have chosen other alternatives. In order to overcome persistent care gaps they prefer (or are forced) to use 'paid informal care' provided mostly by 'self-employed' migrant carers from neighbouring countries. About 30–40,000 formally self-employed domestic assistants, mainly from Slovakia and the Czech Republic, provide twenty-four-hour care with no or very scarce public control or quality assurance in at least 15,000 Austrian households. This area will be a further challenge for quality development over the next few years, at least as long as unemployment and low wages persist in the domestic assistants' home countries.

References

Badelt, C., Holzmann-Jenkins, A., Matul, C. and Österle, A. (1997). *Analyse der Auswirkungen des Pflegevorsorgesystems.* Forschungsbericht im Auftrag des Bundesministeriums für Arbeit, Gesundheit und Soziales. Vienna: BMAGS.

Bahr, C. and Leichsenring, K. (1995). *'leben und pflegen' – Beratung und Koordination im Sozialsprengel. Evaluation eines dreijährigen Modellprojekts im Auftrag der NÖ.* Landesregierung und der Bundesministerin für Frauenangelegenheiten. Vienna: Europäisches Zentrum.

Barth, P. and Engel, A. (2004). *Heimrecht: Heimaufenthaltsgesetz, Heimvertragsrecht mit Musterheimvertrag.* Vienna: Manz.

Biwald, P., Hochholdinger, N., Köfel, M., Gencgel, M. and Haindl, A. (2011). *Pflege und Betreuung in Österreichs Städten. Status Quo, Entwicklung und Reformoptionen.* Vienna: KDZ Zentrum für Verwaltungsforschung.

Bundesministerium für Arbeit, Soziales und Konsumentenschutz/BMASK (2012). *Österreichischer Pflegevorsorge-Bericht* 2011. Vienna: BMASK.

Fasching, P. (2007). Der Heimarzt – Ein Modell zur Verbesserung der ärztlichen Betreuung in Pflegeheimen. Erfahrungen und Stand der Debatte in Österreich [The nursing home physician – a model to improve medical care in nursing homes. Experiences and state of the debate in Austria]. *Ethik in der Medizin,* 19(4): 313–19.

Fischbacher, P. (2011). *Stationäre Langzeitpflege in Österreich: Überlegungen zur Qualität, deren gesetzlicher Grundlage und deren Kontrolle (unv. Masterthesis)*. Salzburg: Universitätslehrgang Executive MBA Healthcare Management.

Ganner, M. (2008). 'Rechtliche Aspekte', in BMSK (ed.), *Hochaltrigkeit in Österreich. Eine Bestandsaufnahme*. Vienna: BMSK, pp. 427–46.

Grundböck, A., Rappauer, A. and Müller, G. (2003). *Evaluation des Dienstleistungsangebotes Entlassungsmanagement durch ambulante Anbieterorganisationen im Kaiser-Franz-Josef-Spital der Stadt Wien*. Research report. Vienna: Dachverband Wiener Pflege- und Sozialdienste.

Hoffmann, F. and Leichsenring, K. (2011). Quality management by result-oriented indicators: Towards benchmarking in residential care for older people. Vienna: European Centre for Social Welfare Policy and Research. Policy brief June 2011/1. Available at: www.euro.centre.org/detail.php?xml_id=1900.

Hofmarcher, M. and Quentin, W. (2013). Austria: health system review. *Health Systems in Transition*, 15(7).

Hofmarcher, M. and Röhrling, G. (2006). Integration of care after the 2005 health reform. *Health Policy Monitor*, April 2006. Available at: www.hpm.org/survey/at/a7/1.

Hofmarcher, M., Röhrling, G. and Walch, D. (2007). Integration of care – follow up. *Health Policy Monitor*, April 2007. Available at: www.hpm.org/survey/at/a9/2.

Kaltenbrunner, G. and Kattnigg, A. (2008). Erfolgskriterien für wirkungsorientiertes Controlling. Eine Reflexion am Beispiel einer öffentlichen Verwaltung. In R. Schauer, B. Helmig, R. Purtschert and D. Witt (eds.), *Steuerung und Kontrolle in Nonprofit-Organisationen, 8. Colloquium der NPO-Forscher im deutschsprachigen Raum, Johannes Kepler Universität Linz, 17–18 April 2008. Eine Dokumentation*. Linz: Trauner Verlag, pp. 285–308.

Laimböck, M. (2008). *Die Zukunft des österreichischen Gesundheitssystems: Wettbewerbsorientierte Patientenversorgung im internationalen Vergleich*. Vienna: Springer.

Leichsenring, K., Nies, H. and van der Veen, R. (2013). The quest for quality in long-term care in Europe – improving policy and practice. In K. Leichsenring, J. Billings and H. Nies (eds.), *Long-term Care in Europe – Improving Policy and Practice*. Basingstoke: Macmillan, pp. 167–90.

Leichsenring, K., Ruppe, G., Rodrigues, R. and Huber, M. (2009). *Long-Term Care and Social Services in Austria. Contribution to the Worldbank Workshop and Study Tour on Social and Long-term Care*. Vienna: European Centre/Worldbank.

Nies, H., Leichsenring, K. and van der Veen, R. (2013). Quality management and improvement in long-term care in Europe. In OECD/European Commission (eds.), *A Good Life in Old Age? Monitoring and Improving Quality in Long-term Care*. Paris: OECD, pp. 223–45.

NÖ Landesakademie/ZeSG – Zentrum für Soziales und Generationen (2010). *Zufriedenheitstudie in den niederösterreichischen Pflegeheimen der ARGE Heime NÖ*. St Pölten: NÖ LAK/ZeSG.

OECD (2005). *Long-Term Care for Older People*. Paris: OECD.

Pass, C. and Hofer, B. (2009). *Evaluierung NQZ-Pilotphase*. Linz/Vienna: Public Opinion/BMASK.

Pochobradsky, E., Bergmann, F., Brix-Samoylenko, E., Erfkamp, H. and Laub, R. (2005). *Situation pflegender Angehöriger*. Studie im Auftrag des Bundesministeriums für soziale Sicherheit, Generationen und Konsumentenschutz. Vienna: ÖBIG.

Pochobradsky, E., Nemeth, C. and Preninger, B. (2008). *Evaluierung und Fortschreibung des Bedarfs- und Entwicklungsplanes für stationäre, teilstationäre und mobile soziale Dienste in Kärnten*. Vienna: ÖBIG.

Prochazkova, L. and Schmid, T. (2009). Homecare Aid: a Challenge for Social Policy and Research. In S. Ramon and D. Zaviršek (eds.), *Critical Edge Issues in Social Work and Social Policy: Comparative Research Perspectives*. Ljubljana: Faculty of Social Work, University of Ljubljana, pp. 139–64.

Rechnungshof/Wirkungsbereich des Landes Kärnten (2008). Altenbetreuung im Bereich der Sozialhilfe. Vienna: RH. Available at: www.rechnungshof.at.

(2011a). Altenbetreuung in Kärnten und Tirol. Vienna: RH. Available at: www.rechnungshof.at.

(2011b). *Belegsmanagement in Akutkrankenanstalten mit dem Schwerpunkt 'Procuratio–Fälle'*. Vienna: Rechnungshof.

Riess, G., Rottenhofer, I., Winkler, P., Busch, M. and Stangl, P. (2007). *Österreichischer Pflegebericht 2007 im Auftrag des Bundesministeriums für Gesundheit, Familie und Jugend*. [Austrian Nursing Report 2007] Vienna: Gesundheit Österreich/ÖBIG.

Rodrigues, R. (2010). Governance and Finance of Long-Term Care in Austria. INTERLINKS National Report. Vienna: European Centre. Available at: http://interlinks.euro.centre.org.

Rosenbaum, U. and Schlüter, W. (2007). *Endbericht Evaluierung E-Qalin®*. Zwickau: Westsächsische Hochschule.

Schmidt, A., Winkelmann, J., Leichsenring, K. and Rodriguez, R. (2013). *Migrant Care Workers in 24-hour Care in Austria*. ECAB Working Paper. Vienna: ECAB.

Schneider, U., Österle, A., Schober, C. and Schober, D. (2006). *Die Kosten der Pflege in Österreich, Ausgabenstrukturen und Finanzierung. Forschungsbericht*. Vienna: WU Wien/Institut für Sozialpolitik.

Scholta, M. (2008). Vom Armenasyl zur Hausgemeinschaft: Gemeinschaftliches Wohnen bei Betreuungs- und Pflegebedarf. In BMSK (ed.), *Hochaltrigkeit in Österreich. Eine Bestandsaufnahme*. Vienna: BMSK, pp. 389–412.

Schrems, B., Dachverband Wiener Sozialeinrichtungen und Fonds Soziales Wien (2007). *Qualitätsprogramm für Wiener Wohn- und Pflegeheime. Zielkatalog und Leitfaden zur Qualitätssicherung und -kontrolle in Wiener Wohn- und Pflegeheimen nach dem Wiener Wohn- und Pflegeheimgesetz (WWPG) [Quality Programme for Viennese Old Age and Nursing Homes. Aims and Guidelines for Quality Assurance and Control in Viennese Old Age and Nursing Homes according to the Viennese Care Home Act]*. Vienna: Dachverband Wiener Sozialeinrichtungen, Fonds Soziales Wien, MA 15 – Gesundheitswesen und Soziales.

Social Protection Committee (2010). A voluntary European quality framework for social services. Brussels: SPC. SPC/2010/10/8 final, available at: ec.europa.eu/social/BlobServlet?docId=6140&langId=en).

Steiermärkischer Landtag/Landesrechnungshof (2002). Bericht betreffend die Prüfung der Gebarung, der Organisation und der Auslastung der Landesaltenpflegeheime Bad Radkersburg, Kindberg, Knittelfeld und Mautern. Graz: Stmk. Landtag. Available at: www.landesrechnungshof.steiermark.at.

Steuerungsgruppe NQZ (2010). *2. Zwischenbericht der Arbeitsgruppe NQZ*. Vienna: BMASK.

Wiener Heimkommission (ed.) (2010; 2011). *Bericht der Wiener Heimkommission*. Annual report. Vienna: Wiener Heimkommission bei der Wiener Pflege, Patientinnen- und Patientenanwaltschaft.

WHO (2000). *Towards an International Consensus on Policy for Long-Term Care for the Ageing*. Geneva: WHO and Milbank Memorial Fund.

3 | Monitoring the quality of long-term care in Germany

VJENKA GARMS-HOMOLOVÁ AND
REINHARD BUSSE

3.1 Introduction

Germany belongs to the group of countries that have undergone, and are undergoing, dramatic demographic changes. The already high life expectancy at birth, of 77 years and 9 months for men and 82 years and 9 months for women, has been continuously increasing (at the rate of around 3 months for boys, and 2 months for girls) since the last count in 2011 (Statistisches Bundesamt, 2011a, 2011b, 2012). Due to the growing birth deficit, which amounted to minus 162,000 in 2008 (equivalent to 0.2 per cent of the population) and which is predicted to reach minus 550,000 (or 0.8 per cent of the population) in 2060 (Statistisches Bundesamt, 2011c), the entire German population is shrinking – from 82 million today to around 70 million in 2060. At the same time, the population structure is changing. Today, 21 per cent of Germans are aged 65 or older (Statistisches Bundesamt, 2011a), but this group will grow to 34 per cent in 2060. In particular, the oldest part of the population aged 80 or over will expand from today's 5 per cent of the population to 14 per cent in 2060 (Statistisches Bundesamt, 2011c). Due to these demographic changes, the need for long-term care will also grow, despite all the progress made in the areas of health promotion, prevention, medical treatment and rehabilitation. Already today, 2.8 per cent of the population (2.3 million people) needs long-term care, up from 2.5 per cent in 1999. Current forecasts to 2030 predict an increase of around 50 per cent to 3.3 million (Statistisches Bundesamt, 2010).

For the 2.3 million people needing long-term care, it is provided in residential facilities in 31 per cent of cases (around 0.7 million people or 0.9 per cent of the total German population). The remaining 69 per cent of those needing care (1.62 million people) live in private, individual housing. Of these, two-thirds (1.07 million) receive informal care by relatives only, while the other third (555,000 people) use formal home care services that are provided by 12,000 home care agencies, or rather, their 269,000 staff members (Statistisches Bundesamt, 2011d). Evidently, the increasing interest in quality of care is a result of the large number of people concerned: users of long-term care, their relatives and members of their social network, and staff of long-term care facilities and home care agencies. Equally important is the fact that there will be an increase in the proportion of the population that will be involved in long-term care in the future (Rothgang et al., 2011).

3.2 The regulatory background to quality management and assurance

3.2.1 Long-term care insurance: legislation, beneficiaries, purchasers and providers

Since the legislation on the long-term care insurance scheme came into effect in 1995 – after two decades of debate on how to ensure broad and financially sustainable access to long-term care in an ageing society – it has become the dominant structural component of long-term care in Germany, a situation similar to healthcare. The German system of social insurance covers sickness (i.e. health insurance), occupational accidents and disease (i.e. accident insurance), old age and disability (i.e. pension insurance), unemployment and, as the fifth pillar, long-term care. The cornerstone of all social insurance legislation in Germany is the Code of Social Law (Sozialgesetzbuch; SGB). It provides the regulatory framework for all of the statutory insurance schemes across the purview of different ministries. Long-term care insurance and the provision of long-term care services fall within the remit of the Federal Ministry of Health, and are regulated primarily by SGB XI, which was added to the Code of Social Law by the Long-term Care Act (Pflegeversicherungsgesetz; PflegeVG) of 1994 (Busse et al., 2013).

All members of statutory sickness funds (including pensioners and the unemployed) as well as everyone with full-cover private health insurance were declared mandatory members. As health insurance has been mandatory for the entire population since 2009, coverage of long-term care is now also universal. Just as in health insurance, two main groups of insurers can be differentiated: (1) the statutory long-term care insurers are known as *Pflegekassen*, or long-term care funds; although legal entities in their own right, the long-term care funds are administered by the sickness funds (which act as payers in the Statutory Health Insurance system) and are located organizationally within them; and (2) private health insurers run long-term care insurance for their insured members alongside health insurance. Most importantly, anyone who has healthcare coverage through a sickness fund automatically has long-term care coverage (Busse et al., 2013).

In contrast to statutory health insurance, long-term care benefits are available upon application only. The medical review boards (Medizinischer Dienst der Krankenversicherung, MDK) – operated jointly by sickness funds and long-term care funds at the state (*Bundesland*) level – evaluate applicants and categorize their long-term care needs and thus their eligibility to receive benefits, while the final decision on entitlements is formally the responsibility of the responsible long-term care fund. Most of the private health insurers purchase this evaluation service from the MDK. Entitlement to insurance benefits is given when limitations in activities of daily living – and thus necessity for care – is expected to last for at least six months (hence 'long-term' care), while short-term nursing care continues to be funded by the sickness funds, and private insurers if included in their benefit packages. The final decision on eligibility is formally the responsibility of the relevant long-term care fund or private insurer. Beneficiaries with a care dependency have a choice either to receive monetary benefits or professional nursing care while living in a private home or in institutional long-term care facilities (mainly nursing homes). Approved beneficiaries have free choice of their care provider based on the principle of self-determination. If in-kind benefits are chosen, long-term care is delivered by a professional organization (either a home care agency or an institutional long-term care facility) which bills the respective long-term care fund directly for the services delivered. Those who choose cash benefits must settle for a comparatively limited amount of money that is intended to compensate for care provided only by relatives as professional caregivers cannot be covered. In such cases family and related informal caregivers are responsible for the quality of care. In 2009, 46 per cent of those entitled to long-term care benefits chose this option.

Long-term care insurance in Germany is financed using a pay-as-you-go approach. As with statutory health insurance, the long-term care insurance scheme is financed, for the most part, through a proportional contribution levied on gross wages. The contribution rate for the long-term care scheme has been 1.95 per cent since 2008 and is split equally between employer and employee; insured people without children pay an additional 0.25 per cent. Starting in January 2013, the contribution will increase up to 2.09 per cent, or 2.3 per cent for childless people (Bundesministerium für Gesundheit, 2012). The long-term care sector in Germany is regulated in much the same way as the healthcare sector, i.e. power is shared between both the federal and state levels as well as between governmental and delegated decision-making entities[1] and negotiations among them.

Within the legal framework provided by the federal Code of Social Law, purchasers and providers (or, more precisely, their 'umbrella organizations' at the state and federal levels) are required to determine the details regarding benefits, providers and quality – which in most other countries would be determined by the Ministry of Health – through negotiation and contractual arrangements ('self-regulation'). The agreements reached in these negotiations have the force of formal rules. In the event that negotiations are unsuccessful, the details are determined through arbitration boards (which include neutral members besides those appointed by the various stakeholders) or, if regulated by law, by the federal government itself (e.g., through the Federal Ministry of Health). Providers and purchasers of care services thus share responsibility for establishing the appropriate basket of available services, their reimbursement, the accessibility of care and its quality (for details see below). This means that stakeholders have to agree upon principles and mechanisms for quality control to fulfil the legal requirements regarding quality (Büscher, 2010). A further mechanism established to ensure quality is that long-term care funds may contract only with eligible providers, i.e., those that have fulfilled various registration criteria, including the quality criteria specified in SGB XI and the implementation of expert guidelines (see Section 3.3).

The main purchasers in the long-term care sector are the long-term care funds, which contract with providers (while private long-term care insurers reimburse their insured for incurred costs). The majority of providers are private for-profit or non-profit entities that have been contracted by the long-term care funds. In 2009, there were approximately 11,600 facilities providing institutional long-term care (with 845,000 nursing home beds, i.e. 1,030/100,000 population)

---

[1] These are public-law, 'corporatist' entities.

and approximately 12,000 home care agencies providing long-term care at home. The principle of subsidiarity applies to long-term care, meaning that in delivering long-term care services, private organizations are given priority over public institutions. This is the case for the whole social care sector. However, for long-term care private for-profit providers are explicitly given the same status as non-profit providers in order to foster competition in the long-term care market (Busse and Riesberg, 2005). Although the share of private for-profit institutional long-term care facilities (mainly nursing homes) has increased at the expense of public providers since 1994, non-profit welfare organizations still dominate institutional long-term care services. Of the institutional long-term care facilities contracted to provide nursing care under long-term care insurance (including day care centres), 55 per cent were owned by non-profit organizations, 40 per cent by private for-profit individuals or companies and 5 per cent publicly, usually by municipalities (for home care agencies, the shares were 37 per cent, 62 per cent and 2 per cent respectively). Institutional long-term care facilities owned by non-profit organizations had on average seventy residents, while private for-profit ones were smaller (fifty-five residents) and public ones larger (seventy-nine residents) (Busse et al., 2013).

3.2.2 *Regulatory responsibilities and powers*

Responsibility for regulating the long-term care sector is spread among different tiers of government and between these and delegated decision makers (i.e., purchasers and providers). That means that the federal-level government (or rather, the parliament) provides the general legal framework to determine the conditions of long-term care and for the long-term care market. This includes measures to increase competition as well as measures to ensure that standards are put in place. In neither the statutory health insurance nor the long-term care insurance schemes does the federal government have the authority to enact detailed measures regarding such issues as the quality of care. Rather, decision-making powers lie with the states, each of which has considerable freedom in shaping its own system, with further devolution granted to the municipalities in some instances. Decision-making jurisdictions are outlined in Box 3.1.

> **Box 3.1 Long-term care decision-making powers by different levels of government in Germany**
>
> **Federal level**
> The federal level of government determines the scope and the general nationwide rules for the provision and financing of long-term care services. Long-term care is regulated under the authority of the Federal Ministry of Health through Social Code Book XI (SGB XI). The education of personnel for nursing homes also is regulated at the federal level.
>
> **State (*Bundesland*) level**
> The responsibility for planning institutionalized care as well as home care lies with the states, which have to guarantee an adequate supply of services. They are prohibited from limiting the number of home care agencies so that competition in the sector may be maintained or increased. Alongside capacity planning and regulatory oversight, the states are also responsible for paying for investments in institutional long-term care facilities (regardless of their ownership status), while recurrent costs are financed by the long-term care funds ('dual financing'). The states may also finance investments in home care agencies – a special feature of the long-term care market (Busse et al., 2013). Furthermore, since 2006 the states have been able to replace federal regulations on homes for people with long-term care needs, for the elderly and the disabled by their own regulations.
>
> **Municipal level**
> Generally, the municipalities are the entities responsible for monitoring and ensuring that regulations regarding long-term care facilities and other homes for the elderly and disabled people are adhered to.

In addition to public (governmental) levels of regulatory oversight, due to the strong influence of long-term care insurance the long-term care sector is governed through delegated decision making by the 'corporatist' actors representing the purchasers and providers that operate the long-term care insurance scheme. In terms of quality measures, they are the ones with the actual power as they – based on requirements

Monitoring the quality of long-term care in Germany 73

defined by federal law – determine the details regarding measures, implementation and enforcement during contract negotiations. These actors are organized at the federal as well as the state level, with the definition of rules and standards mostly determined at the federal level, while implementation and enforcement occurring at the state level.

3.2.3 Current regulation regarding quality

To understand the duality in quality regulation, it is important to understand two separate but overlapping areas of competencies, namely that of the SGB XI/Long-Term Care Act 1994 and that of the Homes Act (Heimgesetz) (Figure 3.1). Entitlements, financing and the provision of long-term care – including quality requirements in both home care agencies as well as institutional long-term care facilities – are regulated by the Long-Term Care Act, while the Homes Act and a set of ordinances regulates all homes, i.e., nursing homes as well as other homes for elderly and disabled people. This means that institutional long-term care facilities fall under both regulatory spheres.

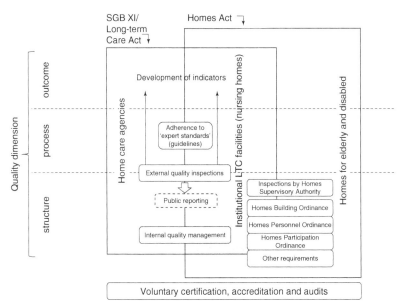

Figure 3.1 Legal responsibilities within the long-term care sector in Germany.
Source: compiled by authors.

As laid down in the SGB XI, long-term care providers (home care agencies and institutional long-term care facilities) are defined as being ultimately responsible for the quality of their services and are required to ensure and continuously improve the quality of these services by (a) implementing their own internal system of quality management and assurance, (b) adhering to expert guidelines developed by stakeholders, and (c) participating in unannounced and routine external quality inspections conducted by the MDK alone or in conjunction with state inspection agencies. The results of these external quality inspections have to be publicly reported (see Section 3.3.5). The details of the measures outlined above are determined by negotiations between the various stakeholders at the federal and state levels, as well as in contractual arrangements between purchasers and providers (see Section 3.3.2).

The Homes Act is the law that regulates housing and the accommodation of individuals in long-term care facilities and homes for the elderly, or for people with disabilities. The law focuses on the protection of residents on the one hand and their participation in decision making related to accommodation issues, on the other (BMFSFJ, 2010). The law regulates the terms of nursing home contracts, the involvement of advisory boards, assessment through the homes' supervisory authorities (Heimaufsicht) and the collaboration of the homes' supervisory authorities, MDK, long-term care funds and welfare organizations. The Homes Act establishes that the introduction of a quality management system according to SGB XI is a prerequisite for running a nursing care institution. Nursing homes have to be assessed regularly by the Homes Supervisory Authority (above all through the municipal organizational units) with or without prior notification. Thus, next to the MDK, the Homes Supervisory Authority is the other important actor performing external quality control in nursing homes (Schmitz and Schnabel, 2006). Its task is to assess and advise the nursing homes with regard to the application of the Homes Act. In addition, the Homes Supervisory Authority and the MDK can coordinate their efforts and perform quality assessments together, which is increasingly the case (MDS, 2011). The Homes Supervisory Authority has certain regulatory measures that it can use to address deficiencies, such as issuing orders, constraints and prohibitions.

Alongside the Homes Act, four complementary regulations exist at the federal level:

Monitoring the quality of long-term care in Germany 75

The Homes Building Ordinance (Heimbauverordnung) specifies minimum requirements with regard to the physical construction of nursing and other homes (e.g. square metres per room or inhabitant, width of doors, number of bathrooms).

The Homes Personnel Ordinance (Heimpersonalverordnung) defines certain qualification requirements for home directors, the ratio of skilled personnel to assistants, the possibility for vocational training etc.

The Homes Participation Ordinance (Heimmitwirkungsverordnung) states that home residents are entitled to elect a board which represents them in decision-making concerning issues such as residence, events, financing and organization (Nies et al., 2010).

The Homes Safe Payments Ordinance (Heimsicherungsverordnung) regulates the responsibilities and obligations of homes with respect to payments made by residents, especially if they finance investments.

In 2006, authority to regulate homes for the elderly and disabled was shifted to the states. Since then each state has been able to replace the federal Homes Act with its own rules and regulations and different states are at various stages of this process (BMFSFJ, 2010). For example, the state of Baden-Württemberg was the first to introduce its own Homes Building Ordinance in 2009. The regulation establishes that an individually utilizable living space or a single room with a private bathroom has to be available for each resident. Furthermore, the number of people in what are known as 'home communities' (*Wohngruppen*) is restricted to fifteen people (Sozialministerium Baden-Württemberg, 2009). Thus, not only is it possible for each state to have its own regulations, but the Homes Supervisory Authority is also organized differently in each state. Two types of organization are possible. The Homes Supervisory Authority is located either at the level of the state government or at the level of the municipal administration. Within both options, many models are possible, which increases the differences in the structure of quality assessment even more. The higher the level of administration at which the Homes Supervisory Authority is established, the greater the number of long-term care institutions it is responsible for. Within this framework, problems such as insufficient numbers of personnel and inadequate training, infrequent and quick assessment of homes, insufficient cooperation with other actors and the limited focus on structural (and certain areas of process) quality, are well known and discussed among stakeholders and policy makers (Schmitz and Schnabel, 2006).

In another development, a new law enacted in the summer of 2012 enables the long-term care insurance scheme to subsidize joint living in group apartments for people who need care (Bundesministerium für Gesundheit, 2012). While experience with the quality of existing group housing has been positive, a formal concept of quality monitoring has not been included into the new Care Redirection Law (Pflege-Neuausrichtung-Gesetz, PNG, Bundesministerium für Gesundheit, 2012).

3.3 The process of quality evaluation

3.3.1 The central role of the Medical Review Boards

Due to their dual role, the MDKs are the most important organizations for anyone who uses or provides long-term care. On the one hand, potential users or their relatives who apply for benefits under the long-term care insurance scheme have to undergo an assessment by MDK staff, who approve or refuse benefit entitlements and recommend the level of payment. The assessment process is problematic in that applicants are aware that decision making is somewhat strict, not really transparent, and not always just. Individuals who already receive long-term care insurance benefits fear periodic reassessment, in particular if their functional dependency is increasing and they need higher-level benefits. It is interesting to note that both potential beneficiaries and people already receiving long-term care benefits are not really aware that the final decision on eligibility is the responsibility of the long-term care fund and not the MDK. On the other hand, care providers and their staff know the MDK as the institution that evaluates their performance and its quality. The evaluation procedure will be described below and with this description we would like to highlight why care providers and their personnel believe that evaluations are often conducted in an inadequate way, following rules and regulations that are not transparent and therefore not just. Consequently, from the point of view of these groups of actors, the MDK does not have a positive image. However, this image is not only the result of the MDK's current functions – it can be traced back to the role of its unpopular predecessor, the medical review commission created in the 1930s, which was responsible for

Monitoring the quality of long-term care in Germany 77

monitoring people who receive benefits for 'unfitness to work' and examined if they were really ill.[2]

The functions of the MDK in long-term care insurance are broader now: among its key tasks are quality assurance and supervision of the adequacy of diagnostics and treatment. Since 1995, the MDK has been supervising not only healthcare provision, but long-term care as well. In practice, the MDK is only responsible for 'operational tasks' – for example the assessment of applicants for long-term care insurance benefits, or visits to long-term care facilities for the purpose of quality assessment. 'Strategic tasks', like the formulation of general principles, development of concepts, and choice of methods for assessments and inspection, are the responsibility of the Medical Review Board of the Federal Association of Sickness Funds (Medizinischer Dienst des Spitzenverbandes, MDS). The range of influence of the MDS stretches across the federal republic: it advises the sickness funds and the long-term care funds in all areas of their medical and nursing competency (MDS, 2011), whereas the MDK operates at the level of single federal states. Consequently, there is not only one Medical Review Board, but regional ones with numerous locations per state. Their line of action differs in some respects from state to state, and the uniform regulations which are set down by the MDS according to the federal law are implemented differently from one state to the other.

Today, Medical Review Boards (MDK) are meant to evaluate not only structural quality but all three dimensions of quality (structures, processes and outcomes) as defined by Donabedian (1982, 1987) according to rules formulated by the MDS (§197a, SGB XI). The range of competencies of the MDS and MDK, their obligations, as well as ways to meet them, are laid down by Section 11 of the Long-Term Care Act (SGB XI) in a very general way. The details are not included in the law itself, but rather in contracts between the contract partners: the long-term care funds, the MDS and providers' umbrella organizations. This type of contract is valid for a defined period only, usually one year. It can be cancelled, or has to be negotiated anew when it expires (Table 3.1).

---

[2] In addition, the MDK, in exercising its function for statutory health insurance, evaluates whether services, e.g., hospital stays, are really appropriate and necessary.

Table 3.1 *Obligations and competences of the Medical Review Boards at the state level (MDK) and the Medical Review Board of the Federal Association of Sickness Funds (MDS)*

Obligation or competence	Relevant sections in SGB XI	Responsibility	Explanation
Advice to care providers	§112(3)	MDK	Aim: prevention of quality deficits, strengthening of long-term care providers' responsibilities.
Participation in defining the principles for quality, quality assurance, and their control	§113; §114a	MDS	The MDS is obliged, through legislation, to collaborate with the long-term care funds and provider umbrella organizations.
Promotion of the development and implementation of 'expert standards'	§113a	MDS	The MDS has to collaborate with the long-term care funds and provider umbrella organizations.
Assessment and quality control of care provision by institutional long-term care facilities, semi-institutionalized settings and home care agencies	§114; §114a	MDK	Since 2011, regular quality assessments take place at least once a year. Both regular assessments and quality deficits assessments legally have to focus on outcomes of care.
Reporting	§114a; §115	MDS and MDK	Each MDK reports on their experiences with quality control and its results to the MDS every three years. The MDS is

Monitoring the quality of long-term care in Germany

Table 3.1 (*cont.*)

Obligation or competence	Relevant sections in SGB XI	Responsibility	Explanation
			obliged to prepare a report on quality and to present it to the federal government as well as to the Federal Association of Sickness Funds/ long-term care funds. Each MDK reports its quality control results to the respective state association of sickness funds/ long-term care funds. Respective state authorities also receive these reports.

Source: Compiled by authors.

3.3.2 Guidelines on Quality Evaluation

Under the Long-Term Care Enhancement Act (PflWG), which took effect in the summer of 2008, the MDS introduced revised guidelines to regulate the monitoring of quality of nursing homes and home care agencies (MDS, 2009a, 2009b). Previously, the medical review boards within the states, which are responsible for on-site quality inspections, became active only when clients or their relatives complained about the care they received (*Anlassprüfung*). Under this framework, the MDK carried out 37,000 quality assessments between 1997 and the implementation of the Long-Term Care Enhancement Act in 2008 (MDS,

2011). In 2008, MDK staff received permission to enter residential facilities or the private homes of service users day or night without prior announcement, and the number of quality assessments rose to 25,000 in just two and a half years (MDS, 2011). This random process of spot-checking nursing homes and home care agencies has now been replaced by a programme of annual quality assessment. In addition, MDK staff follow up on all complaints about quality.

The new guidelines for institutional long-term care facilities (nursing homes), the Guidelines on Quality Evaluation (Qualitätsprüfungsrichtlinien, QPR), describe a total of eighty-two criteria that have to be assessed: thirty-five dedicated to effectiveness in the areas of medically oriented nursing (primarily the communication of nurses with physicians), mobility, pressure ulcers and chronic wounds, nutrition and hydration, and incontinence; ten to management of dementia; ten to social and everyday activities; and nine to rooms, food, cleaning and care of residents' personal hygiene (MDS, 2009a: 137ff). Although the criteria are described in great detail, knowledgeable observers can easily see that all of them capture structures and processes, but none focus on a true outcome. As the basis for the quality assessment, MDK assessors have to use the nursing documentation from the previous four weeks before the assessment takes place (but not of a period longer than six months). It is this aspect that draws criticism from the system's opponents. They argue that it is not appropriate to draw far-reaching conclusions on quality of care from the nursing documentation. The guidelines provide a comprehensive explanation of the meaning of each aspect or assessment item, and recommend how to proceed when extracting the information from the nursing documentation record. Partially, the guidelines also present checklists, scales and recognized assessment methods that can be used to collect the information required. Other sections of the guidelines recommend the use of such instruments without presenting them in detail but corresponding references are made available. On the whole, the guidelines present a semi-structured methodology for the rating and evaluation of an institution's organization, equipment, performance and quality.

However, 'effectiveness and outcomes of care' targets are completely missing as no such measures are presented in the guidelines, and no operationalization of effects and outcomes is available. Thus, MDK assessors focus on the assessment of the structural quality, such as the management of a facility's human resources, environment and

Monitoring the quality of long-term care in Germany 81

equipment, organizational aspects of the facility, bed occupancy and monitoring. The characteristics of the main groups of residents, and the extent to which the facility is able to meet their preferences in terms of the accommodation and social contacts, are also part of the assessment. Another part deals explicitly with the question of whether the facility has an internal quality management system in place. According to the guidelines, MDK assessors have to survey residents on their subjective quality of life and their satisfaction with the facility and service. For this purpose, a fully structured questionnaire with eighteen items is included in the guidelines. The questionnaire covers satisfaction with the behaviour of staff, privacy, visits and opportunities to go outdoors, meals, availability of drinks free of charge, care of personal laundry and handling of complaints (MDS, 2009a). The MDK assessor who carries out the questionnaire has to make sure that no staff member is present during the interview.

The guidelines for home care and home help that are covered by long-term care insurance (SGB XI), as well as those for home nursing – covered by statutory health insurance (§37, SGB V) – do not differ substantially from those that regulate the supervision of quality in long-term care residential facilities (MDS, 2009b). Criteria related to the home environment and equipment are not included: instead, staff home visits are evaluated. As far as the quality of processes is concerned, the proper implementation of medical prescriptions and medical orders plays a major role. The evaluation survey of home care clients contains only twelve items (MDS, 2009b).

Generally, MDK assessors must be qualified nurses, but these can be substituted by 'other authorized experts', for instance, physicians or pediatricians. At least one member of the team has to be trained as an assessor. As far as the assessment of individual residents or clients is concerned, the guidelines require an examination of at least five people in residential facilities and home care agencies with less than fifty customers, or at least 10 per cent of customers of facilities or agencies with fifty or more residents/clients. The mix of these individuals has to reflect the case-mix of the long-term care beneficiaries within the particular facility or agency.

A new achievement of the Long-Term Care Enhancement Act is the effort to increase the transparency of the care market. The corresponding regulation is a part of the guidelines discussed above. Long-term care facilities and home care agencies must present their performance in a way that can be easily understood by customers. In line with this goal, a clear presentation of results from MDK assessments has been published online since July 2009, in a way that enables customers to compare services. The contract partners (i.e., long-term care purchasers and providers) have decided which aspects of the quality and structure of care need to be revealed and separate reports are published on long-term care residential facilities and home care agencies. The reporting contract, called a 'transparency agreement', uses marks (similar to school grades) that go from 1 (excellent) to 5 (insufficient) (MDS, 2009a, 2009b). During the period from 1 July 2008 to the end of 2010, the MDK had to examine about 11,500 home care agencies and 11,000 institutional long-term care facilities. Today, the evaluation results are provided annually.

3.3.3 Implementation of the general commitment to quality at the level of care providers

As mentioned above, care providers are obliged to participate in quality assurance activities (§72, 3 and § 112, 2 SGB XI) and they do, even if it is a struggle (MDS, 2007). For the staff of services and facilities, preparation for MDK monitoring is often accompanied by anxiety, a phenomenon this is not documented by the scientific literature but by a growing market of consultants who offer long-term care facilities and home care agencies professional prep-courses or brochures for trouble-free MDK inspections (PQSG 2012; Pro Pflege-Management, undated). While fear and mistrust are recognized factors hindering good practice, the principle of enabling staff is the most basic requirement of quality management (Crosby, 1992), and yet it carries little weight in the German system of long-term care quality evaluation. At present, quality of care provision is, in fact, mainly externally determined and highly dependent on an external control that should be seen as disadvantageous and counter-productive (Deming, 1982, 1986). A variety of factors is causing problems with quality assurance: firstly, the Long-Term Care Act does not promote care that corresponds with the requirements of the present-day clinical goals of medical and nursing science. In fact, it favours custodial care (Garms-Homolová and Roth, 2004; Wingenfeld, 2008) as demonstrated by the fact that under the long-term care insurance scheme, an improvement in clients' status (e.g., increased physical abilities, greater capabilities to communicate, lower degree of incontinence) leads to a

Monitoring the quality of long-term care in Germany

reduction of benefits, both in terms of money and in-kind services. As a consequence, neither clients or their relatives, nor the service provider are interested in such an improvement – even if the guidelines require the application of preventive care. Secondly, well-qualified staff is scarce in some parts of the long-term care sector. In many facilities employees have very old qualifications, meaning that they graduated a long time ago. Formally, they are considered to be qualified staff, but their real knowledge and competence are limited. Thirdly, while the general shortage of qualified staff has become increasingly noticeable in all business sectors in Germany (Helmrich and Zika, 2010), this is particularly true in the long-term care industry (Helmrich and Zika, 2010; Rothgang et al., 2011), which is not well prepared to compete in the labour market to attract employees. Fourthly, among (qualified) staff, working in long-term care does not have a very positive image or high status (Görres et al., 2010; Ciesinger et al., 2011). Wages are relatively low, and the possibility to hire good staff and to pay high wages is limited within the industry. One reason is that long-term care insurance budgets are fixed, whereas care needs, staff wages and total spending are increasing progressively. Fifthly, quality requirements address nursing staff only. However, many deficiencies in quality result from inadequate medical treatment, lack of coordination and integration of care and lack of collaboration between physicians and nursing care. One example may serve to illustrate this problem. In nursing homes, the hydration of the residents is examined by the MDK. But in some cases a resident receives two or three different diuretics as well as medication that interferes with swallowing, all prescribed by his or her doctor. The nursing home staff has virtually no power to influence the medication regime and is not really entitled to know the reason why a particular medication has been prescribed. While such and similar experiences have not been analysed systematically, they are a common subject discussed in meetings or internet blogs (compare for instance, AWO Bundesverband e.V., 2010; DBFK, 2010, etc.). Recently, the government began efforts to improve collaboration between care staff and physicians in nursing homes. As an incentive for greater cooperation, until the end of 2015, physicians or their organizations contracted to treat nursing home residents will receive special allowances if they do so (Bundesministerium für Gesundheit, 2012). Sixthly, processes that are indispensable to the quality of clinical work are still interpreted as tasks that do not belong to 'true' nursing or 'true' care. Even nursing documentation and care planning are often seen as a purely bureaucratic task. Moreover, the normal documentation systems themselves endorse these beliefs. They are by no means supportive tools that can be used in everyday routines. Documented data or instruments often overlap (Niehörster et al., 1998) and sometimes are unsuitable (Engel, 2008). They are seldom reliable, or precise, hindering their use as a system of triggers to identify risks, problems and strengths. The view that care planning and nursing diagnostics are unnecessary work is supported by the public and the media, which traditionally expect long-term care to primarily entail the provision of physical help and care, and some comfort. Lastly, some long-term care organizations, particularly those providing home care, are very small. Often, they do not have highly developed professional management, leading to considerable deficiencies in the management of human resources, on-the-job training of new staff and staff development; Isfort and Weidner, 2010). In addition, the proportion of temporary contracted staff is increasing (Bräutigam et al., 2010), a development that does not promote the quality of care.

3.3.4 Expert standards

In the late 1990s, the development and implementation of 'expert standards' for nursing started in Germany. The initiators were nurses in academic or leading management positions. They founded the German Network for Quality Development in Nursing (Deutsches Netzwerk für Qualitätsentwicklung in der Pflege, DNQP) as a non-profit organization that is affiliated with the University of Applied Sciences at Osnabrück. The work of the group was funded by the Federal Ministry of Health and its results, the Expert Nursing Standards, were declared to be the 'national nursing standards'. From the very beginning these standards were widely accepted by nursing organizations as well as individual nurses. Most of them felt that in Germany care and nursing had a lot of catching up to do to reach the international level of quality assurance indicated by evidence-based standardizations. The DNQP has developed and tested multiple Expert Nursing Standards in the following areas:

- Pain management (DNQP, 2005)
- Prevention of falls (DNQP, 2006)
- Promotion of bladder continence (DNQP, 2007)
- Discharge management (DNQP, 2009a)

- Care of persons with chronic wounds (DNQP, 2009b)
- Prevention of pressure ulcers (DNQP, recent update 2010a, 2009b)
- Management of nutrition, maintenance and promotion of oral nutrition (DNQP, 2010c).

Generally, these standards, except the one on discharge management, which focuses only on hospitals, have been developed for all care settings. However, long-term care has been underrepresented in field testing these protocols. For instance, the standard on prevention of pressure ulcers has been tested in thirteen hospitals, two nursing homes and four small home care agencies. But implementation is difficult as the rules recommended by the standards are considered to be very general and not specific enough to work with. The main problem is that generally, staff in long-term care facilities and home care agencies do not understand that standards are not incontrovertible orders, but that they 'mark out a corridor' of appropriate nursing/care actions. Thus, more support is needed to increase the practicability of the recommendations included in the standards. Even the MDS suggests using expert standards as a legal norm (MDS, 2009a, 2009b) that can play a decisive role in legal disputes. Another problem with the nursing standards is their mono-disciplinary character. The authors of these standards have neither invited other professions belonging to the multi-disciplinary teams involved in good long-term care nor engaged the clients and their relatives, a shortcoming which also applies to physicians' guidelines.

Not only are the expert nursing standards accepted as the national standards, the DNQP is accepted, too. It collaborates with institutes developing quality measures at the European level and is recognized by the German Nursing Council and other nursing professional organizations. It is surprising however, given the fact that the Long-Term Care Enhancement Act requires the continuing development and updating of the expert standards (§113a, SGB XI), that the DNQP has not yet been elevated to the status of a federal institution, even though many people believe that Germany needs a federal institute for quality of care and nursing. The organization's goals are quality improvement and dissemination of the accepted knowledge base of nursing science. Independent experts have to be called upon to make suggestions on which clinical problems have to be addressed when developing new standards. Moreover, the costs associated with the development of such standards should be covered jointly by the statutory long-term care funds and the private long-term care insurers.

In addition, many care providers, particularly the larger ones, have developed internal standards. If a top-down procedure is used, serious problems may occur when these standards are transferred into everyday care-giving settings. In contrast, standards developed in a bottom-up fashion are more widely accepted, albeit often at the loss of formal scientific evidence in their elaboration.

3.3.5 Public reporting: MDK reports on quality

Before the Long-Term Care Enhancement Act was implemented the MDS published two reports on the quality of long-term care (MDS, 2004; MDS, 2007). The first report was based on data from 793 home care agencies and their 2,700 selected clients, and data on 807 long-term care facilities and their 4,700 selected residents. The data were collected by the MDK during the second half of 2003. Up to 78 per cent of the assessments were completed by MDK nursing staff, and 14 per cent by MDK physicians; 54 per cent of the assessments were compiled during the obligatory evaluation required by law, while 20 per cent of the assessments were undertaken during the course of evaluations initiated by complaints. This first report, which focused on structural data, on nutrition and supply of fluids, as well as on pressure ulcers (MDS, 2004), makes public federal averages but some disaggregated results for the individual states also are presented. The second report covered a longer period (2004 to 2006), more institutional facilities (4,217) and residents (24,648) and a larger number of home care agencies (3,736) and their clients (14,925); 18.8 per cent of the assessments in home care agencies and 23.7 per cent of the assessments in institutional settings were conducted because of complaints. The second report not only presented basic statistics but tried to demonstrate the relationship between structure and the quality of care processes (MDS, 2007).

Both reports were met with strong criticism from different sources. Policy makers complained that many assessments were carried out during regular expected inspections announced in advance. Associations of long-term care providers and healthcare workers criticized the report for painting a gloomy picture that they felt did not reflect the real situation. Indeed, staff felt discriminated against and even vilified. Researchers (e.g., Görres et al., 2009) found fault with numerous aspects of the report. The most

Monitoring the quality of long-term care in Germany 87

heavily weighted arguments were those regarding its methodological inadequacies. These critiques have stressed that the guidelines applicable in those days (MDS, 2007) did not contain a valid and reliable assessment instrument, and assessors were misled into acting arbitrarily. Moreover, no indicators of quality or performance were available in the 2007 version of the guidelines (Görres et al., 2009). Unfortunately, this situation has not changed substantially, despite the reformulated guidelines of 2009 (MDS, 2009a, 2009b), and despite two important initiatives by the government, the first of which is the start of public reporting on long-term care in Germany, and the second the 'Development and Testing of Instruments for the Assessment of Quality and Effectiveness in Institutional Settings for the Elderly' ('Entwicklung und Erprobung von Instrumenten zur Beurteilung der Ergebnisqualität in der stationären Altenhilfe', Wingenfeld et al., 2011). Each of these initiatives is discussed in turn.

Public reporting on the quality of long-term care was introduced by the Long-Term Care Enhancement Act and by the modified guidelines for the evaluation of quality (MDS, 2009a, 2009b). An 'Agreement on Transparency' that is included in the guidelines proclaims that the online public reports (so-called *Pflegenoten*, 'care grades' or 'care marks') aim to provide current or potential customers of care services with transparent, easily understood information on all nursing homes and home care services. The requirement is that customers have to be enabled to compare facilities and care providers (GKV Spitzenverband, 2011). Until May 2011, 18,770 facilities and home care services were included in the care grades online report. After intense public criticism a judicial order stopped publication of further grades for the present time. The critics stressed the following aspects of the public reports as problematic:

- The outcomes are based on nursing documentation only, but not on the real status of clients/residents; moreover, gaps in nursing documentation are interpreted as 'real' problems with the client's well-being (Graber-Dünow, 2011).
- Criteria used for grading are not transparent (Graber-Dünow, 2011).
- The database for the calculation of the care grades is not standardized, and therefore the MDK assessors are not able to reach concordant results.

A scientific evaluation supported the critics in every respect (Weidner et al., 2011). Not only was the database identified as inappropriate, but the weakness of the methods and procedures for deriving care grades also has been criticized. The fact that singular quality problems are generalized by this system was seen as a particular problem. The researchers recognized the failure as 'immanent to the system' (Weidner et al., 2011). However, the care grades are still on the web and the MDS expects to continue with public reporting even though they have been suspended temporarily.

The second government initiative was started by two federal ministries that requested the 'Development and Testing of Instruments for the Assessment of Quality and Effectiveness in Institutional Settings for the Elderly' (Wingenfeld et al., 2011). This undertaking was intended to be an improvement of the quality assessments routinely undertaken by the MDK. In particular, it raises the possibility of measuring effects and outcomes that are not measured as yet. The hasty project fulfilled the expectations of policy makers but from the perspective of the state of the art of long-term care quality measurement (Katz and Green, 1996; Hirdes et al., 2004; Kötter et al., 2011; Mor et al., 2003; Mukamel et al., 2008; Mukamel and Browner, 2003; Mukamel and Spector, 2003; Zimmerman et al., 1995), the results are weak and neither original nor innovative. First of all, many methodological details (such as reliability and risk adjustment) were not revealed by the report. Moreover, the majority of the selected quality indicators (e.g., mobility, falls, weight loss, pressure ulcers, pain management, physical restriction and disruptive behaviour) that are included in other systems of quality indicators (Garms-Homolová, 2008; Hirdes et al., 2004; Zimmerman et al., 1995) were not adopted by Wingenfeld and co-authors (2011). That notwithstanding, inadequacies within the database itself was the major problem: the quality indicators devised by Wingenfeld et al. (2011) rely primarily on normal nursing documentation in residents' records which is different across facilities or agencies and therefore had to be recoded to be unified and used for the calculation of the indicators. This is not only a very time-consuming procedure but also would be subject to reliability problems.

3.3.6 Outcome measurement and performance

Beside the quality obligations required by long-term care legislation, the long-term care funds and the medical review boards (both MDS and MDK), German long-term care providers are discovering their own way to assess, measure and represent the quality of their services. One option is to undergo an audit or certification by an external (commercial) quality organization, such as the European Foundation for Quality Management (EFQM) or Cooperation for Transparency and Quality in Healthcare (KTQ) (see Table 3.2). Other providers use internationally approved quality measurement systems (Zimmerman et al., 1995) that enable them to compare their effectiveness with other providers participating in benchmarking networks. One example is the Berlin Project (www.berliner-projekt.de/Modell.html), a group of thirty-six nursing homes that uses the interRAI Quality Indicators to evaluate performance. The basis of the evaluation process is data from the routinely collected Minimum Data Set (Morris et al., 1995; German version: Garms-Homolová and Gilgen, 2000). Comparisons are accompanied by regular audits, seminars for staff and financial control.

3.3.7 Providers' positioning in the care market, audits and certification

As described, the German 'long-term care market' – a goal proclaimed by the government since the introduction of long-term care insurance – is characterized by a mixture of private for-profit, not-for-profit and, to a much smaller extent, public providers. Despite the fact that the long-term care market is strictly regulated, competition between care providers is high. In some regions, it is almost merciless. The quality of services is one important factor for a provider's positioning in the market. Because the outcomes of care are not (yet) an important factor that influences consumers' choices, the image of services and structural factors (such as the appearance of the residential facility, the possibility to bring one's own furniture and the availability of single room occupancy) are more important. Therefore, many providers, or their umbrella organizations, try to have their quality certified (Gerste and Schwinger, 2004), or as described in Section 3.3.6, to be accredited by a renowned external organization. Increasingly long-term care providers and their services can be found among the winners of quality awards and prizes (such as Germany's Best Employer Award). Large long-term care providers, for instance Diakonie (a large protestant charity organization) and Paritätische Wohlfahrtverband (a large association of independent welfare organizations), have introduced their own quality certificates. Some have modified the trademarked quality systems for

Table 3.2 *Examples of external quality certificates and audits used in the German long-term care sector*

	Institutional long-term care facilities (ILTCF) / nursing homes	Home care agencies (HCA)
Non-sector specific and supra-regional		
DIN EN ISO 9000 ff: Certification from the International Organization for Standardization and the German Institute for Norms. See: www.iso.org/iso/about/discover-iso_isos-name.htm	A large number of ILTCF have been certified and re-certified. For many, ISO is the 'entrance' to quality management.	An increasing number of HCA has been certified. For many, ISO is the 'entrance' to quality management.
EFQM: Audit by the European Foundation for Quality Management: See: www.q-excellence.de	Many ILTCF and groups of ILTCF use the model, fewer apply for actual external auditing.	Relatively few HCA use the model, still fewer apply for actual external auditing.
Award in Germany: Ludwig Erhard Award	Probably no ILTCF has applied for these awards.	Probably no HCA has applied for the awards.
Award at the European level: EFQM Excellence Award		
RAL: Certificate of the 'alliance for goodness' (Gütegemeinschaft), one of the oldest in Germany (founded 1925). See: www.guetegemeinschaft.de	Not available for ILTCF.	A section of the alliance is the 'Alliance of home care agencies assessed for quality' (Gütegemeinschaft qualitätsgeprüfte ambulante Pflegedienste e.V.). At least 10 per cent of HCA have received this certificate. See www.guetegemeinschaft-pflege.de
Non-sector-specific and regional		
Quality Award Berlin Brandenburg (Qualitätspreis Berlin Brandenburg)	Still rare.	No information available.

Based on the EFQM model for excellence and dedicated to local enterprises. The award is funded by the economics ministries in the two federal states of Berlin and Brandenburg. See: www.q-preis.de

Sector-specific (developed specifically for healthcare) and supra-regional

KTQ: Collaboration for transparency and quality in healthcare; and proCumCert: German certification system originally developed for hospitals, but later modified for ILTCF and HCA. See: www.ktq.de	ILTCF have started to use this certification.	Fewer than five HCA are certified under this system.

'Internal' certificates developed by healthcare providers

AQUA: Continuing quality improvement system that relates to the KTQ. Provider specific. www.alexius.de Audits and certificates developed by welfare organizations for their own members, e.g.	Some of the ILTCF that belong to this group use the system.	Very few of the HCA that belong to this group use the system.
a) Diakonie-S-Pflege (Diakonie Qualitätssiegel Pflege) from a major protestant welfare organization. See: www.pflege-und-diakonie.de/qualität/siegel	Up to 86 per cent of all Diakonie ILTCF have received this certificate.	Up to 52 per cent of all Diakonie HCA have received this certificate
b) PQ-sys® developed by the Paritätischer Wohlfahrtsverband on the basis of DIN EN ISO 9001. See: www.sg-cert.de	Less than 2 per cent of ILTCF that belong to this welfare organization have received this certificate.	Less than 5 per cent of HCA that belong to this welfare organization have received this certificate.

Table 3.2 (*cont.*)

	Institutional long-term care facilities (ILTCF) / nursing homes	Home care agencies (HCA)
Certificates, audits and awards certifying excellence in a particular sphere of action		
Job and family (Beruf und Familie). The certificate attests that the company respects the family commitments of its employees. The central issue is quality of human resources management. See: www.beruf-und-familie.de	The number of companies that have received the certificate is increasing.	The number of HCA that have received the certificate is small, but increasing.
Great place to work – Germany's best employer. This supra-regional award is not sector-specific, but the candidates (currently up to 300) are categorized on the basis of the number of employees and affiliation to a certain business sector (e.g. health and long-term care). Companies can apply for the European award as well. See: www.greatplacetowork.de	The number of participants from ILTCF is increasing.	Until now, few HCA have been among the candidates, and those which have been belong to companies that own both ILTCF and HCA.

Source: Compiled by authors.

application to small care facilities and agencies. An overview of certificates and an estimation of their dissemination in long-term care are presented in Table 3.2.

The process of external auditing or certification frequently requires considerable effort in terms of time, resources and money. In the context of the 'official' evaluation of quality by the MDK, the benefits of external certification may be limited. According to the guidelines on the evaluation of quality (QPR) (MDS, 2009a, 2009b), only the assessment of the structural quality can be suspended, if the nursing home or the home care service obtains an external certificate. However, care providers usually list a whole range of advantages for their enterprises, their staff and customers. Most frequently they mention the consulting and advice received by the certifying organization, and the way in which adopting quality management can help redesign their whole business, or networking and exchange of experiences with other candidates. This kind of support is not offered by MDK assessors, even if the QPR states that consulting with providers is one of the prominent goals of the MDS and MDK. Moreover, whereas MDK assessment and the presentation of results are always experienced as negative events, commercial evaluation by certificating institutions and auditing agencies is mainly experienced as a positive gain.

3.4 Conclusions

Although quality assurance has been an integral part of long-term care since its legal inception in 1994, the legislation lacked specifics until the Long-Term Care Quality Assurance Act of 2001, which emphasized the obligation of providers to implement internal quality management. In 2008, further specifics and an even stronger commitment to quality assurance and management were added to the SGB XI by the Long-Term Care Enhancement Act, which followed in the wake of several well-publicized scandals related to the quality of care in German nursing homes. The threat of sanctions for care providers that do not fulfil quality requirements was replaced by real penalties; for instance, the termination of the contract between the care provider and the long-term care fund. In the context of these changes, the importance of Expert Nursing Standards was emphasized. Additionally, unannounced inspections of long-term care facilities as well as of home care agencies were introduced from 2010.

The main issue of quality-related efforts remains the optimization of the structural conditions of care provision. Both, official and private quality assurance activities by commercial companies primarily focus on the structural aspects of quality. Secondly, they focus on quality of processes. Even though the Guidelines on the Evaluation of Quality repeatedly states that outcomes also are assessed, even a superficial glance at the instructions shows that this is not the case. Private activities consist of external audits and certificates that are increasingly popular among long-term care providers. Only a few are able to evaluate outcomes, but most of them explicitly examine structural and process quality, namely organizational aspects, management and processes involving interactions between the management of care companies and staff, customers and collaborating partners.

The measurement of care-relevant outcomes and the comparison of care providers' performance require routine data of good quality, a uniform database and the development of appropriate quality indicators. However, these prerequisites are still not available (or accepted) in Germany. The recent 'Development and Testing of Instruments for the assessment of Quality and Effectiveness in Institutional Settings for the Elderly' (Wingenfeld et al., 2011) has not closed the gap. Thus, the abandonment of current documentation practices and reorientation towards evidence-based data collection are central prerequisites for quality measurement. In addition, German policy makers, long-term care providers as well as researchers need such data collection for the continuous reporting on care, its quality and the changing needs of the ageing population.

The MDK's mandate has been expanded; it is responsible not only for assessing the quality of long-term care but also for giving recommendations on improvement. Terms like 'consultation', 'counselling', and 'counselling-oriented approach' are used very often in the guidelines, but such activities are almost never exercised by the MDK (Görres et al., 2009; Weidner et al., 2011). Instead, the idea of control and supervision dominates quality efforts. This is an approach to quality that is definitely outdated. Founders of the TQM (Total Quality Management) like Deming (1982, 1986) and Crosby (1992) have stressed that investment in staff is key. 'Don't rely exclusively on external quality control' and 'capacitate your staff and your entire company' – these have been the most important principles of contemporary quality management since the introduction of the TQM. But just these principles are missing

Monitoring the quality of long-term care in Germany 95

in the German quality assurance culture in the healthcare sector. A long time ago it was recognized that the intensification of external control has to be replaced by self-monitoring and self-regulation. Training for self-regulation and support of self-efficacy (Bandura, 1994) is an approach that sharpens staff members' perception of the consequences of their own actions. The current system of quality management will not work without this principle. Rather, unilateral external control and threats are paralysing to motivation within services.

All in all, we conclude that the current long-term care policy explicitly claims numerous quality-related activities. As a consequence, the awareness, even knowledge, of quality requirements have increased considerably within the last decade at all levels of the German health-care system. At the same time, the existing regulations set clear limits with regard to the development of quality. It is still the case that long-term care benefits guarantee services that do not meet the standards of excellent or even appropriate care from the point of view of current medicine and nursing science because the prevention, rehabilitation, mobilization and maintenance of the remaining abilities of long-term care clients as well as positive outcomes are neither sufficiently meas-ured nor adequately covered by the long-term care funds. On the con-trary, only clients' full dependency results in higher payment and more benefits in kind. Therefore, positive incentives for care that aim to improve clients' dependency status are low, but perverse incentives that reward the worsening of clients' status are high. A change in this orientation is the most important quality project for the future.

References

AWO Bundesverband e.V. (2010). 14 Verbände klagen gegen eineitige Ausweitung der Qualitätsprüfungsrichtlinie, AWO-Nachrichten-Archiv vom 08.01.2010. Available at: www.awo.org/awo-presse/presse-archiv/archivdetails/article/14-verbaende-klagen-gegen-einseitige-ausweitung-der-qualitaetspruefungs-richtlinie.html (last accessed: February 2012).
Bandura, A. (1994). Self-efficacy. In V. S. Ramachaudran (ed.), *Encyclopedia of Human Behavior*, vol. IV. New York: Academic Press, pp. 71–81.
BMFSFJ / Bundesministerium für Familie, Senioren, Frauen und Jugend (Federal Ministry for Family, Seniors, Women and Youth) (2010). Nursing Home Act. Available at: www.bmfsfj.de/BMFSFJ/aeltere-men schen, did=3270.html.

BMG / Bundesministerium für Gesundheit (2008). Gut zu wissen – das Wichtigste zur Pflegereform 2008. Available at: www.sozialpolitik-aktuell.de/tl_files/sozialpolitik-aktuell/_Politikfelder/Gesundheitswesen/ Dokumente/Pflegereform per cent202008.pdf.

(2012). Pflege-Neuausrichtungs-Gesetz, Stand: nach der dritten Lesung im Bundestag. Available at: www.bundesgesundheitsministerium.de/filead min/dateien/Publikationen/Pflege/Broschueren/Broschuere_Das_Pflege-Neuausrichtungs-Gesetz, Stand nach der 3. Lesung im Bundestag.pdf.

Bräutigam, C., Dahlbeck, E., Enste, P., Evans, M. and Hilbert, J. (2010). *Flexibilisierung und Leiharbeit in der Pflege: eine explorative Studie*. Arbeitspapier 215. Düsseldorf: Hans-Böckler-Stiftung.

Büscher, A. (2010). Public reporting, expert standards and indicators: different routes to improve the quality of German long-term care, *Eurohealth*, 16(2): 4–7.

Busse, R., Blümel, M. and Ognyanova, D. (2013). *Das deutsche Gesundheitssystem. Akteure, Daten, Analysen*. Berlin: Medizinisch Wissenschaftliche Verlagsanstalt.

Busse, R. et al. (2013). *Healthcare Systems in Transition: Germany*. Copenhagen: WHO on behalf of the European Observatory for Health Systems and Policies.

Busse, R. and Riesberg, A. (2005). *Gesundheitssysteme im Wandel: Deutschland*. Berlin: MWV.

Ciesinger, K.-G., Fischbach, A., Klatt, R. and Neuendorf, H. (2011). *Berufe im Schatten: Wertschätzung von Dienstleistungsberufen*. Berlin: LitVerlag AG.

Crosby, P. (1992). *The Externally Successful Organization: the Art of Corporate Wellness*. New York: Mentor.

DBFK (2010). MDK-Qualitätsprüfungen. Infodienst Sonderausgabe, Sektion private ambulante Pflegedienste, 3/2010. Available at: www.nw-ambu lant.de/downloads/sonderinfodienstmaerz2010.pdf.

Deming, W. E. (1982). *Quality, Productivity, and Competitive Position*. Cambridge, MA: MIT, Center for Advanced Engineering.

(1986). *Out of Crisis*. Cambridge, MA: MIT, Center for Advanced Engineering.

Deutsches Netzwerk für Qualitätssicherung in der Pflege (ed.) (2005). Expertenstandard Schmerzmanagement in der Pflege, Entwicklung – Konsentierung – Implementierung. Osnabrück: DNQP, Hochschule Osnabrück. Available at: www.dnqp.de/ExpertenstandardSchmerzmana gement_Akt.pdf.

(ed.) (2006). Expertenstandard Sturzprophylaxe in der Pflege. Entwicklung – Konsentierung – Implementierung. Osnabrück: DNQP, Hochschule Osnabrück. Available at: www.dnqp.de/ExpertenstandardSturzprophyla xe.pdf.

(ed.) (2007). Expertenstandard Förderung der Harnkontinenz in der Pflege. Entwicklung – Konsentierung – Implementierung. Osnabrück: DNQP, Hochschule Osnabrück. Available at: www.dnqp.de/Expertenstandard Kontinenz.pdf.

(ed.) (2009a). Expertenstandard Entlassungsmanagement in der Pflege. 1. Aktualisierung 2009 einschließlich Kommentierung und Literaturstudie. Osnabrück: DNQP, Hochschule Osnabrück. Available at: www.dnqp. de/ExpertenstandardEntlassungsmanagement_Atk.pdf.

(ed.) (2009b). Expertenstandard Pflege von Menschen mit chronischen Wunden. Entwicklung – Konsentierung – Implementierung. Osnabrück: DNQP, Hochschule Osnabrück. Available at: http://www.dnqp.de/ ExpertenstandardChronischeWunden.pdf.

(ed.) (2010a). Expertenstandard Dekubitusprophylaxe in der Pflege. 1. Aktualisierung 2009 einschließlich Kommentierung und Literaturstudie. Osnabrück: DNQP, Hochschule Osnabrück. Available at: www.dnqp.de/ ExpertenstandardDekubitusprophylaxe_Akt.pdf.

(ed.) (2010b). Expertenstandard Dekubitusprophylaxe in der Pflege. Audit-Instrument. Osnabrück: DNQP, Hochschule Osnabrück. Available at: www.dnqp.de/AuditDekubitusprophylaxe.pdf.

(ed.) (2010c). Expertenstandard Ernährungsmanagement zur Sicherstellung und Förderung der oralen Ernährung in der Pflege. Entwicklung – Konsentierung – Implementierung. Osnabrück: DNQP, Hochschule Osnabrück. Available at: www.dnqp.de/ExpertenstandardErnaehrungsma nagement.pdf.

Donabedian, A. (1982). *Explorations in Quality Assessment and Monitoring.* vol. II: *The Criteria and Standards of Quality.* Ann Arbor: Healthcare Administration Press.

(1987). Five essential questions from the management of quality in health-care. *Health Management Quarterly*, 9(1): 6–9.

Engel, K. (2008). *Qualität in stationären Pflegeeinrichtungen: die Anwendung des Resident Assessment Instruments RAI 2.0 als Qualitätsinstruments.* Stuttgart, Berlin, Cologne: Verlag W. Kohlhammer.

Garms-Homolová, V. (2008). Messung der Pflege-Outcomes mithilfe von Routinedaten. *Public Health Forum*, 16: 21–2.

Garms-Homolová, V. and Gilgen, R. (eds.) (2000). RAI 2.0 *Resident Assessment Instrument: Beurteilung, Dokumentation und Pflegeplanung in der Langzeitpflege und geriatrischen Rehabilitation.* Bern: Hans Huber.

Garms-Homolová, V. and Roth, G. (2004). Vorkommen, Ursachen und Vermeidung von Pflegemängeln in Pflegeeinrichtungen im Land Nordrhein-Westfalen: Abschlussbericht zum Projekt der Enquetekommission Zukunft der Pflege in Nordrhein-Westfalen. Available at: www.wernerschell.de/Medizin-Infos/Pflege/Pflegemaengel_NRW.pdf.

Gerste, B. and Schwinger, A. (2004). Qualitätssiegel und Zertifikate. *Gesundheit + Gesellschaft Wissenschaft*, 4(4): 7–15.

GKV Spitzenverband (2011). Veröffentlichung der Pflegenoten. www.aok-gesundheitsnavi.de (AOK), www.bkk-pflege.de (BKK), www.der-pflegekompass.de (Knappschaft, LSV, IKK), www.pflegelotse.de (vdek – Verband der Ersatzkassen). www.pflegenoten.de/Veroeffentlichungen_Uebersicht.gkvnet.

Görres, S., Bomball, J., Schwanke, A., Stöver, M. and Schmitt, S. (2010). *Imagekampagne für Pflegeberufe auf der Grundlage empirisch gesicherter Daten. Einstellung von Schüler/innen zur möglichen Ergreifung eines Pflegeberufes. Zeitraum Juli 2009–Dezember 2009. Im Auftrag des Norddeutschen Zentrums zur Weiterentwicklung der Pflege.* Bremen: Universität Bremen und IPP Bremen.

Görres, S., Hasseler, M. and Mittnacht, B. (2009). Gutachten zu den MDK-Qualitätsprüfungen und den Qualitätsberichten im Auftrag der Hamburgischen Pflegegesellschaft e.V., Bremen: Universität Bremen, Institut für Public Health und Pflegeforschung. Available at: http://www.hpg-ev.de/download/hpg-Gutachten_14_02_20081_1.pdf.

Graber-Dünow, M. (2011). Mogelpackung Pflegenoten. Auswirkungen der Pflegetransparenzvereinbarungen auf die Altenpflege. *Dr. med. Mabuse Zeitschrift für alle Gesundheitsberufe*, 36(189): 50–2.

Helmrich, R. and Zika, G. (eds.) (2010). Beruf und Arbeit in der Zukunft – BIBB-IAB-Modellrechnungen zu den Entwicklungen in den Berufsfeldern und Qualifikationen bis 2025. Bonn: BIBB. Available at: www.qube-projekt.de.

Hirdes, J.P., Fries, B.E., Morris, J.N., Ikegami, N., Zimmermann, D., Dalby, D.M., Aliga, P., Hammer, S. and Jones, R. (2004). Home care quality indicators (HCQIs). Based on MDS HC. *The Gerontologist*, 44 (5): 665–79.

Isfort, M. and Weidner, F. (2010). Pflege-Thermometer 2009: eine bundesweite Befragung von Pflegekräften zur Situation der Pflege und Patientenversorgung im Krankenhaus. Deutsches Institut für Pflegeforschung (dip), Cologne. Available at: http://www.dip.de.

Katz, J. and Green, E. (1996). *Qualitätsmanagement. Überprüfung und Bewertung des Pflegedienstes.* Wiesbaden: Ullstein Mosby.

Kötter, T., Schaefer, F., Blozik, E. and Scherer, M. (2011). Die Entwicklung von Qualitätsindikatoren: Hintergrund, Methoden, Probleme. Z Evidenz, *Fortbildung und Qualität im Gesundheitswesen*, 105(1): 7–13.

Medizinischer Dienst des Spitzenverbandes Bund der Krankenkassen e.V. / MDS (ed.) (2004). *1. Bericht des MDS nach § 118, Abs. 4 SGB XI. Qualität in der ambulanten und stationären Pflege.* Essen: MDS.

(ed.) (2007). *2. Bericht des MDS nach § 118, Abs. 4 SGB XI. Qualität in der ambulanten und stationären Pflege*. Essen: MDS. Available at: http://www.mds-ev.de/media/pdf/2._Bericht_des_MDS.pdf.

(ed.) (2009a). Qualitätsprüfungs-Richtlinien, MDK-Anleitung, Transparenzvereinbarung. Grundlagen der MDK-Qualitätsprüfungen in der stationären Pflege. Available at: http://www.mds-ev.de or http://www.gkv-spitzenverband.de/upload/2010-02-16_stat_Screen_neu_11981.pdf.

(ed.) (2009b). Qualitätsprüfungs-Richtlinien, MDK-Anleitung, Transparenzvereinbarung. Grundlagen der MDK-Qualitätsprüfungen in der ambulanten Pflege. Available at: www.mds-ev.de or http://www.mds-ev.de/media/pdf/2010-04-29_MDK-Anleitung_ambulant_korr.pdf.

(2011). MDK als eigenständige und selbstverwaltete Arbeitsgemeinschaft der Pflege- und Krankenversicherung erhalten. Essen: MDS. Available at: http://www.mds-ev.org/print/3747.htm.

Mor, V., Angelelli, J., Jones, R., Moore, T. and Morris, J. N. (2003). Inter-rater reliability of nursing home quality indicators in the US. *BMC Health Service Research*, 3(20).

Moratorium Pflegenoten (undated). Nein zu Pflegenoten. Available at: www.moratorium-pflegenoten.de/index.php/moratorium.

Morris, J., Murphy, K., Nonemaker, S., Hawes, C., Phillips, C., Fries, B. and Mor, V. (1995). *Long Term Care Resident Assessment Instrument: Users Manual 2.0*. Columbia: interRAI, and Chapel Hill, NC: Research Triangle Institute.

Mukamel, D. B. and Browner, C. A. (2003). The influence of risk adjustment methods on the conclusion about quality of care in nursing homes based on outcome measures, *The Gerontologist*, 38(6): 695–703.

Mukamel, D. B., Glance, L. G., Li, Y., Weimer, D. L., Spector, W. D., Zinn, J. S. and Mosqueda, L. (2008). Does risk adjustment of the CMS quality measures for nursing homes matter? *Medical Care*, 46(5): 532–41.

Mukamel, D. B. and Spector, W. D. (2003). Quality report cards and nursing home quality, *The Gerontologist*, 43(2): 48–66.

Neumann, P. and Klewer, J. (2008). Personalfluktuation und Mitarbeiterorientierung in der ambulanten und stationären Pflege: eine Untersuchung in ambulanten und vollstationären Einrichtungen in Sachsen, *Heilberufe*, 60(1): 13–17.

Niehörster, G., Garms-Homolová, V. and Vahrenhorst, V. (1998). *Identifizierung von Potentialen für eine selbständigere Lebensführung*. Schriftenreihe des BMFSFJ, vol. 147.4. Stuttgart, Berlin, Cologne: Verlag W. Kohlhammer.

Nies, H., Leichsenring, K., van der Veen, R. et al. for Interlinks / Health Systems and Long-Term Care for Older People in Europe (2010). Quality Management and Quality Assurance in Long-Term Care: European

Overview Paper. Utrecht/Vienna: Interlinks. Available at: www.euro. centre.org/data/1278594919_52528.pdf

Pfaff, H. (2011). Pflegestatistik 2009. Pflege im Rahmen der Pflegeversicherung: hrsg. vom Statistischen Bundesamt: Wiesbaden. Available at: www.destatis.de.

PQSG (2012). Die andere MDK-Prüfliste. Available at: www.pqsg.de/seiten/pdf/pqsg-buch.htm.

Pro Pflege-Management (undated). Die optimale Vorbereitung auf die MDK-Prüfung. Available at: www.ppm-online.org/verlag/artikel-lesen/artikel/vorbereitung-mdk-pruefung/.

Rothgang, H., Iwansky, S., Müller, R., Sauer, S. and Unger, R. (2011). Barmer GEK Pflegereport 2011. Schriftenreihe zur Gesundheitsanalyse, vol. 11. Sankt Augustin: Asgard-Verlag.

Schmitz, K. and Schnabel, E. (2006). Staatliche Heimaufsicht und Qualität in der stationären Pflege: Nachrichtendienst des Deutschen Vereins (NDV) No. 4/2006: 170–8. Available at: www.socialnet.de/materialien/54.php.

Sozialministerium Baden-Württemberg / Ministerium für Arbeit und Sozialordnung, Familie, Frauen und Senioren (2009). Heimbauverordnung tritt zum 1. September in Kraft. Available at: www.sozialministerium.baden-wuerttemberg.de/de/Meldungen/214655. html?_min=_sm&template=min_meldung_html&reFerer=80177.

Statistisches Bundesamt (2010). *Demografischer Wandel in Deutschland. Heft 2: Auswirkungen auf Krankenhausbehandlungen und Pflegebedürftige im Bund und in den Ländern. Ausgabe 2010.* Wiesbaden: Statistisches Bundesamt.

(2011a). Bevölkerung uns Erwerbstätigkeit: Lebenserwartung in Deutschland. Durchschnittliche und fernere Lebenserwartung. Wiesbaden: Statistisches Bundesamt. Available at: www.destatis.de/jet speed/portal/cms/Sites/destatis/Internet/DE/Content/Statistiken/Bevoel kerung/GeburtenSterbefaelle/Tabellen/Content100/SterbetafelFBNL, property=file.xls.

(2011b). Bevölkerung und Erwerbstätigkeit: Sterbetafeln früheres Bundesgebiet und neue Länder. 2008/2011. Wiesbaden: Statistisches Bundesamt. Available at: www.destatis.de/jetspeed/portal/cms/Sites/desta tis/Internet/DE/Content/Statistiken/Bevoelkerung/GeburtenSterbefaelle/Tabellen/Content100/SterbetafelFBNL,property=file.xls.

(2011c). Bevölkerung Deutschlands bis 2060. 12. koordinierte Bevölkerungsvorausberechnung. Begleitmaterial zur Pressekonferenz am 18. November 2009. Wiesbaden: Statistisches Bundesamt. Available at: www.destatis.de/DE/Publikationen/Thematisch/Bevoelkerung/Voraus berechnungBevoelkerung/BevoelkerungDeutschland2060Presse51242 04099004.pdf?__blob=publicationFile.

(2011d). Pflegestatistik 2009. Pflege im Rahmen der Pflegeversicherung. Deutschlandergebnisse. Wiesbaden: Statistisches Bundesamt. Available at: www.destatis.de/jetspeed/portal/cms/Sites/destatis/Internet/DE/Content/ Publikationen/Fachveroeffentlichungen/Sozialleistungen/Pflege/Pflege Deutschlandergebnisse5224001099004, property=file.pdf.

(2012). Lebenserwartung in Deutschland erneut gestiegen: Pressemitteilung Nr. 344 vom 02.10.2012. Available at: www.destatis.de/DE/Presse Service/Presse/Pressemitteilungen/2012/10/PD12_344_12621.html.

Weidner, F., Laag, U. and Brühl, A. (2011). Evaluation der Umsetzung der Pflege-Transparenzvereinbarungen ambulant (PTVA) durch den MDK in Rheinland-Pfalz. Cologne: Deutsches Institut für angewandte Pflegeforschung (dip), e.V. Available at: www.dip.de.

Wingenfeld, K. (2008). Stationäre pflegerische Versorgung alter Menschen. In A. Kuhlmey and D. Schaeffer (eds.), *Alter, Gesundheit und Krankheit*. Bern: Huber, pp. 370–81.

Wingenfeld, K., Kleine, T., Franz, S., Engels, D., Mehlan, S. and Engel, H. (2011). Entwicklung und Erprobung von Instrumenten zur Beurteilung der Ergebnisqualität in der stationären Altenhilfe. Im Auftrag des Bundesministeriums für Gesundheit und des Bundesministeriums für Familie, Senioren, Frauen und Jugend. Abschlussbericht, Bielefeld/ Köln. Available at: www.bundesgesundheitsministerium.de or www. bmfsfj.de.

Zimmerman, D. R., Karon, S. L., Arling, G., Clark, B. R., Collins, T., Ross, R. et al. (1995). Development and testing of nursing home quality indicators, *Healthcare Financing Review*, 16: 104–27.

Legislation

Homes Act (Heimgesetz – HeimG)

Social Code Book XI (Sozialgesetzbuch XI – SGB XI)

Social Code Book V (Sozialgesetzbuch V – SGB V)

Long-Term Care Quality Assurance Act (Pflege-Qualitätssicherungs-gesetz – PQsG)

Long-term Care Enhancement Act (Pflege-Weiterentwicklungsgesetz – PflWG)

4 | Quality monitoring and long-term care in Switzerland

GUIDO BARTELT, RUEDI GILGEN,
DANIEL GROB AND THOMAS MÜNZER

4.1 Long-term care and its regulatory context in Switzerland

Care, and especially long-term care, has a long tradition in Switzerland. The first hospices were founded more than 750 years ago and historical documents have revealed that early hospices, which also included care for the aged, were run by monasteries. Over time communities (cities) became responsible for the organization and staffing of such institutions. For example, the Vadiana Library in the city of St Gallen has a well-documented collection of logbooks and financial reports dating back to the mid-sixteenth century that include recommendations for structuring care, such as the number of nursing staff, salaries and food, which can be seen as a very early measure of quality control.

As in many other countries, the Swiss long-term care sector has grown continuously in the last few decades. Between 1995 and 2009, when new legislation was implemented (Federal Health Insurance Regulation Act / Krankenversicherungsgesetz (KVG), 1994) that substantially increased the contribution of national public insurance to financing of both health and long-term care, the cost of long-term care (nursing home and home care) rose by 88 per cent, more than the increase for total healthcare costs (71 per cent) (Bundesamt für Statistik, 2012).

Health and long-term care in Switzerland are regulated by two major political authorities, acting at the federal and/or state (cantonal) level. Primarily, the states (cantons) are responsible for healthcare and therefore Switzerland has twenty-six local healthcare legislation statutes. Nonetheless, the national legislation for public insurance (KVG) regulates many aspects of healthcare financing and delivery, and effectively restricts cantonal action to designing states' healthcare systems. Having

This chapter is dedicated to Dr Ruedi Gilgen, who passed away during the writing of this chapter. Ruedi Gilgen was one of the very few geriatricians in Switzerland who dedicated his work to quality in long-term care institutions.

said that, the twenty-six Swiss cantons differ in their implementation of national legislation based on cultural (French, Italian, German), regional or geographical exigencies and cantonal legislation, and in these respects are not bound by federal law.

People in Switzerland who need nursing care as a consequence of injuries, disease or old age are treated either in an ambulatory/home care setting (i.e., in a non-hospital-based external care setting, known by the acronym SPITEX) or in a traditional nursing home/long-term care institution setting. In this context, ambulatory care means that care is delivered to the person's home by a registered nurse. Treatment and care of people with disabilities who are under 65 years of age are regulated by an additional and separate law and thus will not be discussed in this chapter. Due to Switzerland's ageing population both sectors (SPITEX and long-term care institutions) have expanded significantly in recent years (Table 4.1).

In 2009 a total of 89,679 people lived in institutions caring for people (nursing homes and retirement homes) with the largest proportion of this population aged 80 or over. Differences in the allocation of long-term care resources between Swiss cantons are substantial. As summarized in Figure 4.1, the relative number of nursing home beds per 100 people aged 80 or over, for example, is on average 26 per 100 (or 26 per cent) but varies considerably among the cantons. While there are cantons with a very low rate (e.g., Tessin), other cantons have a rate that is twice as high (Appenzell A.Rh). This may be explained by differences in cantonal regulations and financing, social attitudes towards nursing homes as places to live in older age and resources dedicated to home care. Furthermore, residents of one canton may be living in nursing homes in a nearby canton.

Roughly 30 per cent of long-term care residential facilities in Switzerland are owned by municipalities and are managed by organizing bodies under public law, around 45 per cent are organized as non-profit organizations under private law (foundations, cooperative societies, associations) and 25 per cent are run for profit by large companies and corporations. In contrast, most SPITEX care is organized by non-profit providers whereas only 10 per cent are run by communities. Private SPITEX companies and for-profit services were, until 2010, not covered by the federal SPITEX statistics and are estimated to have a market share of 8 per cent (Gmür and Rüfenacht, 2010).

Table 4.1 *Population growth and trends in long-term care institutions and home-based long-term care in Switzerland, 2000–2009*

	2000	2005	2009	per cent change 2000–2009
Total population	7,204,055	7,459,128	7,785,806	8.1
Aged 65+	1,109,186	1,192,465	1,308,691	18.0
Aged 80+	291,412	336,428	371,604	27.5
Nursing homes				
Number of organizations	1480	1503	1596	7.8
Number of beds	84,031	86,798	91,913	9.4
Number of residents	81,282	84,770	89,679	10.3
Resident days	29,060,468	29,972,630	31,844,879	9.6
Employees (FTE)	54,735	63,483	76,526	39.8
Home-based care				
Number of organizations	787	697	576	–26.8
Number of clients	199,124	195,217	214,443	7.7
Number of hours	10,619,599	11,519,507	12,982,718	22.3
Nursing hours	4,907,022	6,647,723	8,191,951	66.9
Hours for elderly (65+)	8,203,319	9,179,875	10,552,509	28.6
Employees (FTE)	9,855	11,043	12,978	31.7

Source: Bundesamt für Statistik, 2000a, 2000b, 2005a, 2005b, 2009a, 2009b.
Note: FTE: Full time equivalent.

4.1.1 Federal health insurance law

In Switzerland, health insurance, which also covers long-term care services, is mandatory. At the federal level, the Health Insurance Regulation Act (Krankenversicherungsgesetz (KVG)) – enacted in 1994 and since then revised several times, most recently in 2009 – provides the regulatory framework for institutionalized or home-based long-term care. It covers a broad benefit package for the risks of acute and chronic illness, accidents and maternity. By law, any care provided must be effective, appropriate and economical (Paragraph 32, KVG).

Quality monitoring and long-term care in Switzerland 105

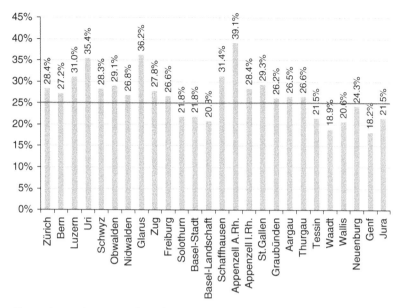

Figure 4.1 Relative number of beds in nursing homes per 100 people aged 80 or over (expressed as a percentage) by Swiss canton, 2008.
Source: authors' calculations based on Bundesamt für Statistik, 2008.

Several sections of the KVG are of interest for an understanding of long-term care. The Act:

- defines the care that has to be covered by mandatory health insurance, such as medical assessments and counselling, clinical examinations and medical treatments and interventions covering basic nursing care, monitoring and support for people who need mental health services;
- lists mandatory criteria (e.g., on staffing and medico-technical equipment) for accreditation as an in-patient care provider and criteria for the cantonal certificate of need. The cantonal certificate of need requires cantons to plan the number of long-term care beds needed, and nursing homes have to apply for their beds to be placed on the cantonal list. Insurance companies are only required to pay for residents in listed nursing homes;
- regulates the contributions to care costs by public health insurance and the maximum amount of co-payment contributed by long-term care

facility residents or home care clients. The Act also obliges the cantons to regulate the coverage of care costs that are not covered by public health insurance, meaning that in effect the (maximum) prices that nursing homes and home care agencies can charge for nursing care are fixed.

Although the KVG provides the major framework for how public health insurance has to cover claims for home-based or residential long-term care benefits at a national level, cantons have discretion to introduce additional regulations in the following areas:

- The cantons regulate licensing for providers of services covered by mandatory health insurance (within federal law requirements).
- The cantons are responsible for the determination of nursing home capacity (certificate of need regulation). Every canton must have a certificate of need process in place but each canton is free to organize its planning, define the number of beds needed and set the criteria deciding which nursing homes (and how many beds) are listed.
- The cantons provide the legal background for financing remaining long-term care costs such as housing, lodging and cleaning. For home-based long-term care this also means cooking and other services. In addition, they define the contributions of the canton and the communities to these costs.
- And finally the cantons are responsible for oversight and defining inspection procedures.

In terms of financing, as of 1 January 2011 new legislation (Art. 25a, KVG, Neuordnung der Pflegefinanzierung) on the financing of nursing care requires that mandatory health insurance should provide fixed contributions that cover roughly 50 per cent of such financing while the remaining costs are to be split between cantons/communities (30 per cent) and clients (20 per cent). In other developments, in 2012 Switzerland introduced the Diagnostic-Related Groups (DRG) funding system for acute hospital care, which, in theory, may lead to shifts to the post-acute and long-term care sector. However, to date, no data on the impact of the new DRG system are available.

At least at a rudimentary level, the long-term care sector in Switzerland is competitively organized. People can choose between different nursing homes, between home care providers and between home-based and institutional care. The choice is made by the client, either alone or in conjunction with family, taking into account existing supply, prices and other factors that are pertinent to the individual. No formal needs assessment takes place. In addition, insured people can switch between insurance companies every year or when the insurance company changes its premiums. Insurance companies are required to offer basic coverage specified by public healthcare legislation to any person applying (community rating) and there are internet-based services that allow consumers to make specific comparisons of the premiums on offer (e.g., www.priminfo. ch). This framework establishes competition between the insurance companies that offer different premiums or add-ons to the basic insurance package.

4.1.2 Quality regulation of long-term care at the federal level

Similarly to healthcare, there are different levels of quality control legislation or quality assurance for long-term care in Switzerland. The KVG formally invests most power in the Swiss federal government (Bundesrat). It allows the federal government to ensure the quality of all benefits covered by mandatory health insurance, including long-term care. The law also allows the federal government to delegate these quality assurance and monitoring tasks to the organizations of health-care professionals or service providers (Art. 58, KVG), and the government has decided to do so. The rationale behind this delegated authority is that, should it fail, the federal government still has recourse to imposing regulations itself. Consequently, quality assurance and control is in the hands of health services providers and professional organizations, respectively. These include, among others, several associations of health service providers, the Swiss Hospital Association, Swiss Home Care Associations and the Swiss Medical Association. These organizations have been assigned the task of developing frameworks and programmes that define the quality of services and requirements for quality improvement.

However, there is some disjunction between what the regulatory framework stipulates and its implementation. Firstly, the modalities to enforce quality assurance programmes should have become part of purchasing contracts between insurance companies and care providers (Art. 77, KVG). Under the KVG, if this does not occur, the federal government can enact the necessary rules directly.

Nevertheless, so far, purchasing contracts which mention quality assurance have been only partly implemented and the government has not yet exercised its powers to impose its own quality regulations. Secondly, neither SPITEX nor the long-term care provider associations have been successful in developing quality criteria in partnership with the insurance companies. The KVG explicitly states that cantonal arbitration boards (*Schiedsgerichte*) can exclude providers that do not participate in quality assurance and improvement programmes from supplying services covered by mandatory healthcare insurance. This has led to the current situation whereby to formally comply with this requirement, at least nominally, each standard contract[1] between a long-term care provider and an insurance company contains a paragraph that requires participation in quality assurance programmes. However, at this juncture, explicit mechanisms or quality assurance systems have not been defined. For example, the latest amendment to the contract between the Swiss Home Care Association and insurance companies regarding administrative procedures for home-based long-term care contains only a declaration that quality assurance will be regulated and that programmes will be implemented by 2014. Effectively, this situation also means that the KVG's system of sanctions for non-compliance with quality assurance programmes cannot be implemented as no quality assurance programmes are in place.

Therefore, although at the federal level, the principles of quality assurance within the health and long-term care system have been broadly established since 1995, there is still no comprehensive definition of quality in long-term care settings nor any consistent nationwide or cantonal implementation of quality assurance measures. Despite this, some national-level quality assurance initiatives are taking place, although none of them tends to integrate long-term care and progress on implementing actual programmes has been slow. For example, in 2011 a Nationwide Quality Control Agency was founded by the federal government, all healthcare insurance companies and Swiss hospitals. This agency now organizes and finances quality measurement in

---

[1] Standard contracts regulate the details of collaboration between providers and insurers, define procedures for assessment, monitoring (not quality) and payment. They also regulate additional price components that are not regulated by national law.

acute care, psychiatry and rehabilitation but not in long-term care. In addition, several national, or at least supra-regional, panels have contributed to the development of general principles for quality assurance and improvement. The government and insurance companies are partially involved in such organizing bodies and they are mostly organized as foundations or incorporated societies and concentrate on patient safety and the quality of providers in acute care or home-based medical services. Again, none of these organizations has a specific focus on long-term care.

To summarize, Switzerland finds itself in a situation where, although there is a clear legal foundation and obligation in national legislation to implement quality assurance measures, the national policy to delegate specific quality regulation to service provider associations and health insurers has not yet been successful in establishing sound quality assurance programmes for the long-term care sector. The slow progress echoes the rather modest advances made in other sectors. For example, in the acute and rehabilitation sectors there is a structure (Association nationale pour le développement de la qualité dans les hôpitaux et les cliniques (ANQ)) that undertakes some quality-related measurement and for hospitals, a federal agency publishes mortality quality indicators. This lack of progress prompted the federal Ministry of Health to state in 2009 that the quality assurance mandated by the federal law across health and long-term care sectors has not been sufficiently developed and that the federal level of government should now become more directly involved in the regulation of quality control (Bundesamt für Gesundheit, 2009).

4.2 Nursing home quality regulation

Historically, in practice, nursing home care has been regulated mainly by state healthcare (cantonal) law, although national law does have some influence. Due to the diversity of the twenty-six states (cantons), healthcare legislation and services differ between cantons. This is especially true for quality issues. The following section provides an overview of the spectrum in terms of regulation related to quality control, summarizes common factors and highlights some interesting solutions.

4.2.1 Licensing and operation rules

For the operation of a nursing home in all cantons there is a requirement to obtain a government licence. In most cantons licensing and quality control regulation are managed by either the cantonal department of health or social affairs. Employees working in licensing departments have degrees in administration, finance and very often in nursing and/or nursing administration. The specific requirements for licensing focus on:

(a) *Infrastructure*. Each canton regulates the operation of a nursing home through specific operational rules which regulate, among other things:
- the minimum size of rooms;
- the size and layout of bathrooms;
- accessibility for people with disabilities or people who need a wheelchair;
- access to special care rooms, e.g., closed gardens for people with dementia or care bathtubs; and
- type and minimum quantity of equipment necessary to provide care.

(b) *Staffing and frameworks*. For licensing purposes most cantons require a framework that covers general operational rules as well as a nursing care framework. However, there are no standards or inter-cantonal agreements about the level of detail and/or itemized contents. Thus, there is considerably high variability between cantons in a number of areas:
- Qualifications of director/administrators. Nursing home directors must have an adequate professional education (e.g., business degree and/or a degree in gerontology).
- Medical care. Medical care normally includes the right to choose a personal physician, or medical care is provided by an employed nursing home (long-term care) physician (medical director). In rare cases, the regulations cover additional issues such as special care needs (e.g., geropsychiatric nursing homes).
- Nursing Care. All cantons regulate the number of registered nurses and nursing aides per nursing home resident and the qualifications of nurses providing care. All nurses have to be trained and registered. Nurses can qualify with a bachelor's or master's degree in

Quality monitoring and long-term care in Switzerland   111

skilled nursing while nursing aides (*Fachangestellte Gesundheit*) have to complete three years of training followed by a theoretical and practical exam. Normally, the number of nursing staff is calculated based on the number of residents and the level of care needed. The head nurse must have a higher degree in nursing and provide leadership skills. Regulations also cover hours of internal and external professional continuing education training per year.

(c) *Organizational and financial requirements*, mainly proof of financial resources. Here the requirement is to provide sufficient equity, in the case of corporate bodies, or to demonstrate the existence of sufficient resources in the case of individuals. In addition, each institution is controlled by a board of directors that is independent of the nursing home administration

(d) *Licensing procedural requirements and data transfer regulations.* Cantons regulate the duration of a nursing home licence (four to six years), during which time the facility can expect to be inspected approximately two to three times, although the norms vary amongst cantons. The licence can be withdrawn if the nursing home violates the above-mentioned regulatory standards. However, there is no public record of any institutions having their licences withdrawn and such cases seem to be extremely rare. A few cantons require an established quality management system for each nursing home, including rules for reporting and monitoring, while other cantons have no regulations.

4.2.2 Definition of quality and quality standards in residential facilities

As federal law only specifies quality-related criteria in a general way, cantons can define such criteria in more detail. Several Swiss cantons have defined quality standards for long-term care institutions. These cover, for example, domains such as organizational structures, qualifications of directors, nursing care, medical services, resident activities, range of motion and use of restraints, dignity, palliative and end-of-life care, dining, house staff services, room and infrastructure and general safety. Other regions have developed quality goals or special areas of focus that change from year to year. All cantons provide online access to lists of licensed nursing homes and the majority also list licensing criteria that are available for download.

4.2.3 Quality control and audits in nursing homes

Several cantons have developed different strategies to establish quality control in long-term care, some of them in an overlapping fashion. These various frameworks or strategies can be characterized as follows:

(a) There is no formal and regular quality monitoring. The authorities normally react and impose sanctions on nursing homes in cases of reported violations of rules. These come about due to a complaint that someone files against the home. In addition, the licensing requirements will be evaluated upon the renewal application process. To our knowledge all cantons provide this basic level of oversight.

(b) The authorities require quality data which are analysed and cases of poor quality trigger an inspection or reinspection. Most cantons, as a minimum, have procedures for checking staffing requirements, and only a few require outcome data. In terms of monitoring staffing levels, the national level collects data annually on the number and qualifications of all nursing home personnel; thus, many cantons have detailed instructions on how to calculate the required staff in nursing care (in relation to case-mix) and submit this data.

(c) The licensing authority (canton) regulates the implementation of quality management systems (such as EFQM, different Swiss systems like Q-Plan and Qualipro) in all nursing homes and monitors such implementation. Only a few cantons require or have specified the use of quality management systems.

(d) The licensing authority performs individual site visits. Most cantons visit institutions, but the content of monitoring and frequencies may differ substantially.

(e) The licensing body (canton) performs regular and systematic audits based on a clearly defined set of licensing criteria and conducted by a professional audit team. Only a few cantons operate such a system and there is no obligation to make the results available publically. Audit results go to the licensing authority, the nursing home and sometimes to the community (city), although some nursing homes may publish their own results if they are favourable.

4.2.4 Summary of nursing home regulation

Our current analysis of quality regulation in nursing home care in Switzerland demonstrates that quality management at the cantonal level focuses primarily on the qualifications requirements for nursing staff, structural quality and in a few instances, procedural quality but only exceptionally on outcome quality. The standards used by cantonal departments offer much space for interpretation and are highly dependent on the monitoring mechanism or the individuals involved in monitoring activities. The results of quality audits (if such audits are done at all) are not systematically analysed and thus do not allow benchmarking. Older Swiss people who need long-term care select residential facilities based on the availability of beds, distance to their previous domicile, the recommendations of friends, social workers or generally on a facility's 'word of mouth' reputation, and in rare cases in line with financial constraints. In some cases, long-term care institutions are selected because they offer specialized services for residents with dementia or visual impairment or because of religious preferences. The results of quality control audits or outcome data are usually not available to the public. In fact, very little information is published that would be useful for people choosing a nursing home.

4.3 Home care quality regulation

Similarly to long-term care institutions, professional home care services (SPITEX) require a licence issued by a designated cantonal agency. Licensing procedures involve the presence of a basic framework for the operation of the service, the availability of nursing staff (normally during daytime hours) and the organization of nursing staff on call, professional requirements for directors, head nurses and nursing staff, and recommendations on required retraining. Therefore, home-based care requirements do not differ significantly from institutional long-term care requirements. Except for a periodic mandate to renew operational licences, there are only a few regulations to monitor quality of care in the home care context. A few cantons recommend the use of a *Quality Manual* issued by the Swiss Home Care Association (SPITEX Switzerland), which can be used for self-evaluation. Other cantons require the use of quality management systems. Similarly to nursing home care, if quality control surveys within SPITEX services are done at all, the results are not published.

The Swiss Home Care Association has launched several initiatives that claim to be relevant for home-based long-term care. However, due to the cantonal structure of the country the Association can only suggest recommendations rather than impose them, a factor which weakens the implementation of a comparable quality assurance system. The Association's *Quality Manual* lists a total of twenty-four standards covering a wide range of topics; for example: evidence-based nursing care, customer satisfaction, ethics of care, critical incidence reporting, case and care management, skill and grade mix, health promotion for staff members and financial management. However, the manual has not been adopted widely. After a pilot project in 2000–2002, SPITEX Switzerland decided to support the nationwide use of the RAI-HC: Resident Assessment Instrument[2] and to recommend it to the cantonal organizations. Since then, RAI-HC has been used in most cantons and it is also mandated by some regulatory authorities at the cantonal level. Based on a survey of users of this instrument, RAI-HC has been demonstrated to have a positive impact on nursing quality (Bartelt et al., 2002; Mylaeus, 2010).

It is possible that RAI-HC may become a solid base for outcome-related quality management in home care. Therefore, SPITEX Switzerland has launched a pilot project to examine the practicability of introducing quality indicators derived from RAI-HC for the purposes of quality improvement. In a report published in 2009, Rüesch et al. (2009) identified nineteen indicators that are feasible. They concluded that a RAI-HC instrument based on these nineteen indicators should be implemented in home-based care as soon as possible. SPITEX Switzerland is currently discussing a nationwide database to collect data and to provide the necessary infrastructure to implement such a system, although in the short term it is unlikely that the results of any subsequent quality measurement exercises would be made public; rather, anonymized benchmarking would be the most likely path taken.

---

[2] The RAI-HC is a comprehensive care and service planning tool for adults in home- and community-based settings. The instrument is generally used with frail elderly or people with disabilities. The tool's focus is on a person's level of functioning and quality of life by assessing needs, strengths and preferences.

4.4 Quality assurance efforts by other players in long-term care

4.4.1 Outcome quality indicators in RAI institutions

The number of long-term care institutions that use RAI-NH (resident assessment in nursing homes) has increased over the last few years.[3] In Switzerland, to date, more than 500 nursing homes in sixteen out of twenty-six cantons have implemented RAI-NH. Once a nursing home has implemented the RAI-NH, the system allows an analysis of quality indicators to take place. Of all originally developed indicators (Zimmerman et al., 1995) twenty-three are currently used in an annual quality report compiled by Q-Sys, the organization that offers RAI System Support in Switzerland. This report is used as an inter-cantonal comparison and also provides the data for quality improvement designed specifically for use within each institution. A quality control group interprets the results, identifies areas of improvement, develops measures and defines ways to re-evaluate implemented measures. Usually, individual nursing homes are supported by external quality indicator coaches that help to evaluate the results and define specific interventions for improvement.

Currently, work with quality indicators differs between cantons and is still voluntary. In three cantons (Solothurn, Basel Stadt and Ticino) the cantonal authorities have calculated indicators for all long-term care institutions in the canton and have provided financial support to institutions working with quality indicators. In several instances, the quality indicators are bundled to cover a specific area, such as pain management or management of restraints, and are integrated into a quality action plan. Figure 4.2 gives an example of the use of one quality indicator (prevalence of severe pain) in participating nursing homes in the Basel Stadt canton over the period 2003–11, while Figure 4.3 shows the recorded prevalence rates for another indicator, the use of restraints, in Ticino canton between 2006 and 2011. In both cases, a reduction in prevalence rates can be seen, although in the case of Ticino canton the reduced prevalence rates for the use of restraints still leaves the Ticino average above the national average.

---

[3] The main motivation seems to be that the RAI-NH is used to generate Resource Utilization Groups (RUGs), along with other systems, to define nursing home reimbursement levels.

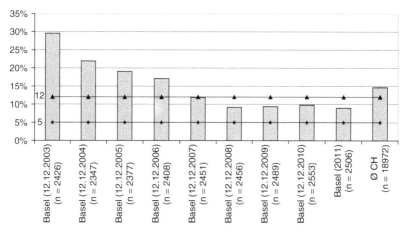

Figure 4.2 'Prevalence of severe pain' quality indicator in the City of Basel canton, 2003–11.
Source: compiled by authors based on Q-Sys AG data, 2011, 2012.
Note: the last bar indicates the average prevalence rate in Switzerland.

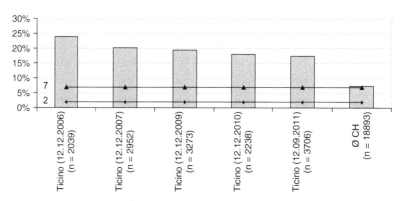

Figure 4.3 Prevalence of restraint use in Ticino canton, 2006–11.
Source: compiled by authors based on Q-Sys AG data, 2011, 2012.
Note: The last bar indicates the average prevalence rate in Switzerland.

In terms of the future direction of these initiatives, the systematic publication of quality outcome measures at the cantonal level does not really feature on the policy agenda. There is an initiative to develop national quality indicators, with a view to publishing these in the same way that hospital indicators are published currently.

4.4.2 *Other quality management systems*

Many care providers, especially long-term care residential facilities, have discussed the possibility of implementing a systematic quality management system. There are several products on the market that range from internationally known standards such as ISO or EFQM[4] to specific Swiss solutions for a systematic quality management system. In addition, the number of customer satisfaction and family members surveys, in both home-based care and residential facilities, is increasing either as a specific part of such quality management systems or as single initiatives. This shows that there have been voluntary efforts to improve quality by service providers, with the ultimate goal of not only improving clients' care but also improving individual providers' market position and attracting future customers. Since monitored outcome measures at the federal or cantonal level are lacking, currently, an evaluation of such individual efforts is not possible.

4.5 Summary and outlook

As in other countries worldwide, in Switzerland the number of elderly people who are treated in home-based and/or institutionalized long-term care settings is increasing.

Unfortunately, in the last fifteen years the delegation of quality assurance regulations to service providers, their associations and healthcare insurers has not induced sufficient progress in achieving a structured quality assurance regime in long-term care. There is increasing evidence that the federal government's delegation strategy has failed. Therefore, there is growing agreement to introduce stronger and more direct governmental involvement in quality monitoring and quality assurance at the federal level. A recent OECD report (OECD/WHO, 2011) points to a general lack of information in the Swiss healthcare sector:

More information is needed to monitor quality of care. The 2006 review highlighted that the Swiss healthcare system combined a high degree of reliance on clinician self-regulation combined with a series of institutional level initiatives to improve quality of care and patient safety.

---

[4] ISO International Organization for Standardization, e.g., ISO 9000, www.iso.org; EFQM European Foundation of Quality Management, www.efqm.org.

The OECD report acknowledges gradual steps since 2006, mainly in the hospital sector. However, additional steps are missing in the long-term care sector. To date, cantonal regulations provide the main framework for quality assurance in long-term care. These regulations primarily focus on rather traditional standards such as licensing and inspection procedures that concentrate on structural quality and human resource qualifications rather than quality outcomes.

Nevertheless, we believe that the level of quality in both home-based care and nursing home care is high in Switzerland, based on a number of factors. First, the financing arrangements to cover long-term care costs are conducive to good levels of care. Since payment is divided up between all of the partners (i.e., national health insurance, direct contributions by cantons and/or communities and long-term care clients) direct payments by service users are kept relatively low and financial support is also provided to low-income residents in nursing homes through the social security system. This shared financing makes it possible to cover high nursing home fees that, in turn, allow the providers to invest in good infrastructure and appropriate staffing levels. Second, there is a wide range of high-quality professional education for all professional groups working in the sector, resulting in a high-quality work force. And finally there is sufficient competition among service providers, including private suppliers, which sets incentives for high quality by service providers.

Having said that, as in the hospital sector, further steps are needed to improve valid quality measurement of outcomes in long-term care. The revised KVG establishes a clear competence at the federal level to collect data for 'medical quality indicators' and to publish them. Publication, defined as making results available to the public, is still poor and needs to be improved. In view of the nationwide implementation of RAI-HC in the home care sector and the voluntary use of quality indicators in many long-term care residential facilities using the RAI system, there is now a strong basis for the implementation of state-of-the-art quality measurement for long-term care. Since there are three different assessment instruments for nursing homes (RAI, BESA, PLAISIR) in use, a consensus on how to proceed needs to be found. The combination of structural input-oriented quality regulation by the cantons, some competition among service providers and generally agreed-upon and publicly available quality measures at the federal level might be a promising way to go.

References

Bartelt, G., Gilgen, R., Dupasquier, J. N. and Staudenmaier, B. (2002). *Pilotprojekt RAI-HC: Zusammenfassender Kurzbericht im Auftrage des Spitex Verbandes Schweiz 1–32, 11–4–2002* [Pilot Project RAI-HC: Short Report Summary for SPITEX Switzerland]. St Gallen: SPITEX.

Bundesamt der Gesundheit (2009). *Qualitätsstrategie des Bundes im Schweizerischen Gesundheitswesen* [Quality Strategy Unit in the Swiss Healthcare System]. N.p.: EDI–BAG.

Bundesamt für Statistik (2000a, 2005a, 2009a). SOMED-Statistik. Available at: https://www.somed.bfs.admin.ch/BusinessModules/Login.

(2000b, 2005b, 2009b). Spitex-Statistik. Available at: http://www.cura viva.ch/index.cfm/48A6FFAB-A21D-299A-2F7223A9C5F8405A/?meth od=dossier.detail&id=32B26C0D-C73C-EC18-6C28FF7F0A6940ED.

(2002). BFS aktuell Standardtabellen 2000 [BFS Current Standard Tables]. Available at: http://www.bfs.admin.ch/bfs/portal/de/index/themen/14/03/02/data/04.parsys.0010.download List.00101.DownloadFile.tmp/ksmtabetnotes2000.zip.

(2007). *Krankenhausstatistik und statistik der sozialmedizinischen Institutionen 2005: Definitive Resultate (Standardtabellen)* [Hospital Statistics and Statistics on Socio-Medical Institutions 2005: Definitive Results. Standard Tables]. BFS News 14, Health. Neuchâtel: BFS.

(2008). Statistik der sozialmedizinischen Institutionen: Standardtabellen. Available at: www.bfs.admin.ch/bfs/portal/de/index/themen/14/03/02/key/01.html.

(2009c). *Statistik der sozialmedizinischen Institutionen 2008: Standardtabellen* [Statistics on socio-medical institutions 2008: Standard tables]. BFS News 14, Health. Neuchâtel: BFS.

(2011). *Statistik der sozialmedizinischen Institutionen 2009: Standardtabellen* [Statistics on Socio-Medical Institutions 2009: Standard tables]. BFS News 14, Health. Neuchâtel: BFS.

(2012). *Kosten und Finanzierung des Gesundheitswesens* (Statistisches Lexikon der Schweiz) [Cost and Financing of Healthcare (Statistical Dictionary of Switzerland)] Available at: www.bfs.admin.ch/bfs/portal/de/index/themen/14/05/blank/key/leistungserbringer.html.

Gmür, R. and Rüfenacht, M. (2010). Spitex. In G. Kocher and W. Oggier (eds.), *Gesundheitswesen Schweiz* [Swiss Healthcare System]. Bern: Huber, pp. 353–64.

Mylaeus, M. (2010). *Umfrage zu den wichtigsten Erkenntnissen bei der Einführung von RAI-HC* [Survey on the most Important Findings during the Introduction of RAI-HC]. Bern: Spitex Verband Schweiz.

OECD/WHO (2011). OECD review of health systems Switzerland. Paris: OECD. Available at: http://dx.doi.org/10.1787/9789264120914-en.

Q-Sys AG (2011). *Qualitätsindikatorenauswertungen 2011* [Indicators of Quality Evaluations, 2011]. St Gallen: Q-Sys AG.

(2012). *Qualitätsindikatorenauswertungen 2012* [Indicators of Quality Evaluations, 2012]. St Gallen: Q-Sys AG.

Rüesch, P., Burla, L., Schaffert, R. and Mylaeus, M. (2009). *Qualitätsindikatoren der ambulanten Pflege (Spitex) in der Schweiz auf der Grundlage von RAI-HC 1–205. 2009* [Quality Indicators of Ambulatory SPITEX Care based on RAI-HC]. SGGP Schriftenreihe No. 96. Bern: SGGP.

Zimmerman, D. R., Karon, S. L., Arling, G., Clark, B. R., Collins, T., Ross, R. and Sainfort, F. (1995). Development and testing of nursing home quality indicators. *Healthcare Financing Review*, 16(4), 107–27.

5 Japan's long-term care regulations focused on structure – rationale and future prospects

NAOKI IKEGAMI, TOMOAKI ISHIBASHI
AND TAKASHI AMANO

5.1 Introduction

Regulations are ostensibly implemented to improve quality and contain public expenditures, and also to show the public that the government is responding to abuses reported by the media. When regulations are revised, professional organizations tend to lobby for upgrading qualification and staffing level requirements because it would advance their status. On the other hand, provider organizations tend to lobby against any revisions that would increase their costs. Their opposing positions could theoretically lead to an ideal balance, skilfully mediated by the government organization responsible for drafting and implementing the regulations. However, in the Japanese context, it has led to a suboptimal compromise that does not necessarily reflect the needs of society. The government organization also has a major stake because its power and budget would be expanded by supporting and leveraging the power of the interest groups (Lowi, 1979). As a practical issue, a phase-in period is needed for the government agency to develop the capacity to enforce new regulations and for the organizations affected by them to be able to comply with the new requirements. Therefore, the regulations on the provision of long-term care services can only be understood from the underlying motives of the parties immediately concerned.

This chapter will begin by presenting the historical background in which long-term care developed in Japan. Next the existing regulations governing long-term care providers will be described, followed by the reasons why they have been focused on the structural aspects of staffing levels, qualifications and facility standards rather than on measurable resident outcomes. The final section looks at the future prospects for monitoring quality in long-term care.

5.2 Background to long-term care in Japan

Long-term care expanded in Japan following four policy decisions made by the government. The first was the enactment of the Welfare Act for Elders (*rōjin fukushihō*) in 1963, which was spearheaded by Shintarō Seto, director of the Institutional Division within the Social Affairs Bureau of the Ministry of Health and Welfare (MHW). He wanted to lay the groundwork for a new government initiative in ageing because post-war poverty issues had been largely resolved by that time (Campbell, 1992). One tangible outcome, though on a very small scale, was the establishment of nursing homes. However, they were not officially referred to as 'nursing homes' because care was not under the direction of nurses, but under the rubric of welfare organizations. The literal English translation is 'special homes for the aged' (*tokubetsu yōgo rōjin hōmu*), and named as such so as to distinguish them from the pre-existing 'homes for the aged' (*yōgo rōjin hōmu*). The latter had been restricted to the indigent but the new type was not: it was for all elders who had more serious physical and mental disabilities. The Act also provided for home-help services but this was initially restricted to the indigent who lived alone. Access to both services was controlled by the local government's social welfare office and means-tested. The services were provided directly either by local governments or by the special welfare organizations, which were almost entirely funded and closely supervised by the government. Care workers employed by the latter had a seniority-based pay scale similar to government employees so that it was possible to attract staff of relatively high quality. The certification and audit processes of nursing homes were similar to other public-sector organizations such as public schools and transport authorities.

The second decision in 1973 was to make healthcare free (with no copayments) to all elders aged 70 and over, and to those with disabilities aged 65 and over. This was when economic growth was at its peak and the expansion of the welfare state was being promoted by progressive prefectural governors. Since there was no limitation on the length of hospital stay, this policy unintentionally opened the door to hospital admissions for 'social reasons'. Patients whose families were unable or unwilling to take care of elders came to be admitted and remained in hospital until they died. Thus, many hospitals were transformed into de facto nursing homes. The proportion of the general population aged 65 and over who were hospital in-patients on the day of the annual survey doubled from 2 per cent in 1975 to 4 per cent in 1990, and came to constitute two-thirds of all elders

Japan's long-term care regulations focused on structure 123

who were institutionalized (MHW, 1975a, 1975b, 1992a, 1992b). The government attempted to remedy this situation by establishing health facilities for the elderly (HFE) (*rōjin hoken shisetsu*) in 1986. The HFE were intended to function as an intermediate care facility between the hospital and the community, and as such, the length of stay of their residents was officially limited to three months.

The third decision was the implementation of the 'Gold Plan' (officially known as the Ten Year Plan to Develop Health and Welfare Services for Elders) in 1989. It was part of the ruling Liberal Democratic Party's strategy to win back votes after nearly losing the election that followed the introduction of the value added tax (VAT) earlier that year. The expansion of long-term care services under the Gold Plan proved so popular it was subsequently revised with higher targets in the five-year 'New Gold Plan' of 1994. By the year of completion in 1999, the number of full-time equivalent home helpers was planned to increase from the 1990 level of 38,945 to 100,000 in the Gold Plan, which was revised to 170,000 in the New Gold Plan. Furthermore, the number of adult day care centres was planned to increase from 1,615 to 10,000 in the first and increased to 17,000 in the next Gold Plan (Kōsei Tōkei Kyōkai, 1996, 2001). The New Gold Plan's goals were generally met (MHLW, 2001a). Although services did expand, they continued to be provided only by local governments or by special welfare organizations. As such, regulatory mechanisms covering the new types of service providers did not develop, and the services tended to remain focused on those with low income. Parenthetically, the expansion of health services such as HFE and visiting nurse agencies was also planned, but, unlike the tax-financed social services, health insurance did not cover the funding of their capital expenditures.

The fourth major policy initiative was the implementation of the public long-term care insurance (LTCI) (*kaigo hoken*) in 2000, which made long-term care services an entitlement, regardless of income level or availability of family support, to all those 65 and over, and to those aged 40–64 with disabilities resulting from age-related diseases such as strokes or Parkinson's (Ikegami, 2007; Campbell et al., 2010). Public awareness of the rapidly ageing society, the growing inadequacy of informal care, problems of 'social admissions' to hospitals, increasing pressure on general revenues and problems with the bureaucratic administration of social services by municipal governments all contributed to the implementation of this new programme. Half of the public expenditures are financed by social insurance premiums levied on all those aged 40 and over, and half by general taxes, with an additional 10 per cent copayment and the partial levying of 'hotel costs' for bed and board by users. Although the LTCI is administered by municipal governments, it is a social insurance programme based on the principle of individual entitlement with guaranteed benefits and free choice of providers. The standards and the LTCI fee schedule are nationally uniform, except for adjustments made in the reimbursed amount reflecting local labour costs, and minor differences in how the prefectural governments disclose the audit reports of providers.

The maximum amount of benefits for purchasing long-term care services is set for each of the seven levels of eligibility. Both eligibility and the level of eligibility are determined by an assessment of the applicant's physical and mental status using a seventy-four-item check list. The assessment is based on universal standards without any provisions for people with special needs, such as being blind. The amount for the highest benefit level is US$4,000 per month, the lowest US$480 (based on the current exchange rate of US$1=100 yen). Benefits are limited to services which must be purchased from certified providers. Cash allowances were excluded because feminist groups opposed them on the grounds that it would not alleviate women's care burden and might conversely increase the social pressure for them to provide care rather than to pursue career opportunities (Campbell, 2002). The fact that the tradition of live-in maids had practically died out and the virtual absence of immigrant labour may also have decreased the public demand for cash benefits.

The providers designated *shitei* by the LTCI can be grouped into the following: the first are those who would have been in the social service sector (nursing homes, day care centres, home helper agencies) prior to the implementation of LTCI; the second are those who would have been in the healthcare sector (hospital long-term care units, HFE, day rehab centres, visiting nurse agencies); the third are the new for-profit and non-profit organizations which were allowed entry into the home- and community-based care market, but not into the institutional care market, following the implementation of the LTCI. To assist beneficiaries in choosing appropriate services, a new quasi-profession of 'care managers' was created. All those who have had five years' experience in health or social services may sit for an examination and, if successful, are given a licence after undergoing forty-four hours of training. Virtually all care manager agencies have been established by home- and community-based

Table 5.1 *Expansion in number of LTCI service users in Japan, May 2001–May 2009*

	2001	2009	Increase rate 2009/2001
Users of home- and community-based care services (thousands)			
Home helper	518.0	1157.7	2.2
Day care	536.7	1267.7	2.4
Day rehabilitation	295.1	474.4	1.6
Rental of assisted devices	288.3	1047.3	3.6
Visiting nurse	188.0	258.0	1.4
Total	1826.1	4205.1	2.3
Users of institutional and quasi-institutional services (thousands)			
Nursing homes	287.3	427.5	1.5
Health facilities for elders	225.4	321.5	1.4
Long-term care hospital beds	104.4	94.5	0.9
Specified facilities	9.8	124.3	12.7
Group homes	8.7	138.5	15.9
Total	635.6	1106.3	1.7

Source: MHLW, 2001b, 2009c.

care provider organizations. Although clients can choose any agency from a list provided by their local government, they have tended to choose the one under the same ownership as the provider that delivers the type of service they are likely to use the most: for example, if these are home-helper services, then the care manager agency usually will be under the same ownership as the home-helper provider.

The LTCI turned out to be very popular. Expenditures doubled from 2000 to 2010 to reach the current level of 1.4 per cent of the GDP (MHLW, 2011a; OECD, 2011). It has crowded out services that are privately purchased so that virtually all long-term care services are provided within the framework of LTCI. As Table 5.1 shows, the number of users of home- and community-based care more than doubled and institutional use increased by 70 per cent in ten years (MHLW, 2001b, 2009c). Despite these increases, waiting lists for admission to nursing homes have continued to lengthen and now exceed twelve months (Nomura Research Institute, 2010). Nursing homes are more popular than home- and community-based care because they provide twenty-four-hour coverage at relatively low out-of-pocket costs (US$700 per month inclusive rate for a standard shared four-bed room, with the amount reduced if the resident is on low income). To meet this excess demand, two new types of quasi-institutions (which are officially categorized as 'housing' and therefore permissible for the entry of new for-profit and non-profit organizations) have increased tremendously. These are the 'specified facilities' (*tokutei shisetsu*) (similar to nursing homes but with better amenities) and the 'group homes' (single rooms with a common living area in units of ten for those with mild to moderate dementia). The reason why these facilities have increased so much is that, in contrast to the formal 'institutions', they do not rely on subsidies for their construction costs and are able to set their own price for bed and board. In addition to these quasi-institutions, there also has been an increase in the number of 'assisted living' housing in which services provided under the LTCI are paid on the same basis as in home- and community-based care.

As has been described above, LTCI in Japan is almost exclusively focused on elders. Long-term care for the disabled or those who are mentally ill has not received much public attention. The underlying reason why elders have been the major social policy issue in Japan lies in the fact that the public is well aware of the rapid ageing of the country: the percentage of the population aged 65 and over was only 12 per cent in 1990, but has nearly doubled to 22 per cent by 2010 and is estimated to become 30 per cent in 2025 (MHLW, 2006).

Following this summary explanation of the historical emergence of the Japanese long-term care system and its financing, this chapter will focus on regulations in the LTCI, but will also briefly refer to regulatory measures for long-term care financed by health insurance. The bulk of the latter is for in-patient care that is still being provided in hospitals. Long-term care services for non-elders with physical and mental disabilities will not be covered; focusing only on elders should facilitate international comparisons because the boundaries of long-term care with other sectors become blurred if occupational training and disability pensions, which have important functions for non-elders, are included (Campbell et al., 2010).

5.3 Regulatory principles in LTCI

Prior to the implementation of the LTCI, regulations in both healthcare and social services had been focused on structural aspects of quality:

Japan's long-term care regulations focused on structure　　127

Table 5.2　*Staffing regulations for institutional care in Japan*

	Nursing homes	Health facilities for elders	LTCI hospital units
Physicians	As needed	1 per 100 residents	3 if < 101 patients plus 1 per 48 patients if > 101 patients
Nurses	1 if < 30 patients 2 if 31–50 patients 3 if > 50 patients	Nurse to aide ratio must be >3:1	1 per 6 patients
Aides	1 aide (or nurse) per 3 residents	1 aide (or nurse) per 3 residents	1 aide per 6 patients
Therapists	1 per facility (could be a nurse or certified masseur)	1 PT or OT or ST per 100 residents	PT or OT as required
Social workers	1 per 100 residents	1 or more	No requirement
Care managers	1 per 100 residents	1 per 100 residents	1 per 100 patients
Pharmacists	No requirement	As needed	1 per 150 patients

Source: MHLW, 2010a.
Note: PT – physiotherapist; OT – occupational therapist; ST – speech therapist.

that is, setting and meeting standards for qualifications and staffing, and standards for physical facilities. After implementation of LTCI, the focus continued to be on the following aspects of quality assurance in both institutional care and home- and community-based care: setting of certification standards, ongoing monitoring of compliance with standards and reporting adherence. Audits of clinical and financial records are generally undertaken by the prefectural government.[1] The mandated staffing levels for the three types of institutional care facilities are shown in Table 5.2 (MHLW, 2010a). It is one full-time-equivalent (FTE) care staff to three residents across all three types. The difference lies in the proportion of qualified nurses: in LTCI hospital units, half of

---

[1] Japan has fifty-seven prefectures or subnational jurisdictions, each of which has a directly elected governor and a single chamber assembly.

the staff must be nurses; in HFE, one-quarter; in nursing homes, only one-tenth. Non-nurses are not required to have any qualifications. Physician staffing requirements differ similarly: twenty-four-hour coverage in LTCI hospital units; one full-time physician per facility in HFE; and one or more physicians contracted to make scheduled weekly visit(s) in nursing homes. Staffing by a physiotherapist or occupational therapist is mandatory only in HFE, a legacy of the fact that they were originally designed to facilitate discharges from hospitals. Parenthetically, nursing home residents must change their physician to the one contracted by the facility but this has not been of major concern because patients are used to changing their physicians as there is no system of registration with general practitioners in Japan.

Table 5.3 shows the facility requirements in the three types of institutions (MHLW, 2010a). The level of amenity, as measured by the floor

Table 5.3 *Facility regulations for institutional care in Japan*

Regulations	Nursing homes	Health facilities for elders	LTCI hospital units
Floor space per bed	$10.65m^2$	$8.0m^2$	$6.4m^2$
Maximum number of beds per room	4	4	4
Width of corridor	At least 1.8m At least 2.7m if rooms are on both sides	At least 1.8m At least 2.7m if rooms are on both sides	At least 1.8m At least 2.7m if rooms are on both sides
Dining room	$3m^2$ per resident	$2m^2$ per resident	$1m^2$ per resident
Therapy room	Dining room can be used	$1m^2$ per resident	$40m^2$
Other	Recuperation room, consulting room, special bathing facilities	Recuperation room, consulting room, special bathing facilities	As for hospitals (special bathing facilities not required)

Source: MHLW, 2010a.

space per bed, the space required for the dining room and so forth, is lowest in LTCI hospital units and highest in nursing homes.

These regulatory requirements reflect the differences in their historical roots, and not necessarily residents' needs. Since nursing homes had been welfare institutions, the staffing of physicians and nurses has remained minimal. On the other hand, although LTCI hospital units provide de facto nursing home care, because they are categorized as hospitals, they are staffed for twenty-four-hour coverage by physicians and nurses. In contrast, the requirements for physical facilities are the opposite: nursing homes have the highest standards while hospitals have the lowest. This is due to the fact that the construction costs of nursing homes are financed separately by the government, while in hospitals they are not, and must be financed from what the hospitals are reimbursed from providing services, with the price set by the fee schedule. The situation is basically the same as HFE but it was possible to set higher physical standards because these were a new type of facility. Care was taken to ensure that the standards for the HFE would be in between nursing homes and LTCI hospital units. Parenthetically, the original idea was that some of the hospitals would be converted to HFE, but none were able to because the physical standards were too high.

Regarding regulations on the processes of care, the only mechanism that has had some effect is the one on physical restraints in institutional settings. There must be documentation that the decision to apply restraints was made after having been discussed by the care team, the objective and the period are clearly stated, and explanations as to why restraints are necessary have been provided to the resident and/or family. Compliance is monitored by auditing the institution's records on the use of physical restraints and interviewing the staff when on-site inspections are made. However, the audit does not include the direct observation of residents. Nor are standard comprehensive resident assessments required. The regulation on physical restraints does not apply to health-insurance-financed hospital long-term care beds, or to any other type of hospital bed.

In home- and community-based care, as shown in Table 5.4, the main focus has been on the number of staff and their qualifications (MHLW, 2010b). Home helper and visiting nurse agencies must have a minimum of 2.5 full-time equivalent (FTE) staff, of which two must be full-time. In home helper agencies, all home helpers must have completed the

Table 5.4 *Regulations for home- and community-based care agencies in Japan*

	Home helper	Day care	Day rehabilitation care
Physicians	N/A	N/A	1 or more
Nurses	N/A	1 or more	N/A
Therapists	N/A	1 (could be nurse or certified masseur)	1 per 10 users (more than 10 per cent FTE must be either PT, OT, ST)
Care workers	Must have completed 130 hours of training Number ≥2.5 of which 2 must be full-time	Must have completed 130 hours of training Number ≥1 (up to 15 users plus 1 per every additional 5 users)	N/A
Supervisors	1 or more	N/A	N/A

Source: MHLW, 2010b.
Note: N/A – Not applicable; PT – physiotherapist; OT – occupational therapist; ST – speech therapist

prescribed 130-hour training course, which is didactic with some classroom practice in caring (completing this course is not required for aides in institutional settings). In addition, every agency must employ at least one designated full-time home helper, who is responsible for providing oversight to part-timers. Part-time workers fulfil a major role: 50.1 per cent of the home helpers' FTE total working hours are provided by part-timers (MHLW, 2007). The number of designated full-time home helpers required increases as the number of part-time workers increases.

Most day care centres had been established by nursing homes, while most day rehabilitation centres were established by HFE. Staffing requirements reflect their origin. For day care centres, they are in between nursing homes and home helper agencies: as in nursing homes, the number of care workers is determined by the number of clients and only one nurse is needed; as in home- and community-based care, all care workers must have completed the 130-hour training course. In day rehabilitation

Japan's long-term care regulations focused on structure 131

centres, there must be one or more physicians on duty and all the staff are categorized as a 'therapist', with the number of therapists determined by the number of clients. However, only 10 per cent of the therapists' cumulative FTE time needs to be provided by a licensed therapist (physiotherapist, occupational therapist or speech therapist). There are no requirements for the remaining 90 per cent. A new regulation was imposed in 2009 for large corporations that have 100 or more agencies. This was introduced in 2006 after the media exposure of COMSN, the largest for-profit chain at that time, which had opened new agencies after being ordered to close the ones not complying with regulations (Yomiuri, 2006). Audits are undertaken by the national government at least once every six years. The focus is the same as the audits performed by the prefectural government except for the fact that cross-checking of records is performed at the national level. If a serious offence is found in any one of its agencies, then all of a corporation's agencies, and not just the offending one, would be ordered to close, thus effectively decertifying the entire organization. This regulation does not exist in the healthcare sector.

5.4 Monitoring and reporting

To designate a provider as a LTCI facility, an application form is submitted showing that it has met the necessary staffing and physical plant requirements. On-site inspections are performed for confirmation. For ongoing monitoring, the staff attendance book is closely inspected. In institutional care, the number of staff per resident must be met both on a daily basis and per calendar month. In home- and community-based care, home helper agencies must show that all their staff has the necessary qualifications, that there are at least two full-time home helpers and that there is the required number of designated full-time carers to supervise the work of part-time workers. Since 50.1 per cent of all FTE home helpers are part time, this could be a considerable hurdle and the violation of this requirement, together with the one on the minimum number of full-time workers required in each agency, were the underlying causes that led to the dissolution of COMSN (Yomiuri, 2006).

The auditing of the LTCI facility or agency for compliance to standards is made in conjunction with that of compliance to LTCI reimbursement rules. The LTCI fee schedule determines the price of all services and the conditions that the provider must comply with in order to be reimbursed. Following the practice set by health insurance, when fees are revised, they are revised individually and not across-the-board at the same rate. This fine-tuning is done so as to provide incentives and disincentives to meet policy goals (Ikegami and Campbell, 1999, 2004). For example, in the 2009 fee schedule revision, which was designed to encourage home helper agencies to hire more experienced workers, the price per visit was set higher for an agency if one-third of its workers had either three or more years of experience, or had the qualification of a certified care worker (MHLW, 2009a). By doing so, the agency's profit would increase because their temporary workers would continue to be paid at the same piecemeal rate. Audits are undertaken to verify that agencies do meet the specifications, should they bill at this higher rate. Non-government, third-party audits focused on user satisfaction surveys and self-evaluation of their management aspects are also performed (Tokyo Metropolitan Government, 2011). However, except for group homes, these surveys are voluntary and providers are allowed to choose the organization conducting the survey, so they have not had much impact.

The ultimate penalty for non-compliance is revocation of an agency's designation as a LTCI provider. During the nine-year period from the implementation of the LTCI to the end of fiscal year 2008, a total of 734 agencies have had their licence revoked, of which about three-quarters were for-profits. On a yearly basis, since the average number of agencies was 964,032 during these nine years, the percentage of total revoked designations averaged 0.076 per cent, varying from 0.03 per cent in 2001 to 0.09 per cent in 2005 (MHLW, 2010c). The more frequently used penalty is ordering the return of the amount inappropriately billed. The amount returned has ranged from 0.02 (2005) to 0.005 per cent (2001) of the total billed (MHLW, 2010a). While these percentages are low, the penalties have had an effect on providers because those having a record of inappropriate billing tend to have all their claims audited more closely. LTCI facilities and agencies must submit an annual report to the prefectural governor, which is then posted on a website. The information is descriptive and consists of the following: name, location, contacting form, number of care workers, facility status and charges. In addition, the results of the prefectural audit are also reported on the web, but the degree to which the reports are disclosed varies across prefectures. Finally, the process for dealing with complaints from clients and their families could be regarded as another means of assuring quality. There are three complaint processes. First, complaints can be made directly to

Japan's long-term care regulations focused on structure 133

the service provider. Every provider must have a designated person to handle complaints and their records are inspected at the time of the audit. The second approach is through a person's care manager, who must follow up on any complaints made. The third option is to lodge a complaint through the long-term care insurer. Should a follow-up be required, it is performed by the prefectural unions of LTCI plans, which have the authority to inspect and order improvements as needed. In the 2009 fiscal year, there were 6,318 consultations, of which 225 were followed up (Kokuho Chuōkai, 2010). According to a survey undertaken in Tokyo, about a quarter of the consultations were related to a complaint (Tokyo CHI Federation, 2010).

5.5 Why are regulations focused on structure?

When Japan made the decision to adopt western institutions in 1868, the central and local governments started to establish hospitals for medical education, for isolating patients with communicable diseases and for treating enlisted men and veterans. However, the majority of hospitals were established by physicians as an extension of their private clinics. The family continued to be responsible for the patient's care even after being admitted to the hospital, while nurses were primarily trained to assist physicians. After the defeat in the Second World War, the occupying forces dictated that hospitals should be made more responsible for patient care. With this objective, the Medical Service Law (*iryōhō*) was legislated in 1948 stipulating that there should be one nurse per four patients. More importantly, the fee schedule started to set higher rates if the hospital met the standard nurse staffing ratio. Since then, as a result of vigorous and successful lobbying by the Japanese Nurses Association, the higher nurse staffing levels have been rewarded by higher reimbursement rates. The staffing level is calculated based on the total number of all nursing staff, including licensed practical nurses and aides, to patients, and also on the proportion of registered nurses to the total nursing staff. Currently, the highest rate is 1 FTE nursing staff to 1.5 patients, with the percentage of registered nurses to the total being 70 per cent and over.

However, the tradition of the family being primarily responsible for providing care to in-patients continued to some degree until 1990. It was particularly prevalent in hospitals providing long-term care for elders, where it took the perverse form of the family hiring a private duty aide.

These aides were on duty twenty-four hours a day, and typically slept on a mattress between the beds of the two patients she cared for. In order to abolish this practice, and also to prevent the excessive use of medication and lab tests under the fee-for-service method of payment, the government introduced an inclusive per diem hospital rate for long-term care patients in 1990. The rate was fairly generous, on condition that the hospital abolished private duty aides and increased the number of hospital-hired aides, so eventually most hospital units with long-term care patients adopted this inclusive rate (Ikegami, 2009).

The quality of hospitals' physical environment was also poor. The Medical Service Law of 1948 set the standard at 4.3 square metres per bed. It was only in 1992, two years after the introduction of the inclusive per diem rate for long-term care patients, that the government introduced a new type of hospital bed, the 'long-term care (convalescent) bed units' (*ryoyō-gata byoshōgun*), with a minimum of 6.4 square metres and with better amenities such as the provision of a dining room. Hospitals with long-term care units were persuaded to invest in upgrading their facilities to meet the new standards by the higher rates set in the fee schedule. The number of these beds increased when hospital beds were formally divided into general beds (*ippan byoshō*) and 'long-term care (convalescent) beds' (*ryoyō byoshō*) in 2003.

In social services, the first step toward imposing qualification and staffing requirements was made in 1982, when the completion of a seventy-hour course was mandated for home helpers. In 1991, the course was expanded into three levels: 40 hours for the third level, 90 hours for the second level and 360 hours for the first level. Obtaining the second level, in which the number of hours was increased to 130 in 1995, became mandatory, and the third level was formally abolished in 2010 (MHLW, 2009b). Independently of this development, the Social Affairs Bureau decided to establish the national qualifications of 'certified care worker' (*kaigo fukushishi*) and 'certified social worker' (*shakai fukushishi*) in 1987. The underlying motive for establishing the former was to professionalize nursing home staff and home helpers. The Bureau officials believed that they should possess caring skills that are distinct from nurses. This might have contributed to the fact that two different words for 'care' are used in Japan: *kaigo*, when provided by care workers, and *kango*, when provided by nurses (Mizukami, 2007). The Bureau encouraged the establishment of special courses in universities, high schools and vocational schools to become a certified care worker and waived the need to sit the national examination for those who have completed them. Parenthetically, the university-level care worker course overlaps extensively with that required for certified social workers. However, because those wanting to become a certified social worker must pass a difficult examination after graduating and, even if they do, there are comparatively few job openings, many are working as care workers. Japan is probably the only country in the world where a significant proportion of certified care workers have received their qualification by completing a four-year university-level course. The Bureau has also encouraged care workers who have five or more years of practical experience to sit the national examination without being required to complete any course work.

5.6 Problems inherent to focusing on structure

Restricting home helpers to those who have completed the 130-hour course and establishing a national licence for certified care workers may have elevated their public image. In home- and community-based care, home helpers tend to be middle-aged housewives who have chosen to work in this field because it is more rewarding and they are paid more than minimum wages. Their comparatively high social status may have facilitated communication with their clients and among themselves, and boosted their morale. In nursing homes, although wages have declined from the public sector seniority-based pay scale which existed in the past (the wage of a care worker about to retire at 60 had been more than three times that of a newly hired care worker), it is still above the minimum level. These factors might explain why the quality of long-term care has been perceived to be relatively high in Japan (Wiener et al., 2007). However, whether or not the course work to become a home helper or a certified care worker is appropriate has not been systematically evaluated (Mizukami, 2007). If certified care workers are to become a profession, then they must have their own professional code and expertise which is distinct from that of nurses. Whether there are career prospects commensurate with such status, and whether care workers have such aspirations also needs to be evaluated. As noted, 50.1 per cent of the FTE home helpers are part-time and do not necessarily seek advancement. There is also the risk of their services being priced out of the market. The fact that the price of a nurse's visit is three times higher than that of a home helper, despite the fact that the care provided by nurses has tended to overlap with home helpers in

Japan (Ikezaki and Ikegami, 2011), is probably the reason why visiting nurse agencies have not expanded to the extent that home helper agencies have. In institutional settings, unlike home- and community-based care, care workers are not required to have any qualifications. However, the split between the requirements for 'social care' and 'healthcare' has led to the convergence of interest between long-term care hospitals and nurses. Because feeding tubes and suctions are defined as 'medical procedures', nurses have insisted that only they should be allowed to implement such procedures. This may be the primary reason why the prevalence of feeding tubes is highest at 36.8 per cent in LTCI hospital units, which are staffed twenty-four hours a day by nurses, and only 7.3 per cent in HFE and 10.7 per cent in nursing homes, which do not have such requirements (MHLW, 2010d).

These differences in staffing and in physical standards would be appropriate if there were a community-based triaging system referring patients to the most appropriate type of care facility. However, none exists and there is a considerable overlap in the functions and populations served because they were introduced on an ad hoc basis to deal with the immediate problem at that time (Ikegami et al., 1994, 2003). Nursing homes were established in 1963 by welfare bureaucrats as a symbol of the Ministry's stake in the welfare of elders (Campbell, 1992). Some hospitals became de facto nursing homes when free medical care was introduced in 1973 as a result of popular pressure. In order to solve the problem created, HFE were established to serve as a bridge between hospital care and home care, and were staffed with one or more therapists for this purpose. However, the HFE have not achieved this objective. Most HFE patients are either admitted for extended respite care, with the residents being transferred back and forth between their homes and the HFE, or as a substitute for a nursing home, because their families are unwilling or unable to provide care (Ikezaki et al., 2005). However, the National Association of HFE (2011) has maintained that they have been fulfilling their original mission. A similar difference in staffing requirements but with little difference in function exists between day care centres and day rehabilitation centres (Iryō Keizai Kenkyu Kikō, 2004). Recent events have added to the confusion on the function that each type of long-term care facility should serve. In 2005, as part of a general policy to contain public expenditures, the government suddenly announced that all LTCI hospital beds would be abolished by the end of 2011. To facilitate this process, a new type of institution, the

Japan's long-term care regulations focused on structure 137

'convalescent HFE' (*kaigo ryoyōkata rōjin hoken shisetsu*), which have staffing and physical standards halfway between LTCI hospital units and HFE, were introduced. However, the National Association of Chronic Care Hospitals (2010), which includes both health insurance and LTCI financed long-term care hospitals, has vigorously opposed the closure of LTCI hospital beds. Very few of the LTCI hospital units have converted to this new type (MHLW, 2010e) and, as part of the LTCI revision legislation passed in 2011, the LTCI hospital beds have been extended for another six years (MHLW, 2011b).

The one government policy that has been consistently applied is the upgrading of structural standards. From 2002, all new nursing homes had to meet the standards for 'unit care' (MHLW, 2002). Unit care is care provided in units of ten residents, all in private rooms, with each unit having its own dining facility. This has not only increased costs, but also has made it more difficult for those on low incomes to be admitted because these rooms have higher out-of-pocket charges. Those on public assistance may not be admitted except on a temporary basis (MHLW, 2005). Improving facility amenity levels are a desirable goal in themselves, but there are already long waiting lists at the pre-existing level.

Regarding qualifications, there were plans to make the requirements to become a certified care worker stricter in 2013: for example, revoking the waiver on the need to sit the national examination for graduates who have taken prescribed courses in university, high school and vocational schools, and, for non-graduates, mandating a six-month course in designated schools before they will be allowed to sit for the examination (MHLW, 2007). These measures were backed by the National Association of Certified Care Workers (MHLW, 2011c). However, the government has since postponed these higher standards, possibly because of pressure from the schools, which are afraid of sharp declines in enrolment, and from providers afraid of labour shortages.

5.7 Prospects for the future

Will quality assurance in Japan remain focused on structure? There are some possibilities for change in the hospital long-term care beds financed by health insurance as a result of the introduction of case-mix based payment in 2006 (Ikegami, 2009). The policy goal behind this change was to encourage the admission of patients with higher medical acuity as well as the discharge of patients with lower acuity. However, providers quickly adapted to the new payment system mainly by reclassifying their patients to higher medical acuity groups. Equally as serious as this gaming behaviour was the fact that some hospitals reported high prevalence rates of urinary tract infection and pressure ulcers. The government responded by issuing directives to providers to calculate the prevalence rates (as quality indicators), and document the care that has been mandated to the patients at risk. However, in order to monitor compliance and to evaluate whether patients are being billed for the appropriate case-mix group, the government must invest in developing a comprehensive patient-level database and in training staff to make on-site inspections. The government has yet to make this investment, partly because it does not have the resources, and partly because it is much more concerned with acute hospital care. Currently, quality indicators for hospital long-term care units financed by health insurance are made available to the patient and the public only when a request is made by an individual. However, since the groundwork has been laid, and the claims review process has become electronically based since 2010, wider dissemination may start in the near future.

Could there be a similar development in LTCI? This is not likely because, unlike in health-insurance-financed hospitals, the risk of up-coding is less for two main reasons: firstly, a patient's eligibility level is assessed by an individual hired by the government, and not by the facility staff, and secondly, ADL and IADL functional status is more difficult to game (as they cannot be hidden under the veil of 'medical need') than the conditions for meeting medical acuity levels. Although the eligibility criteria have been criticized for not paying adequate attention to the needs of those with dementia, these criteria have become the cornerstone of the LTCI, and criticisms have been dealt with by making minor revisions without any changes in the basic structure. Moreover, it is difficult to identify flaws in the eligibility criteria because access to individual-level data has been denied on privacy grounds to all parties. At the care management level, although many feel that there should be better care plans, the auditing so far has focused on checking claims to deny payment for services that are not in line with administrative guidelines, such as the home helper accompanying her client to a beautician (which is only allowed when making visits to physicians). There is no standardized format for assessing clients to draw up care plans, and thus they tend to be impressionistic, especially for the periodic reassessments, which must be performed every six months.

Japan's long-term care regulations focused on structure 139

However, there might be new developments outside of the government's regulatory framework in the large corporate chains providing home- and community-based care and assisted living. These chains would like to expand management control over their agencies and to also publicize their activities in assuring quality so as to promote their services in what has become a fairly competitive market. To meet these objectives, some have joined a project to use interRAI care planning instruments in order to audit and improve quality (InterRAI Japan, 2011). Their interests lie in the fact that quality indicators, calculated from individual assessment data, would provide a basis for comparing the quality, and not just the sales, of their agencies. The introduction of the new suite of assessment instruments would be timely for taking this new initiative (InterRAI, 2011).

5.8 Conclusion

Regulations to assure quality have been focused on the structural aspects of qualifications, staffing levels and physical facilities in Japan. The structural standards have provided a tangible and easy way of auditing quality for the government. By setting different standards, it has allowed social services to develop independently of health services, even after both services were unified in the LTCI. The LTCI, by limiting benefits to services provided by certified agencies, may have galvanized the government bureau responsible for further professionalizing care workers in order to distinguish them from informally hired care workers. The problem lies in the fact that, although the standards have gradually been upgraded, they do not necessarily reflect the needs of society and have led to the following inconsistencies: (i) four types of long-term care facilities providing institutional care; (ii) two types of facilities providing day care; (iii) the co-existence of certified care workers with those who have completed the 130-hour course in home- and community-based care, and with unqualified aides in institutional care; (iv) there are no process-based quality indicators; and (v) public reporting is limited to the summaries of government audits. In the future, market competition outside of government regulations may provide the catalyst for a more consumer-driven pursuit of quality in home- and community-based care and in assisted living where market entry is unrestricted and the price of bed and board is determined by the market.

References

Campbell, J. C. (1992). *How Policies Change*. Princeton University Press.

(2002). How policies differ: long-term-care insurance in Japan and Germany. In C. Harald and L. Ralph (eds.), *Aging and Social Policy: a German-Japanese Comparison*. Munich: Ludicium, pp. 157–87.

Campbell, J. C., Ikegami, N. and Gibson, M. (2010). Lessons from public long-term care insurance in Germany and Japan. *Health Affairs*, 29(1): 87–95.

Ikegami, N. (2007). Rationale, design and sustainability of long-term care insurance in Japan – in retrospect. *Social Policy and Society*, 6(3): 423–34.

(2009). Games policy makers and providers play: introducing case-mix-based payment to hospital chronic care units in Japan. *Journal of Health Politics, Policy and Law*, 34(3): 361–80.

Ikegami, N. and Campbell, J. C. (1999). Healthcare reform in Japan: the virtues of muddling through. *Health Affairs*, 18(3): 56–75.

(2004). Japan's healthcare system: containing costs and attempting reform. *Health Affairs*, 23(3): 26–36.

Ikegami, N., Fries, B. E., Takagi, Y., Ikeda, S. and Ibe, T. (1994). Applying RUG-III in Japanese long-term care facilities. *The Gerontologist*, 34(5): 628–39.

Ikegami, N., Yamauchi, K. and Yamada, Y. (2003). The long-term care insurance law in Japan: impact on institutional care facilities. *International Journal of Geriatric Psychiatry*, 18(3): 217–21.

Ikezaki, S. and Ikegami, N. (2011). Predictors of dying at home for patients receiving nursing services in Japan: a retrospective study comparing cancer and non-cancer deaths. *BMC Palliative Care*, 10(3). Available at: www.biomedcentral.com/1472–684X/10/3.

Ikezaki, S., Yumiko, H., Sakamaki, H. and Ikegami, N. (2005). Kaigo rōjin hoken shisetsu ni okeru zaitaku fukki ni kan suru shisetsu yōin to riyōsha yōin no bunseki [Analysis of facilities and user factors related to returning home in health service facilities for the elderly defined by long-term care insurance]. *Byōin kanri*, 43(1): 9–21.

InterRAI (2011). Instruments: an overview of the interRAI family of assessment systems. Available at: http://interrai.org/section/view/?fnode=10.

InterRAI Japan (2011). InterRAI QI Kenkyukai [InterRAI Quality Indicators Forum]. Available at: www.interrai.jp/.

Iryō Keizai Kenkyu Kikō (Institute for Health Economics and Policy) (2004). *Tsuusyo kaigo rehabilitation ni kansuru tyōsa kenkyu hōkokusyo* [Survey and Research on Day Care Centres and Day Rehabilitation Centres]. Tokyo: Institute for Health Economics and Policy.

Kokuho Chuōkai (The All-Japan Federation of National Health Insurance Organizations) (2010). *Kujyō mōsitate oyobi sōdan uketsuke jyōkyō* [State of Complaints Filed and Received]. Tokyo: Kokuho Chuōkai.

Japan's long-term care regulations focused on structure 141

Kōsei Tōkei Kyōkai (Health and Welfare Statistics Association) (1996). *Kōsei no shihyō* [Health and Welfare Statistics], 43(12).

(2001). *Kōsei no shihyō* [Health and Welfare Statistics], 48(12).

Lowi, T. J. (1979). *The End of Liberalism: The Second Republic of the United States*. New York: WW Norton.

MHW (Ministry of Health and Welfare) (1975a). *1973 Kanja chōsa* [Patient Survey 1973]. Tokyo: Kōsei Tōkei Kyōkai.

(1975b). *1973 Shakaifukushi gyōsei gyōmu hōkoku* [Administrative Report on Social Welfare 1973]. Tokyo: Kōsei Tōkei Kyōkai.

(1992a). *1990 Kanja chōsa* [Patient Survey 1990]. Tokyo: Kōsei Tōkei Kyōkai.

(1992b). *1990 Shakaifukushi gyōsei gyōmu hōkoku* [Administrative Report on Social Welfare 1990]. Tokyo: Kōsei Tōkei Kyōkai.

MHLW (Ministry of Health, Labour and Welfare) (2001a). *1999 Shakaifukushi shisetsuto chōsa* [Survey of Social Welfare Facilities 1999]. Tokyo: Kōsei Tōkei Kyōkai.

(2001b). *Kaigo kyufuhi jittai chōsa 5 gatsu geppō* [Monthly Report of LTCI Benefit Expenditures for May]. Tokyo: MHLW.

(2002). *2002 Kōsei rōdō hakusyo* [Health and Welfare White Paper for 2002]. Tokyo: MHLW.

(2005). Kaigo hoken seido no kaisei ni tomonau seikatsu hogo seido no kaisei [Revision of public assistance following the revision of LTCI]. Available at: www.wam.go.jp/wamappl/bb05kaig.nsf/0/e452fc284a07 9c8e4925707e00192b43/$FILE/siryou1.pdf.

(2006). *Nippon shōrai suikei jinkō* [Future Estimates of Japan's Population] (December 2006 estimates). Tokyo: MHLW.

(2007). *Shakaifukushishi oyobi kaigofukushishihōtō no ichibu wo kaisei suru hōritsu ni tsuite* [On the Partial Revision of the Certified Social Worker and Certified Care Worker Act]. Tokyo: MHLW.

(2009a). *2007 Kaigo service shisetsu, jigyō chōsa* [2007 Survey of Long-Term Care Institutions and Facilities]. Tokyo: MHLW.

(2009b). *2009 Kaigo hōsyu kaitei no gaiyō* [2009 Outline of the Long-Term Care Insurance Fee Schedule Revision]. Tokyo: MHLW.

(2009c). *Kaigo kyufuhi jittai chōsa 5 gatsu geppō* [Monthly Report of LTCI Benefit Expenditures for May]. Tokyo: MHLW.

(2010a). *Kaigohokenhō: Shitei kaigo rōjin fukushi shisetsu· rōjin hoken shisetsu· kaigo ryōyō iryō shisetsu no jinin, setsubi oyobi unei ni kansuru kijun* [LTCI Act Standards for Personnel, Facilities and Administration for Nursing Home, HFE, and Hospital Long-Term Care Beds] (Revision of 30 September 2010). Tokyo: MHLW.

(2010b). *Kaigohokenhō: Shitei kyotaku sa-bisutō no jinin, setsubi oyobi unei ni kansuru kijun* [LTCI Act Standards for Personnel, Facilities and

Administration for Home Care Services] (Revision of 30 September 2010). Tokyo: MHLW.

(2010c). *Kaigo sa-bisu jigyōsho ni taisuru kannsa kekka no jyōkyō* [Audit Results of Care Service Agencies]. Tokyo: MHLW.

(2010d). *Kaigo ryoyō byōshō no genjō ni tsuite* [Present State of Long-Term Care Insurance Hospital Beds. Debriefing Information Presented at the Meeting of the Central Social Insurance Council, 15 October 2010]. Tokyo: MHLW.

(2010e). *Ryoyō byōshō no tenkan ikōto chōsa* [Survey on Attitudes Towards Transferring Long-Term Care Beds. Debriefing Information Presented at the Meeting of the Central Social Insurance Council, 15 October 2010]. Tokyo: MHLW.

(2011a). *Kaigo hoken seido wo torimaku jōkyō* [Situation Faced by Long-Term Care Insurance. Debriefing Information Presented at the Meeting of the Central Social Insurance Council, 7 February 2011]. Tokyo: MHLW.

(2011b). *Kaigo sa-bisu no kibankyōka no tame no kaigohokenntō no ichibu wo kaisei suru hōritsuan* [Draft Act on Revising the Long-Term Care Insurance and Related Acts for Strengthening the Basis of Care Services, 4 April 2011]. Tokyo: MHLW.

(2011c). *Kongo no kaigo jinzai yōsei no arikata ni tsuite* [Future Directions for the Development of Human Resources for Care, 4 January 2011]. Tokyo: MHLW.

Mizukami, S. (2007). Kaigo hukushishi yōsei kyōiku no kadai: kokka shika-kuka wo kaerimite- [Issues surrounding the training programme for certified care worker: upon establishment of the care worker national certificate]. *Shakai Kankei Kenkyu*, 13(1): 75–104.

National Association of Chronic Care Hospitals (2010). Yōbōsho Kan Sōridaijin [Request to Prime Minister Kan]. Available at: http://jamcf.jp/chairman/100720youbou.pdf.

National Association of HFE (2011). Roken = rōjin hoken shisetsu te donna tokoro [What kind of place is a health facilities for elders?]. Available at: www.roken.or.jp/severs/what.html.

Nomura Research Institute, Ltd. (2010). *Tokubetsu yōgo rōjin hōmu ni okeru nyusyo mōshikomisya ni kannsuru tyōsa kenkyu* [Survey and Research on Those Waiting for Admission to Nursing Homes]. Tokyo: Nomura Research Institute, Ltd.

OECD (2011). *OECD Health Data 2011*. Paris: Organisation for Economic Cooperation and Development.

Tokyo CHI Federation (eds.) (2010). *Tokyoto niokeru kaigo sa-bisu no kujyō sōdan hakusho* [Complaints White Paper on Long-Term Care Service in Tokyo]. Tokyo: Tokyoto Kokumin Kenkō Hoken Dantai Rengō Kai.

Tokyo Metropolitan Government (2011). Fukushi sabisu daisansha hyōka [The welfare service third party evaluation]. Available at: www.fuku navi.or.jp/fukunavi/hyoka/hyokatop.htm

Wiener, J. M., Tilly, J., Howe, A., Doyle, C., Cuellar, A. E., Campbell, J. C. and Ikegami, N. (2007). *Quality Assurance for Long-Term Care: the Experience of England, Australia, Germany and Japan.* Washington, DC: AARP.

Yomiuri (2006). Kaigo hōshu COMSN ga kadai seikyu to 50 kasho issei chōsa [COMSN over bills LTCI – Tokyo Metropolitan Government audits 50 agencies]. Tokyo: Yomiuri Shinbun (Newspaper, 27 December, morning edition).

PART III

Long-term care quality systems based on regulatory inspection frameworks

All the case study countries have developed and promulgated regulatory structures detailing the requirements and processes by which private-sector organizations, whether non-profit or for-profit, apply to become providers of long-term care services. However, there is considerable variation in how ongoing provider quality is monitored in the form of regular inspections and audits. We have identified four countries – Australia, England, Spain and the Netherlands – as having regulatory systems structured in such a way that there is a substantial emphasis on ongoing quality monitoring undertaken via inspection. This is not to say that this is not true of other countries as well, it is just that the other countries have some other feature which further distinguishes them, which is why they have been classified into another grouping. As the reader reviews the material in the next four chapters, it is useful to consider the aspects of quality monitoring built into the regulatory structure of the long-term care system in each of these countries. Another challenge common to these countries is the differentiation between social and health-based care models, since both exist in all these countries and are treated differently, in some cases under a common regulatory framework while in others completely differently.

The provision of government-subsidized long-term care in Australia is heavily regulated with regard to supply, prices and quality standards. The government carefully controls the number of providers of a particular type by setting the bar for meeting minimum standards high and limiting approval of new providers based upon the known existing supply and the estimated demand for care in an area. Stringent requirements governing the characteristics of eligible providers are applied and standards are federally mandated and centralized under law with inspections, ongoing monitoring and the application of sanctions tightly controlled by the centre. This hierarchical 'command and control' system emerged following scandals associated with an earlier rapid expansion of the supply of long-term care providers, a phenomenon that is similar to the history of many other countries.

The English long-term care regulatory system has been undergoing repeated reorganization, partially associated with changes in government but also in response to scandals which, when investigated, found the existing structure wanting. Although there have been changes in organization, for some time the English system has been inspection-based and the care standards are set into legislation, not just regulations. While in England, too, there was a period of rapid expansion of providers, current practice is to balance an intensive inspection schedule and high entry standards with rapid response and review of new provider applicants since there is still a sense that service demand outstrips supply. Government vacillation between 'light regulation' and enhanced efficiency and 'crackdowns' in response to public scandals have characterized many countries' experience over the last several decades.

Spain offers its population a universal long-term care entitlement either in the form of a financial subsidy or via specific packages of long-term care services. National legislation on long-term care includes broad quality standards but the autonomous regions are left open to interpret these and to inspect providers. As in many other countries, there is a differentiation between health-related and socially based long-term care services, creating complications at the regional level since the health services are covered under the universal entitlements while the social services may not be. In Catalonia, the region that has been focused on long-term care regulation and quality for the longest time, the inspection system, along with established sanctions, has been operating for decades. Interestingly, there exists a third-party non-governmental agency which offers certification, and that operates in parallel with governmental inspections, a model that is institutionalized in the Netherlands.

The Netherlands guarantees long-term care services coverage, whether in the healthcare sector via nursing homes or home nursing services or in the social homes and/or home care services. An elaborate set of standards and inspection system exists along with a complex set of stepped sanctions for providers that violate care standards and regulations. The national inspectorate is responsible for sifting through the evidence to insure that providers are living up to minimum standards. In addition to the state regulators, and operating completely independently,

Long-term care quality systems

there is a non-governmental entity to which providers apply which attempts to harmonize the multiplicity of quality standards and offers a higher 'certification standard'. There is an elaborate, multi-component system of outcome measurement that includes surveys of care recipients which has recently been incorporated into the Dutch regulatory structure. These data, along with inspection results, are made public, which provides an example of a bridge to the next group of case study countries (see Chapters 10 to 12), those focused on measuring and reporting quality.

6 | *Regulating long-term care quality in Australia*

LEN C. GRAY, DAVID J. CULLEN
AND HAROLD B. LOMAS

6.1 Introduction

This chapter describes the arrangements in Australia for regulating the quality of long-term care services delivered in the community or in a residential setting. Its focus is on the long-term care of 'older people' – 'aged care' in Australian parlance.[1] The chapter begins with an overview of Australia's aged care system and its quality framework, including its place within the broader health and welfare system. It then discusses the arrangements for regulating the quality of residential care, which have been a major focus in recent decades, and the arrangements for regulating the quality of community care, which have a shorter history and are less developed. The chapter then discusses current reforms, which are aimed at better integrating these arrangements within and across programmes, and concludes with some reflections on the key challenges currently facing Australian public policy in this area.

6.2 Overview of Australia's aged care system and its quality framework

Australia's aged care system is funded and regulated through a complex set of arrangements, involving different levels of government and a diverse range of stakeholders, including informal carers and formal care providers from the not-for-profit (religious and charitable), for-profit and government sectors. These arrangements reflect, in part, the broader Australian health and welfare system, involving a similarly complex range of providers, with responsibilities for funding, regulation and service delivery

---

[1] The term 'older people' refers in this chapter to Indigenous Australians aged 50 or older and non-Indigenous Australians aged 65 or older. The life expectancy of Indigenous Australians is currently lower than for other Australians, which means that they often have a need for long-term care at an earlier age (ABS, 2010).

shared between the three levels of government: federal, state and territory ('state'), and local (AIHW, 2010, 2011a).

Aged care services in Australia range from basic care in the community (including assistance with house cleaning and meals) to more intensive care services delivered in both community and residential settings. Government support for these services occurs through a number of programmes, subject to different regulatory arrangements, that have emerged with the evolving roles of different levels of the government in the provision of health services, welfare services and income support (ADoHA, 2010c). In general, lower-intensity aged care services have emerged out of the welfare services sector, which was traditionally the responsibility of state governments, whereas higher-intensity services have their genesis in the federal government's roles in supporting the provision of health services and in providing income support to invalid and older people (Cullen, 2003a).

In 2010–11, total federal government expenditure on the health and welfare needs of older people is estimated to have been 4.3 per cent of GDP and 17.1 per cent of all federal government expenditure. Over the last decade, the level of this expenditure has more than doubled in nominal terms. Within this overall growth in expenditure, there has been a rebalancing from income support to the delivery of services (with income support accounting for 56 per cent of federal government expenditure on the health and welfare needs of older people in 2000–2001 compared to 53 per cent in 2010–11). Within expenditure on aged care there has been a rebalancing of expenditure from residential care towards support for carers and community care, with the latter accounting for 6.2 per cent of federal government expenditure on the health and welfare needs of older people in 2010–11 compared to 3.7 per cent in 2000–01 (ADoHA, 2010d).

Population ageing has been, and continues to be, a key driver of the growth in expenditure on the health and welfare needs of older people. While Australia has a relatively young population compared to other developed nations, it has one of the fastest-growing older populations, particularly people over 85 years, and is projected to develop a similar age profile as other developed nations in the next few decades. In the last twenty five years, the population over 65 has increased from 10.5 to 14.0 per cent of the overall population, and those aged over 85 from 0.8 to 1.9 per cent (ABS, 2008a, 2008b). Increasing life expectancy is expected to lead to continued growth, especially in the very elderly, who represent the largest users of services (Linacre, 2006). As a result of this

Regulating long-term care quality in Australia

population ageing, federal government expenditure on aged care is projected to increase from 0.8 per cent of GDP in 2009–10 to 1.8 per cent of GDP by 2049–50. This is lower in absolute terms than the projected increase in health costs, from 4.0 per cent of GDP to 7.1 per cent of GDP, and on the age pension, from 2.7 per cent of GDP to 3.9 per cent of GDP (Australian Government, 2010). However, the rate of growth is the highest in aged care expenditure (125 per cent compared to 78 per cent for health and 44 per cent for the age pension).

6.2.1 Context – the broader health and welfare sector

With respect to broader health services, regulatory roles and responsibilities are shared between the federal and state governments, but not always in line with funding responsibilities. State governments are primarily responsible for regulating the quality of hospital services, including licensing and registration of private hospitals. The federal government is responsible for regulating the safety and quality of blood and blood products, pharmaceuticals and therapeutic goods and appliances. The registration of health professionals has traditionally been the province of state governments but with a recent movement towards federal government responsibility (AIHW, 2010: 7–11).

Australia's federal government is responsible for funding and managing national subsidy schemes to assist consumers with the costs of private medical services, including the majority of primary care services, specialist medical services including diagnostics and technology and private in-hospital services. The federal government also funds and manages a national scheme for subsidizing pharmaceuticals. These schemes reimburse consumers for part of their fees and provide universal coverage across the population. The majority of acute care is provided through the public hospital system, which is jointly funded by the federal and state governments but with service delivery primarily managed by the states. However, a significant proportion of the population also uses private hospitals, particularly for elective surgery, with more than 40 per cent of the population covered by private health insurance and with user contributions subsidized through a federal government tax rebate scheme.[2]

---

[2] Private health insurance in Australia is directed primarily to private hospital services, in addition to non-hospital benefits such as dental care, physiotherapy and spectacles. Currently, there is no market for long-term care insurance in

In 2009–10, expenditure on health (other than aged care) in Australia accounted for 9.4 per cent of GDP. Almost a third of this expenditure was on the healthcare needs of older people. Across the entire health sector, more than two-thirds of funding is provided by government (69.9 per cent), with the remainder coming from private sources including out-of-pocket payments by individuals and private insurance. Around two-thirds (63.4 per cent) of government funding is provided by the federal government, with state and local governments contributing the other third (AIHW, 2011b).

In 2010–11, total combined expenditures on aged care services by government and consumers was more than 1.0 per cent of GDP, compared to less than 0.5 per cent of GDP in 1986. The federal government is now almost the sole government funder, providing around 70 per cent of funding for long-term care services, with the balance made up primarily through co-contributions paid by care recipients (ADoHA, 2010d).

Looking beyond health, the federal government is responsible for providing income support to unemployed people, age pensioners, people with disabilities, carers (who assist disabled household members by caring for them at home) and people with low incomes requiring rental assistance. In contrast, other community and welfare services have been provided through a range of initiatives funded and regulated by different levels of government. Funding and regulatory arrangements across these community welfare programmes are extremely diverse but in general the pattern has been one of the federal government providing national leadership and contributing funding and the state governments assuming responsibility for direct provision and regulation of services (AIHW, 2011b: 338–57).

6.2.2 The aged care sector

The provision of government-subsidized aged care in Australia is highly regulated, particularly with regard to supply and the prices charged to consumers (Cullen, 2003b). Outside of government programmes, there is only a very small, fully private market for aged care, particularly in

Australia, due in part to supply and demand constraints that have also limited the role of private health insurance internationally, as well as some specific legislative constraints and historical factors (Productivity Commission, 2011: 116–18; Cullen, 2003a).

Regulating long-term care quality in Australia 153

terms of more intensive care services. However, there is a growing market for supported private accommodation or serviced apartments, which are regulated by state governments. This regulation relates primarily to protections for consumers to ensure they are treated fairly in purchasing accommodation from providers and does not extend to the quality of services.

There are two major programme streams through which aged care services are funded and regulated. The first relates to residential and packaged community care programmes, regulated through federal legislation, the Aged Care Act 1997; the second relates to programmes that support the delivery of lower-intensity home and community care services.

Residential and packaged community care programmes account for the majority of intensive, long-term coordinated high- and low-level care delivered to older people in Australia in both residential and community settings. Under these programmes, aged care 'places' are the basic unit of allocation, equating to a bed in a residential care facility or a broadly equivalent package of services delivered to a person in their own home. Providers receive a daily subsidy for every day the place is occupied by, or used to provide services to, an eligible care recipient. Community care packages provide for delivery of individually planned and coordinated care to people living in their own homes, incorporating a range of services broadly comparable to that delivered in a residential setting, including personal and nursing care; social support; transport to appointments; home help; meal preparation; home modifications; and maintenance.

The terms 'low-level care' and 'high-level care' have particular meaning in the Australian regulatory context, with implications for funding, user charges and provider service requirements. Low-level care roughly equates to the level of care historically provided through aged persons' hostels, which emerged out of social housing and retirement village models in the 1950s and were funded separately from nursing homes prior to structural reforms in the late 1990s. High-level care roughly equates to the level of care that was provided through nursing homes, which emerged out of the health and hospital systems in the 1960s, the other element of the residential care programme prior to the structural reforms of the late 1990s (Cullen, 2003a: 74–6).

Low-level care is provided to care recipients who need some care and assistance with, for example, personal hygiene, medications and meals, but do not have an ongoing need for nursing care or specialized therapy services to maintain their independence. Care recipients at this level typically have a significant level of independence, while requiring some assistance from aged care workers other than nurses. High-level care is provided to care recipients who are functionally highly dependent and typically require twenty-four-hour care, including some level of direct nursing care. High-level care includes residents who have a high need for assistance in at least one area – activities of daily living or complex healthcare – or some level of needs in most areas. The exception is behavioural needs. Care recipients who have a high need for behavioural and cognitive support but require little in the way of other support are classified as requiring low-level care, but do receive additional funding in recognition of their high relative level of need for non-nursing care services (ADoHA, 2011c).

The supply of federally subsidized aged care services is tightly controlled. In addition to entry requirements for providers, there are limits on the number of subsidized care places. New places are allocated through a needs-based planning process, providing for growth in services in line with the population aged 70 or over. The current service delivery benchmark is 113 places per 1,000 people aged 70 or over, with a target of forty-four high- and forty-four low-level residential care places, and four high- and twenty-one low-level community care packages. Each year, new places are allocated to areas of relative need, with providers selected using an annual competitive quality-based tendering process (Cullen, 2003b; ADoHA, 2010c).

In Australia, residential care facilities primarily provide permanent care. A small number of places are allocated to (short-term) respite care. Until recently, very few facilities offered formal rehabilitation or restorative programmes, or any form of time limited post-acute care. Residential care funding arrangements have not tended to encourage such activity. In 2005, a national Transition Care Programme was established, which aims to provide time-limited care in the post-acute context for older people requiring low-intensity support and rehabilitation (Gray et al., 2008). Services are jointly funded by the federal and state governments, with the latter managing service delivery. There is flexibility as to whether services are provided in a community or residential setting, with almost a third of services conducted in residential care facilities.

Residential care services are subject to a rigorous accreditation and quality standards monitoring regime, designed primarily to ensure minimum standards are met rather than to provide incentives for higher quality. The quality framework for community care is far less developed than for residential care.

The second major programme stream ('home and community care services') provides a range of care services for older people, people with a disability and their carers, to allow them to continue to live in their own home as long as possible and thus prevent or delay admission into residential care. Until recently, these services were jointly funded by the federal and state governments, with state governments having primary responsibility for establishing new services and managing and regulating service provision.

Home and community care services are generally delivered as individual and uncoordinated interventions, although varying levels of case management are provided, including some intensive and complex care. Services include assistance with gardening, meals, community transport, home modification, personal care and community nursing. Many services have developed from the ground up in response to the needs of local communities and there is considerable variation in service delivery arrangements and associated administrative arrangements not only across, but also within, different states. There is similarly significant variation in the availability and mix of different services. Services are largely funded through fixed grants paid to service providers. Funding is based largely on historical decisions, with allocation of growth funding to service providers each year based on their capacity to meet community needs, taking into account quality issues. A wide variety of organizations is funded to deliver services, ranging from small community groups to large organizations operating a wide range of services, sometimes on a state-wide basis (ADoHA 2010c, 2010e).

The range of quality reporting arrangements has evolved, but varies significantly across different states and service types. Improving consistency in outcomes, including quality, has been a focus since the programme's inception more than twenty-five years ago (ANAO, 2000; Australian Parliament, 1982, 1985a, 1994). These developments are discussed in more detail later in this chapter.

The last few decades has seen a significant growth in services, reflecting in part population ageing but also expanded access both in terms of the range of programmes and geographical coverage of services. In particular, there has been a strong expansion in care available in a person's own home, including both low- and high-level care services.

There has been strong growth in expenditures by both the federal and the state governments, particularly over the last twenty-five years, with the federal government taking on an expanding role in both funding and service delivery over this period.

6.3 Arrangements for regulating the quality of residential care

Residential care services for older people are funded and regulated by the federal government, and provided primarily by the non-government sector, with almost 60 per cent of services provided by the not-for-profit (religious and charitable) sector and 35 per cent by the private for-profit sector. State and local governments are not involved in the regulation of these services to any significant extent, and provide only a very small and diminishing number of services (ADoHA, 2010c: 37). The central role played by the federal government in the provision of residential care and the needs-based framework through which places have been allocated has provided a strong basis for the government to impose quality requirements on residential care providers, as well as creating strong expectations from the community that the government will exercise that power. At another level, the needs-based framework has promoted quality outcomes for older people and their carers by supporting wide and consistent access in terms of the range of services that are available and affordable in different regions, although there is a paucity of data to quantify the impact on health outcomes.

The federal Aged Care Act 1997 provides the legal framework for the funding, regulation and accreditation of aged care services. It provides for a national quality assurance framework for residential care including building certification, accreditation of homes, continuous improvement in service delivery, complaints handling and users' rights. Promoting high-quality care and accommodation is a specific key objective of the Act (Section 2–1(1)(b)). Current arrangements provide for regulation of quality and standards at a number of levels:

- Entry requirements that providers must meet before being approved to provide subsidized care, administered by the Australian government Department of Health and Ageing (ADoHA). These are less focused on quality and more on character and integrity issues,

Regulating long-term care quality in Australia 157

including whether operators have criminal backgrounds, and financial capacity.
- An initial accreditation process, undertaken by an independent Aged Care Standards and Accreditation Agency (ACSAA), through which providers are assessed against specified standards to verify that they have the processes and systems in place to provide adequate care.
- Ongoing monitoring of accreditation standards, also undertaken by the same agency. Accreditation is not a one-off event but rather provides for ongoing monitoring of compliance through announced and unannounced visits (at least one each year) and review of a range of administrative and other information.
- A National Complaints Investigation Scheme, which considers specific individual concerns raised by care recipients or their representatives.
- Compliance activity, undertaken by ADoHA, in response to information from either or both the ACSAA and the Complaints Investigation Scheme.
- Other initiatives, including government-funded advocacy and support services and a community visitors scheme.

Figure 6.1 provides an overview of the major organizations involved.

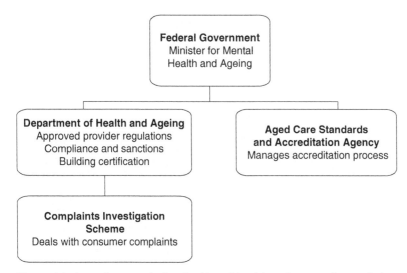

Figure 6.1 Australian agencies involved in residential aged care quality regulation. *Source*: compiled by authors.

The origins of the current quality framework can be traced back to reforms from the mid-1980s to the late 1990s (ALRC, 1995; Australian Parliament, 1985b; Braithwaite et al., 1993; Gregory, 1993, 1994; Ronalds, 1989). Quality of care issues, including specific cases of poor care, were subject to significant public scrutiny and a major ongoing focus for policy makers. As part of reforms in mid-1980s, a standards monitoring process was introduced for nursing homes that focused on quality of care and quality of life for residents, together with more standardized funding arrangements based on hours of care provided to residents at particular frailty levels. Standards monitoring was extended to hostels (aged care homes that provide lower-intensity services, focused on personal rather than nursing care) in 1991 (Cullen, 2003a: 63–7, 71–4).

While these reforms were considered to achieve significant improvements, quality of care issues continued to be an area of significant public concern. In addition, the standard monitoring process, undertaken by ADoHA, proved a source of tension with the residential care industry. Improving these arrangements has been a significant focus for policy makers, with significant changes made in the late 1990s as part of broader structural reforms to integrate the funding of hostels and nursing homes and to streamline accountability requirements for providers (Australian Parliament, 2005; Gray, 2001: 5–8). Another important driver for these reforms was the need to improve the quality of the building fabric, to improve safety and provide a more home-like environment for residents.

Underpinning the changes to quality regulation was a greater emphasis on accreditation and peer review, focusing more on underlying systems than individual cases of poor care, to provide greater incentives for continuous quality improvement and to reduce compliance effort for providers. To support these changes, an independent ACSAA was established, reducing the role of the ADoHA, which instead became focused on compliance action. In addition, building certification arrangements were introduced to ensure that additional capital income provided to industry would translate into investments and improvements in building quality.

6.3.1 Accreditation and compliance arrangements

The accreditation process is the centrepiece of current arrangements for regulating the quality of care in residential care facilities

Regulating long-term care quality in Australia 159

(ADoHA, 2007; ACSAA, 2011; ANAO, 2003). Aged care facilities are assessed against forty-four outcomes, covering four standards, including management systems, staffing and organization development, health and personal care, residential lifestyle, physical environment and safety systems. There are no specific provisions for special needs groups, although the broader funding framework does provide additional recognition in terms of how services are funded.[3] Rather, the framework recognizes that each resident is different, applying general standards to each resident's care needs regardless of race, culture, language, social or religious choices. The Australian government is currently undertaking work to review, improve and streamline these standards. A key objective for this work is increasing the focus on resident-centred care and more clearly articulating care requirements.

The accreditation process provides for aged care homes to undertake a self-assessment and for a team of registered aged care quality assessors, employed by the ACSAA, to conduct a site audit incorporating interviews with residents, their families, staff and management. These audits generally take two to four days to complete. The ACSAA decides whether or not to accredit the service and the period of accreditation, as well as any remedial action, including monitoring and support, taking into account their findings and any other relevant information, including input from the provider and the ADoHA. The outcomes of the decision are published on the ACSAA's website. The ACSAA is also required to undertake at least one unannounced 'support contact' visit for each home. A support contact is usually a shorter visit than an accreditation site audit or review audit, and looks at a smaller sample of the residential care home's systems. It generally involves a visit by two assessors taking between a half and a full day. More generally, the ACSAA plays an important role in working with the ADoHA in ongoing monitoring of compliance and informing and educating industry.

---

[3] The Aged Care Act 1997, Sections 11.2, 72.3. Special needs groups within the Aged Care Act include people from Aboriginal and Torres Strait Islander communities; people from non-English speaking backgrounds; people who live in rural or remote areas; people who are financially or socially disadvantaged; veterans, people who are homeless or at risk of homelessness and care leavers (a person who has been a ward of the state but no longer qualifies for or receives any government assistance). Additional funding is provided through viability and care subsidies in recognition of care needs associated with special needs.

In addition to a central executive office, the ACSAA has five regional offices spread across Australia, each of which has responsibility for particular geographical areas. At 30 June 2011, the ACSAA had 406 registered assessors, 122 of which were permanent employees, with the balance engaged on a contract or casual basis to meet workload demands; 249 or 61 per cent were registered nurses, with assessors also registered based on cultural specific expertise, such as experience of working with indigenous cultures, or language skills. In 2010–11, the ACSAA conducted 5,121 visits, achieving an average of 2.0 visits per home, above the target of 1.75 per home. Of these visits, 3,488 were unannounced.

The ADoHA monitors compliance with the accreditation standards through a network of regionally based compliance officers. It is responsible for taking compliance action, including imposing sanctions as a last resort. Sanctions may include the appointment of an advisor or administrator, a requirement to provide training for its officers at the provider's own expense, a suspension of funding for new residents, or a complete withdrawal of funding. In 2010–11, the Department issued seventy-nine notices of non-compliance in relation to quality of care issues and applied sanctions to eleven homes, four of which remained in place on 30 June 2011. All involved a requirement to appoint an administrator or advisor with nursing experience, in order to avoid their approved provider status being revoked, and all but one involved some suspension of funding for new residents; seven involved requirements to provide training.

The capacity for early identification of 'at risk' services and early action to provide support and address cases of poor care relies on intelligence gathering and sharing between different parts of the regulatory framework. While there is some exchange of information between different parts of the regulatory framework, including between the ACSAA and complaints and compliance management processes, some limitations and potential improvements have been identified as part of recent government reviews. Consumer satisfaction is not systematically taken into account but rather only informs the process when things go wrong and complaints are made, or through information collected through sample interviews by assessors. In addition, both the ACSAA and the ADoHA maintain independent datasets including risk indicators to identify homes of possible concern. In general, current arrangements are considered effective at identifying and addressing individual cases of poor care, identified following specific incidents,

Regulating long-term care quality in Australia 161

visits or complaints, but less so in terms of identifying and addressing risks on a sector-wide basis. Examples of these risk factors include change of ownership; loss of key personnel including senior nursing staff; changes in management systems; rapid growth in resident numbers; rapid change in the mix of residents' needs; building programmes or relocation; changes in processes and procedures not supported by appropriate staff training; change in business strategy or restructuring; and industrial disputation. Improved risk profiling, including strategies for identifying at-risk services, potentially utilizing data collected on all aged care services across the sector, has been identified by the ADoHA as a priority for further work with likely potential for better and more systematic and integrated use of data available on care recipients and care processes.

6.3.2 *Effectiveness of the quality framework*

Reforms to quality arrangements over the last few decades appear to have led to considerable improvements in the quality of both care and buildings. Increased building certification requirements have led to improvements in terms of privacy, space and fire safety, with the proportion of homes compliant with these standards having increased over time to around 99.7 per cent at 30 June 2011. Similarly, while recent reviews suggest a mixture of views as to the effectiveness of arrangements for regulating the quality of care, and there is lack of clear and objective data and measures to assess the performance of the system over time, accreditation is generally considered to have had a positive impact on the quality of care. A 2007 review of the accreditation arrangements, commonly known as the Campbell Report, found that accreditation had been effective, particularly in removing under-performing homes from the sector, setting minimum standards, increasing standards across the sector, improving consistency and developing a focus on continuous quality improvement and resident-focused care (ADoHA, 2007). Measured in terms of compliance with the accreditation standards themselves, it is clear that the last decade has seen a strong and continuing improvement in quality of care, with the number of homes assessed as meeting all outcomes increasing from 63.5 per cent in 2000 to more than 90 per cent in 2010 (Productivity Commission, 2011: 189–95).

However, while the system appears to work effectively in guaranteeing minimum standards are met in the overwhelming majority of homes, there remain deficiencies in terms of incentives for higher-quality care. Because of the highly regulated environment and limited scope for competition, with demand for services exceeding supply, there is limited scope for consumers to exercise power and choice.

Recent years have seen some fall in the average occupancy levels of aged care homes, accompanied by some apparent increase in competition, with some evidence that this may reflect the impact that expanded access to community care is having in reducing the pool of prospective residents in some areas. The national average for occupancy rates declined steadily from round 96 per cent in March 2002 to around 92 per cent in April 2010. While occupancy rates vary significantly by region and remoteness, the gradual trend towards lower occupancy rates has been relatively uniform across regions. In April 2010, the average rate was 92 per cent for major cities, compared to 90 per cent for remote areas and 82 per cent for very remote areas. Occupancy rates are also correlated with size, with smaller services likely to have lower and more volatile occupancy rates (ADoHA, 2011b).

Some recent government initiatives have sought to provide additional information to prospective residents and their families, including on quality outcomes at different homes in their region, to facilitate informed choice. To date, information has been primarily limited to whether service providers comply with the various compliance standards. While the ACSAA makes its decisions and the reports of assessors publicly available, the information available has been criticized as not sufficiently comprehensive and user-friendly to inform choice by consumers. However, there has recently been increasing interest in expanding the quality assurance framework to include additional published quality indicators, so as to assist older people and their families to make informed choices, potentially incorporating input measures such as funding spent on care and nursing and staffing (Productivity Commission, 2011: 207–18).

In general, the framework for measuring performance in quality is under-developed and, beyond compliance with standards, funding is not linked to performance. Provided a service meets the standards or is undertaking action to remedy areas of non-compliance, it is able to receive a comparable level of government funding, based on its resident profile. Recent government reviews have suggested that accreditation arrangements have had a positive impact on quality of care, while also highlighting a paucity of quantitative measures that demonstrate this

Regulating long-term care quality in Australia 163

impact conclusively and a need for further development of sector-wide performance indicators. Development of quality indicators, including surveys of recipients and carers, has been identified as a priority for further work (ADoHA, 2007; ANAO, 2011).

6.4 Arrangements for regulating the quality of community care

Arrangements for regulating quality of care for community care services are far less developed than for residential care and have tended to vary significantly both within and across the multiplicity of programmes that have evolved over time. These programmes include nationally funded community care packages, Home and Community Care services and Veterans' Home Care. Historically, they have involved very different arrangements in relation to quality, assessment, eligibility and user changes.

Regulations across the different community care programmes, and how these compare to residential care, are summarized in Table 6.1.

6.4.1 Community care packages

Community care packages are regulated through the same federal legislation as residential care services. This approach to delivery of community care has become a significant area of focus within the federal government's aged care programme (in 2009–10, care packages represented more than 20 per cent of all federally funded aged care places). The regulatory and funding model is broadly comparable to that applying to residential care. Like residential care, eligibility for care packages is determined by Aged Care Assessment Teams (multi-disciplinary teams of health professionals funded by state governments) and funding is provided through daily subsidies in respect of each care recipient being supported. This contrasts with the Home and Community Care Programme, which includes a variety of assessment arrangements, often applied by individual providers, with funding provided through fixed grants. User charges also differ markedly. Providers of care packages are similarly subject to provider entry requirements, with places allocated through a needs-based planning process. Providers are selected through an annual approval round, which is essentially a competitive tendering process based on quality rather than price. Assessment of quality standards has been based primarily

Table 6.1 *Residential and community care quality regulation in Australia*

	Home and Community Care Programme	Community packages	Residential care services
Provider entry requirements and funding allocation	Varies across states. Federal government to take operational responsibility in most states from July 2012.	Approved provider legislation and needs-based allocation process under the Aged Care Act 1997.	Approved provider legislation and needs based allocation process under the Aged Care Act 1997.
Agency managing quality assurance – prior to March 2011	Prior to March 2011, managed by state governments.	Federal government Department of Health and Ageing – subject to common community standards under the Aged Care Act 1997.	Independent Aged Care Standards and Accreditation Agency, reporting to the federal government – subject to quality and accreditation standards under the Aged Care Act 1997.
Agency managing quality assurance – from March 2011	Subject to common community standards under the Aged Care Act 1997.		
Quality standards – prior to March 2011	Variable arrangements across states.	3 standards (18 outcomes): effective management, appropriate access and service delivery and service user rights and responsibilities.	4 standards (44 outcomes): – management systems, staffing and organisational development – health and personal care – residential lifestyle – physical environment and safe systems.
Quality standards – since March 2011	3 standards (18 outcomes): – effective management, – appropriate access and service delivery – service user rights and responsibilities.		

Complaints processes	Varies across states. Federal government to take operational responsibility in most states from July 2012.	Managed through a Complaints Investigation Scheme that operates within the federal government Department of Health and Ageing. Independent Aged Care Commissioner (statutory officer) reviews outcomes of the Complaints Investigation Scheme.

Source: Compiled by authors.

on reporting requirements and assessments undertaken by providers themselves, with the onus on providers to assess the quality of services provided to individuals in their own home, but with an increased emphasis over recent years on follow-up quality review processes and site visits by the ADoHA, drawing on feedback from users and their carers.

The less rigorous quality framework for community care in part reflects the fact that community care packages are a recent development, with lower-level packages (which support persons with care requirements equivalent to those living in low-care residential care facilities) introduced in the early 1990s, and with higher-level packages only becoming a significant element within the programme in the last decade. It also reflects the less standardized nature and greater variability in intensity of services, which makes measurement of quality more difficult. In addition, while interest in community care quality issues is increasing, they have not attracted the same level of attention or concern as quality of residential care. In part, this is because the formal care provided tends to be seen as just one component of the person's care and there is not the same expectation that the service provider has responsibility for the recipient's overall well-being. The focus of the standards is more on the quality of inputs provided than on the outcomes achieved.

6.4.2 The Home and Community Care Programme

Services provided through the Home and Community Care Programme have been primarily managed by state governments, with decisions around funding and eligible providers generally determined through annual funding rounds which take into account community need and quality issues. State governments have been responsible for monitoring quality, and reporting on progress at a high level, with little information available on quality of services at the national level. Veterans' Home Care includes a similar range of support as the Home and Community Care Programme, but services are funded and provided by the federal Department of Veterans' Affairs, which sets its own quality standards.

Recent reforms have sought to bring these different programmes under a common standards framework. New legislation providing for common standards commenced in March 2011, applying to care packages, Homes and Community Care Services and services provided under the National Respite for Carers programme (ADoHA, 2010b). This legislation effectively standardizes quality arrangements across services historically managed by the states under the Home and Community Care Programme with those applying for community care packages managed by the federal government. The standards include eighteen outcomes covering three broad standards: (1) effective management, (2) appropriate access and service delivery, and (3) service user rights and responsibilities. The quality assurance model is based on the arrangements that have developed for community care packages over recent years. Under this framework, providers of these services are required to report against programme standards and complete a quality review at least once during a three-year cycle. The quality review is a four-step process involving the initial self-assessment report, a desk review, a site visit by a team of two departmental reviewers and notification and appropriate follow-up, including compliance action where necessary. Overall, this process takes around twenty weeks, from first notification to completion of the quality review. Site visits typically take around six to eight hours to complete.

Consumer awareness of services and advocacy and complaints options are supported by a Charter of Rights and Responsibilities for Community Care, which became part of the federal legislative framework on 1 October 2009. The Charter is designed to clarify the rights of care recipients, help them to recognize their responsibilities to service providers and provide them with a greater say in how their services are provided.

6.5 Other regulation

Other regulations relevant to quality that apply to the aged care sector include health, workforce and building and safety requirements, which are additional and applied separately to requirements applied by the federal government as part of the aged care accreditation and building certification arrangements. These areas of regulation have traditionally been the province of state governments, although workforce registration arrangements including skills, qualifications and training requirements is another area where the federal government has been assuming a greater role in recent years with a view to achieving greater national consistency. On 1 July 2010, national registration and accreditation arrangements were established under federal legislation for ten key health professions including chiropractors, dentists, medical practitioners, nurses, midwives, optometrists, osteopaths, pharmacists, physiotherapists, podiatrists and psychologists. These arrangements are governed by the Australian Health Practitioner Registration Agency (see www.ahpra.gov.au). There are also varying requirements under state legislation relating to nurse to patient ratios and twenty-four-hour availability for residents requiring higher levels of care.

The provision of medical services to aged care recipients, including regulation of quality and employment and payment arrangements for medical staff, is managed through a completely separate regulatory framework to that applied to aged care programmes. Most medical care to aged care recipients is provided by privately practising general and specialist medical practitioners, with the support of federal government subsidies provided under a national medical benefits scheme. Operators of residential care services often employ nurses and allied health professionals such as physiotherapists but their focus is on providing ongoing assistance with activities of daily living and therapy rather than medical care. Medical care and treatment for residents, or lack thereof, is not the responsibility of the aged care home. However, while residential care providers have no direct responsibility for provision of medical services to their residents, they are obligated to help facilitate access, for example by assisting with arranging appointments. These arrangements contrast with those in hospitals, where the employment and governance of medical staff is the responsibility of the hospital.

6.6 Current reform initiatives and policy challenges

There is a significant current reform agenda in aged care, focused on creating an integrated national aged care system that has the potential to support more equitable, efficient and consistent outcomes for consumers and their families, including in the regulation of quality.

Reforms since the mid-1980s have focused primarily on addressing issues relating to access, addressing a historical over-reliance on high-level institutional care and under-provision of community care and, to a lesser extent, problems of integration between hostel (now referred to as low-care) and nursing home (high-) care and quality issues in residential care (Cullen, 2003a). Integration and quality are now becoming a greater focus for reform, driven by a broader agenda of encouraging more consumer-centred care (Australian Parliament, 2009). Significant reforms are currently underway, agreed to by both federal and state governments in April 2010 and February 2011, as part of a broader programme of health reform (ADoHA, 2010a). A key direction is moving to consolidate responsibility for aged care at the national level. In response to the perception that the aged care system is complex and confusing for some consumers, the federal government has been moving to create a new front end or single entry point to the system, to simplify access and help older people and their families better navigate the system. Specific directions are being considered in the context of a recent major public inquiry into aged care initiated by government which reported in June 2011. The inquiry was undertaken by the Productivity Commission, an independent government-funded research and advisory body (see www.pc.gov.au). As well as consolidating responsibility for assessment and information services at the federal government level, a key focus has been to create a single channel through which consumers access services and information, uncoupled from service delivery. Another area of focus is supporting greater consumer choice and, where possible, consumer-directed care, with innovative models currently being implemented and evaluated within community care packages and the National Respite for Carers Programme (ADoHA, 2011a: 2–3).

The Australian Government (in 2011) identified the need to make a start on further reform to the aged care system, as a priority for its current term of government. Key themes coming out of the recent inquiry include the need: for greater integration and consistency across aged care programmes; to improve and simplify access to information, assessments and care; for greater flexibility and choice for consumers, particularly in terms of the intensity of care services available if they choose to remain at home; for better linkages between community and residential care; for a greater focus on rehabilitation and restorative care; and improved linkages between aged care and the wider health and community services system (Productivity Commission, 2011: XXVII–LI).

In line with current reform directions, this broad vision of a more integrated aged care system incorporating better links within and across different programme and service types and a single entry point to the system, is gaining increasing community and stakeholder support. Proponents of the single entry point proposal have suggested it could provide a basis for earlier access to services which prevent or delay the functional deterioration of care recipients, with benefits not only in terms of improved health and well-being but also downstream efficiencies in how resources are allocated (Productivity Commission, 2011: 152–5).

A related area of emphasis is the need for better links to other parts of the health system, and access to health services, particularly for people with psychogeriatric and palliative care needs who sit at the point where the aged care, acute, sub-acute care and mental health systems intersect. Concerns have been expressed in the context of recent reviews and inquiries that changes in the acute sector over recent years have increased pressure on aged care homes to care for patients that were traditionally managed in acute care and specialist mental health settings (ADoHA, 2011b: 3, 2011c: 49–50). Conversely, it has also been suggested that these pressures go both ways and that constraints on the aged care sector, including on the supply of places and availability of suitably qualified staff, can result in unnecessary hospital admissions for people whose needs could have been met in an aged care facility (Productivity Commission, 2011: 176–9).

In general, as highlighted in a number of reviews over recent years, the division of responsibility between federal and state governments for the financing and administration of aged care facilities and public hospitals respectively has inhibited a rational, cost effective allocation of care responsibilities between the sectors, with pressures experienced in one sector often attributed to failure of the other (Australian Parliament, 2006; National Health and Hospitals Reform Commission, 2009: 57–8). While recent health reforms are attempting to overcome these problems and create more transparency, overcoming the fragmentation in government roles and services is an ongoing challenge. In the aged care context, there is a growing view in the sector that improved coordination and access to health services, including an expanded role for aged care providers in delivering specialized sub-acute care, could create a basis for improved efficiency and quality outcomes, and that the current reform agenda will provide opportunities to explore innovation in this area. Pressures at the interface of the aged and acute care systems, including psychogeriatric and palliative care, have been identified as possible areas of consideration for future reform (ADoHA, 2011a: 3; Productivity Commission, 2011: 176–9).

Regulating long-term care quality in Australia 171

While this reform agenda could lead to opportunities to improve quality outcomes for consumers, it is also giving rise to a number of challenges for policy makers with specific implications for quality, as outlined below.

6.6.1 Developing integrated quality regulation across community and residential care

Supporting greater choice and efficient allocation of funding between community and residential care will create imperatives for comparable quality measures across both settings. At the same time, these arrangements need to be sensitive to different needs and models of care in each setting, with greater flexibility and less specific standards likely to be necessary in community care. Another difficult issue is how to disaggregate and account for the contribution made by carers, on the one hand, and external providers, on the other. Supporting the contribution of carers is becoming increasingly important with the greater emphasis on community care and in the context of demographic pressures on the supply of informal care including changes in traditional family structures, with increased numbers of people never marrying or being divorced or separated (ABS, 2007), and the trend in younger cohorts towards having fewer children (Productivity Commission, 2008: 34). At the same time the need to encourage this contribution needs to be balanced against the risk of funding services that duplicate their role: a challenge as much for funding and accountability as for quality.

6.6.2 Developing the performance framework and incentives for higher quality

The performance measurement framework is underdeveloped in Australia, not only for aged care but also for primary and acute care and the wider health and community services system. In addition, there are no strong links between funding and performance. Recent health reforms include a strong emphasis on better performance management and transparency, particularly in the acute care sector, with quality and safety a major focus. Key recent initiatives include establishing a National Health Performance Authority and the Australian Commission on Safety and Quality in Healthcare. The Commission officially commenced as an independent, statutory authority on 1 July 2011 (see www.qualityandsafety.gov.au).

Similarly, developing the performance framework is likely to be an increasing focus for aged care in the future, including supporting providers to compare and benchmark their performance against others in the industry, and enabling consumers to compare the quality of alternative providers. There will need to be a cultural shift away from a focus on minimum standards towards continuous innovation and improvement. Improving access to information and quality is likely to be a key area of focus for further work. Some data is already published but is currently limited to information on whether services comply with a variety of standards. There have been recent calls for more comprehensive information to be made available, particularly in relation to staffing levels and skills. At the same time, there are significant challenges in defining appropriate and meaningful input and outcomes indicators. As the Productivity Commission (2011: 214) points out in its recent report, there is potential for moral hazard. For example, an indicator based on reducing the incidence of falls could encourage use of wheelchairs for ambulant residents.

6.6.3 Opportunities and risks associated with the movement towards consumer-directed care

While empowering consumers and supporting consumer-directed care has the potential to drive quality improvements, there are also risks to quality. Current initiatives are revealing many of the positives for care recipients and their carers as well as highlighting some of the significant challenges, particularly for people who are not able to exercise choice, including those who access care on an emergency basis or have cognitive impairment. A large proportion of people entering residential care do so from hospital and many live only a short time afterwards, with 40 per cent surviving less than six months (ADoHA, 2010d: 32).

The nature of the client points to the need for information to be quickly and easily available in a user-friendly format not only for users, but their families, who may have only a very short time to make decisions about care and accommodation options. The inevitable constraints on choice also highlight the limits to the roles that choice and competition can play as drivers for quality, and the need, therefore, for a continuing role for government, particularly for those unable to

Regulating long-term care quality in Australia 173

advocate on their own behalf and with varying level of family support. There will also be quality challenges in terms of allowing greater flexibility in how packages of services are tailored to an individual's needs while at the same time ensuring effective and efficient allocation of resources to services which have an evidence base. In addition, the vulnerable nature of the client group poses challenges in measuring how effectively consumers are involved and provider responsiveness.

6.6.4 *Creating a single entry point and improving the quality and consistency of assessments*

Historically, there has been significant variation in assessment processes, within and across programmes and states. Assessment for eligibility to Home and Community Care services has usually been undertaken by individual service providers, while assessment of eligibility for residential care and care packages has been undertaken by Aged Care Assessment Teams, with the states primarily managing the day-to-day administration of these programmes, supported by federal government funding. Work has been occurring to identify a set of common, validated assessment tools for use by Aged Care Assessment Teams, to improve the consistency of assessment outcomes across Australia (see CHSD, 2010: 4). More generally, work to develop a single entry point to the aged care system and uniform processes for initial assessment and triage could create opportunities to improve quality outcomes for consumers, including timelier referral to services appropriate to their needs.

At the same time, achieving a fully national system and agreement to transfer assessment and programme functions to federal-funded agencies has been a challenging process, with strong support for current arrangements among some local communities and service providers. As of 2 August 2011, when a new National Health Agreement was signed by all governments, there were still two states who had not fully agreed to these reforms.

There are also other challenges relating to broader system design and service delivery capacity. Aged care assessment services, including comprehensive geriatric assessments required to establish eligibility for federally funded community care packages and residential care, historically have been jointly funded by the federal government but managed by state governments. Access to assessment services is highly variable across regions (AIHW, 2011a: 198). Moves towards the federal government taking responsibility for full policy and funding assessment services provides an opportunity to improve access across the country. Unless improved access to assessment is accompanied by improved access and capacity within the sector to respond to the needs of care recipients, there is the potential for greater unmet need to be identified and for waiting lists to increase. In addition, there is the risk that a centralized intake process in some cases may lead to bottlenecks in the system. One advantage of multiple access points is that the assessment workload is spread more widely, reducing the risk of pressure becoming highly concentrated in particular parts of the system. As part of consideration of future directions in this area, there has been increased exploration of information technology solutions and web-based approaches for accessing care that combines central intake processes with local information on availability and service directories. Another area of focus has been call centre models, providing assessments and linking people to services via telephone, which have been trialed extensively in specific regions and already have been employed over recent years, with significant success, for services provided to the war veteran and war widows population (Productivity Commission, 2011: vol. II, 134–5, 143–7).

6.6.5 Better integration of quality arrangements with other parts of the regulatory framework

Better integration of quality arrangements with assessment and funding arrangements, in particular, is likely to be an important challenge as part of the current reform agenda. Largely for historical reasons, these different elements of the regulatory framework have tended to operate separately. The quality and accreditation system relies heavily on regulatory information from inspections or from complaint processes. Information collected through assessment and funding processes is not currently utilized to inform the measurement of quality and inform strategies for quality improvement. Using information gained from assessment of the care needs of care recipients over time to create indicators of quality could potentially contribute to more efficient regulatory processes. Better integration has the potential to improve the quality of clinical care, while reducing administrative processes for providers, creating a more seamless system for both residents and

Regulating long-term care quality in Australia 175

providers. Greater use of information management and information technology could have an important role to play here.

6.6.6 *Integration with the wider health and community services system*

Improving the interface with the wider health system and more seamless transitions between the aged and acute sector is an important element in the current reform agenda. There is a growing recognition that quality outcomes for older people are influenced as much by their access to a wider range of services as they are by access to aged care. For example, people in residential care often find it more difficult to access primary care services which can lead to unnecessary adverse events and hospital admissions. In 2008–9, there were 211,345 people accessing permanent residential care at some time during that year, accounting for 87,827 admissions to hospital from an aged care home and 807,935 days of hospital care.[4] It has been estimated that 31 per cent of transfers from aged care homes to hospitals could be potentially avoidable through better access to basic primary care (Codde et al., 2010). The aversion of some general practitioners (GPs) to providing services in residential care homes, together with the general lack of a culture of patient enrolment in Australia, also inhibits continuity in primary care provider for aged care residents. Access to other health professionals (medical and other specialists) is also problematic, due in part to the relatively small size of aged care facilities, which have an average of around sixty-six places, which means dedicated or co-located services are not feasible and results in the need for the specialist to travel to the facility or for the resident to be transferred with an escort.

The acute-aged care interface is a major pressure point, with significant movement of residents between the sectors. More than half of new admissions to high-level residential care are transfers from hospital. A combination of pressures on hospital budgets (by state governments) and capping of aged care places (through federal allocations) can result in queues of people waiting for a permanent residential care place, in the hospital setting. Recent expansion of community programmes, including growth of packaged care, the introduction of the aforementioned

---

[4] Analysis by the authors based on data provided by the Australian Department of Health and Ageing.

Transition Care Programme and the increasing reluctance of older people to enter residential care, appear to have reduced this problem in some areas.

Access to post-acute and sub-acute care (in the forms of rehabilitation, geriatric evaluation and management and palliative care) is another area of pressure. Access to post-acute care is largely determined by the provision of places by public and private hospitals, and is, for the most part, not subject to any overarching planning. Thus, access is highly variable across states and geographical regions within them. The Transition Care Programme, for which places are allocated on a population-based formula, therefore, tends to operate differently according to the pre-existing provision of post-acute services. In well-supplied regions, it serves mainly to provide community-based support at home, often after an in-patient rehabilitation episode, whereas in others it must fill a gap resulting from a lack of such services within the public hospital system. In such cases, services are more likely to involve more intensive step-down care and are more likely to be provided in a residential or acute institutional setting, with a higher funding contribution from the state health authorities.

Addressing this range of interface problems has been an important recent priority for government, including improving access to primary care through higher financial incentives for GPs. Improving support for aged care providers to meet their regulatory responsibility to facilitate access to health services has also been a recent focus – for example, a recent measure currently being implemented by the federal government extends support for access to specialist medical Telehealth services in residential care homes (see www.mbsonline.gov.au).

6.7 Conclusion

Systems for regulating the quality of long-term care in Australia are at a critical point in development. While residential care services are characterized by a highly regulated quality framework, which recent reviews and increasing rates of compliance suggest has been effective in addressing poor cases of care and promoting wide and consistent achievement of minimum standards, there are increasing imperatives to incorporate incentives for higher quality. There is a growing consensus that consumer choice and empowerment, supported by greater transparency and access to information on quality, is critical to driving these

Regulating long-term care quality in Australia 177

improvements. Regulation of the quality of community care is a work in progress and likely to gain increasing attention given the growing focus on community care in federal government aged care programmes. In addition, while improving quality and access has been an important focus for reform of aged care over the last twenty-five years, there is now an increasing emphasis on achieving better integration within and across different services, which is likely to be accompanied by an increasing focus on integrating and harmonizing quality regulation across the full spectrum of aged care programmes.

References

Aged Care Standards and Accreditation Agency Ltd (ACSAA) (2011). *Annual Report 2010–11*. Canberra: ACSAA.

Australian Bureau of Statistics (ABS) (2007). Lifetime marriage and divorce trends. *Australian Social Trends 2007* (cat. no. 4102.0). Canberra: ABS.

(2008a). *Australian Historical Population Statistics, 2008* (cat. no. 3105.0.65.001). Canberra: ABS.

(2008b). *Population Projections, Australia, 2006–2101* (cat. no. 3222.0). Canberra: ABS.

(2010). *The Health and Welfare of Australia's Aboriginal and Torres Strait Islander Peoples* (cat. no. 4704.0). Canberra: ABS.

Australian Department of Health and Ageing (ADoHA) (2007). *Evaluation of the Impact of Accreditation on the Delivery of Quality of Care and Quality of Life to Residents in Australian Government-Subsidised Residential Aged Care Homes*. Canberra: ADoHA.

(2010a). *Building a 21st Century Primary Healthcare System*. Canberra: ADoHA.

(2010b). *Community Care Common Standards Guide*. Canberra: ADoHA.

(2010c). *Report on the Operation of the Aged Care Act 1997, 1 July 2009– 30 June 2010*. Canberra: ADoHA.

(2010d). *Submission to the Productivity Commission Inquiry Caring for Older Australians*. Canberra: ADoHA.

(2010e). *The 2008 Community Care Census*. Canberra: ADoHA.

(2011a). *Second Submission to the Productivity Commission Inquiry Caring for Older Australians*. Canberra: ADoHA.

(2011b). *Technical Paper on the Changing Dynamics of Residential Care* (prepared to assist the Productivity Commission Inquiry Caring for Older Australians). Canberra: ADoHA.

(2011c). *The Review of the Aged Care Funding Instrument Report*. Canberra: ADoHA.

Australian Government (2010). *Australia to 2050, Future Challenges.* Intergenerational Report 2010. Canberra: Australian Government.

(2011). Media release by the Prime Minister of Australia, the Hon Julia Gillard MP, 8 August 2011. At: www.pm.gov.au

Australian Institute of Health and Welfare (AIHW) (2010). *Australia's Health 2010.* Canberra: AIHW.

(2011a). *Australia's Welfare 2011.* Canberra: AIHW.

(2011b). *Health Expenditure Australia 2009–10.* Canberra: AIHW.

Australian Law Reform Commission (ALRC) (1995). *The Coming of Age: New Aged Care Legislation for the Commonwealth: Review of Legislation Administered by Department of Human Services and Health.* Sydney: ALRC.

Australian National Audit Office (ANAO) (2000). *Home and Community Care.* Canberra: ANAO.

(2003). *Managing Residential Aged Care Accreditation.* Audit Report no. 42. Canberra: ANAO.

(2011). *Report on Monitoring and Compliance Arrangements of Care in Residential Care Homes.* Audit Report no.48. Canberra: ANAO.

Australian Parliament (1982). *In a Home or at Home: Accommodation and Home Care for the Aged.* Report of the inquiry by the House of Representatives Standing Committee on Expenditure. Canberra: Australian Government Publishing Service (AGPS).

(1985a). *In a Home or at Home: Accommodation and Home Care for the Aged: Follow-up Report.* Report of the inquiry by the House of Representatives Standing Committee on Expenditure. Canberra: AGPS.

(1985b). *Private Nursing Homes in Australia: Their Conduct, Administration and Ownership.* Report of the inquiry by the Senate Select Committee on Private Hospitals and Nursing Homes. Canberra: AGPS.

(1994) *Home but Not Alone: Report on the Home and Community Care Program.* Report of an inquiry by the House of Representative Standing Committee on Community Affairs. Canberra: AGPS.

(2005). *Quality and Equity in Aged Care: Report of the Inquiry by the Senate Community Affairs Reference Committee.* Canberra: Australian Parliament.

(2006). *The Blame Game: Report of the House of Representatives Standing Committee on Health and Ageing Inquiry into Health Funding.* Canberra: Australian Parliament.

(2009). *Residential and Community Aged Care in Australia: Report of the Inquiry by the Senate Finance and Public Administration Committee.* Canberra: Australian Parliament.

Braithwaite, J., Makkai, T., Braithwaite, V. and Gibson, D. (1993). *Raising the Standard: Resident Centred Nursing Home Regulation in Australia.*

Aged and Community Care Service Development and Evaluation Reports no. 10. Canberra: AGPS.

Centre for Health Service Development (CHSD), University of Wollongong (2010). *Selecting Tools for ACAT Assessment: A Report for the Expert Clinical Reference Group*. Canberra: ADoHA.

Codde, J., Frankel, J., Arendts, G. and Babich, P. (2010). Quantification of the proportion of transfers from residential care facilities to the Emergency Department that could be avoided through improved primary care services. *Australasian Journal on Ageing*, 29(4): 167–71.

Cullen, D. (2003a). *Historical Perspectives: the Evolution of the Australian Government's Involvement in Supporting the Needs of Older People*. Review of Pricing Arrangements in Residential Care Background Paper no. 4. Canberra: ADoHA.

  (2003b). *The Commonwealth Legislative Framework*. Review of Pricing Arrangements in Residential Care Background Paper no. 2, Canberra: ADoHA.

Gray, L. C. (2001). *Two Year Review of Aged Care Reforms*. Canberra: ADoHA.

Gray, L. C., Travers C. M., Bartlett, H. P., Crotty, M. and Cameron, I. D. (2008). Transition care: will it deliver? *Medical Journal of Australia*, 188(4): 251–3.

Gregory, R. (1993). *Review of the Structure of Nursing Home Arrangements: Stage 1*. Aged and Community Care Service Development and Evaluation Reports no. 11. Canberra: AGPS.

  (1994). *Review of the Structure of Nursing Home Arrangements: Stage 2*. Aged and Community Care Service Development and Evaluation Reports no. 12. Canberra: AGPS.

Linacre, S. (2006). *Caring for an Older Australia – a Presentation to the Economic and Social Outlook Conference: Making the Boom Pay*. Melbourne Institute.

National Health and Hospitals Reform Commission (2009). *A Healthier Future for All Australians*. Canberra: National Health and Hospitals Reform Commission.

Productivity Commission (2008). *Trends in Aged Care Services: Some Implications*. Canberra: Productivity Commission.

  (2011). *Report of the Inquiry into Caring for Older Australians*. Canberra: Productivity Commission.

Ronalds, C. (1989). *Residents' Rights in Nursing Homes and Hostels: Final Report*. Canberra: AGPS.

7 Regulating the quality and safety of long-term care in England

JULIETTE MALLEY, JACQUETTA HOLDER,
RACHAEL DODGSON AND SAMANTHA BOOTH

7.1 Introduction

The focus of this chapter is the regulatory system for quality assurance of long-term care in England.[1] Entry of providers to the long-term care market and their continued operation is currently regulated under the Health and Social Care Act 2008 (HSCA 2008), which also established a single health and social care regulator, called the Care Quality Commission (CQC). Although the current regulatory framework is new, the long-term care sector has been regulated since 1927 with the Nursing Homes Registration Act. However, from 1927 until 2000 regulations varied by long-term care provider type. Thus, there were different regulations and regulators for each care home type (homes with or without nursing); community-based services were unregulated; and publicly owned providers in contrast to independently owned providers were subject only to inspection and not required to register. In addition, there were regional variations since locally based inspection units carried out inspections according to locally defined standards (Day and Klein, 1987; Klein, 1997; Peace, 2003). In 2000, passage of the Care Standards Act (CSA) marked a turning point in the regulation of the sector, beginning a phase of consolidation of the regulatory environment and creating a structure that has largely continued to this day. It established an independent national regulator, with powers to register, inspect and enforce national standards in all care homes and home care agencies, irrespective of ownership status, or region of the country.

By the early 2000s the costs of public sector regulation were rising. There was a widespread perception that regulation and inspection were too burdensome and expensive (Hood et al., 1999; Humphrey, 2003) and that such regimes were not consistent with best practice principles

---

[1] We focus on England not the UK because the devolved administrations for Scotland, Northern Ireland and Wales have significant policy-making powers for both health and social care, and different systems operate.

Regulating the quality and safety of long-term care in England 181

(Better Regulation Task Force, 2003). Legislation was quickly introduced to ensure that all regulators had regard to better regulation principles, namely that regulatory activity should be 'risk-based', with resources targeted towards those organizations seen to be most at risk of failing (Adil, 2008; Black and Baldwin, 2010). The CSA 2000 was amended in line with these principles, regulators were disbanded or merged, and processes for registering providers and monitoring compliance were repeatedly revised in an attempt to rationalize the regulation of health and social care. Risk-based approaches continue to dominate regulatory developments as the double drive to reduce the burden of regulation and ensure its efficiency remains at the forefront of policy makers' minds. Certainly, the most recent statutory revision (the HSCA 2008), which brought together functions previously covered by three different regulators – the Commission for Social Care Inspection (CSCI), the Healthcare Commission and the Mental Health Act Commission – through the creation of the CQC, responded to these concerns (Adil, 2008).

CQC began operating in 2009, the legislation came into effect in 2010, and re-registration of existing providers under the HSCA 2008 was only completed towards the end of 2010. Thus, the newness of the current system means that there is little evidence of how it is working. Furthermore, the system for monitoring compliance with the new regulations is still being developed. The change of government in early 2010 and scandals involving health and social care providers, which provoked criticism of the new system (House of Commons Health Committee, 2011a), have affected how CQC operates. Reflecting on its first two years of operation, CQC has already changed its regulatory approach. We have tried, as far as possible, to incorporate these changes into our description, although at the time of writing (spring 2012) they are not yet implemented. Nevertheless, in such a dynamic regulatory environment, it is likely there will be additional changes to the processes described herein as well as potentially broader changes in terms of strategy or the regulatory model.

7.2 Demand for long-term care and the structure of the market

As the population ages demand for long-term care in England is expected to increase. Continuing improvements in life expectancy suggest that the group over 65 will increase from an estimated 16 per cent of the population in 2010 to 28 per cent by 2032, and those over 85 will increase from 2 per cent in 2010 to 5 per cent (Office for National Statistics, 2007, 2011). The more rapid growth amongst those over 85 is of particular concern for long-term care since it is at the oldest ages that demand for long-term care is the highest. Indeed, to keep pace with demographic pressures and assuming demand is no more constrained by supply than it is at present, the total number of older long-term care users (including residential and non-residential care), is projected to rise from 2.0 million in 2010 to 3.2 million in 2030, an increase of around 60 per cent over twenty years (Wittenberg et al., 2011).

A wide variety of long-term care services are available which fall into two broad types: residential and community-based services. Residential services include nursing homes, where there is twenty-four-hour access to nursing care, and care homes that offer personal care only. 'Extra-care' housing schemes are also available. These offer self-contained accommodation with communal facilities, on-site housing support and access to twenty-four-hour personal care. The availability of community-based services varies by the local administrative area (Local Authority (LA)) but generally include: home care, day centres, supervision services, equipment and minor adaptations, meals and respite for informal carers. A range of other low-level services are also often available, such as domestic help, laundry, transport, befriending and support for informal carers. All these services are considered 'adult social care' (ASC) services, and are not funded by the National Health Service (NHS).[2] Rather, LAs have responsibility for assessing need for these services. The provision of publicly funded social care services is subject to a means test and charges can be levied. One feature of means testing is that around 30 per cent of long-term care is self-funded (Comas-Herrera et al., 2010).

Compared with the situation at the beginning of the 1980s, when the majority of care home providers were publicly owned and community-based services were limited, today there is a mixed economy of care, with the overwhelming majority of ASC providers in the private sector (see Table 7.1), and a large and vibrant home care market. The majority

---

[2] The NHS makes a flat-rate contribution to the fees of all nursing placements in care homes to cover the costs of their nursing care. In some exceptional circumstances care home places are provided by the NHS, under the continuing care policy (Department of Health, 2009).

Table 7.1 *Numbers of providers in England by ownership and type of service at 31 March 2010 (percentage shown in brackets)*[a]

| | Ownership type | | | | |
Service type	Private	Voluntary	LA	NHS	Other[b]
Nursing home	3,831 (88.0)	449 (10.3)	31 (0.7)	11 (0.3)	30 (0.7)
Residential care home	9,535 (68.7)	3,096 (22.3)	1,034 (7.4)	156 (1.1)	61 (0.4)
Home care agency	4,060 (73.0)	765 (14.0)	617 (11.0)	42 (1.0)	42 (1.0)

Source: Care Quality Commission, 2010a.
Notes:
[a] Includes services for all adult client groups, including people with dementia, learning disabilities or autistic spectrum disorder, mental health problems, physical disability, those detained under the Mental Health Act and people who misuse drugs and alcohol and with an eating disorder.
[b] The 'Other' category was included in registration documentation used by the previous regulator.

of publicly funded care is commissioned from the independent (private and voluntary) sector. Estimates for 2009/10 show that 92 per cent of residential care placements and 84 per cent of all home care (by volume) are purchased from the independent sector (The Health and Social Care Information Centre, 2011).

7.3 Regulation of long-term care

The HSCA 2008 provides the regulatory framework for the quality and safety of health and social care but applies only to certain categories of 'regulated activities'. These include 'personal care for people who are unable to provide it for themselves, because of old age, illness or disability, in the place where they are living', and 'accommodation for people who require nursing or personal care'. The definition of personal care includes physical assistance to prompt and supervise, or help or support a person with eating or drinking, toileting, washing or bathing, dressing, oral care, or the care of skin, hair and nails. Thus, the regulations span the premises and care (nursing and personal) provided by care homes for older people (both those with and without nursing care), and the personal care provided by home care agencies supporting people living in their own home, which might be in an extra-care housing scheme (Care Quality Commission, 2010d).

The role of CQC is to 'protect and promote the health, safety and welfare of people who use health and social care services' by registering providers of regulated activities and monitoring their compliance with the regulations. In addition, CQC has powers to enforce compliance with regulations in cases where failures are identified and to prosecute or fine persons who break the law. Compared to its three sector-specific predecessor organizations, which operated under different legislation, the CQC is a very different organization. It is smaller, with reduced resources in terms of funds and staff, and its staff, including inspectors and analysts, work across all regulated health and social care providers. CQC receives a grant from the Department of Health (DH), but it is government policy that the CQC works towards full cost recovery of its regulatory functions from providers by levying fees. Registered providers pay an annual fee to the regulator, which is intended to cover all registration, variation and compliance requirements. Fees are determined according to the type of service and for care homes, they also vary according to the size of the provider. For extra-care housing and home care providers fees vary according to the number of registered locations (Care Quality Commission, 2011a). It is difficult to compare the resources and costs of the ASC functions of the CQC with those of its predecessors, mainly CSCI, because publicly available accounts do not provide a breakdown of CQC resources or expenditure in terms of health, ASC and mental health. In its first year of operation, however, CQC reported a reduction in total expenditure of £58.7 million from the £248.6 million spent by the three previous regulators in 2008/9 (Care Quality Commission, 2010c).

The procedure for both self- and publicly funded service users to make complaints is regulated under the Local Authority Social Services and National Health Service Complaints (England) Regulations 2009. The system aims to resolve problems locally and complaints made to bodies other than the provider will be passed onto the provider, with consent from the individual. If service users are unhappy with the way the provider handles the complaint, they can go to the independent local government ombudsman (LGO), to resolve the complaint without going to court (LGO, 2010). The LGO can hold

Regulating the quality and safety of long-term care in England   185

organizations to account by requiring an apology, financial compensation or repayment, better facilities, better procedures and better instructions for staff. It cannot hold individual workers to account. CQC itself has no statutory investigation function in relation to individual complaints about regulated services, unless they involve the Mental Health Act.

7.4 Registration and certification of providers

All ASC providers of regulated activities (and their managers) are legally required to register with CQC; it is a prosecutable offence to operate without being registered (Care Quality Commission, 2010e). CQC produces guidance for providers explaining how to comply with the HSCA 2008 (Regulated Activities) Regulations 2010 and the Care Quality Commission (Registration) Regulations 2009. The guidance consists of twenty-eight 'Essential Standards of Quality and Safety' related to the regulations, grouped into six 'outcome' areas (see Table 7.2). The registration process has three stages: written application; assessment; and judgement, where providers are notified of the decision and issued with a certificate. Unsuccessful applicants have the right to make written representations to CQC and can appeal to an independent tribunal.

Applicants must declare their compliance with the regulations as part of the registration process. It is a prosecutable offence to knowingly make a false or misleading statement. The application must also provide evidence to demonstrate compliance or evidence to demonstrate how the standards will be met once the provider starts operating; for example, by referring to policies, procedures and systems for staffing levels, reporting and learning from incidents, and safeguarding service users (Care Quality Commission, 2010i). Although assessment of applications is desk-based, in the vast majority of applications CQC make a site visit. All registrations have 'restrictive conditions' attached, specifying, for example, the number of people that can be accommodated in a care home (Care Quality Commission, 2010f). When the provider's circumstances change they must reapply to vary their registration conditions.

During its first year CQC had to register all existing ASC providers under the HSCA 2008 and any new providers. Unsurprisingly, CQC struggled to meet its eight-week target for processing applications

Table 7.2 *The Essential Standards of Quality and Safety and their relationship to the regulations in England*

6 Key outcome domains	Standard	Regulation (year)
Information and involvement	1. Respecting and involving service users	17 (2010)
	2. Consent to care and treatment	18 (2010)
	3. Fees*	19 (2009)
Personalized care, treatment and support	4. Care and welfare of service users	9 (2010)
	5. Meeting nutritional needs	14 (2010)
	6. Cooperating with other providers	24 (2010)
Safeguarding	7. Safeguarding service users from abuse	11 (2010)
	8. Cleanliness and infection control	12 (2010)
	9. Management of medicines	13 (2010)
	10. Safety and suitability of premises	15 (2010)
	11. Safety, availability and suitability of equipment	16 (2010)
Suitability of staffing	12. Requirements relating to workers	21 (2010)
	13. Staffing	22 (2010)
	14. Supporting workers	23 (2010)
Quality and management	15. Statement of purpose*	12 (2009) and Schedule 3
	16. Assessing and monitoring the quality of service provision	10 (2010)
	17. Complaints	19 (2010)
	18. Notification of death of a service user*	16 (2009)
	19. Notification of death or unauthorized absence of a person who is detained or liable to be detained under the Mental Health Act 1983*	17 (2009)
	20. Notification of other incidents* (including injuries, allegations of abuse, police investigations)	18 (2009)

Regulating the quality and safety of long-term care in England 187

Table 7.2 (*cont.*)

6 Key outcome domains	Standard	Regulation (year)
	21. Records	20 (2010)
Suitability of management	22. Requirements where the service provider is an individual or partnership*	4 (2010)
	23. Requirement where the service provider is a body other than a partnership*	5 (2010)
	24. Requirements relating to registered managers*	6 (2010)
	25. Registered person: training*	7 (2010)
	26. Financial position*	13 (2009)
	27. Notifications of absence*	14 (2009)
	28. Notifications – notice of changes*	15 (2009)

Source: Care Quality Commission, 2010d.
Note:
* Asterisked standards are the twelve non-core standards. The sixteen without an asterisk are the core standards.

(House of Commons Health Committee, 2011a). In 2010/11 the median processing time for new registrations was thirteen to fourteen weeks for services and eleven to twelve weeks for managers[3]; applications to vary conditions were taking between nine and eleven weeks depending on application type. This situation was reported to be particularly frustrating for providers who, having invested in new buildings or staff, could not start operations and generate any returns on their investments (House of Commons Health Committee, 2011a). The available data for 2011/12 show that the median processing time is improving, with new applications for services now taking between eight to nine weeks and seven to eight for managers, and applications to vary conditions taking between four to seven weeks depending on application type.

---

[3] In addition to long-term care providers, the managers of care homes and long-term care home service agencies have to register separately.

7.5 Monitoring compliance with the regulations

CQC aims to be outcomes-focused and place the views and experiences of service users at the centre of its regulatory approach. For each of the twenty-eight standards CQC has generated a statement of the 'outcomes' that it expects service users to experience when a provider is compliant with the regulations. These statements, like the regulations, are broadly specified. For example, the statement of outcomes associated with Standard 4, 'the care and welfare of service users', is that service users should 'experience effective, safe and appropriate care, treatment and support that meets their needs and protects their rights' (Care Quality Commission, 2010d: 63). Neither statute nor CQC currently mandate any outcome data collections by providers (e.g., incidence of pressure ulcers, self-reported quality of life or functional ability) to assess the standards. Therefore, the use of the term outcome by CQC and its assessment differ somewhat from traditional evaluation. However, it does mirror the term's use in policy documents (Department of Health, 2011).

CQC encourages providers to take responsibility for assuring their own compliance through self-assessment and improvement activities, and expects providers to collect information that directly demonstrate outcomes for their services users: for example, survey data, complaints and feedback, or other engagement mechanisms. Providers can use any instruments and methods they consider useful. To help providers collate and monitor the data that they collect, CQC has developed a tool known as the 'Provider Compliance Assessment', but does not mandate its use (Care Quality Commission, 2010g). In assuring their own compliance, providers are therefore likely to use a myriad of different instruments filled with unstandardized data that are not easily comparable across providers.

As well as encouraging providers to monitor their own compliance, CQC proactively monitors compliance in two ways: through inspections and 'continuous assessment'. The sixteen core standards, which are considered to have the greatest bearing on the quality and safety of services (see Table 7.2), are monitored continuously, while inspections focus on identifying evidence of non-compliance (although compliance is also reported) in relation to a smaller number of outcomes.

7.5.1 Inspections

Inspections can be scheduled, 'responsive' or themed and are almost always unannounced. Scheduled inspections are carried out on a 'rolling programme', with an inspection between three months and one year after registration and thereafter at least once every year. Responsive inspections are triggered by lack of information about a service, the receipt of 'intelligence' (see the section on continuous assessment below for details of 'intelligence' sources), which the inspector judges to pose a risk sufficient enough to warrant further investigation, or by the need to follow up on enforcement action. Themed inspections are in-depth studies on a specific topic (for example, dignity and nutrition) and involve inspections of a sample of services. All inspections are focused rather than comprehensive; they do not check each of the core standards. Scheduled inspections focus on at least five standards, one of which is always Standard 4 (care and welfare). Inspectors select the other standards to inspect based on either the most relevant areas for the type of service, areas of concern identified during the inspection planning stage (for example, from evidence collected from continuous assessment), or areas that have not been inspected recently. Responsive inspections concentrate on the areas of concern that triggered the inspection. However, should other concerns emerge, the scope can be widened. Following responsive and scheduled inspections, inspectors write a report, which is quality assured within CQC and sent to the provider for comments on factual accuracy before publication (see Section 7.8 below).

For some inspections, CQC uses 'experts by experience' as members of the inspection team. Experts by experience are social care service users, or people with experience of providing informal unpaid care for service users. CQC has continued and expanded this programme, started by its predecessor – the aim being to gain the views of service users and a different perspective. In 2009/10, experts by experience took part in close to 5 per cent of all site visits of registered social care services, just short of the target of including them in 6 per cent of inspections (Care Quality Commission, 2010c) and there are plans to increase this target. A few qualitative interview studies have explored the nature and value of involving lay assessors, service users or 'experts' in the inspection process, with mixed results. One study concluded that lay inspectors provided a useful mechanism for encouraging residents to express their views (Wright, 2005). Another, however, found neither evidence of greater participation by residents nor an increased focus on their views (Barnes, 2003). Simmill-Binning and colleagues (2007) argue that, while there is a strong case for involving non-professionals in regulation to promote public confidence, transparency, independence and a focus on residents' well-being, there is currently no evidence that it improves the quality of inspections.

7.5.2 Continuous assessment

CQC introduced continuous assessment, initially at least, as a way to estimate the risk of non-compliance by a provider with the standards and to direct more in-depth compliance detection activity, then known as 'reviews'. (Reviews, which did not have to include a site visit, have now been replaced by inspections.) Assessment is a desk-based activity, whereby inspectors draw on the available 'intelligence' about a provider to determine whether further regulatory activity is needed. A key source of information is the provider's 'Quality and Risk Profile' (QRP: see Box 7.1 for an explanation and data sources), but inspectors also receive information from other sources, such as their own contacts and whistleblowers. In cases where assessment leads inspectors to suspect non-compliance, they will launch a responsive inspection or bring forward a scheduled inspection. The system is over-ridden in cases where intelligence is indicative of a serious breach of compliance, so that immediate action can be taken.

Continuous assessment is theoretically a significant step forward, when compared to the previous approach developed by CSCI to monitor risk and direct more in-depth activity. Under CSCI, risk of non-compliance was ascertained using the quality rating (from zero to three) that the provider gained on its last inspection. These ratings guided inspection frequency, such that inspections took place annually for one-star providers and more frequently for zero-star, on a biennial basis for two-star providers and a triennial basis for three-star providers. This approach meant that some providers were not subjected to any kind of external monitoring for three years. Whilst the new 'intelligence-based' approach ensures some degree of external monitoring for all providers, its success depends upon how well it predicts non-compliance events. Therefore, the methods and data used for surveillance are critical to the new approach.

Intelligence-based risk monitoring is well established for NHS settings, and has been shown to be relatively effective at identifying

Box 7.1 Explanation of the Quality and Risk Profile and underlying intelligence sources, England

The QRP is a tool for gathering and displaying intelligence about provider in one place to allow inspectors to easily and continuously monitor a provider's risk of non-compliance. Qualitative and quantitative data items are gathered from a variety of sources, analysed and converted to a common scale so they can be combined to generate a single risk estimate per standard. A full explanation of the statistical methods is given in Spiegelhalter et al. (2012). It should be noted, however, that quantitative data are adjusted where appropriate for factors beyond the control of the provider and data items are weighted on aggregation for quality, relevance and how closely they reflect user experience. The individual data items (colour-coded to show whether performance is better or worse than expected) and risk estimates (shown as dials and only presented where there is confidence in the estimate) are both displayed in a provider's QRP. An example profile is shown in Figure 7.1 for a randomly chosen provider for Standard 13. The risk estimate for the standard is shown in the dial towards the top of the screen and the evidence (composed of a number of data items) underlying this estimate is shown below in the table below the dial. Sources of data underlying the ASC QRPs include CQC's own data, such as compliance judgements from registration and/or following inspections, statutory notifications made by providers, complaints and information from whistleblowers (includes information on staffing, safeguarding and availability of activities) as well as other local intelligence shared with CQC. CQC also makes use of data that is publicly available, such as fire enforcement notices (from the Fire and Rescue Services where fire safety is inadequate), Health and Safety Executive Public Register or Enforcement Notices (includes asbestos assessments, controls for legionella bacteria risks, temperature controls on water outlets), and Environmental Health Officer Reports about food hygiene. Additionally CQC has information sharing agreements with suppliers of data, for example, enabling it to utilize data on workforce characteristics from Skills for Care (such as staffing ratios and the proportion of permanent staff) and emergency admissions to acute hospital originating from residential care.

Figure 7.1 An example QRP for Standard 13 in England. © Care Quality Commission 2011.

riskier healthcare providers (Adil, 2008; Bardsley et al., 2009); it is, however, new to ASC. It is arguably more challenging to implement in ASC than in the NHS, largely due to data limitations: fifty data items currently support the QRP in ASC compared to around 500 in healthcare. More specifically, in ASC, data is patchy and some collections are voluntary (e.g., staffing data from Skills for Care)[4] (National Audit Office, 2011a). With the exception of statutory notifications, there are no mandatory provider data collections (on input requirements (e.g., space requirements), process measures or outcomes).

---

[4] Skills for Care is a charitable organization established by an act of Parliament, which aims to ensure that the social care workforce has the right skills to deliver high-quality care. It provides support to employers and grants for training as well as conducting and commissioning research and analysis about the social care workforce.

Most 'intelligence' is qualitative and is either about the provider or specific (not randomly selected) individuals. Despite ongoing discussions about introducing individual-level data collections, the political will required to drive such a change through has not been forthcoming. Given the data limitations, it seems unlikely that the risk model is able to predict non-compliance well across all standards, as even in healthcare, where there is a wealth of data, predictions are better for some standards compared to others (Bardsley et al., 2009). However, there are no reasons to suspect that continuous assessment (and the QRP) is any worse at predicting non-compliance risk than its predecessor, and without studies devoted to determining the predictive ability of either of these approaches it is impossible to draw any conclusions in this regard.

7.5.3 Judging compliance

The standards and 'outcomes' statements are broadly specified so they can be applied flexibly by inspectors, when they assess compliance during an inspection. However, to ensure judgements are consistent and have a solid evidence base, CQC produces guidance known as the 'judgement framework', which is a set of rules and criteria that inspectors follow to decide how the evidence should be interpreted (Care Quality Commission, 2012). The CQC website also contains case studies to further help inspectors match what they see on the ground with 'outcome' descriptions for compliant providers. Since it is impossible to envisage every scenario of non-compliance, the case studies add detail, but there is still room for interpretation and their use is voluntary. The discretionary nature of decision making is seen by CQC as critical to ensuring that judgements about non-compliance are proportionate and take into consideration whether a provider has done all that is 'reasonably practicable' to mitigate any non-compliance. However, discretion combined with the lack of standardized data and regionally based inspection teams can mean decisions are hard to understand and questions have been raised about the consistency of judgements (Cutler and Waine, 2003; House of Commons Health Committee, 2011a). To our knowledge there are no studies that examine the consistency of judgements guided by the judgement framework and therefore the success of such an approach.

Each judgement of non-compliance with a standard has a level of impact attached, which is determined using the judgement framework according to the perceived impact on service users. There are three levels of impact: minor, moderate and major. Non-compliance judged to be of minor impact would be 'not significant' and 'could be resolved quickly'; a moderate impact would or could have a 'significant effect' on the health, safety or welfare of service users and 'may need to be resolved quickly'; a major impact would include incidences of non-compliance judged to have a 'serious current or long-term impact' on the health, safety or welfare of service users and would 'need to be resolved quickly' (Care Quality Commission, 2012). These categories are then used by inspectors to determine the regulatory response (see Section 7.6 below).

7.5.4 Compliance among providers

Current evidence about compliance with the standards is restricted to that generated from 'reviews' over the period October 2010 to July 2011, which in 92 per cent of cases involved an inspection. Over this period, CQC also operated a slightly different procedure for determining the level of concern associated with each incidence of non-compliance and often reacted to minor concerns with informal actions. Most cases were said to have resulted in services quickly becoming compliant, and as such can be considered temporary deficiencies. Despite the differences in methods used and allowing for the fact that many of these reviews were responsive, and therefore likely to exhibit disproportionately high levels of non-compliance, these data are instructive of general levels of compliance. Table 7.3 shows that, for non-nursing homes, compliance rates per standard were 70 per cent or more, and 85 per cent or higher including minor concerns. The exception was Standard 4 on care and welfare. Compliance rates per standard for nursing homes were lower than those observed in homes without nursing. When minor concerns are included only around 73 per cent of nursing homes were judged compliant with Standard Four and 79 per cent with Standard 9 on the management of medicines. In general, comparison of concerns by severity shows that more concerns were judged to be moderate than major. The highest rates of compliance were found for the standard around handling of comments and complaints. In contrast, a recent study for the Office of Fair Trading (2011) found significant deficiencies in this regard: 39 per cent of care homes

Table 7.3 *Findings from CQC reviews of compliance for care homes in England by home type and standard, October 2010 to March 2011[a]*

Standard	Compliant per cent		Major concerns per cent		Moderate concerns per cent		Minor concerns per cent		Number of reviews[b]	
	with nursing	without nursing	with nursing	without nursing	with nursing	without nursing	with nursing	without nursing	with nursing	without nursing
1. Respect and involvement	70	85	3	1	7	5	20	9	591	1170
2. Consent to care and treatment	73	83	2	0.8	9	4	16	12	495	1050
4. Care and welfare	51	68	10	5	17	11	22	16	799	1401
5. Meeting nutritional needs	71	84	4	2	10	5	15	9	599	1139
7. Safeguarding	72	77	6	4	10	8	13	11	648	1277
8. Cleanliness and infection control	70	72	4	3	10	8	16	17	566	1115
9. Management of medicines	61	72	8	3	13	9	18	16	636	1202
10. Safety and suitability of premises	69	73	3	3	10	9	17	15	577	1155

Table 7.3 (*cont.*)

Standard	Compliant per cent		Major concerns per cent		Moderate concerns per cent		Minor concerns per cent		Number of reviews[b]	
	with nursing	without nursing	with nursing	without nursing	with nursing	without nursing	with nursing	without nursing	with nursing	without nursing
11. Safety, availability and suitability of equipment	85	89	3	1	5	3	7	7	507	1033
16. Management of risk, health, welfare and safety	69	78	4	2	10	6	17	14	599	1193 316
17. Handling of comments and complaints	89	91	1	0.2	3	2	7	6	495	1020

Source: Adapted from Care Quality Commission, 2011b.

Notes:

[a] Some care homes may be registered as both 'with nursing' and 'without nursing' so are reported in both columns. These data include care homes for all adult client groups.

[b] The number of reviews is not the same for each standard as reviews do not necessarily focus on all standards.

Regulating the quality and safety of long-term care in England 197

reported that they provided no information on complaints procedures within residents' contracts or statements of terms and conditions, and 41 per cent did not report using posters or other information around the home to provide information on complaints procedures. It is unclear whether this is suggestive of recent improvements or reflects the weight inspectors give to evidence about publicizing complaints procedures when they assess compliance.

Compliance data for home care providers are shown in Table 7.4. Rates of compliance are generally better than those for care homes, at over 70 per cent for all standards. Similarly to care homes, the standards with the lowest levels of compliance were those for the care and welfare of users and the management of medicines. Rates of compliance were much higher when minor concerns were included, reaching over 90 per cent for all standards, save Standard 16 on the management of risk, health, welfare and safety.

7.6 Sanctions and enforcement mechanisms

CQC's approach can be considered an example of 'responsive regulation' (Braithwaite, 2002), since it has at its disposal a palette of sanctions, from which to choose a response that matches the seriousness of the failings. Different sanctions are applied depending on whether non-compliance is judged to be minor, moderate or major. They range from 'compliance actions', to 'warning notices' and finally to criminal and civil actions. Compliance actions are not formal enforcement actions and require providers to submit a report showing how they will achieve compliance, which CQC monitors to see whether improvements are made. Warning notices, by contrast, are the first step on the enforcement ladder. Civil actions consist of the imposition, variation or removal of conditions, suspension of registration and cancellation of registration. CQC monitors responses to each of these conditions, except in the case of cancellation where a provider would need to re-register if it wished to continue to operate. Criminal powers are used when CQC wishes to hold a person to account for causing harm or failing to comply with the law and include fixed penalty notices, cautions, and prosecution for breaching legislation. Civil and criminal powers can be used together, and fines ranging from £300 to £50,000 can be imposed on a one-off basis (Care Quality Commission, 2010j). CQC will escalate its enforcement activity when providers fail to improve or respond.

Table 7.4 *Findings from CQC reviews of compliance of home care agencies in England by standard, October 2010 to March 2011[a]*

Standard	Compliant per cent	Major concerns per cent	Moderate concerns per cent	Minor concerns per cent	Number of reviews[b]
1. Respect and involvement	90	1	3	6	298
2. Consent to care and treatment	87	0.4	4	9	274
4. Care and welfare	73	3	7	17	344
5. Meeting nutritional needs	92	0	2	6	255
7. Safeguarding	83	3	5	9	333
8. Cleanliness and infection control	86	0	5	9	264
9. Management of medicines	75	2	9	15	295
10. Safety and suitability of premises	97	0.5	1	2	222
11. Safety, availability and suitability of equipment	94	0.4	2	4	253
16. Management of risk, health, welfare and safety	78	2	6	15	320
17. Handling of comments and complaints	90	0.4	3	7	284

Source: Adapted from CQC, 2011b.

Notes:

[a] These data include home care agencies providing care to all adult client groups.

[b] The number of reviews is not the same for each standard as reviews do not necessarily focus on all standards.

Regulating the quality and safety of long-term care in England   199

From October 2010 to March 2011, CQC served 671 compliance actions and 156 warning notices. In seven cases CQC imposed a variation of conditions on the location or provider, for example preventing further admissions. There were also ten cases where CQC cancelled the registration. Over the same period, CQC made one prosecution of a home care provider and one of a care home, and in both cases these were for operating without having registered.

7.7 Public reporting of provider quality and safety

CQC reports information about providers on its website for public consumption. The main source of information about providers is the online care directory, which is searchable by the type of service, specialization of the service, area and name of the provider. The search returns a list of providers. For each provider details are shown of the service, any restrictive conditions, notification of whether a scheduled or responsive inspection is in progress and the results of any inspections by outcome area, including whether any compliance or enforcement actions were taken. Inspection reports are also available from a more detailed provider profile page. Detailed information from the QRPs is not published. The directory is not searchable by quality, as was possible under the previous regime, where it was searchable by a quality 'star' rating. It also provides a limited picture of quality, as the new system focuses on ensuring the adequacy of services in the sense that it identifies those providers that comply with the standards, and those that are non-compliant. Quality ratings, by contrast, provided a richer view of quality since they graded providers on a four-point scale and theoretically, at least, identified providers exceeding the standards. There were some criticisms of the quality ratings, notably that they could become rapidly outdated since they were only updated following a key inspection, which could be every three years for the best providers. In addition some people felt that the way it operated did not produce consistent ratings (Care Quality Commission, 2010b; Pitt, 2010b). Nevertheless, research has found some evidence of a relationship between outcomes for users and quality ratings awarded to residential care homes (Netten et al., 2010).

One aim of the quality ratings scheme was to provide purchasers (individuals and LAs) with information about the quality of services, to promote better choices and market efficiency. There is some evidence that the public used quality ratings to choose services, and LAs used them to commission care and in some cases to determine fee payment structures for providers (CSCI, 2009b). A recent study also found that 79 per cent of relatives were aware of inspection reports and of those nearly three-quarters made use of the reports when choosing a home (Darton, 2011). However, to date there is no research showing whether the information provided improved people's choices or quality more generally. There is also anecdotal evidence that the ratings were used by investors, lenders, funds, institutions and property companies to identify sound investments (Laing and Buisson, 2011). There is therefore some disquiet across the sector that this system for marking quality was abandoned, particularly before a new one has been decided upon (Pitt, 2010a; Dunning, 2011; Laing and Buisson, 2011).

Discussions regarding the provision of quality information to help consumer choice are now progressing along very different lines, with interest being expressed by ministers in the development of 'Trip Advisor' style information. A new website, 'The Good Care Guide', has recently been launched, where users of care homes and home care services can rate their provider for its quality of care and staff, facilities and cleanliness and value for money. The Social Care Institute for Excellence (SCIE) is also developing a new website called 'Find Me Good Care', which will cover all social care providers (regulated and unregulated) and will integrate information on compliance from CQC, information from the providers as well as the views of service users, in a 'Trip Advisor' type format.

7.8 Political challenges

Regulating health and social care in England is not an easy task, in part due to the difficult political environment. Despite the necessary and valuable role CQC fulfils, as an arms-length body (ALB) it (like other ALBs) is sometimes stereotyped as inefficient and bureaucratic, drawing on resources that could better be spent on frontline services. The frequent regime reorganizations, introduced to improve efficiency, have been extremely disruptive and have meant that the regulatory system has been in almost constant flux. What is needed now is a period of relative stability; yet more changes abound as the new government elected in May 2010 has announced further restructuring with the creation of HealthWatch, a consumer champion, within CQC (Department of Health, 2010a).

Risk-based approaches have been a feature of long-term care regulation for some years now as a result of calls for greater efficiency. However, developing systems that work continues to be a challenge, and this seems to be particularly true for detecting undesirable or non-compliant behaviour. When CQC developed its new approach under the HSCA 2008, the targeted use of inspections was the established way of detecting non-compliance. Indeed, when it was introduced by CSCI in 2006/07 the number of inspections fell by 44 per cent and continued to fall thereafter, as Table 7.5 shows. However, recent scandals across health and social care, in which critics, and sometimes the public, held CQC accountable for not stopping abuse (Brindle, 2011; Pitt, 2011; Which?, 2011), appear to have prompted policy makers to re-evaluate the wisdom of limited inspection programmes. Although the risk-based approach itself was only a contributing factor, the scandals have tainted 'light-touch' regulation of the sector and have given regulators 'political licence' to conduct a thorough inspection programme – an idea that would have been politically toxic at CQC's inception (Black and Baldwin, 2010).

However, a more thorough inspection regime requires significant resources. In 2011, CQC requested, and was granted, a 10 per cent budget increase from the DH to support compliance monitoring (House of Commons Health Committee, 2011b). Currently, CQC targets its resources by focusing inspections on areas that appear wanting. Nevertheless, in the long run, resource constraints imposed by the tight fiscal climate, or perceptions of burden associated with the regime and further extensions to CQC's regulatory remit, may influence the sustainability of the inspection programme.

7.9 Limitations to the scope of regulations

The regulations do not apply to all types of long-term care provision. Day centres, meals services, equipment services and a variety of low-level non-personal care services that provide support to people in their own homes are beyond the scope of the regulations (Care Quality Commission, 2010h). Although there is no statutory oversight of these services, where the user is publicly funded (and the LA has purchased the service on their behalf) or where the LA funds the service through a grant, as is often the case with day centres, then there is likely to be some monitoring of quality. First, LAs monitor their contracts, and in some LAs this process can involve inspections and the collection

Table 7.5 *Number of inspections or reviews conducted by CQC in England across ASC providers per year, 2002/03 to 2010/11[a]*

Regulator	NCSC	NCSC	CSCI	CSCI	CSCI	CSCI[b]	CSCI	CQC	CQC[c]
Period	2002–3	2003–4	2004–5	2005–6	2006–7	2007–8	2008–9	2009–10	2010–11
Inspections or reviews completed	41,434	46,768	48,062	47,341	26,676	19,059	15,072	11,477	6,481[d]

Source: Adapted from CSCI, 2009a, and data supplied by the CQC in May 2011.

Notes:

[a] Includes inspections of all care homes and home care providers for adults and prior to 2007 services for children.

[b] Reduction in inspection numbers due to the transfer of inspection of children's services to Ofsted from 1 April 2007.

[c] Change in method from inspections to review in October 2010, although at least 93 per cent of reviews included a site visit over this period.

[d] Figures may not match those reported elsewhere as the method for counting reviews changed.

Regulating the quality and safety of long-term care in England 203

of quality data. Second, the DH requires LAs to collect certain information about the quality of care they fund, primarily for public accountability purposes, in the Adult Social Care Outcomes Framework (ASCOF) (Department of Health, 2011). This does mean, however, that if there are any unregulated services serving only self-funded care recipients, they will not be subject to any kind of oversight, which potentially leaves some self-funders in a more vulnerable position than publicly funded users.

The policy drive to expand consumer-directed care schemes, known as Personal Budgets and Direct Payments, also raises problems for CQC. Where a person makes their own arrangements for nursing or personal care, as is the case with Direct Payments, and the nurse or carer works for them without an agency or employer involved in managing or directing the care provided, the nurse or carer is exempt from registration. Whilst nurses and social workers are required to register with, and are regulated by, professional bodies, there is currently no professional or regulatory body for personal care workers. Although some Direct Payment users and self-funders purchase home care from regulated providers, many purchase care from unregulated care workers and, in the case of Direct Payments' users, the worker is often a relative and in some cases a friend, spouse or partner. There are concerns that the lack of regulation will leave self-funders and Direct Payment users exposed and vulnerable to abuse and, conversely, their employees may be vulnerable to abuse and subject to poor working conditions.

In a significant break with the past, on gaining power in 2010, the new government instructed CQC not to use its powers to regularly inspect and monitor the performance of LAs in their role as commissioners and market enablers, in favour of an approach where LAs self-monitor their progress and are held to account by the public (Department of Health, 2010b). The lack of regulatory oversight of LAs and their commissioning practices concerns people in the industry (United Kingdom Homecare Association, 2006; Laing and Buisson, 2011): this is because, unlike the situation in the NHS, where a complex system of tariffs exists for procedures, social care providers also compete on price. As LAs are the biggest purchasers of long-term care services and exhibit significant buyer power, they appear to be using their buyer power to drive down fees for publicly funded users (Price Waterhouse Coopers, 2011) – in some cases, below the price required to maintain longer-term investment and value (Laing, 2008). There is also evidence of cross-subsidization from self-funders to publicly funded residents and requests for top-up fees from third parties for publicly funded residents are common in care homes (Laing and Buisson, 2010). As LAs seek to reduce costs further in the coming years in the face of very significant cuts to their grants from central government, there are concerns about how this will affect the quality of provision, the availability of places for publicly funded clients and the stability of the market, particularly amongst those providers with high proportions of publicly funded clients (Hancock and Hviid, 2010; Price Waterhouse Coopers, 2010).

The possibility of large-scale provider failure is a concern since, currently, no organization has proper oversight of the financial viability of providers, and there are no formal arrangements to ensure continuity of provision for essential services. There is a standard relating to the financial position of providers, but checks at registration are limited and do not involve financial risk assessments. In addition, this financial standard is not one of the core standards and so it is not routinely monitored. The legal requirement for providers to notify CQC within six months if they cease to be financially viable, or will close, is insufficient to ensure an orderly market exit and minimal service disruption. Historically, closures have been monitored and managed by LAs, but these have usually been small homes with limited impact on the market. The disorderly manner in which the recent insolvency of the UK's largest care home provider was dealt with illustrates that these mechanisms are not adequate to protect residents of large-scale providers. Since large care home providers have a sizeable and increasing market share (the largest four represented 25 per cent in 2010 (Laing and Buisson, 2010)), there is a need to develop a system to address serious provider financial failure (National Audit Office, 2011b).

The system for making complaints also raises questions. Complaints are currently resolved and investigated locally, which means that the onus is on providers to conduct thorough investigations and to give adequate information to service users to ensure that they know to whom they should complain. CQC requires providers to create an environment in which users are supported and empowered to complain and conduct thorough investigations, although evidence is contradictory as to whether such an environment is achieved. The focus on local resolution, combined with a lack of regulatory input into investigations of complaints, means that no one seems to consider a provider's capacity to investigate complaints and the circumstances under which it may be inappropriate for the

Regulating the quality and safety of long-term care in England   205

provider to be the first port of call for complainants. For example, where providers have not been open in the past about deficiencies, questions may need to be raised about the honesty of the provider and its ability to investigate complaints. There are also likely to be circumstances where the seriousness of the complaint means that the well-being of service users is at risk, or the anonymity of the complainant is important. In these circumstances, an organization other than the provider may be better placed to conduct investigations.

7.10 Future prospects and challenges

The biggest challenge facing regulation of the sector is the current political and economic climate. The fiscal situation demands a risk-based approach to ensure resources are used in a targeted and effective manner. However, the paucity of data means that there is a need for investment in new (ideally individual-level) data collections to ensure resources are targeted at the right organizations. The recent scandals have also exposed the vulnerability of a targeted use of inspections to criticism, particularly where the regulator lacks solid evidence demonstrating the effectiveness of its methods for predicting the risk of non-compliance events guiding its inspections. Although there is now an appetite for a more comprehensive inspection regime, as public spending cuts continue, given past experience, this regime may need to change. Therefore, it seems important for CQC to improve its ability to predict non-compliance events in ASC, by improving routine data collections and testing its risk model.

Historically, the regulator has been a source of information about the quality of providers and has supported consumers to make choices about their care through its online directory. The current lack of quality information in the online care directory is a challenge for many in the industry. It will be interesting to see whether the 'Trip Advisor' style information from service users on the new websites, combined with CQC's compliance ratings, is able to effectively replace and improve upon the quality ratings.

We have identified several areas where the scope of the regulations is limited and we would expect that these will need to be addressed. The lack of involvement of a regulator in the investigation of complaints may need to be revisited to ensure complaints are properly and appropriately investigated. The continued expansion of the Direct Payments and Personal Budgets programmes seems likely to mean that the amount of unregulated care that is purchased will increase, as people choose to purchase care from whomever they wish. Voices calling for regulation of care workers providing personal care seem likely to become louder and the government will need to respond in a way that is sensitive to the potential for care to be provided by family and relatives and does not affect affordability.

We have been unable to appraise several aspects of the current regulatory approach as it is so new. An important question is whether the emphasis on inspector's discretion, combined with the broadly specified standards, is a source of inconsistency in judgements that could make the chance of successful appeal more likely. Another question is whether a 'one size fits all' regulator for health and social care will prove to be an effective model, or whether the lack of staff and system specialization will need to change to ensure the regulatory approach is sufficiently sensitive to differences between sectors and organizations. There are already suggestions that differences in the availability of data between acute healthcare and ASC have made it more difficult to implement continuous assessment. As the regulatory approach beds in, further areas may emerge.

Acknowledgements

We would like to thank the staff in the Intelligence, Regulatory Development, and Strategic Marketing and Communications divisions of the Care Quality Commission, who provided information and comments; Ann Netten, for her advice and comments; and the editors for their comments, which greatly improved this chapter.

Note: this chapter describes the regulatory framework in place in 2012.

References

Adil, M. (2008). Risk-based regulatory system and its effective use in health and social care. *The Journal of the Royal Society for the Promotion of Health*, 128(4): 196–201.

Bardsley, M., Spiegelhalter, D. J., Blunt, I., Chitnis, X., Roberts, A. and Bharania, S. (2009). Using routine intelligence to target inspection of healthcare providers in England. *Quality and Safety in Healthcare*, 18(3): 189–94.

Barnes, J. (2003). *Inspecting with Lay Assessors: What Value? What Impact?*. London: National Care Standards Commission.

Better Regulation Task Force (2003). *Principles of Good Regulation*. London: Better Regulation Task Force.

Black, J. and Baldwin, R. (2010). Really responsive risk-based regulation. *Law and Policy*, 32(2): 181–214.

Braithwaite, J. (2002). Rewards and regulation. *Journal of Law and Society*, 29(1): 12–26.

Brindle, D. (2011). Regulator to review care system after Winterbourne View abuse scandal. *The Guardian*, 7 June 2011.

Care Quality Commission (2010a). *The Adult Social Care Market and the Quality of Services: Technical Report*. London: CQC.

(2010b). *Analysis of Consultation on Assessments of Quality in 2010/11. Feedback Report*. London: CQC.

(2010c). *Focused on Better Care: Annual Report and Accounts 2009/10*. London: CQC.

(2010d). *Guidance about Compliance: Essential Standards of Quality and Safety*. London: CQC.

(2010e). *A New System of Registration: How to Register under the Health and Social Care Act 2008. Guidance for New Providers*. London: CQC.

(2010f). *A New System of Registration: How We Use Conditions of Registration for New Providers. Guidance for Providers*. London: CQC.

(2010g). *A New System of Registration: Provider Compliance Assessment: Guidance for Providers*. London: CQC.

(2010h). *A New System of Registration: The Scope of Registration*. London: CQC.

(2010i). *A New System of Registration: Using Evidence of Outcomes to Demonstrate Compliance: Guidance for Providers*. London: CQC.

(2010j). *Our Enforcement Policy*. London: CQC.

(2011a). *A New System of Registration: Regulatory Fees for 2011/12. Guidance for Service Providers*. London: CQC.

(2011b). *The State of Healthcare and Adult Social Care in England: An Overview of Key Themes in Care in 2010/11*. London: CQC.

(2012). *Guidance about Compliance: Judgement Framework and Determining our Regulatory Response*. London: CQC.

Comas-Herrera, A., Wittenberg, R. and Pickard, L. (2010). The long road to universalism? Recent developments in the financing of long-term care in England. *Social Policy and Administration*, 44(4): 375–91.

Commission for Social Care Inspection (CSCI) (2009a). *Annual Report and Accounts 2008–09*. London: TSO.

(2009b). *CSCI Quality Ratings Market Research Report*. London: CSCI.

Cutler, T. and Waine, B. (2003). Advancing public accountability? The social services 'star' ratings. *Public Money and Management*, 23(2): 125–8.

Darton, R. (2011). *Study of care home residents' and relatives' expectations and experiences*. Kent: PSSRU, University of Kent and the Registered Nursing Home Association.

Day, P. and Klein, R. (1987). The regulation of nursing homes: a comparative perspective. *The Milbank Quarterly*, 65(3): 303–47.

Department of Health (2009). *The National Framework for NHS Continuing Healthcare and NHS-Funded Nursing Care*. London: DH.

  (2010a). *Liberating the NHS: Report of the Arm's-Length Bodies Review*. London: DH.

  (2010b). *A Vision for Adult Social Care: Capable Communities and Active Citizens*. London: DH.

  (2011). *Transparency in Outcomes: a Framework for Quality in Adult Social Care. The 2011/12 Adult Social Care Outcomes Framework*. London: DH.

Dunning, J. (2011). Adult care providers face less scrutiny, warns ADASS. *Community Care*, 14 February 2011. Available at: http://www.communitycare.co.uk/Articles/14/02/2011/116284/adult-care-providers-face-less-scrutiny-warns-adass.htm.

Hancock, R. and Hviid., M. (2010). Buyer power and price discrimination: the case of the UK care homes market. *CCP Working Paper 10–17*. Norwich: University of East Anglia.

Hood, C., Scott, C., James, O., Jones, G. and Travers, T. (1999). *Regulation inside Government: Waste-Watchers, Quality Police, Sleaze-Busters*. Oxford University Press.

House of Commons Health Committee (2011a). *Annual Accountability Hearing with the Care Quality Commission. Ninth Report of Session 2010–12. HC 1430*. London: TSO.

  (2011b). *Regulatory Bodies: Oral Evidence. Dame Jo Williams DBE and Amanda Sherlock. HC 1203-ii*. London: TSO.

Humphrey, J. (2003). New Labour and the regulatory reform of social care. *Critical Social Policy*, 23(1): 5–24.

Klein, B. (1997). Quality management and quality assurance in Britain and Germany. In A. Evers, R. Haverinen, K. Leichsenring and G. Wistow (eds.), *Developing Quality in Personal Social Services: Concepts, Cases and Comments*. Aldershot: Ashgate, pp. 139–54.

Laing and Buisson (2010). *Care of Elderly People UK Market Survey 2010–2011*. London: Laing and Buisson.

  (2011). After the year that CQC has had, how do you see its future role in the sector? *Community Care Market News*, 17(8): 284–5.

Laing, W. (2008). *Calculating a Fair Market Price for Care. A Toolkit for Residential and Nursing Homes*. York: Joseph Rowntree Foundation.

LGO (2010). *The LGO's New Role in the Independent Care Sector*. Coventry: LGO.

National Audit Office (2011a). *The Care Quality Commission: Regulating the Quality and Safety of Health and Adult Social Care. Report by the Comptroller and Auditor General*. HC 1665 Session 2010–2012. London: TCO.

(2011b). *Oversight of User Choice and Provider Competition in Care Markets*. HC 1458 Session 2010–2012. London: TSO.

Netten, A., Beadle-Brown, J., Trukeschitz, B., Towers, A.-M., Welch, E., Forder, J., Smith, J. and Alden, E. (2010). *Measuring the Outcomes of Care Homes: Final Report*. PSSRU Discussion paper 2696/2. Canterbury: PSSRU.

Office for National Statistics (2007). *2006-based Principal Population Projections, England*. London: ONS.

(2011). *2010 Mid Year Population Estimates*. London: ONS.

Office of Fair Trading (2011). *Evaluating the Impact of the 2005 OFT Study into Care Homes for Older People*. London: Office of Fair Trading.

Peace, S. (2003). The development of residential and nursing home care in the UK. In J. Katz and S. Peace (eds.), *End of Life in Care Homes: A Palliative Approach*. Oxford: Open University Press, pp. 15–42.

Pitt, V. (2010a). Anger over CQC decision to end star ratings. *Community Care*, 21 May 2010. Available at: www.community-care.co.uk/Articles/21/05/2010/114557/anger-over-cqc-decision-to-end-star-ratings.htm.

(2010b). Star ratings end for English care providers. *Community Care*, 19 May 2010. Available at: www.communitycare.co.uk/Articles/19/05/2010/114524/Star-ratings-end-for-English-care-providers.htm.

(2011). Four arrested after panorama exposes disability abuse. *Community Care*, 1 June 2011. Available at: www.communitycare.co.uk/Articles/01/06/2011/116918/four-arrested-after-panorama-exposes-disability-abuse.htm.

Price Waterhouse Coopers (2010). *Fair Care Crisis? An Independent Survey of Social Care Providers for the Elderly*. London: PWC.

(2011). *Understanding Commissioning Behaviours. Commissioning and Competition in the Public Sector*. London: Office of Fair Trading.

Simmill-Binning, C., Clough, R. and Paylor, I. (2007). The use of lay assessors. *British Journal of Social Work*, 37: 1353–70.

Spiegelhalter, D. J., Sherlaw-Johnson, C., Bardsley, M., Blunt, I., Wood, C. and Grigg, O. (2012). Statistical methods for healthcare regulation:

Rating, screening and surveillance. *Journal of the Royal Statistical Society A*, 175(1): 1–25.

The Health and Social Care Information Centre (2011). *Community care Statistics 2009–10: Social Services Activity Report, England*. Leeds: The Health and Social Care Information Centre.

United Kingdom Homecare Association (2006). *A Fair Price for Care. A UKHCA Position Statement. Maintaining the Capacity of the Independent Homecare Sector*. London: UKHCA Ltd.

Which? (2011). Care homes investigated. London: *Which?* 19 April 2011. Available at: www.which.co.uk/news/2011/04/care-home-failings-exposed-by-which-investigation-250910/.

Wittenberg, R., Hu, B., Hancock, R., Morciano, M., Comas-Herrera, A., Malley, J. and King, D. (2011). *Projections of Demand for and Costs of Social Care for Older People in England, 2010 to 2030, under Current and Alternative Funding Systems. Report of Research for the Commission on Funding of Care and Support*. PSSRU Discussion Paper 2811/2. London: PSSRU, London School of Economics and Political Science.

Wright, F. (2005). Lay assessors and care home inspections: is there a future? *British Journal of Social Work*, 35: 1093–1106.

8 Quality monitoring of long-term care for older people in The Netherlands

JOS M. G. A. SCHOLS, DINNUS H. M. FRIJTERS,
RUUD G. I. J. M. KEMPEN AND
JAN P. H. HAMERS

8.1 Introduction

In this chapter we describe the regulatory structure and the monitoring of quality of long-term care in The Netherlands. Firstly an introduction to long-term care for older people is provided, together with some basic information on the position of the long-term care sector within the overall healthcare system, including its capacity, some basic service user characteristics, the services offered and the way the long-term care sector is financed and regulated. In addition, we highlight selected policy and political issues that have emerged over the last decade which have challenged the traditional approach to judging the quality of services. Secondly, we outline the most relevant legislation and regulations related to the rights of long-term care clients as well as those related to the long-term care sector itself, finishing with the most relevant regulatory measures on the quality of care. This is followed by a section on integral quality systems fulfilling ISO 9001 criteria (an internationally accepted standard for quality management systems and certification). Special attention is given to the Dutch Healthcare Inspectorate and its role in the external monitoring of quality of care and to the use of nationally established quality indicators for long-term care. Finally, we focus on the issue of transparency and how the performance of long-term care organizations is communicated to society in general (including service users themselves and insurance companies) through public reporting. In this context, the increasing strength of the role of service users will be addressed. Although this chapter focuses on long-term care for older people, the information provided generally holds for long-term care for young people and for people with chronic somatic, mental or psychiatric diseases as well as for people with mental health disabilities who need chronic care.

8.2 Long-term care for older people

As in many other western countries, the demography of The Netherlands shows an increasing number of older people. Currently, about 16 per cent of the population is 65 years or older, but it is by no means the 'oldest' country in the European Union. In the United Kingdom 16 per cent of the population are aged 65 or over while in Spain this percentage is 17 per cent, in Sweden 18 per cent, in Greece 19 per cent, in Germany 20 per cent and in Italy 21 per cent. In Japan the percentage of people over 65 is 23 per cent, while in the USA it is only 13 per cent (OECD, 2011). In the next twenty years these rates will rise considerably in all countries and will also be associated with a growing number of frail and disabled older persons in need of care.

Table 8.1 presents the most important healthcare, social and housing services that are available for older people in The Netherlands. To set the context, more than 80 per cent of the population aged 65 or over (in 2009) visited a general physician (GP) yearly, with an average of 15 GP-contacts per year; approximately 23 per cent of this population group underwent acute hospital admissions (compared with 6 per cent of the general population), after which most were discharged back home (National Kompas website). General hospitals have no long-stay wards available for older patients with chronic somatic and psychogeriatric diseases or with complex disabilities. Geriatric wards are present today in eighty out of ninety-three general and academic hospitals; they are the province of internal medicine and are mainly meant for short-term, acute geriatric care. Psychiatric hospitals only serve older patients when they display psychiatric or disruptive behaviour. Rehabilitation clinics primarily focus on the rehabilitation of younger patients and older patients are admitted to these clinics only for short and intensive rehabilitation.

Three laws assure that everyone in The Netherlands is insured on a compulsory basis for medical expenses and the basic costs of illness and disabilities – the Health Insurance Act (Zorgverzekeringswet, ZVW), the Exceptional Medical Expenses Act (Algemene Wet Bijzondere Ziektekosten, AWBZ) and the Social Support Act (Wet Maatschappelijke Ondersteuning, WMO). Together they form the legal basis for the health system. Long-term care for older people has undergone dramatic changes since 1968, when a system of public

Quality monitoring of long-term care in The Netherlands 213

Table 8.1 *Healthcare, social services, and housing for older people in The Netherlands*

Domiciliary services	Institutional services
Healthcare	University hospitals
Family physicians (GPs)	General hospitals
Physiotherapists	Psychiatric hospitals
Occupational therapists	Rehabilitation clinics
Speech therapists	Residential homes (old people's
Dentists	homes)
Home care (district nursing and home help)	Nursing homes
Community mental healthcare	
Social and welfare services	
Social work	
Meals on wheels	
Alarm systems	
Sitting services	
Keep-fit exercises	
Social meeting points	
Housing	
Regular housing	
Regular housing with adaptations	
Service flats	

Source: Compiled by authors.

long-term care insurance was introduced. This insurance, based on the AWBZ, covers care not only for older people, but for all individuals with extensive chronic medical and nursing care needs. The AWBZ is funded by social security premiums, taxes and co-payments (Schäfer et al., 2010). This legislation also covers home care and institutional care for older people as well as institutional care for mentally and physically disabled people and for chronic psychiatric patients. The AWBZ covers a broad package of services: personal care, nursing assistance, treatment and stay in an institution. Formal domestic household help used to be part of the AWBZ but in 2007 it was moved to the Social Support Act (WMO), legislation relating to social services and implemented by local councils (municipalities).

The AWBZ scheme involves public insurance, meaning that everyone who is eligible for long-term care, in principle, is entitled to receive care. However, in practice, every new Dutch government establishes budgets for healthcare and long-term care for the four-year period it is in office, which may partly alter the eligibility levels and/or available services. The tax-financed WMO is not an insurance scheme; therefore, the entitlement to social services is dependent on available funds. For domestic household help, in particular, local councils receive a (non-earmarked) budget. In this way municipalities have financial incentives to organize domestic household help efficiently. To protect the rights of people with disabilities, municipalities are obliged to provide all necessary support but they have the flexibility to do this in a manner that they deem to be suitable, as long as they ensure that the end users of services can participate in society. This obligation on local authorities seems to work reasonably well for people with limitations in running a household, especially older people (van Houten et al., 2008).

A request for any type of AWBZ care must be assessed by an independent organization, the CIZ (Centrum Indicatiestelling Zorg/Centre for Care Assessment), which carries out independent, objective and integral assessments to determine eligibility to receive in-kind care and cash benefits. Assessment for household help (WMO) is carried out by the local council. For most of the AWBZ functions, a potential AWBZ user can choose between in-kind care and cash benefits. The cash-reimbursement option is not available for treatment and stays in institutions. Rather, cash reimbursement is given in the form of personal budgets enabling patients to buy care themselves. They are free to choose their caregiver: a care organization, an independent care worker, or a family member, friend, neighbour, etc. For most of the budget, patients are obliged to show that the money was actually spent on care. Patients who prefer in-kind care have some influence with regard to which care organization delivers their services. The responsibility for organizing and purchasing this care remains with regional care offices, called *Zorgkantoren*, which contract with different long-term care providers. Clients can then choose between these contracted providers.

The government bears overall responsibility for the long-term care system. Public care providers must comply with a large number of rules, regulations and guidelines. Providers that deliver care funded by the AWBZ are monitored by an independent supervisory board. The Dutch Healthcare Inspectorate (Inspectievoor de Gezondheidszorg, IGZ)

Quality monitoring of long-term care in The Netherlands 215

supervises not only the quality of care which is regulated by law but also compliance with most governance requirements. Legislation states that the primary responsibility for assuring the quality of care rests with the providers themselves. The Dutch Health Authority (Nederlandse-Zorgautoriteit, NZa), under the Ministry of Health, Welfare and Sport, has a special role as a supervisor and market regulator in health and long-term care. As home-based nursing care is partly deregulated, the NZa monitors competition and determines maximum tariffs. Institutional care is still relatively heavily regulated: the NZa determines tariffs for institutional care, determines the description of the care that should be delivered in order to earn the tariff and monitors whether providers comply with these rules.

Total expenditure for long-term care covered by the AWBZ was €23 billion in 2009, and more than doubled between 1998 and 2009 (an increase of 104 per cent). If WMO expenditure is included, the increase over this period is even greater (121 per cent) (Statistics Netherlands, 2011). As mentioned above, the AWBZ deals with more than care for older people: in 2009 €6 billion was spent on mental healthcare and over €5 billion on care for the mentally and physically disabled. Moreover, over €12 billion was spent on nursing and care for older people, of which about €3 billion covers care outside of institutions. Per capita long-term care expenditure for people aged 65 or over increased from €3,621 in 1998 to €6,262 in 2009. The expected further growth of expenditures for long-term care is a source of great concern.

8.2.1 Available services

In The Netherlands, long-term care services for older people can be classified into three groups: informal care, formal care at home and formal institutional care. Although *informal care* for older people is not as relevant in The Netherlands as in southern and central European countries, it still plays a considerable role. In 2007 there were a total of 3.5 million informal caregivers for all people in need of care, representing nearly a quarter of the total population of about 16 million. About 1.7 million of these 3.5 million people provided help and support during relatively long and intensive periods (de Boer et al., 2009). There are no benefits for informal caregivers but they can receive a payment from an individual's personal budget (see above), which can be used to purchase professional care as well as informal care. As already mentioned, under the WMO municipalities are responsible for supporting informal care-givers (e.g., by providing information and advice) and they do so either directly or indirectly by funding organizations to carry out these tasks. Furthermore, care to relieve the burden of informal caregivers can be funded from the AWBZ (e.g., day care and night care).

Formal care at home (home care) is covered by the AWBZ, except for domestic help and social services, which have been covered by the WMO since 2007. The services available at home covered by the AWBZ include: assistance, personal care, nursing care and treatment. The WMO covers home help, meals on wheels, home adjustments and transport. According to the Ministry of Health, at the end of 2007, some 227,000 older clients received AWBZ care at home (representing 9.4 per cent of the 2.4 million older people in The Netherlands). This involved care for clients aged 65 or over, suffering from a variety of physical or cognitive problems, but who are able to stay in their own homes if adequate informal and formal care were arranged for them. The number of older (those aged 65 or over) users of household help at that time is not known (OECD, 2011).

In The Netherlands, institutional care plays a relatively large role compared to other countries. Prior to 2009, there were two main categories of institutional care – nursing home care offered in nursing homes and residential care offered in residential homes (previously also called 'old people's homes' or 'homes for the elderly'); both were covered by a fixed day-price. Since 2009, ten separate products can be distinguished within institutional care for older people and the chroni-cally ill, and they are referred to as 'severity-of-care packages' (ZZPs; *zorgzwaartepakketten*). Each of these packages represents a combina-tion of different AWBZ care functions. For long-term care for older people, these care packages (ZZPs) range from 'sheltered living with some assistance' (ZZP1) to 'sheltered living with very intensive care due to specific disorders, with an emphasis on care and nursing' (ZZP8) and 'rehabilitation' (ZZP9) and 'palliative care' (ZZP10). Care pack-ages ZZP1 to ZZP4 are mainly offered in all residential homes while care packages ZZP5 to ZZP10 are available in all nursing homes. In daily practice, the original distinction between nursing homes and residential homes therefore still continues. For institutional care, certain hotel services (accommodation, food, cleaning, etc.) are included under AWBZ coverage. However, residents have to make an income-dependent contribution. This co-payment can be considered as a way for older people with sufficient income to pay for their board and lodging.

At the end of 2007, 164,000 older clients (6.8 per cent of the population aged 65 or over)[1] used institutional care, offered in residential homes (100,000 people) and nursing homes (64,000 people) (OECD, 2011). There are about 1,000 *residential homes* in The Netherlands with a total capacity of 100,000 beds. These residential facilities were originally developed following the desire of many older people to leave their own homes for a safer living environment, including having more social contacts with other older people and a basic guarantee to receive nursing care if needed. Older people in residential homes (whose mean age is 84) mostly come directly from their own homes and often have some cognitive deficits or physical disabilities, but they are still able to undertake some of their activities of daily living (ADLs), unlike nursing home residents, who often are more disabled and need a lot of help with regard to their ADLs. Those living in residential homes have a small apartment, with an alarm system, and meals are served either at their apartment or in the home's restaurant. Residents receive some basic nursing and social assistance, and most residential homes also offer a daily recreational programme. As in long-term care in the community, a GP is responsible for providing medical care to residents (Schols et al., 2004).

There are 350 *nursing homes* in the country with more than 64,000 beds (27,000 for patients with mainly somatic, i.e., physical, problems and 37,000 in psychogeriatric wards for patients with mainly cognitive problems, e.g., dementia). Older people who need more complex continuous care and monitoring, which are beyond the range of home care services or the service in residential homes, are often admitted to a nursing home. Every year, 40,000 new somatic patients and 20,000 new psychogeriatric patients are admitted. Most somatic patients (65 per cent) are admitted from hospital and suffer from a stroke, fractures, other locomotor disorders or diseases of the central nervous system (e.g., Parkinson's disease). Most psychogeriatric residents suffering from all types of dementia (53 per cent) are admitted from their own homes (Schols et al., 2004).

---

[1] The total number of people aged 65 and over is approximately 2.5 million.

The development of nursing homes has been influenced by demographic changes in the population and concerns over healthcare costs. In particular, they arose in response to the need to reduce hospital long-term stays, which had become increasingly prevalent among older patients. This led in 1968 to the legal designation of the nursing home as a distinct care facility with its own financing framework in the public domain. Since then, the nursing home has evolved from a place to discharge patients from hospital, for chronic nursing care, to a facility where nursing is integrated with paramedical and medical care and patients are reactivated to their optimal level of functioning. Initially, GPs supported nursing staff in nursing homes on demand, meaning that they only visited the nursing home when they were asked to do so. Today, the 'elderly care physician' (previously known as the 'nursing home physician') is an officially recognized medical discipline, and in addition to physicians and nurses, the nursing home team consists of physiotherapists, occupational therapists, speech therapists, dieticians, psychologists, social workers, pastoral workers and recreational therapists. So, unlike most other developed countries, Dutch nursing homes employ not only nursing staff, but also their own medical, paramedical and psychosocial staff. This allows for the provision of the multidisciplinary, continuous long-term care that most patients require (Schols et al., 2004).

Nowadays, a trend towards scaling down large (hospital-like) nursing homes is taking place with the construction of new, small-scale living facilities and smaller care homes, both of which are mostly part of a large long-term care organization. These new facilities are mainly for residents with dementia and other residents in need of definite, continuing institutional care, to offer them a more homelike living environment, with more personal and independent space. Care is still offered by multidisciplinary teams employed by the long-term care organization, as described above (Verbeek et al., 2009; Schols et al., 2004).

8.2.2 Current issues in long-term care

Over the last decade, some policy and political issues have emerged in long-term care that challenge the traditional approach to judging quality. There is a growing trend to give patients a much more important role in healthcare. Related to this, the development of care services are increasingly moving away from a supply-based approach to a demand-based approach. In this respect, patient experiences have become more important in the overall assessment of the quality of care. Clients are becoming more demanding about the services they require and want to choose between various healthcare options. The relevance of this development is emphasized further by another trend that is becoming more visible – the introduction of competition and other market elements in long-term care and welfare services for elderly clients. The Dutch government has introduced competition in order to stimulate efficiency as well as quality of care and to stimulate demand-based care. Increased attention on taking into account patients' and long-term care users' perspectives also involves a growing focus on the phenomenon of empowering patients. The latter is also important in view of ever-increasing healthcare costs, which, in a country with rising numbers of older people, are a growing concern. The current government wants to introduce more personal responsibility regarding individuals' own healthcare and undoubtedly, in the future, citizens' financial contribution to their healthcare costs will be larger than it is today. In line with this, citizens will place higher demands on the performance and quality of long-term care services. Finally, with regard to developments in the assessment of long-term care quality, over the last decade, several negative incidents of poor quality care or abuse that received considerable media exposure have resulted in a much more active control of the long-term care system by the Dutch Healthcare Inspectorate as well as a broad range of standards for better care, which must be respected (IGZ website).

8.3 Legislation and regulations in the long-term care sector

The laws and regulations related to long-term care are incorporated in various policy papers, guidelines and policy directives. The board of directors of a health or long-term care organization (home care or institutional care) is responsible for the implementation of legal requirements and related policies. Table 8.2 summarizes the remits of the most relevant legislation related to: healthcare organizations (including long-term care organizations), the provision of care, the rights of service users and the accreditation and registration of healthcare professionals. This legislation applies to all long-term care providers, irrespective of whether they provide residential services or home care (Boot, 2010).

Table 8.2 *Health and long-term care legislation in The Netherlands*

Laws regulating the financing of healthcare	*The Health Insurance Act (Zorgverzekeringswet, ZVW), 2006* Everyone in The Netherlands must have basic health insurance. The Health Insurance Act establishes what is included in the basic benefits package and these services must be provided uniformly in the basic benefits package of each health insurer. To cover services/treatments not included in the package (e.g., some dental treatments or plastic surgery) voluntary supplementary insurance can be purchased. For the basic package citizens have to pay an obligatory 'own risk' premium, with an allowance for people on low incomes. Part of the premium is refunded by the tax system. The costs covered under the Health Insurance Act deal with short-term care focused on curing episodes of illness. *The Exceptional Medical Expenses Act (Algemene Wet Bijzondere Ziektekosten, AWBZ), 1968* The Exceptional Medical Expenses Act is compulsory insurance for medical expenses that are not covered by the Health Insurance Act. These include prolonged hospitalization, long-term care for disabled people and long-term rehabilitation or nursing and care of older people in a nursing home or residential home. Care under AWBZ can be obtained in two forms: in-kind or through a personal budget (Persoonsgebonden budget, PGB), where clients directly buy whatever care they require. Health insurers implement the AWBZ from special care offices. Each region has its own care office (Zorgkantoor) whose mission is to implement the requirements of the AWBZ in a customer-focused, efficient, uniform and competition-free way through regionally contracted providers. Care and support must be of high quality. A Zorgkantoor has very close relationships with care providers and patient/client organizations in its region. *The Social Support Act (Wet Maatschappelijke Ondersteuning, WMO), 2007* The Social Support Act reimburses services for people with disabilities. Its purpose is to ensure that all citizens are able to (continue to) participate in society even if they have conditions and impairments that make this difficult. Part of this goal is that everyone has the possibility to continue living independently as long as possible. This aim may imply the involvement of support from family members, neighbours or friends and volunteers. The WMO is implemented by the municipalities. People with disabilities can apply to the municipalities for aids such as wheelchairs, and also for home adjustments or for support such as housecleaning (household help). The WMO also arranges support for volunteers or volunteers' organizations.

Laws related to long-term care – general	*The Care Institutions Accreditation Act (Wet Toelating Zorginstellingen, WTZi), 2005*
Healthcare institutions (including long-term care organizations) need permission and authorization from the Ministry of Health, Welfare and Sport if they want to offer care under the Health Insurance Act (ZVW) or the Exceptional Medical Expenses Act (AWBZ). The Care Institutions Accreditation Act regulates these authorizations, lays down rules on good governance and determines when and what profits may be distributed.

The Medical Treatment Agreement Act (Wet op de Geneeskundige Behandelingsovereenkomst, WGBO), 1994

The Medical Treatment Agreement Act is the main legislation covering patients' rights. It regulates agreements between caregivers and patients for the performance of various medical procedures in all healthcare sectors, including long-term care. Patients' rights under the WGBO consist of the right to information; consent to treatment; confidentiality; privacy while undergoing treatment; and access to one's own patient file or record.

The Psychiatric Compulsory Admissions Act (Wet Bijzondere Opnemingen in Psychiatrische Ziekenhuizen, BOPZ), 1994

The Psychiatric Compulsory Admissions Act regulates the involuntary admission of people with a mental health disorder to psychiatric hospitals, institutions for people with mental health disabilities and psychogeriatric nursing homes. The BOPZ also regulates the legal position of patients once they have been involuntarily admitted. This includes, for instance, rules for (compulsory) treatment and use of restraints. With the introduction of the BOPZ, patients can only be admitted freely, if they show signs of willingness to be admitted (willingness criterion). In all other cases, admission can only take place with 'detention' (In BewaringStelling, IBS) or Judicial Authorization (RechterlijkeMachtiging, RM).

The Healthcare Clients Complaint(s) Act (Wet Klachtrecht Cliënten Zorgsector,WKCZ), 1995

The purpose of the Healthcare Clients Complaint(s) Act is to provide an accessible complaint option and to use these complaints to improve the quality of healthcare. Each client receiving care (including long-term care clients) has the right to complain about the healthcare he or she receives. The care provider must have a complaints procedure and a complaints committee. When the complaint is very serious and the care provider's response is inadequate, the complaints committee has a duty to report it to the Healthcare Inspectorate (IGZ).

Table 8.2 (*cont.*)

	The Participation of Clients in Healthcare Organizations Act (Wet Medezeggenschap Cliënten Zorginstellingen, WMCZ), 1996 The Participation of Clients in Healthcare Organizations Act obliges healthcare organizations (including long-term care organizations) to set up a client council that represents the common interests of their service users/clients. The council provides solicited and unsolicited recommendations to the organization on matters that are important to clients and in cases of important (policy) decisions, the organizations must first ask the advice of the client council.
	The Data Protection Act (Wet Bescherming Persoonsgegevens, WBP), 2001 The Data Protection Act applies to all organizations that collect and process information about people. The law regulates various forms of dealing with personal data such as collection, storage, comparing, linking and providing personal data to third parties.
Laws related to quality of care	*The Quality of Care Act (for Healthcare Organizations) (Kwaliteitswet Zorginstellingen, KWZ), 1996* The Quality of Care Act (for Healthcare Organizations) requires all healthcare providers to adhere to standards regarding the quality of care they offer. Care has to be patient centred and of sound quality, effective in its outcome and cost-effective. Therefore, this legislation forces healthcare organizations to implement a dynamic quality control system and to write an annual report on the status of its quality of care.
	The Healthcare Professionals Act (Wet op de Beroepen in de Individuele Gezondheidszorg, BIG), 1993 The Healthcare Professionals Act aims to promote quality of care and to protect patients against incompetent or careless treatment by caregivers. Only professionals with an approved education are enrolled in a special register. Their titles (e.g., doctor, pharmacist) are protected. Moreover, only qualified professionals may carry out certain medical activities. Compulsory registration in the BIG register covers pharmacists, doctors, physiotherapists, health psychologists, psychotherapists, dentists, midwives and nurses.

Source: Compiled by authors.

8.4 Long-term care quality systems and certification, quality indicators and the role of the Healthcare Inspectorate

8.4.1 *Quality of long-term care*

In this section we provide information about integral quality systems fulfilling the ISO 9001 quality management standard and certification.[2] In addition, we describe the way in which external monitoring of quality of care is performed, with special attention given to the measurement of quality indicators and the role of the Dutch Healthcare Inspectorate (IGZ). The quality of care offered by a long-term care organization is an organized and controlled output and in fact is also an aspect of the organization's performance; the quality of its care reflects how well an organization is able to meet clients' expectations and needs. Table 8.3 outlines the various aspects of an organization's quality of care profile.

Quality improvement includes activities to monitor and improve the quality of the performance of a long-term care organization (both in-patient and out-patient services) and in particular the quality of care it provides. These activities include four categories:

(i) activities focused on the requirement to perform well and to deliver high-quality care, e.g., the availability of all relevant professions and material requirements, training of professionals, efficient procurement procedures, building maintenance, etc.;

(ii) activities aimed at improving the quality of care itself, including the implementation of guidelines, standards and protocols, establishment of an integral 'quality manual' for all employees and the establishment of a complaints procedure for clients;

(iii) activities aimed at the evaluation of care, including satisfaction surveys for clients and employees;

(iv) external assessment in the form of inspection or certification.

The promotion of quality involves a continuous flow of diverse activities. There are many aspects and criteria of quality care related to a large number of processes, both at the level of the professional and at the level of the care organization itself. Quality of care management should follow a 'quality cycle', a cycle of standardizing, assessing and

---

[2] The ISO 9001 is an internationally accepted standard for quality management systems.

Table 8.3 *Main aspects of long-term care organizations' quality of care in The Netherlands*

	General aspects of quality	Relational aspects of quality	Technical aspects of quality
Quality of the long-term care service provider	Effectiveness Efficiency	– transparency and openness to clients – possibilities for client inputs and participation – extent of participation with external parties e.g. networks	– consistency – flexibility – stability
Quality of long-term care professionals	Effectiveness Efficiency	– constructive attitude – general accountability and readiness to provide information – careful and respectful treatment of clients	– expertise – suitability for the job
Quality of the material environment	Effectiveness Efficiency	– usability and user friendliness	– safety
Quality of care	Effectiveness Efficiency Integrated care	– availability – client focus	– customized, tailor-made care

Source: NRV, 1990.

Quality monitoring of long-term care in The Netherlands 225

improving (NRV, 1990; Boot, 2010). Moreover, quality improvement requires the involvement of all employees in long-term care organizations. In daily practice many long-term care organizations have a quality manager who supports, coaches and targets all quality improvement activities. Under the Quality of Care Act (for Healthcare Organizations) (KWZ) (see Table 8.2) all long-term care organizations must have a quality management system that acts as a tool for management to control processes, an organization's performance and its quality of care in a systematic way (Boot, 2010).

In addition, requirements set out by the country's healthcare insurers ensure that long-term care organizations must have their quality management systems certified by an external certification organization. One of the largest is the Foundation for the Harmonization of Quality in the Healthcare Sector (Harmonisatie Kwaliteitsbeoordeling in de Zorgsector, HKZ), founded in 1994. HKZ was established by patient/consumer associations, care providers and care insurers, who agreed on the organization's remit during a Conference in Leidschendam in 1990 (Schellekens et al., 2001).[3] HKZ's goal is the harmonization of quality of care and welfare, by aiming to assess quality in various sectors in the same way. Together with stakeholders, HKZ has developed quality standards (certification schemes) that are available across various sectors, including the long-term care sector. These standards cover the aspects outlined in Table 8.3.

The certification audit of a long-term care provider's quality management system is always performed by a lead auditor and a technical expert from an external certification body who know the long-term care sector and its disciplines well. This ensures that the audit is performed properly and takes into account the situation of an organization's professionals. Depending on the complexity and size of the organization, audits last between one and three days. The quality certification audit, which applies to all healthcare organizations, has two separate aspects.

First, it examines what has been agreed internally about the implementation of care and services (e.g., through available and easily accessible work instructions, guidelines and procedures) and it explores the

---

[3] The Leidschendam conferences have been held regularly since 1990. At these annual conferences healthcare providers, clients and insurers in The Netherlands enter into agreements about quality assurance standards and procedures.

organization's plan for staff education and training activities. Second, the audit explores what actually occurs in practice, covering agreed service provision (e.g., how care tailored to residents' needs is implemented) and planned staff educational activities (e.g., training on how to assess clients' problems in a comprehensive way and how to deliver appropriate care to deal with pressure ulcers and nutrition). The audit also covers to what extent there is regular evaluation in these areas. This is done through a sampling of client records and interviews with executive staff members. If the audit is positive, the long-term care organization receives a certificate and its name is published on one of the many websites that exist for this purpose. After an initial certification, the organization is audited annually by the same external certification body and has to demonstrate that the quality management system in place for all care and service provision systems is maintained and improved. Re-certification takes place every three years. Finally, all healthcare organizations, including long-term care organizations, have to publish an annual report on (the quality of) their care, services and financial performance. This report follows a specific format for both care-related aspects (including aspects shown in Table 8.3) and financial performance.

8.4.2 Monitoring quality of care – the role of the Dutch Healthcare Inspectorate

In addition to the quality certification audits described above, which are obligatory for all long-term care organizations to test the adequacy of their own quality management system, requirements set out by the Ministry of Health (e.g. in laws on care activities and on quality of care) are controlled by regular inspections, performed by the Dutch Healthcare Inspectorate (Inspectie voor de Gezondheidszorg, IGZ), which is an official government body. The Healthcare Inspectorate has the right and duty to inspect all formal healthcare organizations, including long-term care organizations. The Inspectorate promotes public health through effective enforcement of the quality of health services, prevention measures and medical products. It advises the responsible government ministers and applies various measures, including advice, encouragement, pressure and sanctions, to ensure that healthcare providers offer only 'responsible' care. The Inspectorate investigates and assesses the quality of care in healthcare organizations

Quality monitoring of long-term care in The Netherlands

in a conscientious, expert and impartial manner, independent of party politics and is not influenced by current debates.

The Healthcare Inspectorate is part of the Ministry of Health and consists of a main inspectorate and several regional inspectorates, spread across the country. The Inspectorate's work covers all of the Dutch healthcare system and takes place in four domains: general public health, curative healthcare, nursing and chronic care, and drugs and medical technology. As part of its general supervision of the Dutch healthcare system, the Healthcare Inspectorate uses the following methods: (i) phased supervision; (ii) investigation of incidents; (iii) monitoring based on themes; and (iv) enforcement measures.

8.4.2.1 Method 1: phased supervision

Phased supervision is the method by which the Inspectorate ensures efficient and effective enforcement of the legislation for which it is responsible. First, the Inspectorate identifies where the greatest risks to quality of care can be identified. Second, by means of inspection visits, and/or enforcement action, it then prompts care providers to make the necessary improvements. Phased supervision involves three phases:

- Phase 1: identification of risks based on an analysis of the quality information and any additional information about the care provider and its care services, gathered in advance through a pre-structured inspection protocol;
- Phase 2: (protocol driven) inspection visits, assessment and selection of appropriate measures;
- Phase 3: imposition of administrative or disciplinary measures, or instigation of criminal proceedings where appropriate.

In some sectors, such as institutional care, the Inspectorate has considerable experience in this phased supervision approach.

8.4.2.2 The *Zichtbare Zorg* (Visible Care) Programme

Phased supervision, described above, is a refined form of risk-based supervision based on quality indicators as well as other information about healthcare providers and health services. Quality indicators are intended to make the quality of healthcare services measurable and transparent. These indicators were developed by the health and social field itself. In each care sector, the Inspectorate works jointly with healthcare providers, insurers, and representatives of groups of patients, disabled people and older people to produce appropriate indicator sets. Table 8.4 presents an overview of the quality indicators measured in the long-term care sector.

The quality indicator sets, which are available to the public, provide information to support patient choice. They also enable healthcare providers to derive the benefit of a good rating, or stimulate them to improve the quality of their services. Health insurers can use the indicators to substantiate purchasing and contracting. For its part, the Inspectorate uses the indicators to support a system of 'risk-based' supervision, since it is then able to identify areas in which potential risks to quality of care exist. By judging the results on the quality indicators of specific long-term care organizations and comparing them with the overall results of the long-term care sector as a whole, the Inspectorate obtains information about the potential risks related to the quality of care of the specific long-term care organizations being audited and, if necessary, can take disciplinary measures, to force them to improve their performance.

The Minister of Health has requested the Inspectorate to supervise the production of quality indicator sets, resulting in the 'Visible Care' programme. Its website, www.zichtbarezorg.nl, provides information about the care sectors in which quality indicators are already available, and the progress of implementation in other sectors. This information also involves the indicators for long-term care developed in 2007 and which are described below.

In 2007 a steering committee consisting of representatives from provider organizations, insurers, client organizations, the organizations of various healthcare professionals, the Healthcare Inspectorate and the Ministry of Health published a report on what was termed 'appropriate long-term care'. The report, Quality Framework for Responsible Care (Kwaliteitskadervoor Verantwoorde Zorg), covered long-term institutional care (nursing homes and residential homes) and home care (Steering Group on Responsible Care, 2007). Responsible care is not only measured by input and process indicators, but also by care outcome indicators.

There are two categories of indicators (see Table 8.4):

(1) Indicators on the professional content of care (*zorginhoudelijke indicatoren*). Provider organizations are requested to complete a self-evaluation form on these indicators every year. The indicators

Table 8.4 *Overview of quality indicators in long-term care developed by the Steering Group on Responsible Care, The Netherlands*

Themes and indicators	Client indicators		Indicators of professional content of care			
	Client consultation Via CQ-index questionnaire		Self-monitoring at organizational level (from management information)		Self-monitoring at client level (from existing registrations, patient records or from patient self-assessments)	
	Residential care organization	Home care	Residential care organization	Home care	Residential care organization	Home care
Quality of life						
Physical well-being						
Experiences with nursing care	+	+				
Experiences with meals	+					
Living situation						
Experiences with cleaning	+					
Experienced atmosphere	+					
Experienced privacy	+					
Experienced safety of living environment	+	+				
Participation						
Experiences with daytime activities	+	+				
Experienced autonomy	+	+				
Mental well-being						
Experiences related to mental well-being	+	+				
Quality of caregivers						
Experienced professionalism	+	+				
Experienced personal treatment/attitude	+	+				
Experienced reliability of caregivers		+				

230 *Jos M. G. A. Schols, et al.*

Table 8.4 (*cont.*)

Themes and indicators	Client indicators		Indicators of professional content of care			
	Client consultation Via CQ-index questionnaire		Self-monitoring at organizational level (from management information)		Self-monitoring at client level (from existing registrations, patient records or from patient self-assessments)	
	Residential care organization	Home care	Residential care organization	Home care	Residential care organization	Home care
Quality of care organization						
Experiences with individual care plan	+	+				
Experienced possibility for an own voice	+	+				
Experiences with information offered	+	+				
Experienced accessibility by phone		+				
Experienced integration of care		+				
Experienced availability of professionals	+	+				
Availability of specialized nurse			+			
Availability of experienced physician			+			
Experienced (specific) technical skills			+	+		
Quality and safety of care						
Risk assessment of care problems					+	+
Skin lesions (prevalence)					+	
Nutritional status -risk of malnutrition (prevalence)					+	
-malnutrition (prevalence)					+	

Table 8.4 (*cont.*)

Themes and indicators	Client indicators		Indicators of professional content of care			
	Client consultation Via CQ-index questionnaire		Self-monitoring at organizational level (from management information)		Self-monitoring at client level (from existing registrations, patient records or from patient self-assessments)	
	Residential care organization	Home care	Residential care organization	Home care	Residential care organization	Home care
Fall incidents (incidence)					+	+
Incidents related to medication (number)					+	
Use of anti-psychotics (prevalence)					+	
Depressive symptoms (prevalence)					+	
Incontinence						
-prevalence					+	+
-diagnosis (how often established)					+	
Behavioural problems (prevalence)					+	
Freedom restricting measures or restraints						
-prevalence					+	
-application					+	
-effect evaluation					+	
-reduction					+	
Policy on reduction of restraints				+		
Heat protocol			+			
Emergency facilities during electrical power cut			+			

Source: Nivel, 2011.

cover a broad range of topics including the size and quality of medical and nursing staff, prevention, restraints, the care dependency of clients, skin disorders, pressure ulcers, malnutrition, fall incidents, medicine incidents, use of antipsychotics, incontinence and depression. As can be deduced from these examples, the professional content of care is measured both at the organizational and the client level.

(2) Client indicators (*cliëntgebonden indicatoren*), measured by means of the CQ-index (Consumer Quality-Index), through a client-based quality questionnaire, conducted by independent agencies. Areas covered are: physical health, psychological health, participation and living conditions (Nivel, 2011). Data collection for Category 1 indicators takes place every year and for Category 2, every two years. The indicators are constantly being developed, including the proper correction for case-mix and the development of indicators for specific client groups (e.g., clients with dementia, rehabilitation patients and clients with non-congenital brain damage).

The purpose of measuring the quality of long-term care performance is to improve its quality along four different parameters:

- to inform provider organizations about the relative quality of their performance. The organizations can view their own results on the quality measurements and benchmark them with the results of similar institutions around the country to see how well they are doing and to tailor and target their improvement activities in the right way to achieve better performance;
- to inform insurers and enable them to make informed choices when purchasing long-term care. In the near future, healthcare insurers increasingly will follow a strategy of purchasing long-term care services from long-term care providers that offer both cost effective and high-quality care. Data on relevant quality indicators will be used to assess and compare actual quality among competitive suppliers;
- to inform the Healthcare Inspectorate. The Inspectorate uses the quality standards developed by the professional organizations and their stakeholders (self-regulation) for its supervisory activities;
- to inform long-term care users and enable them to make informed choices.

Currently, we may conclude that presenting the details of long-term care performance publicly has an impact and that provider organizations do indeed feel the urge to actually improve their services and also to communicate with their stakeholders on quality improvement issues. Insurers increasingly use data on quality indicators to shape incentives given to healthcare providers during annual negotiations on individual providers' budgets. Every year, the Healthcare Inspectorate produces an overview on the quality of care in the long-term care sector as a whole, also announcing the topics on which it will be undertaking extra monitoring in the year to come. However, it is true to say that long-term care service users or patients and/or their representatives are still getting used to these publicly available quality indicators. As already mentioned, their role in helping client groups to make choices will definitely grow in the future.

8.4.2.3 Method 2: Investigation of incidents

Reports of incidents, unsatisfactory situations and ongoing shortcomings play an important role in the Inspectorate's supervisory and enforcement activities. Some reports may prompt the Inspectorate to take immediate enforcement action. All reports form an important source of information regarding the quality of care. If the Inspectorate receives a report that suggests serious shortcomings in the quality of care, or less serious shortcomings which are nevertheless of a structural, ongoing nature, the Inspectorate will take action. The Inspectorate analyses all the reports it receives, using the results to underpin its opinions regarding the quality of care in the various sectors of the healthcare system. The Inspectorate may also investigate the reports further during its inspection visits. In order to maintain its efficiency and effectiveness, the Inspectorate does not investigate all incoming reports itself. In many cases, it will request the healthcare provider concerned to conduct an internal investigation and to submit a report. However, the Inspectorate does impose certain conditions with regard to the quality and thoroughness of the internal investigation.

8.4.2.4 Method 3: Monitoring based on themes

In addition to phased supervision and investigation of incidents, the Inspectorate occasionally may also perform thematic monitoring across long-term care providers e.g. on issues like drug supply in institutions, the availability of doctors, accessibility to specific care services, and the adherence to specific regulations.

8.4.2.5 Method 4: Enforcement measures

The Inspectorate has various measures at its disposal to ensure compliance with legislation, (professional) standards and guidelines. It can offer advice and recommendations to encourage improvement. It can also impose corrective measures or sanctions. In the most serious cases, the Inspectorate can initiate disciplinary or criminal proceedings. When deciding upon the most appropriate enforcement measure, the Inspectorate will take the following variables into account:

- the 'five Ds': dissatisfaction, discomfort, disease, disability and death (internationally recognized criteria);
- the number of people at risk (i.e., a large, medium or small risk group);
- the manner in which care provision is organized and structured with a view to quality and safety outcomes (poor, moderate, good);
- the attitude of the care provider (ignorance, incompetence, non-compliance).

Supervisory and enforcement activities are generally conducted on the basis of trust. The Inspectorate assumes that care providers are motivated to perform their duties in the best manner possible. However, trust does not mean that the Inspectorate will fail in its own duty to verify that quality and safety standards are being met. At all times, the Inspectorate pursues an appropriate balance between trust in care providers on the one hand, and supervision and inspection on the other. In general, all healthcare organizations that are visited regularly by the Healthcare Inspectorate receive instructions to report on (specific) improvement activities, related to the inspection visit. Yearly, about five to ten hospitals and about ten to fifteen long-term care organizations are sanctioned or held under close watch. Such cases are published on the Healthcare Inspectorate's website. Closing down long-term care organizations occurs rarely.

8.5 Transparency of the performance of long-term care organizations for clients and society – public reporting

Long-term care providers increasingly have to be transparent about their performance to their stakeholders and, especially, to clients themselves. Over the last decade, societal and political changes have encouraged suppliers of long-term care to put their clients at the centre of care and to become more responsive towards client needs and preferences. Putting the healthcare client rather than the care supplier at the centre of processes and structures has been advocated by several proposals on future care provision (Herzlinger, 2004; Mead and Bower, 2000). Hence, the needs and expectations of clients are now being viewed as the starting point in a thorough re-orientation of roles, tasks, operational processes, organizational structures and inter-organizational cooperation in the promotion of a demand-based approach. As a result, care delivery for older people is becoming more demand-based, without sacrificing too much on efficiency and cost containment, which are two other pressing factors that care providers must take into account in day-to-day provision (Bohmer, 2005). To support the development of a demand-based care system, four dimensions should be taken into account simultaneously (De Blok et al., 2009): choice options; variation; client interaction; and joint and coordinated delivery. By increasing the available range of choice options, it becomes more likely that clients will find care and service components that optimally suit their particular circumstances. In addition, it should be possible to combine all choice options provided in any way desired by the client. Combining available care and service components into differing configurations creates variation in the final offering across clients with diverse needs. Furthermore, the interaction between clients and caregivers should be stimulated and managed during the care process so as to consult with clients on their care needs and be able to adapt and customize the care offering accordingly. Finally, whereas many long-term care organizations and even organizational departments work according to autonomous and separate processes and structures, demand-based care provision implies that organizations jointly take care of a client's multiple demands and serve the client in an integrated fashion.

Bearing these factors in mind, since 2008 clients can obtain relevant information about long-term care providers in three ways: a) information published by the Healthcare Inspectorate; b) information published by the long-term care providers themselves; and c) information published on an independent national website.

8.5.1 Information provided by the Healthcare Inspectorate

Virtually all reports about long-term care providers produced by the Inspectorate are made public in accordance with the national Freedom of Information Act (Wet Openbaarheid van Bestuur, WOB). Therefore, the reports can be accessed by anyone who wishes to consult them. In the case of reports concerning specific healthcare institutions, there is no statutory obligation to publish but the Inspectorate will generally do so in accordance with its policy of 'proactive publication'. The latter simply means that the Inspectorate does not wait until it is asked for information about a healthcare institution, but makes its inspection reports available on the website www.igz.nl as soon as they have been finalized. This policy has been in place since 1 July 2008 and applies to the inspection reports for healthcare institutions in many sectors. Each report remains on the Inspectorate's website for a period of three years. The Inspectorate has three reasons for publishing its reports on health-care institutions. Firstly, publication contributes to the transparency of its regulatory activities – the Inspectorate wishes to provide clear infor-mation about its methods and the manner in which it arrives at its conclusions about the quality of care. Secondly, it maintains compliance as publication encourages all healthcare institutions to devote attention to the quality of care, and motivates those that are not currently per-forming as well as they might to make improvements. Thirdly, making reports public serves to inform patients, health insurers and other stake-holders: good information regarding the quality of care assists users and stakeholders to make an informed choice, which is particularly impor-tant now that greater competition has been introduced to the health and long-term care sector.

8.5.2 Information published by long-term care providers

Long-term care providers (institutional care as well as home care organ-izations) also offer transparency to their stakeholders in two ways. Firstly, they are obliged to publish a report every year on their financial performance as well as on their productivity and the quality of the care and services that they have delivered in the year in question. Secondly, most long-term care providers have their own websites and also offer a variety of brochures with client-based information about, among other things, the structure and organization of their services and locations; care modalities and services they offer; accessibility to care and services; availability of long-term care and healthcare professionals; the central role and importance of their clients; the quality of their care modalities and services; and innovative activities.

Quality monitoring of long-term care in The Netherlands

8.5.3 Information published on an independent national website

Of course, the information of the long-term care providers themselves might be self-serving and therefore these days clients can also assess more objective information about the quality of long-term care providers' performances. Specific quality information about long-term care providers is available for all clients via a specific national website 'choose better' (Du Moulin et al., 2010; Meijers et al., 2009). This website contains information about diseases and their treatment, provides adequate patient information on specific cure and care arrangements as well as on healthcare insurance aspects, gives information about where to find professionals and healthcare organizations that may be needed and allows also to compare the services and quality (see Table 8.4) of these organizations and professionals. This national website, therefore, can support and guide clients in making the right choices regarding the care and services they need and prefer and fits nicely in the trend towards a more client-centred care.

8.6 Summary

In this chapter we have tried to show that in the last decade, along with some new legislation and emerging policy and political issues, the approach to judging the quality of long-term care has undergone a dynamic, and perhaps a revolutionary development. Currently, healthcare and long-term care organizations and professionals have become accustomed to the fact that the quality of their performance is no longer an arbitrary matter. Much has been done to make information about the quality of long-term care providers' performance more transparent, even if stakeholders still need to become better acquainted with such developments, especially long-term care users themselves.

In the near future, the role and influence of long-term care consumers themselves will become increasingly important, making the challenge very clear for every long-term care provider tasked with meeting the needs and expectations of their (future) clients. Within The Netherlands, there is still discussion about whether the current way of measuring quality of care is complete and whether the right approach has been adopted. Debate continues on whether further improvements are indicated. In this respect, future research on quality of care might answer these questions. In fact, good long-term care should be the result of the respectful mutual interaction between an empowered client and a highly qualified, continuously learning professional, who is facilitated (in the right way) by the long-term care organization he or she is working in. Therefore, the real challenges lie in developing ways to successfully empower frail and disabled long-term care clients to really demand good-quality care and services, and ensuring that both healthcare organizations as well as healthcare professionals remain self-motivated and ambitious in working continuously to improve their quality of care, instead of doing so only if forced by a regulatory agency.

References

Bohmer, R. M. J. (2005). Medicine's service challenge: blending custom and standard care. *Healthcare Management Review*, 30(4): 322–30.

Boot, J. M. D. (2010). *Organisatie van de gezondheidszorg* [Organization of Healthcare]. Assen: Koninklijke van Gorcum BV.

De Blok, C., Meijboom, B., Luijkx, K. and Schols, J. M. G. A. (2009). Demand-based provision of housing, welfare and care services to elderly clients: from policy to daily practice through Operations Management. *Healthcare Analysis*, 17(1): 68–84.

De Boer, A., Broese van Groenou, M. and Timmermans, J. (eds.) (2009). *Mantelzorg, een overzicht van de steun van en aan mantelzorgers in 2007* [Informal Care, an Overview of the Support from and to Informal Carers in 2007]. The Hague: SPC.

Du Moulin, M. F. M. T., van Haastregt, J. C. M. and Hamers, J. P. H. (2010). Monitoring quality of care in nursing homes and making information available for the general public: state of the art. *Patient Education and Counseling*, 78(3): 288–96.

Herzlinger, R. E. (2004). *Consumer-Driven Healthcare. Implications for Providers, Payers and Policy Makers*. San Francisco: Jossey-Bass.

Mead, N. and Bower, P. (2000). Patient-centeredness: a conceptual framework and review of the empirical literature. *Social Science and Medicine*, 51(7) October: 1087–110.

Meijers, J. M., Halfens, R. J., van Bokhorst-de van der Schueren, M. A., Dassen, T. and Schols, J. M. G. A. (2009). Malnutrition in Dutch healthcare: prevalence, prevention, treatment, and quality indicators. *Nutrition*, 25(5): 512–19.

Mot, E., Aouragh, A., de Groot, M. and Mannaerts, H. (2010). The Dutch system of long-term care. ENEPRI Research Report no. 90. Contribution to WP1 of ANCIEN Project. (Previously published as CPB Document

Quality monitoring of long-term care in The Netherlands 239

no. 204, March 2010. The Hague: CPB Netherlands Bureau for Economic Policy Analysis.) Available at www.ancien-longtermcare.eu/ sites/default/files/LTCSYSteminThe per cent20Netehrlands_RR90.pdf.

Nivel (Netherlands Institute for Health Services Research) (2011). Consumer Quality Index. Available at: www.nivel.nl/en/search/apachesolr_search/ CQ?filters=language per cent3Aen (accessed 28 June 2012).

NRV (1990). *Discussienotabegrippenkader kwaliteit van instellingen* [Discussion paper on the concepts of quality in institutions]. The Hague: Nationale Raad voor de Volksgezondhei.

OECD (2011). *OECD Health Data: Health status, OECD Health Statistics* (database). Paris: OECD.

Schäfer, W., Kroneman, M., Boerma, W., van den Berg, M., Westert, G., Devillé, W. and van Ginneken, E. (2010). The Netherlands: Health system review. *Health Systems in Transition*, 12(1): 1–229.

Schellekens, W. M. L. C. M., van Beek, C. C. and van Everdingen, J. J. E. (2001). *Kwaliteitsmanagement in de gezondheidszorg* [Quality Management in Healthcare]. Houten: Bohn, Stafleu Van Loghum.

Schols, J. M. G. A., Crebolder, H. F. J. M. and van Weel, C. (2004). Nursing home and nursing home physician: the Dutch experience. *JAMDA*, 5(3): 207–12.

Statistics Netherlands (2011). Sharp increase in ABWZ costs. Available at: www.cbs.nl/en-GB/menu/themas/overheid-politiek/publicaties/artikelen /archief/2010/2010-3169-wm.htm?Languageswitch=on.

Steering Group on Responsible Care (2007). *Kwaliteits Kader voor Verant-woorde Zorg* [Quality Framework for Responsible Care]. Available at: www.zichtbarezorg.nl/page/Verpleging-verzorging-en-thuiszorg/Docu menten.

van Houten, G., Tuynman, M. and Gilsing, R. (2008). *De invoering van de Wmo: gemeentelijk beleid in 2007, Eerste tussenrapportage WMO eval-uatie* [The Introduction of the WMO: Municipal Policy in 2007; First Intermediate Report of WMO Evaluation]. The Hague: SCP.

Verbeek, H., van Rossum, E., Zwakhalen, S. M., Kempen, G. I. and Hamers, J. P. (2009). Small, homelike care environments for older people with dementia: a literature review. *International Psychogeriatrics*, 21(2): 252–64.

Websites

Healthcare Inspectorate, www.igz.nl/english/.
National Kompas, www.nationaalkompas.nl/algemeen/menu-rechts/english/.
Nivel (Netherlands Institute for Health Services Research), www.nivel.nl/en/.

9 The regulatory structure of Spanish long-term care: the case of Catalonia's service structures and quality assurance systems

SERGIO ARIÑO BLASCO, MERITXELL SOLÉ,
GLORIA RUBERT, JOSÉ M. SANJUAN AND
JOAN GIL

9.1 Introduction

The rapid ageing of populations in western countries since the mid-twentieth century and the profound social and epidemiological transitions that have occurred over this time are leading us to a new paradigm for dependent elderly people[1] (Lee, 2011) and a new set of guiding principles for contemporary health reform: the importance of increasing accessibility to services, the need to offer quality care and the need to guarantee the financial sustainability of social care schemes (Council of the European Union, 2003; Huber et al., 2011). In the course of history, dependent elderly people in western societies have received care according to a variety of models that have in turn reflected our changing social values (Parkin, 2003; Shahar, 1997; Hirshbein, 2001). Since the mid-twentieth century and mainly as a consequence of the rapid increase in the number of older people in the world, welfare states have been obliged to design more specific social and healthcare policies. In Europe, the implementation of international recommendations after the First World Assembly on Aging (Vienna, 1982) paved the way for a specific plan of action for policy makers responding to the challenges of an ageing society.

In this context, services for long-term care must be understood as the set of activities carried out by informal caregivers (relatives, friends or neighbours) and formal caregivers (health and social service professionals) and intended to provide the best possible quality of life for dependent people

---

[1] The United Nations estimates that the current world population of approximately 7 billion people will increase to 9.3 billion in 2050 and to 10.1 billion in 2100, while the old-age dependency ratio will double by 2050 and triple by 2100.

The regulatory structure of Spanish long-term care 241

according to their individual preferences, allowing them the highest possible degree of independence, autonomy, participation, personal fulfilment and human dignity (WHO and Milbank Memorial Fund, 2000). The definition of long-term care is invariably tied to the concept of dependency – long-term care is about best-quality care, whether formal or informal, and whether provided by health professionals or by professionals in social services. Obviously, dependency is not exclusively a characteristic of the elderly, although it is well documented that in Spain the elderly make up the largest group of dependent people (i.e., 1,462,292 (68 per cent) out of a total of 2,141,404 dependent people are in the 65+ age group). In this chapter, therefore, we will focus on the elderly population and on formal long-term care services rather than informal care (Huber et al., 2011; Rodriguez Cabrero, 1999).

In order to clearly understand the regulatory structure for long-term care in Spain, we should consider its regional political framework. Since the proclamation of the Spanish Constitution in 1978, Spain has been governed as a constitutional monarchy employing a parliamentary system that devolves power to seventeen autonomous communities (hereafter, 'regions') whose governments assume full responsibility for health and social care policies. These regions are responsible for the authorization, certification and accreditation of health and social care providers and are assigned the task of regulating and improving health and social services. Historically, the process of devolving legislative and regulatory authority to the regions has been a gradual one, which began in 1981 and only finished in 2002. During this twenty-year period there was an overlap between central and regional policies across the seventeen regions in both social and healthcare programmes. This long time interval, mainly the result of difficulties in establishing funding agreements, is one of the factors that accounts for the current complexity of Spain's political system[2] (García Armesto et al., 2010).

---

[2] The transfer of power was sequential and took place in two tiers of devolution, progressing at different speeds. Seven regions representing two-thirds of the Spanish population assumed full legislative power between eight and twenty years earlier than the others. It was not until 2001 that a principle of fiscal co-responsibility in the funding of regional health systems was adopted and, two years later in 2003, that the National Health System Cohesion and Quality Act was passed in order to balance equity and efficiency in healthcare between the regional governments.

242 *Sergio Ariño Blasco, et al.*

The case of Catalonia is different, however. By 1981, this region had accomplished the transfer of power by introducing pioneering reforms almost simultaneously for both its social and healthcare policies. In 1986 it created the programme Vida als Anys ('Giving life to years'), which focused on long-term care for frail elderly populations, chronic patients and the terminally ill (CatSalut, 2003). One result was that for the rest of Spain, Catalonia became the region of reference in this field and influenced the subsequent development of the Spanish model of health and social care (providing the perspective for national initiatives such as Spain's First National Plan for Gerontology, the benchmark for social and healthcare policies established in 1991 (Instituto Nacional de Servicios Sociales, 1993)).

It should be noted that in spite of the fact that the Spanish social and healthcare model is not fully integrated, throughout this chapter we will refer to formal long-term care services in terms of both healthcare and social care. Emphasis also will be placed on institutional care rather than home care, since Spanish home care services are still not fully developed. For instance, in January 2008 the mean coverage rate for home care services (within social services) for those aged 65+ was 4.7 per cent (Díaz Martín, 2009). However, this figure actually has doubled since 2002, when home care coverage was only 2.7 per cent. Public spending on home care accounts for 0.2 per cent of Spain's GDP, the lowest spending rate among OECD countries in 2004 (WHO Regional Office for Europe, 2008). Healthcare for long-term care patients in Spain consists of primary care, mental healthcare, hospital care and social and healthcare (the latter addressing the elderly infirm, the chronically ill and terminally ill patients) and is provided by public and private agents in clinics, at home or in hospitals. In 2010, a total of 14,113 beds in Spanish chronic care hospitals were made available to long-term care patients. Social services made available to the Spanish long-term care population consist of domiciliary care (home help, personal care, meals on wheels and telecare), day care (associations, care homes and day centres) and residential care (care homes for the elderly, sheltered housing, family fostering programmes and nursing homes). Residential care provided 329,311 beds in 5,490 centres in 2010, thus covering 4.4 per cent of the Spanish elderly population (see Table 9.1).

With regard to institutional long-term care we find facilities within both the health and social services networks. In certain cases, the

The regulatory structure of Spanish long-term care

Table 9.1 *Socio-demographic indicators and some long-term care services characteristics in Spain and Catalonia, 2010*

	Spain	Catalonia
Territory	505,986 km^2	32,113 km^2
Total Population	47,150,819	7,535,251
Population density (per km^2)	93	234
Population aged 65+	8,092,853	1,265,442
Proportion of total population aged 65+ (per cent)	17.2	17
Population aged 65+ living alone (per cent)	20	22
Life expectancy at birth (average, male and female)	81.5	81.8
Number of hospitals	792	213
Number of beds	161,040	33,793
Skilled nursing facility beds	14,113[a]	8,991[b]
Number of residential home beds	329,311	56,084
Residential Home coverage for those aged 65+ (per cent)	4.4	4.9
Number of people aged 65+ receiving home care services	358,078	57,034
Home Care coverage for those aged 65+ (per cent)	4.7	4.8

Source: Authors' elaboration based on INE, 2011 and Abellán García and Esparza Catalán, 2011.
Notes:
[a] Geriatric and long-term chronic hospital beds.
[b] Skilled nursing facility beds.

Spanish labelling of such facilities can cause confusion: for example, the term 'residential home' can apply to both a healthcare facility and a social services type of care facility (without nursing care). Therefore, we will use the term 'skilled nursing facility for long-term care' to denote institutional facilities provided in the health sector and the terms 'nursing home', 'residential home' and 'home for the aged' to describe residential facilities that depend on the social services sector. This applies to all the regions in Spain.

9.2 The new Spanish framework for long-term care

The turning point for dependency policy and long-term care services in Spain came in 2006 with the Promotion of Personal Autonomy and Care for Dependent Persons Act, otherwise referred to as the Dependency Act, passed on 14 December. This law introduced the Spanish System for Autonomy and Dependent Care Assistance (Sistema para la Autonomía y Atención a la Dependencia, SAAD), which entitles dependent people to receive support and which effectively constitutes the fourth pillar of the Spanish welfare state after education, health and social security benefits (Abellán-García and Hidalgo-Checa, 2011; Observatorio Estatal de la Discapacidad, 2010; Ministerio de Sanidad y Consumo, 2003; Jefatura del Estado, 2006). The system is designed as a network for public use that integrates both public and private centres and services. As regional governments have primary authority in the administration and delivery of long-term care services within SAAD, the 2006 Act also made provisions for the creation of the SAAD Inter-Territorial Council (CISAAD), designed to be its highest instrument of cooperation.[3]

Since January 2007, dependent people have been entitled to either financial aid or in-kind services to cover their personal care needs. Entitlement is determined by each person's status as a Spanish citizen,[4] financial means and degree of dependency. Following an assessment process carried out by regional authorities sharing the cross-national Dependence Assessment Instrument, which grades dependent people on a scale from 0 to 100, applicants are described as having either a moderate, severe or major degree of dependency and each of these three degrees is subdivided in two further dependency levels (Grades I and II), which describe a person's level of autonomy and the degree to which he or she needs help. Once an individual's depend-

---

[3] This approximation to a federal structure makes SAAD similar to the Spanish National Health System. CISAAD is composed of the seventeen regional ministers of social services and the central government's minister of social services. Article 8 lists these ministers' areas and degrees of authority.

[4] Spanish dependent nationals who have resided in Spain for more than five years before filing an application and non-nationals with selection criteria can still apply on the merit of the Law on the Rights and Liberties of Foreigners in Spain and their Social Integration.

ency situation has been assessed, a personalized care plan is drawn up (Plan Individualizado de Atención or Individualized Care Plan) and options for financial aid or in-kind services are discussed. Figure 9.1 provides a flowchart of the assessment process.

Article 15 of the 2006 Act details the catalogue of services to which individuals are entitled. The portfolio includes the following six services: home help, meaning housekeeping tasks and personal care; day centre facilities; night centre facilities; residential care; telecare; and finally, preventive programmes and personal assistance. The network of public institutions belonging to regional governments, local organizations, state reference centres and duly accredited private providers also delivers these services. Financial benefits, which are granted according to the dependent person's degree and level of dependency and economic status, are linked to the acquisition of a service and can be delivered in three ways: financial aid to purchase a service outside the SAAD network; financial aid for a family caregiver, meaning a non-professional caregiver; and finally financial aid for the dependent person to hire a professional caregiver or assistant (Articles 17–19 of the 2006 Act).

Legislative authority in social care is entirely devolved to regional governments, so it is the regions which have to plan, coordinate and allocate their resources and take charge of such areas as managing the register of providers, inspection and evaluation. As far as the central government's responsibility is concerned, Article 7 of the 2006 Act only ensures its provision of a minimum level of protection and financial aid for dependency. CISAAD's central and regional governmental representatives agree upon the second level of protection. Within their territorial boundaries, each regional government may then establish a wider set of benefits. Finally, municipalities can also complement the basket of benefits within their constituencies.

9.2.1 Quality: the core

Quality is a core issue within SAAD. Indeed, Title II of the 2006 Act is entirely devoted to achieving a high standard of quality and efficacy in the provision of benefits through the SAAD system and Article 35 states that quality standards will be established for each of the services that are included in the Catalogue, once agreed upon by CISAAD. Moreover, residential centres will implement internal regulations relative to their

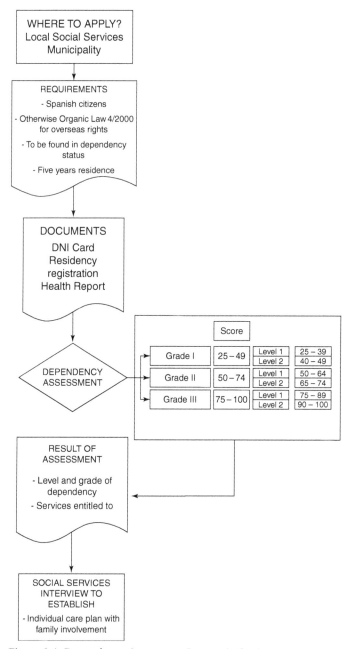

Figure 9.1 Dependency Assessment Process in Spain.
Source: adapted from material from the Spanish Geriatrics and Gerontology Society Working Party.

The regulatory structure of Spanish long-term care 247

own organization and operation, including a quality management system and promoting user participation. The Law outlines common criteria for quality indicators for required services and also suggests which quality assurance tools should be used for the processes of accreditation, professionalization and inspection. Regarding the accreditation of centres, services and providers, the Law aims to move service provision away from the 'administrative model', which is vertical, punitive and inspection- and control-based, to the 'quality model', which addresses integrated and participative total quality management. This new approach, which is perhaps still a theoretical framework, is clearly stated by the Government of Catalonia in its *Social Services Quality Programme 2010*. In order to achieve this model, service providers perform an initial quality evaluation (self-assessment) following directives from standard quality evaluation systems, such as UNE-EN ISO 9001, EFQM, before external evaluation. This approach stresses the importance of collaborative leadership across all agents of the system (Fundación Edad and Vida, 2008; Departament de Benestar Social i Familia, 2010).

Without undermining the power that regional governments have to determine such issues (Article 16), CISAAD agrees upon a common quality assurance framework for the accreditation of centres and quality programmes, as well as quality and safety criteria, quality indicators for continuous improvement and benchmarking, best practices models and the development of quality standards. For instance, CISAAD's 2008 Agreement[5] established cross-regional minimums in quality standards that should be met by the nursing home sector in such categories as staff qualifications and material resources, equipment and documentation (see Table 9.2). And CISAAD's 2009 Agreement[6] established further minimums regarding the accreditation of informal caregivers' expertise and knowledge. This agreement established the basic norms for the training that this type of caregiver would have to receive. At the same time, however, although these agreements on minimums are designed to harmonize the system and reduce the variability of practice, the task of inspecting caregivers and sanctioning those who do not meet the minimums is in the hands of the regional governments.

---

[5] See Resolution of 2 September 2008 (Official State Gazette-BOE no. 303, 17 December 2008).

[6] See Resolution of 4 November 2009 (Official State Gazette-BOE no. 286, 27 November 2009).

248   *Sergio Ariño Blasco, et al.*

Table 9.2 *Global staffing ratio per resident in the nursing home sector in Spain – regional government average in 2008 and mandated ratios in 2011*

	Average (2008)	Dependency Grade II (2011)	Dependency Grade III (2011)
Home for dependent elderly	0.41	0.45	0.47
Day/night centre for elderly	0.23	0.23	0.24
Physical disability home	0.57	0.61	0.64
Intellectual disability home	0.52	0.60	0.63
Day/night centre physical dependency	0.28	0.29	0.30
Day/night centre intellectual dependency	0.29	0.30	0.32

Source: Ministerio de Educación Política Social y Deporte, 2008.
Note: Calculations based on full-time equivalents, taking into account the proportion of annual working hours detailed in collective working agreements for all workers despite their type of contracts.

Although SAAD admits both public and private care providers, the 2006 Act makes no provision for a regulatory apparatus to distinguish between these; in fact, it specifies that the level of quality required of private or subsidized providers' services and centres should be the same as those provided by public organizations.

9.2.2 A note on terminology

Terms such as 'inspection', 'evaluation' and 'accreditation' are often used to refer to different actions in different contexts and so this chapter will adhere to the definitions used in Fundación Edad and Vida, 2008, which are collated from a cross-regional grouping of practices. For each service (day centre facilities, home care services, nursing homes, etc.), the authorization and accreditation process is sequential as well as specific. Most regional governments require authorization by the Social Services Administration, a municipal licence, plus enrolment in the Registry of Social Services in order to be operational. In the Spanish context, we use the following terms:

Authorization:	An action undertaken by the government to determine that a centre meets the necessary conditions to guarantee users adequate care.
Accreditation:	An action undertaken by the government guaranteeing that the accredited services and centres are equal to or exceed the quality minimums required by law. The government requires both public and private or subsidized care providers to meet such minimums.
Certification:	A third-party evaluation that establishes confidence that a product or service meets the requirements of a specific regulation.

9.3 The quality approach in Catalonia

In Catalonia, the ground rules for creating quality standards and reviewing the general terms for authorizing skilled nursing facilities and nursing homes for the aged were first established in the 1980s, well before the new Dependency Law of 2006. In fact, the healthcare sector's skilled nursing facilities and the social services sector's nursing home facilities and services were regulated in the same year, 1987, within months of each other (the former by the Catalan Ministry of Health on 4 August and the latter on 15 July).

9.3.1 Inspection

In this group of social services-based nursing homes, as well as authorization, accreditation and evaluation, the legislation requires random and confidential annual inspections by the Catalan Social Services Department. Act 16/1996 of 27 November regulates actions by inspectors and supervision by the social services authorities. The law specifies that the following general steps should be taken: that the inspection should be conducted *ex officio*; that it should be undertaken periodically, at least annually in the case of residential facilities; that inspectors should be granted free access to the facilities and have the right to inspect them without prior notification; and that inspectors should be given unrestricted access to any information that they consider necessary to determine the centre's compliance with the current regulations.

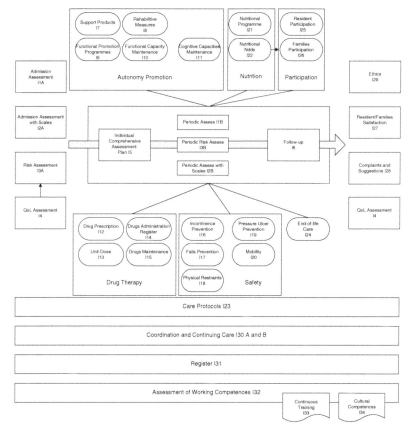

Figure 9.2 Quality indicators and dimensions for nursing homes in Catalonia, 2010.
Source: authors' elaboration of indicators for quality evaluation based on material available from the Generalitat de Catalunya Departament de Benestar Social.

9.3.2 Evaluation

Catalonia's certification process by external evaluation was initiated in 1998, when a series of quality indicators was used to evaluate residential services. The agency charged with this task was the Avedis Donabedian Foundation, which made a series of recommendations for drawing up continuous improvement plans for nursing homes for the elderly. Later, in 2010, newly revised quality indicators were put into practice, for both day centres and nursing homes (see Figure 9.2).

The regulatory structure of Spanish long-term care 251

In the arena of healthcare, the certification process for facilities through external evaluation began in the period 1992–3, with the development of quality indicators. These indicators were subsequently revised in 1996 in order to identify new indicators commonly agreed upon in the sector, focusing at this time on 'patient care' and incorporating improvements in safety at a fundamental level (such as risk assessment for pressure ulcers, falls and malnutrition, abuse, aggression, suicide, adverse drug reactions or delirium). That element was preserved when the indicators were revised in 2006 and the evaluators began the work of incorporating further indicators based on new measurement tools. The last external evaluation in this sector was completed in 2007, when the average performance attainment across all of the indicators was 48.8 per cent (Fundacio Avedis Donabedian and Pla Director Sociosanitari, 2007; Hilarion et al., 2009).

9.4 The customer's perspective in Catalonia: a chronological overview

The Catalan Health Service (Servei Català de la Salut or CatSalut) is characterized by its decentralized and participative nature, which at its most basic level already includes consumer and user representatives working together and creating close ties with local communities. In 1994, the first 'client support units' were launched across different units and territories and two years later the first patient satisfaction surveys on primary and hospital care rated professional expertise as the most important aspect of service while accessibility, information and facility comfort received lower scores. By the end of the 1990s a set of measures were implemented in order to improve the healthcare system's relations with the local community, with proactive and anticipatory actions taken against previous approaches based on responses to complaints. To this end, and through the Catalan Health Service, the Catalan Ministry of Health created in 2000 the Citizen Support Division, a unit aimed at guaranteeing quality of services within public healthcare.

Within a context of increasing integration (i.e., social and healthcare provision) and decentralization (from regional to local governments) in which the Catalan Health Service is attempting to come closer to its clients, that information fulfils its role as the key management tool for healthcare facilities and for the healthcare system as a whole. For instance, the Satisfaction Survey Programme (PLAENSA) was created as an assessment and decision-making tool in order to stimulate improvements in the Catalan healthcare sector by giving voice to patients' preferences (CatSalut, 2007; Generalitat de Catalunya Departament de Salut y CatSalut, 2010b). The programme uses a structured questionnaire of thirty items (some common to healthcare settings and others specifically addressing long-term care) considering aspects such as accessibility, information, professional competence, comfort, coordination, continuum of care, human relationships and psychosocial care and support.

With regard to the healthcare sector there have been annual surveys in 2003, 2007 and 2010 across long-term care units in skilled nursing facilities, some results of which are shown in Table 9.3. In the 2010 survey, a global satisfaction score (from 0 to 10) and a loyalty measure (the percentage of those who said that they would continue to attend the centre) were obtained and showed a score of 8.24 (SD +/–1.47) and 91.7 per cent respectively (Generalitat de Catalunya Departament de Salut y CatSalut, 2012).

Parallel to the development of satisfaction surveys in healthcare settings promoted by the Catalan government, during the mid-1990s social service providers initiated participation mechanisms (questionnaires, committees, senior boards) with residents of care homes for the elderly and nursing homes in order to obtain feedback data on how the centres were operating. Among these we can highlight a twenty-eight-item satisfaction questionnaire completed by 1,910 elderly users of an average age of 81.8 (± 8.2) from eighty nursing homes in 2001. The results show that 30 per cent of these users reported overall satisfaction with their centre, which they described as 'excellent', while 46.5 per cent described their centre as 'above average' (Saura et al., 2001). Interestingly, the dimensions referring to structure, quality of care provision and organizational aspects returned very acceptable results, whereas relationship aspects with care workers, personal exclusion and proactive participation actions would only be improved by receiving immediate attention. This independent study helped to accelerate a further series of actions by the Catalan government to establish quality assurance programmes in the sector (quality indicators for long-term care in residential homes). Among these is a programme to retrieve data on special needs populations. The Catalan Social Services Institute has designed a specific instrument to deal with quality of life dimensions (Verdugo Alonso et al., 2008), which has been validated for social

The regulatory structure of Spanish long-term care

Table 9.3 *Results from PLAENSA survey on the level of residents' satisfaction with skilled nursing facilities in Catalonia, 2003, 2007, 2010*

Survey question	Response categories	Year		
		2003	2007	2010
Patient rating of	Perfect	8.7	5.9	6.8
accessibility to	Very good	35.9	23.9	22.5
healthcare services	Good	35.1	51.7	54.0
(per cent)	Regular	14.1	13.9	12.9
	Poor	6.2	4.6	3.8
		100.0	100.0	100.0
Patient satisfaction	Always satisfied	44.0	44.8	40.7
with professional	Almost always satisfied	23.3	17.8	28.6
competence	Often satisfied	22.7	28.5	24.8
(per cent)	Not often satisfied	7.7	6.8	4.6
	Never satisfied	2.3	2.1	1.3
		100.0	100.0	100.0
Global satisfaction (scale from 0–10)		8.3	8.2	8.2
Loyalty (per cent)		78.40	83.10	91.70
Number of respondents		2,050	2,193	2,322

Source: Generalitat de Catalunya Departament de Salut i CatSalut, 2012.

service users with physical disabilities, intellectual disabilities, sensory impairments, mental health problems, substance abuse problems and for elderly people. At present this instrument is being recommended by the Catalonian Social Services Strategic Programme (2010–13) for individual care planning.

9.5 The nursing home and the acute care hospital network

The Spanish National Health System (SNHS) is characterized by universal coverage. It is almost fully funded by general tax revenue and, with the exception of pharmaceuticals prescribed to those under the age of 65, is provided free of charge at the point of delivery. The SNHS's structure is decentralized, the planning and provision of health services and legislative authority having been devolved to the regional level at the end of 2002. As described in Section 9.1, this devolution led to the creation of seventeen regional ministries of health, each with jurisdiction over the organization and delivery of health services within their territory. Another characteristic of the system is that general practitioners who work at the most local level of the community and who are normally the first contact point for patients, act as the healthcare system's gatekeepers. These GPs then treat patients at the primary care level or refer patients to specialized care according to the clinical complexity of their problem.

Healthcare for long-term care clients is provided in both community and institutional settings such as nursing homes, skilled nursing facilities and acute care hospitals. Regarding home healthcare, there are standard programmes to actively look for and identify people at risk, using both clinical and social approaches. Domiciliary programmes are designed to look for people at risk proactively. Liaison nurses operating between hospitals and primary care are also a common feature in the overall structure and they facilitate communication and help to strengthen the continuum of care. The incidence of case management strategies devised by skilled nurses for patients with chronic and complex needs is becoming higher, helping to attain this objective.

Every nursing home resident has universal healthcare coverage. GPs' lists show that, in addition to people living in their own homes, patients also consist of residents living in private or public nursing homes belonging to the social services network; it is noteworthy, however, that the same does not apply to patients admitted to the healthcare service's skilled nursing facilities network because this is part of the secondary or specialized care scheme. Thus, elderly individuals entering residential long-term care in social sector nursing homes can retain their community-based primary care physician while they live in the same catchment area. However, due to the existence of usually heavy workloads in primary care settings, many nursing homes offer additional medical coverage in a variety of ways, such as having a physician visit on a daily basis, on alternate days or once a week (Fundación Edad y Vida y Applus, 2011; Col·legi Oficial de Metges de Barcelona, 2002). On the other hand, in some cases the healthcare needs of elderly residents are not always appropriately addressed and referral circuits fail to provide rapid responses. Furthermore, progressive increases in the clinical complexity of patients' problems are tipping the scales and

The regulatory structure of Spanish long-term care   255

emergency room referrals during GPs' out-of-office hours are proving to be a challenge to the healthcare system.

Although no global figures are available, data from long-term care patients in skilled nursing facilities would suggest that roughly 16 per cent of discharges are transfers to acute hospital care. Pneumonia (DRG 541) is the most common diagnosis for admission to acute hospitals and also shows the highest in-hospital mortality rate, with up to 33.6 per cent of cases.[7] Winter bed crises, with overcrowded casualty services, occur frequently in western European hospitals. Each year, the media coverage of such crises broadcasts footage of casualty departments where we see people waiting for attention in circumstances that are frankly undignified, and where the message is that the healthcare situation is precarious. The most prominent groups in this scenario are chronic patients: the frail elderly and those with high levels of comorbidity and disability (the 'bed blockers' or 'frequent flyers'), many of whom come from residential or nursing home care. Today, therefore, any level of care that can provide an alternative to hospital admission is considered to be of paramount importance (and particularly for these groups), whether this means hospital-at-home schemes or specialist consultation services such as the deployment of geriatric or palliative care teams.

Targeting policies for the early detection of these patient groups will help to optimize resources. New schemes in the deployment of rapid response teams, hospital-at-home services and in-patient geriatric consultancy for nursing home residents are being piloted in order to help manage the flow of referrals from nursing homes to casualty departments, either facilitating these or finding an alternative solution. Unfortunately, the serious financial problems currently experienced by the Catalan Healthcare System have hampered the development of such initiatives.

9.6 Public reporting

In recent decades, most healthcare systems in developed countries have recognized the need for quality assurance and the assessment of outcomes. The culture of quality assessment and public reporting that was pioneered in the USA (Berwick, 2002) and in the Nordic countries has

---

[7] Unpublished data from the government's Skilled Nursing Homes Repository Unit.

influenced countries like Spain. In 2008, the Executive Council of the Catalan Ministry of Health approved the implementation of the Outcomes Centre (Central de Resultats, 2010) in what can be considered the first Spanish initiative that has been systematically oriented towards quality improvement and public reporting. The Outcomes Centre disseminates healthcare data as this is collated within one database that covers all Catalan hospitals (including long-term care hospitals). The data itself covers such aspects of healthcare as diagnosis, procedures, and patient and centre characteristics. The main goals of the Outcomes Centre are to introduce competence by comparison and cooperation in the system and to promote improvements across the entire board of agents, from members of the community to the government and from professionals to health centres.

The Centre uses a set of quality indicators that are consistent with conceptual frameworks that have been previously defined for and by other countries and systems: these include the Organisation for Economic Co-operation and Development (OECD), the Healthcare Quality Indicators Project (HCQI), the European Community Health Indicators (ECHI) and the Key Indicators from the Spanish National Health System (Helfrich, 2005). These indicators cover socio-demographic factors, lifestyle, healthcare status, resources, service use, quality, economic sustainability and corporate social responsibility. These quality indicators have a heterogeneous nature; some are outcome indicators facilitating comparisons among providers (referring to centres, territories, pathologies and so on) while others aim to give overall information like 'context indicators' about Catalonia. However, indicators potentially related to long-term care beds in healthcare settings are scarce. In this respect, only three main areas of long-term care quality are covered: accessibility and technical quality (*cerebrovascular accident* (CVA) and femur fracture outcomes), efficiency (length of stay) and client satisfaction indicators (common to all healthcare settings) (see Table 9.4). Curiously enough, despite the increased transparency and accountability that we would expect from publishing results on care provision, both generally and particularly from public hospital network healthcare providers, the data retrieved by the Outcomes Centre is aggregated by type of hospital or geographic location and therefore does not allow us to identify specific centres – at least not at the present time. This reluctance to publicly report results may be attributed to fears that providers might acquire negative

The regulatory structure of Spanish long-term care

Table 9.4 *Quality indicators related to long-term care in the Catalan Outcomes Centre's data set*

Quality Indicator		Domain
ES 04	Percentage of population aged 65 years of age and over with limitations in performing some activities of daily life (ADL)	Health status
ES 05	Prevalence of population declaring that they suffer from some type of severe disability	Health status
QU 01	Patients with Cardiovascular Accident referred to Skilled Nursing Facilities (SNF) for rehabilitation	Technical quality
QU 03	Discharge home from SNF, for Cardiovascular Accident patients over 65 years of age	Technical quality
QU 04	Discharge home from SNF, for neck of femur fracture patients over 65 years of age	Technical quality
QU 29	Average Length of stay in SNFs	Efficiency
US 16	Rate of social and healthcare admissions	Resource use
US 17	Percentage of social and healthcare resolution	Resource use
US 18	Percentage of referral's source for social and healthcare	Resource use
US 19	Rate of social and healthcare resource's use	Resource use

Source: Central de Resultats, 2010.

reputations. At the time of writing, the government is planning to extend this outcome assessment scheme to long-term care facilities in order to improve benchmarking that can guarantee confidentiality (proposed for the spring of 2013). Preliminary experiences exist in the acute hospital setting. Every provider is able to use specific software to access a MSIQ webpage (Moduls per al Seguiment d'Inidicadors de Qualitat, or Modules for Monitoring Quality Indicators), which records summaries on different performance indicators compared to the benchmark. This technology is based on In-patient Quality

Indicators from the Agency for Healthcare Research and Quality (AHRQ) in the United States.

Following the rule of 'competence by comparison and collaboration', Catalonia's healthcare regions promote cooperation activities across healthcare providers. It was not until November 2010 that public reporting on social and healthcare results from skilled nursing facilities was presented for the first time, during the VIII Benchmarking Summit hosted by the Barcelona Healthcare Region (Generalitat de Catalunya Departament de Salut and CatSalut, 2010a). In this first experience of benchmarking in the sector, only facilities with mid-term care beds were included. At that time, the Catalan administration published performance results from thirty-five centres (previously asked to participate on a voluntary basis). The domains reported were accessibility (three indicators), effectiveness (seven indicators) and cost-efficiency (four indicators). A ranking order was established using the scores obtained across different centres; on this occasion the results were not anonymous (Figure 9.3).

Figure 9.3 Extract from first public reporting exercise on skilled nursing facilities with mid-term care beds in Catalonia, November 2010.
Source: Catalan Ministry of Health (www.gencat.cat/catsalut/rsb).

In fact, the social services nursing home sector started using External Quality Evaluation Programmes in 1998, taking quality as the defining principle to assess different initiatives and developments in social services. This approach, oriented to quality improvement, is even more clearly highlighted in the new Catalan Social Services Act, in which quality is regarded as an essential tool for the continuous improvement of services, as well as a guarantee for the community. In addition, in its strategic axis on 'quality of service', the 2010–13 Quality Agenda for Social Services in Catalonia emphasizes the need to promote transparency in the social service network, both in terms of regularly publishing results to make them available to the community and in conducting regular surveys to measure the community's knowledge and perception of Catalan Social Services. To date, however, the results of external evaluations have not been published and therefore more progress is needed. In general, we might say that the objective of the present model on public reporting is to obtain reliable data on the quality provided by centres supplying long-term care and about patient satisfaction with those centres. Important progress has been made in both areas; however, it would appear that, to date, the decisions that might determine progress in these two areas have been taken by regulators (and reflect their needs) and not by clients, for whom no information has been provided. In our opinion, this is an important cross-sectional issue in Spanish service provision, particularly in areas such as health and education.

9.7 Conclusions

For many years long-term care in Spain was based overwhelmingly on informal care but social, demographic and epidemiological changes, and a new understanding of care, have obliged us to reconsider the paradigm. If long-term care wishes to provide services to a modern society with quality and efficiency, it faces a challenge. Thirty years ago, Spanish society began to design specific policies and regulations to improve its long-term care services. The complexity of this task was made greater by the changes needed to achieve it: the decentralization of power to the country's seventeen autonomous regions and the gradual devolution of health and social services to these regional administrations, both administratively and financially, in circumstances which sometimes involved duplicating structures and widening the gap between long-term care as it stood and the integrated care model that the country wished to establish. Just five years ago a new law on dependency (regarded as the fourth pillar of the welfare state) was launched in Spain and aimed to provide a basic common framework for all regions, which could establish quality as the backbone of the system.

The success of previous efforts to coordinate health and social services into integrated programmes has been limited. There are clear arguments, however, in favour of the need to forge closer ties between different agents (including the role of citizens) and where the importance of enhanced ICT resources in social and healthcare policies should be stressed. As an example of this, the residential-acute care network has become the focus of recent attention because of concerns about the quality of care provided to frail elderly patients, which is still hampered by a lack of integrated care, with overcrowded casualty services, acute care bed blocking and the overuse, unnecessary duplication and inefficiency of services. Accurate data is of paramount importance for proper analysis and inter-operability across settings and between social and health administrations is a key factor to improving care. However, while a great deal of information is already available, the willingness to undertake public reporting is still lacking. Service providers are still afraid that low scores or ranking positions will affect their reputation and this has constituted an obstacle to progress. Together with community groups and the representatives of service providers, government authorities will have to agree on basic public reporting models that can allow the long-term care system to gain transparency and to facilitate benchmarking and quality improvement.

References

Abellán García, A. and Esparza Catalán, C. (2011). Un perfil de las personas mayores en España, 2011. Indicadores estadísticos básicos [A profile of elderly people in Spain, 2011. Basic statistical indicators]. *Informes Portal Mayores*, 127.

Abellán-García, A. and Hidalgo-Checa, R. (2011). Definiciones de discapacidad en España. *Informes Portal Mayores*, 109. Available at: http://www.espaciomayores.es/InterPresent1/groups/imserso/documents/binario/pm-definiciones-01.pdf.

Berwick, D. M. (2002). A user's manual for the IOM's 'Quality Chasm' report. *Health Affairs (Millwood)*, 21: 80–90.

The regulatory structure of Spanish long-term care 261

CatSalut (2003). *L'atenció socioanitària a Catalunya vida als anys.* Barcelona: Generalitat de Catalunya Departament de Sanitat i Seguretat Social.

(2007). *Pla d'enquestes de sateisfacció d'assegurats del Catsalut per línea de servei.* Barcelona: Atenció Sociosanitaria.

Central de Resultats (2010). Primer informe de la Central de Resultats. Available at: www20.gencat.cat/docs/canalsalut/Minisite/Observatori Salut/ossc_Central_resultats/Informes/Fitxers_estatics/Central_resultats_primerinforme_2010.pdf.

Col·legi Oficial de Metges de Barcelona (2002). *Com prestar una assitènmcia de qualitat a persones que estan en residències geriàtriques. Quaderns de la bona praxis.* Barcelona: Col·legi Oficial de Metges de Barcelona.

Council of the European Union (2003). Joint report by the Commission and the Council on supporting national strategies for the future of healthcare and care for the elderly. Available at: http://ec.europa.eu/employment_social/soc-prot/healthcare/elderly_en.pdf.

Departament de Benestar Social i Familia (2010). *Pla de Qualitiat dels Serveis Socials de Catalunya* [Catalonian Social Services Quality Programme]. Barcelona: Generalitat de Catalunya, Departament de Benestar Social i Familia.

Díaz Martín, R. (2009). *Las Personas Mayores en España. Datos Estadísticos Estatales y por Comunidades Autónomas. Informe 2008,* Madrid: GRAFO, S.A.

Fundacio Avedis Donabedian and Pla Director Sociosanitari (2007). *3ª Avaluació d'Indicadors de Qualitat Dispositius Sociosanitaris* [Third Report on Evaluation of Quality Indicators in Social and Health Care Settings]. Barcelona: Departament de Salut Pla Director Sociosanitari.

Fundación Edad y Vida (2008). *Calidad y acreditación para entidades prestadoras de servicios de atención a las personas mayores en situación de dependencia.* Madrid: Fundación Edad y Vida.

Fundación Edad y Vida y Applus (2011). *Calidad y acreditación para entidades prestadoras de servicios de atención a las personas mayores en situación de dependencia.* Madrid, Fundación Edad y Vida.

García Armesto, S., Abadía Taira, B., Durán, A. and Bernal Delgado, E. (2010). Sistemas Sanitarios en Transición. España: Análisis del Sistema Sanitario 2010 (resumen y conclusiones). *Health Systems in Transition,* 12(4): 1–240.

Generalitat de Catalunya Departament de Salut i CatSalut (2010a) Presentació dels resultats de benchmarking en atenció sociosanitaria. Caixa Forum Barcelona: CatSalut. Available at: www10.gencat.cat/catsalut/rsb/arxius/presentacio_benchmarking_sociosanitari_RSB_2009.pdf.

(2010b). *La veu de la ciutadania.* Barcelona: Departament de Salut.

(2012). *The Voice of Citizens. How the Perception of Citizens Is Linked to the Improvement in Health Services and the Catalan Health System.* Barcelona: Catalan Ministry of Health, Catalan Health Service.

Helfrich, E. (2005). Staffing levels for long-term care. *Cmaj*, 173, 467–8.

Hilarion, P., Suñol, R., Groene, O., Vallejo, P., Herrera, E. and Saura, R. M. (2009). Making performance indicators work: the experience of using consensus indicators for external assessment of health and social services at regional level in Spain. *Health Policy*, 90(1): 94–103.

Hirshbein, L. D. (2001). William Osler and the Fixed Period: Conflicting Medical and Popular Ideas About Old Age. *Archives of Internal Medicine*, 161: 2074–8.

Huber, M., Hennessy, P., Izumi, J., Kim, W. and Lundsgaard, J. (2011). *The OECD Health Project. Long-Term Care for Older People.* Paris: Organization for Economic Co-operation and Development.

INE (Instituto Nacional de Estadística) (2011). *Spain in Figures, 2010.* Madrid: INE.

Instituto Nacional de Servicios Sociales (1993). *Plan Gerontológico Nacional.* Madrid.

Jefatura del Estado (2006). Ley 39/2006, de 14 de diciembre, de Promoción de la Autonomía Personal y Atención a las personas en situación de dependencia [Law 39/2006, 14th December on Promotion of Personal Autonomy and Care for Dependent Persons]. *Boletin Oficial del Estado*, 299: 44142–56.

Lee, R. (2011). The Outlook for Population Growth. *Science*, 333: 569–73.

Ministerio de Educación Política Social y Deporte (2008). Resolución de 2 de Diciembre de 2008. Crietrios comunes de acreditación para garantizar la calidad de los centros y servicios del SAAD [Resolution on common criteria for accreditation and quality assurance of SAAD's centres and services]. *Boletin Oficial del Estado*, 3.

Ministerio de Sanidad y Consumo (2003). Real Decreto de 10 de octubre, por el que se establecen las bases generales sobre autorización de centros, servicios y establecimientos sanitarios. *Boletin oficial del Estado*, 23: 37,893–902.

Observatorio Estatal de la Discapacidad (2010). *El desarrollo y aplicación de la ley de promoción de la autonomía personal y atención a las personas en situación de dependencia.* Olivenza: Informe Olivenza.

Parkin, T. (2003). *Old Age in the Roman World: a Cultural and Social History*, Baltimore: The Johns Hopkins University Press.

Rodriguez Cabrero, G. (1999). *La protección social de la dependencia*, Madrid: Ministerio de Trabajo y Asuntos Sociales (IMSERSO).

Saura, R., Suñol, R., Gil-Origuen, A. and Casals, I. (2001). Estudio de satisfacción en las residencias de personas mayores. *Revista de Calidad Asistencial*, 16: 519–60.

Shahar, S. (1997). *Growing Old in the Middle Ages*. London: Routledge.

Verdugo Alonso, M., Arias Martinez, B. L. G. S. and Schalock, R. (2008). *Escala GENCAT. Manual l'Escala GENCAT de Qualitat de Vida*, Barcelona: Generalitat de Catalunya. Institut Català d'Assisència i Serveis Socials.

WHO and Milbank Memorial Fund (2000). Towards an international consensus on policy for long-term care of the ageing. Available at: http://www.milbank.org/uploads/documents/000712oms.pdf.

WHO Regional Office for Europe (2008). Home care in Europe. Copenhagen: WHO. Available at: http://www.euro.who.int/__data/assets/pdf_file/0005/96467/E91884.pdf.

PART IV

Long-term care quality systems based on data measurement and public reporting

Quality regulation in long-term care is a governmental function rooted in the need to protect members of society who cannot advocate for themselves or who do not have enough knowledge about the services required to make informed choices. Regulation based upon inspection systems relies upon controlling who is allowed to offer services and then sanctioning those providers who do not maintain quality standards. Over the last several decades, some have advocated incorporating 'market forces' into healthcare by providing systematic information about the level of quality care providers attain and sustain. This information is then available for purchasers and consumers of long-term care services. Key to creating a market for quality long-term care is having a systematic approach to measuring quality that can be reliably and readily applied to all providers. Each of the countries in this segment have either moved fully into this model or have put into place a strategy for measuring long-term care clients' outcomes, making it possible to compare the experiences of care recipients across care providers. While some of these countries may also have highly structured and proscriptive inspection-based systems, it is the measurement system and the movement towards reporting quality in a public forum that distinguishes these countries from the other case study countries in this book.

The United States is the prototypical example of a national regulatory system that subsumed earlier state licensure standards that had differed from state to state and which now incorporates regular measures of care recipient outcomes in nursing homes and home health agencies which are publicly reported on the internet by the government for all to see. The availability of common clinical data on all care recipients has been required as a condition of being a government-funded care provider since the 1990s and the availability of these data made it possible to create provider-specific quality measures. These data also influenced the approach to conducting inspections and both these measures and the results of annual inspection results are publicly reported by the federal government. As an example of progressive centralization of authority and policy direction, the US experience in long-term care is highly instructive for other countries which retain a highly regionalized approach to quality regulation.

Long-term care in Canada is a provincial responsibility but over the last decade or more, most of the country's provinces have adopted a common approach for measuring long-term care recipients' experiences and outcomes on a regular basis. In many provinces regulations have been modified to incorporate a requirement that care recipients should be assessed using a common tool and then these data applied to create quality indicators. This process of building quality measures has been associated with efforts to continually improve provider quality rather than as a means of informing the local inspection process and, to date, public reporting of the resulting quality indicators has not been a goal.

New Zealand instituted a mandatory approach to assessing the needs of individuals receiving home care services several years ago, making the local home care agencies, which are funded by local health authorities, responsible for consistently collecting these assessments on a regular basis. These data provided the basis for formulating individualized care plans and made it possible for health policy analysts and central government officials to compare local health authorities on the adequacy of care systems, as evidenced by the level of clients' unmet needs and quality problems. While not used for provider-specific public reporting at this juncture, the availability of comparative reports across regions is almost the same thing, even though only government officials have access to the information for the time being. New Zealand has recently extended the uniform data-based assessment requirement to nursing homes and expects that the same process of gradual implementation and ultimate creation and distribution of quality reports will occur in time.

Finland is the other country in this group; it was classified here because of the major emphasis that both government and non-governmental agencies have given to the voluntary adoption of the uniform nursing home resident assessment. In contrast to the other countries described, a voluntary system makes it difficult to make comparisons across providers throughout the country. However, rather than use these data for public reporting, small consortia of nursing homes that have all volunteered to use a common assessment and to share the resulting quality indicators have emerged to undertake data-guided quality improvement programmes. While these kinds of voluntary consortia also have emerged in the other countries, Finland's voluntary approach makes it somewhat unique.

10 Monitoring the quality of long-term care in Finland

HARRIET FINNE-SOVERI, TEIJA HAMMAR, ANJA NORO, SARI ANTTILA AND PÄIVI VOUTILAINEN

10.1 Setting the context

The constitution of Finland stipulates that society must guarantee adequate social, health and medical services for each of its 5.3 million inhabitants, and promote the health of the population. Due to decentralized governance, responsibility for financing long-term care for older people rests heavily on the shoulders of 336 relatively independent local authorities (municipalities), as does the delivery of long-term care services.[1] Obliged by law to provide long-term care services for older dependent people, these municipalities are free either to provide services themselves or to purchase them from various for-profit or not-for-profit providers. Historically, municipalities have tended to rely on providing their own services.

According to the *Statistical Yearbook on Social Welfare and Healthcare* (National Institute for Health and Welfare, 2010), 87 per cent of all long-term care days[2] in residential facilities were produced in public facilities, 10 per cent in not-for-profit private facilities and only 3 per cent in for-profit private facilities. In contrast, when it comes to sheltered housing for older people, officially known as 'service houses' or 'sheltered housing', only 42 per cent of long-term care days were furnished by public providers while the private sector provided 32 per cent of care days in not-for-profit facilities and 26 per cent in for-profit facilities. Chronic care hospitals, known as 'health centres', are predominantly public (95 per cent). Recent statistics are not available for home care. In all these types of facilities municipalities are responsible

---

[1] Among other things, local authorities also have responsibility for funding and delivering primary and secondary school education.

[2] Long-term care days cover all individuals who formally receive long-term care services while living in residential homes and those who use care services for a period of ninety days or more.

for monitoring care but they are aided in this task by other entities. The National Supervisory Authority for Welfare and Health (known as Valvira), supervised by the Ministry of Social Affairs and Health, undertakes a national supervisory role, together with six Regional State Administrative Agencies (AVI).

Even though no uniform national quality management or improvement programme is mandatory for long-term care providers, this troika of municipalities, Valvira and regional AVIs has been implemented to ensure high-quality health and social services for the population, including chronically ill, older dependent persons. Other important legislative mechanisms aimed at ensuring quality of care and services include the Status and Rights of Patients Act (785/1992) (under healthcare legislation) and corresponding provisions on clients' rights under social care legislation (812/2002) that highlight patients' active roles in decision making. The importance of the latter is accentuated in long-term care institutions or similar settings which mainly are covered by the social sector. Moreover, policies that seek to promote the provision of high-quality care for older citizens are scattered within different parts of other legislation that regulates, among other things, patient payments, care for disabled people, substance abuse and mental health. The aim of these laws is to guarantee reasonable services and clients' rights for care and service recipients, regardless of age. Even though municipalities have wide-ranging freedom to organize long-term care services, they are obliged to adhere to this legislation and to any guidelines issued by Valvira or AVIs.

So far, the policy in Finland has been to improve care and services for elderly people through information and recommendations issued by the Ministry of Health and Social Affairs. However, since 2000 the evidence has increasingly shown that recommendations without any sanctioning powers are too weak a tool to push municipalities to invest properly in the care of older people. For instance, despite official recommendations issued by the Ministry of Health and Social Welfare (see Box 10.1) coverage of formal home care for those aged 75 and over has not reached the recommended level of 13–14 per cent; nor has the level of support available to those receiving informal care reached the recommended 5–6 per cent coverage rate (Figure 10.1).

Concerns over municipalities' willingness to maintain and improve long-term care services for older people and over the sustainability of these services have prompted new legislative proposals. During the

Monitoring the quality of long-term care in Finland 271

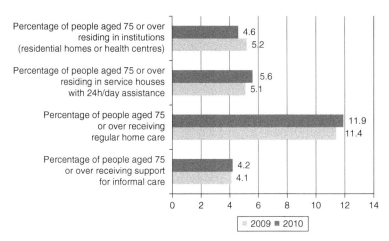

Figure 10.1 Provision of long-term care services in Finland, 2009 and 2010.
Source: National Institute for Health and Welfare, 2011.

Box 10.1 Government recommendations in Finland for long-term care coverage of those aged 75 or older according to type of care

- living in their own home (same services as other adult citizens), 91–2 per cent;
- living in their own home with support for informal care, 5–6 per cent;
- living in their own home with formal[3] home care, 13–14 per cent;
- living in service house apartments with twenty-four-hour/day services, 5–6 per cent;
- living in residential homes (beds) or chronic care hospital, 3 per cent.

Source: Ministry of Social Affairs and Health and Association of Finnish Local and Regional Authorities, 2008.

Note: The recommended coverage rate for each type of care takes into account overlapping of services received by different groups; for example, those living at home receiving the same services as other adult citizens may also be receiving formal home care and those living in their own home with formal home care may also be receiving support for informal care.

---

[3] Formal home care is defined as 'a minimum of one visit per week' by the National Institute for Health and Welfare.

national elections of spring 2011, a draft bill was tabled for comment by stakeholders. In addition, the bill was widely discussed in the media, which focused on the following key points:

- Should there be a subjective right to long-term care and services after a certain age?
- If the answer is yes, should this legally entrenched age be 75 or 80?
- Regarding staffing ratios in long-term care facilities, should minimum ratios be set in legislation?

At the time of writing, the draft legislation is still under discussion. The current national government may modify the content of the draft bill and any revised version would still need to be ratified by parliament.

Last, but not least, an ethics body exists that plays a role in quality assurance and monitoring long-term care. The National Advisory Board on Social Welfare and Healthcare Ethics (ETENE) was established in 1998 with the purpose of discussing ethical issues and publishing recommendations in the field of healthcare. The primary goal is to review and comment on health and social policy issues and to provide an ethical perspective from which such issues can be debated among health and social care professionals, as well as within the forum of public opinion. Among the long list of issues discussed by ETENE are patient autonomy and neglect (2003), care of dying persons (2010), the use of technology in health and social care (2010) and mental healthcare (2010). Currently, ETENE is promoting transparency and ethically sustainable care and service practices.

The rest of this chapter will describe the organization, financing and regulation of long-term care for older people in Finland, as well as the quality improvement mechanisms operating both in community and institutional settings. The chapter mainly concentrates on the residential care sector. National quality monitoring of formal home care mainly has been taking place in municipalities that use RAI-instruments but still, as of 2010, regulatory activities are weak or largely nonexistent.

10.2 Delivery and financing of long-term care

10.2.1 Types of services delivered

Long-term care is delivered in elderly peoples' own homes, in service houses (sheltered housing), either with or without twenty-four-hour

Monitoring the quality of long-term care in Finland 273

assistance, or in institutions, where two alternatives are available: (1) residential homes e.g. nursing homes under social legislation (under revision); and (2) chronic care hospitals e.g. health centres under health legislation (revised May 2011). When care is delivered at home, it includes all kinds of assistance ranging from home help[4] to personal tasks[5] in addition to nursing[6] and medical care.[7] However, current legislation distinguishes between home help under social legislation, and medical care under health legislation. Due to municipalities' independence as to how they organize care and services each town and geographical area has developed its own way of how – and under which law – to package service delivery for home residing clients. Service houses (sheltered housing) usually have their own staffing if care and assistance are available twenty-four hours per day. Such care includes the same variety of services as described in the context of home care. In contrast, service houses without twenty-four-hour services may have their own staffing or partially rely on public or private home care services. Exact figures on the combinations of services in this type of service home are not available.

According to national statistics, in 2009, 9,809 individuals lived in health centres (chronic care hospitals), 17,118 people lived in residential (nursing) homes and 25,684 individuals lived in service houses with twenty-four-hour assistance. Also in 2009, an additional 14,000 older people lived in service houses where twenty-four-hour assistance was not available. Approximately 89,000 people received home care in their own homes, and the majority of them were over 65. Moreover, since 2000, approximately 90 per cent of people in the 75 or over age cohort has been living in his/her own home but the overall number of beds in service houses has been slowly but steadily increasing. Home care services were mainly delivered by public

---

[4] Home help refers to assistance with instrumental activities in daily living (IADLs), e.g., shopping, transport, managing medications, cleaning, washing, making meals, laying and cleaning the table, etc.

[5] Personal tasks refers to assistance with basic activities in daily living (ADLs), e.g., eating, moving around, transfers, dressing, using the toilet, taking care of personal hygiene and bathing.

[6] Nursing refers to tasks performed by licensed nurses, e.g., changing catheters, wound care, IV-treatments, etc.

[7] Medical care refers to tasks performed by physicians and/or nurses, e.g., in addition to nursing, tasks such as diagnosing diseases or prescribing and monitoring medications.

municipalities directly. Few private organizations exist, and these predominantly are not contracted by public municipalities to provide services to their clients.

The supply of long-term care facilities and services has been reviewed in recent years. In 2008, the Ministry of Social Affairs and Health issued recommendations for municipalities stating that an ageing person should have the opportunity to live safely at home as long as possible. According to these recommendations each local authority should plan long-term care and corresponding services for those aged 75 years or older to meet a number of targets, as outlined in Box 10.1. These recommendations, aimed at decreasing levels of institutional care, were largely welcomed by the municipalities. The number of health centre and residential home beds has been rapidly shrinking; however, at the same time, concerns from older citizens about adequate numbers of nursing home beds have been increasing according to discussions mainly raised in the media.

10.2.2 Funding

In 2009, 24 per cent of individuals aged 75 or older received some kind of subsidy or subsided care, help, or accommodation financed from local and/or state taxes. Most local authorities have strict eligibility criteria for long-term care, particularly if twenty-four-hour assistance is available. Moreover, the criteria for eligibility may vary from area to area and authority to authority. Due to the independence of municipalities in providing care, the actual per diem cost of long-term care varies from town to town and area to area. Consequently, the sum paid by older care recipients with the same care needs depends substantially on where he or she lives – in the community (own home), in a service house or in a nursing home, and which of the 336 municipalities happens to be responsible.

In terms of funding, long-term care is divided into two categories: community care and institutional care. Community care covers all care delivered at the person's own home in addition to all care in service houses with or without twenty-four-hour assistance. Institutional care includes residential homes and long-term beds in health centres. The former is theoretically financed by the care recipient and the state, the latter by the care recipient and municipalities. Thus, long-term care is not delivered free of charge to the recipient. The majority of municipalities have created a payment scale to adjust individual payments according to the care recipients' income. In addition, 'a payment ceiling system' sets a maximum payment limit after which no more individual co-payments are made even if more services are provided. This ceiling keeps the total cost at moderate or low levels for care recipients. Despite these precautions, many older people's financial situations will not stretch to cover the actual costs of their care and services. Therefore, two options are available to them:

(1) To live in their own home or in service housing, where they can apply various subsidies from the National Insurance Institution to cover their long-term care costs. Municipalities may grant their own subsidies but this is optional. Additional financial help is often necessary since care recipients pay separately for accommodation, basic services, medication, food and healthcare.
(2) To move into an institution (if eligibility criteria are fulfilled) and pay up to 85 per cent of their individual income until the actual cost of care is covered. Usually, institutional care is all-inclusive, e.g., it includes accommodation, personal care, cleaning, clothing, food, medication and healthcare services.

In theory, the first option is primarily financed by the care recipient. In practice, care recipients cover a smaller proportion of their care, depending on their income. The true bulk of the cost is divided between the state, through the National Insurance Institution (financed by state taxation), and municipalities (financed by local taxation). The costs of the second option are divided between the care recipient and municipalities but not the state. Therefore, the majority of municipalities have found the first option tempting, whereas care recipients with heavy care needs and low incomes prefer the second option, which guarantees at least some monthly income left over even for the poorest individuals.

In summary, organizing and delivering long-term care is a mixture of care and services, guided by legislation that gives municipalities the freedom to organize and monitor on the one hand, but on the other, little means to compare and evaluate against others. It also puts the National Insurance Institute in a difficult position when municipalities can guide the flow of its expenditures by downsizing the number of institutional beds in favour of service housing. Moreover, older citizens in different parts of the country end up in unequal situations regarding co-payments and the long-term care services available.

10.3 Official regulatory mechanisms

Valvira is the central supervisory body that operates directly under the Ministry of Social Affairs and Health. It has primary regulatory tasks, such as licensing, inspection and performance auditing. Valvira also guides the six Regional State Administrative Agencies (AVI). National reforms introduced on 1 January 2010 aim to harmonize regional work and to enhance and ensure the same level of quality in long-term care services across the country's six districts. Close collaboration between the AVIs and Valvira in the areas of health and social care is mandated by legislation and includes monitoring and supervision through joint programmes. One of Valvira's other key roles is to grant (upon application) the right to practise as an authorized healthcare professional. The six Regional State Administrative Agencies have duties that include steering, supervising and monitoring all long-term care, including the services organized by municipalities. These duties also cover occupational health and safety, environmental permits, fire and rescue services and preparedness. Each AVI is responsible for one geographic area.

Unlike private care providers, municipalities can independently decide (without external permission from AVI) whether to build new public nursing homes or service houses, whereas private providers need to apply to the regional AVI for permission. Effectively this constitutes a dual system for authorizing and registering new facilities: a self-licensing system for municipal (public) providers and the AVI for private providers (Supervision of Private and Social Care Providers Act, 1996). According to the legislation governing supervision of private social services, the applicant (if a private provider) must provide his/her name, the name(s) of the care-providing unit(s), detailed contact information, detailed description of the planned care and services, the planned number of beds or clients and detailed information about the professionals responsible for care. This comprises profession, education, job experience and tasks in the unit. Moreover, the number and educational level of all other staff must be given. Other information that needs to be provided includes the planned starting day of the facility, location of client/patient documentation and the main details about the client register, including the name of the responsible register keeper. Information about the employer's register and adequacy, quality and safety of services also must be provided. The AVI is responsible for inspecting the private unit before care provision begins if it has been

Monitoring the quality of long-term care in Finland 277

planned as a twenty-four-hour facility.[8] The inspection comprises all aspects of the requirements outlined in the application (described above) and, if successful, the facility is permitted to start operating. Municipal authorities are responsible for overseeing all the care providers contracted by them, as well as their own facilities, and perform their own inspections. The current aim is to encourage a strong self-regulatory approach so that care providers also audit their care themselves and municipalities would not need to interfere. In cases of complaints by care recipients, AVIs and municipal authorities collaborate and perform the inspections together, with practices varying from area to area.

AVIs have a primary role in inspecting and monitoring the provision of all long-term care services including home care, whether they are public or private. Despite modest capacity, in 2010 AVIs conducted on-site inspections in about 5 per cent of public and private care units (nursing homes, service houses and health centres). The inspections are often systemically directed towards units that have received complaints from clients, their relatives or significant others. For care recipients there is a guided procedure on how to make complaints, assisted by the local ombudsman. Rather than taking the form of a general structured review, inspections focus on the issues stated in complaints, e.g., if the complaint is about medications, medication issues are reviewed, if they are about staffing, the staffing ratios and/or staff skills levels are inspected; if inappropriate care is highlighted, the care processes are assessed. Usually, the care provider first responds to AVIs (and in some cases to Valvira) within a set timeframe by collecting all documentation regarding the issue and providing a written report. Even though municipalities are primarily responsible for overseeing their own long-term care institutions and other care providers from which they purchase services, Valvira and/ or AVIs are permitted to inspect these units without preliminary notification. According to statistics held by Valvira and AVIs, in 2010 a high proportion of decisions in the social sector dealt with the care of elderly people (22 per cent), and over half of these led to further procedures. In Valvira, in 2010, approximately a quarter of complaints in the health sector led to further procedures. However, no statistics are available on the ratio relating to older people in long-term care.

---

[8] Non-twenty-four-hour service homes are usually inspected later by AVIs as part of the quality control process or earlier if something triggers an inspection, such as a complaint.

A new regulatory system that currently is being developed is going to convert some of the previous inspection processes into a more structured and uniform framework. In order to create and renew these processes, a single national review – the first of its kind – targeting all of the 1,500 long-term care facilities in Finland, was conducted by Valvira in 2009. These comprehensive internet-based, facility-level interviews comprised a broad set of questions, ranging from staffing numbers and skills to questions about accommodation and patient documentation. In addition, quality of care (relating to care processes) was examined in the areas of nutrition, rehabilitation, daily programmes for residents and frequency of medication reviews. According to the report based on this review (Valvira, 2010), 1,237 (82 per cent) nursing homes and service houses with twenty-four-hour assistance were included in the analysis, and 190 (15 per cent) did not meet all the criteria for good care. Of those failing to meet all the criteria, most were public providers. All of the failing facilities subsequently underwent more in-depth follow-up inspections.

The main reasons for facilities failing to meet criteria were:

(1) lower staffing levels than recommended by the Ministry of Health and Social Affairs, and the mix of skilled workers was too low or staff were not adequately qualified;
(2) questions about staffing were left blank in the internet survey;
(3) care plans were missing and the facility physician had not reviewed medications within six months;
(4) problems in more than one quality area.

It seems evident, however, that private for-profit and not-for-profit care providers fulfil criteria on staffing ratios and skill-mix because they have been monitored by supervisory bodies. In contrast, before 2009, public care providers had not been systematically monitored by these bodies (unless a complaint had been lodged), and therefore they had the option of deciding whether or not they would follow the Ministry's recommendations on staffing. In this context it is interesting to note that, according to a large study conducted by the National Institute for Health and Welfare (THL), between 2008 to 2010 in 134 service houses and nursing home units, public care providers were cheaper than private for-profit or not-for-profit care providers mainly due to lower staffing ratios. However, case-mix-adjusted quality of care was very similar in all the units examined in this study (Sinervo et al., 2010).

10.4 Quality management and improvement

As Finland has no mandatory quality improvement programmes, and partially due to the relative independence of municipalities in organizing the provision of long-term care, comparing the performance of long-term care facilities has been difficult or almost impossible. However, since 2000, when Resident Assessment Instrument (RAI) benchmarking programmes were launched, concrete data have been made available to allow for such comparisons. In the late 1990s attention was drawn to the RAI, also known as the Minimum Data Set (MDS), which originated in the United States as a mandatory long-term care resident assessment instrument that can be used for quality monitoring in nursing homes there. This instrument was created for long-term care facilities in the mid-1980s to enhance care planning – and through improved care processes to improve outcomes, and thus, the quality of professional care (Hawes et al., 1997). Later on, sister instruments were developed by interRAI, an international not-for-profit research organization and copyright holder of interRAI-instruments. Assessment instruments for home care, community care, acute care, mental health, palliative care and for those with intellectual disabilities[9] have been developed and during the past decade updated to form a fully compatible new suite. This fourth-generation set of assessment instruments is designed to improve the care of vulnerable populations. The new suite also contains a whole set of instruments to assess clients' subjective impressions and thoughts about the care they receive and their quality of life.

Today, each of the basic RAI-instruments comprises a comprehensive questionnaire to assess a person's needs/strengths along with a user's manual. From the variables in the questionnaire numerous well-validated scales can be derived. These include, among other things, cognitive impairment (Morris et al., 1994), basic and instrumental activities in daily living (BADL, IADL) (Morris et al., 1999), depression (Burrows et al., 2000), body- mass index (BMI), pain (Fries et al., 2001) and a scale for Changes in Health, End-stage disease and Symptoms and Signs (CHESS) (Hirdes et al., 2003). The unique features of this system are Clinical Assessment Protocols (CAPs) created particularly for the care planning process, Resource Utilization Groups (RUGs) for payment systems (Fries et al., 1994), and Quality Indicators (QIs) created

---

[9] www.interRAI.org.

for benchmarking between different units, wards or facilities (Zimmerman and Karon, 1995; Hirdes et al., 2004).

In Finland the use of RAI-instruments was launched in 2000 starting with long-term care facilities. Unlike the United States, implementation took place on a voluntary basis. The predecessor of the current National Institute for Health and Welfare (THL), an organization known as STAKES, initiated a pilot project in conjunction with long-term care facilities that were interested in improving their professional care through benchmarking. All the participating facilities and STAKES/THL agreed on the following:

(1) To ensure validity, the RAI questions must not be changed.
(2) Every nurse has to be trained to use the system.
(3) Every client/resident residing in the unit (or receiving home care in the area) has to be assessed. The minimum number of assessments is twice annually.
(4) Software has to be used in the assessment and care planning to ensure that the scales and client assessment protocols are immediately available for the nurse after the assessment. The service provider can either create its own software or purchase it commercially.
(5) Copies of the data have to be sent to STAKES/THL on 31 March and 30 September each year.
(6) In return, within two months of the data delivery STAKES/THL provides each facility with a unit-level benchmarking report in Excel format. This feedback information consists of means and frequencies of socio-demographic data such as age, sex, educational level and length of stay. The feedback report also offers means and frequencies of the main interRAI scales, such as cognition, ADLs, case-mix index and depression, in addition to some clinically meaningful variables, such as pain without pain medication, terminal prognosis, BMI and behavioural problems. Furthermore, the prevalence of twenty-two and the incidence of five quality indicators, developed in the 1990s by Zimmerman and Karon (1995), are presented. These quality indicators cover the following domains: accidents/injuries, mental health and behaviour, clinical care, cognition, continence, infections, nutrition, functional capacity, psychotropic medications, quality of life and skin care. Based on these data each of the units within the facility can compare outcomes of care to other units caring for similar older people and to national averages.

Monitoring the quality of long-term care in Finland 281

(7) STAKES/THL creates and updates bi-annually, a specific Cognos power play cube for benchmarking purposes on the internet, which is available to every RAI-using provider. The participant can see all the feedback information provided in the Excel reports in this Cognos power play cube and can pick any other unit anywhere in the country to make comparisons. This tool has been created for participants to enhance their networks and to learn from best practices.

(8) STAKES/THL organizes a national seminar bi-annually for nurses and other health and social care professionals to compare and discuss care improvement.

The National Institute for Health and Welfare (THL) has collected interRAI data bi-annually from institutions since 2000 and from home care organizations that use RAI-assessments for care planning and quality improvement purposes (since 2003). The mental health RAI-project started in 2006 and the RAI Acute care project in 2009. Moreover, interest in instruments to monitor intellectual disabilities, and palliative care are increasing. New organizations are joining annually, very few resign, and all those who participated in 2000 are expanding their use of RAI to more sophisticated areas, such as eligibility, integration of care and interactions with local politicians.

Today, the use of interRAI tools is still free of charge and voluntary. As the official register holder for health and social care registers, THL contracts with care providers under the same requirements agreed in the RAI pilot phase. Additional dimensions of the interRAI instruments, such as designing payment systems for long-term care facilities and holistic service planning at the local municipality level have entered the picture since 2009. Moreover, a new initiative, 'pay by performance', is currently being discussed.

The use of interRAI instruments has grown steadily since 2000 (see Figures 10.2 and 10.3) and in 2012, 23 per cent of all municipalities were participating in the programme. As Figure 10.3 demonstrates since 2009 interest in home care assessments has slightly overtaken the interest in nursing home instruments but both areas have similar levels of use. Both long-term care institutions and home care organizations are encouraged to use self-auditing methods to monitor and improve the quality of professional care. InterRAI tools, through THL-produced feedback reports, have provided a welcomed opportunity to do this.

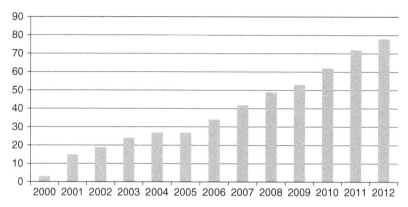

Figure 10.2 Number of municipalities using interRAI instruments, 2000–12.
Source: National Institute for Health and Welfare, 2012.

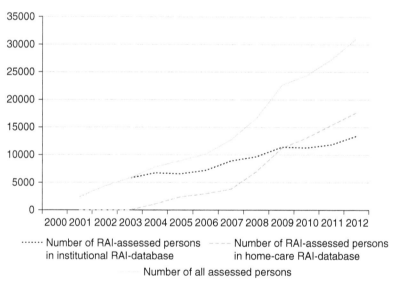

······ Number of RAI-assessed persons in institutional RAI-database   --- Number of RAI-assessed persons in home-care RAI-database
— Number of all assessed persons

Figure 10.3 Number of bi-annually assessed older people in Finland according to long-term care setting, 2000–12.
Source: National Institute for Health and Welfare, 2012.
Note: As the RAI was launched in 2000 no assessments were done in that year.

The possibility to benchmark performance has pushed through a dramatic improvement in care patterns, which is particularly evident in nursing homes' use of psychotropic medications. In 2000, 38 per cent

Monitoring the quality of long-term care in Finland

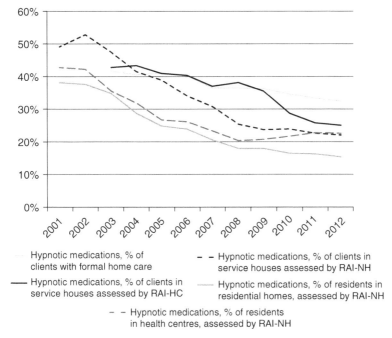

Figure 10.4 Use of hypnotic drugs in long-term care units in Finland, 2001–12. Source: National Institute for Health and Welfare, 2012.

of nursing home residents received hypnotic medication regularly whereas in 2010 the use of these medications was less than 16 per cent (Finne-Soveri et al., 2010). The latter statistic, in contrast to that of 2000, includes the use of melatonin, a natural circadian rhythm regulating hormone from the pineal gland, which comprises a little more than half of the use of hypnotics in 2011 (National Institute for Health and Welfare, 2012). The data for home care is representative from 2006 and reveals a similar trend, as presented in Figure 10.4, which shows a gradual decrease in the use of hypnotic medications in long-term care both at home and in service houses. The same trend also applies to the use of antipsychotic medications in nursing homes, where their use has decreased from 42 per cent to 26 per cent in ten years (Finne-Soveri et al., 2010). The corresponding change in home care within five years was only 2 per cent (from 18 per cent to 16 per cent). There was no change in service houses (26 per cent) (National Institute for Health and Welfare, 2012). Other areas of substantial improvement in nursing homes during the last ten years refer to the following problems: lack of nursing rehabilitation in late loss ADLs (down from 36 per cent to 16 per cent); lack of toileting plans (reduced from 73 per cent to 43 per cent) and lack of activities (down from 66 per cent to 49 per cent). However, the number of residents receiving nine or more medications has increased from 32 per cent to 42 per cent (Finne-Soveri et al., 2010). The reasons behind the increase in extensive poly-pharmacy are the increase in the use of Alzheimer's medications in nursing home settings and the national recommendations to provide vitamin D and calcium to every resident unless contraindicated (National Institute for Health and Welfare, 2012). Other quality areas have improved slowly or not at all. Whether the lack of improvement is due to structural changes in care provision, lack of adequate staffing levels, poor nursing quality or management skills, remains to be investigated.

The multiple uses of RAI long-term care data includes aiding long-term care clients in their decision-making. The national RAI registers have been used, with the written permission of care providers, to raise the visibility of quality of services. The Ministry of Social Affairs and Health, in collaboration with THL and Valvira, has launched a pilot for a collaborative website corresponding to the US website Nursing Home Compare.[10] On this website, information on care providers and some average indicators are presented for potential service users.[11] Since decision-making regarding eligibility for institutional care is still in the hands of municipalities and not all care providers use RAI, information for users is still patchy. However, in the future, competition in the long-term care market may increase, and incentives to gain a good reputation by presenting official data on care quality may tempt additional providers to participate. Other methods for quality management and improvement are sporadically used. Some service houses have been ISO-certified (www.iso.org) but official statistics about quality in long-term care, other than interRAI methods, do not exist.

10.5 Summary and discussion

Quality improvement and the regulatory systems for professional long-term care in elderly people's homes and in institutions are currently

---

[10] www.medicare.gov/NursingHomeCompare/.
[11] www.thl.fi/fi_FI/web/fi/hankesivu?id=22204.

Monitoring the quality of long-term care in Finland 285

undergoing a fundamental change regarding attitudes and operational standards. Clients' voices are being heard better than before through client satisfaction surveys, and client-centred care for older people is created by funding following the person. Consequently, individual care planning, as highlighted in the interRAI instruments, will receive increased attention. In the midst of these changes, there might be several reasons for the sustained voluntary interest in using interRAI tools to achieve quality improvement in long-term care facilities and in-home care.

Firstly, individual long-term care workers were quite alone in dealing with the growing pressure to improve quality before RAI benchmarking stepped into the scene. Professional training was targeted towards nurses in hospitals and palliative care was discussed mainly in the context of cancer patients. InterRAI assessment tools offered, for the first time, an opportunity to identify the needs of clients in a standardized way and to follow up individual outcomes of care in provider units. Nurses could finally substantiate that they were doing good work even if their clients suffered from multiple conditions and died within three years. Moreover, successful work practices and particularly beneficial changes in care patterns could be rewarded both through recognition and by financial incentives or bonuses.

Secondly, care providers found a handy leadership and management tool in interRAI instruments and the benchmarking reports. Resource Utilization Groups (RUG) and the case-mix index are RAI embedded scales to measure care burdens. The higher the index, the more staff with higher skills are needed. It became easier to distinguish leadership problems (which are common) from true lack of staffing resources. In addition, benchmarking reports showed clearly what kinds of skills were needed in different units.

Thirdly, private providers have been entering the field, which historically has been covered by public services. Older individuals very seldom have money to cover all the costs of long-term care. The most important clients for any care provider are municipalities as they purchase services for older citizens. Consequently, both traditional care providers and newcomers have felt an increasing need to 'make one's case' in order to survive the competition in the long-term care market. National benchmarking figures have turned out to be very useful in showing several dimensions of good care. Both central and municipalities in Finland, which has a high degree of decentralized governance, were quite lost without gold (national) standards for quality before RAI indicators were available. Before benchmarking, the care purchasing process and tendering were almost totally based on costs and heavily criticized for not taking quality into account.

Fourthly, voluntary participation still has the effect of putting pressure on those who have not joined the RAI framework. Local politicians increasingly ask for information about quality of care. In the context of Valvira's internet surveys of long-term care facilities, public discussion has pointed out that RAI-users might represent the elite of long-term care services with regard to quality of care. If this really is the case, which is quite likely (but no proper analysis has yet been undertaken), the pressure on more providers to participate will increase.

Fifthly, the entire state can benefit from the registers created through the use of standardized assessments such as RAI, not least in informing recommendations for quality of care. In addition, in Finland, where currently the entire care and service systems are changing and legislation is being revised, such data has been used in political decision making.

In conclusion, the voluntary use of RAI and the benefits of standardized interRAI assessment instruments seem to exceed whatever inconvenience or costs they may create. The most likely explanation for this is to be found in their broad capacity for multiple uses on multiple levels. Regarding the issue of collaboration between THL and Valvira, the former has the role of being the national register holder and overseeing quality improvement, while the latter has the role of being the national regulatory and supervisory body for long-term care. While no facility-level information has been shared, averages have been data-mined from the RAI databases to identify potential weaknesses in quality of care, in order to assist Valvira and AVIs in their tasks. They, too, need national figures to lean on. This collaboration between the two governmental bodies will continue and might expand to areas where data can be used in Valvira's or AVIs auditing processes with permission from the facilities and/or municipalities. The vision of all these governmental organs is to help care providers to self-audit and to develop spontaneous and continuous quality improvement methods – using whatever tool they may choose to achieve positive outcomes. Importantly, electronic documentation and registers with ongoing data collection have created an opportunity to follow up (online) the impact of individual care. National registers offer an opportunity for national and cross-national benchmarking, at least in the countries where interRAI tools are widely used.

References

Burrows, A. B., Morris, J. N., Simon, S. E., Hirdes, J. P. and Phillips, C. D. (2000). Development of an MDS-based Depression Rating Scale for use in nursing homes. *Age and Ageing*, 29: 165–72.

Finne-Soveri, H., Hammar, T. and Noro, A. (2010). Measuring quality of long-term institutional care in Finland. *Eurohealth*, 16(2): 8–10.

Fries, B. E., Schneider, D. P., Foley, W. J., Gavazzi, M., Burke, R. and Cornelius, E. (1994). Refining a case-mix measure for nursing homes: Resource Utilization Groups (RUG-III). *Medical care*, 32(7): 668–85.

Fries, B. E., Simon, S. E., Morris, J. N., Flodstrom, C. and Bookstein, F. L. (2001). Pain in US nursing homes: validating a pain scale for the minimum data set. *The Gerontologist*, 1(2): 173–9.

Hawes, C., Morris, J., Phillips, C. D., Fries, B. E., Murphy, K. and Mor, V. (1997). Development of the Nursing Home Resident Assessment Instrument in the USA. *Age and Ageing*, 26(2): 19–25.

Hirdes, J. P., Fries, B. E., Morris, J. N., Ikegami, N., Zimmerman, D., Dalby, D. M., Aliaga, P., Hammer, S. and Jones, R. (2004). Home care quality indicators (HCQIs) based on the MDS-HC. *Gerontologist*, 44(5): 665–79.

Hirdes, J. P., Frijters, D. H. and Teare, G. F. (2003). The MDS-CHESS Scale: A new measure to predict mortality in institutionalized older people. *Journal of the American Geriatric Society*, 51: 96–100.

Ministry of Social Affairs and Health and Association of Finnish Local and Regional Authorities. (2008) *National Framework for High Quality Services for Older People*. Ministry of Social Affairs and Health, publication no. 5: 1–54.

Morris, J. N., Fries, B. E., Mehr, D. R., Hawes, C., Phillips, C. D. and Mor, V. (1994). MDS Cognitive Performance Scale. *Journal of Gerontology: Medical Sciences*, 49A(4): M174–82.

Morris, J. N., Fries, B. E. and Morris, S. A. (1999). Scaling ADLs within the MDS. *Journal of Gerontology: Medical Sciences*, 54A(11): M546–M553.

National Institute for Health and Welfare (2010). *Statistical Yearbook on Social Welfare and Healthcare 2010*. Helsinki: NIHW.

(2011). *Statistical Yearbook on Social Welfare and Healthcare 2011*. Helsinki: NIHW.

(2012). National RAI-database. THL. Available at: www.thl.fi.

Sinervo, T., Noro, A., Tynkkynen, L.-K., Sulander, J., Taimio, H., Finne-Soveri, H., Lilja, R. and Syrjä, V. (2010). *Yksityinen vai kunnallinen palveluasuminen? Kustannukset, asiakasrakenne, hoidon laatu ja henkilöstön hyvinvointi* [Sheltered Housing – Private or Municipal?

Costs, Clientele Structure, Quality of Care, and the Well-Being of Personnel]. Helsinki: National Institute for Health and Welfare (THL).

Valvira (2010). *Vanhusten ympärivuorokautisen sosiaalihuollon palvelut. Toimintayksiköihin tehdyn kyselyn tulokset ja valvonnan jatkotoimenpiteet* [Twenty-four-hour-a-day Services for Older People in Nursing Homes and Service Houses. Results of a Survey and Further Actions]. Helsinki: Selvityksiä.

Zimmerman, D. R. and Karon, S. L. (1995). Developing and testing of nursing home quality indicators. *Healthcare Financing Review*, 16: 107–28.

11 Regulation of long-term care in the United States

DAVID STEVENSON AND JEFFREY BRAMSON

11.1 Introduction

The market for nursing home care and other long-term care services is one of the most heavily regulated sectors in the US economy. Although long-term care regulations often serve secondary ends, such as controlling provider supply or regulating the price of services, the majority of these rules are designed to ensure the quality and appropriateness of services. There are different theories for the presence of regulation but a standard explanation is that they exist to address some type of market failure, such as consumers' inability to assess, monitor and respond to low-quality care. Thus, government regulation can assist uninformed consumers by developing quality standards, evaluating whether those standards are met, and enforcing improvement when standards are not met. In addition, regulatory standards address the market and political power of nursing facilities and chains relative to residents, who are often sick, elderly and vulnerable.

While similar factors could apply to regulation of other industries, the large degree of public financing for long-term care services in the United States further justifies the extensive governmental intervention. Indeed, although the government itself owns very few long-term care facilities, the federal and state governments are the primary payers for services delivered in these settings. Medicare, a federal entitlement programme of health insurance coverage for the elderly and other protected classes, pays for the majority of post-acute (following acute hospital discharge) nursing home, home health and rehabilitative care. This programme is complemented by Medicaid, a means-tested social insurance programme for certain categories of individuals, primarily regulated and financed by the federal government but administered by the individual states. Medicaid is the primary payer for long-term services and supports, including the large majority of chronic nursing home care, in the United States.

289

Governmental regulation of long-term care services in the US is partly a response to political pressures by both the general public and the long-term care industry. Periodic scandals and revelations about the quality of care in nursing homes have required the US Congress and regulatory agencies in the executive branch to reassess the stringency of the rules iteratively over time. At the same time, reflecting the political strength of the long-term care industry at the state level, some regulations serve more political ends (e.g., state certificate of need programmes, which protect existing facilities by limiting market entry of possible competitor facilities). Whatever the ultimate motivation behind long-term care regulations, the present system boasts a comprehensive regulatory scheme, with a complex interplay of federal, state and voluntary rules controlling and monitoring the quality of nursing homes and, to a lesser extent, other providers. A number of federal laws, including the recent Patient Protection and Affordable Care Act of 2010 (hereafter referred to as the ACA), aim to control access to, and the costs of, long-term care services. Nonetheless, the current regulatory scheme focuses primarily on quality assurance, which will be the focus of this chapter.

Although quality control is a goal in and of itself, long-term care regulations also serve two related functions. First, they are supposed to deter future violations of quality standards – the government cannot identify and pursue every violation, so it instead relies on unannounced inspections and harsh potential penalties to deter lapses in quality. Second, the rules signal to the public that these services are safe to consume, a form of quality assurance important to the maintenance of public confidence in the industry.

In this chapter, we begin with a brief description of the market for long-term care services in the United States, followed by a historical description of how long-term care regulation developed. We move to a three-part explanation of the quality control mechanisms currently in place: (1) the standards for participation, (2) the monitoring and enforcement of compliance, and (3) public reporting and other market-based approaches to improving quality. We focus first and primarily on regulation of nursing home care, given the predominant focus of regulation and the surrounding literature on this sector, before moving to a brief discussion of regulation of other long-term care services. We conclude with a brief discussion of the current state and future of long-term care regulation.

11.2 Demand for long-term care services in the United States

Almost 10 million individuals in the United States have limitations in activities of daily living (ADLs) or instrumental activities of daily living (IADLs), roughly two-thirds of whom are elderly (Tumlinson et al., 2007). The majority (83 per cent) of individuals who need long-term care reside in the community, often supported by unpaid care from family and friends (O'Brien, 2005). For those requiring paid supportive services (either in the community or in a nursing home), the vast majority are uninsured against these potentially catastrophic costs. Private health insurance generally does not cover long-term care, and few elderly people hold specific long-term care policies to cover their expenses (Stevenson et al., 2010). Instead, most individuals in the US rely on one of several governmental programmes to pay for their long-term care services. The federal Medicare programme, an acute care-focused social insurance programme covering almost everyone over age 65 and some under-65 disabled people, provides a range of post-acute care benefits. Although distinct from long-term supportive services, these rehabilitative services – which accounted for more than US$50 billion in spending in 2009 (MedPac, 2010) – are especially important to nursing home and home health providers. The primary source of financing long-term supportive services in the US is the Medicaid programme, a public programme jointly financed and administered by federal and state governments. Medicaid is a means-tested programme covering healthcare services for certain categories of individuals (including aged, blind, and disabled individuals) who meet strict income and asset requirements. Medicaid long-term care spending was almost US$125 billion in 2009, comprising around 62 per cent of all long-term care spending nationwide (NHPF, 2011).

Public funding of the long-term care market historically has gone to the nursing home sector. Since the advent of Medicare and Medicaid in 1965, federal and state policies, as well as a range of political and practical factors, have contributed to what has been labelled an 'institutional bias' in long-term care service delivery, favouring nursing home care over community-based alternatives (Kane et al., 1998). At present, there are around 16,500 nursing homes and 1.6 million nursing home beds in the US (Harrington et al., 2010). Despite substantial support from government-administered programmes, almost all nursing homes are privately operated in the US, with almost two-thirds on a for-profit basis. In addition, more than half of all nursing homes are operated by multi-facility organizations (i.e., they are part of a chain); just over 13 per cent of nursing homes are operated by a hospital. Over the last two decades, a wider range of home- and community-based services have become available to older Americans who need assistance with activities of daily living, some of which have been supported with governmental dollars. Relative to the nursing home sector, oversight mechanisms for home- and community-based providers (e.g., assisted living facilities) are under-developed, despite some overlap in the services provided and populations served.

As discussed below, federal and state governments in the US engage in a partnership to finance, deliver and regulate long-term care services, primarily in the context of state Medicaid programmes. The federal government establishes broad guidelines, specifying mandatory requirements and a range of options available to states. As long as states operate within these guidelines, the federal government is required by law to reimburse states for Medicaid expenditures on an open-ended basis, covering between 50 and 83 per cent of programme costs (depending on a state's per capita income). In addition to covering the remaining programme costs, states set rules regarding eligibility, enrolment and benefits (within federal guidelines). They also contract with and pay providers, and they handle the day-to-day administration of the programmes, including required oversight activities.

11.3 Historical development of long-term care regulation

The history of long-term care regulation in the US consists of three main eras: (1) the paucity of regulations before Medicare and Medicaid were passed in 1965; (2) the uncoordinated attempts to control quality between 1965 and 1987; and (3) the aftermath of the Omnibus Budget Reconciliation Act of 1987, which redefined long-term care quality control.[1] The PPACA of 2010 may initiate a fourth era that focuses on evidence-based techniques and more sophisticated monitoring of quality, but not enough is yet known about the consequences and implementation of this law to determine if such a paradigm shift will occur.

---

[1] For more on this history, several sources provide additional detail: Mendelson, 1974; Vladeck and Twentieth Century Fund, 1980; IOM, 1986; Binstock et al., 1996.

11.3.1 Pre-1965

Before the passage of Medicare and Medicaid in 1965, there was little direct financing of health insurance or healthcare by the US federal government (except for military veterans), and state and local governments provided supportive services only in limited settings, such as mental health hospitals and government-owned facilities for needy individuals ('poorhouses' or 'workhouses'). Instead, government support for long-term care primarily came in the form of welfare payments to elderly and disabled individuals receiving long-term services and supports (e.g., through the Old Age Assistance programme), and through various programmes to support construction of and access to long-term care facilities. By and large, the federal government did not promulgate extensive rules regarding long-term care facilities during this time, and attempts to control quality were undertaken mostly by individual states and municipalities. These rules generally were neither stringent enough to present serious barriers to low-quality facilities nor widespread enough to prevent the aggregation of lower-quality facilities in less-regulated areas.

As a result, ensuring adequate quality of care was a persistent challenge to federal and state policy makers in the decades leading up to the passage of Medicare and Medicaid. In the mid-1950s, for instance, the Commission on Chronic Illness, several states and the Council on State Governments all reported quality-of-care problems (IOM, 1986). Shortly thereafter, the US Public Health Service concluded that few states did an adequate job surveying and inspecting nursing homes, subsequently reporting that 44 per cent of nursing homes failed to meet minimal fire and health standards. With these developments as context, the US Congress expanded the government's involvement in the long-term care sector in 1960, when it passed legislation that was the precursor to today's Medicaid programme (the Medical Assistance for the Aged law, better known as 'Kerr-Mills' legislation). Kerr-Mills provided matching payments to the states to provide medical care to low-income elderly people. Although the programme did not have the national impact that was envisioned by its sponsors, one estimate posits that Kerr-Mills provided assistance to nearly half of all nursing home residents by 1965 (Vladeck and Twentieth Century Fund, 1980), when Congress took up the issue again in the context of the passage of Medicare and Medicaid.

11.3.2 1965–87

By 1965, the US federal government was playing a significant role in financing nursing home care, even though federal standards governing this care essentially did not exist. States receiving federal funds were required to have nursing home licensure programmes, and nursing homes built with federal construction dollars had to meet specific standards. These requirements were largely ineffective, however, and state licensure programmes varied widely in the stringency and implementation of their standards. Medicare and Medicaid would begin to change this inconsistency by establishing uniform conditions of programme participation, under which providers had to meet specific standards to receive payment. However, this transformation would not happen overnight.

The passage of Medicare and Medicaid in 1965 initially did little to affect the toughness of nursing home licensure and other quality control requirements, in large part because few facilities met the standards of care envisioned by the programme. Federal policy makers accommodated this reality, reflecting both a reluctance to face the embarrassment of creating an empty entitlement promise and a response to intense lobbying from states and long-term care providers who feared losing out on federal dollars. Within the Medicare programme, for instance, policy makers created the category of 'substantial compliance', which allowed facilities to participate while they worked toward full compliance. On the Medicaid side, the federal government withdrew a proposal to align Medicare and Medicaid nursing home standards and essentially remanded the issue to the states, thereby delaying the arrival of uniform standards of care. In the immediate wake of Medicaid and Medicare, some felt that the regime of care standards and enforcement was not radically different than it was previously (Moss and Halamandaris, 1977).

Although there were several efforts to strengthen nursing home standards and their enforcement over the subsequent two decades, progress remained slow. This was problematic given the tremendous growth experienced in the long-term care industry, most of which was fuelled by expanded cost-based reimbursement from the government. In many ways, the substantial growth of private, predominantly for-profit facilities during this time established the modern US nursing home industry, with larger, more medically focused facilities becoming the

Regulation of long-term care in the United States 295

industry norm. Between 1963 and 1968, for instance, the number of nursing homes increased from 16,701 to 19,141 (a 15 per cent increase), while the number of beds jumped from 568,560 to 836,554 (a 47 per cent increase) (HEW, 1972).

11.3.3 1987–Present

By the 1970s and 1980s, there was significant evidence that quality failures had become prevalent in the long-term care industry. Two triggering events then compelled Congress to alter the existing obligations of long-term care providers. First, a federal court determined that the Medicare and Medicaid statutes implied that the federal government had an administrative obligation to guarantee that facilities receiving federal money were satisfying legal requirements, including providing high quality medical and patient care (*Smith v. Heckler*, 1984). Second, following failed attempts to reform the standards in the early to mid-1980s, Congress entrusted to the non-governmental Institute of Medicine (IOM) with the responsibility of completing an independent study of nursing home quality and making recommendations as to what reforms were necessary. The IOM report in 1986, *Improving the Quality of Care in Nursing Homes*, offered detailed accounts of widespread quality problems and recommended a drastic overhaul of long-term care regulation (IOM, 1986). Simultaneously, the Government Accountability Office (GAO), the auditing arm of the US Congress, issued its 'Medicare and Medicaid: stronger enforcement of nursing home requirements needed' report, which found that a third of all nursing homes did not meet existing federal quality standards (GAO, 1987).

Following these events – and the broad consumer advocacy associated with them – Congress was forced to act. As part of the Omnibus Budget Reconciliation Act of 1987 (OBRA '87), Congress passed the Nursing Home Reform Act.[2] OBRA '87 significantly altered the responsibilities of long-term care facilities, and to this day it remains the primary source of statutory long-term care requirements, along with the administrative regulations promulgated by government agencies in

---

[2] Long-term care specialists in the US refer to OBRA '87 as the relevant legislation, not the Reform Act itself.

accordance with the statute. The content of these requirements will be explored in later sections of this chapter. While many priorities were realigned by OBRA '87, the most significant high-level change was the shift toward resident-focused, outcome-oriented standards. The new regulations, for the very first time, focused on quality of care, patients' rights, and patient-reported quality of life and satisfaction (more detail on these standards is provided below). OBRA '87 also established the conditions of participation for nursing home providers to receive Medicare and Medicaid reimbursement. For these reasons, the law is considered the foundation of modern-day nursing home regulation.

11.3.4 Current trends

Although OBRA '87 still governs nursing home regulation, the field is experiencing significant flux that could further alter nursing home oversight. Market-driven approaches such as federally mandated public reporting have been growing steadily, emphasizing a supervisory role for the federal government, as opposed to one of only regulation and oversight. Nonetheless, a vast majority of the public believes that *more* regulation of nursing homes is necessary to ensure a higher quality of care (Furrow et al., 2008), a view shared by the majority of specialists within the long-term care research and policy communities as well (Mor et al., 2010).

The recently passed health reform law (ACA) requires the federal government and long-term care facilities to increase the emphasis on evidence-based medicine and information sharing; however, because the regulations pursuant to ACA have yet to be issued, this chapter will not focus on these details except where directly relevant. Moreover, as described below, the regulatory framework for non-nursing home long-term care providers remains relatively undefined, despite more government resources funding care at home and in other residential settings such as assisted living facilities.

11.4 Requirements for nursing home providers

11.4.1 Delineation of responsibility

Low-quality nursing home providers can be excluded from participating in the market through one of two mechanisms: (1) licensure

Regulation of long-term care in the United States   297

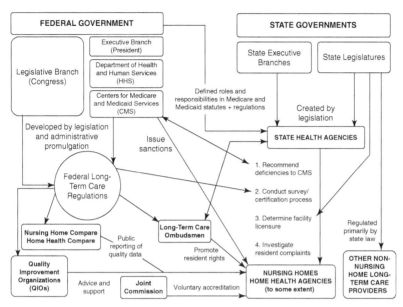

Figure 11.1 Graphical representation of some of the entities involved in long-term care regulation in the United States.
Source: compiled by authors.

requirements that exclude under-performing facilities from delivering care, and (2) quality conditions that must be met for the facility to be eligible for federal reimbursement of services. Although these two functions are fundamentally related, they are sharply divided in the US, with the state governments responsible for licensing nursing home facilities and the federal government responsible for determining the conditions for reimbursement of services delivered to Medicare and Medicaid beneficiaries. Figure 11.1 provides a graphical depiction of the complex interaction of federal and state governments in long-term care regulation, including their relationship with the various entities described in this chapter.

State licensure requirements historically have excluded very few facilities. Loss of licence is considered a drastic remedy that is reserved for very serious breaches of patient safety and quality-of-care standards. Instead, the primary regulatory stringency exists in the federal conditions of participation (Furrow et al., 2008), which stem primarily from OBRA '87.

11.4.2 Federal CMS requirements of participation

11.4.2.1 Regulatory requirements

While OBRA '87 was designed to improve quality in all nursing homes, Congress elected to apply the certification requirements only to those homes that receive payment for services supplied to Medicare and Medicaid beneficiaries. The primary payer for the large majority of the nursing-home-eligible population is the Centers for Medicare and Medicaid Services (CMS), an agency within the Department of Health and Human Services (HHS). Around 95 per cent of all licensed facilities also undergo the CMS certification process and must comply with the federal rules.

The participation requirements in OBRA '87 are quite extensive. Codified in 42 CMS, §483, these rules cover everything from nurse staffing levels to the minimum scope of dental services required. Marshall Kapp, a lawyer and researcher who specializes in long-term care regulation, has identified some of the most important of these hundreds of regulations:

ensuring resident privacy and decisional rights regarding accommodations, medical treatment, personal care, visits, written and telephone communications, and meetings with others [42 C.F.R. § 483.10(e)(1)]; maintaining confidentiality of personal and clinical records [§ 483.10(e)(2)]; guaranteeing facility access and visitation rights to persons of the resident's choosing [§ 483.10(k)]; requiring issuance of notice of rights at the time of admission [§ 483.10(b)]; ensuring proper use of physical restraints and psychoactive drugs [§ 483.13(a)]; protecting resident funds being managed in the facility [§ 483.10(c)]; ensuring transfer and discharge rights, and issuing related notices [§ 483.12(a)]; requiring minimum staffing levels regarding nursing and social work coverage [§ 483.15(g)]; requiring comprehensive resident assessments and individualized care plans drawn in accordance with those assessments [§ 483.20(d)]; requiring state prescreening of all prospective NF admittees [§ 483.20(m)]; and prohibiting admission of individuals with mental illness or mental retardation unless those individuals are found specifically to need nursing services [§ 483.20(f)]. (Kapp, 2000: 712).

11.4.2.2 Minimum Data Set

Among the most crucial of the OBRA '87 requirements, from the perspective of quality assurance, is the mandatory implementation of the Minimum Data Set (MDS). The MDS is a database of information compiled from the standardized Resident Assessment Instrument

Regulation of long-term care in the United States 299

(RAI) forms, which monitor the care plans and quality outcomes for all residents in a given home. The required collection and reporting of these data has had broad consequences, despite the fact that the MDS itself does not have any performance benchmarks. First, there has been a marked improvement in many of the process measures in the MDS, including a decline in catheter and restraint use and an increase in advance medical directives (Rantz et al., 1999). Second, there have been some actual improvements in resident health, with lower incidences of many conditions often associated with poor-quality nursing home care, such as falls, pressure ulcers and malnutrition (Kapp, 2000). Finally, the RAI has triggered more comprehensive discussions between residents and their care providers about their individualized care planning, quality concerns and end-of-life wishes.

The 2010 ACA law leaves in place all of the existing OBRA '87 standards for participation in the CMS programmes, while adding some new requirements. Perhaps most notably, the new law includes provisions around transparency and disclosure of nursing home ownership structures, in order to clarify accountability for care in the context of complex ownership and operating structures, which we discuss in more detail below (Furrow et al., 2010).

11.4.3 State implementation of CMS regulations

Although the participation conditions derive from federal statutory OBRA '87 requirements and CMS regulations, the task of policing compliance with these standards falls on the states. This fragmentation of responsibility has been noted as a potential problem, for it increases bureaucracy without promoting federal-state cooperation, and puts the state agencies in an uncomfortable position of dual accountability. A unified federal approach could be more efficient, but inertia may protect the current framework for the time being (Walshe, 2001).

Under OBRA '87, each state must create a state agency to administer regulatory oversight, maintain health standards for long-term care institutions, provide for regular review of each patient's needs within the nursing home and otherwise comply with the mandates of Congress and CMS (*Smith v. Heckler*, 1984). Although the states are afforded significant discretion in how to create and administer these agencies, some interstate uniformity is nonetheless mandated. For example, the states are required to use federal forms and follow federal inspection protocols during the survey/certification process.

CMS generally defers to state determinations of eligibility for reimbursement. However, the 1965 Medicare and Medicaid statutes do allow the federal government to review state decisions and to overrule them if necessary. This prerogative, known as the 'look behind' provision, guarantees that ultimate control over these federal programmes is held by the federal government, at least formally.

11.4.4 State standards

Although the most important role of states in nursing home regulations ostensibly is in the implementation of federal standards, states that wish to increase the stringency of long-term care regulation do have certain tools available to them. Many states, for instance, have staffing standards that are stricter than the federal guidelines (Harrington and Millman, 2001). The majority of states also have some sort of certificate-of-need (CON) requirement for entry into the nursing home industry (and, to a lesser extent, other long-term care settings), mandating that new facilities address an unmet need. Such programmes are controversial, however, given that they may unduly limit market competition (NCSL, 2011).

11.4.5 Voluntary quality control

While the federal and state regulations discussed above comprise the mandatory requirements of nursing home facilities, many nursing homes elect to undergo additional voluntary scrutiny. Chief among these voluntary programmes is accreditation from the Joint Commission. Importantly, while the Joint Commission's determinations are deemed official for hospitals and some other institutions, they remain strictly voluntary for nursing homes. To date, there is no conclusive evidence that voluntary accreditation results in appreciable quality improvements, and replacement of the current nursing home regime with Joint Commission 'deeming' is unlikely to occur.

Many nursing homes in the US also take advantage of a range of related quality assurance and improvement activities. Almost half of all nursing homes, for instance, participate in the federally supported Advancing Excellence campaign, a programme that has engaged

Regulation of long-term care in the United States 301

provider, advocacy and policy stakeholders and is designed to assist nursing homes in working toward targeted, self-identified goals for quality improvement. Similarly, the federal Quality Improvement Organization (QIO) programme (described below) works with providers in a more consultative way than is allowed in the regulatory process. On the quality control side, nursing home providers, especially larger providers, may engage in internal quality assurance programmes that investigate adverse events, or utilization review programmes to assess whether the services rendered to residents are medically appropriate (Kapp, 2000).

11.5 Monitoring compliance and enforcement mechanisms

11.5.1 *Survey/certification and complaint investigation process*

11.5.1.1 Surveys and certification
In accordance with the federal regulations in 42 CFR, § 483, state survey agencies conduct inspections of all nursing homes seeking reimbursement for Medicare (Skilled Nursing Facilities, or SNFs) or Medicaid (Nursing Facilities, or NFs) services. These inspections take place every nine to fifteen months and are unannounced to the facilities, thus preserving the element of surprise that compels nursing homes to remain vigilant for quality violations. The state agency then determines whether the facility merits a 'certificate of compliance' or whether any deficiencies – instances where facilities are out of compliance – warrant citation. When found, each deficiency is categorized into one of seventeen areas and rated by its scope and severity (on an 'A' to 'L' scale in order of increasing severity). Following inspection, recommendations are submitted to the regional CMS office (for SNFs) or the state Medicaid office (for NFs) for final certification (CMS, 2011a). Facilities that deliver care under both of these programmes, which includes most nursing homes, are subject to both certification requirements.

Based on a recent analysis by the Federal HHS Office of the Inspector General (OIG), almost 92 per cent of all nursing homes had at least one deficiency reported in 2007. Although this proportion has been steady in recent years, it is up from a rate of 81 per cent in 1998. The average number of deficiencies per facility was seven in 2007, with for-profit and chain facilities having higher rates of deficiencies relative to non-profit and non-chain facilities. The most common deficiency types in 2007

302   *David Stevenson and Jeffrey Bramson*

pertained to citations related to quality of care (74 per cent of facilities had a deficiency in this category), resident assessment (58 per cent), quality of life (43 per cent), and dietary services (43 per cent). Most deficiencies received by nursing homes did not involve immediate jeopardy or actual harm to residents (17 per cent). Importantly, substantial cross-state variation exists in the percentage of facilities that receive deficiencies (ranging from 76 to 100 per cent) and in the number of deficiencies per facility (ranging from 2.5 to 14.4 per cent) (OIG, 2008).

11.5.1.2 Complaints

When a nursing home resident suffers an adverse event or is dissatisfied with the quality of care provided by the facility, he or she is entitled to make a formal complaint to the state regulatory agency, which then investigates the complaint. The recent health reform law includes provisions to make the complaint filing process even easier for residents by requiring state agencies to offer standardized complaint forms on their websites and to implement streamlined complaint resolution processes (Furrow et al., 2010).

Consumer complaints data have historically been less widely available than deficiency data, although this has changed in recent years. In 2007, 37,153 complaints were received for nursing home care, 14,394 (39 per cent) of which were substantiated. Although complaints offer useful supplementary data in addition to survey inspections, around 80 per cent of facilities did not have any substantiated complaints in 2007. As with deficiency data, consumer complaint rates vary substantially across states. Based on analyses of 2002 complaints data, for instance, the annual rate of complaints (per 100 residents) ranged from 0.6 to 16.5, while the substantiation rate for investigated complaints ranged from 38 to 66 per cent (Stevenson, 2006).

11.5.2 Available sanctions

11.5.2.1 CMS remedies

Before OBRA '87, the only available sanction against non-compliant facilities was to terminate their eligibility to receive Medicare and/or Medicaid reimbursement. Although this extreme remedy might deter particularly egregious violations, it is an unwieldy tool that has been utilized infrequently by CMS. Since 1987, the availability of other remedies has further decreased the relevance of the termination

Regulation of long-term care in the United States 303

sanction, although this remedy remains available against facilities that pose frequent or immediate jeopardy to their residents. Since the passage of OBRA '87, CMS has had access to a wider array of available sanctions against violating facilities. Upon finding a deficiency, the state (on behalf of CMS) categorizes the seriousness of the violation based on whether any actual harm occurred, the degree of potential harm, the prevalence of the deficiencies and the facility's prior history of noncompliance, as per 42 CFR, § 488.404. The remedies to address deficiencies, laid out in this regulation, range in seriousness from requiring a directed plan of correction, state monitoring of the facility or directed in-service training (Category 1); to denial of payment for new admissions and civil monetary penalties – the latter of which are a relatively recent addition (1999) (Category 2); to further civil penalties, temporary management (receivership) and termination from the Medicare and Medicaid programmes (Category 3).

Another potential remedy that focuses at the level of the corporation rather than the facility is the implementation of a quality-of-care Corporate Integrity Agreement (CIA), a contract with CMS that requires nursing home corporations with identified quality of care problems to consent to additional requirements in exchange for non-exclusion from the Medicare and Medicaid programmes. CIAs, which generally last for three to five years, have been used by CMS in recent years, and there is evidence that these contracts are capable of significantly improving quality of care structures, processes and outcomes (OIG, 2009).

Despite these options, investigations have found that the federal government has been exceedingly lenient in its imposition of penalties, even when they are mandated by the circumstances. In 2006, the OIG found that CMS declined to terminate participation in over half of the facilities that were sufficiently non-compliant to require that sanction. Similarly, CMS failed to apply the Denial of Payment for New Admissions remedy to 28 per cent of the cases that mandated such action, due to both administrative discretion and clerical mistakes such as late referrals (OIG, 2006b).

11.5.2.2 Alternative sanctions

The imposition of penalties is not limited to CMS; the courts are entitled to hold nursing home facilities liable for certain violations, an occurrence that has grown in prominence since the late 1990s (Stevenson and Studdert, 2003). Residents have a private right of action against these facilities for damages in tort and, in some cases, for breaches of contract – such lawsuits resemble traditional medical malpractice cases. Although tort liability is commonly believed to increase incentives for delivering high-quality care, there is much controversy about the authenticity of the link between such liability and care quality. In fact, existing evidence indicates that low-quality facilities are almost equally susceptible to tort claims as are higher-quality homes (Studdert et al., 2011). Furthermore, existing evidence indicates that liability claims have no impact on the subsequent quality of care that facilities provide (see www.ncbi.nim.nih.gov.pubmed/23552438).

Entirely separate from the statutes detailed above, the government may also hold facilities liable under fraud and abuse law, such as the federal False Claims Act, codified in 31 USC, §§ 3729–3733. This law provides for severe sanctions against health providers that defraud the government either by billing CMS for services not actually rendered or, sometimes, for delivering services of such a low quality that they do not meet basic care standards. While this Act is infrequently used to police nursing home quality, it does serve as an additional failsafe against the most egregious violations.

11.5.3 Challenges

Monitoring and enforcing nursing home compliance is an imprecise exercise, particularly in a country as large and diverse as the United States. CMS and the state agencies face a number of challenges and failures, some of which we address here:

11.5.3.1 Survey process is inconsistent and too lenient

An ideal survey/certification process would not vary significantly from state to state. The administration of a federal regulatory scheme ought to be consistent, for both fairness and efficiency reasons. Nevertheless, there is wide variation across and even within states as to the number of facilities cited for deficiencies, the threshold degree of violation necessary to trigger a deficiency citation, the severity of the conditions cited and so forth. While some of this variation can be explained by differences in facilities across states, most of it appears simply to be inconsistency in how the same regulations are applied. There is considerable room for varied interpretations within the current regulations, and in the absence of clarification by federal authorities the outcome is a lack

Regulation of long-term care in the United States 305

Table 11.1 *US State variation in nursing home deficiencies and complaints*

	Low	High	US Average
Deficiencies[1]			
Average number of deficiencies per facility	4.30 (RI)	22.00 (DC)	9.96
Per cent of facilities receiving a deficiency for actual harm or jeopardy of residents	8.17 per cent (FL)	49.37 per cent (ID)	24.67 per cent
Per cent of facilities receiving a deficiency for substandard care	0.00 per cent (DC, DE)	27.95 per cent (OK)	7.34 per cent
Per cent of facilities receiving a deficiency for quality of care violations	2.50 per cent (NH)	84.21 per cent (DC)	35.50 per cent
Per cent of facilities receiving a deficiency for insufficient nursing staff	0.00 per cent (7 states)	12.17 per cent (KS)	2.84 per cent
Complaints[2]			
Annual complaints per 100 residents	0.6 (SD)	16.5 (WA)	4.2
Complaint substantiation rate	8.0 per cent (RI)	65.5 per cent (CT)	37.9 per cent
Average days to investigation	7 (PA)	98 (MN)	43

Sources: [1] Harrington et al., 2010: 87–116. All deficiency statistics are from 2009.
[2] Stevenson, 2006: 355–56. All complaints statistics are from 1998–2002.
Notes: RI = Rhode Island; DC = District of Columbia; FL = Florida; ID = Idaho; DE = Delaware; OK = Oklahoma; NH = New Hampshire; KS = Kansas; SD = South Dakota; WA = Washington; CT = Connecticut; PA = Pennsylvania; MN = Minnesota.

of uniformity (Miller and Mor, 2006). Table 11.1, which shows the variation of several deficiency and complaints statistics across states, demonstrates the wide range of process implementation.

Despite the hundreds of CMS regulations and the broad range of available sanctions, studies have found state inspectors to be overly lenient in investigating and certifying nursing facilities, thereby undermining the enforcement of existing standards. For instance, in a 2003 report addressing nursing home quality, the GAO concluded that surveys suffer from poor investigation methodologies and insufficient documentation, that many surveyors are too inexperienced to evaluate the severity of the deficiencies, that many states lack programmes to double-check the conclusions of the investigators, and that surveys are so predictable that most nursing homes are able to correct or conceal their grossest deficiencies shortly prior to the investigations (GAO, 2003). Other studies have reached similar conclusions (GAO, 2009; GAO, 2007), leading some to conclude that the survey and enforcement processes may need significant overhaul to meet existing quality concerns.

One of the achievements of OBRA '87 was the increased emphasis on outcome measures over the process measures that had dominated regulations after 1965. While such patient-focused and outcome-oriented measures more directly assess the quality of a nursing home, these measures can also be harder to determine, thus having the potential to undermine the effectiveness of the survey process (Stoil, 1994). To address some of its limitations, the federal government launched a demonstration project in five states, known as the Quality Indicator Survey (QIS) programme. This programme aimed to alter inspection methods to target the most serious deficiencies, increase accuracy, improve the usefulness and efficiency of state inspectors and ultimately enhance nursing home quality. Although national rollout of the programme continues (nineteen states are currently implementing the QIS), evaluation results have been mixed to date. A 2007 review by CMS found that the QIS is no more accurate than the traditional survey process and that it has failed to improve documentation or inspectors' speed and efficiency (CMS, 2007). On the other hand, there was a marked increase in the number of deficiencies detected under the QIS, particularly in areas that have historically been under-cited.

11.5.3.2 Complaint process is inconsistent and too lenient

Complaint investigation processes suffer from similar problems to the standard survey process. When the OIG evaluated the process in 2006, it concluded that state agencies failed to investigate many of the most serious alleged deficiencies, did a poor job of following up on complaints after the initial intake and were insufficiently reviewed by CMS (OIG, 2006a). These findings echoed an earlier CMS-sponsored report (Zimmerman et al., 2003). These reports suggest that future quality assurance efforts in the United States should focus not only on the stringency of the regulations, but also on the implementation and enforcement of those regulations.

Regulation of long-term care in the United States

11.5.3.3 Adversarial process prevents progress

Currently, state inspectors function primarily in a policing manner, looking for violations and issuing sanctions to nursing home facilities as punishment. There are several results: first, nursing homes spend considerable time and resources attempting to correct the deficiencies that are most likely to be detected and sanctioned, rather than on improving overall quality. Second, relevant expertise of inspectors could be wasted, as they are able to serve only in a policing role and are restricted from offering information applicable to best practices or quality improvement. Third, when state agencies and CMS issue penalties against long-term care facilities, the fines are generally paid to the government itself, siphoning money away from patient care in those homes that are already having quality difficulties (Miller and Mor, 2006). The regulatory process need not be adversarial to be functional, and the upcoming decade could see a further expansion in the government's role as consultant for nursing homes. Indeed, the Quality Improvement Organization (QIO) programme, discussed below, is an ongoing effort to develop cooperation between regulators and providers. The resource-siphoning problem has also been addressed by the recent ACA law, which allows CMS to remit fines back to nursing homes for certain approved resident-benefitting uses.

11.5.4 Alternate methods of quality monitoring and improvement

Governmental approaches to improving nursing home quality have not been limited to the traditional survey/certification/complaint methodology described above. A range of new and supplemental methods have been used to control quality, a few of which we discuss here.

11.5.4.1 Quality Improvement Organization (QIO) Programme

Medicare's QIO programme utilizes private, non-profit contract entities to form a collaborative bridge between CMS and various healthcare institutions. Begun with an emphasis on controlling utilization and identifying outlier providers, the QIO programme has moved over the last decade towards supporting healthcare decision making, measuring health outcomes and providing technical assistance for improved quality of care. The last decade has also seen an expansion of the programme from acute care settings to a broader range of providers, including nursing homes and home health agencies. In the context of nursing home public reporting efforts, QIOs initially have been directed to help consumers understand and use available quality information, to respond to complaints by and on behalf of Medicare beneficiaries and to work with nursing homes directly to improve performance on clinical measures, many of which were beginning to be publicly reported at the time.

Because QIOs do not function in an official regulatory capacity, they may work with nursing homes in a consultative way. QIOs typically focus on clinical improvement and work with a nursing home's clinical staff, including physicians, offering a range of assistance in both group and individual settings. For example, they may disseminate educational materials that highlight best practices and assist individual homes through on-site visits. Although provider involvement in the QIO programme is voluntary, these entities serve an important role not met by the federal/state regulatory structure, and CMS for the most part has been pleased with their ability to raise and address quality concerns (CMS, 2006). Nonetheless, the net effect of the QIO programme remains unknown, especially relative to the investment.

11.5.4.2 Long-term Care Ombudsman Programme

Authorized under the 1965 Older Americans Act (42 USCA, § 3027) and administered within state agencies by the Federal Administration on Aging, the Long-term Care Ombudsman Programme serves an important extra-regulatory role in nursing home quality assurance. Though they lack legal authority, state ombudsmen are responsible for monitoring and promoting resident rights and for investigating and resolving complaints they receive from nursing home residents.[3] Long-term care ombudsmen also serve as mediators between the government and facilities by communicating best-practices information to nursing homes and informing public agencies of those quality problems that require governmental attention (Kapp, 2000). Although there are no rigorous studies quantifying its impact, experience with the Long-term Care Ombudsman Programme has been largely positive, especially given the modest investment of governmental resources.

---

[3] These complaints and investigations are separate from the legally required complaints mechanism directed by the state regulatory agency, and they essentially constitute another set of eyes and ears to protect and advocate for residents.

11.6 Market-based approaches to quality control

Given the limitations of the current regulatory approach described above, some have questioned whether nursing home care might benefit from a more sceptical, or at least reformed, view of regulation (Kapp, 2000; Walshe, 2001). Further, one paper by two leading long-term care researchers in the United States suggested that 'the current regulatory approach to quality improvement in long-term care should shift its emphasis to utilize a market-driven approach', with a focus on providing information to consumers about quality, effectiveness, and value (Kane and Kane, 2001). Such techniques rely on two related theories: (1) with enough information, nursing home residents and their advocates (as consumers) will select the highest-quality providers at a given cost; and (2) with the right incentives, nursing home providers (as suppliers) will compete on and improve quality in order to increase profits.

11.6.1 Public reporting

Publicizing quality information has been used as a quality improvement strategy in the acute care sector for well over a decade. Despite research showing mixed results of these efforts, publicly reporting quality measures is currently being pursued as a quality-improvement strategy for nursing homes. Designed to empower consumers to make informed choices and to stimulate provider competition on quality, nursing home public reporting began in 1998 with the Nursing Home Compare (NHC) website and has received greater emphasis in the 2002 Nursing Home Quality Initiative (NHQI), both directed by the federal government. Under these initiatives, the federal government publishes quality information about all nursing homes eligible for Medicare or Medicaid reimbursement.

11.6.1.1 Nursing Home Compare

NHC initially included information on facility characteristics, resident characteristics and state inspection reports. For individuals aiming to use NHC in evaluating quality of care across facilities, the measure of survey deficiencies (imprecise as it could be) offered perhaps the most visible way to do this. The initial, modest scope of NHC was bolstered subsequently by the introduction of the NHQI, mentioned above, first on a pilot basis in 2001 and then nationwide in 2002. In particular, the NHQI added to the reported measures a range of MDS-based assessment measures (discussed above) for short- and long-stay nursing home residents.

The federal government has continued to refine the NHC website, most notably via the addition of the Five-Star rating system, through which providers receive star ratings based on their performance on composite measures (in each of several dimensions as well as overall). NHC has also added information about complaints, deficiencies, and enforcement actions against facilities. Table 11.2 provides a list and brief description of the quality indicators available on the NHC website.

In the wake of a renewed focus on the role of ownership in nursing home quality (Stevenson and Grabowski, 2008), the recently passed health reform legislation increased nursing home transparency requirements by mandating that all homes disclose detailed information about the owners and managers of their facilities, as well as anyone else with substantial financial interests. Beyond federal reporting efforts, almost half of all states maintain separate websites that report similar information on nursing homes (Castle and Lowe, 2005).

11.6.1.2 Challenges and evidence to date

Whatever its form and content, public reporting of healthcare quality information is designed to inform and shape the behaviours of key stakeholder groups. For these efforts to succeed decision makers must be aware of the reporting efforts; they must trust the validity of the information; and they must be able to access, understand and act on the information in time to use it. Arguably, certain factors present a barrier to generating a sufficient consumer response to effect changes in provider behaviour. Among these are the level of cognitive impairment common among nursing home residents, uncertainty about the goals of nursing home care itself, and the emergent nature of the nursing home placement decision – in the US, about 70 per cent of all admissions come directly from the hospital, a proportion that approaches 100 per cent of individuals entering nursing homes for post-acute rehabilitative services (Brown, 2011).

In terms of the consumer response to NHC, awareness of the website increased greatly after implementation of the NHQI, at least judging from the number of visits to the website and calls to a toll-free telephone assistance line (OIG, 2004). A recent research study of NHC found that

Regulation of long-term care in the United States 311

Table 11.2 *Information available on the Nursing Home Compare public reporting website, USA*

FIVE-STAR RATINGS	
Overall	Overall rating for the home, out of five stars.
Health Inspections	Also includes information on the number of health deficiencies and the most recent health inspection.
Nursing Home Staffing	Includes the number of residents, as well as the number of nursing hours per resident per day.
Quality Measures	Offers an extensive list of quality measures, broken down by long-stay and short-stay.
OTHER QUALITY INDICATORS	
Fire Safety Inspections	Includes information on fire safety systems, inspections, investigations and deficiencies.
Penalties and Denials of Payment	Number of civil monetary penalties and payment denials against the nursing home.
Complaints and Incidents	Gives explanations and outcomes for any complaints by residents against the home, including information about the number of residents affected and the level of harm.
NURSING HOME CHARACTERISTICS	
Programme Participation	Medicare and/or Medicaid.
Certified Beds	Number of beds in the facility.
Type of Ownership	For-profit, non-profit or government-owned.
Continuing Care Retirement Community	Does the home guarantee lifetime housing with tiered levels of care provision?
Resident and Family Councils	Types of resident feedback available.
Located in a hospital	Is the home associated with a hospital?

Source: Medicare.gov, 2011.

31 per cent of consumers use the Internet in choosing a nursing home, and 12 per cent specifically recall using the NHC website (Castle, 2009). Another recent study found NHC impacted patient sorting on selected measures in response to public reporting, thus improving the match between high-risk patients and high-quality facilities (Werner et al., 2011). While these data points do not indicate universal seeking of quality

information, they do suggest a substantial role for public reporting in the promotion of consumer choice. It is less clear, however, whether the factors underlying the quality indicators are consistent with those criteria that are important to consumers. Quality indicators tend to focus on clinical process-based measures, while resident-centred assessments (such as patient satisfaction and quality of life), despite their frequent measurement and discussion in nursing home evaluation, are absent from NHC (Miller and Mor, 2006). Given the multidimensionality of nursing home quality (Mor et al., 2003), the lack of such indicators might preclude accurate determinations of which facilities are best for the individual, thus undermining a primary purpose of public reporting (Mor, 2005). Public reporting is further complicated by the wide range of services provided within nursing home settings, as the needs and interests of individuals seeking care may be distinct from the general resident population. For example, those needing only short-term rehabilitative services in a nursing home require different care, and therefore different information, than those individuals needing long-term supportive services in the same setting. To date, there is little information about the ability of publicly available quality information to accommodate these diverse aims.

The evidence base on the impact of nursing home public reporting on quality of care generally ranges from mixed to modestly positive. Several studies report that a large majority of homes examine their report cards, and many facilities actively use this information to address quality failures (Mukamel et al., 2007). Similarly, shortly after the unveiling of NHC there was an improvement in certain quality measures, in particular those that most directly contributed to the report card rankings, such as pain treatment and the use of restraints (Konetzka et al., 2010). Other studies have used a range of methodological approaches to investigate the impact of reporting on resident outcomes, with somewhat equivocal results to date (Mukamel et al., 2008; Werner et al., 2009; Grabowski and Town, 2011).

11.6.2 Pay-for-performance

Advances in nursing home payment, such as case-mix adjustment and prospective payment, have improved the efficiency of nursing home provider payments. Nevertheless, most payment schemes in the US provide little incentive to deliver high-quality care. Some have therefore

Regulation of long-term care in the United States 313

proposed altering nursing home reimbursement in order to link payment amounts to performance outcomes, a system known as 'pay-for-performance', or P4P. Such efforts can rely on bonuses for absolute quality outcomes (e.g., pressure ulcers below a specified target) and/or on bonuses for relative quality improvement over time. Although the basic motivations are similar in either method, the latter approach potentially incentivizes (and rewards) mid- and lower-tier facilities.

Several state Medicaid agencies have already begun to implement performance-based compensation in their reimbursement of Medicaid-certified nursing facilities (NFs). Moreover, in order to determine the prudence of applying P4P to Medicare-certified skilled nursing facilities (SNFs), CMS directed the Nursing Home Value Based Purchasing (NHVBP) demonstration to study its implementation in three states, starting in 2009 (Konetzka et al., 2010).

The efficacy of P4P in the US is still unclear. States that have already implemented P4P vary so widely in system design that no standard approach has yet emerged (Arling, 2009). Moreover, although performance-based compensation in other health institutions has had some success, P4P in the long-term care setting is still largely speculative. While some investigations of state approaches to P4P are optimistic (Cooke et al., 2010), the only empirical evidence definitively in favour of the approach is a study from the 1980s in San Diego, California, in which researchers found that incentive payments in long-term care facilities had positive effects on discharge rates and residents' functional status (Briesacher et al., 2009). Meanwhile, there are widespread concerns that P4P, if not carefully designed and overseen, could actually lead to negative consequences. If the risk-adjustment techniques are insufficient, providers will select only healthier, low-risk patients – a technique known as cream-skimming (Konetzka et al., 2010). Similarly, if only certain quality indicators are used in determining performance bonuses, providers may seek improvement in these measures at the expense of others. In short, while P4P is intended to align financial compensation with quality assurance goals, it also opens the door to gamesmanship and other resident-harming quick fixes.

11.7 Non-nursing home long-term care regulations

Although the focus of regulatory and academic attention for long-term care services in the United States has been on nursing homes, home- and community-based services (HCBS) have steadily grown in importance (Kaye et al., 2010). These include home healthcare providers, which provide rehabilitative services in the federal Medicare programme; residential alternatives to nursing homes, such as assisted-living facilities (ALFs); community-based residential care facilities like adult day care; and community-based services such as compensatory home care and personal care attendants. Financing for these other post-acute and long-term care services has similarities to nursing home care, with some important differences. Medicare pays for post-acute services from rehabilitation facilities, home health agencies and other settings. Medicaid, meanwhile, pays for longer-term and chronic long-term care services, such as personal attendants or home- and community-based services, if the states provide for these. Importantly, government financing has played little role in paying for ALF care to date, with the growth in this sector due mostly to private payment (Stevenson and Grabowski, 2010).

Despite some overlap in financing mechanisms and populations served, the OBRA '87 regulation did little to affect non-nursing home providers. Home care services, which are licensed by the state and certified by CMS, are governed largely by state law or unrelated federal laws, such as the Occupational Safety and Health Act. Several other categories of long-term care, such as adult day care and assisted living facilities, continue to be regulated exclusively by state law, which varies widely and is mostly free from federal oversight (Miller and Mor, 2006).

11.7.1 Licensure requirements

Regulations for home health agency participation in CMS reimbursement bear some similarities to nursing home regulations, with CMS making the requirements and the various states administering them. However, the rules for these agencies are significantly less stringent than for nursing homes, and the regulations have focused more on cost and access to care than on quality (IOM, 2001). Furthermore, unlike nursing homes, home health agencies are deemed compliant with CMS if they are accredited by the non-governmental Joint Commission. This allowance could lessen the importance of the CMS requirements and have a deleterious effect if accreditation is too lenient (IOM, 2001).

Regulation of long-term care in the United States 315

Participation requirements for non-nursing-home residential care facilities derive from state law. As such, there is wide variation in the nature of these regulations, including differences in how provider categories are defined, what services they may offer and the licensure requirements themselves. There is also wide variability among states regarding the degree of government involvement as a payer and regulator, with some states clearly specifying the types of services that assisted living facilities can and cannot provide, and others giving providers broader flexibility to meet the needs of residents (Mollica et al., 2008).

Oversight of compensatory home care and other HCBS services is generally performed by the states, again with wide variation. These services are defined in accordance with special Medicaid HCBS waiver programmes, which allow state agencies to define the scope and provision of these services as long as compliance with broad federal guidelines is maintained (CMS, 2011b). Federal requirements apply, however, when the services are provided through a home health agency.

11.7.2 Enforcement and compliance

As with nursing homes, other long-term care providers are monitored by state agencies, and sanctions may be imposed by the state or by CMS, when appropriate. Both the state and federal governments traditionally have been lenient in their enforcement, however. CMS infrequently sanctions facilities for providing low-quality care, and the states themselves have not taken an active role in identifying unlicensed facilities and forcing them into compliance (IOM, 2001). So lax is the regulatory scheme that both the GAO and IOM have called for significantly greater state standard-setting in order to address the consequences of weak governmental oversight (IOM, 2001).

Although these long-term care providers are mostly immune from nursing home compliance regulations, some of the programmes and policies are similar. While only nursing homes must use the MDS system, home health agencies must develop patient care plans and track progress in the Outcome and Assessment Information Set (OASIS), which is a functional analogue to the MDS. The Medicare Long-term Care Ombudsman Programme, discussed above, is also utilized in all non-nursing-home long-term care settings that involve Medicare funds in order to promote patient advocacy and disseminate information about best-care practices.

11.7.3 Market approaches

Market-based approaches also play a role outside of the nursing home setting, primarily for home health agencies. The Home Health Compare (HHC) tool provides detailed quality information on all certified home health agencies in the country, similar to the NHC website described earlier. While HHC does not use the Five-Star ranking system, it does offer numeric information about the track records of the agencies in assisting daily activities, managing pain and other symptoms, treating wounds and preventing pressure sores, avoiding harm, and preventing unplanned hospital care. These numbers are then compared to state and national averages, allowing for a sophisticated quality comparison. The federal government also has sponsored the Home Health Value-Based Purchasing demonstration, similar to the Nursing Home Value-Based Purchasing demonstration described earlier, testing a pay-for-performance approach to provider reimbursement.

11.7.4 Efficacy of non-nursing home long-term care regulation

Little is known of the quality outcomes in long-term care settings outside the nursing home sector, and even less is known about the potential effectiveness of more stringent regulation in these sectors (Zimmerman et al., 2005). The paucity of information in this area stems from a lack of uniform assessment data on assisted living residents, as well as an uncertainty about the range of outcomes for which facilities should be held accountable. Moreover, care in these settings has garnered relatively little attention from researchers and government officials, a feature that could change as more government resources are devoted to them. Indeed, a recent survey of long-term care specialists found that two-thirds of respondents favoured adopting more stringent regulation of assisted living facilities along the lines of requirements for nursing homes (Mor et al., 2010), although assisted living providers themselves have strongly resisted such change.

Home health agencies have been plagued by instances of poor-quality care, although the extent of these problems is unclear (IOM, 2001). Assessing the quality of care delivered in home settings and establishing an oversight strategy for home care presents a substantial challenge. While there is some evidence that the lesser regulatory stringency in these settings has come at the cost of lower care quality, more extensive

Regulation of long-term care in the United States 317

research is required to pinpoint the drawbacks and to identify the appropriate areas for reform, in particular to ensure a continuation of the flexibility and consumer choice that are central to HCBS.

11.8 The current state of long-term care regulation and its future

11.8.1 Performance of current long-term care regulatory approach in the US

The regulatory schemes described in this chapter have had frustratingly mixed results, with some areas performing significantly better than others. Long-term care regulation in the US has been relatively success-ful at improving quality in certain easily measured categories. For example, in the wake of OBRA '87, which emphasized outcome-oriented and patient-centred approaches to quality control, there has been a drastic decrease in the use of restraints and catheters, as well as drops in dehydration rates and pressure ulcers. Patient autonomy has also been bolstered, both by OBRA '87 and by the Patient Self-Determination Act of 1990, which increased advance directives and resident self-determination of care (Kapp, 2000).

On the other hand, quality problems clearly persist in the nursing home sector, which suggests the existence of significant regulatory fail-ures (GAO, 1987, 1998, 1999, 2002; OIG, 1999a, 1999b). The current regulatory system has struggled not only with actual quality control, but also with the detection and reporting of deficiencies. The GAO reported in 2008 that 70 per cent of federal follow-up or 'look behind' surveys (described above) uncovered initial state surveys that missed at least one deficiency with the 'potential for more than minimal harm', a figure that has got worse over the past decade (GAO, 2008). More seriously, 15 per cent of these federal follow-up surveys identified state surveys that missed the most serious deficiencies: those that con-stitute immediate jeopardy or actual harm. Such under-reporting also makes it difficult to determine the true extent of quality problems.

11.8.2 Costs of regulation

The effectiveness of the regulatory scheme must also be evaluated in the context of the costs of regulation, which can be very high. Although no single number encapsulates the total costs of regulating this industry, a 2001 study estimated the annual costs of the nursing home survey/ certification process at US$382 million, or US$22,000 per home (Walshe, 2001). Allowing for inflation, the growth of the market, increases in regulatory stringency and the addition of the complaint, public reporting and quality-improvement features of the long-term care regulatory framework, the direct costs to the government must now surely reach the billions.

On top of these costs are the expenditures by nursing homes to comply with federal and state mandates. These costs include preparation for the surveys, data compilation, responding to complaints and other such measures designed to promote compliance. These costs are difficult to measure, but a recent study calculated the marginal cost of correcting one deficiency in a nursing home at US$3,608, and found that a one-standard-deviation increase in regulatory stringency was associated with a 1.1 per cent increase in nursing home operations costs (Mukamel et al., 2011). Although this study was the first of its kind, this preliminary figure indicates that these indirect costs, in the aggregate, may be substantial (Mor, 2011).

11.8.3 Future of nursing home regulation

Over the last two decades, the federal government has taken many steps to improve the long-term care quality assurance process, especially for nursing homes. The current system is considerably improved relative to the insufficient and uneven regulation in place before 1987. Nonetheless, the current level of regulatory stringency in the US has not consistently led to the safe, effective, patient-centred nursing home care that was envisioned by OBRA '87. In light of these results, some scholars and policy makers have argued for even tougher standards and more effective enforcement; others have cited this outcome as evidence that the regulatory system is ineffective and should be replaced by simpler, less punitive measures (Walshe, 2001). It is hard to predict future regulatory changes but given the current political climate and optimism about the effects of P4P and public reporting, a continued emphasis on market-based approaches is likely to endure. Other suggested reforms could gain traction in the future, including strengthening oversight and enforcement, considering a facility's past quality performance in setting the frequency of inspections, and allowing QIOs and

Regulation of long-term care in the United States 319

survey agencies to work together in integrating quality assurance and quality improvement. However, long-term care regulation is a politically charged topic with high stakes, a feature which entrenches the status quo and makes substantial reform unlikely.

Perhaps the most important change in the future of long-term care regulation will be a greater incorporation of consumer voice in how long-term care is delivered, evaluated and reported. More specifically, quality measures and indicators may begin to integrate core issues of patient satisfaction, quality of life, and care experience. If this shift occurs, long-term care in the US may finally fulfil the vision of person-centred care envisioned by OBRA '87 and embodied by the current disability rights and nursing home culture change movements.

References

Arling, G. (2009). Medicaid nursing pay-for-performance: where do we stand? *The Gerontologist*, 49(5): 587–95.

Binstock, R. H. et al. (1996). *The Future of Long-Term Care: Social and Policy Issues*. Baltimore: The Johns Hopkins University Press.

Briesacher, B. A. et al. (2009). Can pay-for-performance take nursing home care to the next level? *Journal of the American Geriatrics Society*, 56(10): 1,937–9.

Brown: Alpert Medical School (2011). Create custom reports on long-term care. Available at: http://ltcfocus.org/.

Castle, N. G. (2009). The nursing home compare report card: consumers' use and understanding. *Journal of Aging and Social Policy*, 21(2): 187–208.

Castle, N. G. and Lowe, T. J. (2005). Report cards and nursing homes. *The Gerontologist*, 45(1): 48–67.

CMS: Centers for Medicare and Medicaid Services (2006). Report to Congress on the evaluation of the Quality Improvement Organization (QIO) Program for Medicare beneficiaries for fiscal year 2006. Available at: https://www.cms.gov/QualityImprovementOrgs/downloads/2006RtCQIO.pdf.

(2007). Evaluation of the Quality Indicator Survey (QIS). Available at: https://www.cms.gov/CertificationandComplianc/Downloads/QISExec Summary.pdf.

(2011a). Certification and compliance: nursing homes. Available at: https://www.cms.gov/CertificationandComplianc/12_NHs.asp.

(2011b). HCBS waivers – section 1915(c). Available at: http://www.cms.gov/MedicaidStWaivProgDemoPGI/05_HCBSWaivers-Section1915 per cent28c per cent29.asp.

Cooke, V. et al. (2010). Minnesota's nursing facility performance-based incentive payment program: an innovative model for promoting care quality. *The Gerontologist*, 50(4): 556–63.

Furrow, B. R. et al. (2008). *Health Law: Cases, Materials and Problems* (6th edn). St Paul: West.

   (2010). *Healthcare Reform Supplement to Health Law: Cases, Materials and Problems*. St Paul: West.

GAO: Government Accountability Office (1987). Medicare and Medicaid: stronger enforcement of nursing home requirements needed. Available at: http://gao.justia.com/department-of-health-and-human-services/1987/7/medicare-and-medicaid-hrd-87-113/HRD-87-113-full-report.pdf.

   (1998). California nursing homes: care problems persist despite federal and state oversight. Available at: http://www.gao.gov/archive/1998/he98202.pdf.

   (1999). Nursing homes: additional steps needed to strengthen enforcement of federal quality standards. Available at: http://www.gao.gov/archive/1999/he99046.pdf.

   (2002). Nursing homes: more can be done to protect residents from abuse. Available at: http://www.gao.gov/new.items/d02312.pdf.

   (2003). Prevalence of serious problems, while declining, reinforces importance of enhanced oversight. Available at: http://www.gao.gov/new.items/d03561.pdf.

   (2007). Efforts to strengthen federal enforcement have not deterred some homes from repeatedly harming residents. Available at: http://www.gao.gov/new.items/d07241.pdf.

   (2008). Nursing homes: federal monitoring surveys demonstrate continued understatement of serious care problems and CMS oversight weaknesses. Available at: http://www.gao.gov/new.items/d08517.pdf.

   (2009). Medicare and Medicaid participating facilities: CMS needs to reexamine its approach for funding state oversight of healthcare facilities. Available at: http://www.gao.gov/new.items/d0964.pdf.

Grabowski, D. C. and Town, R. J. (2011). Does information matter? Competition, quality, and the impact of nursing home report cards. *Health Services Research*, 46(6pt1): 1,698–1,719.

Harrington, C. and Millman, M. (2001). *Nursing Home Staffing Standards in State Statutes and Regulations*. San Francisco: Henry J. Kaiser Family Foundation. University of California, San Francisco.

Harrington, C. et al. (2010). *Nursing, Facilities, Staffing, Residents, and Facility Deficiencies, 2004 through 2009*. San Francisco: Department of Social and Behavioral Sciences. University of California, San Francisco.

Regulation of long-term care in the United States 321

HEW: Department of Health, Education, and Welfare (1972). In-patient health facilities as reported from the 1967 MFI Survey. Available at: http://www.cdc.gov/nchs/data/series/sr_14/sr14_004.pdf.

IOM: Institute of Medicine (1986). *Improving the Quality of Care in Nursing Homes*. Washington: National Academy Press.

(2001). *Improving the Quality of Long-Term Care*. Washington: National Academy Press.

Kane, R. A., et al. (1998). *The Heart of Long-Term Care*. New York: Oxford University Press.

Kane, R. L. and Kane, R. A. (2001). What older people want from long-term care, and how they can get it. *Health Affairs*, 20(5): 114–27.

Kapp, M. B. (2000). Quality of care and quality of life in nursing facilities: what's regulation got to do with it? *McGeorge Law Review*, 31(3): 707–31.

Kaye, H. S., Harrington, C., and LaPlante, M. P. (2010). Long-term care: who gets it, who provides it, who pays, and how much? *Health Affairs*, 29(1): 11–21.

Konetzka, R. T., et al. (2010). Applying market-based reforms to long-term care. *Health Affairs*, 29(1): 74–80.

Medicare.gov (2011). Nursing Home Compare. Available at: http://www.medicare.gov/nhcompare.

MedPac (2010). *A data book: healthcare spending and the Medicare Program*, pp. 129–53. Available at: http://www.medpac.gov/chapters/Jun10DataBookSec9.pdf.

Mendelson, M. A. (1974). *Tender Loving Greed: How the Incredibly Lucrative Nursing Home 'Industry' is Exploiting America's Old People and Defrauding Us All* (1st edn). New York: Knopf.

Miller, E. A. and Mor, V. (2006). *Out of the Shadows: Envisioning a Brighter Future for Long-Term Care in America*. Chapter 6: Modernizing regulation. Report for the National Commission for Quality Long-Term Care. Providence, Rhode Island: Brown University, Center for Gerontology and Healthcare Research.

Mollica, R., Sims-Kastelein, K., and O'Keefe, J. (2008). Assisted living and residential care policy compendium, 2007 update. Portland: National Academy for State Health Policy. Available at: http://aspe.hhs.gov/daltcp/reports/2007/07alcom.htm.

Mor, V. (2005). Improving the quality of long-term care with better information. *Milbank Quarterly*, 83(3): 333–64.

(2011). Cost of nursing home regulation: building a research agenda. *Medical Care*, 49(6): 525–36.

Mor, V., et al. (2003). The quality of quality measurement in United States nursing homes. *The Gerontologist*, 43(SII): 37–46.

(2010). The taste for regulation in long-term care. *Medical Care Research Review*, 67(4): 38S–64S.

Moss, F. E. and Halamandaris, V. J. (1977). *Too Old, Too Sick, Too Bad: Nursing Homes in America*. Germantown: Aspen Systems Corporation.

Mukamel, D. B., et al. (2007). Nursing homes' response to the Nursing Home Compare report card. *Journals of Gerontology Series B: Psychological Sciences and Social Sciences*, 62B(4): S218–S225.

(2008). Publication of quality report cards and trends in reported quality measures in nursing homes. *Health Services Research*, 43(4): 1,244–62.

(2011). Does state regulation of quality impose costs on nursing homes? *Medical Care*, 49(6): 529–34.

NCSL: National Conference of State Legislatures (2011). Certificate of need: state health laws and programs. Available at: http://www.ncsl.org/IssuesResearch/Health/CONCertificateofNeedStateLaws/tabid/14373/Default.aspx.

NHPF: National Health Policy Forum (2011). National spending for long-term services and supports (LTSS). Available at: http://www.nhpf.org/library/the-basics/Basics_LongTermServicesSupports_03-15-11.pdf.

O'Brien, E. (2005). *Long-term care: understanding Medicaid's role for the elderly and disabled*. Kaiser Commission on Medicaid and the Uninsured. Available at: http://www.kff.org/medicaid/upload/Long-Term-Care-Understanding-Medicaid-s-Role-for-the-Elderly-and-Disabled-Report.pdf.

OIG: Office of the Inspector General (1999a). Nursing home survey and certification: overall capacity. Available at: http://oig.hhs.gov/oei/reports/oei-02-98-00330.pdf.

(1999b). Quality of care in nursing homes: an overview. Available at: http://oig.hhs.gov/oei/reports/oei-02-99-00060.pdf.

(2004). Inspection results on Nursing Home Compare: completeness and accuracy. Available at: http://oig.hhs.gov/oei/reports/oei-01-03-00130.pdf.

(2006a). Nursing home complaint investigations. Available at: http://oig.hhs.gov/oei/reports/oei-01-04-00340.pdf.

(2006b). Nursing home enforcement: application of mandatory remedies. Available at: http://oig.hhs.gov/oei/reports/oei-06-03-00410.pdf.

(2008). Memorandum report: 'Trends in nursing home deficiencies and complaints'. Available at: http://oig.hhs.gov/oei/reports/oei-02-08-00140.pdf.

(2009). Nursing home corporations under quality of care corporate integrity agreements. Available at: http://oig.hhs.gov/oei/reports/oei-06-06-00570.pdf.

Rantz, M. J., et al. (1999). Minimum data set and resident assessment instrument: can using standardized assessment improve clinical practice and outcomes of care? *Journal of Gerontological Nursing*, 25(6): 35–43.

Smith v. Heckler: *In re the Estate of Michael Patrick Smith v. Heckler*, 747 F.2d 583 (10th Cir. 1984).

Stevenson, D. G. (2006). Nursing home consumer complaints and quality of care – a national view. *Medical Care Research and Review*, 63(3): 347–68.

Stevenson, D. G. and Grabowski, D. C. (2008). Private equity investment and nursing home care: is it a big deal? *Health Affairs*, 27(5): 1,399–408.

(2010). Sizing up the market for sssisted living, *Health Affairs*, 29(1): 35–43.

Stevenson, D. G. and Studdert, D. M. (2003). The rise of nursing home litigation: findings from a national survey of attorneys. *Health Affairs*, 22(2): 219–29.

Stevenson, D. G. et al. (2010). The complementarity of public and private long-term care coverage. *Health Affairs*, 29(1): 96–101.

Stoil, M. J. (1994). Surveyors stymied by survey criteria, researchers find. *Nursing Homes*, 43(4): 58.

Studdert, D. M. et al. (2011). Relationship between quality of care and negligence litigation in nursing homes. *New England Journal of Medicine*, 364(13): 1,243–50.

Tumlinson, A. et al. (2007). Long term care in America: an introduction. National Commission for Quality Long-Term Care. Available at: http://www.newschool.edu/ltcc/pdf/ltc_america_introduction.pdf.

Vladeck, B. C. and Twentieth Century Fund (1980). *Unloving Care: The Nursing Home Tragedy*. New York: Basic Books.

Walshe, K. (2001). Regulating United States nursing homes: are we learning from experience? *Health Affairs*, 20(6): 128–44.

Werner, R. M., Konetzka, R. T. and Kruse, G. B. (2009). Impact of public reporting on unreported quality of care. *Health Services Research*, 44(2.1): 379–98.

Werner, R. M. et al. (2010). State adoption of nursing home pay-for-performance. *Medical Care Research and Review*, 67(3): 364–77.

(2011). Changes in patient sorting to nursing homes under public reporting: improved patient matching or provider gaming? *Health Services Research*, 46(2): 555–71.

Zimmerman, D. et al. (2003). *Nursing Home Complaint Investigation: Building the Model System*. Baltimore: CMS.

Zimmerman, S. et al. (2005) How good is assisted living? Findings and implications from an outcomes study. *Journals of Gerontology, Series B: Psychological Science Sciences and Social Sciences*, 60(4): S195–S204.

12 Long-term care for the elderly in Canada: progress towards an integrated system

JOHN P. HIRDES AND VAHE KEHYAYAN

12.1 Introduction

Hospital and physician services for Canadians of all ages are shared responsibilities of the federal government and the governments of ten provinces and three territories. However, long-term care is regulated, funded and delivered only under the auspices of provincial/territorial governments with no major role for the federal government. Therefore, one cannot accurately refer to the 'Canadian healthcare system' as a singular entity. Rather healthcare, and long-term care, is delivered by thirteen different systems with national legislation guiding some, but not all, aspects of service delivery, regulation and administration (Beland and Shapiro, 1994). In addition, healthcare in Canada is provided by a mixture of public and privately funded services, and the balance between those sources of payment varies by region. The complexity of the Canadian healthcare mosaic has increased further with the introduction of regional authorities responsible for 'local' management of health services in the last two decades.

Rather than provide an encyclopedic summary of the regulatory structure of healthcare for the elderly in all regions of Canada, this chapter will focus on the experience of the province of Ontario to illustrate the experience of the country's most populous province. It is also the province with the most fully integrated health information system across the continuum of care for older people, which is intended to improve clinical practice, quality, public accountability and funding of health services. That said, one must remain aware that this overview represents a single province's experience that shares much, but not all, in common with other regions of the country. The chapter begins with a brief overview of the three levels of government (federal, provincial, regional) that have an influence over healthcare in Canada. The remainder deals specifically with the continuum of care for the elderly in Ontario.

324

12.2 The wider health system context and the roles of government

The Government of Canada bears national responsibility for health protection and public health, but it provides healthcare services only to selected sub-populations (aboriginal peoples, the Royal Canadian Mounted Police, Canadian Armed Forces and inmates in federal prisons). For the most part, its role is limited to co-payment of provincially managed healthcare services through the 2004 Canada Health Transfer and the administration of the Canada Health Act (CHA), 1984.

The transfer of funds from federal to provincial or territorial governments is subject to compliance with the requirements of the 1984 *Canada Health Act* (Flood and Choudhry, 2004). That act set national standards to govern the provision of medically necessary physician and hospital services, but it does not apply to home care, nursing homes or pharmacare. The five principles of the CHA are that the covered services must be: (a) publicly administered; (b) comprehensive – covering all medically necessary hospital, physician and surgical dental services; (c) universal – providing equal coverage to all citizens; (d) portable – to ensure coverage if citizens move between provinces; and (e) accessible to allow reasonable access to those services. Policies and regulations related to long-term care services are set only by provincial governments without linkage to the CHA and with no accountability to the federal government.

A federal report on the future of healthcare in Canada prepared by a commission led by a formal provincial premier (Romanow, 2002) recommended a number of additions to the CHA, including the introduction of a sixth principle of public accountability and the inclusion of home care as a type of service subject to the Act. However, both recommendations failed to translate into legislation as a result of considerable opposition from provincial governments. Several provinces established organizations with responsibilities for monitoring healthcare quality and safety. In addition, the Health Council of Canada (HCC) was formed with a mandate to report on progress toward goals established in a 2004 First Ministers' Accord on health funding.

12.2.1 Ontario healthcare system

According to estimates of health expenditures made by the Canadian Institute for Health Information (CIHI) (CIHI, 2010), the total per capita expenditure on health in Ontario in 2010 was CAN \$1,524 representing about 12.2 per cent of GDP, which is slightly higher than the national expenditures (11.4 per cent GDP). Expenditures on 'other institutions', which include nursing homes and similar residential care facilities, accounted for about 10 per cent of total national expenditures (individual provincial rates were not reported by CIHI). Public expenditures represent about two-thirds of Ontario's total expenditures. Hospitals accounted for 34 per cent of public expenditures, followed by physicians (23 per cent), other health spending (19 per cent) and drugs (10 per cent) (CIHI, 2010). The bulk of private expenditures in Ontario are accounted for by health professionals other than physicians (e.g., dentists, physical therapists) and drug costs (34 per cent and 33 per cent, respectively) (CIHI, 2010). However, medications for the elderly are publicly funded under the Ontario Drug Benefit Program. Drug costs have been the most rapidly increasing source of health expenditures in Canada over the last two decades (Morgan, 2004). Although Ontario has lower per capita expenditures than the Canadian average on hospitals and fewer health professionals per 100,000 population (CIHI, 2009a), it has the highest level of drug expenditures per capita in the country (CAN \$346 compared with CAN \$308 for Canada as a whole) (CIHI. 2010).

12.2.2 Healthcare funding in Ontario

Ontario began the transition from global funding for healthcare organizations toward case-mix-based funding methodologies with the introduction of Case Mix Groups, a Canadian adaptation of Diagnosis Related Groups (Ladak, 1998) in 1983 as a basis for acute hospital funding. By 2002, the Resource Utilization Groups (RUG-III) case-mix system (Fries et al., 1994; Hirdes et al., 1996) was used in the funding methodology for complex continuing care hospitals.

Until recently, home care has been funded through global budgets allocated to Community Care Access Centres (CCACs). Case managers are expected to contract healthcare services from home care provider agencies without capping services supplied to an individual level while adhering to a prescribed overall case management budget. In 2005 the Ministry of Health and Long Term Care (MoHLTC) and CIHI jointly funded a research project to validate the Resource Utilization Groups

Long-term care for the elderly in Canada 327

for Home Care (RUG-III/HC) case-mix system (Poss et al., 2008). A province-wide study of over 440,000 clients demonstrated that the RUG-III/HC would be an appropriate case-mix system for long-stay home care. However, case-mix-based funding has not yet been introduced to that sector.

Long-term care homes in Ontario have been funded with case-mix adjustments since the early 1990s, when the Alberta Resident Classification System (ARCS) was introduced to that sector (Hirdes, 2001). ARCS was a relatively simple classification system with eight groups differentiated primarily on the basis of functional status, continence and behaviour. However, over time, the distributions of ARCS groups within long-term care homes began to converge (for a variety of reasons, including problematic coding practices) such that almost all long-term care residents fell into one of two ARCS categories. By 2010, the ARCS system was abandoned in favour of the RUG-III as the case-mix system for long-term care homes.

12.2.3 Local Health Integration Networks

Most provinces have regional health authorities that provide management and oversight of health services at the local level. The Government of Ontario established fourteen Local Health Integration Networks (LHINs) in 2005 (Ministry of Health and Long-Term Care, 2011c) with the aim of creating an integrated healthcare system that improves quality of care and is more responsive to local needs. The authority and mandate of LHINs are defined under the Local Health System Integration Act, 2006 (LHSIA 2006).

12.2.4 LHIN governance and accountability mechanisms

Each LHIN is governed by a board of directors appointed through a mechanism established by the Ontario government. The relationship between the Ministry and LHINs is governed by an accountability agreement known as a Ministry/LHIN Accountability Agreement (MLAA). The MLAA requires LHINs to: (a) establish performance goals, objectives and standards, performance targets and measures for the network and the local health system; (b) report on the performance of the network and the local health system; (c) plan for spending the funding that the network receives from the Ministry; and (d) establish a performance management process for the network. In addition to MLAAs, the Ministry and LHINs enter into a Ministry-LHIN Performance Agreement (MLPA) with a focus on system performance and financial accountability (Waterloo Wellington LHIN, 2010). The MLPA includes fourteen performance indicators and LHIN targets and sets out Ministry and LHIN obligations.

Given that the Ministry has entered into accountability agreements with the LHINs, each LHIN, in turn, has entered into accountability agreements with health services providers such as hospitals, long-term care homes, community care access centres (CCAC), community support services (CSS), community health centres (CHC) and community mental health and addiction (CMHA) services. These agreements enable LHINs to provide funding to health services providers for the delivery of health services. They are intended to support 'a collaborative relationship ... to improve the health of Ontarians through better access to high quality health services, to co-ordinate healthcare in local health systems and to manage the health system at the local level effectively and efficiently' (Central East Local Health Integration Network, 2010).

12.2.5 Long-term care settings across the continuum

In each province/territory elderly persons and adults with disabilities receive services from a broad spectrum of community- and facility-based agencies across the continuum of care. While the Canada Health Act reflects the basic components of primary care and hospital services that represented the bulk of healthcare services when publicly funded Medicare was established in the 1960s, the breadth of continuum of healthcare has grown dramatically since that time. The lack of a national legislative framework governing many of the services provided to older adults means that there is tremendous heterogeneity in the structure, intensity and nature of long-term care services provided to the elderly. Ontario shares numerous aspects of its continuum of care with other provinces; however, it is also distinctive in some aspects of long-term care (e.g., model of case management, delivery of post-acute care, separate social services in the community from clinically oriented home care). The remainder of this chapter provides an overview of each of the major components of Ontario's continuum of care.

12.3 Care for the elderly in Ontario

12.3.1 Long-term care homes

Expenditures on 'other institutions', which are primarily comprised of nursing homes, represent about 10 per cent of total Canadian health expenditures. On a per capita basis, Canada spends more than four times as much on institutional care than on home care (CIHI, 2007, 2011). In Ontario, about two-thirds of long-term care homes services are provided on a for-profit basis (facilities owned by private corporations) and the remaining third are provided by not-for-profit organizations (e.g., municipal governments or charitable organizations). The for-profit homes include individual homes owned and managed as a family business, as well as those that are part of corporate chains. There are about 750 nursing homes in the province with 75,000 beds, and the rate of institutionalization of the elderly in 2006 was 6.3 per cent for persons aged 65 and over (Hirdes et al., 2011) compared with 6.7 per cent in 1981 (Forbes et al., 1987).

All long-term care homes are subject to provincial regulation and monitoring. These facilities are licensed by the province. The Ministry of Health and Long Term Care (MoHLTC) provides public funding for the healthcare portion of long-term care home services; however, the user is responsible for a co-payment to cover accommodation costs. In 2010, the co-payment was between CAN $50 and $70 per day (for basic to preferred accommodation) and the Ministry portion was about CAN $90 per day for a total of about CAN $140 per day compared with CAN $997 per day for an acute hospital stay (Ontario Hospital Association (OHA), 2010).

Long-term care homes offer both long-stay (with an indefinite duration) and short-stay (expected to be less than ninety days) accommodation. However, publicly funded short stay beds are very limited in supply and access to privately funded respite beds is only slightly greater. About 6 per cent of residents are discharged within ninety days of admission compared with 57.0 per cent of patients in complex continuing care hospital settings (Hirdes et al., 2011). The median length of stay among persons discharged from long-term care is about 155 days, which is substantially shorter than that in other Canadian provinces. This may be explained, at least in part, by the two to three times higher rate of discharges to hospital in Ontario compared with other provinces/territories (Hirdes et al., 2011). Given that about half of all discharges from Ontario long-term care homes are to hospital settings, the length of stay differential may reflect regional differences in approaches to end-of-life care in nursing home settings. About one-third of discharges are due to death, and returning to home accounts for only about 1 per cent of long term care discharges in Ontario.

Until recently, there was no provincially mandated standardized clinical assessment system for Ontario nursing homes. Under a previous approach, chart reviews were done by external staff employed by the MoHLTC to document resident characteristics using the Alberta Resident Classification System (Hirdes, 1997). These records were used only for case-mix classification and played no role in care planning or quality improvement initiatives. However, following the mandated introduction of interRAI assessment instruments[1] into numerous other healthcare sectors (Bernabei et al., 2009; Hirdes, 2006; Hirdes et al., 2003), the Resident Assessment Instrument 2.0 (RAI 2.0) and its associated Resident Assessment Protocols (RAPs) for care planning were mandated as the provincial standard for assessment in long-term care homes. The aim was to improve quality of care at the individual and population levels and to provide information that could be used at the facility level to inform the nursing home payment system. All residents in these facilities are assessed within fourteen days of admission and every ninety days thereafter. Data from these assessments are submitted nationally to CIHI's Continuing Care Reporting System, which is used for national statistical reporting on nursing homes across the country. Implementation of the RAI 2.0 was done on a phased-in-basis beginning in 2005 with complete implementation in all homes by 2010.

12.3.2 Retirement homes and assisted living

Retirement homes and (more recently developed) assisted living facilities are privately funded organizations that have historically been

---

[1] interRAI assessment instruments are comprehensive clinical assessment tools used as part of normal clinical practice to assess medical, psychosocial and environmental aspects of a person's functioning (www.interrai.org). They also track interventions, services and medication use. These assessments may be used to support multiple applications for multiple audiences (Hirdes et al., 1999, 2008; Gray et al., 2009), including care planning, outcome measurement, quality monitoring and case-mix-based funding.

Long-term care for the elderly in Canada 331

accountable to the Ministry of Community and Social Services. Their accountability was transferred to the purview of the MoHLTC in 2008, but they are not subject to the same regulations as long-term care homes and residents bear the full costs for services they provide. Only a portion of these organizations belong to a professional association (Ontario Retirement Centres Association (ORCA)), and there is no requirement for accreditation or external inspection of health services. Growth in the retirement home industry has been substantial, particularly since it is often considerably more profitable than the operation of long-term care homes.

Ontarians can apply directly for admission to retirement homes and there is no minimum level of care required for entry. As a result of sometimes prolonged waiting times for entry into long-term care homes for persons deemed eligible for placement, retirement homes have begun to offer an expanded array of privately purchased health services as an alternative to publicly funded long-term care. The lack of a standardized, mandatory assessment approach for retirement homes and assisted living makes it almost impossible to determine the needs of residents in these settings. However, the belief that these homes house an increasingly frail population with little or no oversight, no public accountability framework and no service quality standards has led to the introduction of proposed legislation for a regulatory authority for these homes (Ontario Government, 2010f). There is a sense that more expensive retirement homes targeting affluent seniors provide good-quality care that may be comparable to or better than long-term care homes, but there is no evidence base to evaluate this assumption. In contrast, anecdotal stories of poor quality in lower-cost retirement homes (Toronto Star, 2010) have become cause for heightened public concern.

12.3.3 Home care

Home care is provided through publicly funded agencies known as Community Care Access Centres (CCACs). These were established to serve as a single point of access to healthcare services in the community, including admission to long-term care homes, in-home services and school services (Ministry of Health and Long-Term Care, 2011a). The authority of CCACs is derived from their designation as placement coordinators under the Long Term Care Homes Act, 2010. In this capacity, placement coordinators determine individuals' eligibility for community support services such as home care, transportation, meals-on-wheels or admission into long-term care homes based on criteria set out under the Act.

There are fourteen CCACs in Ontario with geographic boundaries directly aligned with their LHINs. CCACs are funded by the LHINs through the MoHLTC and are accountable for the delivery of services and funding received on the terms and conditions of their respective Multi-Sector Accountability Agreements (MSAAs) (Central East Local Health Integration Network, 2010). CCACs are also governed by the Community Care Access Corporations Act, 2001, which establishes them as service agencies and sets out their mandate, governance and accountabilities (Ontario Government, 2010a). Other legislation that governs CCACs includes: Home Care and Community Services Act, 1994; Health Insurance Act, 1990; Commitment to the Future of Medicare Act; Long-Term Care Homes Act, 2010; and Accessibility for Ontarians with Disabilities Act, 2005.

CCACs serve at least five populations of home care clients: (a) long-stay clients expected to be on service for sixty days or more requiring maintenance level or supportive care; (b) short-stay post-acute clients discharged from hospital, typically requiring wound care, intravenous therapy or other nursing services; (c) rehabilitation clients requiring short-term physical or occupational therapy; (d) palliative home care clients, half of whom are expected to live six months or more; and (e) medically fragile children receiving care at home or in school settings. Case managers are responsible for evaluating the needs of all types of clients, and they contract services (mainly personal support/homemaking, rehabilitation and nursing) with home care provider agencies through a competitive bid process. Successful home care service providers enter into accountability agreements with CCACs for the delivery of these services.

In 2009–10, approximately 603,000 Ontarians received approximately 29.4 million visits/hours of care at home (Ontario Home Care Association, 2011). These included personal support/homemaking (69 per cent), nursing (26 per cent) and therapy services (5 per cent). While case management and the contracted services provided through CCACs are fully funded by the MoHLTC, many Ontarians choose to supplement CCAC allocated services with privately purchased home care services. These supplemental services include clinical services by licensed health professions (e.g., physical therapy, nursing) or unlicensed personal support services. These supplemental services may be

Long-term care for the elderly in Canada 333

paid by 'privately-insured employment and/or government pro-grammes (such as respite programmes) and/or direct private purchase' (Ontario Home Care Association, 2011). It is estimated that the 150,000 individuals in Ontario 'purchase an additional 20 million visits/hours of home care services annually in order to remain at home' (Ontario Home Care Association, 2011).

Due largely to economic constraints, the number of individuals served by home care agencies fell by about 2.8 per cent from 2005–2006 to 2009–2010. However, the total number of units of services in the same period has increased 14.2 per cent, indicating an increase in the care demands of the smaller home care population receiving services in later years (Ontario Home Care Association, 2011). Although nursing visits, personal support services and homemaking increased in that time period, rehabilitation services, including occupational therapy, physi-otherapy and speech-language therapy visits declined by 9.1 per cent (Ontario Home Care Association, 2011).

12.3.4 *Admission and assessment processes*

Following its mandated adoption in 2003 as the standard assessment system for home care, case managers assess long-stay home care clients with the RAI-Home Care (RAI-HC) (Canadian Home Care Association, 2008) on intake and every six months thereafter in order to determine service eligibility and needs. In addition to allocation of home care services, CCAC placement coordinators also are responsible for the nursing home placement process. The RAI-HC (or Hospital version of RAI-HC if the client is in hospital) is used to inform decisions about nursing home eligibility and priority levels for admission. Although case managers may support clients who are admitted into retirement homes, those facilities do not require an assessment for entry. As mentioned above, historically, retirement homes were governed by another minis-try and were not regarded as 'healthcare facilities'. The evolution of retirement homes into unregulated alternatives to nursing homes will probably result in a change in these practices over time.

Persons who seek admission to a long-term care home must contact the CCAC in their geographic community. Placement coordinators determine eligibility for long-term care home admission by criteria set out in Section 155 of Regulation 79 under the Long Term Care Homes Act, 2010 (LTCHA). The criteria for long-stay residency include:

(1) the person is at least 18 years old; (2) the person is an insured person under the Health Insurance Act; (3) the person requires nursing care be available on-site 24 hours a day, requires, at frequent intervals throughout the day, assistance with activities of daily living, or requires, at frequent intervals throughout the day, on-site supervision or on-site monitoring to ensure his or her safety or well-being; (4) the publicly-funded community-based services available to the person and the other caregiving, support or companionship arrangements available to the person are not sufficient, in any combination, to meet the person's requirements; and (5) the person's care requirements can be met in a long-term care home (Ontario Government, 2010e).

Nursing homes have the right to refuse a resident who has applied for admission; however, the right to refuse is not open-ended. Concerns about potential behavioural problems are a relatively common reason for refusal of potential residents, and these individuals often experience prolonged hospital stays because of difficulties in gaining admission to long-term care.

To date, there have been no mandated CCAC assessments for short-stay post-acute or rehabilitation clients. If these individuals remain on service for more than sixty days they receive a RAI-HC assessment. However, in 2010 CCACs began province-wide implementation of the interRAI Contact Assessment (CA) as a preliminary screening assessment for all home care clients at the first point of contact to determine their need for more comprehensive assessment with RAI-HC. While the RAI-HC has been used for about 200,000 assessments per year to date, the interRAI CA is expected to be applied to over 400,000 intakes annually. In addition, CCACs began implementation of the interRAI Palliative Care (interRAI PC) (OACCAC, 2011) in 2011 as the standard assessment for all community-based palliative care services managed by CCACs. This also includes some services offered by CCACs to persons in residential hospices. Hospice care in Ontario is provided by community-based volunteer organizations funded by LHINs to provide a range of compassionate end-of-life support and care to persons living with a life-threatening illness and their families. Hospice services include respite care, drop-in programmes and outreach, education and bereavement counselling. For pain and symptom management, professional services, including medicine and nursing, are available from and funded through CCACs. Additional funding is raised through fund-raising and benefactors. While some hospice programmes stand alone, others are integrated into other service organizations.

12.3.5 Community Support Agencies

There are over 800 community support agencies across Ontario that provide services to a lighter-care community-based population than typically seen by CCACs. However, there is considerable overlap between the populations targeted by each, and it is not uncommon for frail older adults to receive services from both. Both types of agency are accountable to the Ontario MoHLTC. The main aim of community support agencies is to help older adults and persons with disabilities remain independent and to continue to live in their homes and communities (Ministry of Health and Long-Term Care, 2011b). These agencies are fully or partially funded by the provincial ministry. The services that they provide include: professional services, personal support and homemaking, meals, community transportation, acquired brain injury services, assisted living services in supportive housing, and elderly persons' centres (Ministry of Health and Long-Term Care, 2011b). Individuals can access these services directly through self-referral.

In 2010, community support agencies were mandated to use the interRAI Community Health Assessment (CHA) as the standard assessment for their caseload, unless the person is already assessed with RAI-HC. A lack of coordination and communication between some CCACs and community support agencies is a current problem affecting business processes for assessment practices and information sharing. In addition, because they are considered community support agencies, some hospices are currently implementing the inter-RAI CHA system rather than the interRAI PC, even though it would be more clinically appropriate to adopt the latter instrument.

12.3.6 Hospital-based care

Hospitals are subject to the terms of the Canada Health Act, 1984. As such, they are managed under the direction of public boards of directors and the majority of their services are funded by the MoHLTC with no additional fees to the patient. However, a co-payment equivalent to that charged for basic nursing home services (about CAN \$50) is levied on patients declared by the attending physician to require an Alternative Level of Care (ALC). ALC patients are those who no longer have a condition requiring acute care, but they are not considered able to return home safely. They therefore typically are awaiting placement in a long-term care home. ALC patients are typically elderly, but they may include persons with disabilities or mental health needs combined with chronic health conditions that limit their ability to live independently. Other non-ministry revenues include relatively modest commercial sources such as parking fees and gift shop sales. In 2010, 86 per cent of hospital revenues came from the MoHLTC, and 68 per cent of their expenditures were for compensation and benefits. The balance of expenditures was roughly equally divided between equipment, medical supplies, drugs, general supplies and other expenses (OHA, 2010).

The share of national expenditures accounted for by hospitals has fallen from almost half of total health expenditures in 1975 to about 25 per cent in 2010. Nonetheless, it remains about 2.5 times greater than expenditures on nursing homes and about double the expenditures on physicians (CIHI, 2011). Ontario has the lowest rate of age-standardized acute in-patient hospitalization at 7,160 per 100,000 compared with 7,837 for the national average (CIHI, 2010). The average length of stay in acute hospitals is 6.4 days in Ontario, compared with 7.7 days in other provinces (OHA, 2010). Rates of emergency department visits in Ontario have declined somewhat from 454 per 1,000 population in 1997 to 431 per 1,000 population in 2009 (OHA, 2010).

There are four types of hospital beds in Ontario that are available either in a stand-alone facility or in specialized units within acute care hospitals. In 2010, there were 18,355 acute hospital beds staffed and in operation compared with 5,798 complex continuing care (CCC), 4,335 psychiatric and 2,322 rehabilitation hospital beds. The supply of rehabilitation and psychiatric beds rose by 13 per cent and 70 per cent, respectively, whereas the supply of CCC and acute beds fell by 50 per cent and 45 per cent, respectively between 1990 and 2010 (OHA, 2010).

12.3.6.1 Complex Continuing Care Hospitals/Units

Complex continuing care (CCC) hospitals/units provide care to medically complex frail older persons who do not require acute hospital services, but are too medically unstable to go to long-term care homes. The number of CCC beds dropped substantially in the last two decades as a result of a change in the role of these facilities. In the early 1990s there was a sense that there was too much overlap in the populations covered, and services provided, by CCC hospitals/units and long-term care homes. The Health Services Restructuring Commission (1996–2000) engaged in an extensive review of all health services in the province. It recommended a reorientation of CCC service to place a greater emphasis on rehabilitation and medically complex populations with the majority of lighter-care patients to be redirected towards long-term care homes (Hirdes et al., 2003). A comparison of case-mix distributions in these facilities also shows a pronounced reduction of the percentage of patients with light care needs in response to the directives of the Commission.

Since that time lengths of stay in CCC hospitals/units have declined dramatically as the emphasis switched towards short-term post-acute care (CIHI, 2004). In the early 1980s the average length of stay in chronic hospitals was over two years, but by 2011 the average length of stay among discharges was ninety days with a median length of twenty-nine days. More than half of CCC admissions are discharged within ninety days and about one-third of those discharges are persons returning to their homes (Hirdes et al., 2011).

As part of the process of restructuring the mandate of CCC hospitals/units there was an interest in establishing a case-mix-based payment system that would reflect the resource requirements of patients in post-acute hospital settings. Following an extensive review by the Ontario Joint Policy and Planning Committee (JPPC), the Resident Assessment Instrument ((RAI 2.0) (Hirdes et al., 1997) was mandated in 1996 as the standard assessment for CCC settings in order to support the introduction of the Resource Utilization Groups (RUG-III) case-mix system (Fries et al., 1994). The assessment is done on admission and on a quarterly basis; however, only basic tracking and disposition information is gathered at discharge.

Although the RAI 2.0 was originally designed to be used to support clinical practice and care planning, it was mainly introduced as a case-mix tool for funding purposes. By 2002, the provincial funding formula included a modest case-mix adjustment for CCC; however, the RUG-III case-mix system is now being more fully incorporated into the province's Health Based Allocation Method (HBAM) payment system that is being introduced across multiple healthcare sectors.

About four years after its implementation in CCC settings, the RAI 2.0 and its associated quality indicators (Jones et al., 2010; Mor et al., 2003) began to be used to support greater public accountability in that sector. The Hospital Report (OHA, 2003) initiative was a partnership of CIHI, the JPPC, OHA and the MoHLTC, which produced the first public, balanced score card on the performance of different types of hospitals in Ontario. By 2003, the first hospital-specific data were publicly released on CCC hospital performance with respect to issues like restraint use, pressure ulcers and functional decline. In subsequent years, both CCC hospitals/units and long-term care homes have RAI 2.0 quality indicators publicly reported by Health Quality Ontario (see below).

12.3.6.2 Psychiatric hospitals/units

Psychiatric hospitals/units in Ontario provide a broad range of in-patient mental health services to populations of all ages, including acute, forensic, long-stay and geriatric psychiatry. Persons aged 65 and over comprise about 14 per cent of the psychiatric hospital population (CIHI, 2009b); however, there are two distinct elderly populations: (a) community admissions with mental health needs comparable to the general adult population; and (b) admissions from long-term care homes that tend to have severe behavioural disturbances. Although discharges to psychiatric hospitals account for only about 1 per cent of long-term care discharges, these individuals comprise the bulk of patients in geriatric psychiatry units in those hospitals. In addition, there are notable differences in length of stay between older persons admitted to psychiatry from community and long-term care home settings. The median length of stay for the general adult population is eight days in psychiatric units in general hospitals compared with twenty-four days in specialty psychiatric hospitals (CIHI, 2009b); however, the median length of stay for elderly patients ranges from about ten days for those aged 65+ in acute psychiatric units to thirty-five days in geriatric units and fifty-seven days in long-stay units. About 75 per cent of discharges among those admitted to in-patient psychiatry from long-term care homes return the person to a nursing home setting (CIHI, 2009b).

All persons admitted to an adult mental health bed in Ontario are assessed with the RAI-Mental Health (RAI-MH) (Hirdes et al., 2001; Hirdes et al., 2002; Martin et al., 2009) on admission and discharge. In addition, those with stays longer than ninety days are reassessed on a quarterly basis. The RAI-MH was developed to support clinical practice, quality monitoring and case-mix classification through a collaborative research project between interRAI, the JPPC and the MoHLTC. It was mandated for use in all adult psychiatric in-patient settings in 2005. To date, over 400,000 assessments have been completed. The System for Classification of In-patient Psychiatry (SCIPP) case mix system will be incorporated into the HBAM payment system to inform funding decisions for mental health services, including geriatric psychiatry.

12.3.6.3 Acute hospitals

Acute hospitals provide general hospital care to an increasingly elderly population in Ontario. By 2009–10, elderly persons accounted for about 38 per cent of acute hospital discharges (CIHI, 2011), even though they represent only about 13 per cent of the population. The majority of older persons have relatively straightforward health needs that are managed effectively through hospital and they are then discharged home in a relatively predictable manner. However, Alternate Level of Care (ALC) patients have been a major concern in Canada because of the belief that they impede flow through the hospital and cause overcrowding of emergency departments (CIHI, 2009c; Costa and Hirdes, 2010). The designation as ALC is based on a physician judgement that the person no longer needs acute care, and the person requires care in another setting (typically a long-term care home). However, there is not a clear operational definition that is reliably administered across the province, resulting in substantial facility-level variations that may reflect definitional rather than clinical differences (Costa and Hirdes, 2010).

A reduction of ALC days has been an important policy priority in the last five years, but progress has been relatively modest in that time. This is due to a variety of factors, including an increase in the length of time for admission to long-term care homes among those who have been assessed as requiring that level of care (Health Quality Ontario, 2011). As part of a CAN $1 billion investment in community services, the province's Aging at Home Strategy was introduced in 2007 as an initiative to support independent living of seniors in Ontario. However, by the second year of the strategy, much of its funding was reallocated to support initiatives aimed at reducing ALC days in hospitals. One promising initiative known as 'Home First' involves supporting a return to the community from hospital prior to making decisions about long-term care placement.

The intent of this type of programme is to increase the possibility of return to the person's home with appropriate supports and to remove the pressures of decision making in a hospital environment. It is expected that future provincial quality reports will use the percentage of long-term care home admissions directly from hospital as an indicator of health system quality.

Persons in acute care hospitals who have been designated as ALC patients awaiting nursing home placement are assessed by CCAC case managers with an adapted 'Hospital version' of RAI-HC. However, the assessment is currently used only for placement purposes and clinical findings are not shared with hospital staff and care plans are generally not developed in response to the assessment. This means that an important opportunity to improve outcomes for hospital-based frail older adults is often missed.

Costa and Hirdes (2010) provide a comprehensive comparison of ALC patients and long-stay home care clients using Hospital RAI-HC and RAI-HC data, respectively. The ALC population is substantially more impaired in domains like functional status, cognition and continence, compared with the general home care population. In addition, they have notably higher rates of mental health problems including depressive symptoms and behaviour disturbance.

Persons discharged to home care from hospitals are assessed in hospital by CCAC case managers using the interRAI Contact Assessment to determine the urgency of their need for initiation of service provision and the need for comprehensive assessment. In addition, the assessment is intended to provide a basic clinical assessment of persons with less complex needs that may not receive the full RAI-HC assessment. Implementation of the interRAI CA began in 2010 with most CCACs completing the implementation phase in 2011. CIHI added the capacity to manage and report on both the Hospital Version of the RAI-HC and the interRAI CA as part of the Home Care Reporting System. CIHI's Discharge Abstract Database and National Ambulatory Care Reporting System have both been important sources of information on acute hospital and emergency department utilization for persons of all ages, including the elderly. However, the interRAI instruments provide a more comprehensive clinical view of older persons than those two systems. In addition, they provide the first assessment and screening systems in acute hospitals compatible with those used in other sectors.

Long-term care for the elderly in Canada 341

12.3.6.4 Rehabilitation

Rehabilitation services are provided through a variety of organizations with different types of funding, oversight and accountability. Physical, occupational and speech language therapists are all regulated health professionals accountable to colleges governing professional practice. Rehabilitation assistants are not currently licensed, although formal educational and credentialling programmes are emerging. A College of Kinesiologists of Ontario was recently established to regulate that discipline; however, no comparable college exists for rehabilitation assistants.

Acute, CCC and stand-alone rehabilitation hospitals provide a full range of physical therapy, occupational therapy and speech language pathology services that are publicly funded and delivered directly by the hospitals. Designated rehabilitation beds represent about 8 per cent of all hospital beds in the province. Rehabilitation departments in hospitals tend to be staffed mainly by licensed therapists. In contrast to hospital settings, access to rehabilitation in long-term care homes has been relatively limited historically. In part, this was a consequence of the Health Services Restructuring Commission directive for rehabilitation services to be provided in hospital settings rather than long-term care. However, it is being increasingly realized that residents of these homes have rehabilitation potential which has not been met with commensurate service provision. Recent legislation has been put in place to expand access to restorative care in long-term care homes (Ontario Government, 2010c, 2010e). The relatively modest level of rehabilitation provided in these homes has come from external agencies contracted by CCACs to provide a limited number of visits or from external for-profit rehabilitation provider companies. On average, long-term care residents receive less than five minutes of rehabilitation per week and over 90 per cent of that therapy comes from aides rather than licensed rehabilitation professionals (Hirdes et al., 2010; Hirdes et al., 2011).

In community-based settings, home care provider agencies may be contracted through CCACs to provide in-home rehabilitation services for long-stay home care clients, but these are typically capped at four visits after intake. Only about 10 per cent of long-stay home care clients receive physical therapy or occupational therapy, and about 75 per cent of those considered to have rehabilitation potential do not receive these therapies (Hirdes et al., 2004; Dalby et al., 2005). Moreover, according to the Ontario Home Care Association (OHCA, 2010) access to publicly funded rehabilitation in Ontario has declined in home care settings with a drop of 9 and 25 per cent in physical therapy and occupational therapy visits contracted by CCACs, respectively. A recent report commissioned by the MoHLTC (Walker, 2011) called for the expansion of 'Assess and Restore' service to help improve the independence of the elderly and reduce the burden of ALC days in acute hospitals. However, the lack of a coherent approach to rehabilitation to date was noted as an important barrier, and several recommendations dealt with the need to establish clear programme standards and admission criteria for these services.

12.4 Health Information Systems and public reporting across the continuum of care

The interRAI family of assessment instruments (Hirdes et al., 1999, 2008; Gray et al., 2009) have become the de facto national standards for assessment in home care and nursing home settings in Canada. Eight provinces and territories are implementing interRAI instruments for those two settings, and several of them are also in the process of adopting other instruments (e.g., interRAI Contact Assessment, interRAI Palliative Care). The remaining provinces/territories currently use locally developed solutions unique to their region. Health Canada, the federal Department of Health, is now exploring using the RAI-HC with First Nations and Inuit populations on a national basis. Compared with other jurisdictions in Canada and internationally, Ontario has the most extensive implementation of interRAI instruments, covering home care, nursing homes, CCC hospitals, psychiatric hospitals, community support services, deaf, blind intervenor services and community-based palliative care (Hirdes, 2006). Ontario was the first province to adopt an interRAI instrument with the mandated use of the RAI 2.0 in CCC hospitals/units beginning in 1996. In addition, it has collaborated with interRAI in the development of new instruments and applications, including the RAI-Mental Health and interRAI Contact Assessment.

A major consideration in Ontario's adoption of numerous interRAI instruments has been recognition of the value of an integrated health information system based on assessments with common standards across care settings. The interRAI instruments are unique because they share common items, terminology, assessment methods, outcome

Long-term care for the elderly in Canada

measures and care planning protocols across multiple care settings (Gray et al., 2009). In addition, the possibility of using data from interRAI assessments for multiple applications serving multiple audiences has been an important feature of interest to Ontario policy makers. A recent initiative led by the MoHLTC to establish an Integrated Assessment Record (IAR) has the promise of more fully exploiting the use of multiple interRAI assessments as a common clinical record. The IAR will function as a common registry of all mandated assessments for an individual, which can then be accessed by clinicians to obtain a longitudinal view of the person's status. The IAR is expected to be fully operational in 2013.

At the national level, the Canadian Institute for Health Information compiles data from interRAI as part of the Continuing Care Reporting System (CCRS) (www.cihi.ca/ccrs) and Home Care Reporting System (HCRS) (www.cihi.ca/hcrs) to support national statistical reporting on residential and community-based long-term care. In addition, the Ontario Mental Health Reporting System (OMHRS) (www.cihi.ca/omhrs) serves a similar function for in-patient mental health data from Ontario and interRAI Community Mental Health data from Newfoundland. CIHI produces standard reports to submitting organizations that allow them to compare themselves with regional, provincial and national indicators. In addition, those organizations can access facility-identifiable data through CIHI's electronic portal to support internal quality improvement initiatives. CIHI also produces substantive reports from the data housed in CCRS, HCRS and OMHRS that are released to the general public as 'Analyses in Brief'. In addition, participating organizations can access restricted databases for limited facility-level comparisons that are not publicly available. CIHI reports tend to receive extensive media coverage, so they play an important role in raising public awareness about the quality of residential and community services in Canada. Some recent examples include reports on caregivers in home care, restraint use in psychiatry and depression among nursing home residents.

There is currently no national standard survey dealing with personal preferences, satisfaction or the 'patient experience'. Several pilot studies have been conducted, but most uses of these surveys remain at the local or individual province level. For example, Ontario CCACs have adopted a common client survey that was implemented in all regions by 2012. The survey is administered by an external polling firm and involves random samples of discharged clients on a quarterly basis and annual samples of active clients. End-of-life clients are excluded from the survey pool; however, there are plans to expand the survey process to current caregivers and family members of deceased clients.

12.5 Improving quality of care in home care and long-term care

Improvement of health system quality and accountability has been a priority for health policy makers and service providers nationally for at least the last two decades. Ontario has played a leadership role in this area with the introduction of clinical data standards, creation of public reporting mechanisms, and establishment of accountability agreements with health service professionals. Quality improvement is regarded as a shared priority and responsibility of numerous stakeholders in the province, and the mechanisms to improve quality are multifold.

12.5.1 Regulatory framework and inspection of long-term care homes

In Ontario, the primary regulatory framework for the quality of care and quality of life of residents in long-term care homes is provided by the Long Term Care Homes Act (LTCHA), 2010 (Ontario Government, 2010c). An overarching fundamental principle of the Act is that 'a long-term care home is primarily the home of its residents and is to be operated so that it is a place where they may live with dignity and in security, safety and comfort and have their physical, psychological, social, spiritual and cultural needs adequately met' (LTCHA, 2010, Section 2). This fundamental principle guides the application and administration of the Act.

The LTCHA and its regulations provide several measures for safeguarding residents from abuse, neglect, or risk of harm, including a:

- bill of rights;
- mechanism for the reporting of improper treatment or care that result in harm or a risk of harm to a resident, abuse of a resident by anyone or neglect of a resident by the licensee or staff that resulted in harm or a risk of harm to a resident, and unlawful conduct that resulted in harm or a risk of harm to a resident; and
- mechanism for the reporting and investigation of complaints.

Long-term care for the elderly in Canada 345

12.5.1.1 Standards of care, services and programmes

The LTCHA and its regulations set out requirements for safety and security, including locking devices for doors and stairways, use of elevators, floor space for both residents and staff, furnishings, privacy curtains, bed rails, communication and response systems, use of generators and lighting and temperature control systems. Specific services and programmes include nursing and personal support services, falls prevention and management, skin and wound care, continence care and bowel management, pain management, care and management of residents with behaviour problems, restorative care, recreational and social activities, nutrition care and hydration programmes, weight management, dietary and food services, medical services, religious and spiritual practices, accommodation services such as housekeeping, laundry and maintenance and volunteer programmes.

12.5.1.2 Compliance inspection and enforcement

Trained inspectors, who are registered nurses, registered dietitians and environmental health specialists by profession, inspect long-term care homes to ensure their compliance with the requirements set out in the LTCHA and its regulations. These inspectors are appointed by the Minister of Health and Long Term Care. Every long-term care home must be inspected at least once annually on a randomized schedule. With a few exceptions (e.g., inspections for compliance with a closure plan), all inspections occur without prior notice.

The Long-Term Care Home Quality Inspection Program (LQIP) provides the structure and process for the inspection of long-term care homes. Under this scheme, inspectors conduct structured interviews with residents, family members and staff members. They make direct observations of how care is provided, and review residents' records of personal health information (including RAI 2.0 assessments and facility-level reports). Inspection Protocols are used to evaluate compliance with specific aspects of care or treatment. Some examples of Inspection Protocols include: continence care and bowel management, falls prevention, restraint minimization, pain management and skin and wound management. All non-compliances are documented and reported to the long-term care home.

The severity and scope (i.e., pervasiveness throughout the long-term care home) of the non-compliance, and the long-term care home's history of compliance determines inspectors' decisions or actions.

These actions range from a voluntary response to correct minor issues to more extreme responses including: ordering that funding to be returned or withheld, ordering the licensee to retain one or more persons acceptable to the director to manage or assist in the management of the long-term care home, and making an order revoking the licence for the operation of a long-term care home.

12.5.1.3 Complaints reporting and investigation

The LTCHA requires long-term care homes to have written procedures for making complaints and to post these procedures where people can see them. Long-term care homes are required to acknowledge a complaint within ten business days where possible and to advise the complainant when a resolution could be expected. Complaints or incidents involving abuse or neglect of residents must be investigated immediately. All written complaints must be forwarded to the designated director under the LTCHA.

An alternative approach available for making complaints is a toll-free ACTION Line established by the MoHLTC. Residents, family members, employees of the long-term care home, anyone providing services to the resident or any member of the general public may call the ACTION Line with their complaints or concerns. Any information that is received by the director pertaining to improper treatment that resulted in a risk of harm to a resident, abuse or neglect of resident, unlawful conduct, or any apparent retaliation against a resident for reporting or disclosing to the director or an inspector, is investigated by a compliance inspector.

12.5.2 Accreditation of health services

Accreditation Canada is a not-for-profit national organization independent of government and health service providers (Accreditation Canada, 2011). It provides peer review evaluation of organizations' performance in Canada and internationally based on standards set by expert advisory committees. It also provides education services on accreditation standards and processes, patient safety and quality.

The accreditation process is tailored to different types of organizations and provides different standards for over thirty sectors including hospitals, home care and long-term care homes. In 2010, long-term care homes were the most common site for accreditation surveys (34 per cent) followed by acute hospitals (18 per cent). Home care agencies accounted for 9 per cent of accreditation activities that year (Accreditation Canada, 2010). Organizations interested in being accredited contact Accreditation Canada and request to be accredited. Accreditation surveys are peer reviews conducted by experienced members of health and social service professions (e.g., physicians, nurses, occupational therapists, social workers) and health executives. The focus of accreditation surveys is patient safety and quality practices.

Accreditation Canada surveyors assess the performance of organizations against national standards related to governance, administration, clinical practice and risk management. Surveys usually take several days depending on the size of the organization. Organizations may be awarded full accreditation after the survey, but typically they receive accreditation contingent on conditions specified by the surveyors. In 2010, only 3 per cent of organizations surveyed in Canada and internationally were not accredited.

In addition to Accreditation Canada, long-term care homes could also receive accreditation from the Commission on the Accreditation of Rehabilitation Facilities (CARF) as of October 2008. CARF's accreditation consists of a two-step process: (1) a self-assessment by the organization; and (2) an external third-party peer review (CARF International, 2011). CARF supports organizations such as long-term care homes that are interested in being accredited through coaching to initially complete a self-assessment of their care and services against CARF's applicable standards. Following this step, and based on this self-assessment, the long-term care home endeavours to conform to CARF's standards for a period of six months. Once the long-term care home demonstrates a substantial conformance with CARF's standards, the organization is ready for the next phase, which is an accreditation survey by a team of external peer surveyors from their own field. Recommendations are identified by the surveyors. The long-term care home is required to submit a Quality Improvement Plan (QIP) to CARF to show how it will address the gaps identified (CARF International, 2011). CARF's accreditation awards include: (1) three-year accreditation for full conformance; (2) one-year accreditation for conformance with many standards; (3) provisional accreditation for organizations which after one year are still functioning at the one-year accreditation level; (4) non-accreditation for major deficiencies, which impose a risk to the health, wellness or safety of those served.

12.5.3 Professional associations and quality improvement

The professional associations for each major sector of healthcare also play important roles in quality improvement and accountability of the healthcare system. While each association serves an advocacy role acting on behalf of its member organizations as stakeholder representatives interacting with the MoHLTC, these associations also engage in broader activities that have an impact on healthcare quality.

Long-term care homes in Ontario typically belong to one of two professional associations – the Ontario Long Term Care Association (OLTCA) representing the for-profit providers and the Ontario Association of Non-profit Homes and Services for Seniors (OANHSS) representing the not-for-profit homes. Both associations participate actively in provincial-level working groups or committees, and they also host annual conventions that include quality improvement as a major focus. Recently, OLTCA launched a Quality Improvement Recognition Program for organizational achievements in quality improvement.

The Ontario Hospital Association (OHA) represents all hospitals in the province. The OHA and Ontario Medical Association have been the most influential voices affecting Ministry policy. The OHA supports a broad range of educational activities for its members, hosts the largest annual healthcare conference in Ontario and supports a variety of applied research efforts in collaboration with other organizations. For example, in 2000 the OHA and MoHLTC launched the Hospital Report collaborative, representing the first major initiative to provide facility-level balanced score cards to report on the performance of the hospital sector. Recently, the OHA established a strategic alliance with the Ontario Association of Community Care Access Centres (OACCAC) to increase the level of collaboration between the hospital and community care sectors.

The OACCAC is the professional association representing Community Care Access Centres. In addition to its work representing those stakeholder organizations, OACCAC provides IT services and reporting for all home care agencies. It manages the Client Health and Related Information System (CHRIS), which is the provincial home care information system, including data for multiple interRAI assessment instruments and administrative data. OACCAC provides internal decision support services and sets IT standards for all CCACs in the province. It manages the RAI-HC, interRAI CA and interRAI PC data

Long-term care for the elderly in Canada 349

in the province and it has the authority to mandate province-wide assessment practices within CCACs. As part of its information management role, OACCAC has also begun to release public reports on the quality of home care and it led to the creation and implementation of a common client experience survey. At its annual meeting the OACCAC also recognizes outstanding organizational performance through its Awards for Excellence Program.

Home care and community support service providers are represented by the Ontario Home Care Association (OHCA) and Ontario Community Support Association (OCSA), respectively. Both organizations host annual professional conferences that include information on innovations, quality-related initiatives and educational programmes. OHCA members are expected to adhere to the Association's Standards for Home Healthcare Service Agencies. In addition, they conduct an annual self-evaluation of adherence with those standards using the OHCA Quality Template. This template is intended to function as a publicly reported balanced scorecard measuring four dimensions of service: customers, learning and growth, internal business, financial management.

12.5.4 *Health Quality Ontario*

Health Quality Ontario (HQO; Ontario Government, 2010d) was established as an independent, arms-length agency under the Commitment to the Future of Medicare Act on 12 September 2005, and its mandate was later expanded under the Excellent Care for All Act, 2010 (Ontario Government, 2010b). In its current role, HQO is charged with three major responsibilities:

(a) monitoring and publicly reporting on the quality of care with a particular focus on access to public services; health human resources; consumer and population health; healthcare outcomes across care settings, including home care, long-term care homes and hospitals;
(b) supporting continuous quality improvement (for example, through the Residents First initiative that provides quality improvement education to long-term care homes);
(c) promoting evidence-informed care by providing recommendations on clinical practice guidelines and funding for healthcare and medical devices.

Since 2010, HQO has published public reports on health system performance and quality for long-term care homes, CCC hospitals and CCACs (HQO, 2011). These reports provide information at least at three levels: overall health system performance with no disaggregation of results; LHIN-level findings; and organization-specific results that may be searched through the Internet. The HQO reports use a variety of administrative databases, but they also employ clinical data gathered through the various interRAI assessment instruments mandated for different healthcare sectors. Many of HQO's quality indicators and associated risk adjusters are those developed by interRAI for home care and long-term care homes (Hirdes et al., 2004; Mor et al., 2003; Jones et al., 2010). In addition to cross-sectional views of regional and facility-level variations, the reports include longitudinal data representing historical changes in health system performance.

With the initial introduction of public reports for long-term care homes, participation in the site-specific reporting was optional. About 100 homes participated in that first phase; however, public reporting will be mandatory for all homes by 2013.

12.6 Concluding comments

Ontario's health and long-term care systems have made important strides over the last three decades in improving the quality of care provided to older citizens. Although much more needs to be done, important innovations have occurred in many domains. The implementation of standardized health information systems that span multiple sectors holds the promise of yielding insights into the needs of vulnerable populations that were commonly overlooked. New quality improvement and public accountability initiatives mean that quality is becoming a shared commitment, with evidence and transparent reporting as its foundation. Payment systems that aim to allocate resources equitably based on the needs of healthcare service recipients rather than on the basis of historical power differences between organizations are important from both the perspective of the rights of individuals to receive equal treatment and the sustainability of the healthcare system. Finally, the recognition that healthcare must function as an integrated system rather than a collection of independent entities focused on narrowly defined clinical activities is moving from being a platitude towards an expectation.

Long-term care for the elderly in Canada 351

Even though each province/territory is administratively autonomous and relatively distinct from others, there are aspects of the Ontario experience that could be useful if adopted elsewhere. Ontario's leadership in the adoption of comprehensive assessment systems across the continuum of care and public reporting with data from those assessments are important innovations that have led to tangible improvements in accountability and quality of care. The fact that Canada's federal structure distributes, rather than centralizes, authority for healthcare means that no single government can set the national standard in this regard. However, Canada has never been closer to a consensus on assessment standards for home care and nursing homes than it is today. It is reasonable to expect that within the next decade only Quebec will remain outside of the interRAI standard. As implementation of these instruments nears completion, increasing attention will move towards use of the data to support reporting at the provincial level; however, the publication of comparative data for eight provinces/ territories (Hirdes et al., 2011) represents the most comprehensive picture to date of the nursing home sector. A similar report was released by the Health Council of Canada (2012) using RAI-HC and other data to describe home care nationally.

Tommy Douglas, the founder of Canadian Medicare, said, 'Courage, my friends; 'tis not too late to build a better world.' Policy makers and the general public today have more evidence available about the quality of nursing homes and home care than at any prior point. Although perfection has by no means been achieved, Ontario's health system for the elderly has indeed progressed towards a better world.

References

Accreditation Canada (2010). Annual report 2010. Available at: www.accreditation.ca/uploadedFiles/Annual per cent20Report per cent202010.pdf. Accessed 5 January 2012.

    (2011). Accreditation Canada: driving quality health services. Available at: www.accreditation.ca/. Accessed 29 August 2011.

Beland, F. and Shapiro, E. (1994). Ten provinces in search of long term policy. In V. Marshall and B. McPherson (eds.), *Aging: Canadian Perspectives*. Peterborough, ON: Broadview Press, pp. 245–67.

Bernabei, R., Gray, L., Hirdes, J., Pei, X., Henrard, J.C., Jonsson, P.V., Onder, G., Gambassi, G., Ikegami, N., Ranhoff, A.H., Carpenter, I.G., Harwood, R.H., Fries, B.E., Morris, J.N. and Steel, K. (2009).

International gerontology. In J. B. Halter, J. G. Ouslander, M. E. Tinetti, S. Studenski, K. P. High and S. Asthana (eds.), *Hazzard's Geriatric Medicine and Gerontology* (6th edn). New York: McGraw Medical, pp. 69–96.

Canadian Home Care Association (CHCA) (2008). *Portraits of Home Care in Canada*. Toronto: CHCA.

Canadian Institute for Health Information (CIHI) (2004). *Complex Continuing Care in Ontario: Resident Demographics and System Characteristics*. Ottawa: CIHI.

(2007). *Public-Sector Expenditures and Utilization of Home Care Services in Canada: Exploring the Data*. Ottawa: CIHI.

(2009a). *Healthcare in Canada 2009: a Decade in Review*. Ottawa: CIHI.

(2009b). *Analysis in Brief: Exploring Hospital Mental Health Service Use in Ontario, 2007–2008*. Ottawa: CIHI.

(2009c). *Analysis in Brief: Alternate Level of Care in Canada, 2009*. Ottawa: CIHI.

(2010). *National Expenditure Trends, 1975–2010*. Ottawa: CIHI.

(2011). *Healthcare in Canada 2011: a Focus on Seniors and Aging*, Ottawa: CIHI.

CARF International (2011). Commission on Accreditation of Rehabilitation Facilities. Available at: www.carf.org.proxy.lib.uwaterloo.ca/providers. aspx?Content=Content/Accreditation/Opportunities/AS/toc.htm. Accessed 8 August 2011.

Central East Local Health Integration Network. (2010). Multi-Sector Accountability Agreement (MSAAs). Available at: www.centraleastlhin. on.ca.proxy.lib.uwaterloo.ca/report_display.aspx?id=12684. Accessed 26 August 2011.

Costa, A. P. and Hirdes, J. P. (2010). Clinical characteristics and service needs of alternate-level-of-care patients waiting for long-term care in Ontario hospitals. *Healthcare Policy*, 6(1): 32–46.

Dalby, D. M., Hirdes, J. P. and Fries, B. E. (2005). Risk adjustment methods for home care quality indicators (HCQIs) based on the minimum data set for home care. *BMC Health Services Research*, 5(1): 7.

Flood, C. M. and Choudhry, S. (2004). Strengthening the foundations: modernizing the Canada Health Act. In T. McIntosh, P. G. Forest and G. P. Marchildon (eds.), *Romanow Papers: The Governance of Healthcare in Canada*. University of Toronto Press, pp. 312–45.

Forbes, W. F., Jackson, J. A. and Krause, A. S. (1987). *Institutionalization of the Elderly in Canada*. Toronto: Butterworths.

Fries, B. E., Schneider, D. P., Foley, W. J., Gavazzi, M., Burke, R. and Cornelius, E. (1994). Refining a case-mix measure for nursing homes: Resource Utilization Groups (RUG-III). *Medical Care*, 32(7): 668–85.

Gray, L. C., Berg, K., Fries, B. E., Henrard, J. C., Hirdes, J. P., Steel, K. and Morris, J. N. (2009). Sharing clinical information across care settings: the birth of an integrated assessment system. *BMC Health Services Research*, 29(9): 71.

Health Council of Canada (2012). *Seniors in Need: Caregivers in Distress*. Toronto: Health Council of Canada.

Health Quality Ontario (HQO) (2011). *Quality Monitor: 2011 Report on Ontario's Health System*. Toronto: HQO.

Hirdes, J. P. (1997). Development of a cross-walk from the Minimum Data Set 2.0 to the Alberta Classification System. *Healthcare Management Forum*, 10(1): 27–9, 32–4.

(2001). Long term care funding in Canada: a policy mosaic. *Journal of Aging and Social Policy*, 13(2–3): 69–81.

(2006). Addressing the health needs of frail elderly people: Ontario's experience with an integrated health information system. *Age and Ageing*, 35(4): 329–31.

Hirdes, J. P., Botz, C. A., Kozak, J. and Lepp, V. (1996). Identifying an appropriate case-mix measure for chronic care: evidence from an Ontario pilot study. *Healthcare Management Forum*, 9(1): 40–6.

Hirdes, J. P., Fries, B. E., Morris, J. N., Ikegami, N., Zimmerman, D., Dalby, D. M., Aliaga, P., Hammer, S. and Jones, R. (2004). Home Care Quality Indicators (HCQIs) based on the MDS-HC. *The Gerontologist*, 44(5): 665–79.

Hirdes, J. P., Fries, B. E., Morris, J. N., Steel, K., Mor, V., Frijters, D., Jonsson, P., LaBine, S., Schalm, C., Stones, M. J., Teare, G., Smith, T., Marhaba, M. and Perez, E. (1999). Integrated health information systems based on the RAI/MDS series of assessment instruments. *Healthcare Management Forum*, 12(4): 30–40.

Hirdes, J. P., Ljunggren, G., Morris, J. N., Frijters, D. H., Finne Soveri, H., Gray, L., Björkgren, M. and Gilgen, R. (2008). Reliability of the interRAI suite of assessment instruments: a 12-country study of an integrated health information system. *BMC Health Services Research*, 8: 277.

Hirdes, J. P., Marhaba, M., Smith, T. F., Clyburn, L., Mitchell, L., Lemick, R. A., Curtin Telegdi, N., Pérez, E., Prendergast, P., Rabinowitz, T. and Yamauchi, K. (2001). Development of the Resident Assessment Instrument – Mental Health (RAI-MH). *Hospital Quarterly*, 4(2): 44–51.

Hirdes, J. P., Mitchell, L., Maxwell, C. J. and White, N. (2011). Beyond the 'iron lungs of gerontology': using evidence to shape the future of nursing homes in Canada. *Canadian Journal on Aging*, 30(3): 371–90.

Hirdes, J. P., Poss, J. W., Fries, B. E., Smith, T. F., Maxwell, C. J., Wu, C. and Jantzi, M. (2010). *Canadian Staff Time and Resource Intensity*

Verification (CAN-STRIVE) Project: Validation of the Resource Utilization Groups (RUG-III) and Resource Utilization Groups for Home Care (RUG-III/HC) Case-mix Systems. Final Report to Ontario Ministry of Health and Long Term Care. Waterloo, ON: University of Waterloo.

Hirdes, J. P., Sinclair, D. G., King, J., McKinley, J. and Tuttle, P. (2003). From anecdotes to evidence: complex continuing care at the dawn of the information age. In B. E. Fries and C. J. Fahey (eds.), *Implementing the Resident Assessment Instrument: Case Studies of Policymaking for Long-Term Care in Eight Countries*, New York: Milbank Memorial Fund. Available at: www.milbank.org/uploads/documents/interRAI/030222interRAI.html#canada. Accessed 21 August 2013.

Hirdes, J. P., Smith, T. F., Rabinowitz, T., Yamauchi, K., Pérez, E., Curtin Telegdi, N., Prendergast, P., Morris, J. N., Ikegami, N., Phillips, C. and Fries, B. E. (2002). The Resident Assessment Instrument-Mental Health (RAI-MH)©: inter-rater reliability and convergent validity. *Journal of Behavioral Health Services and Research*, 29(4): 419–32.

Jones, R. N., Hirdes, J. P., Poss, J. W., Kelly, M., Berg, K., Fries, B. E. and Morris, J. N. (2010). Adjustment of nursing home quality indicators. *BMC Health Services Research*, 10: 96.

Ladak, N. (1998). *Understanding How Ontario Hospitals Are Funded: An Introduction (RD#6–11)*. Toronto: Joint Policy and Planning Committee.

Local Health System Integration Act (2006). Available at: www.search.e-laws.gov.on.ca/en/isysquery/9fccc650-88b5-4de3-9240-934499d67202/1/doc/?search=browseStatutes&context=#hit1. Accessed 26 August 2011.

Martin, L., Hirdes, J. P., Morris, J. N., Montague, P., Rabinowitz, T. and Fries, B. E. (2009). Validating the Mental Health Assessment Protocols (MHAPs) in the Resident Assessment Instrument Mental Health (RAI-MH). *Journal of Psychiatric and Mental Health Nursing*, 7: 646–53.

Ministry of Health and Long-Term Care. (2011a). Community care access centres. Available at: www.health.gov.on.ca/english/public/contact/ccac/ccac_mn.html. Accessed 26 August 2011.

  (2011b). Community care access centres: client services policy manual. Available at: www.health.gov.on.ca/english/providers/pub/pub_menus/pub_ccac.html. Accessed 15 August 2011.

  (2011c). Local health integration networks. Available at: www.lhins.on.ca/home.aspx?LangType=4105. Accessed 26 August 2011.

Mor, V., Angelelli, J., Gifford, D., Morris, J. and Moore, T. (2003). Benchmarking and quality in residential and nursing homes: lessons from the US. *International Journal of Geriatric Psychiatry*, 18(3): 258–66.

Morgan, S. (2004). Drug spending in Canada: recent trends and cause. *Medical Care*, 42(7): 635–42.

Ontario Association of Community Care Access Centres (OACCAC) (2011). ICCP Palliative Care Impact Assessment Framework. Available at: www.ccac-ont.ca/Upload/on/General/ICCP/ICCP_Impact_Assessment_Framework_Sep2011.pdf. Accessed 27 August 2012.

Ontario Government (2010a). Community Care Access Corporations Act, 2001. Available at: www.search.e-laws.gov.on.ca/en/isysquery/3a091197-663c-438f-bd99-165e9a043d70/2/doc/?search=browseStatutes&context=#hit1. Accessed 26 August 2011.

(2010b). Excellent Care for All Act. Available at: www.search.e-laws.gov.on.ca/en/isysquery/b4d0278e-8c19-48a1-949f-f68939d6e921/1/doc/?search=browseStatutes&context=#hit1. Accessed 26 August 2011.

(2010c). Long-Term Care Homes Act, 2010, S.O. 2007, Chapter 8. Available at: www.search.e-laws.gov.on.ca/en/isysquery/0da8b45c-c26e-45b3-843b-9e56fc49b55c/2/doc/?search=browseStatutes&context=#hit1. Accessed 26 August 2011.

(2010d). Ontario health quality. Available at: www.ohqc.ca/en/mandate.php. Accessed 14 September 2011.

(2010e). Ontario Regulation 79/10 made Under the Long-Term Care Homes Act, 2007. Available at: www.search.e-laws.gov.on.ca/en/isysquery/2305b97b-92dc-459b-bcd2-73ddf2cd0e64/1/doc/?search=browseStatutes&context=#hit1. Accessed 26 August 2011.

(2010f). The Retirement Homes Act, 2010. Available at: www.seniors.gov.on.ca/en/retirement_homes/index.php. Accessed 27August 2012.

Ontario Home Care Association (OHCA) (2010). Report on the OHCA roundtable on rehabilitation in home care. Available at: www.homecareontario.ca/public/docs/news/2010/november/report-on-the-ohca-roundtable-rehabilitation-in-home-care.pdf. Accessed 10 September 2011.

(2011). Home care in Ontario: facts and figures. Available at: www.homecareontario.ca/public/docs/publications/2011/home-care-facts-and-figures.pdf. Accessed 10 September 2011.

Ontario Hospital Association (OHA) (2003). *Hospital Report: Complex Continuing Care Hospital-Specific Results*, Toronto: OHA.

(2010). Health system facts and figures. Available at: http://www.healthsystemfacts.com/Client/OHA/HSF_LP4W_LND_WebStation.nsf/Index.html?ReadForm. Accessed 10 September 2011.

Poss, J.W., Hirdes, J.P., Fries, B.E., McKillop, I. and Chase, M. (2008). Validation of Resource Utilization Groups Version III for Home Care (RUG-III/HC): evidence from a Canadian home care jurisdiction. *Medical Care*, 46(4): 380–7.

Romanow, R. (2002). *Building on Values: the Future of Healthcare in Canada – Final Report*. Ottawa: Commission on the Future of Healthcare in Canada.

Toronto Star (2010). Seniors at risk in retirement home, investigation reveals. Available at: www.thestar.com/news/investigations/article/869045--seniors-at-risk-in-retirement-home-investigation-reveals. Accessed 27 August 2012.

Walker, D. (2011). Caring for our aging population and addressing alternate level of care. Available at: www.homecareontario.ca/documanager/files/news/report--walker_2011--ontario.pdf. Accessed 27 August 2012.

Waterloo Wellington Local Health Integration Network (2010). Ministry LHIN Performance Agreement (MLPA). Available at: www.waterloo-wellingtonlhin.on.ca/uploadedFiles/Home_Page/Board_of_Directors/Board_Meeting_Submenu/WWLHIN per cent20MLPA per cent20April per cent2022 per cent202010 per cent20Board per cent20pres per cent20final.pdf. Accessed 26 August 2012.

13 Regulating the quality of long-term aged care in New Zealand

BRIGETTE MEEHAN AND NIGEL MILLAR

13.1 Introduction

New Zealand is still a relatively young country, but by 2026 it is anticipated that 20 per cent of its projected population of 4.7 million will be over the age of 65, the currently adopted definition of being an 'older person'. By 2051 the number of people over 85 years and older is expected to increase and will make up 22 per cent of all New Zealanders aged 65 years and over. Statistics from 2010 show New Zealand has a population of 4.39 million, the majority of whom are Pakeha (New Zealanders of European descent). The most recent (2006) census records 15 per cent of the population as Maori, 9 per cent as Asian, and 7 per cent as Pacific peoples (OECD, 2010).

In New Zealand, long-term care is treated as part of the general healthcare system. All permanent residents are eligible for services but criteria for accessing services exist and generally involve means assessment to determine individual eligibility; the family (apart from the person's spouse / partner) is not required to make a contribution. Long-term publicly funded care includes community support and aged residential care. For older people, community support consists mostly of home-based support services which include personal care (such as dressing, showering and medication management), household support (such as cleaning and meal preparation), equipment to help with safety at home, carer support and respite care. Specialist and therapy services may be available also, according to assessed need. Aged residential care is defined as long-term care hospitals/specialist hospitals (psychogeriatric), specialist dementia units and rest homes. Home-based services are provided with the aim of meeting the expectation of most New Zealanders to remain in their homes and also delaying entry into aged residential care (Ministry of Health, 2002).

The authors thank Maria Williamson for her contribution to this chapter.

This chapter explains how long-term care services for older people are administered in New Zealand. It describes how the services are organized, regulated, funded and audited. Finally, it reports on changes to improve the quality of care for older people by introducing comprehensive clinical assessment to improve care delivery while also providing information for future planning and funding.

13.2 The management of long-term care services

Long-term care is integrated into the health system. Overall administration systems apply as with primary, secondary, tertiary and public health systems. The Minister of Health, along with the cabinet and the government, develops policy for the health and disability sector. The Ministry of Health (MoH) is the principal advisor to the government on health and disability matters and is responsible for leading and supporting the sector. Most of the day-to-day business of the system, and the majority of the funding, are administered by district health boards (DHBs). DHBs plan, manage, provide and purchase health services for the population of their district to ensure that services are arranged effectively and efficiently for all of New Zealand. This includes funding for primary care, hospital services and aged care services, and services provided by other non-government health providers including Maori and Pacific providers. Primary health organizations (PHOs) are funded by DHBs to support the provision of essential primary healthcare services through general practices. Funding and purchasing of long-term care for older people in New Zealand is managed through the DHBs, supported by policy developed through the MoH.

Annually the MoH sets out an Operational Policy Framework for DHBs. Essentially, this is a set of rules, policies and principles which describe operating functions and accountability requirements. The DHBs sign a Crown Funding Agreement which signifies agreement with the national Operational Policy Framework. Although the Operational Policy Framework does not prescribe a specific model for DHBs' service delivery, there is an expectation that older people with similar needs will receive similar services regardless of where they live (Office of the Auditor-General, 2011).

13.3 Long-term care services; home-based and aged residential care

Currently, around 586,000 people in New Zealand are 65 years or over, or approximately 12 per cent of the total population. Most older people live at home without assistance; approximately 58,000, or 10.5 per cent of people over 65, have their support needs assessed each year (internal Ministry of Health estimates). The proportion of people needing assistance increases with age, so support services are primarily relevant to approximately 155,000 older people aged over 80. In total approximately 75,000 individuals who are 65 years or over receive some home-based services (Office of the Auditor-General, 2011) and about 32,000 older people are permanently living in just under 700 aged residential care facilities (New Zealand Aged Care Association, 2011).

DHBs contract mostly with private providers to provide home-based support services or aged residential care for their district. The number of contracts and service specifications for home-based services vary by DHB. For aged-related residential care (ARRC) there is a national agreement for providing these services that governs DHB contracts with ARRC providers. In order to access funding for home-based or residential care an older person first must be assessed by a Needs Assessment Service (Ministry of Health, 2011a). These agencies are often referred to as 'NASCs' (Needs Assessment and Service Coordination services). Needs assessment is provided according to the individual DHB service delivery model. For example, it may be performed directly by a dedicated service of the DHB, a dedicated third-party assessment agency, or by a combination of providers according to the perceived complexity of need. If client complexity is perceived to be low, third-party providers of home-based support services may complete the assessment. The complex/ non-complex decision can be monitored at local and/or national levels via new standardized software described later in this chapter.

13.3.1 Home-based services and supports

The twenty DHBs provide needs assessment and service coordination services to older people through NASCs, or through a variety of similar service delivery agencies and play a key role in allocating home-based support services and determining entry into residential care for older people. There are approximately fifty home-based support providers delivering services to older people around New Zealand, ranging from large national organizations to smaller local providers. DHBs negotiate contracts with providers based on the needs of their older population, market forces and specific requirements of the provider. Arrangements vary according to individual DHB priorities and the way their services are configured. Local approaches to contracting and quality assurance can reflect tailored responses to local conditions or be an innovative response to common issues that all providers and DHBs face. Although in recent years some DHBs have actively reduced the number of home-based providers, it is generally acknowledged that DHBs may tolerate a wide variety and number of contracts with home-based providers because this increases their ability to provide flexible solutions for local needs (Office of the Auditor General, 2011).

13.3.2 Funding home-based support services

Funding for home-based support services is devolved to DHBs through the Crown Funding Agreement. In 2009–10 about NZD $224 million was spent on home-based support services for about 75,000 older people, funding an estimated 9.2 million hours of support (Office of Auditor-General, 2011). In 2010–11 the actual amount spent, NZD $221 million, was less than the forecast of NZD $232 million due in large part to the disruption caused by the two large earthquakes in the Canterbury district. The total home-based support services spent in 2011–12 was NZD $246 million. In addition to home-based support there are both public and private sources of payment. Information on how much is privately paid for home-based services is unknown but is not expected to be significant; however, as the number of older people increase this is likely to change. In addition to New Zealand government superannuation, some funding to support older people in the community is also provided through the social benefits system.

Payment arrangements differ across the country. The arrangements of DHBs with their providers may be either individualized (per client) funding or bulk funding. Individualized funding varies from client to client, primarily based on need but also taking into account the level of support available from family and close others. A few DHBs pay providers via bulk funding to provide a range of services tailored to the older person's assessed need. Payment rates across the country also differ. Differences are usually due to historical practices and local differences

Regulating the quality of long-term aged care in New Zealand   361

in demand and other market forces. DHBs have begun working towards a regional approach in some areas where more commonality is possible and desirable, while retaining sufficient flexibility to allow DHBs to be innovative and responsive (Internal Ministry of Health document: 20110488, 2011).

If an older person is receiving services their income is means tested via eligibility for the Community Services Card (CSC), which is only available to people below an income threshold, essentially a proxy for low income. DHBs individually manage the level of home-based support services that are provided free of charge to the older person, and over the last few years, they have ceased providing household cleaning services unless the older person is entitled to a CSC (Ministry of Health, 2011a; Internal Ministry of Health document: 20110488, 2011). Home-based personal care services with household management (cleaning) services, when allocated, are all free of charge. Equipment and home modification services that are low cost (under NZD \$50) are not funded but more expensive equipment may be provided on permanent loan or housing modification costs can be subsidized depending on a means assessment and on a co-payment basis (Ministry of Health, 2011b).

DHBs can make autonomous decisions about thresholds for access to services and there is variety in service provision for home care services by region of the country, according to the DHB's service delivery model for needs assessment (Office of Auditor-General, 2011). Older people who are ineligible for publicly funded support services in the home, or those people whose needs assessment does not meet the DHB threshold for funded support, are free to purchase home support services privately. All secondary care services such as therapy (for example, occupational therapy), and medical specialists are free upon assessed need. Waiting lists are a feature of these types of services at most DHBs. Some services may be available privately in certain localities.

13.3.3 Aged residential care services

In 2009, approximately 5.6 per cent of the over-65 population received long-term care in an institutional setting. Data suggests that today, residential care episodes are shorter than twenty years ago, with people entering long-term care facilities at a later age and with more health problems (OECD, 2010). Four categories of residential care are available. Rest home care is designed for older people with greater levels of independence compared to hospital-level care. Dementia care includes specialist dementia units and there is specialist hospital-level psychogeriatric care for those older people who have both medical and psychogeriatric care needs. Originally, entry into rest home care was a choice made by individuals often while still reasonably independent and mobile. For example, rest homes in the 1970s made provisions for residents parking their cars. Aged residential care services had a social welfare rather than a health focus and the system was administered by the Department of Social Welfare. Because the rest home was considered to be a permanent substitute for home, residents were partially subsidized and expected to pay relevant costs. Income and asset testing was implemented to ensure that those people who could afford to pay for the costs of living at home continued to contribute to this cost in the residential care setting. Another kind of residential facility emerged during the late 1980s, when independent forms of community housing and lifestyle living for older people, known as retirement villages, were developed by private companies and designed for active independent older people with some assets to choose rest home care as a housing option. An attractive feature for many older people is the availability of a long-term residential care facility within the village so that the village residents can stay within the community they know when their care needs increase. Depending on the income and assets of the resident, the initial private arrangements may become publically funded as the older person's care needs increase.

Of the 32,000 older people living in aged residential care, 64 per cent of residents are subsidized by the government. Although 32 per cent of residents do not receive the residential care subsidy it is estimated that almost half of this number access a 'top-up' which is not means tested. 'Top-ups' are described later in this chapter. In terms of distribution, 57 per cent of residents are in rest homes, 31 per cent in private hospitals and 8 per cent in dementia units, with 37 per cent of rest homes located within retirement villages (Grant Thornton New Zealand, 2010: 76, 8).

Providers of home-based services and long-term aged residential care are overwhelmingly privately owned companies. According to the Grant Thornton Review (2010), approximately two-thirds (68 per cent) of aged residential care facilities in New Zealand are owned by for-profit operators (p. 32). Over time, religious and welfare organizations have largely sold out and private corporate interests have purchased home-based service agencies or residential care facilities. A study by Boyd et al. (2009) shows

Regulating the quality of long-term aged care in New Zealand 363

very distinct changes in the characteristics of residential care residents in Auckland between 1988 and 2008. Although the older (65+) population in the area has increased by 43 per cent, the number of aged care beds overall has increased by only 3 per cent. Rest home care has seen the largest decrease in residents when compared to the proportion of the total older adult population. For those aged over 85 the proportion living in rest homes dropped from 27 per cent in 1988 to 16 per cent in 2008. Over the same period the proportion of people in rest home assessed as 'independent' has decreased from 23 per cent to 7 per cent. Dependency, as indicated by mobility, continence and cognitive function, has significantly increased for the total population living in aged care facilities. Those with high dependency have increased from 36 per cent of the total residential aged care population in 1998 to 56 per cent in 2008. The authors attribute many of these changes to changes in policy and the associated increase in the availability of community care services.

Once in residential care the older person should expect to live in a resident-centred environment that promotes their independence and quality of life. Services that must be provided include: accommodation (including access to toilet and shower), food services, laundry, nursing care, general equipment for mobility and personal care, General Practitioner (GP) visits, prescribed medication, continence products, diversional (recreational) activity and all healthcare prescribed by a GP (Ministry of Health, 2010b).

13.3.4 Funding residential care services

Until 1993 hospital-level aged residential care was available in public hospitals and was free to patients, although after thirteen weeks they ceased to receive any pension payments from the government, except for a small personal allowance. There was also some private hospital provision (income-tested only) for those with age-related conditions who were not able to be accommodated in public hospitals. In 1993, Disability Support Services funding was transferred from Social Welfare to Health. At the same time, income and asset testing was extended to those people needing hospital-level care whether in public or private facilities because they had similar care needs.

In order for older people to access long-term residential care, the older person's needs must first be assessed. Even older people who privately pay must be assessed if they wish to live in a residential care facility that also provides DHB contracted care services. If their assets are below the defined asset threshold they qualify for the Residential Care Subsidy (RCS) which is paid by the resident's DHB. They may then enter a facility and contribute most of their New Zealand Superannuation[1] and also any other income they received. The RCS applies to those aged 65 years and over; 83 per cent of those cared for in residential care settings received the subsidy in 2009–10. If a person does not qualify for a subsidy the person pays the cost of care up to the maximum of the care home cost.[2] Those whose only asset is their former home may qualify for an interest-free residential care loan. In total DHBs pay around 60 per cent of the cost of long-term residential care provided.

Asset and income testing for long-term aged residential care continues today. However, in 2005, the government amended the Social Security Act, 1964 to remove incrementally the asset test which older people viewed as inequitable. The associated Social Security (Long-term Residential Care) Regulations of 2005 increased the asset exemptions. In 2005, older people could retain up to NZD \$150,000 before the older person has to pay the full cost of their rest home care. This increased by NZD \$10,000 each year (on 1 July) and by July 2011 the asset threshold was NZD \$210,000. The asset test applies fully to single people or couples where both are in care. Where only one of a couple has been assessed as needing aged residential care, an alternative test that fully exempts the home and car is available (Ministry of Health, 2010b). In the 2012 Budget the Government reduced the annual increase in the asset threshold from \$10,000 a year to the annual rate of inflation. The asset threshold from 1 July 2012 was \$213,297.

There are limits to what aged residential care providers can charge for DHB-contracted rest home care if the older person has met needs assessment criteria. This is known as the 'maximum contribution'. The maximum contribution is set by each Territorial Local Area (TLA)[3] annually

---

[1] New Zealand Superannuation is a universal pension paid to people aged 65 and older, with payment rates varying depending on household situation (e.g., single, sharing accommodation or married).

[2] In 1994 a maximum weekly payment level was established for long-term care and any costs above that amount are met by the government.

[3] Territorial authorities are the second tier of local government in New Zealand and are based on community of interest. The territorial authorities administer local roads and reserves, sewerage, building consents, the land use and subdivision aspects of resource management and other local matters.

Regulating the quality of long-term aged care in New Zealand   365

and published in all newspapers and on the MoH website. Hence, the subsidy paid by the DHBs for eligible residents is the difference between the resident's contribution and the published price of rest home care. The price is applied to rest-home-level care, covering all rest homes in each district and for all residents assessed as needing this level of care. Those residents with higher acuity needs are provided for and funded at the higher levels of care, for example, at a dementia unit, hospital or psychogeriatric facilities. All needs-assessed residents, whether subsidized or private payers, residing in DHB contracted facilities at higher levels of care, receive a 'top-up' subsidy for costs above the rest home price paid by the relevant DHB.

Providers may offer services additional to those in the ARRC Agreement at additional cost should residents choose these. Should an older person elect not to be needs assessed they may purchase residential care privately but in that instance there will be no price control and the arrangement will be outside of the legislation. However, private payers who have met the needs assessment criteria are also protected under the legislation by the maximum contribution (price of rest home contracted care services) as long as they remain in a DHB-contracted care facility (Ministry of Health, 2010b).

13.4 Regulation of long-term aged care services

13.4.1 Regulation of home-based support services

The requirement to provide home-based support services (HBSS), should an older person wish to receive long-term support services, is contained in a Crown Funding Agreement between the MoH and each of the twenty DHBs. Each DHB describes how it will meet these obligations via its District and Regional Annual Plans. There are no national mandatory regulatory requirements for service provision. Furthermore, home support workers are not regulated or certified in the way that allied health professionals are under the Health Practitioners Competency Assurance Act; all regulatory controls are incorporated into the contract between DHB and the provider. DHBs can require that providers comply with the voluntary Standards, New Zealand Home and Community Support Sector Standards NZS8158:2003 governing staff training should they choose. In 2011 half of the DHBs made the Standards a requirement of their contracts (Office of the Auditor-General, 2011).

The voluntary Home and Community Support Sector Standards (NZS 8158:2003) establish the minimum requirements that should be attained by HBSS providers. The Standards are limited to health and disability services provided in a person's home and/or in the setting of a community support service provider. Standards New Zealand released revised Home and Community Support Sector Standard NZS 8158:2012 on 19 April 2012. The Standard sets out what people receiving support in a home or community setting can expect from the services that they receive and the minimum requirements to be attained by provider organizations. There is a phased approach to their use and from 1 September 2013 certification against the previous voluntary standard (NZS 8158:2003) will no longer be recognized, in essence making the revised standard mandatory. The New Zealand Home Health Association (an association of home-based providers) supports mandatory standards for the provision of home-based support services to older people and currently requires its members, as a minimum, to be certified as complying with the voluntary Standards (see the New Zealand Home Health Association website www.nzhha.org.nz).

13.4.2 Regulatory oversight of home-based support services

HBSS provider contracts with DHBs usually include service specifications, sector and employee standards, quality plans, management of risks and contract reporting. DHBs monitor providers via performance monitoring reports consistent with their individual DHB contracts which include the ability to audit for compliance with their contracts. These audits may cover a range of matters such as recruitment practices and risk management processes. The DHB also works with providers if any quality improvement actions are needed as a result of audits or complaints.

DHBs arrangements vary. Many have collaborated to develop regional shared service agencies (RSSA) to complete quality audits of providers on behalf of DHBs; however, the different RSSA approaches reflect the different requirements. A MoH work programme is underway (Internal Ministry of Health document: 20110488, 2011) to reduce variability between audits across DHBs and region by developing common tools and approaches for audits to achieve greater consistency. One aim is that providers that contract with more than one DHB are supposed to be treated more consistently, reducing the compliance burden of having different audit requirements for the same or similar services. If the example of residential care is followed once the home care provider community is experienced with the quality audits, public reporting could follow.

Providers are being encouraged to complement DHB audits with providers' own actions to assess and improve performance. Providers collectively have developed a self-assessment schedule (with input from DHBs). Self-assessment is used as a voluntary method of determining provider performance and adherence to the Standard and contract and could form part of overall performance monitoring, potentially reducing the frequency of DHB audits (Internal Ministry of Health document: 20110488, 2011).

13.4.3 Regulation of aged residential care services

All private and public providers of rest home or hospital levels of care are required by legislation to fulfil certification requirements under the Health and Disability Services (Safety) Act (HDSS (Safety) Act, 2001) managed by the MoH. Under the Act the service is certified, not the premises. However, as certified services are provided on the premises, the adequacy, appropriateness and state of the premise is of significance in determining if the service is being provided in a safe manner. The criteria for certification of prospective, or actual, providers are contained in section 27 of the Act. Auditing of providers' compliance with this Act is described in greater detail below.

The service specifications are described in the national Age Related Residential Care (ARRC) Agreement. The service specifications follow the generally standard format of service philosophy, objectives, policies and clinical recording. Regular comprehensive assessment and a personalized care plan for each resident are required. Although they must adhere to the standardized national contract, aged residential care facilities may vary widely, allowing providers the flexibility to market their services.

Under the ARRC contract staff ratios must meet the needs of residents in aged care facilities. Compliance with certification requirements under the HDSS (Safety) Act, 2001 means quality control systems are in place to support adequate staffing levels. Providers must have a rationale for staffing that includes consideration of the skill and competency of staff, and staff numbers, in relation to the care required by the facility's configuration of residents. Providers are able to use the handbook *Indicators for Safe Aged-care and Dementia-care for Consumers* (SNZ HB 8163:2005) to help them determine the number of staff required (Ministry of Health, 2010b).

The Retirement Villages Association (RVA) represents about 80 per cent of the registered retirement village industry and is governed by the Retirement Villages Act (2003) and associated Code of Practice (2008). The Association reports that they cover 270 member villages with approximately 17,800 dwelling units which are home to more than 20,000 older New Zealanders. Retirement villages that belong to the Retirement Village Association are required to have a verification audit every three years (Retirement Villages (General) Regulations, 2006). Those villages that have a long-term care facility must also comply with the legislative requirements for the provision of health and disability services. This includes certification and audits under the HDSS (Safety) Act, 2001. One interesting aspect of a retirement village being certified to provide aged residential care is the development of supported living apartments which can also be used to provide rest-home- or hospital-level care. The certification arrangements are the same as for rest homes and this means that the resident who opts to purchase the use of the room under a licence-to-occupy arrangement can live independently just like elsewhere in the community until such time as they are assessed as needing aged residential care, at which stage the care can be provided to them in their own apartment.

13.4.4 Regulatory oversight of residential care services

Certification of aged care residential facilities is a requirement whether the service is publically or privately funded or whether the service is contracted by a DHB or not. HealthCERT, a division of the MoH, certifies a range of services such as mental health services, surgical services and hospital and rest homes services to ensure that services are provided at safe and reasonable levels for consumers as required under the HDSS (Safety) Act, 2001. HealthCERT designates audit agencies (DAAs) that inspect places providing healthcare services and monitors DAA performance. The administration for certification of providers is outlined in sections 26 to 31 of the HDSS (Safety) Act, 2001. The Act requires any operator providing healthcare service that is required to be certified under the Act to comply with any conditions subject to which the operator was certified. Certification can be for periods up to five years but is generally for only twelve months for a new provider, with a verification audit required. At the end of each certification period a new certificate will be issued if all is satisfactory and this is likely to be for the longer periods.

In 2009 the Office of the Auditor-General turned its attention to rest home care and completed an audit of those services. The Auditor-General's role in New Zealand is to provide independent assurance that public entities are functioning as intended, and accounting for their performance. The Office of the Auditor-General carries out annual audits for about 4,000 public entities in the public sector, and also may select to investigate any area in detail, as in this case, the area of rest home services. In the final audit report (Office of the Auditor-General, 2009) the Auditor-General recognizes that audits of rest homes can never eliminate the risk of poor care. Audits can only establish whether, at a particular point in time, rest homes have the systems and processes in place to minimize that risk. The information that audits provide is limited to a period of a few days (during business hours) and is conducted after the rest home has had several months (or longer) to prepare. Not only is audit inherently limited as a tool, the Auditor-General's investigation found that auditing by designated auditing agencies (DAAs) was inconsistent and sometimes of poor quality (Office of the Auditor-General, 2009).

In 2010, the government made significant changes to aged residential care auditing, introducing 'spot' auditing procedures where there is no prior warning to the facility and made audit results publicly available on the MoH's website. Spot surveillance audits are used to help identify undesirable practices. They are also used when serious complaints are made, either to the MoH, a DHB, or the Health and Disability Commissioner. Audits are completed by DAAs at the provider's expense. Recent attention has been given to improved procedures for auditors, to make the approach to auditing more consistent. The ARRC contract provides for instances whereby aged care providers fail to meet their obligations identified via audit. For serious breaches under the ARRC contract the DHB may send in a temporary manager or remove residents, effectively closing the facility. Since 2010, audit reports have been made available on the HealthCERT website as a first foray into public reporting.

13.4.5 Consumer choice and voice

In New Zealand, in theory at least, clients at home receiving services and older people in residential care are free to change their care provider. In practice, some older people's choice may be influenced by the availability of a service or facility within the area in which they wish to live. Support for the older person to select a home-based provider is generally available through the assessment agency, which may advise which providers are available and may help match their preferences. The ability to select a residential care provider may be limited by urgency, access to a social worker and the number of beds available in the desired area at the time of need. Groups such as Age Concern may help older people and their families with their choice of rest home or hospital and, as mentioned above, family can now access a summary audit report on each facility from the HealthCERT's website.

Depending on the services that the residential care facility offers, older people may select rooms to meet their preferences such as size, aspect, additional services or the availability of an ensuite toilet and bathroom. Providers will generally charge for optional choices; however, they must give residents the choice to not receive extra services, and therefore not have to pay more than the standard contract rate. The MoH's guide to long-term residential care for older people (Ministry of Health, 2010b) states 'it's ok to change your mind and move to another facility. Your admission agreement will state what advance notice your current place requires' (p. 8); however, the number of older people who take up this option is unknown. Informal Ministry of Health records indicate that in 2011/12, 1,447 residents moved from a facility to one in the same service category and 636 facilities had someone leave. Reasons for these changes in residents are not known. Choosing to return to community living may be problematic as well, particularly if the older person's home has already been sold to support permanent residential care.

As part of consumer choice, older people in residential care may retain their own GP. In practice, however, this may not be practical and most residential care operators try to develop a relationship with specific GPs. If residents choose to be attended by their own GP, they may have to pay extra fees for this service if the rest home provider has a GP that provides a dedicated service to the facility for a fixed fee. The GP has medical responsibility for the residents as though they are living in the community. There is no barrier for a resident to access acute services. Across the country, DHBs have developed services, such as dedicated gerontology nurses available to visit and provide advice, to reduce unplanned entry to hospital. Other efforts include allowing GPs direct access to hospital beds for planned interventions in order to reduce the need to admit via the emergency department.

The ARRC contract requires providers to survey consumers (residents and their families) about their satisfaction with the long-term care provided by the facility. The findings of these surveys are not managed centrally and national reporting is unavailable. For those at home, advocacy services such as Age Concern or Grey Power are available; however, there is no formal 'voice' for older people receiving home support services. Although still in the consultation phase, the MoH is proposing that home care providers take a more consistently robust approach to designing and administering user satisfaction surveys (Internal Ministry of Health document: 20110488, 2011). This includes providers and DHBs reaching agreement regarding the content of the survey tool, the survey methodology and who administers it. It also assumes that funders and providers should collectively explore the viability of a recurring national satisfaction survey that will provide information at a higher level on satisfaction and issues across the sector. All health-based services, including the performance of health professionals or other care staff, may be reviewed by the Health and Disability Commissioner who will also receive complaints from individuals.

13.5 Future long-term care policy directions

13.5.1 Aged residential care

Over the last few years long-term care in New Zealand has been scrutinized by two formal national investigations. In 2010 an Aged Residential Care Service Review (ARCS Review) was released and in 2011 a performance audit of home-based support services for older people was published. The ARCS Review was led by a New Zealand project team from Grant Thornton Ltd (a business advisory company), overseen by a Steering Group including representatives from DHBs, Aged Residential Care providers and the Ministry of Health, and co-sponsored by New Zealand Aged Care Association and the twenty District Health Boards of New Zealand. This review provided an opportunity for stakeholders to collaborate and contribute to a sustainable future. It had the highest provider participation rate of any comparable international study undertaken to date (Grant Thornton New Zealand, 2010). The review assessed the cost, capacity and service delivery implications of the growing number of aged residential care services. The report made projections regarding demand through to 2026, projecting significant increased demand for beds (78–110 per cent), for new, upgraded or replacement of current facilities and an increased demand for workforce (50–75 per cent). The report asserts that one of the greatest barriers to meeting future demand is that providers' current financial returns for subsidized service delivery are insufficient for building new capacity and replacing existing stock (Grant Thornton New Zealand, 2010). Despite this some providers have continued to build new facilities, particularly in conjunction with retirement villages. The report makes fifteen recommendations, ranging from increased public awareness through to piloting new models of care, including changing economic models such as those that recognize differing performance of providers. The recommendations informed the development of an integrated workplan for the Steering Group to progress.

The care needs of the aged residential care population are clearly changing. Residents are older and more dependent than ever before. As the population of those aged over 85 increases there will be a rise in the prevalence of neurodegenerative diseases such as Alzheimer's Disease (Boyd et al., 2009). The Minister of Health, alert to this potential issue, has recently required the DHBs to develop 'Dementia Pathways' to focus services across the continuum of care, to meet the needs of this increasing group of older people and their families.

13.5.2 Home-based care

The Auditor-General released a performance audit of home-based support services for older people in 2011. A stated objective of the review was to ascertain whether the current processes used to manage and deliver home-based support services ensure that services are available to those who need them, are of an appropriate quality and are able to meet current and future demand. The Auditor-General concluded: 'generally, services appear to be delivered adequately' (Office of the Auditor-General, 2011: 3). The report noted when considering DHBs' progress on implementing the New Zealand Positive Ageing

Strategy (2001) that the integration of support services, especially with health services, showed that some progress had been made (p. 15) and gave as an example the implementation of a consistent approach to assessment (detailed later in this chapter). The Auditor-General provided five recommendations to support effective and efficient home-based support delivery.

The Auditor-General's report has triggered a number of responses within the sector. Among these, the MoH, aware of the dissatisfaction with the level of variability in service contracting, has begun a programme of work intending DHBs and the Ministry to identify broad shared requirements (e.g., philosophy, service definition, access criteria, transfer and exit from services) in a national service specification (Internal Ministry of Health document: 20110488, 2011). If this proposal is adopted DHBs would progressively align their HBSS service specifications to the core components agreed to in the national specification, with any local additions specified separately. Individual DHBs will continue to negotiate the purchase price with providers as occurs at present.

13.5.3 Changing policy directives in assessment

In common with other international trends, increasing proportions of older people are choosing to remain in their homes until the end of their lives and in New Zealand they expect that health services will be provided to support them to do so. The desire to 'age in place' was noted by researchers about twenty-five years ago when discussing how to provide long-term support services into the future (Wetherall et al., 2004). By the early 1990s a service model had developed explicitly separating a service that assessed people for home-based services from the service that allocated and coordinated care. The service coordination and the home-based services were also separated from services that provided treatment and rehabilitation for people with disease, impairment and activity limitation. According to Wetherall et al. (2004) the motivations for this policy were complex, but included an assumption that a social model of disability management would reduce costs by assisting the older person to remain at home as long as possible.

To implement this policy, NASC agencies were created. The perception was that NASCs became involved only after all health interventions had been considered and the 'goal' was to provide home supports for as long as the older person required them. NASC assessors were encouraged to prioritize the older person's 'voice' in relation to their needs, even if the assessors held a health professional qualification and had a clinical opinion that might have differed from the clients' wishes. Indeed, in some Health Districts the decision was made to actively avoid recruitment of health professionals, or, if appointed, they were not encouraged to maintain ties with their professional disciplines. Wetherall et al. (2004) note that the assessment designed by the MoH excluded a clinical evaluation of the older person, and as such omitted consideration of issues that are important to older people such as urinary incontinence, and mobility issues such as falls and dementia (Campbell, 2004). Campbell notes that 'no proper clinical assessment of the utility of the instrument was ever performed and that the "separation" policy was implemented to a varying extent throughout New Zealand and has not been subjected to any serious scientific scrutiny' (Campbell, 2004: 2).

By the late 1990s concerns were emerging about the need to improve the health of older people, particularly about the unsatisfactory integration of health and social services and information sharing (Keeling et al., 2005). Millar (2000) describes poor outcomes for older people in long-term care arising from a disjointed continuum of care, services across the continuum of care not communicating with each other, and omissions or duplication of information. In addition, there was no formal dialogue with older people about how improved health outcomes might be achieved (Millar, 2000). In response to many of these concerns, major policy documents focused discussion on considering what 'best practice' meant for older people's assessment and their resulting care. For example, the Health of Older People Strategy (2002) provided direction to DHBs and strengthened the policy goal of increasing integrated care to support older people at home rather than in residential care (Ministry of Health, 2002).

13.6 Monitoring and regulating quality of care

13.6.1 Quality issues in assessment

The New Zealand Guidelines Group (NZGG) shifted the focus of assessment and support provision from 'social' to what Keeling et al. (2005)

Regulating the quality of long-term aged care in New Zealand 375

termed 'the inextricable linkage between assessing the health and social needs of older people, and the services designed and delivered to meet these needs' (p. 236); in other words, assessing needs in a way which leads to improving the outcomes for older people, by improving the fit between assessed needs and service effectiveness, and required agreement on 'outcomes that matter to older people' (New Zealand Guidelines Group, 2003). The NZGG wanted to find a common language to express costs and benefits, to identify outcome measures and to begin the challenge of local and national benchmarking. The introduction of comprehensive clinical assessment was one outcome of the Guidelines.

In 2004, five DHBs successfully piloted the use of a comprehensive clinical assessment, the interRAI home care assessment (MDS-HC) assessment as a substitute for the non-validated, subjective assessment in use at the time. However, the pilot evaluation identified that a significant training exercise was required to increase the skill levels of staff involved in the assessment process (Weidenbohm et al., 2006). In 2007, a business case was agreed to as a priority by all the DHB chief executive officers and during 2008 and 2009, the government allocated NZD $19 million in additional capital and operating funding for DHBs to introduce the assessment, including an associated training initiative. All DHBs were expected to be fully using interRAI home care assessments within four years (by 1 July 2012) to support the determination of eligibility for long-term care services: either home-based support or aged residential services (Ministry of Health, 2010a).

13.6.2 Quality challenges in community assessment; training, Maori acceptance and software

The home care assessment project included three major areas of focus: training, Maori strategy and software. Under the new policy in New Zealand, in order to be trained assessors must have a professional discipline where assessment is part of the scope of practice, and have a current practising certificate (Ministry of Health, 2010a). A National Training Service is embedded within the DHBs and an expert practitioner approach is used to train assessors. Quality is monitored at a national level by a competency-based curriculum, standardized training materials and associated e-learning, including a mandatory annual coding examination programme.

Maori stakeholders have provided a positive cultural review of the assessment, the scope of the items and the process of assessment, particularly from the point of view of non-Maori assessors assessing Maori clients. Their review, completed as a core part of the implementation project, emphasized that the competency of the assessor is critical to the process. A cultural framework for the assessment of Maori clients has been identified and specific guidelines for assessing this group have been incorporated into the training programme. At this stage, whether the interRAI assessment should be supplemented by a specialist Maori cultural assessment remains unclear. Further cultural work will be undertaken as required.

New Zealand has developed a national software host platform that provides the interRAI assessments and associated care plans for older people in the community over the internet to all members of the older persons care team. Assessors input assessment information directly online or into a disconnected laptop during the assessment in an older person's home, thus supporting data quality. If in disconnected mode they then synchronize and update the database when they return to the office to complete the care plan. The older person's assessments and their plans can be viewed by the care team and also be easily transferred from one care location to another or between staff.

Improved assessment and the use of software is expected to support community-focused care and care integrated across primary, secondary and tertiary areas as information sharing for the providers improves and the need for duplication and fragmented assessments decreases. The purpose of the national host is to provide the software to all New Zealand DHBs, and, where agreed, their associated service providers. To date, this includes all DHBs, 38 home care providers and 400 (out of the 690 potential) aged residential care facilities. A national data warehouse of assessment data for reporting purposes, and a national Decision Support System (DSS) data warehouse for local and national analytical reporting purposes are also available. The software is integrated with the National Health Identifier and integration work is under way with the most commonly used secondary care software product. Interoperability with the major software systems used by residential care providers is also in active preparation. The work will then move to support integration with major primary care products. A repository of de-identified data is available for research purposes, access to which is governed by an information governance policy.

13.6.3 Quality issues in aged residential care assessment

Some DHBs are beginning to question the effectiveness of relying on audits to monitor the age-related care contract and some are beginning to shift their monitoring to focus more on quality improvement (Office of the Auditor-General, 2009). The advantages of Quality Indicators (QIs) generated from an interRAI assessment have been recognized by DHBs and provider organizations alike and in mid-2011 a four-year national project of voluntary introduction of the interRAI long-term care facility tool (LTCF) for enabling comprehensive clinical assessment into residential care began. In October 2012 the Minister of Health announced that all aged care facilities were required to be participating in training by June 2014 and that using comprehensive clinical assessment would be mandatory to achieve certification by July 2015. The implementation project, budgeted at close to NZD $11 million, is funded by DHBs and is developed and managed in collaboration with the New Zealand Aged Care Association and the MoH. Implementation of comprehensive clinical assessment brings together a response to two current critical issues in the residential care sector; delivering high-quality care to individual residents and developing systems for measuring, monitoring and improving quality of care across the whole sector over time.

QIs are elements within interRAI client assessments which are used to establish a measure that can be translated into a statistical summary which is aggregated over all clients being served. While QIs are defined in terms of individual characteristics, they only take on meaning when expressed as averages at the facility or agency level and when aggregated to the facility level they produce summary measures reflecting presumed quality of care. Each QI has an explicit definition and inclusion/exclusion criteria. There is strong evidence that the QIs capture meaningful aspects of nursing home performance (Morris et al., 2003). Morris et al. (2003) advocate that it is important to present different indicators across multiple domains for a full view of facility quality performance. QIs have been shown to influence the performance of care providers in improving quality of care; of governments in monitoring care; and of the sector in reporting to the public (Mor et al., 2003; Mor, 2005).

There are other significant advantages to using interRAI as the comprehensive clinical assessment within the residential care context.

Introduction will support the continuum of care from home, the quality of assessment and heighten early alerts to risks for unexpected admission to emergency departments, provide an opportunity for improving quality monitoring and developing facility risk rating systems within aged residential care. Because the QIs are derived directly from the assessment instrument they can be calculated without the need for additional data collection.

13.7 Conclusion

Long-term aged care is funded and delivered throughout New Zealand by the twenty DHBs to their populations. DHBs are charged with ensuring that services are available to meet the needs of their population groups, including older people. The MoH provides policy and regulations which support DHBs in various ways. DHBs are also required to ensure that the Minister has agreed and signed off on their Annual and Regional Plans, which ensures that direction and leadership is provided by central government.

Home-based support services are provided through individual DHB contracts with individual providers and may differ in price and other conditions for services, whereas aged residential care is provided under a national contract with agreed conditions which apply to all providers and which flow through to all residents. The national ARRC contract is provided for in legislation and agreed annually between representative DHBs and providers.

A major change has been made to improve the quality of assessment in New Zealand as the basis for delivery of home-based support services and considering alternatives to permanent placement into aged residential care. The rollout of comprehensive clinical assessment by the adoption of interRAI assessment instruments to all DHBs in New Zealand has been the catalyst for other changes, such as requiring a professional assessment workforce, an expert practitioner approach to ensure the quality of the service continues, software support for a continuum of care for the older person and a cultural consideration of the assessment process. The decision support aspect of the interRAI assessments facilitates early identification of health risks for the older person or highlights clinical opportunities for the client, allowing services to be delivered to those who are most likely to benefit. The automatically aggregated data obtained during

Regulating the quality of long-term aged care in New Zealand 379

comprehensive clinical assessment will inform planners and funders at both local and national levels.

MoH and DHB responses to the recent Office of the Auditor-General report (Office of the Auditor-General, 2011) are driving a proactive approach to HBSS planning, and in delivering their services for those who would benefit. In addition the 'Dementia Pathways' work programme and the Community Pharmacy Project, which supports appropriate medication use, are examples of a variety of initiatives underway that focus support for older people living in the community.

While in recent years concern has been expressed about conditions and services in residential care, the government has put stricter controls in place to ensure auditors are well qualified and understand their role in ensuring safe services for older New Zealanders. Families are now able to obtain audit reports on any facility that they may be considering for their family member. The introduction of the interRAI LTCF Assessment (2011–15) is anticipated to bring similar benefits as the home care implementation. In particular, the assessment will assist the nurses to develop a care plan targeted to the older person's needs and will allow for more explicit and comparable understanding of service quality within facilities across New Zealand.

References

Boyd, M., Connolly, M., Kerse, N., Foster, S., von Randow, M., Lay-Yee, R., Chelimo, C., Broad, J., Whitehead, N. and Walters-Puttick, S. (2009). *Changes in Aged Care Residents' Characteristics and Dependency in Auckland 1988 to 2008: Findings from OPAL 10/9/8 Older Persons' Ability Level Census.* Auckland: University of Auckland, Faculty of Medical and Health Sciences.

Campbell, J. (2004). Assessment prior to institutional care: time to move past the Support Needs Assessment Form (SNAF). *The New Zealand Medical Journal*, 117(1202) (September): U1072.

Grant Thornton New Zealand (2010). *Aged Residential Care Service Review (ARCS Review) Summary of Findings.* September. Available at: http://nzaca.org.nz/publication/documents/ARSCR.pdf.

Gray, L., Berg, K., Fries, B., Henrard, J., Hirdes, J., Steel, K. and Morris, J. (2009). Sharing clinical information across care settings: the birth of an integrated assessment system. *BMC Health Services Research*, 9: 71.

Internal Ministry of Health document (2011). Health Report 20110488.

Keeling, S., Larkins, B. and Millar, N. (2005). Changing assessment processes in older person's health: some Canterbury Tales. *New Zealand Family Physician*, 32(4): 234–7.

Millar, N. (2000). A model of aged care reform. In A. Bloom (ed.), *Health Reform in Australia and New Zealand*. Melbourne: Oxford University Press, pp. 338–47.

Ministry of Health (2001). *The Health and Disability Services (Safety) (HDSS) Act, 2001*. Wellington. New Zealand.

(2002). *Health of Older People Strategy: Health Sector Action to 2010 to Support Positive Ageing*. April. Available at: www.health.govt.nz/publication/health-older-people-strategy.

(2010a). *Establishment of interRAI Assessments within New Zealand (2008–2010)*. Wellington: Ministry of Health (internal document available on request).

(2010b). *Long-term Residential Care for Older People. What You Need to Know*. Wellington: Ministry of Health.

(2011a). *Needs Assessment and Support Services for Older People. What You Need to Know*. Wellington: Ministry of Health.

(2011b). Equipment for disabled people of all ages. Available at: www.health.govt.nz/publication/equipment-disabled-people-all-ages.

Mor, V. (2005). Improving the quality of long term care with better information. *Milbank Quarterly*, 83(3): 333–64.

Mor, V., Angelelli, J., Jones, R., Roy, J., Moore, T. and Morris, J. (2003). Inter-rater reliability of nursing home quality indicators in the US. *Health Services Research*, 3(20): doi:10.1186/1472–6963–3–20.

Morris, J., Moore, T. and Jones, R. (2003). Validation of Long-Term and Post-Acute Care Quality Indicators. Available at: http://interrai.org/applications/qireport2.pdf.

New Zealand Aged Care Association (2011). The future of aged care. Discussion Paper. 27 September. Wellington: New Zealand Aged Care Association. Available at: www.whocares.org.nz/documents/The per cent20Future per cent20of per cent20Aged per cent20Care per cent2027 per cent20September per cent202011.pdf.

New Zealand Guidelines Group (2003). Assessment processes for older people: an evidence based best practice guideline. Available at: www.nzgg.org.nz/resources/57/Assess_Processes_GL.pdf.

Office of the Auditor-General, New Zealand (2009). Effectiveness of arrangements to check the standard of services provided by rest homes. Available at: www.oag.govt.nz/2009/rest-homes.

(2011). *Performance Audit Report. Home Based Support Services for Older People*. Wellington: Office of the Auditor-General.

Organization for Economic Co-operation and Development (OECD) (2010). New Zealand long term care fact sheet. Available at: www.oecd-ilibrary.org.

Standards New Zealand (2003). Home and community support sector Standard NZS 8158:2003. Available at: www.standards.co.nz/.

(2012). Home and community support sector Standard NZS 8158:2012. Available at: www.standards.co.nz/.

Weidenbohm, K., Parson, M., Dixon, R., Keeling, S., Brant, T. and Kilpatrick, J. (2006). *The Exploration of the interRAI Training Programme Implemented across Five District Health Boards in New Zealand.* Auckland: University of Auckland, Uniservices.

Wetherall, M., Slow, T. and Whiltshire, K. (2004). Risk factors for entry into residential care after a support needs assessment. *Journal of the New Zealand Medical Association*, 117(1202), 24 September: U1075.

Websites

InterRAI: www.interRAI.org.
Ministry of Health: www.health.govt.nz.
New Zealand Home Health Association: www.nzhha.org.nz.
Retirement Villages Association: www.retirementvillages.org.nz.

PART V

Long-term care quality systems and developing regulatory systems

The final two case study countries are still in developmental stages and have been furiously working to develop legislation, followed by guidelines that local or regional authorities can implement. The populations of both South Korea and China have been ageing rapidly, meaning that their need for formal long-term care is relatively recent and is expected to grow dramatically in the next several decades. South Korea recently enacted universal long-term care service eligibility but is still grappling with what kinds of organizations can serve recipients of this new healthcare benefit. China, which until recently had only government-operated long-term care facilities, has adopted a policy to stimulate the private sector to develop institutional long-term care by subsidizing construction and operation. This policy has been coupled with a policy of 'light touch' regulation meant to further encourage investment by the private sector. How these two countries develop their long-term care quality regulatory systems over the next several decades will be of considerable interest to other rapidly ageing developing countries.

14 Quality monitoring of long-term care in the Republic of Korea

HYE-YOUNG JUNG, SOONG-NANG JANG,
JAE EUN SEOK AND SOONMAN KWON

14.1 Introduction

South Korea's rapid emergence as an industrialized nation with migration to urban centres and a declining fertility rate has led to increasing demand for long-term care services as the population continues to age. Informal care provided by family members has traditionally been the primary source of long-term care in the country. However, as the elderly constitute a larger percentage of the population, family size declines and women participate in the workforce in larger numbers, the government have been pressed to stimulate the growth of long-term care services and to develop a national insurance programme to fund them. Escalating healthcare expenditures for the elderly, driven by acute hospital stays used in lieu of long-term care services, further increased the pressure and pushed the issue to the forefront of the nation's policy agenda.

In July 2008, South Korea introduced national Long-Term Care Insurance (LTCI). The programme mainly covers services for individuals age 65 and over and is independent of the National Health Insurance (NHI). Although NHI and LTCI maintain separate accounts, administrative services for both programmes are handled by the National Health Insurance Corporation (NHIC) to minimize overhead costs. NHI covers medical care for all citizens of the country and participation is mandatory. The intent of LTCI is to cover all elders in South Korea who need long-term care with contributions from public funding. Before the implementation of the dedicated insurance scheme, long-term care services were very limited and available only to the very poor and disabled through government welfare programmes, or expensive private institutions that served wealthy clients. Once the programme was initiated, an emphasis on increasing the number of providers of long-term care services led to an enormous expansion of the industry. Currently, about 6 per cent of the nation's elders participate in LTCI and receive care from nearly 4,000 residential care providers and almost 20,000 home care agencies (NHIC,

385

2011: 15). This represents remarkable growth given that only 0.4 per cent of elders received formal long-term care services from approximately 200 facilities less than a decade ago (Cho et al., 2004). However, regulation and oversight have not developed commensurately, prompting concerns over the quality of care provided. These concerns have changed the focus of policy makers to improved quality assurance and away from merely increasing the supply of providers.

LTCI acted as a catalyst for South Korea's long-term care industry and hasty development of its regulatory infrastructure followed. The country's system of oversight for long-term care is still in its infancy, but has recently begun to make large strides toward improving the quality of care provided to the programme's participants. The purpose of this chapter is to introduce the newly implemented formal long-term care system in South Korea, including its regulatory and oversight system. The chapter consists of two sections. The first introduces the LTCI programme, which created the foundation for South Korea's formal long-term care system, and discusses the societal influences that led to its initiation. The second section describes details of the regulatory and inspection system for long-term care services following the implementation of LTCI.

14.2 Long-term care insurance

14.2.1 Background

South Korea's population is rapidly ageing at a time when the dynamics of the traditional family structure are evolving. The country has experienced a rapid transition from an ageing to an aged society driven by increased life expectancy and a significant decline in its fertility rate. The population's proportion of elderly (aged 65+) was estimated to be 10.7 per cent in 2010, which is expected to grow to 38.2 per cent by 2050 (Statistics Korea, 2010). South Korea's ageing structure means that the country is facing the extensive care needs of elders with multiple chronic diseases and conditions. For example, more than 86 per cent of elders have been diagnosed with at least one chronic disease, nearly 23 per cent have one or more instrumental activity of daily living (IADL) limitations, and over 8 per cent have limitations with activities of daily living (ADL) (Cho et al., 2004; Chung and Seok, 2005).

However, South Korea's ageing population has unique features compared to other developed nations due to significant social changes, such as an evolving family structure and the changing role of women. Traditionally, adult children have served as informal caregivers. Societal values such as respect for elders and care for aged parents are strongly entrenched in Korean culture and are reflected in the informal care system. However, the traditional family structure has been changing over time with a decline in the proportion of elderly living with their children. Industrialization and urbanization have contributed to this trend along with waning family size and more women participating in the workforce. The population of elders living alone in South Korea increased over 85 per cent from 2000 to 2010 (Statistics Korea, 2010: 11). Elder care has traditionally been provided by female family members. Up to 80 per cent of the care for elders is provided by female family members, with spouses carrying the most responsibility, followed by daughters-in-law and daughters (Seok, 2010a). However, among dispersed families, daughters-in-law are more likely to serve as primary caregivers. Therefore, increasing female participation in the labour force has led to diminishing resources available for caregiving.

Influences other than an ageing society or changing family structure have also driven the need for long-term care services. For instance, a rapid increase in national health expenditures due to high utilization rates of in-patient care among elders, in addition to substantial out-of-pocket expenses, have contributed to the need for long-term care services. Despite South Korea having a universal health insurance programme, the plan covers less than 60 per cent of charges (Kwon, 2007). Given the health needs of the elderly and the high prevalence of chronic disease in this population, the restricted benefits create a substantial financial burden for the elderly with chronic diseases. Elders in South Korea typically have limited disposable income. For instance, in 2009 the national pension plan only covered 27.6 per cent of the elderly population and 7.5 per cent of all elders relied on government assistance. Most elders depend on financial support from their adult children (Statistics Korea, 2010: 26–7).

Moreover, many elders were relying on acute care hospital beds as a means to obtain long-term care services, which led to substantial increases in national health expenditures. This phenomenon has been termed 'social admission'. The situation is exemplified by the long average length of stay for hospital visits for chronically ill elders and the share of national health expenditures that go toward in-patient care for these individuals. In 2001, the average length of stay in acute hospitals was 17.1 days for elders, which is more than 30 per cent longer than the average length of stay for all hospitalizations in the country (Cho et al., 2004). The portion of NHI expenditures spent on the elderly increased from 9.3 per cent in 1990 to 30.5 per cent in 2009 (Statistics Korea, 2010: 18).

The fiscal burden of long-term care on the NHI and mounting social pressure acted as the impetus for the government to implement a national insurance plan for these services and to initiate additional programmes to develop an adequate system for the country's growing needs. In July 2008, South Korea introduced national LTCI, which mainly covers individuals age 65 and older with no income eligibility requirement. LTCI is a contribution-based single payer insurance system financed separately from the NHI. The intent of the programme is to cover all elders who need long-term care regardless of income, financed with minimal contributions from all citizens. As of 2011, approximately 6 per cent of elders in South Korea were covered by LTCI, with 3,929 residential care facilities and 19,948 home care agencies providing long-term care services (NHIC, 2011: 15). On average, contributions are about US$4 per person monthly. There are no private insurers for long-term care services in South Korea and the federal plan through the NHIC is the only coverage available. NHIC is responsible for all provisions of LTCI including collection of contributions, recipient assessment and monitoring of providers.

Developing a more substantial long-term care system has been a concern of previous presidential administrations. The idea of creating a public long-term care system was proposed by two earlier administrations, those of Presidents Kim Dae Jung and Rho Moo Hyun, during the early 2000s. This resulted in the initiation of the first elderly long-term care pilot programme in July 2005, which was followed by two more pilot programmes in 2006 and 2007. Legislation to add LTCI to the national health plan was passed by the National Assembly in April 2007 and came into effect in July 2008.

Prior to LTCI implementation, there were few formal long-term care services available in the country and minimal regulation. Services were only available to the very poor as part of a government welfare programme or to wealthy clients willing to pay for services in expensive private facilities. The government programme mostly provided services for physically and mentally impaired elders with limited residential care services. In 2002, there were only twenty-six specialized hospitals for elder care and 171 residential care facilities, which covered only 0.3 per

Quality monitoring of long-term care in the Republic of Korea 389

cent of the total population aged 65 and over (which amount to approximately 3.6 million people) (Kwon, 2007).

14.2.2 Financing

Financing for LTCI comes from multiple sources. Mandatory premium contributions from NHI participants provide 60 to 65 per cent of the funding for LTCI, government subsidies amount to 20 per cent, and out-of-pocket copayments account for 15 to 20 per cent, depending on whether individuals use institutional care or home-based services. Low-income elderly participants are exempt from the individual contribution. The threshold is approximately US$900 per month for a family of two.

14.2.3 Beneficiaries

Once the programme was implemented, enrolment grew rapidly (Figure 14.1). As of 2011, over 318,000 elders were eligible for the programme and more than 286,000 received LTCI benefits (residential care or home care), with the programme covering approximately 6 per cent of elders in the country (NHIC, 2011: 15). Among all LTCI beneficiaries, 65.9 per cent receive home care services, 33.9 per cent

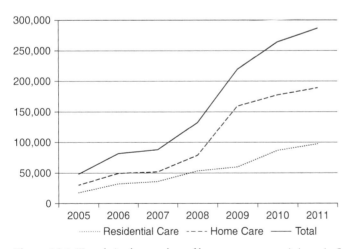

Figure 14.1 Trends in the number of long-term care recipients in South Korea, 2005–11.
Source: National Health Insurance Corporation, 2011.

receive residential care, and 0.2 per cent collect cash benefits. Residential care was utilized more by elders with the most severe functional status and elders with moderate functional status were the largest users of home care.

14.2.3.1 Eligibility

All elders age 65 and over in need of long-term care services qualify for LTCI benefits regardless of income level. LTCI also provides coverage for those under 65 with selected conditions. However, benefits are primarily driven by the need for care among the elderly population, with a focus on those with severe ADL limitations. Substantial coverage gaps remain for the non-elderly disabled. In order to receive services, pre-authorization is required. This is based on an assessment of a recipient's functional status following a recommendation from a general physician or specialist. Eligibility status and severity grades are assigned to recipients based on levels of physical functioning. Grades 1 to 3 qualify recipients for services covered by LTCI, with Grade 1 representing the most severe functional needs (Table 14.1). Assessments cover fifty-two items characterizing functioning and need for assistance,

Table 14.1 *Assessment grades for long-term care eligibility status in South Korea*

	Grade 1 (Most severe)	Grade 2 (Severe)	Grade 3 (Moderate)
Activities of Daily Living (ADL) Measures	Completely dependent > = 6 ADL	Partially dependent > = 5 ADL	Partially dependent > = 3 ADL
Functional status description	Patient is bedridden, cannot move without assistance	Can maintain daily life in a wheelchair	Use a walking frame to move
	Completely dependent on assistance ADLs such as having meals, dressing and toileting	Tends to stay in bed during the day	Can go outside only with assistance

Source: Ministry of Health and Welfare, 2007.

Quality monitoring of long-term care in the Republic of Korea 391

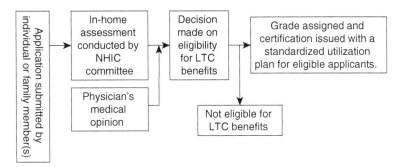

Figure 14.2 Assessment process in South Korea to determine long-term care needs.
Source: National Health Insurance Corporation website: www.longtermcare. or.kr/portal/longtermcare/sub03_01.jsp.

which are reviewed by a committee that gives final approval and assigns a grade for functional status level.

Figure 14.2 depicts the details of the assessment process. Assessment of LTCI needs occurs at the local level by an NHIC eligibility assessment committee. Once elders with functional difficulty apply through local agents in the NHIC for LTCI benefits, the committee visits the applicant and assesses their long-term care needs. Members of the committee include a nurse, a social worker and a medical doctor from NHIC. The assessment committee decides on the eligibility for benefits and issues a long-term care certification. The certification states the beneficiary's severity level (grade), benefit amounts and associated costs.

14.2.3.2 Benefits
LTCI benefit levels are differentiated by the severity of a patient's condition with the maximum benefit for each category being set by national guidelines. Residential care benefits are paid in a flat monthly sum, which is approximately US$1,400 for Grade 1. Home care benefits have a lower monthly limit on benefit coverage of roughly US$1,000 per month. Individuals are free to choose any home care benefits (e.g., bathing, home help) within the monthly limit (Table 14.2). Beneficiaries are required to pay 20 per cent co-insurance for residential care and 15 per cent for home care. Meals and private rooms for residential care services are not covered by LTCI.

Table 14.2 *Residential care benefits and home care limits in South Korea, 2011*

Severity	Grade 1	Grade 2	Grade 3
Residential care benefits	1,487,375 won/month	1,377,571 won/month	1,267,463 won/month
Home care monthly limit	1,140,600 won/month	971,200 won/month	814,700 won/month

Source: National Health Insurance Corporation, 2011.
Note: US$1 = 1,050 won (at August 2011).

Lastly, a specific cash benefit is available for family caregiving. Recipients residing in rural areas with no facilities and persons with certain psychological conditions that make admission to long-term care settings difficult are eligible. However, the government has put stringent guidelines in place to qualify for cash benefits. The monthly maximum benefit is about US$140 regardless of severity grade. Reasons for the strict requirements and limited payment include the potential for misuse of cash payments, worries that the benefit may impede development of the formal long-term care system and concerns over leaving the burden of care with families, particularly women. Currently, only 0.2 per cent of LTCI participants receive cash benefits (Seok, 2010b).

14.2.4 Providers

The number of providers has soared since LTCI was implemented (Figure 14.3). In 2011, there were 3,929 residential care facilities and 19,948 home care agencies that provided long-term care services. On average, there are about twenty-five residents per facility, while each home care agency manages roughly twenty elders (NHIC, 2011: 15). Given that only 0.4 per cent of elders (13,907 elders) were served by approximately 200 facilities in 2002, this represents a vast increase in the number of long-term care service providers and individuals receiving services from them (Cho et al., 2004; Kwon, 2007).

The majority of long-term care providers are private agencies (99.5 per cent) that are reimbursed and overseen by the NHIC. Providers must meet national minimum standards in order to provide LTCI benefits and receive reimbursements, which are defined by law based

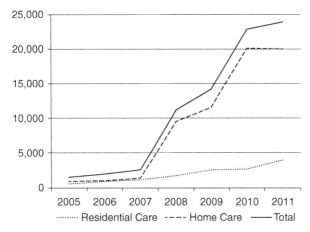

Figure 14.3 Trends in the number of long-term care providers in South Korea, 2005–11.
Source: National Health Insurance Corporation, 2011.

on the types of services provided. Although the NHIC is responsible for ongoing inspection of providers, local government approves initial accreditation and has authority to terminate the operation of LTCI providers. Market entry for providers is unrestricted with no control over ownership or the number of sites, as long as they meet minimum requirements. Details of provider qualifications and inspection systems are explained in the next section.

14.2.4.1 Types of services
There are two types of services available to beneficiaries based on their needs: residential care services and home care services. Long-term care services offered under LTCI are designed to be flexible so that they meet recipients' specific needs and preferences.

Residential care services include licensed nursing homes (10+ beds) and licensed group homes (5–9 beds). Residential care facilities are meant to provide services for long-term nursing care, which supplies room and board. Although recipients are not restricted in their selection of residential care or home care benefits, residential care services are generally recommended only for elders with higher severity (Grades 1 and 2) due to insufficient facility infrastructure. Most residential long-term care facilities do not have separate special care units. For instance, dementia patients receive care in the same facility as other residents. However, facilities often designate separate rooms for residents needing special care. New policy options addressing special care have been discussed by policy makers, but none has come to fruition. For example, adjusting reimbursements to providers for beneficiaries with special care needs has been under consideration. Currently, facilities are not paid more for patients requiring special care.

Home care agencies provide services that include home help, bathing, day/night care and short-term care. Home care services are intended to help recipients with activities of daily living, which is mainly provided by certified care aids.

14.2.4.2 Staffing

Residential care facilities are required to have minimum staffing levels that include one geriatric nurse for every twenty-five residents, one certified care aide (*yoyang bohosa*) per 2.5 residents, one physical therapist and one social worker per forty residents. The head (geriatric) nurse is responsible for monitoring and observation, checking vital signs and dispensing medication. Certified care aides provide the majority of daily care for residents such as bathing, toileting and assistance with eating. Social workers help with any needs relating to residents' well-being and social support. All required staff are full-time-equivalent positions.

Home care services are provided mostly by certified care aides. However, certified care aides who provide home care services have unique characteristics. Many are individuals who became certified to care for their own family members and have been dubbed 'family care aides'. Family members are allowed to provide home care services and be paid as long as they undergo training in formal government programmes and receive certification as a care aide. In 2011, about 40 per cent of all registered certified care aides were working for relatives (Ministry of Health and Welfare, 2011a). The government has limited the time that family care aides are allowed to care for elders due to difficulty in monitoring the quality of care provided and to prevent potential misuse of funds. Certified nurse aides can only provide services to their own family members for a maximum of two hours per day, which is only 50 per cent of the time allowed for non-family members. More recently, the government implemented further restrictions on home care services provided by family care aides, reducing the allowed time to one hour per day.

Quality monitoring of long-term care in the Republic of Korea   395

In terms of staffing, overlapping roles and conflicting responsibilities among registered nurses, nursing aides, and certified care aides are issues requiring attention. Moreover, one of the main problems related to care aides in South Korea concerns the poor conditions in which they work. This situation results in low job satisfaction and high turnover rates (Cho, 2009). Details on the certification process and other requirements for long-term care workers are detailed in the long-term care workforce section below.

14.2.4.3 Reimbursement

Providers are reimbursed by NHIC. After beneficiaries make their copayment, the provider bills NHIC directly for the balance. Residential care providers are paid per diem rates that are differentiated by the severity of a patient's condition. Home care services are reimbursed on an hourly, or per visit, basis depending on the type of home care tasks provided (e.g., bathing, housework, etc.). Fees are set by the government with no geographic variation in reimbursements to providers.

14.2.4.4 Clinical care

LTCI is designed to pay for custodial care, not medical care. By law, residential care facilities and home care agencies are prohibited from providing medical services. LTCI beneficiaries must receive clinical care, including in-patient and ambulatory services, from designated hospitals paid by NHI. While the policy that residents cannot retain their primary care doctors has not changed, more leeway has been given since 2010 due to patients voicing a strong interest in receiving care from hospitals or doctors of their choice. Physicians often work on a part-time basis in residential facilities even though they are not allowed to treat patients or prescribe medications. They only check on patients' status and refer them to designated hospitals. Residents receive prescriptions from hospitals, which nurse aides dispense to residents under a nurse's supervision.

There is some overlap in services covered by NHI and LTCI. In principle, LTCI covers only custodial care based on ADL needs and NHI covers medical needs for elders, but accountability is ambiguous since the roles overlap in practice. For instance, NHI covers services such as home-based skilled nursing care or specialty long-term care hospitals for those with dementia. Interestingly, some of these same services are also covered by LTCI. Although patients are free to choose services through NHI or LTCI, benefits and the out-of-pocket expenses are similar for both programmes, most beneficiaries select LTCI agencies for long-term care services. This is partially due to custodial care being included in the price of services covered by LTCI. Despite long-term care experts and policy makers voicing concerns over the potential for adverse consequences resulting from fragmentation of services and redundant government spending on certain types of care, there is a dearth of research or reporting that addresses these issues.

14.3 Regulatory and inspection system for LTCI providers

The NHIC and local governments are jointly responsible for quality management and oversight of long-term care providers. Although the current oversight system is fragmented, the NHIC and local governments each play an important role in quality control of long-term care providers. While local governments play a vital role in the certification process and have the authority to terminate a provider's business operations, the NHIC controls the quality of long-term care providers through regular assessments and inspections.

14.3.1 Provider certification / market entrance

Local government approves accreditation of long-term care service providers. Only residential and home-based services that meet minimum national standards can be certified as providers. These standards have been legally defined by the NHIC based on the types of services provided and the credentials of the service providers. Potential providers who want to become accredited must submit an application to the local government that describes the general characteristics of their facility, its staffing and its physical environment. A representative of the local government reviews the submitted documentation and approves certification. Service providers need to obtain permission from the local government to establish and expand facilities. Thus, local governments rather than the NHIC regulate the establishment of care services. Certification can also be revoked by local governments for committing fraudulent acts, failing to meet specified standards, changing the business type without properly reporting it or not complying with requests from officials for records and other materials. However, a hearing must take place before a provider's certification status is withdrawn.

Providers have unrestricted access with respect to entrance into the market, and no control over the ownership or the number of facilities is exerted as long as they meet the minimum requirements. After providers have satisfied the minimum national standards in terms of staffing and the physical environment, they can obtain accreditation as long-term care agencies. All for-profit and non-profit private facilities can be reimbursed for the services they provide in this domain. Efforts to manage the supply of long-term care began with very limited authority in response to high consumer demand, which led to a rush to establish service agencies. In this context, the government focused on expanding capacity in terms of the number of private-sector providers and beds. Recently, with supply generally in place, quality assurance has become a higher priority and has emerged as a central concern of the Ministry of Health and Welfare.

14.3.2 Oversight of long-term care providers by NHIC

The NHIC acts as an independent inspector that oversees unfair practices, abuse, and serious deficiencies of providers through interviews of top-level staff and audits of provider records. In 2009 and 2010, the NHIC implemented a new oversight system, the 'long-term care assessment system' for long-term care providers. The new system was implemented for residential-based care in 2009, with home care added the following year. Initially, participation in the new inspection system was voluntary, but assessments became mandatory for all providers in 2011.

The rapid increase in long-term care providers, combined with a rudimentary assessment system, raised a significant amount of public concern prior to 2009 and heightened awareness for the need to develop an adequate assessment tool to reflect quality based on patient outcomes. The assessment tool used in South Korea before 2009 was not as rigorous as the current system. It placed little emphasis on measuring patient outcomes or processes of care and focused heavily on management and infrastructure of facilities (Jung et al., 2010).

The NHIC assesses the quality of facilities based on the results of evaluations. The system utilizes pay-for-performance and public reporting as quality control mechanisms. High-performing facilities receive incentives in the form of refunds, and less-qualified facilities are put at a disadvantage. The intent of the policy is to control provider quality through incentives based on performance. Additionally, providers who rank in the top 30 per cent and those falling into the bottom 10 per cent are publicly reported on NHIC websites. The policy incentivizes autonomous efforts toward quality improvement and promotes competition in the industry.

14.3.2.1 Inspection schedule

Regular inspections are conducted every two years by type of service and the size of each entity. Periodic follow-up inspections are conducted of providers found to have performed poorly on the standard inspection and of those in the bottom 10 per cent based on NHIC assessment results. As part of the inspection and auditing process, each facility must participate in an initial review as well as regular follow-up reviews.

14.3.2.2 Inspection tools and content

The inspection tool has five sections that consist of a total of 106 measures for residential care providers, while measures for home care range from 56 to 98 depending on the service type (Table 14.3).

The five sections include operations, environment and safety, satisfaction and personalized care, delivery of services and outcomes of services. The number of measures differs by type of service, with some of the items designed for specific services. Examples of measures in each section follow. The operation section includes questions on organizations' management issues such as whether regular staff meetings are held, whether sufficient staff benefits and training are provided and confidentiality of recipients' personal information. The environment and safety section focuses on questions related to patient safety and securing the environment: for example, proper sanitation and climate control in the facility, and ensuring that bathrooms have handrails or slip-resistant floors. Additionally, the satisfaction and personalized care section includes questions addressing resident-centred care. For instance, issues of patient satisfaction, personalized care, respect for personal items and space and conflict resolution are included. Examples of items in the delivery of care section include proper storage and dispensing of medications, whether processes are in place to prevent pressure sores and any improper use of restraints. Lastly, the 'outcomes of care' section consists of patient quality outcome measures. These include the percentage of residents who had pressure sores, falls or ostomy care, and ADL improvement in the first six months following admission.

Table 14.3 *Domains of long-term care evaluation and weighted scores in South Korea**

Categories	Residential		Home visits		Home bathing		Home nursing visits		Day care		Short-term stay	
	Number of items	Weighted score	Number of items	Weighted score	Number of items	Weighted score	Number of items	Weighted score	Number of items	Weighted score	Number of items	Weighted score
Total score	106	100	56	100	56	100	60	100	92	100	98	100
Operation	17	18	17	32	17	32	17	30	16	20	16	18
Environment and safety	26	23	6	9	9	13	7	11	23	23	25	25
Satisfaction and personalized care	15	13	11	17	12	19	11	16	13	13	15	14
Delivery of care	43	38	21	39	17	33	24	40	39	42	41	41
Outcomes of care	5	8	1	3	1	3	1	3	1	2	1	2

Source: Ministry of Health and Welfare, 2011b.
Note: * Scores can be classified according to the size of the agency.

Each measure has a specific number of points assigned to it that contributes to an overall scale with a maximum of 100 points. Weights are assigned to each item based on its importance relative to other domains. Provider performance is evaluated by the total points they receive.

The assessment tool covers a broad range of indicators for quality measures, but a large portion of them, and their weights, are still focused on providers' operational performance or management. Accommodating and modifying the assessment tool to improve measures of patient outcomes are at the heart of ongoing debates to improve quality efforts.

The system relies on self-administered evaluations by providers without direct input from clients or residents. On-site assessments are conducted by a two-person team from NHIC over the course of six to seven hours in the case of residential agencies, and three to four hours for community-based agencies. Although inspectors from NHIC are trained for the assessment process, they are not necessarily long-term care experts. This has raised concerns over the effectiveness and consistency of inspections.

14.3.2.3 Rewards and penalties

The NHIC pays an additional 5 per cent over the regular full payment to agencies ranked within the top 10 per cent according to the previous year's evaluations. Rewards are paid based on a relative rank, not by absolute points. In other words, incentives are paid according to the rank of each facility among all providers of the same type and not by specific score-related criteria. However, if the agency commits an administrative violation, or if the NHIC determines that there is another reason for withholding the reward, it can be excluded as a potential recipient. The top 30 per cent of providers are listed on NHIC's long-term care website as highly qualified agencies (www.longtermcare.go.kr). Those ranked within the upper 30 per cent of providers receive special ribbons bearing their names to highlight their rankings and agencies can display these achievement ribbons in their buildings. The NHIC also provides a list of high-quality long-term care agencies to local governments, and the top five are given the opportunity to make a presentation about their services. This presentation enables them to promote their business and share their knowledge of quality assurance with other providers. The bottom 10 per cent of providers, as determined by assessment rankings, is put at a disadvantage through public disclosure of their names and closer monitoring. However, there are no specific monetary fines applied to poorly performing facilities or agencies.

Quality monitoring of long-term care in the Republic of Korea 401

Based on 2009 and 2010 assessment results, the average score for residential care providers was about 77 points while the mean score of home care providers was a little over 81 points, ranging from 15 points to 100 points. The scores showed large disparities among home care agencies in the assessments (Ministry of Health and Welfare, 2011a).

14.3.2.4 Evaluation committee

The NHIC long-term care evaluation committee plans the assessment process annually. The committee decides what information from the assessment results to disclose and how it will be disseminated. It also determines the levels of rewards and penalties, and specifies other issues that are important in the evaluation of long-term care. The long-term care evaluation committee consists of one chairman and thirteen committee members appointed by the director of the NHIC according to the following six criteria:

1. four people nominated by non-governmental organizations, including organizations for older individuals, consumers, and citizens;
2. four individuals representing long-term care agencies;
3. one academic professional with knowledge and experience related to long-term care;
4. one official from the Ministry of Health and Welfare;
5. one official affiliated with a municipality;
6. the executive director and one additional official from the NHIC. The executive director serves as the chair of the long-term care committee.

When providers do not submit required reports or documentation, submit a false report, or are uncooperative in the evaluation process, the long-term care evaluation committee can order the suspension of an organization's business operations. Although the NHIC has the authority to impose a temporary suspension, it cannot permanently close down providers. In situations where the NHIC feels that a provider's operations should be terminated, it may recommend that the local government revoke the business's certification.

14.3.3 *Regulation of the long-term care workforce*

Local governments are responsible for accreditation and oversight of training programmes for the long-term care workforce. Although private institutions provide training, the government administers the exams for certification. Long-term care workers can be categorized into several groups: professional geriatric nurses, visiting nurse aides and care aides.

14.3.3.1 Geriatric nurses

Nurses with more than three years of professional nursing experience who have received specific education and training can be certified as professional geriatric nurses (according to the Medical Law enacted in 2003). Colleges, departments of nursing and schools of public health can be accredited as educators for these programmes by the Ministry of Health and Welfare. Professional geriatric nurses can serve as representatives of long-term care agencies and/or work as head nurses in residential care facilities. Geriatric nurses working in home care agencies provide visiting nursing services, support medical treatment, offer health counselling, and provide care related to oral hygiene.

14.3.3.2 Visiting nurse aides

Nursing aides with more than three years of clinical experience during the last ten years can serve as long-term care nursing aides after completing an educational programme designed for visiting nurse aides. The nursing services provided by geriatric nurses and nursing aides overlap somewhat in the context of agencies offering long-term care services. This potential role conflict between the two jobs sometimes emerges as an organizational problem.

14.3.3.3 Certified care aides

Certified care aides (known as *yoyang bohosa*) work within long-term care agencies and assist elders with activities of daily living. These workers must be certified by passing a national examination that is offered once a year after completion of mandated training. Only those who receive scores of 60 per cent or higher on the exam are permitted to become certified care aides unless there are other reasons for disqualification, such as having a criminal record (Figure 14.4). New care aides are required to attend eighty hours of classes, eighty hours of technical training and eighty hours of practical training through hands-on experience, yielding a total of 240 hours. Local governments determine the number of educational facilities, their distribution, the supply–demand ratio and the prerequisites for care aides in each area.

Quality monitoring of long-term care in the Republic of Korea   403

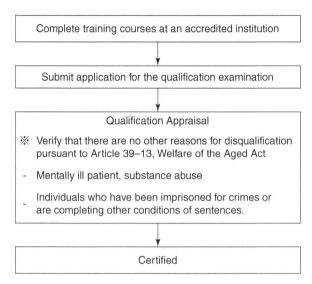

Figure 14.4 The qualification process for certified care workers in South Korea. *Source:* compiled by authors.

In response to a substantial number of complaints regarding the adequacy of training, the government plans to improve the curriculum both qualitatively and quantitatively. Until recently, more than 1,400 educational facilities trained approximately 810,000 care aides (data from April 2010). This number reflects an oversupply with respect to demand for these workers. Thus, since April 2010, the government has attempted to enhance the quality of care aides by various means, including amending the law governing the accreditation of educational facilities. During the early stages of development of long-term care services in South Korea, any educational institution that applied for accreditation received it. Local governments have now become more discerning in awarding accreditation.

14.3.4 *Information for consumers*

Consumers can obtain general information about providers from the NHIC website and identify high performing providers. This includes information about the location, size and other structural characteristics of facilities. The list of high-performing agencies is available at www.longtermcare.go.kr. After providers participate in an NHIC mandatory assessment process, the final report is made available to the public so that LTCI beneficiaries can make informed choices about providers. No particular strategy has been designed to provide a 'voice' for consumers. The Korea Consumer Agency, the government entity charged with protecting consumer rights and interests, is concerned with beneficiaries' satisfaction with the care they receive and the competence of caregivers. At present, patient-level claims data are collected by the government, but no systematic process is in place to collect data reflecting satisfaction with both institutional and home-based services. The claims data are not used for assessment of quality measures.

14.4 Challenges and conclusion

Implementation of LTCI established a foundation for the formal long-term care system in Korea. The percentage of the elderly population that benefits from long-term care services has increased substantially from 0.4 per cent in 2002 to 6 per cent in 2011. As the programme grows, the number of providers is increasing rapidly, with the industry creating over 225,000 jobs since LTCI began. The programme has significantly reduced the burden on informal caregivers and has created a framework with the goal of providing universal coverage for all elders who require long-term care services regardless of income.

According to early evaluations, a majority of the beneficiaries responding have expressed satisfaction with services. In a 2009 survey of long-term care services, over 90 per cent of respondents reported that LTCI had reduced psychological stress on caregivers in their families and that the financial burden of care had been reduced by over 50 per cent (Seok, 2010b). Another survey indicated that 80 per cent of LTCI beneficiaries expressed satisfaction with services (Kwon et al., 2010). But despite the success of LTCI in expanding access to long-term care services, there are numerous policy issues that remain to be addressed. Fragmentation in services and oversight, in addition to problems of access in rural areas, and inconsistencies between consumer preferences and the government's objectives still need to be resolved.

Healthcare services for elders are fragmented. LTCI is designed to provide access to custodial care, but the NHI is responsible for clinical care and is funded through a separate mechanism. These factors have the potential to negatively affect the care provided to beneficiaries. The current financial scheme creates incentives to shift costs between the two public programmes, which hinders efforts to improve the quality of care. Further, elders with functional problems and multiple chronic diseases generally require comprehensive health services. These individuals often encounter many problems arising from fragmentation of services. For instance, inadequate administrative coordination between the NHI and LTCI and a lack of smooth transitions between services are issues that plague elders participating in both programmes. Combining NHI and LTCI funding into a single pool to serve LTCI beneficiaries may be an option. Integrating the funding into a single entity may eliminate any conflicting financial incentives between the two programmes while improving efficiency and coordination of care. However, to date, reports of adverse consequences have not surfaced. Given the limited time that the programme has been operating, this may change as it matures and more data are available.

In addition, oversupply of long-term care providers has led to problems. The number of providers exceeds demand and there is intense competition among them to recruit long-term care beneficiaries. One common strategy used by providers is to offer beneficiaries reduced copayments. The majority of long-term care providers are small, privately owned, for-profit entities that make minimal initial investments in infrastructure, and financial stability is a concern. On the other hand, the government is optimistic that market forces will distinguish higher-quality providers from ones of lower quality. Other suggestions to address the oversupply of providers have also been offered, such as converting small group homes into facilities for beneficiaries with dementia or other conditions that require specialty care. Although an oversupply of long-term care providers has become a chief policy concern in regard to quality control, the regional distribution of providers is characterized by a disparity in the availability of services between rural and urban areas (Lee, 2010). In particular, home care and day care services are concentrated in large cities. Thus, issues of accessibility and the right to access disproportionately affect elders residing in rural areas.

The current evaluation of long-term care services is complex, involving multiple administrative agencies, and the debate over whether to create a single-evaluator system drawn from the NHIC and local governments persists. For instance, despite the leverage yielded by the NHIC through its role in the evaluation process, it has no authority over the renewal of accreditation of long-term care agencies. Only local governments have the authority to permit and prohibit business operations. Additionally, all authority related to the evaluation of providers, insurance claims and management of long-term care services is assigned to the NHIC, which has raised concerns among healthcare professionals about the institution's excessive control. Separating the authority for accreditation from the entity responsible for inspections may not be ideal. The effectiveness of the inspection system could potentially be increased if the NHIC were also given authority over accreditation of providers. However, given that local governments are unlikely to voluntarily yield power to NHIC, intervention on the part of federal lawmakers would be needed for this to occur.

Lastly, current policy changes in the 'family care aide' benefit warrants discussion. In June of 2011 the government announced that reimbursements for family care aides would be restricted to sixty minutes a day for a maximum of twenty days per month. The benefit previously reimbursed up to ninety minutes a day for as many as thirty-one days per month. Given the considerable number of certified care aides working for family members, the reduction was met with harsh rebuke from families utilizing the benefit. Initially the government limited cash benefits to very small amounts. The intention was to prevent cash assistance from hindering the development of the formal long-term care industry in addition to concerns over misuse of the benefit. However, beneficiaries and their families started using the 'family certified care aide' as a parallel to the cash benefit. This led to more people being certified as care aides with the purpose of providing care for their own family members. As more family members have become certified care aides there have been increasingly more cases of misuse reported, confirming the government's initial fears. Many of these include family care aides applying for reimbursements without having provided proper care or grossly over-reporting the amount of care. However, the family care aide benefit appears to be the best option for some families. For elders who need twenty-four-hour care, particularly those with dementia, or who exhibit violent behaviour, receiving care through other LTCI benefits may be challenging. Given the monthly limit of LTCI benefits (about US$900 to US$1,300), combined with a relatively high copayment and a preference for receiving care from family members, it is not surprising that the family care aide benefit is popular. It may be a practical option for families that have a relative in need of constant care while providing a source of income.

The formal long-term care system in South Korea continues to evolve rapidly. Policy makers are constantly seeking improved ways of accommodating long-term care needs. Although financial sustainability is a concern, the government is considering expanding LTCI eligibility to allow higher-functioning elders with fewer ADL limitations to participate in the programme. The need for special care services has been considered with other possible options, such as higher reimbursement rates for those with special care needs or converting small group homes to special care facilities. The importance of developing an enhanced assessment tool that reflects quality based on beneficiaries' outcomes has also been discussed, along with the need for a more stringent inspection system that oversees providers.

Despite swift growth, South Korea's formal long-term care system remains in its early development. The country's regulatory and oversight system is still maturing and substantial concerns exist among consumers, providers and policy makers. Given the amount of time the programme has been in operation, experience is limited and few data are available for evaluation. As more time passes, inefficiencies and other unintended consequences of policies may come to light. However, the country has made substantial progress in expanding access to long-term care services among its elderly population.

References

Cho, C. Y. (2009). Current and challenge of care aides in long term care. *Korean Academy of Care Welfare*, 10: 83–105.

Cho, K. H. et al. (2004). Healthcare for older persons: a country profile – Korea. *Journal of the American Geriatrics Society*, 52(7): 1,199–204.

Chung K. et al. (2005). *Development of Assessment Tool and Unit Cost for Korean Long-Term Care Services*. Seoul: Ministry of Health and Welfare and Korea Institute for Health and Social Affairs.

Chung, K. and Seok, J. (2005). *Development of Korea's Long Term Care Oversight and Inspection System*. Seoul: Korea Institute for Health and Social Affairs.

Jung, H. Y. et al. (2010). A health outcomes approach to evaluating long-term care facilities: lessons from the United States. *Journal of the Korean Geriatrics Society*, 14(2): 61–9.

Kwon, S. (2007). Future of long-term care financing for the elderly in Korea. *Journal of Aging and Social Policy*, 20(1): 119–36.

Kwon, J., Han, E. J., Kang, I. O. (2010). An analysis of the relationship among quality, satisfaction and purchase intention perceived by home help service users. *Journal of the Korean Gerontological Society*, 30(2), 355–68.

Lee, Y. K. (2010). Time series analysis of geographical equity in the long-term care service for the elderly in Korea from 2003 to 2008. *Social Welfare Policy*, 37(2): 201–16.

(2011). Living to one hundred: how to improve elderly long term care. *Health and Welfare Forum*, 195: 28–38.

Ministry of Health and Welfare (2007). *Main Contents of the LTCI for the Elderly*. Seoul: Ministry of Health and Welfare.

(2011a). Korean Long Term Care Law 2011. December.

(2011b). *Manual for Long Term Care Evaluation*. Seoul: Ministry of Health and Welfare.

National Health Insurance Corporation (NHIC) (2011). *Long-Term Care Insurance for the Elderly Monthly Statistics Report*, May 2011. Seoul: NHIC.

Seok, J. (2010a). Public long-term care insurance for the elderly in Korea: design, characteristics, and tasks. *Social Work in Public Health*, 25(2): 185.

(2010b). *Family and Care: Basic Analysis Report on First Wave (2006–2007) of Korean Longitudinal Study of Aging (KLoSA)*, pp. 129–43. Seoul: The Ministry of Labour.

Statistics Korea (2010). *2010 Korean Elderly Census*. Daejeon: Korean Office of Statistics.

15 Long-term care in China: reining in market forces through regulatory oversight

ZHANLIAN FENG, XINPING GUAN,
XIAOTIAN FENG, CHANG LIU, HEYING
JENNY ZHAN AND VINCENT MOR

15.1 Introduction

Traditionally, elder care in China has been confined to the familial sphere, long enshrined by the Confucian norm of filial piety. However, in recent years demographic shifts and rapid socioeconomic changes have escalated concerns about whether Chinese families will still be able to take care of a rapidly growing elderly population. These concerns are compounded by China's one-child policy, which has been in effect for more than thirty years, further straining the capacities of family caregivers. Against this backdrop, formal long-term care services have emerged and expanded rapidly in China, a process catalysed both by government policies and private-sector initiatives.

In this chapter, we begin with an outline of the unprecedented challenges for Chinese elder care in the context of population ageing and profound socioeconomic transformations, followed by an overview of the evolving long-term care landscape in China. Next, we document the rise of formal long-term care services for the elderly, and summarize major policy efforts mounted by the Chinese government in spurring the growth of these services over the last decade. This is followed by a description of the current regulatory structure and process from the perspectives of both central and local government authorities. We conclude by highlighting the need for strengthening regulatory oversight through the building of an information infrastructure in this rapidly growing long-term care service sector.

The writing of this chapter was supported, in part, by a grant from the US National Institutes of Health (R03TW008142).

15.2 Perfect storm: ageing, socioeconomic changes and the elder care challenge

Portrayed as an ageing giant, China is facing unprecedented challenges in the care of a rapidly growing older population (Flaherty et al., 2007). According to China's most recent (sixth) census, by 2010, the population aged 65 years old and over reached 119 million, accounting for 9 per cent of the total population, up from 7 per cent in 2000 (Haub, 2011). Current projections suggest that the proportion of older population (65+) in China will more than double in the next thirty years, to 22.6 per cent in 2040, while the proportion aged 80 or more will grow even faster, from just 1.4 per cent today to 5.0 per cent by 2040 (Kinsella and He, 2009). Given China's enormous population base, these proportions translate into the largest absolute numbers of older people in the world, from 119 million aged 65+ and 19 million aged 80+ today to 329 million and 73 million, respectively, by 2040. The older population is also living longer: at age 65, older Chinese today can expect to live an average of sixteen additional years for women and fourteen additional years for men (United Nations, 2007). The rapid ageing of China's population and continuous gains in life expectancy, together with a shrinking working age population, results in a steady rise in old age dependency (Harwood et al., 2004). In 2008, the old age dependency ratio (i.e., the number of people aged 65 and over per 100 people aged 20–64) in China was about 13, and it is projected to increase to 19 by 2020 and 40 by 2040 (Kinsella and He, 2009).

Aggravating these trends are profound socioeconomic transformations which are set to gradually erode the traditional family-based safety net system for the aged (Flaherty et al., 2007; Jiang, 1995; Zhan, 2002; Zhang, 2007). Due in large part to China's rigorous family planning policies over the past few decades, the total fertility rate (average number of children born to a woman of childbearing age over a lifetime) has declined rapidly, from 5.8 in 1970 (Banister, 1987) to 1.5 at present (PRB, 2011). As a result, family size is diminishing and multigenerational households waning (Logan et al., 1998; Zeng, 1986). Across Chinese cities, the emerging '4:2:1' family structure is increasingly of concern. This structure consists of four grandparents, two adult children, both without siblings, and one grandchild and is a consequence of China's one-child policy that has been in effect for more than thirty years (Flaherty et al., 2007). Meanwhile, historically, female labour force participation in China has been high and continues to rise (Lee, 1995), which, combined with rising divorce rates, further constrains the availability of family caregivers for the aged (Zhan, 2002).

The acceleration of urbanization and industrialization in China has led to increased population mobility. In 2010, the proportion of the urban population in China approached 50 per cent. Driven by migration from rural areas, the urban population increased by 207 million from 2000 to 2010, while the rural population declined by 133 million (Haub, 2011). Young people are increasingly on the move to follow employment opportunities far away from home (Fan, 2008; Liang, 2001). As a result, Chinese families and generations are separated more than ever, straining the ability (if not so much the willingness) of adult children to care for ageing parents. A recent national survey indicates that 'empty-nest' households account for more than 50 per cent of all elderly households in both urban and rural areas, and the rate could be as high as 70 per cent in some big cities (Xinhua, 2011). Apart from the geographic dispersion of adult children, the high rate of 'empty-nesters' among the Chinese elderly also reflects the general preference of independent living over intergenerational co-residence among both the older and younger generations today.

The confluence of these ongoing trends has fuelled rising demands for aged care services. One estimate suggests that as many as 6.5 million elderly Chinese currently may require a level of care similar to that provided in nursing homes, and this number is projected to jump to 16.8 million by 2030 (Flaherty et al., 2007). A recent national survey reveals that currently there are about 33 million (or 19 per cent of total) elderly people who need partial or full assistance with activities of daily living; among them, 10.8 million (or 6 per cent of total elderly population) are totally disabled and dependent on others (Zhang, 2011). By 2015, according to projections, the number of elderly Chinese who are incapable of self-care will increase to 40 million, of which, about 12.4 million will be totally disabled/dependent (Zhang, 2011). Thus, the challenges are daunting for Chinese families and society to meet the care needs of a rapidly growing elderly population.

15.3 Long-term care in the Chinese context: tradition and change

For millennia, Chinese families have relied on the traditional practice of filial piety (*xiào*) to provide elder care by adult children at home (Davis, 1993; Ikels, 1989; Sher, 1984; Treas, 1977). Based on this Confucian doctrine, older parents are cared for physically, financially and emotionally by their adult children. In modern China, all adult children are required by law to take care of their parents in old age, as codified in Article 49 of the Constitution of the People's Republic of China: 'Parents have the duty to rear and educate their minor children, and children who have come of age have the duty to support and assist their parents' (State Council Information Office, 2006). The cultural mandate of filial piety, now reinforced by law, is all but natural given the absence of a national social security system in China (Chu and Chi, 2008; Flaherty et al., 2007; Gu et al., 2007; Wu et al., 2009).

Currently, no national health insurance programme for older people (like Medicare in the US) exists in China, nor do publicly funded safety net programmes covering health and long-term care for the needy (like Medicaid in the US). Hospital care for elders is paid primarily out-of-pocket on a fee-for-service basis and following long hospital stays patients are discharged home without institutional or community-based post-acute care (Flaherty et al., 2007). As is the case in the US and elsewhere, most elderly Chinese prefer living in their own homes rather than institutions (Chu and Chi, 2008). Despite recent government policy initiatives promoting the development of home- and community-based elder services, such as cash allowances for paid home care, community health centres, senior housing, recreational facilities and adult day care programmes (State Council Information Office, 2006; Wu et al., 2005), so far, such services have not yet emerged as a viable long-term care option for most elderly people. Consequently, there is little help outside of the family that Chinese elders can count on when the need for long-term care arises. As has been observed – quite fittingly – 'for thousands of years, filial piety was China's Medicare, Social Security and long-term care, all woven into a single family value' (Levin, 2008).

In spite of the long-standing cultural mandate of filial piety and the fact that family norms are still strong in contemporary China, they are by no means immune to change. As described earlier, demographic

Long-term care in China 413

shifts, coupled with a rollercoaster of socioeconomic and cultural changes in Chinese society over the past few decades, have made the fulfilment of this cultural tradition increasingly difficult for many families in both urban and rural China (Zhan et al., 2006b). The traditional concept of *xiào*, indeed, has constantly been adapted and reinterpreted by both elderly parents and their adult children in the face of a rapidly changing social reality (Chow, 1999; Zhan, 2004; Zhan et al., 2008, 2011). This can be reflected in shifting attitudes among both the older and younger generations toward more tolerance of institutional placement (Guan et al., 2007; Lam et al., 1998; Zhan et al., 2006a, 2006b).

Not long ago, elder care homes were virtually unheard of in China. The few facilities that existed were state social welfare institutions serving exclusively childless elders, orphans and people with mental health problems or learning difficulties but without families (Gu and Liang, 2000; Ikels, 1993; Wu et al., 2008). Older adults who were institutionalized were strongly stigmatized (Chen, 1996; Shang, 2001). Few families with adult children would have imagined placing an elderly parent in an institution to be cared for by strangers. With China's economy expanding in the private sector and demands for social services for the aged rising, a service sector for elder care started to emerge and has grown rapidly since the mid-1990s (Shang, 2001; Wong and Tang, 2006). So now, adult children who are unavailable or unable to provide adequate care, but who have the means, have the option of placing their parents in an elder care facility. Thus, it would appear that the changing social contexts are altering the cultural meaning of institutional elder care. Indeed, open discussions in China about living in an elder care home as an acceptable option or lifestyle are increasingly common (Fan, 2006; Zhan and Montgomery, 2003). At times, the ability of placing an elderly parent in a high-quality, costly care home may have brought with it a sense of pride and privilege rather than shame and stigma as has been felt traditionally; in such circumstances, adult children's willingness to make such financial arrangements are seen as a clear indication of *xiào* behaviour (Zhan et al., 2008).

It may also be the case that the increased availability of alternative care options has induced 'latent' demand for such care by meeting the needs of some elders that would have otherwise gone unmet. This, coupled with demographic imperatives, shifting cultural norms regarding filial piety and rising purchasing power among potential consumers,

414   *Zhanlian Feng, et al.*

has led to the emergence and rapid growth of a long-term care service sector in China, as documented in the section that follows.

15.4 The rise of formal long-term care for the aged

Studies on formal long-term care in China have been limited, not surprisingly since this newly emerging sector is still in its early stage of development. Although elder care services provided in the home and community-based settings have begun to develop in a few major urban centres like Shanghai (Wu et al., 2005), such services remain quite spotty across most cities and towns and virtually non-existent in rural areas, despite a strong policy stance in recent years in favour of their development (as described in detail later in this chapter). In contrast, institutional elder care services have emerged with greater visibility and have expanded more rapidly. In this section, we briefly review the evolution of formal long-term care services, with a focus on the growth of long-term care facilities.

Traditionally, Chinese institutional care was limited to the 'three nos' (*sān wú*), namely, those with no children, no income and no relatives (Chen, 1996).[1] Social welfare institutions in many small or medium-sized cities generally lumped childless elders, mentally ill patients and orphans together under the same roof (Zhan, 2002). In 1988, there were only 870 welfare institutions for elders, caring for 46,837 individuals nationwide, out of a population already exceeding one billion (Chen, 1996). Childless elders were placed by the government in institutions and government paid the costs. The vast majority of elders, those with children, at that time had no choice in terms of their care, as their adult children were required by law to take care of them financially, physically and emotionally. In the mid-1990s, the Chinese government implemented welfare reform, which decentralized the operation and financing of welfare institutions (Croll, 1999; Wong and Tang, 2006). For instance, the government budget for social welfare services and social relief had been reduced from 0.58 per cent of Gross Domestic Product (GDP) in 1979 to 0.19 per cent in 1997 (Shang,

---

[1] The current definition of the 'three nos' (*sān wú*) is worded differently, referring to those who 'have lost the ability to work, have no source of income, and have no legal guardians to support them or their guardians do not have the ability to support them' (State Council Information Office, 2006).

2001). Consequently, state welfare institutions gradually changed their financial bases from total reliance on state resources to having more diversified resources from the government, the business sector, local communities and families or individuals (Shang, 2001). In recent years, the government has actively encouraged the development of elder care services in the private sector (State Council Information Office, 2006; Xinhua, 2005). As a result, the number of elder care facilities has proliferated.

According to official statistics, by 2005, there were 39,546 residential institutions nationwide providing long-term care services for seniors, with approximately 1.5 million beds in total; among them, 29,681 (75 per cent of the total) were rural elderly people's homes, with 895,000 beds (60 per cent of the total), virtually all financed and run by local governments (State Council Information Office, 2006). By 2009, the total number of elder care institutions nationwide was about the same (nearly 40,000), but the total number of beds expanded substantially, to 2.66 million; these facilities housed 2.1 million elderly residents (Zhang, 2011). Despite this growth, on a per capita basis China still has far fewer long-term care beds than most developed countries. One estimate indicates that between 1.5 and 2 per cent of the Chinese older population (aged 65+) lives in residential institutions, compared to rates of 5 to 8 per cent in western countries (Chu and Chi, 2008; Gu et al., 2007).

The low rate of institutionalization among elderly Chinese is attributed in part to a wide gap between the rising demands for institutional care and the limited capacity of existing facilities (Wong and Tang, 2006). In response, the central government called for an additional 3 million new elder care home beds to be built and a total of 1.8 million related jobs to be created during the period of China's *11th Five-Year Plan (2006–2010) for Socioeconomic Development*, but this added capacity is believed to be still less than half what is required (Xinhua, 2007). The current, *12th Five-Year Plan (2011–2015)* urges the addition of another 3.42 million beds in the next five years to reach a total of 6.6 million beds, with the goal of boosting capacity to at least thirty beds per 1,000 elders by 2015, up from roughly eighteen beds per 1,000 elders at the present (State Council, 2011).

Our recent research work in China provides a glimpse into the dramatic growth and character of elder care homes across Chinese cities (Feng et al., 2011). In Tianjin, for instance, there were only four

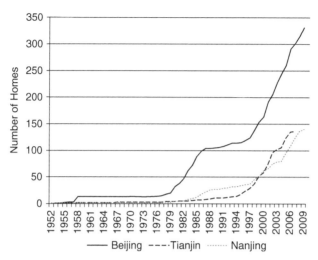

Figure 15.1 Growth of elder care homes in selected Chinese cities, 1952–2009.
Source: authors' calculations based on original research data.

facilities in 1980 (all government-run), but there were thirteen by 1990, sixty-eight by 2000 and 157 by 2009 (twenty government-run and 137 privately run). Similar rates of growth were also observed in Nanjing and Beijing (Figure 15.1). The private sector has dominated this growth. In Nanjing, government ownership dominated homes built before 1990 (96 per cent) but was increasingly rare in the 1990s (60 per cent) and diminished significantly in the 2000s (23 per cent), a pattern that was also observed in several other cities where data are available. In Nanjing, the average home now draws over 80 per cent of its operating revenues from private payments or other non-government sources, and this share increases sharply the more recent the establishment of the facility. The majority (85 per cent) of non-government owned homes receive ongoing per-bed subsidies from the government. The lack of clinical staff characterizes the majority of facilities that were studied, and most care staff in Nanjing facilities are rural migratory workers. There is considerable variability across homes in the case mix of residents in terms of functional dependence and acuity levels. The type of facilities cover a wide spectrum, ranging from 'mom-and-pop' style board-and-care homes (i.e., small homes typically owned and run by members of a family) and senior apartments providing little professional care (the majority)

Long-term care in China 417

to modern nursing homes equipped with nursing and medical care capacity (relatively few) – reminiscent of what US nursing homes were like back in the 1960s or 1970s, when hospital length of stay was longer and a post-acute industry had yet to develop. These findings portray the emergence and rapid growth of a nascent industry of institutional long-term care in urban China and a fundamental shift in institutional ownership, financing and clientele.

Government subsidies for private-sector homes are becoming increasingly common. In Nanjing, for instance, the municipal government provides financial inducements for new constructions to the amount of 2,000–4,000 yuan (roughly US$300–600) per new bed and an ongoing operating subsidy of 80 yuan (*c.* US$12) per occupied bed each month (Jiangsu News, 2010; Xinhua, 2009), but the amounts actually allocated may vary across districts within the city depending on local resources. In Beijing, the government currently provides a construction subsidy of between 8,000 and 16,000 yuan (*c.* US$1,250–2,500) per new bed and an operating subsidy of 100–200 yuan (*c.* US$15–30) per occupied bed for privately run facilities (Ministry of Civil Affairs and China National Committee on Ageing, 2010b). These amounts, especially the operating subsidies, are modest but since most residents are paying privately as well, these construction and operating inducements are clearly enough to have underpinned a lot of the observed growth. Thus far, however, there has been little regulatory oversight over the kinds of services and quality of care provided in this rapidly growing sector of long-term care facilities. We turn to these policy-relevant issues in the remainder of this chapter.

15.5 Policy engineering: the government's role in building long-term care services

The year 1999 marked a critical point in Chinese population ageing. That year, the proportion of China's older population aged 60 and over exceeded 10 per cent, which, according to international standards, marks the ageing phase of a population (State Council Information Office, 2006). That same year, the China National Committee on Ageing was established, which is responsible for coordinating national policy efforts in planning, developing and improving ageing services and now involves twenty-eight (initially twenty-six) ministerial-level government agencies. Since then, policy initiatives by Chinese central government have built momentum to spur the development of a system of social services for the elderly. The overall framework of this emerging system, as laid out in the central government's *12th Five-Year (2011– 2015) Plan* (State Council, 2011), can be characterized as three tiers of social support services for the aged: home-based care as the *foundation* (*jī chǔ*), community-based services as *backing* (*yī tuō*) and institutional care as *support* (*zhī chēng*).[2]

The Chinese government has always been actively promulgating home-based care as the primary pillar of long-term support of the elderly. As has always been the case, much of the care within an elder's home is informal care provided by family members, and for those who can afford it, supplemented by paid care. This policy stance is not surprising given the cultural mandate of filial piety and the lack of a public safety net in China. Thus, family caregivers will continue to shoulder the major responsibility of elder care in the foreseeable future, although their availability and ability are increasingly strained. Recognizing the growing needs for social care of the elderly, the Chinese government has begun to invest in the development of various community-based services for the aged, primarily in urban areas. These efforts are catalysed by a series of national policy directives and documents promulgated in the last decade, such as *Opinions on Promoting Urban Community Construction Nationwide* (Ministry of Civil Affairs, 2000b) and *Opinions on Strengthening and Improving Community Services* (State Council, 2006). The goal is to provide diversified and more convenient services to community residents, including the aged, and to improve the social service environment for them.

---

[2] It is interesting to note that the last tier of the social service system for the aged – institutional services – has always been emphasized and officially was termed as a *supplement* (*bǔ chōng*) instead of *support* (*zhī chēng*) in the previous, *11th Five Year (2006–2010) Plan for Socioeconomic Development* and in all major policy documents until 2011, including the 2006 *White Paper on the Development of China's Undertakings for the Aged* (State Council Information Office, 2006). This nuance could be significant, because the Chinese word *zhī chēng* conveys a much stronger sense of 'support' than the word *bǔ chōng*, the latter clearly denoting a peripheral role of 'support'. A personal communication from a key policy maker at the Ministry of Civil Affairs confirmed that this wording change does not reflect a real shift in policy direction or focus. Rather, it is more of a tactic in order to make a stronger case for requesting more funds for developing aged care services – in competition with many other government agencies – from the central government's budgets for the next five years.

Long-term care in China 419

In another major policy initiative, the Chinese government invested a total of 13.4 billion yuan (roughly US$2.1 billion) in the so-called 'Starlight Programme' to build community welfare service centres for seniors over a three-year period, 2001–4. By 2005, the programme helped to set up 32,000 'Starlight Senior Centres' nationwide which are intended to provide family visit, emergency aid, day care, health and healing services, and to organize recreational activities, benefiting over 30 million elderly people (State Council Information Office, 2006). However, no rigorous assessment of the short-term impact of this programme has been reported. The extent to which these community-based senior centres are built to serve the intended functions also remains unclear. Since 2005, partly due to dwindling financial input from the government, the 'Starlight Programme' has gradually lost momentum, raising questions about its long-term sustainability. To date, self-sustaining, community-based long-term services for the elderly have remained very limited and largely invisible except in a few large cities like Shanghai and Beijing.[3]

In contrast, the government has stepped up efforts to build institution-based elder care services by actively promoting the construction of senior citizens' lodging houses, homes for the aged and nursing homes to serve seniors with different financial and physical conditions, especially those who are frail, sick and disabled (State Council Information Office, 2006). This development has followed two separate tracks, leading to a dual system of institutional elder care – one that is directly invested, owned and managed by the government and the other which is market driven and developed, owned and run by the private sector. In cities, state-run social welfare institutions target elderly people who qualify as 'three nos'. In rural areas, government-subsidized homes for the elderly target those who are 'three nos' qualifying for 'five guarantees', namely guarantees for food, clothing, housing, medical care and burial expenses. Unlike

---

[3] The fate of the Starlight Programme is typical of many government-sponsored, large-scale projects in China: with strong political will and effective mobilization of resources, they can be physically built very quickly but leave much to be desired in terms of persistent and quality performance. In this particular case, more than funding disruption or anything else, the lack of a qualified workforce and a well-defined set of quality services tailoring to the care needs of community-dwelling elders is to blame for the fading of Starlight.

their predecessors in the planned economy era, which served exclusively childless elders and other state welfare recipients, however, all government-funded institutions now also take elders with families who must pay for their care out-of-pocket. In urban public facilities the majority of residents are private payers (Feng et al., 2011): in contrast, the vast majority of residents in rural facilities are still welfare recipients, just as they have always been (Wu et al., 2009; Zhang, 2011). In the meantime, the government has been actively encouraging the development of elder care homes by the private sector. This policy stance has been driven by several concerns. The first and foremost is a growing consensus among Chinese policy makers about the severe shortage of long-term care bed supply vis-à-vis escalating demand. Thus, building more beds – and quickly – to fill this perceived supply-demand gap becomes an immediate and high priority on the policy agenda. In the words of a central government official:

After assessing the current situation of aged care services, our strategic judgement is that we should focus on expanding the total volume of supply. This is what is needed the most right now. The core approach to achieving this is via encouraging the entry of private-sector capital . . . There used to be no rules regarding entry, because in the past all facilities were state-run welfare institutions. For private capital seeking entry into this sector, the bar should not be set too high now; that is, there should not be too many hurdles for entry. (Interview with official from the Ministry of Civil Affairs, 2011)

Second, Chinese policy makers have increasingly realized that it is imperative to reposition the government's role in the provision of social services for the elderly, from direct 'supplier and provider' of services to 'purchaser and regulator' of services. Traditionally, the government has assumed all these roles in a centrally planned economy, which has proved to be utterly ineffective and unproductive. A central government official has put it quite clearly:

From a macro, strategic perspective, we ought to encourage *guó tuì mín jìn*, that is, 'retreat of state functions and advancement of civil society engagement'. Our core principle is that we shall not become the direct supplier of aged care services, but rather, become the purchaser and regulator. The government should not directly build and manage such services. History has already proved that this is a mode that is of low efficiency and wasteful. (Interviews with official of the Ministry of Civil Affairs, 2011)

Long-term care in China   421

Thus, promotion of 'socialized' services is seen as an important reform of Chinese social welfare policy provision and management (Ministry of Civil Affairs, 2000a). In a broad sense, the government's call for increased private-sector involvement in the development of formal long-term care services for the elderly is analogous to the transition from a planned economy to a market economy, which has led to remarkable economic growth in China over the past thirty years. Guided by this strategic shift in policy making, a series of national policy directives have been issued, such as *Opinions on Accelerating Socialized Welfare Services* (Ministry of Civil Affairs, 2000a), *Opinions on Supporting Non-government Entities in the Development of Social Welfare Institutions* (Ministry of Civil Affairs, 2005) and *Opinions on Accelerating the Development of Social Services for the Aged* (China National Committee on Ageing, 2006), to speed up private-sector development of institutional social services for the aged. Various approaches are encouraged to mobilize social resources for this purpose, such as state-built and privately run, privately operated with government support, government subsidies, and services purchased by government (State Council Information Office, 2006). All of these policy documents urge preferential policy treatments, such as tax exemption, government subsidies for new and existing beds, land appropriation or leasing for new construction and reduced rates for utilities (water, electricity, gases, telephone services, etc.).[4] Some have explicitly encouraged people who are laid off or unemployed to open 'mom-and-pop' style elder care homes or adult day care facilities (China National Committee on Ageing, 2006). All these policy efforts are believed to have accelerated the growth spurt in long-term care facilities in China in the last decade, especially in the private sector, as documented above.[5]

---

[4] Although the national policy guideline urges local government authorities to put such stimulus measures in place, the actual form of incentives and number of subsidies available to private-sector facilities vary substantially from place to place depending on local needs and resources. Generally, these incentive structures are more common in the economically more developed provinces and municipalities on China's east coast than in inland regions.

[5] Interviews with government officials suggest that favourable and encouraging policy directives from the central government authority, commonly known in China as 'red-headed documents', literally – are widely seen as a necessary stimulus to attract private-sector investment which has spurred the rapid growth of long-term care facilities in recent years.

Accompanying the rise of institutional elder care, recent years have seen the emergence of voluntarily organized trade associations representing long-term care facilities in China. Most of these associations are locally based, but some have a national reach. A prominent example is the National Union for Long-Term Care, which was established in 2009 and currently has a membership of over 1,000 elder care service providers nationwide, mostly in the private sector (www.czlm.org). This organization is led by a vanguard long-term care provider group named Hetong, a non-government, not-for-profit organization founded in the city of Tianjin in 1995, which now operates seven long-term care facilities, a geriatric hospital, two vocational training schools and one institute authorized to appraise and certify occupational skills and qualifications for elder care workers. The Union serves as a platform to facilitate networking and information sharing among member organizations, promote professionalism in this rapidly expanding industry and to advocate for their collective interest via a variety of venues such as websites, trade journals and national forums. Naturally, these trade associations have a vested interest in government policies concerning social services for the aged. The rise of these voluntary trade associations is a reflection of the emergent civil society structure in China as a natural consequence of broad-scale privatization (Shang, 2001; Wong and Tang, 2006).

As this new sector of institutional long-term care services is emerging and expanding rapidly, the challenge of how to channel its development into an appropriate regulatory framework also arises. The remaining sections of this chapter are devoted to describing the regulatory structures and mechanisms currently in place with regard to the entry, registration, inspection and quality monitoring of long-term care facilities – at both the central and local government levels.

15.6 Regulatory oversight: central government perspectives

Under the jurisdiction of the State Council, the Ministry of Civil Affairs is responsible for domestic social and administrative affairs in China. It is the central government agency in charge of social welfare and services for the aged, disabled, veterans, and other special populations. Specifically, the national regulatory authority over aged care services rests with the Division of Social Welfare for the Elderly and Disabled, under the Ministry of Civil Affairs' Department of Social Welfare and

Long-term care in China

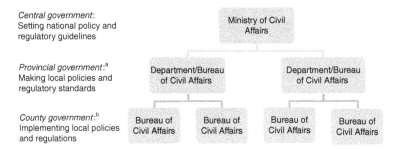

Figure 15.2 Administrative and regulatory structure of aged care services in China.
Source: Ministry of Civil Affairs of the People's Republic of China (http://www.mca.gov.cn/).
Notes:
[a] Currently, there are 33 provincial-level administrative units in China, including 22 Provinces, 5 Autonomous Regions, 4 Direct-controlled Municipalities (Beijing, Shanghai, Tianjin and Chongqing) and 2 Special Administrative Regions (Hong Kong and Macau).
[b] Currently, there are 2,858 county-level administrative units in China, including 1,464 counties, 855 municipal districts and 539 other county equivalents.

Charity Promotion. As is typical of the policy-making process in other areas in China, the Ministry of Civil Affairs sets national policies, regulatory guidelines and standards which are to be followed and implemented by provincial-level Departments (or Bureaus) of Civil Affairs. Then, this process trickles down locally to cities and counties within each province. The administrative and regulatory structure of aged care services in China is depicted in Figure 15.2.

At the national level only minimal standards currently exist with regard to the licensing and regulation of aged care service providers. In 1999, the Ministry of Civil Affairs released the *Provisional Measures for the Management of Social Welfare Institutions* (Ministry of Civil Affairs, 1999).[6] This is the first national policy effort aimed at formalizing the regulation of all types of social welfare institutions, including both government and privately run facilities serving the elderly, the

---

[6] The term 'provisional' to denote 'temporary' is common in the titles of Chinese regulatory documents and statutory laws even if the regulatory measure remains in place for quite a long time.

disabled, orphans or abandoned infants.[7] This regulation stipulates that county or higher-level civil affairs government agencies assume the regulatory authority for supervision, monitoring and inspection of all social welfare institutions within the local government jurisdiction. It provides broad outlines of the application and registration process including required procedures, qualifications and documentation of supporting materials in order to open an elder care facility. Once approved, registered and in operation, a facility should be inspected annually by the local authority. Towards the end of this regulation (Appendix Article No. 28), the following provision is offered: 'Those social welfare institutions which were already in operation before this regulation takes effect should file an application to the county or higher-level government agency of civil affairs within six months to obtain a *Certificate for Approval of Opening a Social Welfare Institution* pursuant to requirements set herein.' This suggests that up to this point some facilities had presumably operated without proper registration.[8] This set of regulatory measures is augmented by several concurrent or subsequent regulations which together form the regulatory framework currently in place, as further detailed below.

In simple terms, the current regulatory structure for long-term care facilities in China is underpinned by three major policy documents commonly known as 'Two *guī fàn*, One *biāo zhǔn*' by policy makers and providers.[9] Each of these national policy documents is briefly described below.

---

[7] Before 1999, only one broadly related policy document, entitled *Assessment Standard for State Social Welfare Institutions for the Aged*, was identified. Released in 1993, this Standard was applicable only to state social welfare institutions (for the elderly, children or persons with psychiatric/mental health conditions) managed by county or higher-level governments. The intended purpose was to evaluate applications by eligible institutions to become 'nationally recognized state social welfare institutions' (Class I or Class II), to be approved and named by the Ministry of Civil Affairs.

[8] Interviews with both central and local government officials confirm that even today an unknown (presumably small) number of privately run elder care facilities (most likely 'mom-and-pop' style homes) are operating without proper official registration.

[9] The two Chinese terms *guī fàn* and *biāo zhǔn* are almost interchangeable for the English word 'standard'. In this case, it is challenging to translate each into a different equivalent in English. It should also be noted that efforts are now underway to revise and update these three key policy documents. At the time of writing, however, they are the prevailing official guidelines.

15.6.1 Code for the Design of Buildings for Elderly Persons (guī fàn *no. 1*)

The *Code for Design of Buildings for Elderly Persons* (JGJ 122–99) was jointly promulgated by the Ministry of Construction (now renamed the Ministry of Housing and Urban-Rural Development) and the Ministry of Civil Affairs in 1999. Obviously, this Code addresses the 'bricks and mortar' of facilities housing the elderly. The guiding principle of the Code recognizes the need for building designs that meet older persons' special requirements for 'safety, hygiene and comfort' (Ministry of Construction and Ministry of Civil Affairs, 1999). The Code is applicable to newly built, expanded or renovated residential buildings and public facilities in cities and towns that cater exclusively to the elderly. The Code outlines detailed specifications on virtually all design features of a seniors building, ranging from the surrounding environment to net width of the doorway, usable area of the kitchen, position of grab bars in the bathroom and bed-size dimensions. It should be noted that virtually all specifications contained in the Code are framed as *desired* options 'under normal circumstances' or 'if conditions permit' (as indicated by the use of such words as 'should' or 'may'), rather than mandated requirements. Indeed, the word 'must', which denotes strict compliance in all circumstances, is mentioned only once throughout the Code, in Section 4.4.6, which stipulates that in elderly facilities equipped with elevators, 'the waiting area and space inside the elevator *must* ensure convenient access for wheelchairs and gurneys during emergencies'. As such, this leaves much room for discretion in actual implementation of the Code. This may be a significant issue particularly because most senior care facilities in Chinese cities are operated on leased properties which were built originally for various functions other than senior care (e.g., factories, schools, office buildings).[10]

---

[10] Relatively few senior care facilities in Chinese cities are newly built because of the difficulty in obtaining permits to lease land for this purpose. In virtually all major cities across China, land has become one of the most expensive commodities. The crowded nature of urban housing and the recent real estate boom have aggravated this situation.

15.6.2 Basic Standards for Social Welfare Institutions for the Elderly *(guī fàn no. 2)*

The *Basic Standards for Social Welfare Institutions for the Elderly* (MZ008-2001) was released by the Ministry of Civil Affairs in 2001. It stipulates the guiding principles, terminology, basic service standards, facility operations and 'bricks and mortar' requirements for facilities and equipment. Since this is the first ever national policy guideline and the only one currently in effect regarding the minimum standards for institutional elder care services, a brief description of its main features is warranted.

The Basic Standards were instituted in order to 'strengthen formalized management of social welfare institutions for the elderly, uphold the rights of the elderly, and promote the healthy development of social welfare services for the elderly' (Ministry of Civil Affairs, 2001). These Standards are applicable to social welfare institutions of all types which provide nursing, rehabilitative or custodial care for the elderly. The elderly refer to people 60 years old and over. The Standards distinguish three broad groups of elderly people according to their care needs: *zì lǐ* – referring to those who are independent or capable of self-care; *jiè zhù* – those who need assistive devices, such as handrails, canes, wheelchairs and lifters, for activities of daily living; and *jiè hù* – those who require nursing care and are dependent on others for activities of daily living.[11] Partially based on the types of residents served, all elder care facilities are classified into eight categories, as summarized in Table 15.1.[12]

After defining the terminology, the Basic Standards provide some guidelines on the basic standards for services provided in the various facilities. The services cover the following categories: meals, personal care, rehabilitation and psychosocial services. Personal care services vary depending on the type of residents. For *zì lǐ* elders, only a few housekeeping services are prescribed, such as 'room cleaning once a

---

[11] The Basic Standards do not provide further details regarding exactly what criteria are used to differentiate the three elderly groups.

[12] As is the case with the levels of care used to categorize the elderly into three broad groups, the Basic Standards stop short of providing more detailed criteria based on which facilities are classified into the eight types. Accordingly, there appears to be a great deal of ambiguity in the character of facilities across different categories.

Long-term care in China

Table 15.1 *Officially classified types of elder care facilities in China*

Type[a]	Definition/Description
1. Social Welfare Institutions for the Aged	Facilities funded and managed by the government that serve 'three no' elders and others (*zì lǐ*, *jiè zhù* or *jiè hù*),[b] providing daily living, recreational, rehabilitative and healthcare services.
2. Homes for the Aged	Facilities serving exclusively *zì lǐ* elders or those serving all elders (*zì lǐ*, *jiè zhù* or *jiè hù*), providing daily living, recreational, rehabilitative and healthcare services.
3. Hostels for the Elderly (Seniors Apartments)	Congregational, apartment-style senior homes, providing meals, housekeeping, recreation and healthcare services.
4. Homes for the Elderly Aided by Assistive Devices	Facilities serving exclusively *jiè zhù* elders, providing daily living, recreational, rehabilitative and healthcare services.
5. Nursing Homes	Facilities serving exclusively *jiè hù* elders, providing daily living, recreational, rehabilitative and healthcare services.
6. Homes for the Elderly in Rural Areas	Facilities located in rural townships, towns or villages serving 'three no', 'five guarantee' elders and others, providing daily living, recreational, rehabilitative and healthcare services.
7. Nurseries for the Elderly	Facilities providing short-term (day, boarding, or temporary) care for the elderly, including daily living, recreational, rehabilitative and healthcare services.
8. Elderly Service Centres	Community-based service centres for the elderly, providing a variety of services such as cultural and recreational activities, rehabilitative and healthcare, delivered on-site or at home.

Source: Ministry of Civil Affairs, 2001.

Note: [a] Currently, there is no information available on the distribution of existing facilities across the different facility types defined here.

[b] *zì lǐ* refers to residents who are independent or capable of self-care; *jiè zhù* refers to those who need assistive devices, such as handrails, canes, wheelchairs and lifters, for activities of daily living; *jiè hù* refers to those who require nursing care and are dependent on others for activities of daily living.

day, no flies, mosquitoes, mice, cockroaches or bugs in sight' and 'bathing twice a week in the summer, and once a week during other seasons'. There is also a vague requirement stating that 'service staff should be on duty twenty-four hours a day, individualized care should be implemented following certain procedures, and care plans should be adjusted depending on circumstances'. For *jiè zhù* elders, in addition to the housekeeping services for *zì lǐ* elders, a few additional items are specified, such as 'support residents by the arm to the bathroom' and 'prevalence of Degree-I pressure ulcers should be kept below 5 per cent and no Degree-II pressure ulcers should exist (except for patients suffering severe hypoproteinemia prior to admission, high-degree swelling of the whole body, late-stage cancer or cachexia)'. For *jiè hù* residents, a few extra requirements are added, such as providing basic dental care, delivering meals to rooms, feeding residents with food and water, assisting residents with toileting, and taking residents for outdoor activities for one hour every day (weather permitting).

Rehabilitative services are very sketchy and prescribed in very general terms, such as 'perform physical checkup for residents once a year' and 'make annual rehabilitative plans and organize residents for rehabilitative activities three times a week'. Psychosocial services are outlined in a similarly sketchy and vague manner, such as 'provide opportunities for able-bodied residents to participate voluntarily in public service or other activities, and organize healthy residents to attend one public service activity every quarter' or 'have a targeted "admission adjustment plan" to help newly admitted residents make a smooth transition through the early period of facility residence'. For either rehabilitative or psychosocial services, no distinction is made according to the type of residents or type of facilities. Regarding facility operations, the Basic Standards outline general requirements with regard to facility permit and naming rules, personnel and human resources, organizational management and documentation systems. Finally, some general, bricks and mortar requirements on the facilities and equipment are specified, consistent with the building Code described above.

15.6.3 National Occupational Standards for Old-Age Care Workers *(One* biāo zhǔn*)*

The *National Occupational Standards for Old-Age Care Workers* was drafted by the Ministry of Civil Affairs and approved and promulgated

Long-term care in China

by the Ministry of Labour and Social Security (now renamed the Ministry of Human Resources and Social Security) in 2002 (Ministry of Labour and Social Security, 2002).[13] The establishment of these standards was based on the *Classification of Occupations of the People's Republic of China*, which was released in 1999. This classification system has come about in response to a growing need to revamp the outdated job classification system developed and implemented during the era of China's planned economy. In a rapidly developing, market-oriented economy, Chinese occupational structures have undergone profound changes. Many new occupations and job categories have emerged that need to be recognized and classified. Accordingly, it is also necessary to define and update related standards for occupational skills and vocational qualifications. The category of 'old-age care workers' (*yǎng lǎo hù lǐ yuán*) is just one example of newly emerging job categories.

Under the official definition given in the *National Occupational Standards for Old-Age Workers*, an 'old-age care worker' is a person who 'provides daily living assistance or nursing for the elderly'. Four ranks of old-age care workers are classified according to experience, training and skills level: entry (equivalent to National Occupational Qualification Grade V), intermediate (Grade IV), advanced (Grade III) and technician (Grade II). The basic educational requirement for this occupation is middle school graduation (nine years of schooling). Basic training requirements include at least 180 hours for entry-level workers. At least 150 hours of additional training are required for promotion to the intermediate level, 120 additional hours to the advanced level and 90 additional hours to be a technician. All training is to be completed at a full-time vocational school. To receive a certificate at each level, an applicant needs to pass two separate exams, one concerning 'theoretical' knowledge (a closed exam for ninety minutes) and the other concerning actual operational skills (a test taking between 90 and 120 minutes). Evaluated on a 100-point scale, each exam covers six broad training components: daily living assistance; technical care; rehabilitative care; psychological care; training and supervising; and

---

[13] These standards are now under review and revision by an expert panel jointly convened by the Ministry of Civil Affairs and Ministry of Human Resources and Social Security. The 4th Draft Revision was discussed by the panel in March, 2011, and a finalized version is expected to be released in the future.

care management. To help vocational schools with their training programmes, a companion training guideline with more detailed instructions was published in 2006 by the Ministry of Labour and Social Security.

In summary, the regulations described above serve as national policy guidelines, and as such, they are necessarily limited in the extent to which they are directly implementable by local authorities, given substantial variations in socioeconomic development and the growth of formal long-term care services across provinces and municipalities. The real challenge, therefore, lies in how to operationalize and enforce these national regulatory guidelines locally.

15.7 Regulatory oversight: challenges for local implementation

Once national policy guidelines are issued and transmitted down the administrative hierarchy, local government authorities are responsible for following these guidelines to introduce and implement specific policy measures that best fit local conditions. Government subsidies and other forms of policy inducements are also formulated and implemented at the local level. In the spirit of the national guidelines described above, a wide variety of local policies and initiatives concerning the development of community-based or institutional elder care services have been put into place across provinces and municipalities in China (Ministry of Civil Affairs and China National Committee on Ageing, 2010a). In this section, we highlight major challenges local government policy makers face in the exercise of regulatory oversight over institutional elder care providers, using the city of Tianjin as an example and drawing on insights gained from recent interviews with officials of the Tianjin Municipal Bureau of Civil Affairs.

15.7.1 Current regulatory structure

The *Measures for the Management of Elder Care Institutions in Tianjin* took effect on 1 March 2007, following approval by the Municipal Government of Tianjin (Tianjin Municipal Government, 2007). It designates the Tianjin Municipal Bureau of Civil Affairs as the supervisory authority for all elder care facilities in the city. However, it is the subordinate department of civil affairs in each district or county that has the administrative responsibility of actually

Long-term care in China 431

monitoring and inspecting facilities within the local jurisdiction – a practice known as *shǔ dì guǎn lǐ*, literally meaning 'territorial management'.[14] It should be noted that many of the provisions contained in this supposedly local policy document largely mimic those outlined in the national policy guideline, *Provisional Measures for the Management of Social Welfare Institutions*, with few specific or quantifiable requirements stipulated. Indeed, only two places in the provisions mention numeric requirements. One concerns the staff-resident ratio: 'One direct-care worker should be available for no more than eight residents who are capable of self-care and no more than four residents who are not capable of self-care.' The other concerns the level of fines for violations of certain provisions.

According to the rules, a prospective elder care facility operator should meet all of the following requirements before filing an application: (1) if the applicant is an organization, that organization must possess the status of an independent legal entity; if the applicant is an individual, that individual must have full capacity for civil conduct; (2) the facility to be opened should fit the government's planning for aged care facility development; (3) the applicant should have assets commensurate with facility size; (4) there should be fixed facilities and service equipment commensurate with facility size, which should further comply with requirements set out in the *Code for Design of Buildings for Elderly Persons* as well as requirements for fire safety, public hygiene, heating and cooling systems; and (5) there should be administrative personnel, professional staff and direct-care workers commensurate with services rendered in the facility.

Upon approval of the application, the applicant should proceed to registration at the local (district/county) department of civil affairs. If the facility is non-government and not-for-profit in nature, then the registration should be filed with the local government agency in charge of licensing non-government, non-enterprise (*mín bàn fēi qǐ yè*) organizations. If the facility is government-run and not-for-profit, then the

---

[14] The same pattern of administration is followed by other provinces and municipalities in China. Generally, the provincial or municipal department of civil affairs is the authority that makes policies, but it is the county- (or district-, in municipalities like Beijing, Tianjin and Shanghai) level agency of civil affairs that actually implements those policies and assumes the responsibility of licensing and inspecting elder care facilities.

registration should be with the local government agency supervising all public-sector, non-enterprise organizations. Finally, if the facility is non-government and for-profit, registration should be sought at the local government office for commerce and taxation. Almost all private-sector elder care facilities currently in operation are registered as non-government, non-enterprise and not-for-profit providers because this status makes them eligible for government subsidies and other policy benefits which are not conferred to for-profit facilities. No facilities are allowed to take elders with infectious diseases or psychiatric/mental problems (such patients should be placed in specialized institutions or medical facilities).

Once registered and in operation, a facility is subject to annual inspection by multiple government agencies led by the Municipal Department of Social Organization Administration (which is affiliated with the Municipal Bureau of Civil Affairs) and its local office in each district or county. Other agencies include the department of health, the fire department and department of public safety. Depending on availability of resources and personnel, some districts or counties may conduct inspections more frequently. As yet, the current regulations do not contain any specific measures to monitor the quality of care supplied in elder care facilities.

15.7.2 Enforcement of regulatory rules is far from rigorous

Officials of the Tianjin Municipal Bureau of Civil Affairs acknowledge many practical difficulties in exercising regulatory oversight, due to the lack of specificity in current regulatory standards, and more importantly, due to inadequate capacity (including personnel and budget) for regulatory enforcement. Let us consider facility size, in terms of number of beds, as one criterion for licensure and market entry: neither the Ministry of Civil Affairs nor the Tianjin Municipal Bureau of Civil Affairs has specified the minimum number of beds in order for a facility to be registered and licensed. As a result, Tianjin Municipal officials noted, just a few years ago, quite a number of small-sized facilities (with twenty to thirty beds) were approved to operate. Led by the belief that small-sized facilities lack the necessary space, resources and personnel to deliver essential services, officials soon realized the need to raise the bar. Currently, the general requirement is at least fifty beds for facilities located in suburban counties

Long-term care in China 433

and 100 beds for those operating in urban districts.[15] The lack of regulatory capacity, such as a routine team of qualified personnel, is particularly notable. In the words of a municipal government official:

The problem is that right now a regulatory system, by the Ministry of Civil Affairs down to localities, has not yet been established. Suppose an elder care facility violates certain rules, it should be penalized according to provisions in the regulation. But with inadequate enforcement personnel how can you impose those penalties? In the end, although the regulations and laws are all well stated, their implementation is an issue. (Interview with official of the Tianjin Municipal Bureau of Civil Affairs, 2011)

Compliance with the required building code also appears to be a challenge. In Tianjin, as in other major cities across China, most elder care facilities are rented or leased facilities, retrofitted from residential buildings, factories or even school classrooms. Since there are certain limits to renovating existing building structures to meet the special requirements for senior care, an issue arises as to how many elder care facilities are up to or in substantial compliance with the mandated standards. In the eyes of officials in Tianjin, the answer is less than reassuring:

So, for these rented facilities the foremost concern is safety, particularly fire safety. Because the house was initially built not for elderly people, it doesn't conform to the *Code for Design of Buildings for Elderly Persons*. But this is the reality. If you don't renovate and use old buildings but rather build new ones, fewer new beds will be added . . .There is a big deficit [of beds]. There is a shortage of space. And now, the control over land use is very tight. (Interviews with official of the Tianjin Municipal Bureau of Civil Affairs, 2011)

As for facility staffing, officials in Tianjin noted that recruitment and retention are significant concerns. Direct-care workers in elder care facilities are poorly paid and inadequately trained. In current Tianjin elder care facilities almost 40 per cent of direct-care staff are laid-off workers from local factories and nearly 12 per cent are migrants from adjacent rural areas (Feng et al., 2012). National figures are difficult to come by, but even in the best possible estimate, less than one-third of front-line workers providing aged care services have received any professional training (Zhang, 2011).

---

[15] In one of the central districts of Tianjin where there is already a high density of facilities, an even higher requirement of at least 150 beds is currently in effect.

15.7.3 *The tension between conflicting policy goals*

Echoing the sentiment of central government policy makers, local officials of the Tianjin Municipal Bureau of Civil Affairs are keenly aware of the tension between potentially conflicting objectives of government policies, such as how to strike a balance between expediting the growth of long-term care services and bringing regulations up to speed. At the end of the day, however, it seems quite clear that growth has always trumped regulation on the policy agenda:

Generally speaking, this whole system of elder care, from facility construction and operation to the provision of services and regulation, is still at its early stage of development. As of now, development is the most urgent need, and management and regulation are not the focus yet. It is always said that development should go hand in hand with regulation, but now the issue of development is more important. (Interview with official of the Tianjin Municipal Bureau of Civil Affairs, 2011)

Another recent example illustrates the conflict of interest between different government agencies with regard to the allocation of land for building elder care facilities. The case involves a China-US joint venture which sought to build an elder care facility on a parcel of land located in a downtown district of Tianjin. The planned facility was intended to be non-enterprise and not-for-profit (thus entitled to tax exemption and other favourable policy treatments), and the application received approval by the Municipal Bureau of Civil Affairs.[16] However, since the planned building site is located in a block designated as an 'industrial development zone', only for-profit enterprises are permitted. In a letter to the applicant the local district government indicated disapproval of the plan by both its civil affairs and commerce departments. Considering the shortage and escalating cost of land, it is not entirely surprising that local government have little incentive to parcel out land to non-profit, non-governmental entities that do not provide tax revenue, as a local official put it clearly:

There are policy documents issued by the central government which stipulate favourable treatments in land allotment for non-profit elder care facilities, but

---

[16] According to the current *Measures for the Management of Elder Care Institutions in Tianjin*, a joint venture with foreign capital involved in building an elder care facility must seek approval by the Municipal Bureau of Civil Affairs and the Municipal Bureau of Commerce before proceeding for registration and licensure at the district level.

Long-term care in China 435

in reality it's not doable. For local government, the amount of GDP to be produced from every piece of its land has been carefully calculated. So a piece of land that is given away means a loss of GDP to the government. (Interview with official of the Tianjin Municipal Bureau of Civil Affairs, 2011)

The issues and challenges in regulatory oversight at a local level, as described here, are not unique to Tianjin. One must keep in mind that Tianjin is among the most developed municipalities in China and has experienced a dramatic growth of elder care facilities in the private sector over the last decade. The weaknesses and limitations of the current regulatory apparatus and capacity in Tianjin would be expected to be very similar, or even worse, in other areas across China.

15.8 Rising scandals and calls to strengthen regulatory oversight

Partly due to the lack of rigorous enforcement of regulatory oversight, scandals in Chinese long-term care facilities have already surfaced. Media exposés on two recent tragic incidents highlight this emerging concern poignantly. On 3 December 2008, a fire erupted in a privately run seniors apartment block in the city of Wenzhou, Zhejiang Province, killing seven elderly residents (Xinhua, 2008). It was later found that the doors of the building were locked when the fire broke out shortly after midnight, and that the facility had failed previous fire safety inspections – yet still remained in operation until the fire. In another scandal making national news, a nightshift caregiver of a privately run Senior Care Home in Zhengzhou, capital city of Henan Province, was caught on video on 30 May 2011 forcing a seventy-nine-year-old resident to drink his own urine (Xuyang, 2011). When the resident refused he was hit with a slipper and whipped with strips of cloth that were also used to tie him to his bed. Authorities later found many residents in the home were suffering from dementia and were often tied to their beds. These are just two examples and abuses, neglect, safety concerns and resident care problems may have gone unnoticed in many other facilities across the country, stressing the need for more rigorous and effective regulation and quality monitoring. Governments are increasingly at stake here, given the significant state and local investment in public-sector elder care facilities and also in the private sector through financial subsidies.

Prompted by rising concerns about scandals and mishaps of all sorts in elder care facilities, the Ministry of Civil Affairs issued a circular in 2009 urging all provincial/municipal government authorities to conduct a thorough inspection on the actual implementation of 'Two *guī fàn*, One *biāo zhǔn*' in local facilities (Ministry of Civil Affairs, 2010). Although the inspection form includes as many as eighty-seven items, each to be rated on a three-level Likert-type scale (complied, basically complied, failed), most of the items appear to be conceptual rather than quantifiable or operational, raising questions about the utility and effectiveness of the inspection.[17] The circular required that local authorities carry out this inspection once a year (between 10 October and 30 November) and transmit summary inspection results to the Ministry (by 15 December). This effort seems to resemble many of the large-scale, campaign-style policy initiatives frequently seen in China. Whether this effort and its related instrument will be refined and institutionalized to have a lasting impact remains to be seen.

Scandals aside, currently there is little publicly available information about the characteristics of and quality of care in existing long-term care facilities to inform consumer choices. Because public financing of private-sector long-term care facilities is still quite limited, there is little incentive for the government to invest in systematically collecting such information and making it transparent. As a result, the burden of information gathering is entirely on the elderly and their family members. Typically, it takes multiple visits to a number of facilities before a final choice is made. A few cities (e.g., Beijing; Wuhan, Hubei Province; and Qingdao, Shandong Province) have in recent years experimented with a system of star-rating local elder care facilities similar to that used for hotel rankings (Ministry of Civil Affairs and China National Committee on Ageing, 2010c), but participation in the system is

---

[17] By and large, the eighty-seven items included on the inspection form reflect a mere breakdown of major provisions as stipulated in the three national regulatory policy documents, the 'Two *guī fàn*, One *biāo zhǔn*'. On many items, especially those other than 'bricks-and-mortar' requirements, what actually constitutes 'complied', 'basically complied' or 'failed' remains ambiguous. For example, it is not clear how to determine compliance on the requirement that a facility 'have a targeted "admission adjustment plan" to help newly admitted residents make a smooth transition through the early period of facility residence'. There also is a notable lack of quality of care indicators on the inspection list. Furthermore, at the local level, it is not known who makes up the inspection team and whether the inspection items have been interpreted in a consistent manner across localities.

Long-term care in China 437

voluntary and neither the validity nor the impact of the system has been evaluated.

15.9 Building an information infrastructure

Since formal long-term care in China is still in its early stage of development, an overly ambitious or heavy-handed approach to regulation may not be advisable, for two reasons. First, it can be too costly to be financially feasible or appealing to policy makers. Second, it may have the unintended effect of stifling private-sector initiatives to further the growth of the industry (Feng, 2011). Instead, a well calibrated, lighter approach, informed by sound and credible information, will provide a crucial launching point. This calls for the building of an information infrastructure to foster an evidence-based approach to policy making, quality improvements and regulation. It entails the periodic collection of good-quality information on long-term care facilities and their residents. In the US, all Medicare/Medicaid certified nursing homes are mandated to report both facility- and resident-level data electronically and on a regular basis (Mor, 2005). This is achieved through a uniform survey instrument for annual facility inspections and a standardized resident-level assessment instrument (reported upon admission, and at least quarterly thereafter, for all residents in a facility). It will take time and substantial resources to build a similar infrastructure in China. Chinese policy makers should consider launching a demonstration project in a few advanced provinces or major cities to pilot a 'reduced' form of an online information gathering system, following a two-step strategy. As an initial step, it would be easier to start building a facility-level data collection system. All prospective and existing facilities participating in the demonstration would be mandated by the local government authority to report some basic facility-level information (e.g., ownership, size, services provided, staffing levels and mix, and aggregate health conditions of current residents, etc.) on a regular basis (e.g., once a year). Facilitated by a web-based data reporting and retrieval system, information on all individual facilities could be made available to both the central government authority and local regulatory agencies on a timely and ongoing basis. With this type of information, the government would be able to implement targeted monitoring and interventions focusing on a small number of facilities where problems are most likely to occur (for example, facilities that house much sicker than average patients yet have much lower than average staffing levels).[18] In the second step, a similar pilot programme could be initiated to pilot a resident-level assessment instrument designed to garner key information on care processes and outcomes. In the long run, the ultimate goal of these demonstrations, if successfully implemented, is to build a comprehensive data system for long-term care facilities across the country.

15.10 Conclusion

China's population is ageing rapidly and pressures are building to grow formal long-term care services as a policy. In recent years, Chinese governments at all levels have stepped up efforts toward building a long-term care system for the elderly. Chinese policy makers envision a three-tiered elder care system which consists of in-home care as the primary pillar, community-based services as the second pillar, and institutional care as the last pillar. Yet, current policy initiatives and priorities seem to be tilting toward increasing the stock of long-term care facility beds more rapidly in years to come. As such, an 'institutional bias' is set to work its way into the nation's fledgling long-term care system right from the beginning. While home and community-based services in China remain spotty and have a long way to go to define their niche in shaping China's long-term care landscape, a booming industry of residential care facilities is already shaping up across the country. The growth of this industry is particularly fast in urban areas and concentrated in the private sector.

Currently, there is little rigorous regulatory oversight for this rapidly developing sector of institutional elder care, partly resulting from policy makers' zealous pursuit of increasing the number of beds more quickly in order to fill a widely perceived gap between overwhelming demands for long-term care and limited bed capacity. In addition, existing regulations focus on structure and do not explicitly consider quality of care issues. The obstacles and challenges for effective regulation of aged care services, such as conflicting policy objectives, fragmentation of the

---

[18] It is encouraging that the Ministry of Civil Affairs has recently embarked on pilot testing a facility-level information system, though the interest now is focused on gauging the information needs of individual facilities.

regulatory system, inoperable regulatory policy and lack of capacity for regulatory enforcement, are also seen in the regulation of the country's medical care and health services (Wang et al., 2007), which have a higher priority than long-term care services on the policy agenda, but still leaves much to be desired. This notwithstanding, it is imperative for Chinese policy makers to institute a formalized regulatory structure as soon as possible. To this end, it is essential to build an ongoing and transparent information infrastructure in order to enhance regulatory oversight and quality monitoring in Chinese residential long-term care facilities.

References

Banister, J. (1987). *China's Changing Population.* Stanford University Press.

Chen, S. (1996). *Social Policy of the Economic State and Community Care in Chinese Culture: Aging, Family, Urban Change, and the Socialist Welfare Pluralism.* Brookfield, VT: Avebury.

China National Committee on Ageing (2006). *Opinions on Accelerating the Development of Social Services for the Aged* (in Chinese). Beijing.

Chow, N. (1999). Diminishing filial piety and the changing role and status of the elders in Hong Kong. *Hallym International Journal of Aging*, 1(1): 67–77.

Chu, L. W. and Chi. I. (2008). Nursing homes in China. *Journal of American Medical Directors Association*, 9(4): 237–43.

Croll, E. J. (1999). Social welfare reform: trends and tensions. *The China Quarterly*, 159: 684–99.

Davis, D. S. (1993). Financial security of urban retirees. *Journal of Cross-Cultural Gerontology*, 8: 179–96.

Fan, C. C. (2008). *China on the Move: Migration, the State, and the Household.* London and New York: Routledge.

Fan, M. (2006). In China, aging in the care of strangers: one-child policy changes tradition. *Washington Post*, p. A01.

Feng, Z. (2011). Charting an inevitable course: building institutional long-term care for a rapidly aging population in China. *China Health Review*, 2(2): 2–5.

Feng, Z., Zhan, H. J., Feng, X., Liu, C., Sun, M. and Mor, V. (2011). An industry in the making: the emergence of institutional elder care in urban China. *Journal of American Geriatrics Society*, 59(4): 738–44.

Feng, Z., Zhan, H. J., Guan, X., Feng, X., Liu, C. and Mor, V. (2012). The rise of long-term care facilities in urban China: emerging issues of access disparities (in Chinese). *Population and Development* 18(6): 16–23.

Flaherty, J. H., Liu, M. L., Ding, L., Dong, B., Ding, Q., Li, X. and Xiao, S. (2007). China: the aging giant. *Journal of American Geriatrics Society*, 55(8): 1,295–300.

Gu, D., Dupre, M. E. and Liu, G. (2007). Characteristics of the institutionalized and community-residing oldest-old in China. *Social Science & Medicine*, 64(4): 871–83.

Gu, S. and Liang, J. (2000). China: population aging and old age support. In V. L. Bengtson, K. Kim, G. C. Myers and K. Eun (eds.), *Aging in East and West: Families, States, and the Elderly*. New York: Springer, pp. 59–93.

Guan, X., Zhan, H. J. and Liu, G. (2007). Institutional and individual autonomy: investigating predictors of attitudes toward institutional care in China. *International Journal of Aging and Human Development*, 64(1): 83–107.

Harwood, R. H., Sayer, A. A. and Hirschfeld, M. (2004). Current and future worldwide prevalence of dependency, its relationship to total population, and dependency ratios. *Bulletin of the World Health Organization*, 82(4): 251–8.

Haub, C. (2011). *China Releases First 2010 Census Results*. Washington, DC: Population Reference Bureau.

Ikels, C. (1989). Becoming a human being in theory and practice: Chinese views of human development. In D. I. Kertzer and K. W. Schaie (eds.), *Age Structuring in Comparative Perspective*. Hillsdale, NJ: L. Erlbaum Associates, pp. 109–34.

   (1993). Chinese kinship and the state: shaping of policy for the elderly. In G. Maddox and M. P. Lawton (eds.), *Annual Review of Gerontology and Geriatrics*. New York: Springer, pp. 123–46.

Jiang, L. (1995). Changing kinship structure and its implications for old-age support in urban and rural China. *Population Studies*, 49(1): 127–45.

Jiangsu News (2010). Subsidies of 80 yuan per resident per month to non-government owned elder care homes (in Chinese). Available at: http://jsnews.jschina.com.cn/nj/201003/t346244.shtml. Accessed 18 September 2010.

Kinsella, K. and He, W. (2009). *An Aging World: 2008*. International Population Reports (P95/09–1). Washington, DC: US Census Bureau.

Lam, T. P., Chi, I., Piterman, L., Lam, C. and Lauder. I. (1998). Community attitudes toward living arrangements between the elderly and their adult children in Hong Kong. *Journal of Cross Cultural Gerontology*, 13(3): 215–28.

Lee, C. K. (1995). Engendering the worlds of labor: women workers, labor markets, and production politics in the south China economic miracle. *American Sociological Review*, 60(3): 378–97.

Levin, D. (2008). A tradition under stress: who will care for the nation's elders? *AARP Bulletin*. Available at: www.aarp.org/politics-society/

Long-term care in China 441

around-the-globe/info-07-2008/aging_in_china_a_tradition_under_stress. html. Accessed 2 September 2013.

Liang, Z. (2001). The age of migration in China. *Population and Development Review*, 27(3): 499–524.

Logan, J. R., Bian, F. and Bian, Y. (1998). Tradition and change in the urban Chinese family: the case of living arrangements. *Social Forces*, 76(3): 851–82.

Ministry of Civil Affairs (1999). *Provisional Measures for the Management of Social Welfare Institutions* (in Chinese). Beijing: Ministry of Civil Affairs.

(2001). *Basic Standards for Social Welfare Institutions for the Elderly (MZ008-2001)* (in Chinese). Beijing: Ministry of Civil Affairs.

(2000a). *Opinions on Accelerating Socialized Welfare Services* (in Chinese). 13 February. Beijing: Ministry of Civil Affairs.

(2000b). *Opinions on Promoting Urban Community Construction Nationwide* (in Chinese). 3 November. Beijing: Ministry of Civil Affairs.

(2005). *Opinions on Supporting Non-government Entities in the Development of Social Welfare Institutions* (in Chinese). 16 November. Beijing: Ministry of Civil Affairs.

(2010). Circular on conducting inspections on the implementation of 'Two *guī fàn*, One *biāo zhǔn*' in aged care institutions (issued: 10 September 2009). In Ministry of Civil Affairs and China National Committee on Ageing (eds.), *Policy Documents on the Standardization of Aged Care Services Nationwide: A Collection* (in Chinese). Beijing: China Society Publishing House.

Ministry of Civil Affairs and China National Committee on Ageing (2010a). *Basic Situation of Aged Care Services Nationwide: A Collection* (in Chinese). Beijing: China Society Publishing House.

(2010b). *Policy Documents on Aged Care Services Nationwide: A Collection* (in Chinese). Beijing: China Society Publishing House.

(2010c). *Policy Documents on the Standardization of Aged Care Services Nationwide: A Collection* (in Chinese). Beijing: China Society Publishing House.

Ministry of Construction and Ministry of Civil Affairs (1999). *The Code for Design of Buildings for Elderly Persons (JGJ 122–99)* (in Chinese). 1 October. Beijing.

Ministry of Labour and Social Security (2002). *National Occupational Standards for Old-Age Care Workers* (in Chinese). 11 February. Beijing.

Mor, V. (2005). Improving the quality of long-term care with better information. *The Milbank Quarterly*, 83(3): 333–64.

PRB (2011). *2011 World Population Data Sheet*. Washington, DC: Population Reference Bureau.

Shang, X. (2001). Moving toward a multi-level and multi-pillar system: changes in institutional care in two Chinese cities. *Journal of Social Policy*, 30(2): 259–81.

Sher, A. E. (1984). *Aging in Post-Mao China: The Politics of Veneration.* Boulder: Westview Press.

State Council (2011). *The 12th Five-Year Plan for the Development of Social Services for the Aged (2011–2015)* (in Chinese). Beijing.

(2006). *Opinions on Strengthening and Improving Community Services* (in Chinese). 9 April. Beijing.

State Council Information Office (2006). China publishes a White Paper on its undertakings for the aged. Available at: www.china.org.cn/english/China/191990.htm. Accessed 21 August 2013.

Tianjin Municipal Government (2007). *Measures for the Management of Elder Care Institutions in Tianjin* (in Chinese). Tianjin.

Treas, J. (1977). Family support systems for the aged: some social and demographic considerations. *The Gerontologist*, 17(6): 486–91.

United Nations (2007). *World Population Prospects: The 2006 Revision.* New York: Population Division of the Department of Economic and Social Affairs of the United Nations Secretariat.

Wang, H., Ge, Y., Gong, S. and Mem, M. (2007). *Regulating Medical Services in China.* New York: Milbank Memorial Fund.

Wong, L. and Tang, J. (2006). Non-state care homes for older people as third sector organisations in China's transitional welfare economy. *Journal of Social Policy*, 35(2): 229–46.

Wu, B., Carter, M. W., Goins, R. T. and Cheng, C. (2005). Emerging services for community-based long-term care in urban China: a systematic analysis of Shanghai's community-based agencies. *Journal of Aging and Social Policy*, 17(4): 37–60.

Wu, B., Mao, Z. and Xu, Q. (2008). Institutional care for elders in rural China. *Journal of Aging and Social Policy*, 20(2): 218–39.

Wu, B., Mao, Z. F. and Zhong, R. (2009). Long-term care arrangements in rural China: review of recent developments. *Journal of American Medical Directors Association*, 10(7): 472–7.

Xinhua (2005). Beijing encourages private nursing homes. Available at: www.china.org.cn/english/Life/126277.htm. Accessed 2005.

(2007). More personnel needed in Chinese nursing homes. Available at: http://english.peopledaily.com.cn/200701/23/eng20070123_344000.html. Accessed 2007.

(2008). Fire killed 7 in a Wenzhou senior apartment alleged in operation illegally (in Chinese). Available at: http://news.xinhuanet.com/society/2008-12/04/content_10454544.htm. Accessed 2008.

(2009). Converting a community hospital into elderly rehab centre should not be that difficult (in Chinese). Available at: www.js.xinhuanet.com/xin_wen_zhong_xin/2009-08/28/content_17527859.htm. Accessed 2009.

(2011). Vast 'empty nests', disabled aging population challenging China's social network. Available at: http://news.xinhuanet.com/english2010/china/2011-03/02/c_13756275.htm. Accessed 2011.

Xuyang, J. (2011). Age old issues. Available at: http://special.globaltimes.cn/2011-06/663228.html. Accessed 2011.

Zeng, Y. (1986). Changes in family structure in China: a simulation study. *Population and Development Review*, 12(4): 675–703.

Zhan, H. J. (2002). Chinese care giving burden and the future burden of elder care in life-course perspective. *International Journal of Aging and Human Development*, 54(4): 267–90.

(2004). Willingness and expectations: intergenerational differences in attitudes toward filial responsibility in China. *Marriage and Family Review*, 36(1/2): 175–200.

Zhan, H., Liu, G. and Guan, X. (2006a). Willingness and availability: explaining new attitudes toward institutional elder care among Chinese elderly parents and their adult children. *The Journal of Aging Studies*, 20(3): 279–90.

Zhan, H. J., Feng, X. and Luo, B. (2008). Placing elderly parents in institutions in urban China: a reinterpretation of filial piety. *Research on Aging*, 30(5): 543–71.

Zhan, H. J., Feng, Z., Chen, Z. and Feng, X. (2011). The role of the family in institutional long term care – cultural management of filial piety in China. *International Journal of Social Welfare*, 20: S121–S134.

Zhan, H. J., Liu, G., Guan, X. and Bai, H. G. (2006b). Recent developments in institutional elder care in China: changing concepts and attitudes. *Journal of Aging and Social Policy*, 18(2): 85–108.

Zhan, H. J. and Montgomery, R. J. V. (2003). Gender and elder care in China: the influence of filial piety and structural constraints. *Gender and Society*, 17(2): 209–29.

Zhang, H. (2007). Who will care for our parents? Changing boundaries of family and public roles in providing care for the aged in urban China. *Care Management Journals*, 8(1): 39–46.

Zhang, K. (2011). News release on the National Study of Disability and Functional Limitations of the Elderly. 1 March. Beijing: China National Committee on Ageing.

PART VI

Conclusion

16 Regulating quality of long-term care – what have we learned?

TIZIANA LEONE, ANNA MARESSO AND VINCENT MOR

16.1 Introduction

In this chapter we summarize key findings from the fourteen case studies, following the themes set out in Chapter 1. In particular, we aim to highlight features of the regulatory functions operating in each country, namely what type of long-term care regulatory system is in place (e.g., data-oriented or professionally oriented), its level of centralization or decentralization and, most importantly, whether any information on quality is collected and, if so, how it is used in efforts to assure and improve long-term care quality.

16.2 Long-term care regulatory approaches

The variation in approach to long-term care quality regulation characterized in the chapters of this book makes it very challenging to develop a coherent yet concise system to classify the different approaches that countries have adopted. We have attempted to classify the countries by broad regulatory approach (Table 16.1) based on the general characteristics that they share. We understand that the classifications may not be a 'snug' fit for each of the different systems we've proposed. However, the classification scheme offers a reasonably close account of the streams of regulations and quality assurance processes found in the countries represented in this book. One of the most striking things to emerge from our comparative work is that the Austrian, German, Japanese and Swiss approaches to specifying the educational levels, training and even staff certification requirements for their long-term care workforces underpins the regulatory framework operating in these countries. From our perspective, these governments cede the main responsibility for upholding standards to professional and/or provider organizations. Government sees itself as a partner in assuring quality.

447

Table 16.1 *Classification of countries by broad regulatory approach*

Regulatory Approach	Associated country characteristics			
Professionalism-based regulatory system	**Austria** Professional organizations participate in formulating regulations. State variation includes long-term care nurses and geriatric aides	**Germany** Expert nursing standards required of all nursing staff	**Japan** National qualification of 'certified care worker' established	**Switzerland** Nursing staff professional qualifications. Professional and provider organizations assume responsibility for identifying standards for quality assurance
Inspection-based regulatory system	**Australia** Network of regional inspectors for random or periodical inspections	**England** Focused inspections: intelligence-based approach with qualitative/quantitative data on providers' risk of non-compliance information	**The Netherlands** Effective enforcement of the quality of health services (including long-term care), prevention measures and medical products	**Spain (Catalonia)** Random and confidential annual inspections by the Catalan Social Services Department
Data measurement/public reporting regulatory system	**Canada** interRai[a] Instruments covering both home care and nursing	**Finland** interRai, voluntary self-auditing methods for both	**New Zealand** HealthCERT website with information on facilities. Nationally administered	**USA** RAI Minimum Data Set – Nursing Home public reporting website

| | homes. Data are used for national statistical reporting on nursing homes across the country | nursing homes and home care | consumer surveys; no public reporting but interRai assessments required |
| Developing long-term care regulatory systems | South Korea Minimum national standards are in place, with inspections designed to monitor compliance. | China National guidelines and standards on structural elements of residential facilities with limited inspection – but little regulation of home care. | |

Source: compiled by authors.

Notes: [a] interRAI assessment instruments are comprehensive clinical assessment tools used as part of normal clinical practice to assess medical, psychosocial and environmental aspects of a person's functioning (www.interrai.org).

This approach is quite distinct from that of the more empirical, inspection-based approaches in place in Australia, England, the Netherlands and Spain, which focus much more on government authorities monitoring providers' compliance with statutorily defined regulations. It is even more different from the inspection-oriented systems in countries that have added a data-intensive quality measurement and public reporting approach, as is in place in Canada, Finland, New Zealand and the US. With their relatively newer long-term care systems, we've classified South Korea and China as having 'developing' regulatory approaches. Time will tell whether they will more naturally fall into any of the other three broad categories that we have created to classify the different approaches countries have adopted.

Table 16.1 presents the country-specific basis for classifying each of the countries represented in the book into one of the four general regulatory classification schemes. The paragraphs which follow provide a conceptual framework for each of these four types of systems and how they differ from one another in the regulatory philosophy that seems to underpin them.

Professionalism-based systems: we include in this category those regulatory systems that make professional development and control over the regulatory standards of what constitutes acceptable care and even 'self-policing', a primary feature of the regulatory approach. In these countries the state works in collaboration with professional associations to define standards, expectations and minimums of educational attainment that stipulate who can work in these settings or with this population and who cannot. This approach could signify that these societies have placed great trust in the professions to police their own, and to monitor adherence to standards, thereby assuring quality even for workers that historically were less professionally trained. Indeed, in these countries the social institutions of the professions are acknowledged to have unique expertise which the state cannot and should not replicate and therefore the state relies upon this expertise and the professions' commitment to their training and codes of ethical practice to assure the quality of care provided to the frail elderly population.

Professionalization of long-term care has been evolving in Austria, Germany and Japan over the last two decades. In particular, in Germany quality requirements address nursing staff through the introduction of Expert Nursing Standards which cover nurses working in all areas of the health sector. Although these are difficult to implement in long-term care

Regulating quality of long-term care – what have we learned? 451

settings because quality standards are not fully understood, there is evidence of a growing sensitivity to this issue through an increasing awareness of the lack of professional skills among long-term care staff and the critical need to remedy this situation. In Japan, a great deal of attention has been given to the professionalization of care. As far back as 1987, the Social Affairs Bureau decided to establish the national qualification of 'certified care worker' with the specific goal of professionalizing nursing home staff and home care helpers. These long-term care workers work alongside qualified nurses in both nursing home and home care settings. Although more recent, in Austria professional organizations are considered when it comes to the preparation of laws or other regulations, and they make themselves heard and are proactive in the formation of legislation and regulations enacted pursuant to these laws (e.g., the Federation of Austrian Care Homes was heavily involved in the development of the National Quality Certificate). Switzerland's long-term care regulatory system also is characterized mainly by the professionalization of nursing staff and long-term carers. In particular, licensing procedures rely heavily on stipulating the number of nursing staff and their respective qualifications as well as retraining head nurses, nursing staff and nursing home directors in new standards and requirements.

However, the importance of professional groups is not limited to the group of countries we have identified here. For example, although Canada's key regulatory feature is the data measurement of outcomes and standards, professional associations representing nursing homes as well as home care providers have played an important role in quality improvement, including through annual conferences that include quality as a focus, educational programmes, management of inter-RAI assessment data (in home care), the development of other self-assessment surveys and the launching of organizational achievement awards in quality improvement. The difference, however, can be seen in the extent to which the government in Canada is driving the quality improvement focus versus the formalized structure of the professions as distinct from providers' 'trade' organizations.

Inspection-based approaches: the regulatory, inspection-oriented approach is characterized by government assuming the primary role of rule making and ongoing inspection to insure that rules are being adhered to by the providers of long-term care services. Obviously, in all countries it is the province of the government to establish regulations pursuant to the laws that are passed governing long-term care services.

In these countries, while society appears to trust the government to manage this process, there is much less confidence in the professions to 'get it right' and look out for the needs of the frail who are in need, much less the providers of care who are viewed as only interested in providing the minimum care. This is why the need for inspection and close oversight of providers is stressed. Even if society does not trust government, other social institutions like the professions have chosen not to engage in the world of long-term care even though they may run the acute medical care system. That is to say, while society may cede considerable authority and discretion over what constitutes quality of care in the operation of hospitals and primary care, no such implicit trust of long-term care service agencies exists.

The countries we have categorized within this group have strong inspection-based regimes. Australia's system is based on inspections, starting with the accreditation process. Accreditation is not a one-off event; rather, repeated inspections are carried out on an unannounced basis as well. Monitoring is undertaken by the Department of Health through a network of regional officers who can resort to sanctions if necessary. In England, inspections can be scheduled, responsive or focused on particular themes of care problems and are almost always unannounced. Most inspections are focused on a particular area rather than being comprehensive. The reforms conducted in the last few years (some of which were prompted by scandals over poor care in residential facilities) have meant that the long-term care regulatory system has changed substantially and the current system is entering a phase of stabilization. The Dutch have a very well-developed regulatory framework; inspections in the Dutch long-term care system are undertaken by the Healthcare Inspectorate, which uses a series of data collection instruments to guide the process and phased inspection processes, including phased supervision; investigation of incidents; monitoring based on thematic areas of problems; and enforcement measures. In Spain, the inspection system varies across the regions, which have to plan, coordinate and allocate their resources and take charge of such areas as registration and control of providers, inspection and evaluation. In the Catalan system, which is used as an example, legislation requires random and confidential annual inspections by the Catalan Social Services Department. Inspections are usually conducted annually with no warning and inspectors must be given access to all areas of the elder care home.

Data measurement and public reporting-based approaches: we include in this group those countries that have emphasised standardization and data reporting as key features of their system. Consumer-based approaches, as well as market competition, characterize many of the countries in this group. Obviously, in all cases, these data-intensive and market competition approaches are built on top of standard regulatory-based systems with licensing, inspections and complaints investigation.

The USA has been at the forefront of public reporting. Using the RAI Minimum Data Set (MDS),[1] the Nursing Home Compare website reports information on a range of MDS-based assessment measures for short- and long-stay nursing home residents. Recently, a five-star rating system has been added which integrates rankings based upon inspection results as well as staffing levels with the MDS-based quality measures. In Switzerland, despite the general lack of standards within the long-term care sector, some of the Swiss cantons seem to have started using RAI assessment tools in nursing homes (RAI-Nursing Home) and in home care (RAI-Home Care). While these are not publicly reported at present, they are used as the basis for multi-institution quality improvement systems. Canada increasingly has been relying on a Resident Assessment Instrument, with Ontario having the broadest array of uses and is the Province with the most experience using these instruments for care planning, comparative reporting and organizational and programme care planning in the nursing home and home care context. However, no patient survey detailing consumer experience is systematically available as yet. The last country in this group, New Zealand, at least in theory, has a consumer-choice-based system founded on a number of factors, including quality and price. However, in the residential care sector, it is most likely that the elderly might choose their preferred facility according to where the service is located (i.e., vicinity to relatives) rather than based on publicly reported quality information. A national survey with consumer experiences is available but it is not standardized, nor is it publicly available. However, there are plans in the future to address both issues.

Developing regulatory systems: the countries included in this group are characterized by a rapidly growing demand for long-term care as a result

---

[1] The MDS is a Resident Assessment Instrument (RAI) which is required in all US nursing homes in order to ensure that a resident's care plan is based upon a comprehensive assessment of their needs.

of major demographic and cultural changes in the organization of familial responsibilities and the dearth of social institutions or structures to address these needs. In China, society and government are still struggling with their approach to providing and assuring quality of services in the acute and ambulatory healthcare system. For example, China is grappling with the rising prevalence of long-term care needs well before other western societies had to do so relative to the emergence of a well-functioning and regulated acute healthcare system. China is experiencing a booming private long-term care industry without much regulation. While guidelines and directives have been issued from the central government, provincial authorities are loathe to enforce quality standards since they worry that targets for building new elder care home beds could be missed. The key issue remains the uncontrolled growth of the long-term care sector. Policy makers seem to be more interested in structural investment (i.e., increasing the stock of long-term care beds) rather than regulating facilities. South Korea, like China, has seen the sector grow rapidly to the extent that the current over-supply of long-term care providers is presenting concerns about maintaining quality levels in a very competitive market that prefers to use financial incentives (reduced co-payments) above other inducements to recruit potential service users.

16.3 Regulatory centralization or decentralization

Another major differentiation that we were able to discern in our review of the fourteen country cases included in the book is the extent to which the regulatory function is centralized or decentralized. We consider centralization vs. decentralization both with respect to geo-political boundaries within the country and the level of local discretion available in interpreting regulatory provisions regardless of whether they are nationally or regionally standardized. Most countries have different levels of government at which different functions are undertaken to assure a smoothly functioning and regulated economy and society. Indeed, almost all of the contributing authors in the case studies had difficulty integrating the somewhat different approaches that different geo-political units within their countries employ in regulating long-term care services. Some chose to focus on one region, province or area, occasionally contrasting the chosen region's approach with the country as a whole.

Table 16.2 provides a snapshot of how regulatory functions are either centralized or decentralized in the fourteen countries in our sample. By

Table 16.2 *Centralization and decentralization in the regulation of public long-term care*

	Country	Responsibility for Licensure/ Registration of facilities	Responsibility for Inspection/Quality monitoring
Professionalism based regulatory systems	Austria	*Residential care:* De-centralized to federal states (*Länder*) and municipalities based on 'Needs and Development Plans' *Home care:* De-centralized to the states (*Länder*)	*Residential care:* De-centralized to the states or counties. At the national level care homes may apply voluntarily for a third-party audit to acquire the 'National Quality Certificate' (NQZ) *Home care*: De-centralized to the states (*Länder*)
	Germany	*Residential care and home care:* De-centralized. Contracts between providers and statutory health care funds/long-term care funds in the federal state (*Länder*) of location	*Residential care*: De-centralized. Medical Review Boards at the state level (*Länder*), communities, and 'corporate' stakeholder agency umbrella groups (voluntary external audits) *Home care*: De-centralized. Medical Review Boards at the state level (*Länder*), communities, and voluntary external audits
	Switzerland	*Residential care and home care:* De-centralized to regions (cantons)	*Residential care and home care:* De-centralized to regions (cantons)
	Japan	*Residential care and home care:* De-centralized to prefectural (sub-national) government applying national Long-term Care Insurance regulations	*Residential care and home care:* De-centralized to prefectural (sub-national) government applying national Long-term Care Insurance regulations

Table 16.2 (*cont.*)

	Country	Responsibility for Licensure/ Registration of facilities	Responsibility for Inspection/Quality monitoring
Inspection based regulatory systems	Australia	*Residential care:* Centralized within Federal Government *Home care:* Mainly centralized. Since July 2012, responsibility lies with the Federal Government in the six states and territories that have agreed to participate in the national scheme while in the other two states, responsibility is shared between the federal and state governments	*Residential care:* Centralized within Federal Government *Home care:* Mainly centralized. Since July 2012, responsibility lies with the Federal Government in the six states and territories that have agreed to participate in the national scheme while in the other two states, responsibility is shared between the federal and state governments
	England	*Residential care and home care:* Centralized within a national agency, the Care Quality Commission	*Residential care and home care:* Centralized within a national agency, the Care Quality Commission
	The Netherlands	*Residential care and home care:* Centralized at national level	*Residential care and home care:* Centralized. National health care inspectorate and external certification organizations
	Spain	*Residential care and home care:* De-centralized to the autonomous regions (*comunidad autónoma*)	*Residential care and home care:* De-centralized to the autonomous regions (*comunidad autónoma*)

Data measurement and public reporting based regulatory systems	Finland	*Residential care:* Mixed. A national agency (Valvira), through regional branches for private facilities; and municipalities license their own public, local facilities *Home care:* Mixed. Centralized for health care authorities while decentralized for social authorities providing long-term care	*Residential care:* Mixed: A national agency (Valvira), through regional branches for private and public facilities; municipalities also perform inspection and monitoring functions. *Home care*: Centralized for strictly private facilities. Mixed for public facilities – locally-owned facilities and those private organizations that sell services to municipalities
	USA	*Residential care and home care*: De-centralized to state governments. Although residential care (and to a lesser extent skilled home health care) follows a uniform minimum national set of standards, minimal licensure standards for community-based long-term care providers are established at local level	*Residential care and home care*: De-centralized. For residential care state governments are responsible, but follow a uniform minimum national set of standards. Home care standards are less extensive or uniform across states.
	Canada	*Residential care and home care*: De-centralized to provincial governments	*Residential care and home care*: De-centralized to provincial governments
	New Zealand	*Residential care and home care:* Centralized via the National government, through District Health Boards	*Residential care and home care:* Centralized via the National government, through District Health Boards

Table 16.2 (*cont.*)

	Country	Responsibility for Licensure/ Registration of facilities	Responsibility for Inspection/Quality monitoring
Developing regulatory systems	South Korea	*Residential care and home care:* De-centralized to local governments	*Residential care and home care:* Centralized through a national agency
	China	*Residential care:* De-centralized. Provincial and sub-provincial local authorities are meant to implement national policies, regulatory guidelines and standards but do so variably. *Home care:* De-centralized. Little regulation in the formal home care sector. No known national guidelines exist so where regulation occurs, this is at the local level.	*Residential care:* De-centralized. Provincial and sub-provincial local authorities are meant to implement national policies, regulatory guidelines and standards but do so variably. *Home care:* De-centralized. Little regulation in the formal home care sector. No known national guidelines exist so where regulation occurs, this is at the local level.

Source: Authors' compilation.

Regulating quality of long-term care – what have we learned? 459

centralization we mean an administrative structure where responsibility for setting standards or guidelines is vested in a central, usually national, agency or level of government, even if such standards are then implemented by more local branches. In contrast, decentralization refers to situations where authority for regulatory decision-making, including standard-setting and quality monitoring, lies with dispersed units, either geographical administrative entities such as autonomous regions or municipalities or more diffusely with other external organizations.

Interestingly, all four countries that we have identified as having regulatory systems based on professionalism – Austria, Germany, Japan and Switzerland – also have decentralized administrative systems for operationalizing licensure and inspection of long-term care providers and/or quality monitoring. In some cases (Austria, Germany and Switzerland) this decentralization echoes the federal structure of the countries' political architecture, where sub-national regions or cantons enjoy extensive administrative, legislative and policy-making autonomy. In the case of Germany, Health Medical Boards in each state play a crucial role in inspections and monitoring standards, along with other state-level inspection agencies and external quality certification bodies.

Conversely, three out of the four countries that have inspection-based regulatory models – Australia, England and The Netherlands – tend to centralize licensure, inspection and quality monitoring functions for long-term care within national agencies or inspectorates, either directly or through regional branches. In the case of The Netherlands, this process occurs in parallel to the substantial use of voluntary external certification organizations that attest to provider quality and which serve to boost the profiles of providers in the long-term care market. In the fourth country in this group, Spain, regulatory functions, including quality monitoring, are decentralized to the Autonomous Communities (regions) in accordance with the country's strong regional political structure. However, at least within the Catalan region, the regulatory structure is centralized within the regional government's health inspection regulatory structure.

Finally, the rest of the countries in our sample follow a heterogeneous pattern in terms of their administrative configurations. Sharing regulatory systems based on data management and public reporting, and being nations with federal structures, Canada and the United States also have decentralized administrative systems to regulate long-term care, directed by the provinces and states respectively. However, in the case of the US, for residential care in particular, a uniform minimum national set of standards is in place, established by the federal agency responsible for paying nursing homes and home care agencies. These are highly centralized and uniform standards and inspection procedures in spite of the fact that they are not implemented uniformly. On the other hand, New Zealand, whose regulatory system also emphasises data collection and has an emerging public reporting framework, centralizes all of its long-term care regulatory functions, including quality monitoring, at the national level via the Ministry of Health, with implementation via District Health Boards. Finland employs a mixed scheme, with functions largely shared between the historically autonomous municipalities and the National Supervisory Authority for Welfare and Health (Valvira) and its regional branches. Lastly, with their nascent and developing long-term care regulatory systems, China and South Korea have largely decentralized arrangements with local authorities bearing most responsibilities for regulatory functions, although in the case of South Korea, the National Health Insurance Corporation is responsible for monitoring quality and in China, at least in the residential sector, local authorities are meant to adhere to nationally set policy guidelines and standards.

Whatever the administrative configuration of regulatory functions, the main issue is whether standards are implemented effectively and quality assurance meets appropriate benchmarks. In this respect, an almost universal concern expressed in countries with decentralized systems is the challenge of implementing regulatory processes in a uniform manner and in maintaining quality levels across geographical divisions, particularly in countries where local authorities exercise significant autonomy in the management and provision of long-term care, creating a greater potential risk of uneven standards being applied depending on a person's area of residence. For example, in Austria, the diffuse nature of quality management among the regions means that there are different regimes across the country, ranging from the minimal to the more extensive, with developments in quality assurance being very much dependent on regional initiatives and priorities.

Some countries have addressed this challenge by developing national guidelines on structural requirements and quality standards that need to be implemented by sub-national authorities, or by having minimum national framework legislation in place. This is the case in China,

Regulating quality of long-term care – what have we learned? 461

Germany, Japan and the United States, although in Germany, states implement standards differently and, since 2006, states have been able to replace federal regulations on homes for people with long-term care needs with their own regulations. On the other hand, in Finland, national guidelines are not compulsory for municipalities even though there are financing implications that provide an incentive for municipalities to adopt national guidelines.

A stronger centralizing trend is evident in England. After decades during which regulatory functions were dispersed among the local authorities that organize and deliver most long-term care services, inspection and quality monitoring functions were centralized into a unitary national organization, now called the Care Quality Commission. Other countries such as Australia, New Zealand, The Netherlands and South Korea also have national bodies that either take on monitoring functions directly or exercise a supervisory role over local implementation. However, this does not mean that merely promulgating national standards is a panacea for regulatory oversight, much less does it guarantee effective quality monitoring. China, which is still only just starting to develop its long-term care system, initially is focusing on rapid expansion of residential facilities, the majority of which are privately owned. Getting local authorities to implement national regulatory guidelines adequately and to ensure provider compliance is proving difficult since local authorities have to balance the competing demands of implementing regulations and quality standards while also achieving quite ambitious targets to increase the number of residential facilities. Since entrepreneurs who are building facilities want a healthy return on their investment, they interpret the application of stringent regulations as limiting their goal.

Another policy challenge for systems that devolve quality assurance responsibilities is the potential for inaction. One such example is Switzerland, which is experiencing difficulties implementing quality standards nationally. Perhaps because Swiss cantons enjoy extensive autonomy, the government decided to delegate the task of developing a nationally mandated quality assurance programme to long-term care provider associations, in partnership with health insurer organizations. Thus far, however, the strategy has not been very successful, with significant delays and no quality assurance framework in sight. While national legislation allows for the government to step in with its own centrally imposed quality guidelines, to date the government has refrained from doing so.

16.4 Monitoring long-term care

In all of the case-study countries included in this study, we see that regulatory frameworks and monitoring activities for residential facilities (nursing homes) are in place, no matter how developed or under-developed the sector is. In contrast, homecare remains the most neglected sector from a quality assurance perspective, although Finland reports a growing interest in monitoring home care quality and a few countries such as New Zealand (voluntary) and Switzerland (in the cantons where they are applied) have more advanced indicators. One other phenomenon, confirmed by all of the case studies, is the key issue of data availability. This is often patchy in nursing homes and is generally lacking for home care services, although some countries (such as The Netherlands, New Zealand, Canada, the US and Switzerland) have made inroads into monitoring the quality of home care.

A related issue is that, even if data are collected for quality assurance purposes, often they are not made publicly available, mostly due to the opposition of providers (e.g., in England and Germany) because they are sensitive to sharing information with competitors or feel uneasy about the reputational risk involved in publicly releasing information about poor performance. This applies to information that is assembled during the course of regulatory inspections as well as other data about the providers' quality performance. It is still the case that many European countries do not routinely assemble standardized information that emerges from the inspection process. This is far less cumbersome than collecting and aggregating and then reporting resident-level data, but apparently raises as much consternation among providers. Indeed, in England the lack of consistency in inspectors' inspection assessments has created legal problems and in the US inspection results have been frequently challenged in the courts. Some countries have started collecting data from their inspections (Australia, England, The Netherlands and Catalonia), but only a few are considering releasing these data publicly to facilitate consumers' making choices based on these data such as the US or New Zealand, where market competition stimulated by public reporting has led to small, but statistically significant, shifts, in which facilities patients choose. However, many of the country cases presented in this volume have highlighted the difficulty of standardizing inspections or assessments across different regions or even individual assessors. This lack of consistency makes it

Regulating quality of long-term care – what have we learned? 463

difficult to compare providers and therefore to use collected data in a meaningful way.

A policy lesson that can be gleaned from this experience is that effective data gathering and monitoring activities are central to assuring the quality of long-term care. While the overriding purpose of measuring long-term care structures, processes and outcomes is to ensure the safety and dignity of service users, this objective is very closely linked with the secondary aim of informing provider organizations (or ultimately the public) about the relative quality of their performance. With meaningful data and effective information systems, provider organizations can view their own results in terms of these quality measurements and benchmark them against the results of similar institutions around the country to see how well they are doing and to tailor their improvement activities accordingly. Data on long-term care providers are also used to inform insurers, enabling them to make informed choices when purchasing long-term care services. In the near future, health insurers will increasingly follow a strategy of purchasing long-term care services from providers that offer both cost-effective and high-quality care. Thus, data on relevant quality indicators will be used to assess and compare actual quality among competitive suppliers. Indeed, we are already seeing this process taking place in the US, Canada, Finland and New Zealand.

16.5 The reach of regulatory functions

Table 16.3 presents a synthesis that characterizes and compares the adoption of regulatory functions and the status of long-term care regulation in our case study countries. A wide range of different regulatory functions (seventeen in total) are listed in the rows in the table. The check marks in each country column provide a gross indicator that a particular function is an integral part of the regulatory apparatus in that country. The table also orders the country columns from left to right, starting with the countries that have the greatest number of check marks (USA, Canada and The Netherlands), through to the one with the fewest (China). This ordering scheme provides a somewhat crude, but nevertheless illuminating, 'league table' of the relative regulatory responsibilities encumbering each country. It is important for the reader to recognize that this 'league table' refers to the scope and intensity of regulatory oversight and intervention rather than to the effectiveness of

Table 16.3 *Long-term care regulatory function undertaken by countries*

Regulatory Function	USA[a]	Canada	Netherlands	England	Australia	Finland	Japan	Germany	Austria	Spain	New Zealand	South Korea	Switzerland	China
1. Registration/Licensure	X	X	X	X	X	X	X	X	X[b]	X	X	X	X	X
2. Structural (physical) standard setting	X	X	X	X[c]	X	X	X	X	X[b]	X	X	X	X	X
3. Professional education and training standards	X	X	X	X[d]	X	X	X	X[b]	X	X		X	X	X
4. Long-term care professional associations	X	X[e]	X	X	X		X	X	X		X			
5. Care Process minimum standards	X	X	X	X[f]	X[g]	X	X	X	X[b]	X	X	X	X[b]	
6. Resident/Client outcomes measures	X	X	X	X	X	X		X	X[b]	X	X			

7. Routine inspection	X	X	X	X	X		X	X	X[b]	X	X	X	X[b]	X[b]
8. Random/ unannounced inspections	X	X	X	X	X	X		X		X	X			
9. Data- and experience-based inspection	X	X	X	X		X	X	X					X[b]	
10. Monetary penalties for non-compliance	X	X	X	X	X[i]	X	X	X	X[b,j]	X		X		
11. Sanction and warning system	X	X	X	X	X	X	X	X[k]	X	X		X	X	
12. Legal appeals process	X	X	X	X[l]	X[m]		X							
13. Complaint collection and monitoring system	X	X	X	X	X	X	X		X[b]	X		X		
14. Telephone or web-based action-line complaint process		X	X		X	X	X	X	X					
15. Public reporting	X	X	X	X		X	X[n]			X	X	X		
16. Consumer choice data	X		X			X					X			

Table 16.3 (*cont.*)

Regulatory Function	USA[a]	Canada	Netherlands	England	Australia	Finland	Japan	Germany	Austria	Spain	New Zealand	South Korea	Switzerland	China
17. Pay-for-performance quality assurance	X	X												

Source: compiled by authors from case study chapter information.

Notes: [a] Functions can vary slightly across nursing homes and community based options.

[b] Varies across regions.

[c] Regulations pertaining to structural aspects are very broadly specified for the most part.

[d] Standards for all groups exist but enforceability depends on the staff group (e.g., nurse, social worker, care worker).

[e] Industry associations of aged care providers and nursing professional bodies.

[f] Some provider regulations refer to aspects of the care process but these are broadly specified. Within the regulations, cross-references are made to best practice guidelines but inspectors seem to have a good deal of leeway on how to interpret this standard. NICE is developing quality standards which set out care process minimum standards but it is not yet clear to what extent these are enforceable or merely guidelines.

[g] Legislation sets out a Schedule of Specified Care and Services and requires providers to deliver care of 'an appropriate standard'. However, the legislation does not set out minimum staff-resident ratios or hours of care.

[h] Poorly or variably enforced.

[i] There are no fines for poor care per se. However, poor providers can be sanctioned by having government funding withheld for new residents until they meet care standards. This is a form of financial sanction.

[j] These exist but are poorly enforced and with very low level of fines.

[k] Contracts can be terminated by the Long-term Care Fund.

[l] Appeals can be brought against registration or outcome of inspections.

[m] Providers have appeal rights against regulatory decisions. Care recipients have appeal rights against a decision by the government not to approve them for subsidized care.

[n] Limited to inspections.

Regulating quality of long-term care – what have we learned? 467

regulations or to the quality of care, the goal of all such systems. We are a long way from being able to reliably and validly rank countries, or even regions within a country, on the basis of the effectiveness of the regulatory systems designed to assure the quality of care offered to long-term care service recipients.

The top-most row of Table 16.3 indicates that all countries have some form of licensure structure in place. Even in China, the least developed country among our case studies, there is a formal regulatory process in which long-term care providers must register with the regional office of the Ministry of Social Welfare. The second row is also universally indicated since regulations govern characteristics of the physical plant ranging from fire and safety considerations to quality-of-life considerations such as room size, etc.

The role of professional standards can be formalized within national or regional regulations or imposed less formally via generally accepted professional standards maintained by professional associations. The third row in Table 16.3 pertains to the existence of formal regulations governing the level of education and training that certain groups of long-term care workers must attain in order to be employed in facilities and/or agencies providing long-term care services to the elderly. Please note that this table does not indicate the *level* of training required. For example, nurses aides working in certain European countries (e.g., Finland) require up to three years of specialized training and supervision, whereas in the US, the federal requirements are less than one month's training. Furthermore, market conditions can also have an enormous influence on the extent to which these kinds of professional standards are adhered to by providers. That is, the local unemployment rate, the availability of excess labour (e.g., illegal immigrants from eastern Europe or Mexico or rural immigrants from China), the prevailing government reimbursement rates as well as the level of regulatory enforcement all contribute to whether training standards are actually applied and adhered to in practice.

The fourth row provides an indication of the role of professional associations and/or independent, non-governmental, organizations in setting standards for long-term care providers. For example, in Austria, the professional associations of physicians, nurses and even long-term care providers seem to be the critical actors determining what regulations and standards are adopted. Similarly, in Japan, the professional associations have been very important in setting minimal standards for the different types of long-term care workers. Additionally, the provider associations have been at the forefront of advocating for care standards and ongoing differentiation between the different types of long-term care providers. On the other hand, in the US, associations of long-term care providers are generally seen as advocating for more limited minimum training requirements or other externally imposed restraints, arguing that rigid standards undermine creative adaptation to new circumstances. Conversely, while China and South Korea have introduced minimal training standards for long-term care workers, professional associations have not independently been incorporated into the standards setting process.

The fifth and sixth rows of Table 16.3 focus on the existence of non-structural aspects of quality incorporated into the regulatory apparatus. Process standards can be applied to encourage positive aspects of care as well as to prohibit processes that are known to have a negative impact on care quality. For example, process quality issues that have been stressed in many countries include efforts to reduce the use of physical restraints as well as anti-psychotic medications. Process standards exist in several countries to minimize the use of these behaviour control schemes by requiring extensive documentation to justify their use. Provisions to discourage these types of care processes can be incorporated into regulations and care standards, which are then the subject of inspection. These process standards then focus regulators on these issues during inspections, either observing patients or reviewing residents' medical records, and therefore send a clear message to providers to limit these processes.

To incorporate the requirement that residents' outcomes be measured and assessed as an aspect of quality control is a relatively advanced regulatory oversight approach since it implies that the regulations stipulate what constitutes 'outcomes' for frail older individuals who are expected to deteriorate, albeit not too quickly. The challenge in regulating improvement, or even maintenance, of residents' outcomes in long-term care is establishing a system to document that these quality standards have been met. While regulators inspecting a long-term care programme are able to review residents' records covering an extensive period of time and to determine whether care processes were introduced to improve residents' well-being, it is difficult to establish whether the introduction of a given intervention 'caused' or 'prevented' subsequent outcomes observed in patients. The issue of instituting

Regulating quality of long-term care – what have we learned? 469

measurement systems to document the extent to which the long-term care recipients achieve desirable outcomes is addressed in the lower rows of Table 16.3.

Rows 7, 8 and 9 deal with the approach to inspections that is adopted by the regulatory agency after a provider has been registered, licensed or certified. Routine inspections are virtually universal in our study countries, although in China the regularity of inspections is limited and completely the responsibility of the regional authority in spite of the fact that guidelines for what constitutes regulations are promulgated by the central government. In some countries, like Finland and Austria, the inspection schedules may be dictated by a combination of central government and regional or state government authority even though the inspection authority may be more locally based. This can mean, as in the Tyrol region in Austria, that despite inspections being required on a regular basis by law at the state level, they might not be regulated. The differences between regularly scheduled versus randomly conducted inspections presents an interesting opportunity to compare the influence of expectations. For example, in the US, after years of regularly scheduled inspections of long-term care providers, revised regulations require a certain proportion of inspections to be 'unannounced', or done at random times, since these are expected to observe providers engaged in normal behaviour, viz. patient care. In England most inspections, regardless of the scope and focus, are unannounced and appear to have been structured in this way for quite some time. In any event, it was reported in the US that regulators tended not to observe substantial differences as a function of type of inspection. As fundamental as this issue of inspection type is to understanding effective regulatory practices, there is no empirical data supporting one approach over the other in terms of stimulating better care for recipients.

In addition to unannounced inspections, it is also conceivable to condition inspections based either upon historical performance or a desk audit of data that the provider submits in advance. Inspection schedules based upon historical performance in past inspections is undertaken in selected cantons in Switzerland, where, instead of being inspected annually, a provider that did well in several consecutive inspections might not be inspected for several years on the assumption that they have mastered the requisite functions to meet all the regulatory requirements. On the other hand, in the US there is no linkage between inspection frequency and/or intensity and the quality reporting system that is in place. In England, there are thematic and focused inspections depending upon the providers' performance in their last inspection.

One regulatory provision that directly links quality to provider financing is to levy a fine against providers that perform poorly. One approach is to fine the provider directly and another is to restrict admissions. The latter means the provider loses money every day until the quality problem is resolved while the former is a fine which is levied and then has to be collected. The ability of government to levy fines and/or restrict admissions requires that this power exist in the law. As can be seen in Row 10, regulatory authorities in some countries, including England, Finland, Austria and Japan, have the power to levy fines but the frequency with which this is done varies considerably. In the US both the federal and most state governments have the authority to levy fines and to restrict admissions of one sort or another and the evidence suggests that over the past decade these discretionary regulatory actions have been applied increasingly more often.

Over and above financial sanctions, most regulatory authorities have the ability to sanction long-term care providers in ways that compromise their ability to retain their licence. This could entail a warning system in which deficient providers are told to return to regulatory compliance within a certain period of time or risk losing their licence to operate (Row 11). Unfortunately, while these provisions are in place in most countries, they are extremely difficult to apply, particularly in the case of residential care providers. This is largely because frail older persons live in these facilities and the act of relocating them places a heavy burden on the regulatory agency precisely because it requires the availability of many empty beds in the area and because of the potential burden of 'relocation' stress borne by the residents. It is therefore not surprising that few of our case study countries have documented the rate of provider 'closure'. Even in the US, where falling demand for nursing home care beginning in the late 1990s makes closure more feasible, orders for a home to close (revocation of licensure) directly due to regulatory action are quite rare.

In some countries the regulatory authority must ultimately rely upon the legal system to determine whether they are entitled to apply sanctions to providers that have transgressed. That is, the law that authorizes the regulator to set standards and to regulate provider behaviour may sometimes include provisions for that provider to appeal the rulings of the regulator. This can apply to the denial of an operating licence

Regulating quality of long-term care – what have we learned? 471

in the first place or to the threat of closure and licensure revocation. The appeals process generally requires the regulator to appear before a judge whose job it is to ensure that all rules have been adhered to and all the processes for notifying the provider of the pending regulatory action have been complied with. Results of such appeals are not often documented and there is limited evidence as to whether providers win these appeals more often than they are lost (Row 12).

Consumers' complaints are another mechanism for judging providers' quality. Several countries (Row 13) have highly diverse systems in place that allow consumers, their families and special consumer advocacy groups to submit complaints about the treatment of long-term care recipients. In some countries there are special toll-free telephone numbers and/or Internet-based complaint filing websites (Row 14). In the US, all such complaints must be investigated as a matter of course whereas in England complaints are resolved locally and complaints made to bodies other than the provider will be passed on to the provider with the individuals' agreement. Investigations into the validity of consumers' complaints may be minimal or substantial, depending upon the nature of the complaint and who made it. Unfortunately, there are limited data available as to the scope and frequency of 'legitimate' complaints in the countries that have complaint monitoring systems, partially because of the minimal documentation that seems to be required and partially because of the variability in determining what constitutes a 'legitimate' complaint.

Rows 15 to 17 all involve the availability of systematic data on provider quality performance. Public reporting entails making information about providers' quality performance available to consumers. The most rudimentary approach to this is requiring that the results of regulators' inspections be available to consumers upon their request. Having publicly reported data that goes beyond this requires the collection, assembly and ultimately posting of this information in places where interested parties can readily access systematic information about provider quality. Such systems exist in the US, where various measures of quality, ranging from staffing levels, to inspection results, to indicators of process and outcome quality are computerized and posted on government websites. Several Canadian provinces are engaged in similar kinds of public reporting. In Finland, data on residents' outcomes are voluntarily reported and fed back to providers with the intention that ultimately this information might be appropriate to inform consumers' choice as to which provider in a given area should be visited. A similar structure is in place in New Zealand for their home care agencies and is slated to be put into place in New Zealand residential care facilities. It should be noted that the data infrastructure necessary to implement this kind of a system is nowhere near as complex and difficult as it was a few decades ago due to the rapid advance of the Internet and the increasing sophistication of all manner of individuals in dealing with Internet-based information. Nonetheless, moving toward a resident outcomes public reporting system requires a shared understanding of what constitutes indicators of care quality. While this may appear to be a technical problem, to the extent providers are not interested in having their performance publicly reported, technical objections can mask other more fundamental and political objections.

16.6 Where to now?

Methodologically, the term quality, it seems, can assume different meanings in settings where there is no agreement on a common framework. Often, quality refers to institutional structures such as the number and training of staff and the cleanliness and appropriateness of the physical plant. Quality, in terms of process and outcomes, is harder to obtain; many of the measures currently available still need to be checked for reliability and validity. Once the hurdle of trying to measure quality in long-term care is overcome, the next step should be to make data publicly available and, if feasible, potentially to adopt uniform, clinically relevant, patient information systems for both nursing homes and home health services. As two recent international meetings showed,[2] a big gap remains in the literature with respect to home care, which, in most cases, has not been assessed.

In terms of monitoring compliance with standards as well as quality benchmarks, the English experience shows there are no reasons to suspect that continuous assessment (and using a provider's Quality Risk Profile – QRP) is any worse at predicting non-compliance risk than its predecessor,

---

[2] A seminar on long-term care organized at the London School of Economics and Political Science in May 2010 (see www2.lse.ac.uk/LSEHealthAndSocialCare/ LSEHealth/eventsAndSeminars/Measuring per cent20the per cent20Quality per cent20of per cent20Long-Term per cent20Care.aspx) and an OECD meeting held in November 2012 (see www.rcplondon.ac.uk/sites/default/files/documents/ oecd_agenda.pdf).

Regulating quality of long-term care – what have we learned? 473

which used a provider's quality rating (based on its last inspection). Without studies devoted to determining the predictive ability of either of these approaches to quality assurance, it is impossible to draw any conclusions as to which should be retained as part of the regulatory structure in England. Regardless of inspection regime, one of the most promising developments across quite a few countries in our sample is the voluntary adoption of inter-RAI assessment instruments. Rooted in the need to adequately assess a frail older person to properly develop an individualized care plan, the resulting data, updated on a regular basis, form the basis for monitoring care quality in the organization across all service recipients and to inform service providers of where improvements in care processes are necessary.

Administratively, there is a clear 'conflict' of responsibilities between different levels of government. In most countries the national government sets standards and policies and then delegates the authority to a local or state government to do the operational work. Depending upon the country, this might be setting standards, guidelines and/or requirements which the states or local entities have to implement. While these different levels of authority can be confusing, other related factors sometimes may make matters worse. For example, there are situations where there are conflicting fiscal incentives between different levels of government, as in the case where national (health) insurance pays for hospital care but the local authority pays for nursing home care. In such cases, a cost-shifting incentive exists for the sickest long-term care recipients to be hospitalized, particularly if the payment rates in nursing homes are not higher for sicker patients.

An additional challenge in providing quality long-term care is presented by the sometimes complicated balancing act of providing the correct mix of residential long-term care services and home care services. On the one hand, the elderly in most countries would prefer to remain at home for as long as possible and, indeed, many are there by default. However, until recently most investment has traditionally been in the residential care services realm (Colombo et al., 2011). With home care, family members and the elderly themselves may end up receiving fewer services compared to residing in a nursing home. This reduces states' financial obligations, saving money, at least insofar as long-term care services go. However, such considerations must be counterbalanced with the need to provide safe and appropriate services, especially for frail people living alone, since it is harder to monitor care quality and to detect fraudulent service provision in the many thousands of individual community homes where these at-risk clients reside. While nursing homes are easier to regulate and inspect, one alternative to large-scale, institution-like facilities is to have many small providers, although it is much harder to regulate and to automate for outcomes since such homes may not be big enough to have dedicated information systems, etc.

The future of long-term care regulation is probably one of the most challenging to predict. Many countries seem to feel that quality of long-term care is a 'weak link' (Brodsky et al., 2000). Some of the key issues that may explain the lower quality of care commonly thought to exist in the long-term care sector may relate to a weak 'quality improvement' approach, provider fragmentation and lack of common standards. One basic policy recommendation is that countries' regulatory systems should establish minimum standards for long-term care facilities, including such structural indicators as the level and qualifications of staff, the minimum staffing levels and skill-mix, procedural standards and infrastructure specifications. Some countries may wish to regulate the rights of patients to long-term care, both in terms of technical care and in terms of civil rights. Above all, compliance with standards should be enforced.

The lessons learned from the case studies in this volume include some possible insights: standards or protocols should be established where sufficient evidence is available, and research encouraged in order to expand the knowledge base necessary for quality long-term care. Professionalism and continued education should be at the forefront of the field; and where technically feasible, outcomes assessment may need to be implemented in order to measure the extent of performance in terms of quality and to improve care accordingly. What might be more challenging and where less agreement is likely to be reached is on the standardization of outcomes. In this respect, even in healthcare, the science of performance measurement is still in its infancy (Smith et al., 2009).

In terms of consumer choice, often these programmes are still experimental, covering only a small part of the population. But in Austria and Germany, for example, a large part of the public scheme to provide publicly funded long-term care is built around these concepts. These initiatives enable more people with care needs to stay at home as long as possible, by mobilizing or sustaining the contributions of clients' natural informal care systems. Across the long-term care spectrum, consumer choice can improve the self-determination and satisfaction of older persons and increase the degree of independent living, even in cases of dependency on long-term care. Without a doubt, the availability of information in the public domain is critical here, not only so potential long-term care users can know what services are available to them and at what cost, but ideally to gauge the quality of the services they may wish to use.

In general, having a choice is appreciated by older people because it gives them greater control over their own lives. Greater choice and consumer direction could contribute to better quality of life at similar cost compared with traditional services. Where home care services are the preferred option, it is essential that sufficient additional resources to support caregivers are available, such as respite care and counselling.

It is probably safe to predict that data will increasingly become available in the public domain as scandals and pressure groups demand greater transparency. In line with this development, staffing issues will not only be in the headlines due to (predicted) shortages but also since in many countries the adequacy of staff training in long-term care is called into question. Moreover, increasing quality standards in long-term care and publicizing their existence may translate into higher expectations and discrimination on the part of service users, who, after all, are required to contribute towards the cost of such services.

In summary, this volume has attempted to describe and compare the long-term care systems of a number of developed and developing countries around the world with a particular emphasis on the regulatory structure under which formal long-term care service providers operate. As expected, we observe considerable heterogeneity across these countries in terms of the regulatory structures that are in place. While all countries' laws acknowledge a governmental responsibility for assuring that those who care for the frail and vulnerable elderly meet minimal standards, the way in which each country interprets and implements that responsibility varies widely, presumably reflecting the cultural values, ideological perspective and political history of each country. We hope that future efforts will build upon this start by documenting the structure of long-term care systems in more countries, thereby greatly enhancing our ability to empirically understand how society's efforts to assure the quality of social institutions translates into the outcomes experienced by the frail and dependent members of our societies.

References

Brodsky, J., Habib, J. and Mizrahi, I. (2000). *Long-Term Care in Five Developed Countries. A Review*. Geneva: World Health Organization.

Colombo, F., Llena-Nozal, A., Mercier, J. and Tjadens, F. (2011). *Help wanted? Providing and paying for long-term care*. OECD Health Policy Studies. Paris: OECD Publishing. Available at: http://dx.doi.org/10.1787/9789264097759-en.

Smith, P.C., Mossialos, E., Leatherman, S. and Papanicolas, I. (eds.) (2009). *Performance Measurement for Health System Improvement: Experiences, Challenges and Prospects*. Cambridge University Press.

Index

adversarial vs. consensual approaches to regulation 17–18
age statistics xviii
Australia
  ACSAA (Aged Care Standards and Accreditation Agency) 157, 158–61, 162
  acute-aged interface 175–6
  ADoHA (Australian Government Department of Health and Ageing) 156–7, 158–61, 166
  aged care
    federal government expenditure 150, 152
    health service links 170, 175–6
    performance framework development 171–2
    policy challenges 168–76
    population ageing 150–1
    Productivity Commission enquiry 169, 172
    reform initiatives 168–76
  Aged Care Act 153, 156
  Aged Care Assessment Teams 163, 173
  aged care sector 152–6
    acute-aged interface 175–6
    medical services 167–8
    post-acute care 176
    relevant regulations 167–8
    sub-acute care 176
    system overview 149–56
  Australian Commission on Safety and Quality in Health Care 171–2
  behavioural needs care 154
  Campbell Report 161
  care service control 154
  care service growth 155–6
  carers/providers separation 171

centralized monitoring 461
Charter of Rights and Responsibilities for Community Care 167
community care
  integration, quality regulation 164–5, 171
  integration with other services 170, 175–6
  packages 163–6
  programmes 153, 155
  quality regulation 163–7, 171, 174–5
consumer-directed care, and quality 172–3
Department of Veterans' Affairs 166
eligibility assessment 173–4
federal/state responsibilities 151–2, 156, 170
health and welfare sector 151–2
high-level care 153–4
home and community care
  common standards legislation 166–7
  funding 155
  providers 163
  services 153, 155
  single entry point 169–70, 173–4
Home and Community Care Programme 163, 166–7
inspection data 462–3
inspection-based regulatory system 459
long-term care
  command and control system 145
  government subsidized 145–6
  inspection-based systems 452
  low status of 15–16
low-level care 153–4
National Complaints Investigation Scheme 157

477

478   *Index*

Australia (cont.)
  National Health Agreement 173
  National Health and Hospitals
      Reform Commission 170
  National Health Performance
      Authority 171–2
  National Respite for Carers
      Programme 167, 169
  performance framework development
      171–2
  quality framework effectiveness
      161–3
  quality and regulatory framework
      174–5
  quality reporting 155
  regulatory framework 447–50
  residential care
      funding 156
      occupancy levels 162
      programmes 153, 154–5
  residential care quality regulation
      156–63, 164–5
      at risk services 160–1
      complaints investigation 157
      compliance 157, 158–61
      integrated 171, 175–6
      peer review 158
      provider accreditation 157,
          158–61, 162–3
      provider requirements 156–7
      reforms 158
      support contacts 159
  single entry point 169–70, 173–4
  Transition Care Programme 154, 176
  Veterans' Home Care 166
  welfare expenditures 152
Austria
  acute health care, quality assurance
      53–4
  ADL (activities of daily living) 34
  allowance entitlement 34–5
  allowances payment 34
  audit commissions 52
  Austrian Institute for Training and
      Education in Public Health 56
  care home
      administrator certification 21–2,
          59–60
      application/authorization 42–3
      competition 61–2

  incentives 61–2
  inspection 48–53, 469
  medical care 46
  monitoring 48–53
  Patient and/or Resident Advocate
      52
  quality assurance 48–53
  quality standards 43–8
  regional differences 48–53
  regulatory structure 40–1, 447–50
  resident place limits 42–3
  residents' representation 52
  residents' rights 41, 59–60
  staff ratios/structures 44–5
  staff standards 45–6, 59–60
  standards 43–8
  Care Home Habitation Act 41
  Care Home Treaty Act 41
  care structure 29–30
      in Vienna 47–8
  community-based care
      application/authorization 42–3
      criteria 54
      regulations 47
      regulatory structure 42–3
  decentralized administrative system
      459
  decentralized governance 33
  E-Qalin (European Quality
      Improvement and Innovative
      Learning) 55, 56–8
  extra-government regulators 21
  Federal Audit Commission 52
  Federal Government responsibilities
      40–1
  Federal Health Care Agency 53–4
  Federal Institute for Quality in Health
      Care 53–4
  Federation of Care Homes 54, 56, 59
  Federation of Viennese Health and
      Social Care Services 55
  grey/black market care 35
  Health Care Reform 54
  Health Quality Act 53–4
  home care 37–8
  IADL (instrumental activities of daily
      living) 34
  inspection schedules 469
  inter-agency working 62–3
  intermediary care 37–8

ISO 9000 standard 55
long-term care
and federal constitution 33–6
performance management 59–63
professionalization of 450–1
transparency 59–63
migrant carers 35, 48, 63
Ministry for Social Affairs and
Community Protection 56, 58
NQZ (National Quality Certificate)
for care homes 58–9
nursing associations and care 15, 467
nursing home standards 21–2
provider quality management/
development 54–5
public/private funding 60–1
QAP standard 55
quality management systems 460
quality measurement by public
authorities 55–6
regional government responsibilities
40–1
regional health care funds 53
residential care *see* care home
respite care 39
social insurance 33
subsidiarity 33
systematic quality approach 53–4
universal long-term care allowances
33–4
Viennese Care Home Act 47
Viennese Care Home Commission 47,
52
Working Group for Long-term Care
52–3

Braithwaite, J. 11–12

Campbell Report 161
Canada
Accreditation Canada 346–7
ALC (Alternative Level of Care)
patients 335–6, 339–40
ARCS (Alberta Resident
Classification System) 327, 330
Canadian Institute for Health
Information 343
CARF (Commission on the
Accreditation of Rehabilitation
Facilities) 347

CCACs (Community Care Access
Centres) 291, 328, 331–3,
341–2, 343
home care clients served by 332
legislation governing 332
CCRS (Continuing Care Reporting
System) 343
CHA (Canada Health Act), principles
of 325, 328, 335–6
CHC (community health centres) 328
CIHI (Canadian Institute for Health
Information) 325–6, 330
CMHA (community mental health
and addiction) services 328
CSS (community support services)
328
decentralized administrative system
459–60
government roles 325
HBAM (Health Based Allocation
Method) 337
HCRS (Home Care Reporting
System) 343
Health Canada 342
health information systems 342–4
Health Quality Ontario 349–50
health service accreditation 346–7
Health Services Restructuring
Commission 337
IAR (Integrated Assessment Record)
343
JPPC (Joint Policy and Planning
Committee) 331, 337–8
LHINs (Local Health Integration
Networks) 327–8, 332
long-term care 266, 328
low status of 15–16
professionalization of 450–1
LQIP (Long-Term Care Home
Quality Inspection Program) 345
LTCHA (Long Term Care Homes
Act) 333–4, 344–6
Medicare 328, 351
MLAA (Ministry/LHIN
Accountability Agreement) 327–8
MoHLTC (Ministry of Health and
Long Term Care) 329, 330, 331,
335–6, 343
national health service overview
324–5, 350–1

480 *Index*

Canada (cont.)
 OMHRS (Ontario Mental Health
  Reporting System) 343
 Ontario *see* Ontario
 ORCA (Ontario Retirement Centres
  Association) 331
 public reporting 342–4, 471–2
 quality performance transparency
  23–4
 RAIs (Resident Assessment
  Instruments) 330, 333–4, 337–8,
  340, 342–4, 351
 RAPs (Resident Assessment
  Protocols) 330
 RUG (Resource Utilization Groups
  for Home Care) 326–7, 337–8
 SCIPP (System for Classification of
  Inpatient Psychiatry) 339
care homes
 appropriate care assessment xix–xx
 enforcement/regulation xviii,
  xxii–xxiii, 7
 key-performance indicators 58
 Medicare/Medicaid financing
  18–19
 monitoring/inspection xviii, xxi, xxii,
  7, 9–12
 NQZ (National Quality Certificate)
  for care homes 58–9
 occupancy levels xix
 openness to consumers xxiii, 58–9
 punishment of xxii–xxiii
 residents
  capacity of xix
  fear of abuse xix
  rights 41, 59–60
  vulnerability of xix, 3–4
 scandals 3–4, 146
 see also individual countries
care providers *see* provider
care quality *see* quality of care
caregiving organizations 5–6
Catalonia *see* Spain
Catholic charities 5–6
centralization vs. decentralization of
  care regulation 15–16
China
 ageing population 410, 417
 Basic Standards for Social Welfare
  Institutions for the Elderly 426–8

care homes
 building standards 425, 433
 care facility operator inspection
  432, 435–7, 469
 care facility operator registration
  431–2
 care facility operator requirements
  431
 eligibility for 419–20
 expansion 413–14, 415–17,
  419–20
 facilities 416–17, 425
 housekeeping services 426–8
 land allocation for 434–5
 National Occupational Standards
  for Old-Age Care Workers
  428–30
 personal care services 426–8
 private sector 415, 419–20,
  421
 private-sector government
  subsidies 417
 private sector in market economy
  421
 private-sector policy directives 421
 psychosocial services 428
 regulatory oversight *see* regulatory
  oversight
 rehabilitative services 428
 scandals 435–7
 social welfare standards 426–8
 staffing 416, 428–30, 433
China National Committee on Aging
  417–18, 430
Code for the Design of Buildings for
  Elderly Persons 425
decentralized administrative system
  460
Department of Health 19
development goals 17
elder care
 government role in development
  417–22
 government role as purchaser/
  regulator 420
 state funding 6–7
empty-nest households 411
inspections 432, 435–7, 469
local government responsibility 5,
  430–5

Index

long-term care 17, 19
  budget reduction 414–15
  changing attitudes 412–14
  community-based care policy 418
  demand levels 411
  dual system of institution-based
    care 419–20
  family duty 412
  government subsidies 430
  growth rate/government policy
    conflicts 434–5, 461
  home-based care policy 418
  information infrastructure
    development 437–8
  lack of public/insurance funding
    412
  low institutionalization rate 415
  official classifications of 427
  Ministry of Social Welfare 19
  national guidelines 460–1
  National Occupational Standards for
    Old-Age Care Workers 428–30
  National Union for Long-Term Care
    422
  one child policy 6, 409
  policy engineering 417–22
  population mobility 411
  professional associations 468
  regulatory oversight 417, 473
    building standards 425, 433
    care home scandals 435–7
    care home staffing 433
    central government 422–30
    current regulatory structure (local)
      430–2
    local government 430–5
    standards 432–3, 435–7,
      438–9
  regulatory system development
    453–4
  rise of formal care 414–17
  senior citizens' lodging houses 419
  socioeconomic change 410–11
  Starlight Programme 419
  Starlight Senior Centres 419
  territorial management 431
  three-tiered care system policy 438
  Tianjin case study 430–5
  traditional institutions 414–15
  voluntary trade associations 422

complaint process 11, 22, 471
  see also individual countries
consensual vs. adversarial approaches to
  regulation 17–18
Costa, A. P. 340
cream-skimming 313
Crosby, P. 94–5

data measurement-based long-term
  regulatory approach 453
Day, P. 24–5
Deming, W. E. 94–5
Diakone 89–93
DNQ (German Network for Quality
  Development in Nursing) 84–6
documentation 13
Douglas, Tommy 351

E-Qalin (European Quality
  Improvement and Innovative
  Learning) 55, 56–8
EFQM (European Foundation for
  Quality Management) 89
elder care service regulations 16–20
enforcement and monitoring *see*
  monitoring and enforcement
England
  ageing population 181–2
  ASC (adult social care) 182–3, 185–7
  care ombudsman 22
  centralized monitoring 461
  complaints procedures 184–5, 204–5,
    471
  continuous assessment 188, 190–3
  core standards 188
  CQC (Care Quality Commission)
    180, 181, 184–201
  CSA (Care Standards Act) 180
  CSCI (Commission for Social Care
    Inspection) 181
  enforcement/regulation xxii–xxiii
  Essential Standards of Quality and
    Safety 186–7
  Experts by Experience 189
  Healthcare Commission 181
  HealthWatch 200
  HSCA (Health and Social Care Act)
    180, 183
  inspection data 462–3
  inspection-based regulatory system 459

Index

England (cont.)
 LA (local authority) providers 182, 203–4
 LGO (Local Government Ombudsman) 184–5
 Local Authority Social Services and National Health Service Complaints (England) Regulations 184–5
 long-term care
  community-based 182
  complaints procedures 184–5, 204–5, 471
  compliance monitoring 188–97, 205
  compliance monitoring judgement framework 193–4
  consumer-directed care schemes (Personal Budgets and Direct Payments) 203, 205–6
  demand for 181–3
  enforcement mechanisms 197–9
  inspection 188, 202
  inspection discretion 10
  inspection documentation 13
  inspection of Local Authorities 203–4
  inspection-based systems 452
  intelligence-based risk monitoring 190–3
  market structure 181–3
  monitoring, risk-based 190–3
  political issues 200–1, 205
  provider certification 185–7
  provider compliance 188–97
  provider failure 204
  provider ownership/types data 183
  provider quality ratings 199–200
  provider registration 185–7
  provider standards 7–9
  provider standards public reporting 199–200
  provider star rating 190
  regulation xxii–xxiii, 146, 183–5
  regulation exemptions 201–3
  regulation limitations 201–5
  residential 182
  risk-based approach to inspection 17–18
  risk-based regulation 181, 201, 205

 sanctions 197–9
 services available 182
 Mental Health Act Commission 181
 Nursing Homes Registration Act 180
 personal care, definition 183–4
 Provider Compliance Assessment tool 188
 quality performance transparency 23–4
 Quality and Risk Profile 190, 191
 regulatory framework 447–50
 requirement for payment 9
 responsive regulation 197
 scandals 181, 205
 SCIE (Social Care Institute for Excellence) 200
 Trip Advisor-style information 200, 205
European Association for Directors and Providers of Residential Care Homes for the Elderly 54
European Association for Directors and Providers of Residential Care Services for the Elderly 56
European Union Leonardo da Vinci Programme 56
extra-government regulators 21–3

Finland
 AVIs (Regional State Administrative Agencies) 270, 276–7, 286
 chronic care hospitals (health centres) 269, 273–4
 ETENE (National Advisory Board on Social Welfare and Health Care Ethics) 272
 home care 273–4, 462
 individual care planning 285
 inspection schedules 469
 legislative proposals 270–2
 long-term care
  eligibility 274
  funding 274–5, 285–6
  government targets 274–1
  older people's options 275
  payment ceiling system 275
  private providers 285–6
  recipient charging 274–5, 285–6
  services delivered 272–1
  structure 269–72

Index

MDS (Minimum Data Set) *see* RAI
mixed centralized/decentralized
  administrative system 460
municipalities' responsibilities
  269–72, 276–7
national guidelines, non-compulsory
  460–1
nursing home care assessment 266–7
nursing standards 285
provider supervision 276–7
quality assurance 270–2
quality management/improvement
  279–84
quality performance transparency
  23–4
RAI (Resident Assessment
  Instrument) performance
  benchmarking 279–84, 285, 286
regulatory failures 278
regulatory mechanisms 276–8
RUG (Resource Utilization Groups)
  285
sheltered housing (service houses) 269
STAKES/THL 280–1
Status and Rights of Patients Act 270
Supervision of Private and Social Care
  Providers Act 276
THL (National Institute for Health
  and Welfare) 278, 280–1, 286
trade craft exchange 24
Valvira (National Supervisory
  Authority for Welfare and
  Health) 270, 276, 277, 278, 284,
  286
First World Assembly on Ageing
  (Vienna) 240
funding, by state 6–7
funding limitations xxi
  monitoring/inspection xxii
  staffing xxi

Germany
  Berlin Project 89
  care home administrator certification
    21–2
  Care Redirection Law 76
  care structure 30
  Code of Social Law 68, 70
  decentralized administrative system
    459

demographic changes 67–8
Development and Testing of
  Instruments for the Assessment
  of Quality and Effectiveness in
  Institutional Settings for the
  Elderly 88, 94
DNQ (German Network for Quality
  Development in Nursing) 84–6
E-Qalin (European Quality
  Improvement and Innovative
  Learning) 58
Expert Nursing Standards 84–5, 93
external quality audits/certificates
  89–93
extra-government regulators 21
Federal Ministry of Health 68, 72
health insurance 68–9
home communities 75
Homes Act 73–6
Homes Building Ordinance 75
Homes Participation Ordinance 75
Homes Personnel Ordinance 75
Homes Safe Payments Ordinance 75
Homes Supervisory Authority 73–6
insurers 20
Long Term Care Act 30, 73–6, 77, 82,
  89–93
long-term care
  benefits 69
  effectiveness and outcomes of care
    targets 80–1
  expert standards 84–6
  federal level 71–2
  financing 17
  insurance 68–71, 76
  insurance (pay-as-you-go) 69–70
  MDK (Medical Review Boards) 69,
    76–7, 83, 86–8
  medical care 83–4
  municipal level 72
  outcome measurement/
    performance 88–9
  professionalization of 450–1
  providers 70–1, 77, 89–93
  public reporting of 87–8
  quality control 70
  quality evaluation 76–93, 94
  quality evaluation care provider
    commitment 82–4
  quality evaluation guidelines 79–82

484   *Index*

Germany (cont.)
   quality regulation 73–6
   regulatory powers 71–2
   regulatory responsibilities 71–2
   state level 71–2
   structural conditions 94
   Long-term Care Enhancement Act
     79–80, 81, 85, 87–8, 93
   Long-term Care Quality Assurance
     Act 93
   MDK (Medical Review Boards) 69,
     76–7, 78–9, 82, 86–8, 93, 94–5
   MDS (Medical Review Board of the
     Federal Association of Sickness
     Funds) 77–81, 82, 85, 86–7, 93
   national guidelines 460–1
   nursing home standards 21–2
   regulatory framework 447–50
   requirement for payment 9
   Social Code Book XI 72
   staff qualification 83–4
   staff shortages 83
   TQM (Total Quality Management)
     94–5
   transparency agreement 82, 87–8
Grant Thornton Ltd. 371–2

healthcare needs xix
healthcare regulation vs. social welfare
   18–20
health and safety xx
Hirdes, J. P. 340

inspection-based long-term regulatory
   approach 451–2, 469–70
inspections
   and complaints 11
   discretion 10–11
   documentation 13
   inspection team composition 10
   risk-based 12, 17–18
   see also individual countries
insurers 20
Italy, E-Qalin (European Quality
   Improvement and Innovative
   Learning) 58

Japan
   assisted living housing 126
   care process requirements 129

care structure 30, 137
care worker qualifications/
   certification 127, 134–6, 137,
   139
community-based care regulations
   130
Convalescent HFE 136–7
day care centres, staffing levels 130–1
decentralized administrative system
   459
free healthcare for elders 122–3
future policy changes 137–9
HFE (Health Facilities for the Elderly)
   123, 124, 127–8, 136–7
home care 129–30, 218
home care regulations 130
home care staffing levels 129–30, 218
hospital environments 134
hospital prevalence rates/quality
   indicators 138
institutional care regulations 128–9
institutional facility requirements
   128–9
Japanese Nurses Association 133
long-term care
   background 122–6
   benefits eligibility levels 124–5
   care worker quality 122
   convalescent bed units 134
   Gold Plan 123
   nursing associations and care 15,
     135–6, 467
   professionalization of 450–1
   Special Homes for the Aged
     (nursing homes) 122, 137
LTCI (long-term care insurance) units
   123–6, 136–7
   auditing 127, 131–2, 232
   complaints procedures 132–3
   medical staff cover 127–8
   monitoring/reporting 131–3
   patient eligibility 114, 138
   penalties 132–3
   regulatory principles 126–31
   service user numbers 125–6
Medical Service Law 133
MHW (Ministry of Health and
   Welfare) 122
National Association of Chronic Care
   Hospitals 136–7

Index

national guidelines 460–1
overlapping functions/responsibilities
136–7, 139
private duty aides 133–4
RAI care planning instruments 139
regulations and structural standards
133, 139
problems with 135–7
regulatory framework 447–50
requirement for payment 9
social hospital admissions 122–3
specified facilities 126
staffing levels 127, 131–3
staffing regulations data 127
structural standards upgrade 137
Welfare Act for Elders 122
Jewish homes for the aged 5–6

Kapp, Marshall 298
Klein, R. 24–5
KTQ (Cooperation for Transparency
and Quality in Health Care) 89

Leonardo da Vinci Programme 56
licensed providers 8–9, 11
licensure structures, by country 455–8,
467
living alone, elderly 6
local government responsibility 5
long-term care
consumer choice 474–5
financing 17, 60–1
future regulation issues 474
low status of 15–16
monitoring 462–3
national/regional government care
regulation 16
nursing associations 15
regulated professionals 14–16
residential/home care balance
473–4
social welfare model 18–19
see also individual countries; quality
of care
long-term regulatory approach
data measurement-based 453
inspection-based 451–2
professional-based 450–1
public reporting-based 453, 475
regulatory functions 463–72

regulatory system development
453–4
long-term regulatory function, by
country 464–6
Lutheran homes 5–6
Luxembourg, E-Qalin (European
Quality Improvement and
Innovative Learning) 58

market forces in healthcare 265
Medicare/Medicaid 18–19, 20
migrant carers 35, 48, 63
monastery hospices 5–6, 102
monitoring and enforcement xviii, xxi,
xxii–xxiii, 7, 9–12
adversarial vs. consensual approaches
17–18
multi-generational households 6

national/regional government care
regulation 16
Netherlands
available services 212, 215–18
formal care at home 216, 462
informal care 215–16
institutional care 216–18
AWBZ (Exceptional Medical
Expenses Act) 212–15, 216
centralized monitoring 461
CIZ (Centre for Care Assessment)
214
extra-government regulators 21
Freedom of Information Act 235–6
government responsibility 214–15
healthcare legislation 212–15, 220–2
HKZ (Foundation for the
Harmonization of Quality in the
Health Care Sector) 225
IGZ (Health Care Inspectorate) 106,
214–15, 223, 226–7, 228, 232,
233, 234, 235–6
information supplied by 235–6
proactive publication 236
independent national website
information 237
indicators
client 232
professional content of care
228–32
inspection data 462–3

486   *Index*

Netherlands (cont.)
  inspection-based regulatory system
    459
  long-term care
    ageing population 212
    certification 146–7
    competition 219
    current issues 218–19
    demand-based 234–5
    enforcement measures 234
    incident investigation 233
    inspection-based systems 452
    legislation 219
    for older people 212–19
    performance/public reporting
      234–7
    phased supervision 226–33
    provider certification 225–6
    providers, information published
      by 236
    quality 223–6
    quality aspects 224
    quality improvement activity
      categories 223
    quality indicator sets 228
    quality monitoring 226–7, 233
    quality parameters 232
    quality parameters and Health
      Care Inspectorate 106, 232
    quality parameters and insurers
      232
    quality parameters and providers
      232
    quality parameters and users 232
    regulation 146–7, 447–50
    risk-based supervision 226–33
    themes and indicators 230–1
  nursing homes 217–18
    medical/multidisciplinary staffing
      218
  NZa (Dutch Health Authority) 215
  Quality of Care Act 225
  quality of care legislation 222, 225
  Quality Framework for Responsible
    Care 228
  quasi-consultative regulatory
    structure 18
  regulatory framework 447–50
  visible care programme (Zichtbare
    Zorg) 227–33

  WMO (Social Support Act) 212–14,
    216
  Zichtbare Zorg (Visible Care)
    Programme 227–33
  ZVW (Health Insurance Act) 212
  ZZPs (severity-of-care packages)
    216–17
New Zealand
  aged residential care services *see*
    residential care
  ageing population 357, 359
  ARCS (Aged Residential Care
    Service) Review 371–2
  ARRC (aged-related residential care)
    contract 359, 367–8, 369, 371,
    378
  Auditor-General home-based support
    audit 372–3
  Auditor-General rest home audit 369
  care legislation 364, 365,
    367, 368
  centralized administrative system
    459–60
  clinical assessment 373–4
  Community Pharmacy Project 379
  Crown Funding Agreement 360–1,
    365
  CSC (Community Services Card) 361
  DAAs (designated auditing agencies)
    369
  dementia care 362, 379
  DHBs (district health boards) 358,
    359–61, 363–5, 366–7, 371,
    376, 378
  DSS (Decision Support System) 376
  HBSS (home-based support services)
    assessment quality 266, 378–9
    Auditor-General audit 372–3
    contracts with DHBs 366–7, 378
    funding 360–1
    as preferred policy 373–4
    privatization 362
    provider assessment 367
    regulation 365–7
    regulatory oversight 366–7
    and supports 359–60
  HealthCERT 368–9, 370
  home care advocacy services 371
  Home and Community Support
    Sector Standards 366

Index

inter-RAI LTCF 377, 379
long-term care
  consumer choice-based system 453
  low status of 15–16
  overview 357–8
  services management 358
LTCF (long-term care facility) tool 377
Maori care assessment 376
MoH (Ministry of Health) 358, 377–8
NASCs (Needs Assessment and Service Coordination services) 359–60, 373–4
Needs Assessment Service 359
New Zealand Home Health Association 366
New Zealand Positive Ageing Strategy 372
Operational Policy Framework 358
PHOs (primary health organizations) 358
policy directive changes 373–4
privatization 362
psychogeriatric care 362
quality
  assessment issues 374–5
  community assessment issues 375–6
  home care 266, 378–9, 462, 472
  Maori clients 376
  monitoring/regulation 374–8
  performance transparency 23–4
  software 376
  training issues 375
RCS (Residential Care Subsidy) 363–4
residential care 361–3
  assessment quality issues 377–8
  audit effectiveness issues 377
  Auditor-General audit 369
  Auditor-General service audit 369
  funding 360–1, 363–5
  future policy 371–2
  maximum contribution 364–5
  medical provisions 370–1
  needs assessment 363–4
  QI (Quality Indicators) 377–8
  regulation 367–9
  regulatory oversight 368–9
  residents' characteristics 362–3

residents' consumer choice/voice 370–1
residents' GP choice 370–1
rest home audits 369
rest home certification 368–70
rest homes 362
retirement villages 362, 368
satisfaction surveys 371
retirement village certification 368–9
RSSAs (regional shared services agencies) 366
RVA (Retirement Villages Association) 368
service coordination 359–60, 373–4
nursing associations, and care 15, 21–2
nursing homes *see* care homes

Ontario
  Ageing at Home Strategy 339–40
  care for elderly
    admission/assessment 333–4
    assisted living 330–1
    community support agencies 335
    see also home care; hospital-based care; long-term care homes
  Case Mix Groups 326
  healthcare funding 325, 326–7
  healthcare system 325–6
  health expenditure estimates 325–6
  Health Quality Ontario 349–50
  home care 326–7, 331–3
    accreditation 346–7
    admission/assessment 333–4
    client groups served by CCACs 332
    quality improvement 344–50, 462
  hospital-based care 335–42
    CCC (complex continuing care) hospitals/units 336–8, 342
    acute hospitals 339–40
    psychiatric hospitals/units 338–9
    rehabilitation services 341–2, 347
  long-term care 266, 328
  long-term care homes 327, 329–30
    accreditation 346–7
    admission/assessment 331, 333–4
    associations 348–9
    care standards, services and programmes 345

488   *Index*

Ontario (cont.)
  clinical assessment 330
  complaints reporting/investigation
    346
  enforcement 345–6
  funding 329
  inspection 344–6
  length of stay 329–30
  LQIP (Long-Term Care Home
    Quality Inspection Program) 345
  LTCHA residents' safeguards 344,
    345–6
  quality improvement 344–50
  regulatory framework 344–6
  retirement homes 330–1
  nursing homes *see* long-term care
    homes
  professional associations 348–9
  see also Canada
Ontario Drug Benefit Program 326
Open Method of Coordination 62
outcome measurement 13–14
over-65 population 6

Paritätische Wohlfahrtverband 89–93
pay-for-performance programmes 14
PDCA (plan-do-check-act) cycle 57
performance, reporting and rewarding
    12–14
poor-house 5
process standards 468
professional associations
  by country 467–8
  and care 15
  care-enhancing activities 21–2
professional judgement 15
professional regulation 14–16
provider organizations 21
  trade craft exchange 24
provider standards
  competition 23–4
  establishment of 7–9
  sanctions xxii–xxiii, 11, 470–1
  transparency of 23–4
  see also individual countries
public reporting 453, 471–2, 475
public scrutiny 23–4
punishment, of care homes xxii–xxiii,
    11
purchasing power regulation 20

quality of care xx–xxiii
  centralization vs. decentralization of
    care regulation 15–16, 451–4,
    473
  and data collection/provision 463,
    471–2
  E-Qalin (European Quality
    Improvement and Innovative
    Learning) 55, 56–8
  elder care service regulations 16–20
  elusiveness of idea 24–5
  good practice 59
  institutional structures 472
  minimum levels xxii
  openness to consumers xxiii, 462–3
  outcome measurement 13–14
  pay-for-performance programmes 14
  processes and outcomes 472
  public reporting 472
  and quality of life xxi
  Quality Risk Profile 472
  standard setting xxi–xxii, 7
  standards compliance 472–3
  transparency 23–4
  see also individual countries;
    regulation
quality of life xx
  and quality of care xxi
quality management, PDCA (plan-do-
    check-act) cycle 57
quality monitoring 145
quality regulation *see* regulation
quality standards xxi–xxii

regulated professionals 14–16
regulation
  adversarial vs. consensual approaches
    17–18
  by purchasing power 20
  in care homes xviii, xx–xxiii
  centralized/decentralized 15–16,
    451–4, 473
  complaint process 11
  compliance/deterrence-based 10–11
  country characteristics 448–9
  extra-government regulators 21–3
  family responsibility 5
  historical basis 4–7, 54–5
  inspection-based 265
  regulated professionals 14–16

Index

489

reporting/rewarding performance 7, 12–14
rise in caregiving organizations 5–6
risk-based regulation 12
standard setting 7, xxi–xxii
state responsibility 4–5
transparency 23–4
see also individual countries
regulatory components xviii
regulatory functions 463–72
   structure of 7–14
regulatory league table, by country 463–7
regulatory pyramids 11
regulatory structures
   effectiveness of 25
   quasi-consultative 18
regulatory systems
   design issues xx–xxiii
   inspection-based 451–2
   long-term regulatory approach 447–54
   professional-based 450–1
   public reporting-based 453
religious societies 5
Republic of Korea
   ageing population 386–8
      and hospital beds 387–8
   centralized monitoring 461
   clinical care 395–6
   decentralized administrative system 460
   family care aides 394, 406
   family structure 386–7
   home care 392, 394
      staffing 394
   Korea Consumer Agency 403–4
   long-term care
      care system 388–9
      eligibility assessment 390–1
      evaluation 399, 405–6
      workforce regulation 401–3
   LTCI (Long-Term Care Insurance) 385–6, 388–9
      background 386–8
      beneficiaries 389–92
      benefits 391–2
      clinical care 395–6
      eligibility 390–1
      financing 389

information to consumers 403–4
staffing 394–5
staffing roles/responsibilities 395, 404–5
sustainability 407
types of services 393–4
NHIC (National Health Insurance Corporation) 385, 389, 395–6
   evaluation committee 401
   information to consumers 403–4
   inspection schedule 398
   inspection tools/content 398–400
   on-site inspections 400
   overlapping roles/responsibilities 395, 404–5
   quality management/oversight 396–401
professional associations 468
providers 392–6
   beneficiary satisfaction 404
   certification/market entrance 396–7
   certified care aides 394, 402–3, 406
   competition between 405
   geriatric nurses 402
   NHIC oversight 397–401
   numbers of 404, 405
   provider inspection 395
   provider reimbursement 395
   rewards/penalties 400–1
   visiting nurse aides 402
residential care 393–4
   benefits 392
   eligibility 390–1
   special care 393–4, 407
   staffing 394
social admission 387–8
residents' outcomes 468–9
risk-based regulation 12, 17–18
Rüesch, P. 114

scandals 3–4, 146, 181, 205, 290, 435–7
sectarian traditions 5–6
Seto, Shintaro 122
Simmill-Binning, C. 190
Slovenia, E-Qalin (European Quality Improvement and Innovative Learning) 58
social welfare vs. health care regulation 18–20

South Korea *see* Republic of Korea
Spain
  Catalonia
    VIII Benchmarking Summit 258
    Catalan Health Service 251–3
    Citizen Support Division 251
    client support units 251
    competence by comparison and
      collaboration rule 258
    External Quality Evaluation
      Programmes 259
    Giving Life to Years programme 242
    inspection data 462–3
    long-term care, inspection-based
      systems 452
    long-term care participation
      surveys 252–3
    long-term care services data 243
    MSIQ (Modules for Monitoring
      Quality Indicators) 257
    Outcomes Centre 256–8
    pioneering reforms 242
    PLAENSA (Satisfaction Survey
      Programme) 251–2, 253
    Quality Agenda for Social Services
      259
    quality approach 249–51
    quality approach evaluation 250–1
    quality approach inspection 249
    quality evaluation systems 247
    quality indicators 250–1, 256, 257
    satisfaction surveys 252
    Social Services Quality Programme
      247
    socio-demographic indicators 243
  CISAAD (SAAD Inter-territorial
    Council) 244, 245–8
  Dependence Assessment Instrument
    244–5
  Dependency Act (Promotion of
    Personal Autonomy and Care for
    Dependent Persons Act) 244
    Article (7) 245
    Article (15) 245
    Article (16) 247, 248
    Article (17) 245
    Article (18) 245
    Article (19) 245
    service provision 247
    Title II 245

elderly population 6
First National Plan for Gerontology
  242
home care 242, 254
inspection-based regulatory system
  459
long-term care
  acute hospital care 255
  bed blockers 255
  care services data 243
  central/regional government
    legislative authority 245, 259–60
  certification 146, 249
  chronic patients 255
  framework 244–9
  frequent flyers 255
  government accreditation 249
  government authorization 248
  inspection-based systems 452
  institutional 242–3, 254–5
  nursing home care 254–5, 259
  nursing home staffing 255
  quality as core issue 245–8
  regulation 146, 447–50
  residential home terminology
    242–3
  terminology 242–3, 248–9
  types of 242
political framework 241
public reporting 255–59
regulatory framework 447–50
SAAD (Spanish System for Autonomy
  and Dependent Care Assistance)
  244, 245–8
SNHS (Spanish National Health
  Service)
  free at point of delivery 253
  regional health ministries 254,
    259–60
  universal coverage structure 253–4
  socio-demographic indicators 243
staffing levels xxi
staffing standards 467
Swiss Home Care Associations 107
Swiss Hospital Associations 107
Swiss Medical Association 107
Switzerland
  acute/rehabilitation sectors 109
  care homes 103
  care structure 29–30

Index 491

decentralized administrative system 459
extra-government regulators 21
home care
  non-hospital external care setting
    see SPITEX
  Quality Manual (SPITEX) 113
  quality regulation 113–14, 462
inspection schedules 469
KVG (Federal Health Insurance
    Regulation Act) 30, 102–3,
    104–7
  care defined 105
  financing 106, 118
  mandatory staff/equipment 105
  public health insurance 105–6
long-term care
  cantonal arbitration boards 108
  cantonal certification 105
  cantonal financing 106
  cantonal nursing home certification
    106
  cantonal oversight/inspections 106,
    108, 469
  cantonal regulations 106
  federal level 102–3, 117–18
  patient choice 106–7
  population trends 104
  state level 102–3, 117–18, *see also*
    cantonal
medical quality indicators 118
monastery hospices 5–6, 102
Nationwide Quality Control Agency
  108–9
nursing home quality regulation
  109–13
  assessment instruments 118
  data transfer rules 111
  financial requirements 111, 118
  framework 110
  infrastructure 110
  licensing 110–11
  medical care 110
  nursing care 110
  operational rules 110–11
  organizational requirements 111
  staff qualifications 110, 118
  staffing 110
OECD report 117–18
Q-Sys 115

quality assurance
  delegation to service providers
    117–18
  nationally mandated programme
    461
quality regulation 107–9
  and health providers 107
  and insurers 108
  lack of consistency 108–9
  long-term care, purchasing
    contracts 107–8
RAI quality indicators 115–16
RAI-HC (Resident Assessment
    Instrument – Home Care) 114,
    118
RAI-NH (Resident Assessment
    Instrument – Nursing Homes)
    115–16
regulatory framework 447–50
residential facilities
  nursing home regulation 113
  quality control/audits 112
  quality standards 111
SPITEX (Swiss Home Care
    Association) 103, 108, 113–14
standard setting 30

terminology 36
total institutions xix
TQM (Total Quality Management)
  94–5
transparency 23–4
transparency agreement 82

United States
  ADL (activities of daily living)
    limitations 291
  ALFs (assisted-living facilities) 314
  Assisted Living Facilities 19
  care home financing 18–19
  CIA (Corporate Integrity Agreement)
    303–4
  CMS (Centers for Medicare and
    Medicaid Services) regulations
    298, 299–300, 302–3, 313,
    314–15
  Commission on Chronic Illness 293
  complaints 302, 305, 306, 471
  CON (certificate-of-need) entry
    requirement 300

United States (cont.)
  decentralized administrative system
    459–60
  Department of Health 19
  enforcement/regulation xxii–xxiii
  False Claims Act 304
  government programmes 291–2, *see
    also* Medicaid; Medicare
  HCBS (home and community-based
    services) regulations 313–17
    efficacy of 316–17
    enforcement and compliance 315
    financing 314
    licensure requirements 314–15
    market approaches 316
    monitoring xxi
    oversight 315
    quality care standards 316–17, 462
    structure and services 314
  HHC (Home Health Compare) 316
  Home Health Value-Based
    Purchasing 316
  IADL (instrumental activities of daily
    living) limitations 291
  *Improving the Quality of Care in
    Nursing Homes* 295
  insurers 20
  IOM (Institute of Medicine) 295
  Joint Commission for the
    Accreditation of Health Care
    Organizations 21, 314–15
  long-term care
    cost of regulations 317–18
    current performance 317
    data measurement approaches
      453
    demand for 291–2
    institutional bias 291
    low status of 15–16
    Medicare/Medicaid *see* Medicaid;
      Medicare
    non-nursing home *see* HCBS
    nursing homes *see* nursing homes
    Ombudsman Programme 308
    regulation, 1965–1987 294–5
    substantial compliance category
      294
    uninsured recipients 291
    see also HCBS (home/community
      care); nursing homes

long-term care regulation 292–6
  pre-1965 293
  1987–present day 295–6
  current trends 296
MDS (Minimum Data Set) *see* RAI
Medicaid 18–19, 20, 289, 291–2,
  294, 295, 297, 298, 300, 301,
  302–3, 309, 313, 314, 315
Medical Assistance for the Aged law
  (Kerr-Mills) 293
Medicare 18–19, 20, 289, 291–2,
  294, 295, 297, 298, 300, 301,
  302–3, 307–8, 309, 313, 314,
  315
national guidelines 460–1
national regulatory system 265–6
NFs (Medicaid-certified nursing
  facilities) 313
NHC (Nursing Home Compare)
  public reporting 309–10, 311,
  312
NHQI (Nursing Home Quality
  Initiative) 309, 310
NHVBP (Nursing Home Value Based
  Purchasing) 313
Nursing Home Reform Act (1987) 8,
  295–6
nursing homes
  Advancing Excellence campaign
    300–1
  certificate of compliance 301
  certification 10, 298, 301–2
  certification costs 318
  CMS remedies 302–3
  complaints 302, 305, 306, 471
  compliance/enforcement 296–7,
    301–8
  cream-skimming 313
  deficiencies 301–2, 305
  incentive payments and discharge
    rates 313
  inspection failings 307
  Joint Commission accreditation 300
  legislation 298
  P4P (pay-for-performance)
    312–13, 318
  providers 291, 296–301
  public reporting 309–12, 318
  quality control, market-based
    309–13

Index

quality indicators 312
regulation compliance costs 318
regulation future 318–19
resident-centred assessments 312
risk-adjustment techniques 313
sanctions 302–4
star ratings 310
state standards 300
survey process failings 304–6
surveys 301–2
voluntary quality control 300–1
OASIS (Outcome and Assessment Information Set) 315
OBRA (Omnibus Budget Reconciliation Act) 292, 295–6, 298–9, 299–300, 303, 306, 318–19
Old Age Assistance programme 293
Older Americans Act 308
Ombudsman Programme 308, 315
overview/background 289–90
poorhouses/workhouses 293

PPACA (Patient Protection and Affordable Care Act) 290, 292, 296, 299
professional associations 468
provider standards 7–9
QIO (Quality Improvement Organization) programme 300–1, 307–8, 318
QIS (Quality Indicator Survey) programme 306
RAI (Resident Assessment Instrument) performance benchmarking 298–9
regulation costs 317–18
requirement for payment 9
scandals 290
Smith v. *Heckler* 299
SNFs (Medicare-certified nursing facilities) 313
state funding 6–7

Wetherall, M. 373–4
Wingenfeld, K. 82–3, 88

For EU product safety concerns, contact us at Calle de José Abascal, 56–1°, 28003 Madrid, Spain or eugpsr@cambridge.org.

www.ingramcontent.com/pod-product-compliance
Ingram Content Group UK Ltd.
Pitfield, Milton Keynes, MK11 3LW, UK
UKHW020348060825
461487UK00008B/579